THE RIGHT TO HEALTH IN INTERNATIONAL LAW

The Right to Health in International Law

JOHN TOBIN

UNIVERSITY PRESS

OXFORD
UNIVERSITY PRESS

Great Clarendon Street, Oxford OX2 6DP

Oxford University Press is a department of the University of Oxford.
It furthers the University's objective of excellence in research, scholarship,
and education by publishing worldwide in

Oxford New York

Auckland Cape Town Dar es Salaam Hong Kong Karachi
Kuala Lumpur Madrid Melbourne Mexico City Nairobi
New Delhi Shanghai Taipei Toronto

With offices in

Argentina Austria Brazil Chile Czech Republic France Greece
Guatemala Hungary Italy Japan Poland Portugal Singapore
South Korea Switzerland Thailand Turkey Ukraine Vietnam

Oxford is a registered trade mark of Oxford University Press
in the UK and in certain other countries

Published in the United States
by Oxford University Press Inc., New York

© John Tobin 2012

The moral rights of the author have been asserted
Database right Oxford University Press (maker)

Crown copyright material is reproduced under Class Licence
Number C01P0000148 with the permission of OPSI
and the Queen's Printer for Scotland

First published 2012

All rights reserved. No part of this publication may be reproduced,
stored in a retrieval system, or transmitted, in any form or by any means,
without the prior permission in writing of Oxford University Press,
or as expressly permitted by law, or under terms agreed with the appropriate
reprographics rights organization. Enquiries concerning reproduction
outside the scope of the above should be sent to the Rights Department,
Oxford University Press, at the address above

You must not circulate this book in any other binding or cover
and you must impose the same condition on any acquirer

British Library Cataloguing in Publication Data
Data available

Library of Congress Cataloging in Publication Data
Library of Congress Control Number: 2011939857

Typeset by SPI Publisher Services, Pondicherry, India
Printed in Great Britain
on acid-free paper by
CPI Group (UK) Ltd, Croydon, CR0 4YY

ISBN 978–0–19–960329–9

1 3 5 7 9 10 8 6 4 2

Preface

In 2008 my partner, Lorraine, gave birth to twins, Will and Tess, in a private hospital. Five midwives, an obstetrician, and a paediatrician assisted her. She was administered with a cocktail of drugs to prevent haemorrhaging and the resuscitation equipment was present just in case the twins suffered any complications. After the birth Lorraine was provided with 24-hour care from midwives for five days and the twins, who were too small and weak to feed from the breast or bottle, were placed in the special care nursery for 16 days, where they fed via a gastric nasal tube.

As I reflected on this experience, it reminded me how access to effective health care is a lottery. But for living in a developed country like Australia, Lorraine, Will, and Tess may well have been deprived of the medical care necessary to meet their health needs. It forced me to recall an experience 20 years earlier when, volunteering in Tanzania, I watched a woman in the back of truck lie in a pool of her own blood as she was rushed to a community hospital. My colleagues told me that her condition was most likely the result of a 'backyard' abortion. Naively, I recalled seeking their assurance that the woman would be okay. She was after all going to a hospital. 'Unlikely' was the reply as the hospital had no medicine to stop the haemorrhaging.

The WHO estimates that every day approximately 1000 women[1] and over 17,000 infants under five die due to complications that could have been prevented or treated with simple medical interventions.[2] A child born in a developing country is over 10 times more likely to die within the first five years of life than a child born in an industrialized country like Australia.[3] In sub-Saharan Africa a woman's risk of dying from treatable or preventable complications of pregnancy and childbirth over the course of her lifetime is 1 in 22 compared to 1 in 7,300 in the developed regions.

There is no equity in global health.[4] In 2007 the world spent US$5.3 trillion on health. Of this expenditure, 86 per cent was spent on OECD countries, which represent 18 per cent of the world's population. In 40 WHO member States, total health spending by the state, households, the private sector, and external donors was less than US$46 per year per person—the minimum spending per person per year to provide basic life saving services.[5] Of course, the health divide is not simply between developed and developing states, and within developed states there remain huge gaps

---

[1] WHO, UNICEF, UNFPA and World Bank, *Trends in Maternal Mortality 1990 to 2008* (WHO, 2010).

[2] WHO, 'Children: Reducing Mortality' (WHO Fact Sheet 178, November 2009) <http://www.who.int/mediacentre/factsheets/fs178/en/index.html> accessed 14 June 2011.

[3] ibid.

[4] See: World Bank, *World Development Indicators 2011* (World Bank, 2011) 94–97 (provides comparative figures for states in relation to health expenditure, number of health workers, and hospital beds which illustrates the level of inequity between states).

[5] WHO, 'Spending on Health 2007—Global Update' (WHO Fact Sheet, 2010) <http://www.who.int/nha/use/global_fact_sheet_2007-Jun_2010.pdf> accessed 14 June 2011.

in access to affordable and accessible health care and the social determinants of health.

These problems are not unknown. Globally they have inspired the Millennium Development Goals (MDGs) to reduce infant mortality, improve maternal health, and combat HIV/AIDS, malaria, and other diseases. Locally, sophisticated and effective measures are being taken by States, households, civil society, medical professionals, health economists, bioethicists, policy makers, and the private sector to improve health outcomes. Indeed, the photo on the cover of this book captures an example of a collaborative initiative to provide primary health care to Ghanaian women and their children. But there is still considerable distance to be travelled. Globally, none of the health MDGs are on track to be met by 2015[6] and within Ghana itself, notwithstanding examples of good practice, the malaria infection rate is 48 per 100,000, only 28 per cent of females between 15–24 have comprehensive knowledge of HIV/AIDS, the maternal mortality ratio is 350 per 100,000 live births, and the probability of dying under age five is 69 per 1000 live births.[7] And for just about every country in the world there is a series of statistics that paint a depressing picture with respect to various health indicators. Indeed, in my own country, Australia, the state of indigenous health remains appalling, the level of childhood obesity remains a grave concern, as do unwanted teenage pregnancies and sexually transmitted diseases, and mental health is only starting to receive the funding it has long been denied.

Given the vast and complex nature of these issues, the question I found myself asking as I set about the task of writing this book was, what role, if any, can the right to health play in contributing to effective health outcomes?

Professor Bryan Stevenson, the Director of the Equal Justice Initiative in New York, has said that 'words can save lives'.[8] As a lawyer, I have professional inclination to embrace this sentiment. But I am acutely aware of the limitations of my profession and recognize that it is the actions of doctors and the provision of medicine and the social determinants of life, that actually save lives. Words do, however, have a role to play. But it is the meaning we give them and the actions that are inspired by their meaning that have the capacity to determine whether lives will be saved or, indeed, lost. Thus, the right to health in international law remains a benign idea unless it can be animated with a meaning that persuades those with the capacity to improve the health of individuals to take appropriate measures to achieve this end. It is my hope that this book might make a modest contribution to developing such an understanding of the right to health in international law.

---

[6] World Bank (n 4) 5–6.
[7] WHO, *World Health Statistics 2011* (WHO, 2011) 24, 26, 34, 36.
[8] Bryan Stevenson, 'Confronting Injustice' (Public Lecture, NYU Law School, 23 September 2009) <http://www.youtube.com/watch?v=EVD9Zdz8NBo> accessed 14 June 2011.

Acknowledgements

This book could not have been completed without the assistance and contributions of a vast number of people. I would especially like to thank Professor Philip Alston whose inbox was all too frequently flooded with my requests to comment on draft chapters. Despite his significant commitments, he always managed to provide me with insightful advice and constructive criticism. Professor Anne Orford was also generous in her support of my work on this project when it began its life as a PhD. And my PhD examiners, Professor David Kinley and Professor Matthew Craven, challenged me with their comments to develop a stronger and more persuasive account of the right to health in international law.

Thanks are also extended to my colleagues in the Law School at the University of Melbourne—Associate Professor Alison Duxbury, Associate Professor Bruce Oswald, Dr Wendy Larcombe, and Dr Chris Dent—who generously agreed to read parts of this book at various stages in its formation. I am further indebted to Professor Hilary Charlesworth, Professor Dorothy Schroder, Professor Michael Freeman, Dr Ara Keys, Jonathan Liberman, Jason Pobjoy, Henrietta Zeffert, and the anonymous referees who all made time to provide invaluable comments on my work.

I have been especially fortunate to enjoy the benefit of the research assistance provided by the Melbourne Law School Research Office and the Melbourne Law School Law Research Service. Under the guidance of Alissa Sputore, Robin Gardener, and Louise Ellis, a vast number of students, especially Claire Kelly, Jenny Huynh, and Nahal Zebarjadi, have diligently attended to a constant stream of research requests. The work this service has provided has been truly extraordinary. I have also been fortunate to have the benefit of two exceptional research assistants, Kristen Anderson and Mary Quinn, whose work was of the highest standard and without which this book would never have been completed.

A special note of thanks must also be extended to Merel Alstein, from Oxford University Press, whose patience with me was unending the Centre for Human Rights and Global Justice at NYU Law School which very generously provided me with the facilities and support to complete the final stages of this book.

Finally, to my partner Lorraine and my children Grace, Charlie, Tess, and William, thank you for your constant support and remarkable understanding when the demands of writing placed significant stress on our family life.

Aspects of this book have appeared in other publications. Chapter 3 is largely based on J Tobin, 'Seeking to Persuade: A Constructive Approach to Human Rights Treaty Interpretation' (2010) Harv Hum Rts Rev 1, and Chapter 8 is largely based on J Tobin, 'The International Obligation to Abolish Traditional Practices Harmful to Children's Health: What Does It Mean and Require of States?' (2009) 9 HRL Rev 373. A special thanks to the editors of these journals for allowing the publication of these articles in this book.

Contents

Table of Cases	xiv
Table of Treaties	xvi
List of Abbreviations	xviii

Introduction	1
I Clarifying expectations	6
II Constructing a meaning for the right to health	8
A The history of the right to health	8
B The conceptual foundations of the right to health	9
C The need for a persuasive methodology	10
D The meaning of health	11
E The obligation of states to recognize the right to health	11
1 Charting the History of the Right to Health	14
I Introduction	14
II From invisible to inalienable: the recognition of the right to health	16
III The origins of the right to health	19
A The need to navigate the dangers of excessive liberalism and collectivism	19
B The nexus between war, rights, health, and peace	23
C The WHO and the right to the highest attainable standard of health	27
D The adoption of the UDHR and its aftermath—a common enemy unites then the Cold War divides	30
E Using history to understand the meaning of the right to health	33
IV The role of public health in delivering the right to health	34
A The ancient commitment to collective action to protect health	34
B The reality of mixed motivations underlying collective health measures	35
C The rise and fall of the Enlightenment	36
D State expansion and the Industrial Revolution—towards an instrumentalist vision of public health	37
E The rebirth of rights and the struggle for justice	38
F Transforming national differences into an international commitment	39
V Conclusion: looking into and beyond the history of the right to health	41

2 The Right to Health—Its Conceptual Foundations	44
I Introduction	44
II The preliminary question: the need to interrogate the conceptual foundations of the right to health?	47
III The conceptual foundations of the right to health	49
A Looking for foundations in incompletely theorized agreements	49
B The idea of a human right to health	50
C Grounding rights in interests	52
D A social interest theory of rights	54
E Dignity as both coterminous and foundational	56
F Beyond individualism	57
G Dynamic but not arbitrary	59
IV Dealing with the detractors: a defence of the right to health	60
A The libertarian objection	60
B The status objection	63
C The formulation objection	65
D The relativist challenge	67
E The resource allocation dilemma	69
V Conclusion—an imperfect but good justification	73
3 A Methodology to Produce a Meaning for the Right to Health	75
I Introduction	75
II The act of interpretation: from intentionalism to persuasion	78
III Defining the interpretative community—moving beyond states towards a communitarian model	81
IV Seeking to persuade by constructive engagement	86
A Providing a transparent account of the interpretative process	86
B The features required for constructive engagement	88
V Conclusion—towards a common understanding	118
4 The Meaning of the Highest Attainable Standard of Health	121
I Introduction	121
II The scope of the interest in which the right to health is grounded	123
A The distinct nature of the international formulation	123
B The meaning of health	125
C Moving beyond a biomedical definition of health	126
D The danger associated with inflating the right to health	130
III The freedoms associated with health	132
A The right to sexual and reproductive freedom—an adolescent perspective	133
B Freedom from medical experimentation	144
C Freedom from non-consensual medical treatment	144

IV The qualitative nature of the entitlements under the right to health	158
A Availability	159
B Accessibility	167
V Conclusion—a socially manageable meaning of health	173

5 The Obligation to Recognize the Right to Health by All Appropriate Means — 175
I Introduction	175
II The obligation to 'take steps'	177
III The meaning of 'all appropriate means'	178
A A margin of discretion	178
B Legislative measures	179
C Using the tripartite typology to identify 'other appropriate measures'	185
D Using the work of the human rights treaty monitoring bodies to develop an understanding as to the nature of 'appropriate measures'	197
IV Conclusion—moving towards a sufficiently specified account of the measures required to secure the right to health	224

6 The Progressive Obligation to Realize the Right to Health — 225
I Introduction	225
II The meaning of 'maximum available resources'	226
A Towards a dynamic understanding of available resources	226
B Developing social resources	230
C Seeking international co-operation as a source of resources	231
III The progressive nature of a state's obligations and the process for prioritization	232
A The need for a dialogue	232
B Addressing the resource allocation dilemma	235
IV The concept of minimum core obligations	238
A Genesis and inflation	238
B In search of a principled basis for minimum core obligations	241
C In search of a practical content for the minimum core obligations under the right to health	243
V Conclusion—progressive as a pragmatic and principled process	252

7 Specific Measures Required to Secure the Right to Health — 254
I Introduction	254
II The obligation to diminish infant and child mortality	255
III The obligation to provide medical assistance and health care, especially primary health care	261
A Introduction	261
B The emphasis on primary health care	263

IV	The obligation to combat disease and malnutrition	267
	A Introduction	267
	B Disease prevention	269
V	The obligation to ensure occupational health and safety	286
VI	The obligation to provide pre-natal and post-natal health care for mothers	287
	A A progressive or immediate obligation	287
	B The meaning of 'appropriate' pre- and post-natal care	289
VII	The obligation to raise awareness and ensure access to information concerning health	291
	A Introduction	291
	B The information about health which all segments of society are entitled to receive	293
VIII	The obligation to develop preventive health care, guidance for parents, and family planning education and services	296
	A Introduction	296
	B The obligation to develop preventive health care	297
	C The obligation to develop guidance for parents	298
	D The obligation to develop family planning education and services	299
IX	Conclusion—deference with limits	301

8 The Obligation to Abolish Traditional Practices Harmful to Health — 303
  I Introduction — 303
  II The nature of a state's obligation—making progress towards effective abolition — 305
  III The practices to be abolished: 'traditional practices prejudicial to the health of children' — 306
    A Prejudice to health as a contested concept — 306
    B The identification of those practices to be abolished — 307
  IV Measures to abolish traditional practices prejudicial to a child's health — 314
    A Case study: female genital cutting — 314
    B The problem of classification — 315
    C The nature and health consequences of the practice — 316
    D The measures to be adopted by states — 317
  V Conclusion—the need for a culturally sensitive approach — 323

9 The International Obligation to Secure the Right to Health — 325
  I Introduction — 325
  II The nature and scope of the international obligation to co-operate — 327
    A A vision of qualified solidarity — 327
    B The obligation to promote and encourage co-operation under the CRC — 329
    C A tripartite international obligation — 331

III Case study: the impact of the international obligation to co-operate on access to medicines	351
A The dilemma: Intellectual property rights v access to medicines	351
B Can TRIPS be justified?	354
C Trade law and human rights—in search of system coherence	364
D TRIPS and access to medicines—adjusting and reviewing expectations	366
IV Conclusion	368
Conclusion	371
Appendix	376
Select Bibliography	381
Index	403

Table of Cases

Alex, Re (2004) 180 FLR 89 (FamCt, Aust) 149
Alyne de Silva Pimental v Brazil CEDAW/C/49/D/17/2008 (10 August 2011) . . . 222, 228, 289
Asylum Case (Colombia v Peru) [1950] ICJ Rep 266 (ICJ) 91
B (a Minor), Re [1988] 1 AC 199 (HL, UK). 153, 157
Bellotti v Baird, 443 US 622 (1979) (SC, USA) 148
Buck v Bell, 274 US 200 (1927) (SC, USA) 153
Chan v Korean Airlines Ltd, 490 US 122 (1989) (SC, USA). 115
City of Akron v Akron Center for Reproductive Health Inc, 462 US 416 (1983) (SC, USA) . . . 148
Consumer Education and Research Centre v Union of India (1995) 1 SCR 626
 (SC, India). 187, 203
D v United Kingdom ECHR 1997–III (ECtHR) 204
DAS v Victorian Human Rights and Equal Opportunity Commission (2009) 24 VR 415
 (VSC, Aust). 72, 183
Drug Action Forum v Union of India (1997) 6 SCC 609 (SC, India). 203
*Effect of Reservations on the Entry into Force of the American Convention on Human
 Rights (Arts 74 and 75)*, Advisory Opinion OC-2/82 of 24 September 1982,
 Inter-Am Ct HR (Ser A) No 2 (1982) (Inter-Am Ct HR) 92
Eve, Re [1986] 2 SCR 388 (SC, Canada) 153, 156
Exchange of Greek and Turkish Populations under the Lausanne Convention VI [1925]
 PCIJ (ser B) No 10 177
Francis Mullin v Administrator, Union of Delhi (1981) 2 SCR 516 (SC, India) 187, 203
Gabčikovo-Nagymaros Project (Hungary/Slovakia) [1997] ICJ Rep 7 (ICJ) 107
*General Secretary, West Pakistan Salt Miners Labour Union, Khewra, Jhelum v Director
 Industries and Mineral Development, Punjab Lahore* [1994] SCMR 2061 (SC, Pakistan) . . 203
Gillick v West Norfolk and Wisbech Area Health Authority [1986] 1 AC 112 (HL, UK) 139
Government of the Republic of South Africa v Grootboom [2001] 1 SA 46
 (CC, Sth Afr). 97, 240, 245
Henao v The Netherlands App No 13669/03 (ECtHR, 24 June 2003) (ECtHR) 204
International Centre for the Legal Protection of Human Rights 'Interights' v Croatia,
 Decision No 45/2007 (30 March 2009) (European Committee of Social Rights). 201
Interpretation of Peace Treaties (Second Phase) (Advisory Opinion) [1950] ICJ 221 (ICJ) 91
Ireland v United Kingdom (1978) Series A no 25 (ECtHR) 92
Judgment No SU-225/98 (1998) (CC, Columbia) 2, 205
Judgment No SU-337/99 (1999) (CC, Columbia) 147
Judgment No T-551/99 (1999) (CC, Columbia) 147
Kjeldsen Busk Madsen and Pedersen v Denmark (1976) Series A no 23 (ECtHR) 142
KNLH v Peru, Communication No 1153/2003, UN Doc CCPR/C/85/1153/2003
 (22 November 2005) (HRC) 143, 164, 204
Konrad v Germany ECHR 2006-XIII (ECtHR). 142
Land Island and Maritime Frontier Dispute (El Salvador v Hondouras) (Judgment)
 [1992] ICJ Rep 351 (ICJ). 90
*Legal Consequences for States of the Continued Presence of South Africa in Namibia
 (South West Africa) Notwithstanding Security Council Resolution 276
 (Advisory Opinion)* [1971] ICJ Rep 16 (ICJ) 104

*Legal Consequences of the Construction of a Wall in the Occupied Palestinian
   Territory (Advisory Opinion)* [2004] ICJ Rep 136 (ICJ)........................ 325
Loizidou v Turkey ECHR 1996–VI 2220 (ECtHR)................................ 93
Maharjan v His Majesty of Government NKP, 2053, vol 8, 627 (SC, Nepal) 203
Marion (No 2), Re (1992) 17 FamLR 336 (FamCt, Aust) 153, 156
Minister of Health v Treatment Action Campaign (No 2) [2002] 5 SA 721
   (CC, Sth Afr)... 2, 97, 99, 240
Mohiuddin Farooque v Bangladesh (1996) 48 DLR 438 (HC, Bangladesh) 203
Olga Tellis v Bombay Municipal Corporation [1986] AIR SC 180 (SC, India) 187
Osman v United Kingdom ECHR 1998–VIII 3124 (ECtHR)........................ 192
P v P (1994) 181 CLR 583 (HC, Aust) 153
Paschim Banga Khet Majoor Samity v State of West Bengal (1996) 4 SCC 37 (SC, India) 203
*Pharmaceutical Manufacturers' Association of South Africa v President of the Republic
   of South Africa*, Notice of Motion, Case Number 4183/98 (February 1998)
   (HC, Sth Afr) 355
Planned Parenthood v Danforth, 428 US 52 (1976) (SC, USA)....................... 139
R v Momcilovic (2010) 25 VR 436 (VSCA, Aust) 72, 183
R v Oakes [1986] 1 SCR 103 (SC, Canada) 72, 182–3
*Restrictions to the Death Penalty (Arts 4(2) and 4(4) of the American Convention on
   Human Rights)*, Advisory Opinion OC-8/83 of 8 September 1983, Inter-Am
   Ct HR (Ser A) No 3 (1983) (Inter-Am Ct HR)................................. 92
*Rights of Nationals of the United States of America in Morocco (France v United
   States of America)* [1952] ICJ Rep 176 (ICJ) 90
Secretary, Department of Health and Community Services v JWB & SMB (Marion's Case)
   (1992) 175 CLR 218 (HC, Aust) 148, 149, 153, 155
Selmouni v France (2000) 29 EHRR 403 (ECtHR)............................. 64, 75
Skinner v Oklahoma, 316 US 535 (1942) (SC, USA)............................. 153
*Social and Economic Rights Action Center and the Center for Economic and Social
   Rights v Nigeria*, Communication No 155/96 (27 October 2001) (African
   Commission on Human and Peoples' Rights) 185, 240
Soobramoney v Minister for Health [1998] 1 SA 765 (CC, Sth Afr) 85, 102, 205–6, 218, 241
*South-West Africa Cases (Ethiopia v South Africa; Liberia v South Africa) (Joint Dissenting
   Opinion of Sir Percy Spender and Sir Gerald Fitzmaurice)* [1962] ICJ Rep 465 (ICJ)..... 79
Szijjarto v Hungary, Communication No 4/2004, UN Doc CEDAW/C/36/D/4/2004
   (14 August 2006) annex (CEDAW Committee) 154, 163
The Amiable Isabella, 19 US (6 Wheat) 1 (1821) (SC, USA) 115
The Rainbow Warrior (New Zealand v France) (1990) 82 ILR 449 (France–New
   Zealand Arbitration Tribunal)... 332
*The Right to Information on Consular Assistance in the Framework of the Guarantees of the
   Due Process of Law*, Advisory Opinion OC-16/99 of 1 October 1999, Inter-Am
   Ct HR (Ser A) No 16 (1999) (Inter-Am Ct HR)................................. 93
Tyrer v United Kingdom (1978) Series A no 26 (ECtHR)........................... 93
Vincent Panikulangura v Union of India (1987) 2 SCC 165 (SC, India) 203
Waite and Kennedy v Germany App No 26083/94 (ECtHR, 18 February 1999) (ECtHR) ... 338
Wemhoff v Germany (1968) Series A no 7 (ECtHR)............................. 93
Yanomami v Brazil, Resolution No 10/85, Case No 7615 (1985) (Inter-American
   Commission on Human Rights)... 202

Table of Treaties

Additional Protocol to the American Convention on Human Rights in the Area of
  Economic, Social and Cultural Rights (Protocol of San Salvador) (San Salvador,
  17 November 1988, entered into force 16 November 1999, OAS Treaty Series
  No 69 (1988), 28 ILM 156) 19, 123, 263, 265, 267, 292, 326, 356, 380
African Charter on Human and Peoples' Rights (African Charter)
  (Banjul Charter) (Nairobi, 27 June 1981, entered into force 21 October 1986,
  1520 UNTS 217) 8, 19, 123, 262, 326, 379
African Charter on the Rights and Welfare of the Child (Addis Ababa,
  11 July 1990, entered into force 29 November 1999, OAU Doc
  CAB/LEG/24.9/49) 19, 123, 256, 262, 263, 379
American Convention on Human Rights (Pact of San José, Costa Rica) (San José,
  22 November 1969, entered into force 18 July 1978, 1144 UNTS 123)............ 326
Convention on the Elimination of All Forms of Discrimination against Women
  (CEDAW) (New York, 18 December 1979, entered into force 3 September
  1981, 1249 UNTS 13)........... ....18, 60, 134, 137, 168, 185, 255, 262,
                                                    288–9, 291–2, 299, 300, 304, 377
Convention on the Rights of Persons with Disabilities (CRPD) (New York,
  30 March 2007, entered into force 3 May 2008, UN Doc A/RES/61/106)........18, 59,
                                                    109, 123–4, 154, 157, 161, 168, 169,
                                                    172, 215, 255, 262, 326, 377
Convention on the Rights of the Child (CRC) (New York, 20 November 1989, entered
  into force 2 September 1990, 1577 UNTS 3) 7, 12, 18, 24, 56, 59, 66, 69,
                        83, 85, 95, 105, 112, 123, 131–2, 140, 144, 146–7, 176, 178–9,
                        186–9, 191, 194, 198, 204, 212, 214, 219, 224, 231, 242, 247–9,
                        254–6, 262–3, 267, 286, 288, 291–2, 293, 297, 299–300, 305–9,
                                                    325–30, 341, 347–8, 376
European Convention for the Protection of Human Rights and Fundamental Freedoms
  (European Convention on Human Rights) (Rome, 4 November 1950, entered
  into force 3 September 1953, 213 UNTS 221) 75, 93, 142, 313, 356
European Social Charter (Turin, 18 October 1961, entered into force 26 February
  1965, 529 UNTS 89)........................ 19, 123, 202, 255, 267, 291–2, 379
International Convention on the Elimination of All Forms of Racial Discrimination
  (CERD) (New York, 21 December 1995, entered into force 4 January 1969,
  660 UNTS 195) 18, 168
International Convention on the Protection of the Rights of All Migrant Workers
  and Members of Their Families (CMWF) (New York, 18 December 1990,
  entered into force 14 March 2003, 2220 UNTS 3) 18, 168, 255, 378
International Covenant on Civil and Political Rights (ICCPR) (New York,
  16 December 1966, entered into force 23 March 1976, 999 UNTS 171) 31, 72, 84,
                                                    106, 141, 144, 157, 162, 164–5, 175, 181, 188,
                                                    191, 215, 240, 286, 305
International Covenant on Economic, Social and Cultural Rights (ICESCR)
  (New York, 16 December 1966, entered into force 3 January 1976,
  993 UNTS 3) 6, 12–13, 18, 24, 31–2, 51, 56, 58–60, 66, 72, 85,
                        95, 97, 105, 108–9, 112, 114, 123–6, 130–4, 144, 167, 175–81, 187, 194,
                        198–9, 204, 212, 215, 222, 224, 225, 237–49, 254–63, 267–8, 281, 286–92,
                                                    297, 301–2, 303–6, 325–30, 339–48, 356–70, 371

International Health Regulations 343
Marrakesh Agreement Establishing the World Trade Organization (Marrakesh,
    15 April 1994, entered into force 1 January 1995) 1867 UNTS 3) annex 1C
    (Agreement on Trade-Related Aspects of Intellectual Property Rights)............... 352
Optional Protocol to the International Covenant on Economic, Social and Cultural
    Rights (Optional Protocol to the ICESCR) (New York, 24 September 2009,
    UN Doc A/63/435) (not yet in force) 179, 234–5, 340
Paris Convention for the Protection of Industrial Property (Paris, 20 March 1883,
    entered into force 26 April 1970, 828 UNTS 305) 356
Protocol to the African Charter on Human and Peoples' Rights on the Rights of
    Women in Africa (Maputo, 13 September 2000, entered into force
    25 November 2005, OAU Doc CAB/LEG/66.6)...................134, 166, 318, 322
Protocol to the Convention for the Protection of Human Rights and Fundamental
    Freedoms (Paris, 20 March 1952, entered into force 18 May 1954, 213 UNTS 262) .. 141
Vienna Convention on the Law of Treaties (VCLT) (Vienna, 23 May 1969,
    entered into force 27 January 1980, 1155 UNTS 331)........... 76–7, 86–100, 104–8,
                                                118–119, 177, 277, 240, 242, 373
WHO Framework Convention on Tobacco Control (Geneva, 21 May 2003,
    entered into force 27 February 2005, 2302 UNTS 166)........................ 343

List of Abbreviations

A Fem LJ	Australian Feminist Law Journal
A J Primary Health	Australian Journal of Primary Health
Ahfad J	Ahfad Journal
AIPJ	Australian Intellectual Property Journal
AJIL	American Journal of International Law
AJLM	American Journal of Law and Medicine
Am J Bioethics	American Journal of Bioethics
Am J Psych	American Journal of Psychiatry
Am J Pub Health	American Journal of Public Health
Annals Am Acad Pol & Soc Sci	The Annals of the American Academy of Politics and and Social Science
ASIL	The American Society of International Law
Aus Dis Rev	Australian Disability Review
Aus J Primary Health	Australian Journal of Primary Health
Aus J Pub Health	Australian Journal of Public Health
Aust	Australia (jurisdiction)
BMJ	British Medical Journal
Buff L Rev	Buffalo Law Review
Bull WHO	Bulletin of the World Health Organization
BYBIL	British Year Book of International Law
Cam Q Health Ethics	Cambridge Quarterly of Healthcare Ethics
CAT	Convention against Torture
CC	Constitutional Court (South Africa)
CEC	Commission for Environmental Cooperation of North America
CEDAW Committee	Committee on the Elimination of All Forms of Discrimination against Women
CEDAW	Convention on the Elimination of All Forms of Discrimination against Women
CERD	Committee on the Elimination of Racial Discrimination
Chi-Kent L Rev	Chicago-Kent Law Review
Child Dev	Child Development (journal)
Child	Child: Care Health and Development (journal)

List of Abbreviations

CIS	International Occupational Safety and Health Information Centre
CJLJ	Canadian Journal of Law and Jurisprudence
CMAJ	Canadian Medical Association Journal
CMWF	International Convention on the Protection of the Rights of All Migrant Workers and Members of Their Families
CO CAT	Concluding Observations of the CAT Committee
CO CEDAW	Concluding Observations of the CEDAW Committee
CO CRC	Concluding Observations of the CRC Committee
CO ESC	Concluding Observations of the ESC Committee
CO HRC	Concluding Observations of the Human Rights Committee
Cochrane Database Syst	Cochrane Database of Systemic Reviews Rev
COE	Council of Europe
Colum L Rev	Columbia Law Review
Copyright Bull	Copyright Bulletin
Cork OL Rev	Cork Online Law Review
Cornell Intl LJ	Cornell International Law Journal
CRC Committee	Committee on the Rights of the Child
CRC	Convention on the Rights of the Child
CRPD	Convention on the Rights of Persons with Disabilities
CRR	Center for Reproductive Rights
CSDH	Commission on Social Determinants of Health
Dev Pol'y Rev	Development Policy Review
DFID	Department for International Development (UK)
Duke LJ	Duke Law Journal
ECOSOC	United Nations Economic and Social Council
ECtHR	European Court of Human Rights
EIA	Ethics and International Affairs (journal)
EJIL	European Journal of International Law
Emory Intl L Rev	Emory International Law Review
Enviro Health Perspectives	Environmental Health Perspectives (journal)
ESC Committee	Committee on Economic, Social and Cultural Rights
Eur Psych	European Psychiatry (journal)
Expert Op Therapeutic	Expert Opinion on Therapeutic Patents Patents

FamCt	Family Court (Australia)
FAO	Food and Agriculture Organization
GA	United Nations General Assembly
Geo LJ	Georgetown Law Journal
GNP	Gross National Product
Harv Hum Rts J	Harvard Human Rights Journal
Harv L Rev	Harvard Law Review
HC	High Court
Health & Hum Rts	Health and Human Rights (journal)
Health Matrix	Health Matrix: Journal of Law and Medicine
Health Pol'y & Planning	Health Policy and Planning (Journal)
HELI	Health and Environment Linkages Initiative
HL	House of Lords
HRC	United Nations Human Rights Committee
HRL Rev	Human Rights Law Review
HRLJ	Human Rights Law Journal
Hum Rts Brief	Human Rights Brief
Hum Rts Q	Human Rights Quarterly
IACHR	Inter-American Commission on Human Rights
ICCPR	International Covenant on Civil and Political Rights
ICDC	International Child Development Centre
ICESCR	International Covenant on Economic Social and Cultural Rights
ICF	International Classification of Functioning, Disability and Health
ICJ	International Court of Justice
ICLQ	International and Comparative Law Quarterly
ICON	International Journal of Constitutional Law
ICPD	International Conference on Population and Development
IDS Bull	IDS Bulletin
IILJ	Institute of International Law and Justice (New York University School of Law)
ILC	International Law Commission
ILO	International Labour Organization
IMCI	Integrated Management of Childhood Illness (WHO)
IMF	International Monetary Fund

Ind Intl & Comp LR	Indiana International and Comparative Law Review
Inter-Am Ct HR	Inter-American Court of Human Rights
Intl Affairs	International Affairs (journal)
Intl J Child Rts	International Journal of Children's Rights
Intl J Gyn & Obs	International Journal of Gynecology and Obstetrics
Intl J Health Services	International Journal of Health Services
Issues L & Med	Issues in Law and Medicine (journal)
J Contemp'ry HL & Pol	Journal of Contemporary Health Law and Policy
J Cultural Div	Journal of Cultural Diversity
J Dis Pol'y Studies	Journal of Disability Policy Studies
J Epidemiology	Journal of Epidemiology and Community Health & Comm Health
J Fam L	Journal of Family Law
J Generic Med	Journal of Generic Medicines
J Health Econ	Journal of Health Economics
J Hum Dev	Journal of Human Development
J Hum Lactation	Journal of Human Lactation
J Hum Rts Practice	Journal of Human Rights Practice
J Med Ethics	Journal of Medical Ethics
J Med Phil	Journal of Medicine and Philosophy
J Pediatrics	Journal of Pediatrics
J Pub Health Pol'y	Journal of Public Health Policy
J Transnat'l L & Pol'y	Journal of Transnational Law and Policy
J World Invest & Trade	Journal of World Investment and Trade
J World Trade	Journal of World Trade
JL Med & Ethics	Journal of Law, Medicine and Ethics
JLM	Journal of Law and Medicine
JWIP	Journal of World Intellectual Property
LJIL	Leiden Journal of International Law
LON	League of Nations
LS	Legal Studies (journal)
MDG	United Nations Millennium Development Goal
Med & L	Medicine and Law (journal)
Med L Rev	Medical Law Review
Ment Retard Dev Disabil Res Rev	Mental Retardation and Developmental Disabilities Research Reviews

Mich J Intl L	Michigan Journal of International Law
MJIL	Melbourne Journal of International Law
Mt Sinai J Med	Mount Sinai Journal of Medicine
New Eng J Med	New England Journal of Medicine
NILR	Netherlands International Law Review
NQHR	Netherlands Quarterly of Human Rights
NZAID	New Zealand Agency for International Development
OAU	Organization of African Unity
OECD	Organisation for Economic Co-operation and Development
OHCHR	Office of the High Commissioner for Human Rights
Ohio NUL Rev	Ohio Northern University Law Review
OJLS	Oxford Journal of Legal Studies
PAHO	Pan American Health Organization
PCH	Primary Health Care
PHAST	Participatory Hygiene and Sanitation Transformation Approach
PHE	Public Health Ethics (journal)
Phil & Pub Aff	Philosophy and Public Affairs
Phil Q	The Philosophical Quarterly
Pol & Life Sci	Politics and the Life Sciences (journal)
Pol Theory	Political Theory (journal)
Prim'ry HCR & Dev	Primary Health Care Research & Development (journal)
PSRH	Perspectives on Sexual and Reproductive Health (journal)
RCADI	Recueil des Cours de l'Académie de Droit International
Reg & Governance	Regulation and Governance (journal)
SAJ Hum Rts	South African Journal of Human Rights
Sask L Rev	Saskatchewan Law Review
SC	Supreme Court
Soc Sci & Med	Social Science and Medicine (journal)
Stan L Rev	Stanford Law Review
Sth Afr	South Africa (jurisdiction)
Stud Transnat'l Legal Pol'y	Studies in Transnational Legal Policy
SUL Rev	Southern University Law Review
Syd LR	Sydney Law Review

TRIPS	Trade-Related Aspects of Intellectual Property Rights
U Pa L Rev	University of Pennsylvania Law Review
UC Davis L Rev	UC Davis Law Review
UDHR	Universal Declaration on Human Rights
UN	United Nations
UNC	United Nations Charter
UNDG	United Nations Development Group
UNDP	United Nations Development Programme
UNECE	United Nations Economic Commission for Europe
UNFPA	United Nations Population Fund
UNICEF	United Nations Children's Fund
UNSWLJ	University of New South Wales Law Journal
VSC	Victorian Supreme Court (Australia)
VSCA	Victorian Supreme Court of Appeal (Australia)
Wake Forest L Rev	Wake Forest Law Review
WHA	World Health Assembly
WHO	World Health Organization
WIPO	World Intellectual Property Organization
WMA	World Medical Association
Yale J Intl L	Yale Journal of International Law
Yale JH Pol L & Eth	Yale Journal of Health Policy, Law, and Ethics
Yale JL & Hum Rts	Yale Journal of Law and Human Rights
Yale JL & Human	Yale Journal of Law and the Humanities
YB Intl L Comm'n	Yearbook of the International Law Commission
Youth Studies Aus	Youth Studies Australia

Introduction

In recent years the right to health has come into its own in terms of recognition by states, active promotion by key international organizations, grassroots level campaigns, and general scholarly engagement. This book recounts the historical, philosophical, and theoretical journey of the concept as a prelude to identifying its normative content and the nature of the obligations that flow from it.

One of the greatest challenges in undertaking such an assessment is to navigate between the extremes of great enthusiasm and optimism, manifested by many of the proponents of the right to health, and the deeply pessimistic views of those who doubt that the concept has sufficient traction in terms of coherence, definability, political viability, economic sustainability, or justiciability. This book mounts a strong defence of a middle course that sees the right to health as a concept that has matured dramatically over the past decade or two and holds immense promise as both a normative framework and an operational framework, but which will continue to confront many challenges of a legal, political, economic, and cultural nature.

The greatly enhanced visibility of the right to health over the past decade can be seen in many contexts—political, social, institutional, legal, medical, and academic. The end of Cold War created the opportunity for recognition of the interdependence and indivisibility of civil and political rights and economic social rights at the Vienna World Conference on Human Rights in 1993.[1] Around the same time, the development community began to see the advantages in terms of political economy in invoking the language of human rights to enhance its cause. And a diverse range of groups began to actively exploit what they recognized as the complementarity of the human rights and development agendas.[2] The right to health thus became something of value to a constituency well beyond a limited group of human rights advocates. In the late 1990s, the Committee on Economic Social and Cultural Rights (ESC Committee) adopted its General Comment on the right to health[3] and the Commission on Human Rights appointed the first Special Rapporteur on the right to

---

[1] *Vienna Declaration and Programme of Action*, UN Doc A/CONF.157/23 (12 July 1993) para 8.

[2] Mac Darrow and A Tomas, 'Power, Capture and Conflict: A Call for Human Rights Accountability in Development Cooperation' (2005) 27 Hum Rts Q 471, 472; Philip Alston, 'Ships Passing in the Night: The Current State of the Human Rights and Development Debate Seen through the Lens of the Millennium Development Goals' (2005) 27 Hum Rts Q 755, 798–807; Peter Uvin, 'From the Right to Development to the Rights-Based Approach: How "Human Rights" Entered Development' (2007) 17 Development in Practice 597; *Report of the Special Rapporteur on the Right to Health to the Human Rights Council 2011*, UN Doc A/HRC/17/25 (12 April 2011) paras 7–13.

[3] ESC Committee, *General Comment No 14: The Right to the Highest Attainable Standard of Health*, UN Doc E/C/12/2000/4 (11 August 2000).

health in 2002 with a mandate to develop a collaborative understanding of the measures required to promote and protect the right to health.[4] Parallel to these developments, academics and practitioners started to explore the linkages between health and human rights;[5] dedicated journals started to engage with the idea and consequences of perceiving health as a human right;[6] civil society started to integrate the right to health into their advocacy;[7] universities began to teach courses on health and human rights;[8] and domestic courts in jurisdictions such as South Africa, India, and Columbia delivered decisions guaranteeing access to medicines and emergency medical treatment.[9] Internationally, the right to health began to infuse the work of bodies such as the World Health Organization (WHO),[10] the United Nations Children's Fund (UNICEF),[11] and the Millennium Development Project.[12] Thus, after remaining largely dormant for several decades after its initial recognition in the WHO Constitution in 1946 and the Universal Declaration of Human Rights (UDHR) in 1948, the right to health has begun to assert a role for itself in debates over health policy, service delivery, and development policy generally.

This is not to say that the right has conquered all of the obstacles that have for so long stood in its way. However, in a recent analysis John Harrington and Maria Stuttaford suggest that:

the human right to health has moved to the centre of political debate and social policy across the globe. Civil society organizations have put this right at the heart of campaigns for health justice at national and global levels. It features prominently in the output of the United

---

[4] Commission on Human Rights, *The Right of Everyone to the Highest Attainable Standard of Health*, Res 2002/31, UN Doc E/CN.4/RES/2002/31 (22 April 2002) para 5.

[5] See, eg, Jonathan Mann and others (eds), *Health and Human Rights: A Reader* (Routledge, 1999); Sofia Gruskin and others (eds), *Perspectives on Health and Human Rights* (Routledge, 2005); Paul Farmer, *Pathologies of Power: Health, Human Rights and the New War on the Poor* (University of California Press, 2005) ch 9; Elizabeth Fee and Manon Parry, 'Jonathan Mann, HIV/AIDS and Human Rights' (2008) 19 J Pub Health Pol'y 54.

[6] See, eg, 'Health and Human Rights: An International Journal' <http://www.hhrjournal.org/index.php/hhr> accessed 14 June 2011; 'International Health and Human Rights' <http://www.biomedcentral.com/bmcinthealthhumrights> accessed 14 June 2011. *The Lancet*, one of the world's leading medical journals, has for some years included papers on health and human rights.

[7] See generally *Report of the Special Rapporteur on the Right to Health to the Human Rights Council 2007*, UN Doc A/HRC/4/28 (17 January 2007) paras 12–17.

[8] See Daniel Tarantola and Sofia Cruskin, 'Health and Human Rights Education in Academic Settings' (2006) Health & Hum Rts 297.

[9] See, eg, *Minister of Health v Treatment Action Campaign (No 2)* [2002] 5 SA 721 (CC, Sth Afr); *Paschim Banga Khet Mazdoor Samity v State of West Bengal* (1996) 4 SCC 37 (SC, India); Judgment No SU-225/98, 10.3.1998 (CC, Columbia).

[10] See Benjamin Meier, 'Global Health Governance and the Contentious Politics of Human Rights: Mainstreaming the Right to Health for Public Health Advancement' (2010) 46 Stan J Intl L 1, 35–42. See also WHO, 'Health and Human Rights' <http://www.who.int/hhr/en/> accessed 7 June 2011.

[11] Marta Santos-Pais, *A Human Rights Conceptual Framework for UNICEF* (Innocenti Essays No 9, UNICEF and ICDC 1999).

[12] Lynn P Freedman and others, UN Millennium Project Task Force on Child Health and Maternal Health, *Who's Got the Power? Transforming Health Systems for Women and Children* (Earthscan, 2005) 31.

Nations (UN) and regional human rights bodies, as well as national courts and legislatures; national constitutions increasingly include explicit recognition of the right to health. Long neglected in the legal academy, many scholars now labour to develop its normative content, to contextualize its application and to evaluate it from the point of view of moral philosophy and theories of justice.[13]

As a result of what they describe as 'this remarkable transformation',[14] they conclude that we have 'moved beyond the period of defensiveness when most discussion of the right to health was detained by the existential question of whether it could ever exist in the first place'.[15]

The claims of Harrington and Stuttaford suggest that the right to health is playing a central and prominent role in shaping the development of health policy and delivery of health services around the globe; that an understanding as to the meaning and implementation of the right to health has been developed and accepted. But are their claims as to the impact of the right to health and its meaning justified? Is it true that we have moved beyond a period of defensiveness and have arrived at the point where we can collectively explore the potential of this right to deliver just and equitable health outcomes? Have we developed an adequate foundation for its moral and philosophical basis? Have we developed an account of its normative content that moves beyond an empty aspirational slogan? And have we developed a sufficient understanding of the measures required to translate this account into practice—what is increasingly referred to as a rights-based approach to health?[16]

But for all of the dramatic progress that has been achieved, it is not at all clear that the right to health has in fact 'moved to the *centre* of political debate and social policy across the globe'. The empirical evidence that is reviewed in this book would suggest that the status and relevance of the right to health is much less secure and far more marginalized than such a claim would indicate. In anecdotal terms, this is illustrated by the major health care debate that took place in the United States in 2009–10. While candidate Barack Obama endorsed the concept of a right to health care,[17] President Obama opted instead to locate the underpinnings of his health reform

---

[13] John Harrington and Maria Stuttaford, 'Introduction' in John Harrington and Maria Stuttaford (eds), *Global Health and Human Rights* (Routledge, 2010) 1.
[14] ibid 2.   [15] ibid 5.
[16] See, eg, Alicia Yamin, 'Will We Take Suffering Seriously? Reflections on What Applying a Human Rights Framework to Health Means and Why We Should Care' (2008) 10 Health & Hum Rts 45; Alicia Yamin, 'Suffering and Powerlessness: The Significance of Participation in Rights-Based Approaches to Health' (2009) 11 Health & Hum Rts 5; John Tobin, 'Beyond the Supermarket Shelf: Using a Rights Based Approach to Address Children's Health Needs' (2006) 14 Intl J Child Rts 275; *Report of the Special Rapporteur on the Right to Health to the Human Rights Council 2011* (n 2).
[17] See 'The Second Presidential Debate', *New York Times* (New York, 7 October 2008) <http://elections.nytimes.com/2008/president/debates/transcripts/second-presidential-debate.html> accessed 14 June 2011 ('Brokaw: "Quick discussion. Is health care in America a privilege, a right, or a responsibility?" ... Obama: "Well, I think it should be a right for every American. In a country as wealthy as ours, for us to have people who are going bankrupt because they can't pay their medical bills—for my mother to die of cancer at the age of 53 and have to spend the last months of her life in the hospital room arguing with insurance companies because they're saying that this may be a pre-existing condition and they don't have to pay her treatment, there's something fundamentally wrong about that."')

agenda in the principles of cost effectiveness and economic sustainability.[18] In Australia, although policy makers have accepted the linkage between health and human rights, the idea of the right to health was conspicuously absent in shaping the adoption of health care reforms in 2011.[19] Similarly, in the United Kingdom the right to health was not included in the list of 10 principles that underlie its global health strategy.[20] Moreover, as the privatization of health care assumes a greater role in the provision of health care within states, there is little evidence to suggest that the impact of this development on the right to health has been taken into account. At the international level, institutions such as the WHO still struggle to make the transition from a biomedical model of health to a rights-based approach and the 'human rights agenda has remained marginal, contested and severely under-resourced'.[21] And where health concerns intersect with international trade and intellectual property rights, the right to health has remained relatively marginalized.[22] Indeed, Upendra Baxi has gone so far as to suggest that the disregard by the global pharmaceutical industry of the health needs of the South 'mocks' the very idea of a human right to health.[23]

On the domestic front, effective constitutional protection of the right to health remains the exception rather than the norm. And enthusiasm for the right to health is far from universal within the academic literature or among professional bodies. Recent expositions of the relationship between justice and health care tend to assign the right to health a relatively minor or non-existent role.[24] Philosophers such as James Griffin are scornful of what they perceive as the weak philosophical foundations of the right to health in international law;[25] while economists such as William Easterly believe a right to health will skew resources to benefit politically

---

[18] See, eg, 'Text: Obama's Speech on Health Care Reform', *New York Times* (New York, 15 June 2009) <http://www.nytimes.com/2009/06/15/health/policy/15obama.text.html?_r=1> accessed 13 July 2010, cf Edward Kennedy, 'Health Care as a Basic Human Right: Moving from Lip Service to Reality' (2009) 22 Harv Hum Rts J 165.

[19] See Australian Labor Party, 'Health Reform—A Healthy System for the 21st Century' <http://www.alp.org.au/agenda/health-reform> accessed 10 June 2011. The right to health is also absent from other Government strategies and inquiries in relation to health issues. See, eg, Department of Health and Ageing, *Primary Health Care Reform in Australia: Report to Support Australia's First National Primary Health Care Strategy* (Australian Government, 2009); House of Representatives Standing Committee on Health and Ageing, *Weighing It Up: Obesity in Australia* (Parliament of Australia, 2009).

[20] UK Department of Health, *Health is Global: A UK Government Strategy 2008–2013* (UK Government, 2008) 8.

[21] Paul Hunt, 'The Health and Human Rights Movement: Progress and Obstacles' (2008) 15 JLM 714, 723.

[22] See Chapter 9, Part III.

[23] Upendra Baxi, 'The Place of the Human Right to Health and Contemporary Approaches to Global Justice' in Harrington and Stuttaford (n 13) 12, 19.

[24] See, eg, Norman Daniels, *Just Health: Meeting Health Needs Fairly* (CUP, 2008) 15; Yvonne Denier, *Efficiency, Justice and Care: Philosophical Reflections on Scarcity in Health Care* (Springer, 2007). cf Jennifer Ruger, *Health and Social Justice* (OUP, 2010) 118; Amartya Sen, 'Why and How is Health a Human Right?' (2008) 372 The Lancet 2010.

[25] James Griffin, *On Human Rights* (OUP, 2008) 208.

effective advocates at the expense of the most needy.[26] Even in the medical literature, and especially in those journals where the central role of the right to health would most likely be affirmed such as the American Journal of Public Health and the European Journal of Public Health, articles embracing the right to health remain rare. Indeed, within the medical profession and among public health professionals generally, the right to health remains a relatively novel concept. For the most part, preference continues to be given instead to the notion of equity as the foundation or cornerstone of a just health care system.[27]

This reluctance to embrace the right to health by non-lawyers is linked, in part at least, to its legal origins and creates an urgent need to think about ways of developing an interdisciplinary understanding of the right. But even within legal circles there remain serious reservations as to the legitimacy of the right to health that stem from concerns regarding its capacity to hold a determinate meaning and its justiciability before courts. South Africa, Colombia, and Brazil may have included a right to health in their constitutions, but many other jurisdictions, including Australia and the United Kingdom, have steadfastly refused to do so.[28] And despite attempts over the last decade or so to articulate a vision of the right to health and a deeper understanding of its core principles, concerns as to its meaning and implementation in practice remain widespread. For example, the notion that the right to health has some sort of minimum core has been criticized,[29] and its overall normative content remains heavily contested. Insistence on the centrality of the principle of non-discrimination and on the indivisibility of the right to health with other human rights have been a source of deep frustration for many policy makers who must deal with the reality of scarce resources.[30] This inevitably demands that tough choices be made to give priority to some rights over others and to the claims of some rights-holders over others. Such conflicts and dilemmas arise in a great many contexts such as between young and old, between those living in urban areas and those in remote rural areas, and those with chronic diseases that are costly to treat and those whose interests are best served by an emphasis on basic primary care. The question is always whether the concept of a right to health is helpful in resolving such dilemmas.

---

[26] William Easterly, 'Human Rights are the Wrong Basis for Healthcare', *Financial Times* (London, 12 October 2009) <http://www.ft.com/cms/s/0/89bbbda2-b763-11de-9812-00144feab49a.html#axzz1PDNbqlAS> accessed 14 June 2011.

[27] Hunt (n 21) 714 (notes that 'many health professionals have never heard of the right to health').

[28] See, eg, UK Joint Committee on Human Rights, *Twenty First Report* (UK Parliament 2004) ch 4, paras 52–5 ('The Status of Economic Social and Cultural Rights') <http://www.publications.parliament.uk/pa/jt200304/jtselect/jtrights/183/18307.htm> accessed 10 June 2011; *National Human Rights Consultation Report* (Commonwealth of Australia 2010) 355–6.

[29] See, eg, Katharine Young, 'The Minimum Core of Economic and Social Rights: A Concept in Search of Content' (2008) 33 Yale J Intl L 113.

[30] Lauchlan Munro, '"The Human Rights-Based Approach to Programming": A Contradiction in Terms?' in Sam Hickey and Dianas Mitlin (eds), *Rights-Based Approaches to Development: Exploring the Potential and Pitfalls* (Kumarian Press, 2009) 187, 197–201. Indeed, Richard Horton, as Editor of the Lancet in 2004, suggested that the obsession with the indivisibility of rights was undermining child survival: Richard Horton, 'UNICEF Leadership 2005–2015: A Call for Strategic Leadership' (2004) 364 The Lancet 2071.

Moreover, the concept of participation—invoked as a mantra with respect to all rights including the right to health—has been criticized for bypassing the hard problems associated with those whose situation or status effectively preclude them from any meaningful participation.[31]

A picture therefore emerges of the right to health that is far more contested and much less central to political and social debates concerning health care than its most enthusiastic advocates would suggest. But this is a far cry from concluding that the right to health is irrelevant. On the contrary there is no doubting that it is increasingly an unavoidable part of public health discourse. The central challenge now is to move the right from the periphery to the centre of such debates, a challenge that will require far more sophisticated and hard-headed analysis on the part of lawyers, health professionals, and public policy makers. This book aims to contribute to meeting that challenge.

I Clarifying expectations

In responding to this challenge, no attempt is made to traverse the relationship between the right to health and the broad range of specific health sector issues confronting contemporary societies. Such an approach would simply descend into an eclectic and subjective collection of issues that would inevitably be treated superficially and add little to the existing literature. Instead, the approach adopted in this book is to anchor the analysis to a discussion of the core principles that inform the status, content, and implementation of the right to health in the hope that the reader will be able to apply these principles to specific health sector issues. This is not to say that there will be no discussion of specific issues—the centrality and prominence of issues such as the privatization of health care, the role of non-state actors, access to medicines, and reproductive health demand inclusion in any book on the right to health in international law. However, rather than devote separate chapters to these issues, their treatment will be designed to illustrate the application of the core principles that are the central focus of this book.

Moreover, no attempt is made to comprehensively examine the meaning of the right to health as it appears in international, regional, *and* domestic contexts. Instead, the focus of this book is on the right to health in international law and primarily the formulation adopted in the International Covenant on Economic, Social and Cultural Rights (ICESCR)[32] and the Convention on the Rights of the

---

[31] Baxi (n 23) 18.

[32] International Covenant on Economic Social and Cultural Rights (ICESCR) (New York, 19 December 1966, entered into force 3 January 1976, 993 UNTS 3) art 12:

1 The States Parties to the present Covenant recognize the right of everyone to the enjoyment of the highest attainable standard of physical and mental health.
2 The steps to be taken by the States Parties to the present Covenant to achieve the full realization of this right shall include those necessary for:
   (a) The provision for the reduction of the stillbirth-rate and of infant mortality and for the healthy development of the child;

Introduction 7

Child (CRC)[33] because these two instruments offer the most comprehensive expression of the right in international law.[34] Attention will be drawn to other international, regional, and domestic instruments that address the right to health but only for the purpose of highlighting the way in which such instruments expand, inform, or deviate from the nature of this right in international law.[35] As a consequence this book does not provide a detailed examination of the regional and domestic case law

---

    (b) The improvement of all aspects of environmental and industrial hygiene;
    (c) The prevention, treatment and control of epidemic, endemic, occupational and other diseases;
    (d) The creation of conditions which would assure to all medical service and medical attention in the event of sickness.

[33] Convention on the Rights of the Child (CRC) (New York, 20 November 1989, entered into force 2 September 1990, 1577 UNTS 3) art 24:

1. States Parties recognize the right of the child to the enjoyment of the highest attainable standard of health and to facilities for the treatment of illness and rehabilitation of health. States Parties shall strive to ensure that no child is deprived of his or her right of access to such health care services.
2. States Parties shall pursue full implementation of this right and, in particular, shall take appropriate measures:
   (a) To diminish infant and child mortality;
   (b) To ensure the provision of necessary medical assistance and health care to all children with emphasis on the development of primary health care;
   (c) To combat disease and malnutrition, including within the framework of primary health care, through, inter alia, the application of readily available technology and through the provision of adequate nutritious foods and clean drinking-water, taking into consideration the dangers and risks of environmental pollution;
   (d) To ensure appropriate pre-natal and post-natal health care for mothers;
   (e) To ensure that all segments of society, in particular parents and children, are informed, have access to education and are supported in the use of basic knowledge of child health and nutrition, the advantages of breastfeeding, hygiene and environmental sanitation and the prevention of accidents;
   (f) To develop preventive health care, guidance for parents and family planning education and services.
3. States Parties shall take all effective and appropriate measures with a view to abolishing traditional practices prejudicial to the health of children.
4. States Parties undertake to promote and encourage international co-operation with a view to achieving progressively the full realization of the right recognized in the present article. In this regard, particular account shall be taken of the needs of developing countries.

[34] As at 12 August 2011, 160 states were party to the ICESCR and 193 states were party to the CRC. No state has entered a general reservation to art 12 of the ICESCR upon ratification or accession. Three states—Argentina, the Holy See, and Poland—have entered reservations upon ratification or accession to the CRC in relation to those aspects of art 24 which concern family planning. However, no state has entered a broad reservation to the obligation to recognize the right of a child to the highest attainable standard of health.

[35] See Appendix 1 for a listing of the right to health as it appears in other international and regional treaties. For a more detailed listing of international instruments relevant to the right to health see: *Report of the Special Rapporteur on the Right to Health to the Commission on Human Rights*, UN Doc E/CN.4/2003/58 (13 February 2003) annex 1. For a comprehensive examination of the history and development of the international normative structure see Brigit Toebes, *The Right to Health as a Human Right in International Law* (Hart Publishing, 1999) 27–85. For a timeline of the significant international developments relevant to a child's right to health see WHO, *The World Health Report 2005: Make Every Mother and Child Count* (WHO, 2005) 5.

on the right to health as appears for example in the African Charter on Human and People's Rights or the South African and Colombian constitution. Such case law is relevant to the extent that it demonstrates the justiciability of a right to health. But a detailed examination of the right to health in regional or domestic legal systems is beyond the scope of this book.

II Constructing a meaning for the right to health

It has been said that 'one would be hard pressed to find a more controversial or nebulous human right than the "the right to health"'[36] which 'is characterized by conceptual confusion as well as a lack of effective implementation'.[37] This characterization presents a significant problem for a project that seeks to deploy the right to health as a strategy to influence health outcomes and provide guidance for states seeking to implement their obligations under international law.[38] Although significant work has been done in recent years to 'unpack'[39] various aspects of the right to health by bodies such as the Special Rapporteur on the Right of Everyone to the Enjoyment of the Highest Attainable Standard of Physical and Mental Health, the Committee on Economic Social and Cultural Rights (ESC Committee), the Committee on the Rights of the Child (CRC Committee), and academic commentators, the contours of this right are far from fully mapped.

A The history of the right to health

Rather than leap straight into the task of developing the normative content of the right to health, the approach taken here is to begin with an account of the historical, philosophical, and theoretical journey of this concept. This is because an examination of the history of the right to health has the potential to reveal insights into the intended meaning of this right and clarify debates as to the source of its origins. The idea of a right to the highest attainable standard of health is, after all, a bold exhortation, and its inclusion in international instruments was not the result of some divine act of intervention. It carried expectations for its authors but what were they and why were states, sovereign bodies accountable to no other entity at the time, prepared to accept such an obligation?

---

[36] Jennifer Ruger, 'Toward a Theory of a Right to Health: Capability and Incompletely Theorized Agreements' (2006) 18 Yale JL & Hum Rts 273.

[37] Toebes (n 35) 259–60.

[38] Lawrence Gostin, 'Global Health Law Governance' (2008) 22 Emory Intl L Rev 35, 36 (identifies lack of definition as a serious structural problem within international law); *Report of the Special Rapporteur on the Right to Health to the Human Rights Council 2007* (n 7) para 8 (notes that the gap in understanding of the right to health placed a significant constraint on all those working in the field of health and human rights especially during the 1990s).

[39] *Report of the Special Rapporteur on the Right to Health to the General Assembly 2007*, UN Doc A/62/214 (8 August 2007) para 70.

The examination of the history of the right to health undertaken in Chapter 1 reveals that this right is not, as is often assumed, the product of Communist ideology. On the contrary the lineage of this right is interwoven with the genes of a diverse range of actors—the legacy of the Enlightenment, the failings of the Industrial revolution, the development of a distinct Latin American philosophy that was heavily steeped in Catholic values about justice, the impact of the Great Depression, the emergence of the modern welfare state, and the personality of individuals such as Franklin D Roosevelt. It is also deeply interconnected with the history of public health, which reveals an ancient acceptance of the need for states to take measures to protect the health of their people. Significantly, this is the basic premise that underlies the right to health. Historically, the motivations for public health measures tended to shift in a pendulum-like way from instrumentalism to humanitarianism—an excessive swing towards instrumentalism always proving counterproductive to both the interests of the state and individual because of increased poverty, disease, and sickness thus necessitating a counter swing towards humanitarianism. However, the horrors of World War II provided both the impetus and window of opportunity in which states agreed upon a conception of the right to health that recognized the interdependence of humanitarian and instrumental motivations. Thus, far from being an abstract ideology or utopian dream, the history of the right to health reveals this idea to be endowed with deeply pragmatic origins.

B The conceptual foundations of the right to health

An examination of the conceptual foundations of the right to health, which is the focus of Chapter 2, is warranted for both strategic and substantive reasons. For many philosophers, the right to health simply cannot be justified. It is said to lack a convincing theoretical account of its conceptual foundations[40] and is a 'vacuous concept' that should be demoted from the list of human rights recognized under international law.[41] Such a position not only has a destabilizing effect on the legitimacy of the right to health, but if correct, it makes any attempt to interpret this right look like a futile exercise. As a consequence, there is a need to see if a philosophical defence of the right to health can be offered. If such a defence can be mounted, it has the potential to both ward off the skeptics and provide a stronger theoretical foundation upon which to erect the normative content of the right.

The conclusion to be drawn is that such a justification does exist. This defence is based on what is described as a social interest theory of rights. The fundamental tenet of this theory is that human rights are not essential or inherent but socially constructed and it is 'interests' that ground human rights. However, it rejects the idea that the interests which ground a right must be determined by reference to a comprehensive theory as to when a particular interest will constitute the foundation for a legitimate human right. It also rejects the suggestion that the international instruments that protect the right to health offer no agreement on the conceptual

---

[40] Daniels (n 24) 15.   [41] Griffin (n 25) 208.

foundations of human rights such as a right to health.[42] Instead, it will be argued that, although not completely theorized, there is an overlapping consensus as to the conceptual foundations of the right to health in international law, which is derived from the social process that led to the recognition of a person's interest in achieving the highest attainable standard of health as the basis for a human right. Hence the idea of a 'social interest' theory of rights as opposed to other explanations, such as an 'urgent'[43] or 'basic' interest theory.[44]

Chapter 2 also interrogates those arguments commonly used to challenge the legitimacy of the right to health, which are described as the libertarian objection; the status objection; the formulation objection; the relativist challenge; and the resource allocation dilemma. This discussion reveals that much of the conceptual opposition to the right to health is based on a theory of rights that is inapposite to the theory of human rights adopted in international law. Moreover, most of the opposition based on implementation of the right to health is informed by assumptions as to the scope of the right to health and the nature of a state's obligations, which pay no regard to the actual obligations of a state as expressed within the relevant human rights treaties. A careful examination of the text of these treaties, which is the focus of the discussions in Chapters 4 to 9, reveals that such objections are without foundation.

C The need for a persuasive methodology

All too often the process of defining the content of a human right, such as the right to health, is unaccompanied by any explanation, or at best a scant explanation, as to the methodology used to generate the interpretation offered. This gives rise to allegations of 'sloppy' humanitarian argument[45] and a tendency towards 'result driven jurisprudence', which reflects the personal preferences of the interpreter.[46] In response to these concerns, Chapter 3 is dedicated to outlining the methodology to be adopted with respect to the meaning of the right to health in international law. The fundamental premise of this methodology is that the act of interpretation is not simply the process of attributing *a* meaning to the right to health but ultimately an act of persuasion—an attempt to persuade the relevant interpretative community that a particular interpretation of the right to health is the most appropriate meaning to adopt. Importantly, this community extends beyond states, their agents, and international lawyers towards a more communitarian model in which the interests *and* insights of a much wider range of stakeholders who have an interest in the right to health, must be taken into account in the interpretative exercise—a process described as constructive engagement. Ultimately it is argued that a persuasive

---

[42] Griffin (n 25) 16.
[43] Charles Beitz, *The Idea of Human Rights* (OUP, 2009) 109–10.
[44] Allen Buchanan and Kristen Hessler, 'Specifying the Content of the Human Right to Health Care' in Allen Buchanan (ed), *Justice and Health Care: Selected Essays* (OUP, 2009) 213.
[45] David Kennedy, 'The International Human Rights Movement: Part of the Problem?' (2001) 14 Harv Hum Rts J 101, 120.
[46] Jeremy Waldron, 'Judges as Moral Reasoners' (2009) 7 Int J Constitutional Law 2, 6.

interpretation of a right such as health will be enhanced if it satisfies four criteria—it must be principled, practical, coherent, and context sensitive.

D The meaning of health

Chapter 4 commences the task of applying the methodology outlined in Chapter 3 to develop a meaning of the right to health in international law. The focus in this chapter is on the meaning and scope of the interest in which this right is grounded namely, the highest attainable standard of physical and mental health. It advances four arguments. First, far from guaranteeing a right to be healthy, as suggested by some commentators, the phrase 'highest attainable standard' recognizes that the level of health enjoyed by an individual will be dependent on factors peculiar to an individual and the resources available to a state. Second, the actual meaning of health, which has been largely overlooked by the human rights treaty supervisory bodies, should extend to a biopsychosocial model, which recognizes the potential for social factors, and not merely a pathological condition, to limit the functioning of an individual within society. This approach provides better guidance for states in identifying the measures necessary to secure the right to health relative to the traditional biomedical definition. Third, a persuasive case can be made to extend the scope of the right to health to freedoms the implications of which will be examined in the context of sexual autonomy for adolescents, consent to medical treatment, and the practice of non-consensual sterilization of women and girls with intellectual disabilities. Finally, the four qualitative elements of the right to health—that health care and related services be available, accessible, acceptable, and of appropriate quality—support an understanding of this right that is practical, or to borrow the words of Beitz and Griffin, 'action guiding'[47] and 'socially manageable'[48] for states.

E The obligation of states to recognize the right to health

An adequate normative account of a human right requires that it have a well-specified counterpart obligation. Chapters 5 to 9 offer a response to this challenge. Chapter 5 examines the meaning of the requirement under international law that states must take steps by all appropriate means to secure the right to health. It draws significantly on the work of the treaty supervisory bodies, principally the ESC Committee and the CRC Committee, to inform the scope of this obligation. Although this work is shown to be unreasonably conflated at times, a persuasive case can still be made to support the calls of the treaty supervisory bodies that states must adopt the following measures to secure the effective enjoyment of the right to health—the development of national health plans; the creation of effective accountability mechanisms; the collection of appropriate data and development of relevant indicators and benchmarks; the facilitation of effective participatory strategies; the

---

[47] Beitz (n 43) 163.   [48] Griffin (n 25) 37–8.

encouragement of multisectoral and interdisciplinary initiatives; and the development of targeted health policies for especially vulnerable groups.

Chapter 6 examines the meaning of the obligation to secure the right to health progressively subject to available resources. It argues that despite the apparently amorphous nature of this obligation, it remains possible to articulate a persuasive account of how states can implement this obligation in a way that is principled, practical, coherent, and context sensitive. A process will also be outlined by which to guide states in the resolution of the macro/micro resource allocation dilemma, outlined in Chapter 2. It will be shown that international law accommodates the reality of the need for states to prioritize the allocation of scarce resources provided that the state is able to demonstrate that the process for allocating these resources can be shown to be reasonable. This standard will be satisfied where the decision-making process is shown to be principled, evidence based, consultative, transparent, and evaluative. The chapter concludes with an analysis of the controversial concept of minimum core obligations. It will be argued that the ESC Committee has inflated this concept as it applies to the right to health in a way that fails to satisfy any of the requirements outlined in the interpretative methodology to be used in this analysis. But rather than abandon this concept, it will be argued that a principled and practical defence can be advanced to justify its use as a tool to assist in understanding the nature of a state's obligation to secure the right to health within the context of limited resources.

Chapter 7 examines the nature of the obligation imposed on states with respect to the specific measures listed in article 12 of the ICESCR and article 24 of the CRC which range from an obligation to diminish child mortality to an obligation to develop preventive health care including family planning education and services. The central theme to emerge from this analysis is that considerable deference must be given to states' margin of appreciation to allow for a context sensitive implementation of the specific measures required to secure the right to health in international law. However, this margin remains subject to the overriding caveat that whatever measures are adopted by states they must be undertaken in a manner that is directed towards securing the effective implementation of the right to health and pursue coherence with the other obligations imposed under the ICESCR, the CRC, and the broader system of international law. Moreover, the requirement that the measures be 'appropriate' demands that they must also be effective—as assessment that requires extensive engagement with research from a broad range of non-legal disciplines such as public health and pediatrics.

It is now widely acknowledged that a person's health is not merely compromised by gaps in medical knowledge, a lack of health services, or inadequacies in the social determinants of health. Many traditional practices are also maintained despite their prejudicial impact on the health of individuals. As a consequence, the right to health in international law imposes an obligation to abolish such practices. The nature and scope of this obligation is the focus of Chapter 8 and the conclusions to be drawn are as follows. First, the obligation to abolish harmful traditional practices is a progressive one which requires states to take a combination of whatever measures are necessary—legislative, administrative, social, and education—to ensure the effective eradication of such practices. Second, an assessment as to the prejudice of a particular practice to the health of a child cannot be reduced to a simple biomedical assessment and the broader psycho-social impacts and significance of a practice must be taken into account. Third, an examination of the treatment of corporal punishment and male circumcision by the CRC Committee provides evidence of both a cultural and gender bias in the identification of practices deemed harmful to the health of a child. Fourth, the practice of female genital cutting will be used to demonstrate that rather than adopt a simple legislative regime based on zero tolerance, a multifaceted approach, which is generated through dialogue with the communities that tolerate harmful practices, must be adopted if the effective elimination of harmful practices is to be achieved. Finally, although the right to health under the ICESCR does not include a specific obligation to abolish harmful traditional practices, it is reasonable to imply such an obligation in the general obligation of states to take measures to protect the health of individuals from the practices of non-state actors.

Chapter 9 examines the highly contested and elusive nature of the international obligation to cooperate for the purpose of securing the realization of the right to health in international law. The overarching conclusion to be drawn is that although the 'parameters of international assistance and cooperation are not yet fully drawn',[49] it remains possible to articulate 'a convincing account' as to the scope of the obligation 'in order to articulate its concrete implications' for states with respect to the areas and means by which co-operation should take place.[50] Central to this account is the requirement that states must take reasonable measures subject to available resources to *respect, protect,* and *fulfil* the right to health of individuals in other states. This typology of obligations is illustrated by way of a case study, namely access to medicines within the context of the international system for the protection of intellectual property under the Trade-Related Aspects of Intellectual Property Rights (TRIPS) regime, to assess the legitimacy of a state's involvement in this regime. It concludes that, on balance, involvement in TRIPS does not necessarily violate the *respect* and *protect* elements of a state's international obligation to secure the right to health. But this regime is not an effective mechanism by which to facilitate access to medicines in developing states and the international obligation to *fulfil* the right to health requires that states must make bona fide efforts to develop a complementary system that is more likely to achieve this end.

---

[49] *Report of the Special Rapporteur on the Right to the Highest Attainable Standard of Health to the General Assembly 2005*, UN Doc A/60/348 (12 September 2005) para 60.

[50] Allen Buchanan and David Golove, 'The Philosophy of International Law' in Jules Coleman and Scott Shapiro (eds), *The Oxford Handbook of Jurisprudence and Philosophy of Law* (OUP, 2002) 868, 906.

1
Charting the History of the Right to Health

I Introduction

If, as has been suggested, the writing of the history of human rights has become the 'new fashion',[1] then the history of the right to health, which is yet to attract any close attention, is decidedly out of vogue. This treatment sits in stark contrast to the claim that 'the human right to health has moved to the centre of political debate and social policy across the globe'.[2] If it were true that the right to health had assumed such pre-eminence, it would be reasonable to assume that its status would have attracted greater interest from historians. But the reality is that the right to health remains relatively marginalized in political and social debates across the globe and this is partly because it is so poorly understood.[3] So if, as some historians suggest, the history of human rights can help us better understand the meaning of a right,[4] a study of the history of the right to health is both necessary and appropriate.

This chapter seeks to commence this task. Its aim is to reveal some insights into the factors that motivated the adoption of the right to health in international law and the anticipated consequences for states in accepting such a right. It consists of three parts.

---

[1] Samuel Moyn, 'On the Genealogy of Morals' (2007) 284 (15) The Nation 25, 31. This enterprise has largely emerged over the last decade or so. See, eg, Lynn Hunt, *Inventing Human Rights: A History* (Norton & Co, 2007); Samuel Moyn, *The Last Utopia: Human Rights in History* (Harvard University Press, 2010); Paul Lauren, *The Evolution of International Human Rights: Visions Seen* (3rd edn, University of Pennsylvania Press, 2011); Roland Burke, *Decolonization and the Evolution of International Human Rights* (University of Pennsylvania Press, 2010); William Korey, *NGOs and the Universal Declaration of Human Rights: A Curious Grapevine* (St Martin's Press, 1998); Michelle Ishay, *A History of Human Rights: From Ancient Times to the Globalization Era* (University of California Press, 2004); Roger Normand and Sarah Zaidi, *Human Rights at the UN: The Political History of Universal Justice* (Indiana University Press, 2008); Johannes Morsink, *The Universal Declaration of Human Rights: Origins, Drafting and Intent* (University of Pennsylvania, 1999); Thomas Buergenthal, 'The Normative and Institutional Evolution of International Human Rights' (1997) 19 Hum Rts Q 703; Stephen Marks, 'From the "Single Confused Page" to the "Decalogue for Six Billion Persons": The Roots of the Universal Declaration of Human Rights in the French Revolution' (1998) 20 Hum Rts Q 459.

[2] John Harrington and Maria Stuttaford, 'Introduction' in John Harrington and Maria Stuttaford (eds), *Global Health and Human Rights: Legal and Philosophical Perspectives* (Routledge, 2010) 1.

[3] See Introduction.

[4] Hunt, *Inventing Human Rights* (n 1) 19. See also Neil Stammers, 'A Critique of Social Approaches to Human Rights' (1995) 17 Hum Rts Q 488, 488 (argues that 'ideas and practices concerning human rights are *created* by people in particular historical, social, and economic circumstances'); cf Moyn, *The Last Utopia* (n 1) 225 (argues that '[i]nstead of turning to history to monumentalise human rights by rooting them deep in the past, it is much better to acknowledge how recent and contingent they really are').

First, it offers a chronological overview of the emergence of the normative expression of the right to health in various international and regional legal instruments. This discussion affirms that the right to health, like other economic and social rights, is now recognized as an *inalienable* international human right along with traditional civil and political rights. It does not, however, explain how the right to health came to be a twentieth century 'graft' on what is an 'essentially eighteenth century tree'.[5] This issue is the subject of examination in Part III of the chapter, which traces the complex factors that led to the inclusion of the right to health in international law. This discussion reveals that during World War II and its immediate aftermath, humanitarian concern and the activities of civil society combined with domestic and regional political agendas and global strategic considerations to provide the opportunity for the inclusion of health within international law.

Importantly, during this time the right to health was not simply seen as a noble aspiration or utopian goal—a perception that characterizes its contemporary understanding. On the contrary it was intimately linked, more so than other economic and social rights, with maintaining peace and security and was therefore considered to be of significant instrumental value. Moreover, the realization that the state had a duty to secure an individual's *right to health* was not—again as is often assumed—the product of communist ideology. On the contrary, the lineage of this right can be traced to a Latin American philosophy that sought to navigate between the consequences of extreme liberalism and collectivism to produce a form of social liberalism. It is also reflected in the values of the modern welfare state, which were affirmed most famously by Roosevelt in his Four Freedoms Speech in 1941. The genealogy of right to health is therefore tied less to an abstract ideology and more to the organic outcome of political struggles that were intent on delivering a pragmatic vision by which states could mitigate human suffering.

Part IV of this chapter deepens this understanding as to the role of the state with respect to its citizens by connecting the *history of the right to health* with the *history of public health*. The striking feature of this discussion is that throughout civilization there is evidence of an acceptance of the need for collective action to address the health of individuals. Such a sentiment alone did not necessitate the adoption of a right to health and much of the history of public health is actually motivated by anterior political and/or economic interests. Ultimately, it was the legacy of the Enlightenment period, especially the French revolutionaries, when combined with the subsequent failings of the Industrial revolution to deliver equality and alleviate poverty that inspired the clamour for public health measures to be provided as a human right. However, what the *history of public health* still reveals in terms of insights into the *history of the right to health*, is that societies have long accepted the necessity—whether for humanitarian, economic, and/or political reasons—of taking measures to protect the health of individuals.

Importantly, the transformation of this sentiment into a *human right* to health was not inevitable. On the contrary, the acceptance of the right to health in international

---

[5] Johannes Morsink, 'The Philosophy of the Universal Declaration' (1984) 6 Hum Rts Q 209, 310.

law was the product of a fragile and tentative international consensus that emerged in the wake of World War II, regarding the relationship between a state and its citizens. Under this model, the actions of states with respect to health were not to be reduced to mere instrumentalist considerations that served the interests of the state (or indeed elite groups). At the same time, it was never anticipated that the right to health would demand that the broader interests of states could be completely disregarded—a reality that is sometimes overlooked by over-enthusiastic advocates.[6] But the adoption of a human right to health in international law was still intended to radically transform and elevate the status of an individual within a state's decision-making process by imposing an obligation on states to take measures to protect and promote health as a matter of entitlement and not simply because it was in the state's interests to do so.

II From invisible to inalienable: the recognition of the right to health

In *Inventing Human Rights: A History*, Lynn Hunt starts her investigation into the history of human rights with Thomas Jefferson's first draft of the Declaration of Independence in 1776 in which he wrote:

We hold these truths to be sacred & undeniable, that all men are created equal & independant [sic], that from equal creation they derive rights inherent & inalienable, among which are the preservation of life, & liberty, & the pursuit of happiness.[7]

For other commentators the origins of contemporary human rights are to be found in the French *Declaration on the Rights of Man and of the Citizen* (1789), which declared that all men 'are born equal and remain free and equal in rights', such rights being 'natural and imprescriptible'.[8] Neither of these instruments, however, made

---

[6] See *Universal Declaration of Human Rights*, GA Res 217A (III), UN Doc A/810 (10 December 1948) art 22 (UDHR) (makes the realization of socio-economic rights, such as the right to health, conditional on the resources available to a State); art 29(2) (provides that all human rights are subject to limitations that are necessary for securing the rights and others and of meeting the just requirements of morality, public order, and the general welfare in a democratic society). See also Therese Murphy and Noel Whitty, 'Is Human Rights Prepared? Risk, Rights and Public Health Emergencies' (2009) 17 Med L Rev 219, 242 (challenges advocates to consider the adoption of an instrumentalist vision of rights to complement a normative vision of rights in the context of health); Hurst Hannum, 'Human Rights in Conflict Resolution: The Role of the Office of the High Commissioner for Human Rights in Peacemaking and Peacebuilding' (2006) 28 Hum Rts Q 1, 16 (discusses tendency of human rights advocates to be moralistic and unsympathetic to social and political realities); David Kennedy, *The Dark Side of Virtue: Reassessing International Humanitarianism* (Princeton University Press, 2004) (discusses the dangers that accompany enthusiasm in humanitarian endeavours and human rights advocacy).

[7] Hunt, *Inventing Human Rights* (n 1) 15. The final version of the *Declaration of Independence*, which was adopted by the US Congress on 14 July 1776, provides that:

We hold these truths to be self-evident, that all men are created equal, that they are endowed by their Creator with certain unalienable Rights, that among these are Life, Liberty and the pursuit of Happiness.

[8] *Declaration of the Rights of Man and of the Citizen* (France, 1789) preamble; art 1. See, eg, Marks (n 1) 459; Frede Castberg, 'Natural Law and Human Rights' in Asbjørn Eide and August Schou (eds), *International Protection of Human Rights* (Almquist & Wiksell, 1968) 19; Morsink, 'The Philosophy of

any reference to a right to health. The US Bill of Rights of 1791 was similarly silent, as were the English Magna Carta of 1215 and the English Bill of Rights of 1689, which excluded the right to health from the 'true, ancient and indubitable rights and liberties of the people'.[9] Although the French *Declaration* of 1793 did include what are now considered to be economic and social rights, such as education and social assistance, the right to health was not listed among them.[10]

Moving forward to 1946—170 years after Jefferson's Declaration—the Constitution of the World Health Organization was adopted.[11] This instrument expanded the list of inalienable rights by providing that:

The enjoyment of the highest attainable standard of health is one of the fundamental rights of every human being without distinction of race, religion, political belief, economic or social condition.

This broad formulation was subsequently overlooked when the *American Declaration on the Rights and Duties of Man* was adopted in 1948, but the idea of a right to health was still embraced in article XI, which provides that:

Every person has the right to the preservation of his health through sanitary and social measures relating to food, clothing, housing and medical care, to the extent permitted by public and community resources.[12]

When the *Universal Declaration of Human Rights* (UDHR) was adopted by the UN General Assembly in December 1948, although the right to health was not included as a specific right, it was not abandoned.[13] Instead, it was bundled together with a series of economic and social rights in article 25(1), which states:

---

the Universal Declaration' (n 5) 310–11 (notes comments of representatives to the Third Committee of the UN General Assembly that support the influence of eighteenth century declarations, especially the French Declaration); James Griffin, *On Human Rights* (OUP, 2008) 8. Other commentators commence their history of human rights by drawing parallels between human rights and the values underlying various systems of religious belief or ancient cultures. See, eg, Lauren (n 1) 5–17. There is, however, a danger in equating every vision of justice with human rights: Normand and Zaidi (n 1) 11. Moreover, the focus of this chapter is on understanding the emergence of the right to health as a *legal* concept. cf Moyn, 'On the Genealogy of Morals' (n 1) 29 (rejects placement of French Declaration at the origins of human rights today because 'it gave rise to nothing like the contemporary human rights movement').

[9] Hunt, *Inventing Human Rights* (n 1) 114.

[10] The *French Declaration of the Rights of Man and Citizen of 1793* does address matters that would now be classified as economic and social rights. For example, article 21 provides that '[p]ublic relief is a sacred debt. Society owes maintenance to unfortunate citizens, either procuring work for them or in providing the means of existence for those who are unable to labor'; article 22 provides that '[e]ducation is needed by all. Society ought to favor with all its power the advancement of the public reason and to put education at the door of every citizen' and article 23 states that '[t]he social guarantee consists in the action of all to secure to each the enjoyment and the maintenance of his rights: this guarantee rests upon the national sovereignty'. But there is no explicit reference to the right to health or access to medical care.

[11] Constitution of the World Health Organization (New York, 22 July 1946, entered into force 7 April 1948, 14 UNTS 185).

[12] *American Declaration of the Rights and Duties of Man*, OAS Res XXX (Ninth International Conference of American States, 1948) (emphasis added).

[13] *Universal Declaration of Human Rights*, UNGA Res 217A (III), UN Doc A/810 (10 December 1948).

Everyone has the right to a standard of living adequate for the *health and well-being of himself* and of his family, including food, clothing, housing and medical care and necessary social services...[14]

In 1966, when the International Covenant on Economic, Social and Cultural Rights (ICESCR) was adopted, the 'right to the highest attainable of health' asserted its independent status on the international stage in the following formulation:

1. The States Parties to the present Covenant recognize the right of everyone to the enjoyment of the highest attainable standard of physical and mental health.
2. The steps to be taken by the States Parties to the present Covenant to achieve the full realization of this right shall include those necessary for:
   (a) The provision for the reduction of the stillbirth-rate and of infant mortality and for the healthy development of the child;
   (b) The improvement of all aspects of environmental and industrial hygiene;
   (c) The prevention, treatment and control of epidemic, endemic, occupational and other diseases;
   (d) The creation of conditions which would assure to all medical service and medical attention in the event of sickness.[15]

This normative commitment to the right to health in international law was maintained in the subsequent adoption of other international human rights treaties such as the CERD,[16] the CEDAW,[17] the CRC,[18] the CRMWF,[19] and the CRPD,[20] which affirm and expand the application of the right to health as it applies to discrete groups.[21]

---

[14] See Brigit Toebes, *The Right to Health as a Human Right in International Law* (Hart Publishing, 1999) 36–40 (provides an overview of the drafting history of the right to health in the UDHR; notes that although consideration was given to adopting the formulation used in the WHO Constitution this approach was rejected on the basis that it was too general and too vague; the focus was therefore shifted to an inclusion of several social determinants of health).

[15] International Covenant on Economic, Social and Cultural Rights (ICESCR) (adopted 16 December 1966, entered into force 3 January 1976, 993 UNTS 3) art 12. See Benjamin Meier, 'Global Health Governance and the Contentious Politics of Human Rights: Mainstreaming the Right to Health for Public Health Advancement' (2010) 46 Stan J Intl L 1 (provides detailed examination of the drafting history of article 12 albeit with a focus on the role of the WHO).

[16] International Convention on the Elimination of All Forms of Racial Discrimination (CERD) (New York, 21 December 1995, entered into force 4 January 1969, 660 UNTS 195). See also *Declaration on the Rights of Indigenous Peoples*, GA Res 61/295, UN Doc A/RES/61/295 (13 September 2007) annex, arts 17 (2), 21, 23, 24, 29.

[17] Convention on the Elimination of All Forms of Discrimination against Women (CEDAW) (New York, 18 December 1979, entered into force 3 September 1981, 1249 UNTS 13) arts 12(1), (2).

[18] Convention on the Rights of the Child (CRC) (New York, 20 November 1989, entered into force 2 September 1990, 1577 UNTS 3) art 24. See also the *Declaration of the Rights of the Child*, UNGA Res 1386 (XIV), UN Doc A/4354 (20 November 1959) 19, principles 2, 4, 5, 9.

[19] International Convention on the Protection of the Rights of All Migrant Workers and Members of their Families (CRMWF) (New York, 18 December 1990, entered into force 1 July 2003, 2220 UNTS 3) arts 25, 28, 43(1)(e), 45(1)(c).

[20] Convention on the Rights of Persons with Disabilities (CRPD) (New York, 13 December 2006, entered into force 3 May 2008, UN Doc Doc A/61/611) art 25.

[21] See Appendix 1 for the full text of the relevant articles. See Toebes (n 14) 40–62 (provides an overview of the drafting history of these instruments).

Moreover, at the regional level the right to health can also be found in various formulations—its inherent, essential, or inalienable status acclaimed—within instruments such as the European Social Charter;[22] the African Charter on Human and People's Rights;[23] the African Charter on the Rights and Welfare of the Child;[24] and the Additional Protocol to the American Convention on Human Rights in the area of Economic, Social and Cultural Rights, which is generally referred to as the Protocol of San Salvador.[25]

But what caused this revelation whereby health emerged from virtual obscurity within rights discourse to become an inalienable human right? In the time that elapsed between Jefferson's *Declaration* and the WHO Constitution, fierce debates had raged among Western philosophers about the significance of rights—consider for example, Mary Wollstonecraft's *Vindication of the Rights of Women*;[26] Thomas Paine's *Rights of Man*;[27] Jeremy Bentham's often quoted disdain of natural rights as 'nonsense upon stilts';[28] and Pasquale Fiore's *Le droit international codifie et sa sanction juriduque*.[29] But these debates, which had all but disappeared by the end of the nineteenth century as 'the consolidation of state power took precedence over theories of the individual',[30] never engaged with the idea of a right to health. Thus, the question remains, what factors led to its debut and repeat appearances in international legal instruments in the middle and later part of the twentieth century?

III The origins of the right to health

A The need to navigate the dangers of excessive liberalism and collectivism

As has already been noted, scholars have tended to overlook the history of the right to health and indeed the broader class of economic and social rights to which it

---

[22] European Social Charter (Turin, 18 October 1961, entered into force 26 February 1965, 529 UNTS 89) art 11.

[23] African Charter on Human and Peoples' Rights (African Charter) (Nairobi, 27 June 1981, entered into force 21 October 1986, 1520 UNTS 217) art 16.

[24] African Charter on the Rights and Welfare of the Child (Addis Ababa, 1 July 1990, entered into force 29 November 1999, OAU Doc CAB/LEG/24.9/49) art 14.

[25] Additional Protocol to the American Convention on Human Rights in the Area of Economic, Social and Cultural Rights (Protocol of San Salvador) (San Salvador, 17 November 1988, entered into force 16 November 1999, OAS Treaty Series No 69 (1988), 28 ILM 156) art 10. See Appendix 1 for the full text of the relevant articles. See Toebes (n 14) 63–73 (provides a brief overview of these instruments).

[26] Mary Wollstonecraft, *A Vindication of the Rights of Women* (1792) (2nd edn, Penguin Books, 1992).

[27] Thomas Paine, *Rights of Man* (1791) (Penguin Books, 1984).

[28] Jeremy Bentham, 'Anarchical Fallacies; Being an Examination of The Declarations of Rights Issued during the French Revolution' in John Bowring (ed), *The Works of Jeremy Bentham* (William Tait, 1843) vol II, 501.

[29] Cited in Martii Koskenniemi, *The Gentle Civiliser of Nations: The Rise and Fall of International Law from 1870–1960* (CUP, 2001) 54 (notes that Fiore identified six fundamental rights—personal freedom and inviolability; the right to civil liberty and nationality; the rights to emigration, commerce, property, and the freedom of conscience).

[30] Normand and Zaidi (n 1) 15.

belongs.[31] For example, Hunt's history of human rights provides no insight into the emergence of this class of rights.[32] She manages to identify the remarkable expansion in the list of inalienable rights under the UDHR, but offers no insight into how this came to pass and fails to even mention the right to health.[33] Paul Lauren at least links, albeit in a very cursory way, the existence of contemporary economic and social rights to the legacy of the social entitlements provided for under the 1791 French *Declaration*.[34] He also makes some passing references to the right to health, but he provides no real explanation as to how this concept actually emerged.[35] Johannes Morsink's examination of the history of the UDHR in *The Universal Declaration of Human Rights: Origins, Drafting and Intent* (1999) is slightly more helpful. He suggests that the inclusion of the right to medical care in the UDHR, like the rights to food and shelter, 'came from the Latin American socialist tradition'.[36] In doing so he seeks to displace the common assumption that economic and social rights were largely the result of communist influence.[37]

---

[31] Some commentators offer some discussion as to the history of the right to health. See, eg, Toebes (n 14) 7–16 (provides a rudimentary overview); Dorothy Porter, *Health, Civilisation and the State: A History of Public Health from Ancient to Modern Times* (Routledge, 1999) 63–162 (offers a more sophisticated examination of the history of public health within the context of the modern state but the treatment of the right to health as a legal concept is overlooked); Lauren (n 1) 75, 115 (offers some passing references to the right to health); Christopher Hamlin, 'The History and Development of Public Health in Developed Countries' in Roger Detels and others, *Oxford Textbook on Public Health Volume 1: The Scope of Public Health* (5th edn, OUP, 2009) 20, 28 (simply notes that the history of the right to health was gradual, piecemeal, complicated, and even fundamentally conflictual); Benjamin Meier, 'The World Health Organization, the Evolution of Human Rights and the Failure to Achieve Health for All' in John Harrington and Maria Stuttaford, *Global Health and Human Rights: Legal and Philosophical Perspectives* (Routledge, 2010) 163 (examines the contribution of the WHO to the development of the right to health); Ruth Roemer, 'The Right to Health Care' in Hernán Fuenzalida-Puelma and Susan Connor (eds), *The Right to Health in the Americas: A Comparative Constitutional Study* (PAHO, 1989) 17, 18. Although there is as yet no comprehensive treatment of the history of economic social and cultural rights, it has received some limited attention from scholars. See, eg, Normand and Zaidi (n 1) 98–9; 188–92, 200–8; Marks (n 1) 502–8; Daniel Whelan and Jack Donnelly, 'The West, Economic and Social Rights and the Global Human Rights Regime: Setting the Record Straight' (2007) 29 Hum Rts Q 908 (discuss adoption of economic and social rights in the UDHR and impact of the welfare state on the emergence of economic and social rights); Alex Kirkup and Tony Evans, 'The Myth of Western Opposition to Economic, Social, and Cultural Rights? A Reply to Whelan and Donnelly' (2009) 31 Hum Rts Q 221 (examine history of Western resistance to economic and social rights); Daniel Whelan and Jack Donnelly, 'Yes, a Myth: A Reply to Kirkup and Evans' (2009) 31 Hum Rts Q 239 (challenging the claim that West is resistant to economic and social rights); Lauren (n 1) 294 (notes that the 'energies expended to advance economic and social rights first resulted from the extent of massive suffering on the part of men, women and children exploited by the industrial revolution').

[32] See Moyn, 'On the Genealogy of Morals' (n 1) 26 (criticizes Hunt's focus on bodily integrity and her failure to address the pressure for economic and social rights).

[33] Hunt, *Inventing Human Rights* (n 1) 204.

[34] Lauren (n 1) 18.

[35] ibid 74, 116, 117, 125, 213 (most of the references are superficial and unaccompanied by references to any supporting documentation).

[36] Morsink, *The Universal Declaration of Human Rights* (n 1) 192.

[37] See, eg, Matthew Craven, *The International Covenant on Economic Social and Cultural Rights: A Perspective on its Development* (Clarendon Press, 1995) 9 (suggests that Soviet Union championed the cause of economic and social rights but omits any reference to the Latin American influence); Aryeh Neier, 'Social and Economic Rights: A Critique' 13 Hum Rts Brief (2006); Ruth Gavison, 'On the Relationship

Morsink's link between economic and social rights and the experiences of Latin America is well founded but his association of these rights with socialism is problematic. A more complex explanation is required which reveals that the ancestry of the right to health is deeply wedded to the need to adopt a pragmatic vision of how best to alleviate human suffering and address inequality. The rise of communism and socialism during the nineteenth century may have been the result of the 'perceived limitations of constitutionally framed' civil and political rights.[38] But neither of these movements embraced the idea of rights as a mechanism to address economic and social considerations. Marx was dismissive of the concept of rights[39] and early socialist ideology, with its focus on the interests of the collective, was no more enthusiastic.[40] At the same time, as Hunt points out, these movements did raise 'two enduring questions about rights: were political rights enough and could the individual's right to protection of private property co-exist with society's need to foster the well being of its less fortunate members?'[41] It was the need to resolve these questions that helped shape the emergence of a distinctive philosophy of rights within Latin American nations as they gained independence in the nineteenth century.

Contrary to what has been suggested by Morsink, this philosophy cannot be reduced to a form of Latin American socialism.[42] Mary Ann Glendon's examination of the history of human rights in Latin America reveals a much more complex explanation in which a variety of sources are relied upon—comparative legal systems, political thought, philosophy, religious beliefs, historical developments, and local values—to produce a distinctive Latin American approach to human rights.[43] Significantly this approach was not the product of Marxist or socialist ideology. Instead, it relied heavily on Catholic teachings with respect to human dignity and

---

between Civil and Political Rights and Social and Economic Rights' in Jean-Marc Coicaud, Michael W Doyle, Anne-Marie Gardner (eds), *The Globalization of Human Rights* (United Nations University Press, 2003) 54 n 46; Maurice Cranston, 'Human Rights, Real and Supposed' in DD Raphel (ed), *Political Theory and the Rights of Man* (MacMillan, 1967) 43–53.

[38] Hunt, *Inventing Human Rights* (n 1) 196.

[39] Karl Marx, 'On the Jewish Question' (1843) ('None of the supposed rights of man go beyond the egoistic man ... that is, an individual withdrawn into himself, into the confines of his private interests and private caprice, and separated from the community') <http://www.marxists.org/archive/marx/works/1844/jewish-question/> accessed 26 August 2010. See also Kenneth Baynes, 'Rights as Critique and the Critique of Rights: Karl Marx, Wendy Brown and the Social Function of Rights' (2000) 28 Pol Theory 451; Marks (n 1) 474–9.

[40] Hunt, *Inventing Human Rights* (n 1) 197; Tom Campbell, *The Left and Rights: A Conceptual Analysis of the Idea of Socialist Rights* (Routledge, 1983) ch 6 (provides analysis of the competing visions of human rights within socialist ideology).

[41] Hunt, *Inventing Human Rights* (n 1) 197.

[42] Morsink, *The Universal Declaration of Human Rights* (n 1) 130.

[43] Mary Ann Glendon, 'The Forgotten Crucible: The Latin American Influence on the Universal Human Rights Idea' (2003) 16 Harv Hum Rts J 27. See also Paolo Carozza, 'From Conquest to Constitutions: Retrieving a Latin American Tradition of the Idea of Human Rights' (2003) 25 Hum Rts Q 281, 288 (offers detailed history of the development of human rights within Latin America).

social justice which sought to avoid what Pope Pius XI described as the 'twin rocks of shipwreck', namely extreme individualism and collectivism.[44]

The first normative expression of this endeavour within Latin America was the adoption by Mexico of a Constitution in 1917, which included provisions that dealt with economic and social entitlements. It did not include a specific right to health, but it did include provisions which entitled women 'to medical and obstetrical attention', medicines, nursing aid, and infant care services; medicines and medical attention for members of a worker's family;[45] an obligation on the part of the state to take preventive measures in relation to diseases and epidemics;[46] and the 'prohibition of unhealthful (sic) or dangerous work'.[47] Although this Constitution is often seen as reflecting socialist ideology,[48] again, such a perception is misleading and simplistic.[49] An examination of its drafting history provides no evidence of a commitment to such a vision.[50] Indeed, if a theme can be said to exist, it is that all individuals are to have rights, *including civil and political rights*, which are provided with extensive protection under the Mexican Constitution.[51] Moreover, as Carozza has pointed out, the principles adopted under the Mexican Constitution were 'borrowed or imitated in varying degree by virtually every Latin American constitution... and made themselves felt in the next wave of European constitutionalism too'.[52] Thus, they were not confined to socialist states, and countries such as Bolivia, Brazil, Chile, Cuba, Honduras, Panama, Paraguay, Peru, and Uruguay adopted constitutions that 'either stated an explicit right to health care or had such a right imbedded in clauses about the duties of the government.'[53]

The emergence of economic and social rights, and more specifically the right to health as a contemporary *legal concept*, therefore owes much to the Latin American philosophy of human rights. Importantly, this philosophy was not, as Carozzo has argued, 'the product of a general theory nor the mechanical importation of foreign ideas but rather the tangible experience of the Revolution' and the need to respond to address the human needs of the poor and working class.[54] It was an organic movement born out of a local struggle and the desire to achieve and deliver an alternative vision of justice and equality. This vision of 'social liberalism'[55] produced a form of constitutionalism that was quite different to the Western tradition that had been spawned by the American and French declarations. However, this *national* and *regional* trend within Latin American does not explain how health came to be accepted as an inalienable human right in *international law*—a more detailed explanation is required.

---

[44] Cited in Glendon (n 43) 36. See also Carozza (n 43) 311 (refers to the need to navigate between 'brutally atomistic liberal capitalism' and 'excessive socialist collectivism').
[45] Constitution of Mexico 1917, art 123 B. XI (1).
[46] ibid art 73 XVI (2).   [47] ibid art 123 A II.
[48] See, eg, Glendon (n 43) 35.
[49] Carozza (n 43) 305.
[50] ibid 305–6.   [51] ibid.   [52] ibid 304.
[53] Morsink, *The Universal Declaration of Human Rights* (n 1) 192. See also Fuenzalida-Puelma and Connor (n 31).
[54] Carozza (n 43) 307.   [55] ibid 311.

B The nexus between war, rights, health, and peace

1 World War I—the seeds of a rights revolution

The explanation for the ultimate adoption of the right to health in international law is intimately connected with the occurrence of war and the strategic role of health in achieving and maintaining global peace. The Great War of 1914 to 1918 provided the stimulus for the creation of the League of Nations (LON) whose Covenant was adopted on 28 April 1919.[56] Although human rights were not part of the League's vision for a peaceful world, the need to attend to the health of individuals was considered to be central. Article 23 of the Covenant of the LON required states to provide humane conditions of work and 'take steps in matters of international concern for the prevention and control of disease'. Article 25 provided that:

> The Members of the League agree to encourage and promote the establishment and co-operation of duly authorised voluntary national Red Cross organisations having as purposes the improvement of health, the prevention of disease, and the mitigation of suffering throughout the world.[57]

The primary purposes of the LON were strategic and political—namely to achieve peace and security and preserve state sovereignty. But the call to mitigate suffering in article 25 also reflected humanitarian concerns in relation to the appalling state of health in war-ravaged countries.[58]

Among the various bodies created under the auspices of the LON was the Health Organisation—a body which was established in 1920 and co-existed with the Office International d'Hygiène Publique, which had been set up in 1907 largely to address the spread of communicable diseases.[59] (Both bodies were effectively absorbed into and replaced by the World Health Organization after World War II.)[60] Significantly, the Health Organisation of the LON enjoyed 'unstinted support' among nations and

---

[56] See FP Walters, *A History of the League of Nations* (OUP, 1960).

[57] ibid 60 (notes that this provision was included at the request of the International Committee of Red Cross societies).

[58] WHO, *The First Ten Years of the World Health Organization* (WHO, 1958) 22.

[59] For a detailed history of both bodies see WHO, *First Ten Years* (n 58) 15–27. Lauren has suggested that the mandate of the International Office of Public Health was to advocate for a global right to health: Lauren (n 1) 74. But he provides no evidence to support this claim and the better view is that the role of the Office was to disseminate to States information on public health, especially communicable diseases: WHO, *First Ten Years* (n 58) 17. This is because at the time, international measures in the field of public health were not motivated by the idea of an inalienable right to health. Rather it was the needs of Western states to guard against the 'exotic diseases' that 'are or may become a permanent threat to civilised states' that inspired such collective action: Professor Rocco Santoliquido, President of the Office, cited in WHO, *First Ten Years* (n 58) 18. The same rationale had informed the international sanitary movement and global health governance which emerged in 1851 with the first International Sanitary Conference: David Fidler, 'Fighting the Axis of Illness: HIV/AIDS, Human Rights and US Foreign Policy' (2004) 17 Har Hum Rts J 99, 108; Toebes (n 14) 12. For a history of this movement see: Norman Howard Jones, *The Scientific Background of the International Sanitary Conferences 1851–1938* (WHO, 1975).

[60] Walters (n 56) 182.

'showed the way' in terms of the capacity for international collaboration and support in relation to public health matters.[61] It adopted a 'broad outlook on health questions' and looked beyond issues such as the control of epidemics to consider issues such as non-communicable diseases, housing, physical fitness, rural hygiene, medical and public health training, and social diseases such as malnutrition.[62] The seeds of concern for the social determinants of health, which characterize contemporary understandings as to the nature of the right to health as expressed in the ICESCR and the CRC, were therefore sown well before the right to health was adopted in international law.

With the onset of World War II, the suspicion of many that the LON was incapable of maintaining international peace and security was confirmed. However, the work of its Health Organisation demonstrated not only an awareness among states of the need to address health concerns collaboratively, but also the capacity to undertake the measures required to achieve this purpose. Such measures may not have been motivated by the existence of an explicit human right to health or indeed an international obligation to co-operate to secure the enjoyment of this right. Other factors such as political and strategic interests and advances in medical knowledge inspired such collaborative measures. But the foundations from which the right to health were to emerge had been established. The first signs of this development can be seen in the adoption of the Declaration on the Rights of the Child by the LON in 1929, in which states accepted their duty to ensure that the hungry child is fed, the sick child helped, and the orphaned child sheltered.[63] Unfortunately it was to take the catastrophic events of World War II to catapult these tentative beginnings into a right to health for all individuals in international law.[64]

2 World War II—a rebirth for rights

In the context of World War II and the history of human rights, special significance is attached to the contribution of the US President Franklin D Roosevelt in his State of the Union address in 1941.[65] This speech, which was motivated by the

---

[61] ibid 182–3. See also Lauren (n 1) 116 (notes that the Health Organization 'became one of the most successful operations' of the LON).

[62] WHO, *First Ten Years* (n 58) 29–30.

[63] The LON also established an Advisory Committee for Child Welfare, which examined matters pertaining to the health of children in early infancy, starvation and homelessness, blindness and sickness: Lauren (n 1) 116.

[64] See Morsink, *The Universal Declaration of Human Rights* (n 1) 36–91 (examines the role of World War II as a catalyst for the UDHR and the rights which were included in this instrument); John Humphrey, *Human Rights and the United Nations: A Great Adventure* (Transnational, 1984) 10–13; Normand and Zaidi (n 1) 81–106; Louis Henkin, *The Age of Rights* (Columbia University Press, 1990) 1.

[65] Franklin D Roosevelt, *The State of the Union Address to Congress*, 6 January 1941, in Samuel Rosenman (ed), *The Public Papers and Addresses of Franklin D Roosevelt* (Random House, 1938–1950) 672. See Daniel Whelan and Jack Donnelly, 'Setting the Record Straight' (n 31) 911–13 (discuss significance of Roosevelt's speech); cf Alex Kirkup and Tony Evans (n 31) 226 (argue that the reference to freedom from want did not advocate economic and social rights but the need to adopt a particular economic order). The approach of Kirkup and Evans, however, tends to overlook the fact that the speech is deeply embedded not only in the need to adopt a particular global economic order but the need to protect human rights. In the mind of Roosevelt, freedom meant 'the supremacy of human rights everywhere'.

'unprecedented' threat to American security posed by the war,[66] outlined Roosevelt's famous Four Freedoms including:

freedom from want—which, translated into world terms, means economic understandings which will secure to every nation a *healthy peacetime life* for its inhabitants—everywhere in the world.[67]

Roosevelt's vision, which included a call to 'widen the opportunities for adequate medical care',[68] struck a chord with the American people as they emerged from the Great Depression. But its significance exceeded its resonance within the US domestic political economy. It radically transformed the nature of the relationship between the state and its people 'by establishing a system of public responsibility to provide individuals with entitlements to unemployment compensation, social security and other matters of general welfare'.[69] An acceptance was therefore growing that states had an obligation to attend to the economic and social needs of their constituents not simply for instrumentalist considerations but as a matter of human rights.[70] Moreover, the protection of human rights, including economic and social rights, was not simply seen as an abstract utopian goal but a precondition for global peace and security.[71]

Importantly, this vision was not confined to the USA and Latin American nations, which had already come to this realization many years earlier. It was also extending to Europe. For example, the British historian EH Carr wrote of an empty form of democracy which recognizes 'the right to vote but forgets the right to work and the right to live'.[72] The work of Sir Hersch Lauterpacht—one of the most influential international law scholars of his generation[73]—was especially relevant in this regard when he proposed in 1943 an International Bill of Rights, which covered both civil and political rights and economic and social rights including an obligation on states

---

Thus the better view is that the protection of human rights and the adoption of a particular economic order were considered to be complementary rather than mutually exclusive.

[66] Franklin Roosevelt, *The State of the Union Address to Congress* (n 65).
[67] ibid (emphasis added).   [68] ibid.
[69] Normand and Zaidi (n 1) 88.
[70] Whelan and Donnelly, 'Setting the Record Straight' (n 31) 913 (argue that the US and indeed Britain 'placed economic and social rights at the center of their post war visions of domestic and international order'). cf Kirkup and Evans (n 31) 226.
[71] Humphrey (n 64) 32 (notes that of the four principles that had been proposed for the preamble—no peace unless human rights are respected; man does not only have rights but duties; man is a citizen not only of the state but the world and there can be neither human freedom nor dignity unless war and the threat of war are abolished—only one was included in the UDHR, the 'the one which said that respect for human rights is the foundation of peace'). See also Normand and Zaidi (n 1) 23. But note that when the US, UK and USSR met in 1940 to chart a new international organization, human rights were dropped from the agenda only to be reinstated 'after concerted lobbying by civil society groups and smaller nations especially the Latin Americans': Normand and Zaidi (n 1) 23.
[72] Normand and Zaidi (n 1) 98.
[73] Marks (n 1) 474.

'within the limits of their economic capacity' to make provision for employment, education, and public assistance in the case of sickness and disablement.[74]

A tide was therefore surging and with it was being carried the promise of an international bill of human rights including economic and social rights. A critical contribution of this movement was the preparation of a statement of *Essential Human Rights* by a committee appointed by the American Law Institute (ALI) in 1944.[75] This committee drew heavily on national constitutions, including those of Latin American states, to produce a declaration in 1946 that was intended to reflect universal trends and have broad appeal.[76] Although many draft texts of the UDHR were submitted to the UN, John Humphrey, the man tasked with the responsibility for preparing the first draft as head of the UN Human Rights Division, has written that, '[t]he best of the texts from which I worked was the one prepared by the American Law Institute and I borrowed freely from it'.[77] Moreover, this text cannot be reduced to an expression of the 'visionary aspirations of the political left' and instead reflected 'a mainstream elite exposition of the emerging pattern of American and broader Western ideals and practice'.[78]

With respect to the history of the right to health, the ALI statement may not have included such a right explicitly, but the right to social security did include a requirement that:

The state has a duty to maintain or insure that there are maintained comprehensive arrangements for the promotion of health, for the prevention of sickness and accident and the provision of medical care...

Roosevelt's vision as to the role of the state and the Latin American philosophy of human rights loom large both in the formulation of this right and the following 'comment' which accompanied the ALI statement:

The duties imposed upon the state by this article are to see that resources of society are organised:
to raise standards of health
to prevent sickness and accident
to provide medical care wherever needed including maternity cases...[79]

---

[74] Hersch Lauterpacht, *An International Bill of the Rights of Man* (Columbia University Press, 1945) 155. See also Hersch Lauterpacht, *International Law and Human Rights* (Archon Books, 1968) 354–5. See Normand and Zaidi (n 1) 99 (note that 'the acceptance of social and economic rights by a prominent liberal jurist such as Lauterpacht demonstrated the changed mood throughout Europe'); Korey (n 1) 34 (notes that the American Jewish Committee also supported Lauterpacht's work and called for an international bill of rights including an appeal that was signed by 1,300 'distinguished Americans of all faiths and races').

[75] Whelan and Donnelly, 'Setting the Record Straight' (n 31) 917–19.

[76] Committee of Advisors on Essential Human Rights, American Law Institute, 'Statement of Essential Human Rights' (1946) 243 Annals Am Acad Pol & Soc Sci 18.

[77] Humphrey (n 64) 32.

[78] Whelan and Donnelly, 'Setting the Record Straight' (n 31) 919.

[79] *Statement of Essential Human Rights*, art 15, in Committee of Advisers on Essential Human Rights, American Law Institute (n 76) 24–5.

Given the influence of the ALI statement on Humphrey's thinking, it is not surprising that his first draft of the UDHR included a right to medical care, especially given his admission in his biography that he already determined to include economic and social rights in his draft text before undertaking this task.[80]

Ultimately these factors—the national constitutions of Latin American states, the vision of Roosevelt, the enthusiasm of civil society and religious groups,[81] the work of the ALI members, and the preferences of Humphrey—were not sufficient to guarantee the right to health and other economic and social rights safe passage into the final text of the UDHR. But before turning to a discussion of how the right to health came to find a place in the UDHR, which was adopted in 1948, it is necessary to examine the impact of another intervening act which is of major significance to the emergence of the right to health in international law—namely the adoption of the Constitution of the World Health Organization in 1946.

C The WHO and the right to the highest attainable standard of health

As the work of the LON demonstrates, states had accepted the instrumental significance of health in maintaining international peace and security. This understanding was not abandoned when the UN Charter was adopted in 1945. Among those areas listed under article 55 of the UN Charter, in which international cooperation between states is necessary to ensure conditions for peaceful and friendly relations between states, is the need to find solutions to health problems.[82] In order to achieve this goal it was recommended in a declaration from Brazil and China to the San Francisco Conference in 1945, which was unanimously approved, that proceedings be commenced for the establishment of an international health organization.[83]

The product of these further proceedings was the creation of the World Health Organization in 1946. It is the preamble of the WHO Constitution that introduces for the first time into international law, the idea of the right to the highest attainable standard of health. The origins of this phrase can be traced to drafts of the preamble *and* the aims and objectives of the WHO Constitution, which were prepared in March 1946 by sub-committees of the Technical Preparatory Committee for the International Health Conference held in June–July 1946. The draft preamble included the phrase; '[t]he right to health is one of the fundamental rights to which every human being, without distinction as to race, sex, language or religion, is entitled'; and the draft aims and objectives included, '[t]o improve physical and

---

[80] Humphrey (n 64) 2.

[81] Normand and Ziadi (n 1) 127–9 (note that Jewish and Christian groups were the most organized of the civil society and faith-based organizations).

[82] The inclusion of health in art 55 is said to have been a direct result of a memorandum submitted by the Brazilian delegation in which it quoted Cardinal (then Archbishop) Spellman that: 'Medicine is one of the pillars of peace': WHO, *First Ten Years* (n 58) 38 ('health of all peoples ... seen to be fundamental to the attainment of peace and security.')

[83] WHO, *First Ten Years* (n 58).

mental health in order to establish "positive health" amongst all peoples'.[84] There is nothing in the Official Minutes of the meetings of the Preparatory Committee to suggest that either of these proposals were considered to be contentious by any members of the Committee. Indeed, in the final draft of the WHO Constitution submitted by the Preparatory Committee to the Economic and Social Council, the reference to the right to health was retained in the preamble and the proposal for the aims and objectives of the WHO was modified to read, 'to achieve the highest possible state of physical and mental health for all peoples'.[85]

The Official Records of the WHO indicate that this commitment to the ideas of the right to health and achieving the highest possible state of health for individuals, were maintained when states met and adopted the final constitution of the WHO at the International Health Conference. President Truman of the USA, in an opening message to representatives at the conference, declared that:

The right to adequate medical care *and* the opportunity to achieve and enjoy good health should be available to all people. For this objective I can assure you the interest and the support of the United States.[86]

Again, as with the preparatory meeting, nothing is recorded in the minutes of the meetings for the conference to suggest that the idea of a right to health was considered to be controversial.[87] Moreover, the extension of this right to something more than medical care was confirmed by the adoption of a recommendation by the Canadian representative that a simple formula for expressing the overarching objective of the WHO be reduced to the following phrase:

The objective of the World Health Organization ... shall be the attainment by all peoples of the highest possible level of health.[88]

---

[84] WHO, *Official Records of the World Health Organization No 1: Minutes of the Technical Preparatory Committee for the International Health Conference Held in Paris from 18 March to 5 April 1946* (UN WHO Interim Commission October 1947) annexes 10, 11. The Preparatory Committee was comprised of State representatives who were drawn from the field of public health in Belgium, Mexico, Canada, Argentina, Czechoslovakia, France, Egypt, Norway, England, Poland, Greece, India, USA, Brazil, Yugoslavia, and China. It is unclear from the Official Minutes which member of the sub-committee responsible for drafting the preamble initiated the reference to the right to health (this sub-committee was comprised of representatives from China, Canada, Argentina, and Czechoslovakia). Similarly there is no indication of dispute as to the scope of the WHO's intended aims within the sub-committee responsible for drafting the aims of objectives of the WHO (this sub-committee was comprised of representatives from Belgium, France, Egypt, Norway, England, Poland, Greece, India, USA, Brazil, and Yugoslavia). Interestingly of the four states that submitted draft proposals for consideration by the Preparatory Committee (France, USA, England, Yugoslavia), none made any reference to a right to health.

[85] ibid annex 23.

[86] WHO, *Official Records of the World Health Organization No 2: Proceedings and Final Acts of the International Health Conference Held in New York from 19 June to 22 July 1946* (UN WHO Interim Commission June 1948) 31.

[87] ibid 44–6.

[88] ibid 16, 49 (indicates that this recommendation was approved without any discussion).

Charting the History of the Right to Health

This degree of consensus is quite remarkable and contrasts sharply with the status of the right to health in contemporary settings.[89]

However, an examination of the history of the WHO Constitution also reveals that the commitment to the idea of a right to the highest attainable standard of health for individuals was accompanied by a strong appeal to the instrumentalist dimensions of health. This is evident in the draft of the WHO Constitution prepared by the Preparatory Committee which included in the preamble a statement that '[h]ealth is an essential factor in the attainment of security and well being for individuals and nations'.[90] Moreover, this sentiment carried favour with the delegates to the International Health Conference as illustrated by the inclusion alongside the right to the highest attainable standard of health in the final preamble to the WHO Constitution of the ideas that 'The health of all peoples is fundamental to the attainment of peace and security and is dependent upon the fullest co-operation of individuals and States' and 'The achievement of any State in the promotion and protection of health is of value to all.'[91]

The right to health was therefore considered to be both normative and instrumental. It imposed an obligation on states to act individually and collectively in order to fulfil not only the right to health of individuals but also to satisfy the strategic interests of states *and* the broader community. Interestingly, the history of the WHO is not suggestive of any concerns among states as to the potential for interests within this model to come into conflict. The interdependence of these potentially conflicting interests could possibly be seen as a reflection of the goodwill and commitment by states to harness their collective capacities and work collaboratively to improve global health outcomes in the post war era.[92] Indeed, it is worth noting that the drafting of the WHO Constitution was dominated by public health and medical experts who shared a strong commitment to collaboration[93] and a confidence in the capacity of medical science to provide the means by which to service the interests of all parties.[94] In any event, the consensus about the significance of the right to health during the drafting of the WHO Constitution was replaced in

---

[89] WHO, *First Ten Years* (n 58) 44–5 (notes that delegations from all 51 members of the United Nations were present at the Conference in addition to 13 non-Member states and managed to reach agreement within four and a half weeks).

[90] WHO, *Official Records No 1* (n 84) annex 10.

[91] WHO Constitution, preamble.

[92] This commitment to collaboration was noticed by the Observer from Ireland, Dr MacCormack, who remarked that the International Health Conference 'had not only had a common objective, but also something more—a real faith in a love of their life's work. The sacrifices made for the sake of unanimity had not gone unnoticed...': WHO, *Official Records No 2* (n 86) 90. See also the closing address to the Conference from the President who described the WHO Constitution as a Magna Carta for health: 94–6.

[93] All the members of the Technical Preparatory Committee were public health experts (see WHO, *Official Records No 1* (n 84) 5) as were a large number of the delegates at the International Health Conference (see WHO, *Official Records No 2* (n 86) 7–13).

[94] WHO, *First Ten Years* (n 58) 38 (is suggestive of an expectation and faith in the capacity of scientific advancements to address post war concerns).

the years that followed by a greater level of anxiety during the drafting of the UDHR and beyond.[95]

D The adoption of the UDHR and its aftermath—a common enemy unites then the Cold War divides

The final text of the UDHR makes it clear that both sets of rights are included and thus considered to be inalienable in international law. But as Humphrey has explained, the reality is that '[t]here was significant opposition in the drafting committee' to the inclusion of economic and social rights especially from the USA and United Kingdom.[96] Ultimately this opposition was muted, not simply by the influence of the Latin American and Soviet voting blocs, but a common and resolute commitment by all states to denounce in the strongest possible terms the atrocities committed by Nazi Germany and a determination to offer an alternative vision of a just and peaceful world.[97]

Human rights, including economic and social rights such as the right to health, became central to this vision. This was reflected in the first preambular paragraph of the UDHR, which states:[98]

Whereas recognition of the inherent dignity and of the equal and inalienable rights of all members of the human family *is the foundation of freedom, justice and peace in the world.*

Morsink has explained that the initial reluctance of the delegations from the West to give the 'new rights' full status during the drafting of the UDHR was 'in part due to the gaps in their own constitutions.'[99] Humphrey has also claimed that '[i]t is by no means certain that economic and social rights would have been included in the final text if I had not included them in mine'.[100] What is telling, however, is that despite the fragile status of the concept of economic and social rights within some Western states, the anxiety of these states was not sufficient to translate into a resistance to the inclusion of such rights in the UDHR. Indeed, Morsink's analysis of the drafting history of the UDHR led him to conclude that 'for the great majority

---

[95] It is also important to recall that there was a level of resistance to the inclusion of human rights within the UN Charter in 1945 by the UK, USA, and Russia despite the fact that Declaration of the United Nations signed by Roosevelt and Churchill in 1941 had explicitly referred to human rights. This resistance however was ultimately overcome by persuasive lobbying from civil society and the influence of Latin American states. See generally Morsink, *The Universal Declaration of Human Rights* (n 1) 1–3; Hunt, *Inventing Human Rights* (n 1) 202–3; Korey (n 1) 29–42; Normand and Zaidi (n 1) 107–38.

[96] Humphrey (n 64) 32, 45. See also Normand and Ziadi (n 1) 188–92 (for example, Mrs Roosevelt argued that the US Government 'did not believe that the economic, social and cultural rights listed in the latter part of the UDHR implied the need for direct government action': cited Normand and Ziadi (n 1) 191.)

[97] Humphrey (n 64) 53 (recounts a conversation with the head of the Yugoslav delegation in which he writes that 'What they wanted most of all ... was a condemnation of warmongering. If they got that they would be willing to compromise on other things.')

[98] UDHR, first preambular paragraph (emphasis added).

[99] Morsink, *The Universal Declaration of Human Rights* (n 1) 192.

[100] Humphrey (n 64) 32.

of drafters' the distinction between the two sets of rights 'was a benign one'.[101] Both sets of rights were cut from the 'same moral cloth'[102] and possessed what he describes as an 'organic unity'.[103]

This unity, however, was actually more fragile than Morsink[104] and other commentators[105] have conceded, and was significantly disturbed by the deepening of the Cold War in the 1950s and 60s.[106] The common enemy that had united the allied powers in the aftermath of World War II had been defeated. As such there was no longer a need to suppress the battle between the competing ideologies of market power and centralized state planning.[107] The casualty of this new war was the shattering of the intention to transform the commitments under the UDHR into a single binding international legal instrument.[108] Political compromise and realpolitik demanded the adoption of two separate Covenants by the UN General Assembly—the ICCPR and the ICESCR in 1966, neither of which came into force until 1976.

The right to health may have been given a separate legal identity by its inclusion in the ICESCR—an identity that was affirmed in subsequent international treaties. But subject to a few exceptions,[109] it remained a relative recluse during the Cold War

---

[101] Morsink, *The Universal Declaration of Human Rights* (n 1) xiv.
[102] ibid 191.
[103] ibid xiv. See also ibid 232–8.
[104] See Normand and Zaidi (n 1) 189–90 (noting the opposition of the USA and UK to the inclusion of economic, social, and cultural rights and arguing that the secondary status of these rights was reflected in the debates about the order of these articles in the UDHR and in the comments of Cassin, the French representative on the drafting committee, who championed their inclusion yet conceded that 'economic social and cultural rights were "almost as important" as civil and political rights' representing a logical development from rather than an equal part of the human rights foundation.)
[105] Whelan and Donnelly, 'Setting the Record Straight' (n 31) 915 (arguing that nothing in the UDHR 'suggests even the slightest denigration of economic and social rights'); Whelan and Donnelly, 'Yes, a Myth' (n 31) 255 (arguing that the US and UK were 'the driving force' behind the incorporation of economic and social rights in the global human rights regime).
[106] See Kirkup and Evans (n 31) 232 (arguing that every effort was made to reject economic and social rights in the years after the adoption of the UDHR).
[107] Normand and Zaidi (n 1) 201.
[108] Kirkup and Evans (n 31) 226–32 (tracing the steps which they believe led to the bifurcation of the two sets of rights into separate covenants), cf Whelan and Donnelly 'Yes, a Myth' (n 31) 246–54 (challenging the account offered by Kirkup and Evans).
[109] For example, in 1978 the Carter Administration adopted a policy on international health, *New Directions in International Health Cooperation*, in which the right to health was stated for 'form an integral part of the foreign policy of the Carter Administration': P Bourne, *New Directions in International Health Cooperation: A Report to the President* (US Government Printing Office, 1978) 1. See also 'Human Rights', Presidential Directive/NSC-30 (17 February 1978) (states that promotion of human rights, including 'basic economic and social rights', 'shall be a major objective of US foreign policy') <http://www.fas.org/irp/offdocs/pd/pd30.pdf> (accessed 22 June 2011). Subsequent regimes in the US however rejected the legitimacy of the right to health in their response to the global HIV/AIDS pandemic. See Fidler (n 59) 116–23. In the same year the idea of the right to health was also affirmed as a fundamental right in the *Declaration of Alma Ata*, which was adopted at an international conference on primary health care organized by the WHO and UNICEF: *Declaration of Alma Ata* (International Conference on Primary Health Care, Alma Ata USSR, 6–12 September 1978) para 1. The *Declaration* also affirmed that 'Governments have a responsibility for the health of their people which can be fulfilled only on the provision of adequate health and social measures': para V.

when neither Western nor Communist states had any real incentive or determination to promote or nurture its development in international law.[110] This ideological conflict also proved toxic to the capacity of the WHO, which had been instrumental in the initial discussions to shape the formulation of right to health in the ICESCR,[111] to embrace and develop the idea of a right to health in practice. This is because despite signs of initial enthusiasm for this endeavour, a change in leadership saw the WHO adopt a functional biomedical approach to discrete health problems as a way of avoiding the politicization of its work in the bipolar world.[112] Meanwhile, developing states were preoccupied with the decolonization enterprise and efforts to assert their right to development.[113] The welfare state expanded during this period. But it would be wrong to interpret this development as an explicit commitment to economic and social rights, such as the right to health, because it was not driven by this paradigm.[114] Thus, it is only since the 1990s that any substantive interest in the meaning and content of the right to health in international law has emerged so as to enable it to take a visible place within the lexicon of international human rights law.[115]

[110] Korey (n 1) 7 (explaining that the isolationism of the 1950s, McCarthyism, and xenophobia reversed enthusiasm for human rights within the USA and although Carter's presidency saw the elevation of human rights their understanding was confined to the foreign policy context); Whelan and Donnelly, 'Setting the Record Straight' (n 31) 945 (arguing that neglect of economic and social rights by the West during the Cold War years is exaggerated and Western states maintained a commitment to economic and social rights during this period); cf Kirkup and Evans (n 31) 222–32 (arguing that after the adoption of the UDHR, a domestic movement within the US increased resistance to the inclusion of economic and social rights in a binding international covenant largely because of fears that such rights reflected communist ideology and would increase government intervention; the effect of this movement was to force the US administration under Eisenhower to push for the adoption of two separate covenants); cf Whelan and Donnelly, 'Yes, a Myth' (n 31) 251–2 (arguing that domestic opposition within the US was primarily fuelled by concerns about US sovereignty and the impact of international law rather than economic and social rights per se; further arguing that the period of latency was also a consequence of the Third Committee of the UN General Assembly shifting its attention to ending colonialism and apartheid); Moyn, *The Last Utopia* (n 1) 222 (arguing that civil and political rights dominated and preoccupied Western conceptions of rights and their opposition to totalitarian and authoritarian regimes). Indeed in such a context the collapse of totalitarianism and authoritarianism regimes meant that consciousness of economic and social rights 'could not help but surge').

[111] Meier, 'Global Health Governance and the Contentious Politics of Human Rights' (n 15) 15–25 (provides a comprehensive account of the role of the WHO in the development of the right to health under the ICESCR and demonstrates that the inclusion of the specific measures listed in para 2 of art 12 of the ICESCR was largely attributable to the influence of the WHO).

[112] ibid 25–35 (notes that the WHO would not return to the idea of a right to health as a means to achieve global health policy until the 1970s but for a variety of reasons its capacity to shape and influence the status and content of the right to health had been comprised by its earlier neglect of this norm). See also Meier, 'The World Health Organization, the Evolution of Human Rights and the Failure to Achieve Health for All' (n 31) 163.

[113] See generally Burke (n 1) (provides an historical account of the influence of decolonization on the international human rights program).

[114] Kirkup and Evans (n 31) 237 (argue that the emergence of the welfare state 'did not conform to the expectations of international law but to the structures of the global political economy').

[115] See Paul Hunt, 'The Health and Human Rights Movement: Progress and Obstacles' (2008) 15 JLM 714, 714–16. Although the reasons for its emergence are complex, the collapse of the Soviet Empire was certainly a contributing factor. It meant that there was no longer a geopolitical need to insist on the divide between civil and political rights and economic and social rights—not that Western States could

E Using history to understand the meaning of the right to health

The preceding discussion provides several insights into the history of the right to health that are important to the contemporary understanding of this right. First, the first normative expression of rights was inspired by the perceived need to provide protection for individuals against the unjustified actions of the state. Within Anglo–American thinking, which expressed a strong preference for civil and political rights such as freedom from torture, equality, and freedom of religion,[116] health was excluded from this early conception of rights. Second, the legal recognition of economic and social rights, including the right to health, emerged as a pragmatic and humanitarian response to human suffering and the need for Governments to take measures to alleviate this suffering. Importantly, this philosophy of rights cannot be reduced to an expression of communist or socialist ideology. Instead, the better view is that represents a pragmatic attempt to navigate a centre path between the excesses and failings of both liberalism and collectivism.

Third, the social context that facilitated the adoption of declarations that transformed political and moral conceptions of rights into legal instruments that guaranteed rights was defined by conflict—local conflicts in the case of the US, France, and Latin American countries, and World War II in the case of the WHO and UDHR. This suggests that rights were not 'born in antipolitics' as some commentators have claimed.[117] On the contrary, the protection of rights was seen

---

always wrestle themselves from their addiction to civil and political rights as the panacea for global suffering: see, eg, Fidler (n 59) 101 (discusses how the Bush Administration rejected thinking about health in terms of human rights and preferred to reconceptualize it as being dependent on the achievement of civil and political rights). Scholars, such as Moyn, have also suggested that the 'collapse of alternative institutionalisms' such as communism and 'the crisis of other utopias' provided the opportunity for human rights to fill the void and provide the dominant vision for addressing global wrongs: Moyn, *The Last Utopia* (n 1) 213, 222. Indeed, in such a context the collapse of totalitarian and authoritarian regimes meant that consciousness of economic and social rights 'could not help but surge': ibid 223. But the explanation for the rise of the right to health and other economic and social rights is more complex than Moyn suggests. NGOs from the developing world, now emerging in competency and capacity in the aftermath of decolonization, started to call on the international community, and indeed international NGOs, to 'pay greater attention' to economic and social rights, which, for too long, had been subordinated to civil and political rights: Korey (n 1) 15–16. See also Paul Hunt, 'The Health and Human Rights Movement: Progress and Obstacles' (2008) 15 JLM 714, 715–17 (examines contributions of NGOs to relationship between health and human rights). And the work of Jonathan Mann cannot be overlooked. During the 1980s, as the HIV/AIDS pandemic took hold, Mann pioneered the use of a rights-based approach to health. Importantly the adoption of this approach was driven not by commitment to some utopian vision of human rights but by the need to find a pragmatic solution to human suffering. Critically, in Mann's mind, the human rights framework was considered to offer 'public health a more coherent, comprehensive and practical framework of analysis and action on the societal root causes of vulnerability to HIV/AIDS than any framework inherited from traditional health or biomedical science': Jonathan Mann, 'Human Rights and AIDS: The Future of the Pandemic' in Jonathan Mann and others (eds), *Health and Human Rights* (Routledge, 1999) 216, 223. It is important to stress that Mann's concern was with the interdependence between health as a medical concept and the entire range of human rights—civil, political, and economic and social. Thus, his focus was not the right to health per se. His work did, however, raise the profile of the relationship between health and human rights generally.

[116] See generally Hunt, *Inventing Human Rights* (n 1); Hamlin, 'The History and Development of Public Health in Developed Countries' (n 31) 28.
[117] Moyn, *The Last Utopia* (n 1) 213.

ritical to not only providing a new way of government, but also maintaining
ce.[118] Rights claims were certainly inspired by a humanitarian sentiment. But
the impact of such sentiment must not be overstated because, as Moyn has observed,
humanitarianism does not in and of itself 'always take the form of revolutionary
rights assertions or the search for legal guarantees'.[119] What can be said, however, is
that post-conflict and transitional settings tended to provide fertile social conditions
in which the three elements of human rights discourse—the political, moral, and
instrumental—could be aligned and crystallized into a legal form. Significantly when
this window of opportunity opened at the international level, the right to health was
included in this vision.

IV The role of public health in delivering the right to health

A The ancient commitment to collective action to protect health

How health came to be swept up in the revolutionary understanding of human rights at the international level is explained in part by the factors that have been identified above.[120] But there is a further element to the history of its emergence as a human right that remains to be told. This element is linked with the history of public health. Much has been written about this topic since the pioneering works of scholars such as George Rosen in *A History of Public Health* and Rene Sand in *The Advance to Social Medicine*.[121] These discussions need not be repeated here and it sufficient to acknowledge that this history, like that of human rights, is both complex and contested.[122] There are, however, common themes within this literature that are relevant to understanding the development of the idea of a right to health.

---

[118] See Fidler (n 59) (describes this change as a shift from a Westphalian system of governance with its emphasis on State interests to a post-Westphalian system in which the status of the individual is centralized).

[119] Moyn, 'On the Genealogy of Morals' (n 1) 26. Moyne also warns against the ambiguous consequences of humanitarianism and its potential to legitimize imperialist activities: ibid 28, 30.

[120] cf Moyn, 'On the Genealogy of Morals' (n 1) 29 (argues that the UDHR was less about revolution and more about restoration). However, Moyn fails to acknowledge the transformative expectation that accompanied the drafting of the UDHR. See generally Humphrey (n 64). Nor does he address the significance of the departure from the Westphalian model of governance that was ushered in by the adoption of the UDHR (albeit, it could be argued, more by way of rhetoric than substantive action): Fidler (n 59).

[121] See, eg, George Rosen, *A History of Public Health* (MD Publications, 1958) (traces the history of public health in Europe and the USA); Rene Sand *The Advance to Social Medicine* (Staples Press Ltd, 1952). See also C Fraser Brockington, *A Short History of Public Health* (J & A Churchill, 1956).

[122] Detels and others (n 31) 3–64 (trace history of public health in developed, low, and middle income countries); Porter, *Health, Civilisation and the State* (n 31); Dorothy Porter (ed), *The History of Public Health and the Modern State* (Rodopi, 1994) (provides a collection on the history of public health in specific jurisdictions). The very definition of 'public health' itself is not without controversy. But for the purposes of this chapter I have adopted a broad approach which is 'concerned with the general questions of how, why and in what manners states came to take an interest in peoples' health': Detels and others (n 31) 20.

First, threats to the health of individuals whether in the form of transmissible disease, poor sanitation, inadequate drinking water, or lack of access to medical care, have been a social concern throughout human history. There is, as Dorothy Porter explains a 'history of collective action in relation to the health of populations'.[123] Ancient Indian cities provided bathrooms and drains with covered sewers;[124] the 'Creten-Mycenan culture had large conduits';[125] 'impressive ruins of sewerage systems and baths testify to the achievements of the Incas in public health engineering'.[126] Moreover, as Porter also explains '[f]rom ancient times, political states have been involved in the organisation of medical services and the institutionalisation of medical practice and education'.[127] Thus, for example, 'the provision of public physicians by Greek city states was imitated and expanded with the Hellenization of the defeated Persian Empire and later the Roman Empire'.[128] In addition, '[t]he Romans were aware that disease could result from occupational hazards'[129] and 'by the second century AD...a public medical service was constituted' with the principal duty of its doctors 'to give medical attention to poor citizens' including the provision of free care.[130] During the Middle Ages 'communal activities in the interest of health were undertaken under the aegis of the Church'.[131] Medieval communities did not have an organized public health system as we know it today but they did have administrative machinery for disease prevention and sanitary supervision.[132] These measures provide evidence of a long held understanding by those occupying positions of power of the need to address the social determinants of health for those persons subject to their jurisdiction and the need to provide them with access to health care—keeping in mind that, in relative terms, early collective health measures would have lacked the scientific knowledge to prevent or treat many illnesses.

B The reality of mixed motivations underlying collective health measures

However, the existence of collective action to address the health concerns of communities throughout civilization, does not mean that the right to health was some nascent concept simply awaiting germination. On the contrary, the collective health measures taken throughout history in areas such as sanitation, water supply, education, access to medical care, and nutrition were motivated by complex and often competing factors. Humanitarian concerns of secular philanthropists were relevant along with the desire of religious organizations to provide charity and welfare to the sick and destitute. But economic and political considerations are also recurring and dominant forces in the history of public health.

---

[123] Porter, *Health, Civilisation and the State* (n 31) 4.
[124] Rosen (n 121) 1.   [125] ibid 2.   [126] ibid 3.
[127] Porter, *Health, Civilisation and the State* (n 31) 17.
[128] ibid 11.   [129] Rosen (n 121) 121.   [130] ibid 23.
[131] ibid 29. See also Porter, *Health, Civilisation and the State* (n 31) 12.
[132] Rosen (n 121) 47.

Indeed from the sixteenth to the eighteenth century public health became shaped by the emergence of the modern nation state.[133] With this development, the social and religious considerations which had motivated public health initiatives were replaced by the political need to expand the power of the state.[134] As Rosen explains, '[p]roblems of health and disease were considered chiefly in connection with the aim of maintaining and augmenting a healthy population and thus in terms of their significance for the political and economic strength of the State'.[135] The concept of an individual right to health was not what motivated states to secure the health of individuals. Indeed, for Foucault and others who have built on his work, the creation of government-sponsored publication health initiatives was associated with an expansion in the regulatory power of the state. This expansion was facilitated by the rise of scientific knowledge and subsequent privileging of public health experts who, in turn, dominated public health governance and 'enhanced the professional power of medicine to police health and illness'.[136] Such a position is hardly the bedrock on which to establish a right to health.

C The rise and fall of the Enlightenment

For other commentators, however, there is evidence of an alternative and less repressive interpretation of the history of public health.[137] Rosen, for example, suggests that there was a growing understanding among political leaders of their responsibility to create 'conditions and facilities that would promote health, prevent disease and render medical care easily accessible to those in need of it'[138]—such measures could not 'be left to the uncertainty of individual initiative'.[139] The idea that the state—as opposed to local councils or authorities—had obligations with respect to the health of an individual's health was beginning to emerge. In understanding this development, Porter has argued that 'the most important ideological influence on late eighteenth century rhetoric about health and the political state was the Enlightenment philosophy of democratic citizenship' associated with the US and French revolutions.[140] This movement had radical implications for the purpose of

---

[133] ibid 85 ('whose outlines slowly appear out of the storm sea of politics like a whale coming to the surface').

[134] ibid 86.   [135] ibid 90.

[136] Porter, *The History of Public Health* (n 122) 3. See also N Rose, 'Governing "Advanced" Liberal Democracies' in A Barry, T Osborne and N Rose (eds), *Foucault and Political Reason: Liberalism, Neo-Liberalism and Rationalities of Government* (UCL Press, 1996) 54. It should be noted however the privileging of the knowledge of experts can also be used by such experts to counter the health policy decisions of the (elected) government—further impacting on the role of individuals to have a say in such policy, as their vote does not necessarily contribute to the debate. Terry Johnson briefly refers to conflict between health professionals and government policy in England in his piece 'Expertise and the State' in M Gane and T Johnson (eds), *Foucault's New Domains* (Routledge, 1993) 150.

[137] Detels and others (n 31) 25–7 (discuss the emergence of the concept of medical police throughout Europe in the 18th century in which the issue of public health was approached through an emphasis on regulation and social control but trace the subsequent emergence of a liberal welfare model in which the interests of individuals became more prominent).

[138] Rosen (n 121) 91.   [139] ibid 92.

[140] See Porter, *Health, Civilisation and the State* (n 31) 57.

public health and demanded a shift from a model whereby public health initiatives were intended to serve the interests of a state to a focus on the role of the state in securing the health of an individual.[141]

Jefferson, it will be recalled, failed to include a right to health in his list of inalienable rights. But he still remained acutely aware of the relationship between the political system of a state and the health of its citizens. For Jefferson, 'sick populations were the product of sick political systems'.[142] But this did not entitle them to a right to health. Instead, in Jefferson's mind the guarantee of the right to liberty and the pursuit to happiness would automatically lead to a healthy life. This of course is a classic or libertarian position with respect to human rights which sees no active role for the state in taking measures to secure the happiness that Jefferson believed all individuals were entitled to.[143]

In contrast the French did perceive the need for the state to take on a greater role with respect to the health of individuals.[144] The French revolutionaries may not have included health in the original *Declaration on the Rights of Man* in 1789, but in '1791 the Constitute Assembly's Committee on Salubrity did add health to the state's obligations to its citizens'[145] and in 1793 and 1794 'passed a series of laws that established a national system of social assistance including medical care'.[146] The implementation of these initiatives was initially thwarted by a lack of resources and a divergence of opinion about how to secure the right to health[147]—themes that still characterize the contemporary understanding of the right to health. More problematic, however, was the perceived tension between the revolutionaries' commitment to libertarian values, such as economic freedom and protection of private property, and the interventionist strategies required to protect the right to health.[148]

D State expansion and the Industrial Revolution—towards an instrumentalist vision of public health

Thus, the promise of the bold new social order that had been anticipated by the revolutionaries was quickly quashed. Equality before the law was to be protected but 'the communitarian promises of the Revolution' were discarded in the nineteenth

---

[141] Detels and others (n 31) 27.

[142] Porter, *Health, Civilisation and the State* (n 31) 57.

[143] Henkin (n 64) 87, 99 (suggests that for Jefferson and his time, there was no expectation that government provide people with the benefits commonly associated with the modern welfare state or economic and social rights). A similar sentiment was expressed by Mrs Roosevelt during the drafting of the UDHR when she proclaimed that the US government 'did not believe that the economic social and cultural rights in the latter part of the declaration implied the need for direct government action': cited in Normand and Zaidi (n 1) 191.

[144] Matthew Ramsey, 'Public Health in France' in Dorothy Porter (ed), *The History of Public Health and the Modern State* (Rodopi, 1994) 45, 48–9.

[145] Porter, *Health, Civilisation and the State* (n 31) 57; Rosen (n 121) 144.

[146] Rosen (n 121) 145.

[147] Ramsey (n 144) 49. [148] ibid 50.

century as 'utopian and subversive'.[149] The seeds for the idea of a right to health may have been sown in France and migrated abroad, but they were quickly trampled upon. This was caused not only by the rise of the Nation State and its imperial agenda, but by a raw 'utilitarian political economy' that accompanied the advance of the Industrial Revolution.[150] Under this vision the prevention of infant mortality was not a right, but an economic imperative to prevent the loss of human capital; the prevention of disease by the provision of sanitation and water was not a right but a measure to ensure the supply of healthy workers.

As a consequence, instrumentalism in the form of political power and economic utility came to be the primary factor motivating states to take measures to secure the health of their populations.[151] During the mid-nineteenth century there was a growing awareness that 'it would be good economy to undertake measures for the prevention of disease'[152] and 'it was this recognition of the economic and social costs of preventable disease which provided the stimulus for action for better public health'.[153] The Enlightenment preoccupation with rights—while 'still burning in the hearts of the German and French revolutionaries'[154]—became, if not irrelevant, then effectively suppressed in the development of health policies.

E The rebirth of rights and the struggle for justice

Somewhat ironically the Industrial Revolution, characterized as it was by appalling working conditions and the reality that poverty was often exacerbated rather than eliminated, actually provided the platform from which rights discourse, especially economic and social rights, could reemerge.[155] Poverty and ill health came to be recognized as constant companions which prompted 'socially minded citizens, physicians, clergymen, social workers and government officials to found a common ground of action'.[156] These collaborative efforts and local movements took up causes such as the prevention of communicable diseases, industrial safety, and the reduction of infant mortality.[157] More significantly in terms of the history of the right to health, the humanitarian sentiment that informed such initiatives, was increasingly being informed by a growing political movement that took 'seriously the democratic

---

[149] ibid 51. See also Normand and Zaidi (n 1) 14–15 (note that 'The Napoleonic era ended France's flirtation with individual rights and ushered in a period of nationalization in Europe in which the consolidation of state power took precedence over theories of the individual').

[150] Porter, *Health, Civilisation and the State* (n 31) 57.

[151] Porter, *The History of Public Health* (n 122) 8.

[152] Porter, *Health, Civilisation and the State* (n 31) 185.

[153] Rosen (n 121) 188. For example, the adoption of the Poor Laws in early nineteenth century England was motivated, not by a right to health, but a desire to promote the health of workers and keep them off welfare: Caroline Kaufmann, 'The Right to Health Care: Some Cross-National Comparisons and US Trends in Policy' (1981) 15F Soc Sci & Med 157, 159.

[154] Porter, *The History of Public Health* (n 122) 8.

[155] Lauren (n 1) 294.

[156] Rosen (n 121) 325.

[157] ibid.

implications of liberalism in terms of human rights and human dignity'.[158] Workers became organized and started to demand 'various kinds of social services including health services.'[159] This movement eventually led to the creation of the International Labour Organization in 1919. The trajectory of public health generally, however, was far less linear with 'historical diversities and continuities, contrasts and convergences' informing how states went about the development and delivery of public health initiatives.[160]

F Transforming national differences into an international commitment

It is not the place to examine the complex history of public health in individual states here.[161] It is important, however, to draw attention to the fact that the history of public health within a particular jurisdiction may have a potential impact on the contemporary understanding of the right to health within that jurisdiction. In the case of what was the USSR, for example, the obligation to provide health care services to all its citizens was achieved through the creation of a centralized state controlled system which provided services free of charge. But there were little or no private sector medical services and patients were not entitled to their choice of physician.[162] Within the United Kingdom, public health innovation was also 'driven through the expansion of an interventionist central state',[163] which lead to the creation and subsequent expansion of a national health insurance scheme as early as 1911.[164] But this model was underpinned by the values of justice and rationality in that it was seen to be 'right and good'[165] to assure medical services of sufficient quality and quantity to citizens.[166] Centralization of public health was also a feature of the French model but it was tempered by 'the reality of voluntarism (and) localism'.[167]

In contrast, in the USA the dominance of the *laissez faire* political philosophy meant that there was staunch resistance to centralized public health reforms throughout the nineteenth century.[168] Americans simply recoiled from collective community policies required for health reform because they were seen to be associated with a

---

[158] ibid 203.   [159] ibid.
[160] Porter, *The History of Public Health* (n 122) 10.
[161] See ibid.   [162] Kaufmann (n 153) 158.
[163] Porter, *Health, Civilisation and the State* (n 31) 147.
[164] See the National Health Insurance Act 1911 (UK) (extended provision of health care to the indigent). This scheme was subsequently extended to include dental care, nursing care, and other services by the mid-1930s and in 1948 the National Health Service Act extended services to all residents and not just the indigent.
[165] Christopher Hamlin, 'State Medicine in Great Britain' in Dorothy Porter (ed), *The History of Public Health and the Modern State* (Rodopi, 1994) 32, 132.
[166] Kaufmann (n 153) 159 (notes that the expansion in the UK health system did not follow from 'an explicit adherence to the concept of a right to treatment' but the ultimate creation of a National Health Service 'underscores a national commitment to the right to health care for all British citizens').
[167] Ramsey (n 144) 102.
[168] Porter, *The History of Public Health* (n 122) 10–11; Elizabeth Fee, 'Public Health and the State: The United States' in Dorothy Porter (ed), *The History of Public Health and the Modern State* (Rodopi, 1994) 224.

paternalistic model of government that had been 'replaced by a system of values which were wedded to the virtues of the absolute sovereignty of the individual'.[169] Reform, where it did occur within the USA in the nineteenth century, was therefore often ad hoc and 'promoted by Puritan model codes regarding social cleanliness and godliness'.[170] Although as Porter explains, 'a new technocratic ideal of social progress became influential... this never succeeded in overcoming the persistent American suspicion of central government paternalism and a belief in the superior claims of local rights.'[171]

At the end of the century, however, the idea of public health as social reform emerged in the USA as a pragmatic response to the distress caused by the extremes in wealth and privilege, relative to the social misery and deprivation that had been brought on by industrialization and urbanization.[172] The resultant movement brought together an eclectic group which included scientists, municipal officers, physicians, engineers, architects, lawyers, and women 'seeking to escape the bounds of domestic responsibilities' in a campaign for improved public health services and greater attention to the social determinants of health such as housing.[173]

As to why this movement was successful, Elizabeth Fee has suggested that it offered 'a middle ground to the cut throat principles of entrepreneurial capitalism and the revolutionary ideas of the socialists, anarchists and utopian visionaries.'[174] The experience within North America, therefore, offers an interesting parallel with the emergence of economic and social rights within Latin America where states were seeking to navigate between the dangers of extreme individualism and collectivism. Many North Americans, like their South American counterparts, were increasingly coming to the realization that Jefferson's liberty may have been necessary, but it was not a sufficient guarantee of a life of happiness and well being. The state had to do more than simply avoid interfering with civil and political rights if it were to secure the health of its citizens and ensure a life of happiness.

As America entered the twentieth century, other events helped shape a national consciousness as to the importance of the relationship between public health and the state. It came to be seen as 'good economics' that would help conserve 'national vitality';[175] it was necessary to ensure that young men would be fit for combat[176] and in the aftermath of the Great Depression, federal funding of public health was a fundamental part of Roosevelt's New Deal.[177] Significantly, it is at this point that the history of public health collides with the history of human rights to produce the idea of the right to health in international law. A moment had arrived in time when the nations of the world—admittedly not universal in their gathering—stood united in

---

[169] Porter, *Health, Civilisation and the State* (n 31) 161. See Pat Milmoe McCarrick, 'A Right to Health Care' (National Reference Centre for Bioethics, Literature Scope Note No 20) 1 (notes that as early as 1798 Congress passed a law providing medical care for merchant marines under the Relief of Sick and Disabled Seaman Act and over time extended the delivery of health services to other groups such as war veterans, Native Americans, prisoners, and federal employees).
[170] Porter, *Health, Civilisation and the State* (n 31) 147.
[171] ibid.   [172] Fee (n 168) 233–5.
[173] ibid 234.   [174] ibid.   [175] ibid 241.
[176] ibid 242.   [177] ibid 246.

their conviction to deliver a new vision of peace of justice for humanity—as the preamble to the UDHR proclaims, 'a common standard of achievement of all peoples and all nations.'[178] Human rights, including the right to health, considered to be 'a spent political force' that 'barely retained any intellectual currency' at the turn of the twentieth century,[179] were central to this vision.

The history of public health had demonstrated that in the absence of collective action to deliver health services and protect health, the humanitarian, economic, and political consequences were profoundly negative for both states and individuals. It is this conclusion that led Rosen to proclaim that the history of public health demonstrates that 'the promotion of health and the prevention of disease in a community' had come to be recognized as 'clearly the responsibilities of government'.[180] The notion within public health discourse that the state is responsible for the protection and promotion of the health of its citizens is therefore intimately connected with and mutually supportive of the idea within human rights discourse that states have an obligation to recognize the right of every individual to the highest attainable standard of health. That there is a right to health in international law is not simply a legacy of the political struggle to deliver a particular vision of justice in the post war world. It is also the culmination of a complex interplay of factors—political, economic, philosophical, humanitarian, and religious—over thousands of years within the field of public health that coalesced to produce a particular vision as to the role of the state with respect to the health of individuals at a particular point in time.

V Conclusion: looking into and beyond the history of the right to health

The historian Samuel Moyn has warned of the dangers in looking to the past to understand contemporary human rights standards because for him the very concept of human rights is a relatively new invention.[181] At the same time, he has conceded that an examination of 'prior languages and practices' can provide an insight into the conditions that gave rise to the emergence of a human right in the first instance.[182] The discussions in this chapter have sought to identify these 'prior languages and practices' in order to provide the scaffolding from which contemporary ideas and understandings as to the nature of the right to health have emerged or indeed diverged from the past. No attempt has been made to offer a comprehensive history of the right to health—such an ambitious task is well beyond the scope of this book.

---

[178] The significance of the adoption of the UDHR must be tempered by the reality that only 58 nations were involved in its drafting and 8 states abstained: the Communist Bloc (which included Russia, Ukraine, Byelorussia, Poland, Czechoslovakia, Yugoslavia), South Africa, and Saudi Arabia. Yemen and Honduras were absent. At the same time those non-Western states that provided their assent included Afghanistan, Egypt, India, Liberia, Pakistan, the Philippines, Taiwan, and Thailand. In terms of ideological breakdown, 37 states represented the Judeo-Christian tradition; 11 Islamic; 6 Marxist and 4 the Buddhist tradition.
[179] Normand and Zaidi (n 1) 15.
[180] Rosen (n 121) 358.
[181] Moyn, 'On the Genealogy of Morals' (n 1) 30.
[182] ibid 30.

The aim, however, was to commence this project and in doing so, it was possible to reveal that many of the assumptions that characterize contemporary debates as to the nature and status of the right to health are misplaced.

In the first instance it is not, as it routinely suggested, the product of—and nor can it be reduced to—an expression of communist ideology. On the contrary, its origins in the Enlightenment period and the emergence of a Latin American philosophy of human rights, indicate that the ideological foundation of the right to health combines an embrace of liberal values with an acceptance of the need for states to take measures to mitigate the harm caused by excessive liberalism and capitalism. Moreover, the right to health cannot be reduced to a mere aspiration that reflects a utopian vision that is impractical and unrealistic. To reduce the history of human rights to the 'history of utopianism', as some commentators have done,[183] is to overlook the reality that its foundations are deeply interwoven with pragmatic and instrumentalist considerations. A state that fails to attend to the health of its population undermines its economic potential, creates the risk of social instability, and threatens its global strategic capacity. Indeed, the history of public health tells us that, absent a right to health, all civilizations have long recognized the need for communal action to protect the health of their populations.[184] The emergence of the right to health did not displace the complex considerations that motivated such actions. It did, however, seek to elevate the status of the individual within the decision making matrix of states to demand actions to protect and promote the health of individuals as a matter of entitlement rather than mere instrumentalism. It demands that greater consideration must be given to the questions of for whom (the answer is all individuals) and why (the answer is because health is an entitlement) these actions are undertaken.

At the same time, it would be misleading to suggest that the inclusion of the right to health in international law was uncontroversial. Its history, like that of the right to public heath, is deeply connected to the 'dialectics of political power'.[185] Just a few years after Roosevelt had embraced the right to medical care in his State of the Union address, the US Department of State 'barely mentioned economic and social rights' when it prepared its draft international bill of rights.[186] Moreover, the US resistance to the inclusion of these rights in a binding covenant only intensified in the years

---

[183] Moyn, *The Last Utopia* (n 1) 225.
[184] The same understanding exists within respect to the need for State to take action with respect to issues that are the subject of other economic and social rights such as education and housing. Moreover, this is reflected in the development of the modern welfare state, which offers a particular vision with respect to the functions and legitimacy of a State. But caution should be exercised in taking the existence of a welfare state as evidence of support for economic and social rights as some commentators have suggested. See, eg, Whelan and Donnelly, 'Setting the Record Straight' (n 31) 919–27, especially 921. A welfare state remains a political entity that does not necessarily protect and promote the health of an individual as a matter of legal entitlement. Indeed, Evans and Kirkup have argued that the expansion of the welfare state in the West after World War II reflected, not a commitment to economic and soical rights, but 'a particular configuration of the global political economy in which a high level of economic and social entitlement guaranteed by the state was viewed as essential to the survival of the capitalist world order': Kirkup and Evans (n 31) 233.
[185] Porter, *The History of Public Health* (n 122) 24.
[186] Normand and Zaidi (n 1) 102.

after the adoption of the UDHR.[187] Indeed anxiety, apathy, and antagonism have always been, and remain, its constant companions. The aftermath of World War II somewhat ironically provided a narrow window of opportunity through which to navigate these constraints and embed the right to health within the international system for the protection of human rights. Critically, the antagonists that exploited this opportunity where drawn from a broad and diverse coalition of social actors and the history of the right to health is anything but the exclusive domain of lawyers—a point that must not be overlooked in any attempts to map out the contemporary understanding as to the nature of this right.

Ultimately the inclusion of the right to health in international law reflected an attempt to create a governance structure that was not based solely on the traditional Westphalian system of state sovereignty whereby state interests provided the overriding rationale for undertaking domestic and international health measures.[188] In contrast, the post-Westphalian governance framework ushered in by the adoption of the United Nations Charter, the UDHR, and indeed the WHO Constitution elevated the status of the individual and his or her human right to health.[189] As a consequence, the fact that there is a right to health in international law is now beyond dispute. As to whether there should be such a right in international law, what it might mean as a legal concept, and how it should be implemented in practice remain questions that are far from settled. It is the discussion of these issues that will occupy the remainder of this book and it is to the first question—the philosophical basis of the right to health—that I now turn.

---

[187] Kirkup and Evans (n 31) 226 (examine drafting history of the covenants to identify three primary reasons for this resistance—the perception that such rights were mere aspirations, hollow in content because so few states had the capacity to protect them and, unlike civil and political rights, an inappropriate subject of international law); cf Whelan and Donnelly, 'Yes, a Myth' (n 31) 246 (challenge the interpretation of the drafting history offered by Kirkup and Evans).

[188] Fidler (n 59) 108–9.

[189] ibid. As such it did not, as has been suggested by Moyn, seek to 'transcend politics': Moyn, *The Last Utopia* (n 1) 227. Rather it sought to promote an alternative political vision of governance.

2
The Right to Health—Its Conceptual Foundations

I Introduction

Historians may have shown little interest in the historical origins of the right to health, but its conceptual foundations have been the subject of attention amongst bioethicists and philosophers in the field of justice and health care for many years.[1] This attention should not be mistaken as evidence of a sophisticated and rigorous discussion regarding the justification of the right to health as expressed in international law. On the contrary, the relevant literature has tended to focus on the legitimacy of a narrower conception of the right to health, which encompasses only the right to a minimum level of health care in the context of achieving just health outcomes.[2] Only recently has there been any sustained consideration of the

---

[1] See, eg, Allen Buchanan, 'Justice: A Philosophical Review' in Earl Shelp (ed), *Justice and Health Care* (D Reidel Publishing Co, 1981) 3; Martin Golding, 'Justice and Rights: A Study in Relationship' in Earl Shelp (ed), *Justice and Health Care* (D Reidel Publishing Co, 1981) 23; Edmund Pellegrino, 'The Social Ethics of Primary Care: The Relationship between a Human Need and an Obligation of Society' (1978) 45 Mt Sinai J Med 593; Caroline Kaufmann, 'The Right to Health Care: Some Cross-National Comparisons in US Trends in Policy' (1981) 15F Soc Sci & Med 157; Norman Daniels, *Just Health Care* (CUP, 1985) 4–9; Allen Buchanan, 'The Right to a Decent Minimum of Health Care' (1984) 13 Phil & Pub Aff 55; Thomas Bole and William Bonderson (eds), *Rights to Health Care* (Kluwer, 1991); Tom Beauchamp and Ruth Faden, 'The Right to Health and the Right to Health Care' (1979) 4 J Med & Phil 118; William Ruddick, 'Why Not a General Right to Health Care?' (1989) 56 Mt Sinai J Med 157; James Drane, 'Justice Issues in Health Care Delivery' (1990) 24 Bull PAHO 566, 575–6; Allen Buchanan and Kristen Hessler, 'Specifying the Content of the Human Right to Health Care' in A Buchanan (ed), *Justice and Health Care: Selected Essays* (OUP, 2009); H Tristram Engelhardt, 'Rights to Health Care' in H Tristram Engelhardt, *Foundations of Bioethics* (OUP, 1986) ch 8.

[2] See, eg, Beauchamp and Faden (n 1) 128 (argues that it is 'hard to imagine that we are not obliged by a string of moral principles to provide a decent minimum of health care'); Buchanan, 'The Right to a Decent Minimum of Health Care' (n 1) 55 (notes 'a consensus that there is...a right to a decent minimum of health care pervades recent policy debates'); Gary Johns, 'The Right to Health Care and the State' (1983) 132 Phil Q 279, 279; Charles Fried, 'Equality and Rights in Health Care' (1976) 6 Hastings Center Report 29–34; Ronald Bayer and others, 'Toward Justice in Health Care' (1988) 78 Am J Pub Health 583; Buchanan and Hessler (n 1); Ruddick (n 1) 161. See also John Rawls, *The Laws of Peoples* (Harvard University Press, 2002) 50 (argues that a state must assure basic health for all its citizens so as to ensure a just stable and democratic society but does not derive this conclusion from a right to health and prefers to confine the notion of human rights to international political relations). cf H Tristram Engelhardt, *Foundations of Bioethics* (OUP, 1986) 336 (argues that '[a] basic human right to the delivery of health care, even the delivery of a decent minimum of health care does not exist').

formulation of the right to health as used in international law—*the right to the highest attainable standard of health*—within the justice and health paradigm.[3] Moreover, where the right to health has featured in the emerging discourse of philosophy and human rights, its treatment has been more incidental than the subject of specific concern. Thus, for example, the right to health has been identified by James Griffin as an example of a specific claim that cannot be justified within his particular theory of human rights[4] and it has been used by Onora O'Neill to demonstrate that the entire class of economic and social rights is without justification.[5]

Scepticism is a constant companion of all human rights[6] and the right to health is no exception. Indeed, despite the increasing attention this right has received from philosophers, agreement on a persuasive account of its conceptual foundations remains elusive. Thus, while Jennifer Ruger may have recently advocated a model to justify the formulation of the right to health in international law,[7] Norman Daniels, one of the world's leading scholars on justice and health, has maintained the position he first advanced in the 1980s—that in the absence of a theoretical account of its foundations, an 'appeal to a right to health or to health care is not an appropriate starting point for an inquiry into just health'.[8] The aim of this chapter is to address the first part of Daniels' concern, namely the absence of a theoretical account of the foundations of the right to health.[9] It seeks to determine whether this right, as expressed in international law, can be justified within a theory of human rights or is simply a 'vacuous concept'[10] that should, as James Griffin has suggested, be demoted from the list of human rights recognized under international law.[11]

---

[3] See, eg, Jennifer Ruger, 'Toward a Theory of a Right to Health: Capability and Incompletely Theorized Agreements' (2006) 18 Yale JL & Human 273; Jennifer Ruger, *Health and Social Justice* (OUP, 2010) 118 (argues that a 'health capability paradigm offers a philosophical justification for a right to health'); Norman Daniels, *Just Health: Meeting Health Needs Fairly* (CUP, 2008) 144, 216–18; Maria Merritt, 'Bioethics, Philosophy and Global Health' (2007) 7 Yale JH Pol L & Eth 273, 276–300.

[4] James Griffin, *On Human Rights* (OUP, 2008) 208. The reasons for Griffin's rejection of the right to health are discussed below in Part IV (C).

[5] Onora O'Neill, 'The Dark Side of Human Rights' (2005) 81 Intl Affairs 427, 429. For O'Neill, economic and social rights, like the right to health, are aspirational and abstract rights whose justification is 'muddled' and 'vague' largely because of a perceived failure to address the obligations that are attendant on the realization of such rights. O'Neill, however, makes no attempt to interrogate the text of the relevant instruments to assess the nature of the obligations imposed on states—a characteristic, which as detailed in Part IV, is common to many critiques of economic and social rights.

[6] See generally Charles Beitz, *The Idea of Human Rights* (OUP, 2009) 3–7; John Tasioulas, 'The Moral Reality of Human Rights' in Thomas Pogge (ed), *Freedom From Poverty as a Human Right: Who Owes What to the Poor?* (OUP, 2007) 75, 79–82.

[7] Ruger, *Health and Social Justice* (n 3) 118.

[8] Daniels, *Just Health: Meeting Health Needs Fairly* (n 3) 15. See Daniels, *Just Health Care* (n 1) 5. Daniels does however provide a justification for a right to health 'as a special case of a right to fair equality of opportunity [which is his model for a just health system] since the protection of health it affords helps to protect opportunity': Daniels, *Just Health: Meeting Health Needs Fairly* (n 3) 144.

[9] It is beyond the scope of this project to provide a comprehensive account of just health. With respect to this issue, see, eg, Daniels, *Just Health: Meeting Health Needs Fairly* (n 3) and Ruger, *Health and Social Justice* (n 3).

[10] Raymond Guess, *History and Illusion in Politics* (CUP, 2001) 144.

[11] Griffin (n 4) 208.

Part II of this chapter considers the preliminary question of whether an inquiry into the conceptual foundations of the right to health is necessary. It is, after all, already recognized in international law, it is reflected in various national constitutions, and it is increasingly used both as a policy tool by governments and as an advocacy tool by groups worldwide. The view taken here, however, is that an examination of the conceptual foundations of the right to health has the capacity to assist in resolving broader issues as to the relevance, scope, and meaning of the right to health in practice. It also has the potential, if not to rebut, at least to dampen the scepticism with which it has been greeted by some.

Part III explores the question of whether a persuasive account of the conceptual foundations of the right to health can be offered. It concludes that such a justification does exist, based on what is described as a social interest theory of rights. This theory rests on the premise that human rights are not essential or inherent but are socially constructed and it is 'interests' that ground human rights. However, this theory rejects the idea that the interests which ground a right must be determined by reference to a coherent and internally consistent normative theory as to when an interest will constitute the foundation for a legitimate human right. It also rejects the suggestion that the international instruments that protect the right to health reflect no agreement on the conceptual foundations of human rights.[12] Instead, it will be argued that, although not completely theorized, there is an overlapping consensus as to the conceptual foundations of the right to health in international law, which is derived from the social process that led to the recognition of a person's interest in achieving the highest attainable standard of health as the basis for a human right.[13] Hence the idea of a 'social interest' theory of rights as opposed to other explanations, such as an 'urgent'[14] or 'basic' interest theory.[15]

Part IV explores the arguments that are commonly used to challenge the legitimacy of the right to health. These arguments are described as the libertarian objection; the status objection; the formulation objection; the relativist challenge; and the resource allocation dilemma. This discussion reveals that much of the conceptual opposition to the right to health is based on a theory of rights that is inconsistent with the theory of human rights adopted in international law. Moreover, most of the opposition based on implementation of the right to health is informed by assumptions as to the scope of the right to health and the nature of a state's obligations, that pay no regard to the actual obligations of a state as expressed within

---

[12] Griffin (n 4) 16.
[13] This model places significant emphasis on the deliberative process that led to the creation of the international instruments that protect the right to health. But it would be wrong to compartmentalize it in what Marie-Benedicte Dembour has labelled as the deliberative school of human rights thought: Marie-Benedicte Dembour, *Who Believes in Human Rights? Reflections on the European Convention* (CUP, 2006) 248. This is because for Dembour, deliberative scholars view human rights as 'no more than legal and political standards; they are not moral . . . standards': 248. In contrast, an interest theory of rights interprets the agreement that gives rise to the adoption of human rights instruments as reflecting significant moral content albeit imperfect and contested. See David Gautier, *Morality by Agreement* (OUP, 1986).
[14] Beitz (n 6) 109–10.
[15] Buchanan and Hessler (n 1) 213.

the relevant human rights treaties.[16] A careful examination of the text of these treaties, which is the subject of detailed discussion in the remaining chapters of this book, reveals that such objections are unconvincing.

II The preliminary question: the need to interrogate the conceptual foundations of the right to health?

When confronted with the issue of the conceptual foundations of human rights, one of the world's pioneering human rights academics, Louis Henkin, wrote, '[t]he justification of human rights is rhetorical, not philosophical. Human rights are self evident, implied in other ideas that are commonly intuited and accepted'.[17] It is an appealing sentiment and offers an easy exit strategy from the need to engage with the intellectual complexities, or potential harm as some would say,[18] associated with philosophical inquiry. Richard Rorty favours a similar course. For him the success of the human rights enterprise is not dependent on grand theories that seek to justify the very existence of the concept of human rights—such 'foundationalism' is said to be outmoded.[19] Pragmatism and sentiment, not theory and reason, are the ingredients he considers necessary to 'bring about the utopia sketched by the Enlightenment'.[20] Thus, given that there is already a right to health in international law, and advocates are increasingly enlisting this right in their struggle to address the health needs of individuals, a question arises as to whether there is any need to interrogate its conceptual foundations.

The view taken here is that to evade this question is to give up on a fundamental element of the human rights idea, thus jeopardizing its legitimacy and potential for implementation. This argument rests on the proposition that an international human right, such as the right to health, can be seen to consist of three interconnected dimensions—legal, political, *and* moral.[21] The justification of the legal dimension of the right to health rests on the premise that it has been recognized as a legitimate standard within international law.[22] Thus, it complies with what Griffin calls the 'rule of recognition' as to when the term 'human rights' has been used

---

[16] See Merritt (n 3) 280 (uses the idea of problems of conception and problems of implementation to examine the philosophical status of the right to health).

[17] Louis Henkin, *The Age of Rights* (Columbia University Press, 1990) 2 (further notes that '[t]he contemporary version does not ground or justify itself in natural law, in social contract, or in any other political theory').

[18] John Humphrey, *Human Rights and the United Nations: A Great Adventure* (Transnational Publishers, 1984) 44 (argues in his account of the drafting of the Universal Declaration of Human Rights, that 'the greatest harm which resulted from the introduction of unnecessary philosophical concepts was the needless controversy and useless debate they invited').

[19] Richard Rorty, 'Human Rights, Rationality and Sentimentality' in Stephen Shute and Susan Hurley (eds), *On Human Rights* (Basic Books, 1993) 111.

[20] ibid 118, 122.

[21] Rainer Frost, 'The Justification of Human Rights and the Basic Right to Justification: A Reflexive Approach' (2010) 120 Ethics 711, 711 (refers to the moral, political, and legal *life* of a human right).

[22] Griffin (n 4) 203.

correctly or incorrectly in international law.[23] The political dimension of the right relates to the way in which it is invoked by advocates as a tool to assess the legitimacy of measures that impact on the health of individuals within a state and between states.[24] The justification for such an approach draws on the claim that human rights is a global enterprise that provides the 'settled norms of political discourse',[25] whereby states have voluntarily accepted the obligations under the relevant treaties that protect the right to health as the standards by which to assess the legitimacy of their efforts to address the health needs of their citizens.

But relying solely upon the legal and political justifications of the right to health risks overlooking the reality that, despite states' ostensible acceptance of human rights through ratification of international treaties, there remains widespread disagreement as to the status of economic and social rights, including the right to health.[26] Moreover, even if agreement can be reached on the idea of a right to health, there is an absence of widespread consensus as to its implications. In such circumstances, Henkin's claim as to the self-evident legitimacy of human rights looks very fragile in a pluralistic world and Rorty's exhortation to 'concentrate our energy on manipulating sentiments' becomes deeply problematic.[27] In the absence of agreement as to the meaning of the right to health and its underlying values, the right risks becoming invisible to those for whom it is not self-evident. It also remains especially vulnerable to manipulation, whether consciously or unconsciously, by those who wish to use it as a rhetorical device with which to agitate, not for an *international* right to health, but for their own subjective vision of what such a right should entail.[28]

In such circumstances, the need to better understand the conceptual foundations of, and to provide a moral justification for, the right to health becomes more

---

[23] ibid. cf Ronald Dworkin, 'Human Rights and International Law: Political Legitimacy' (unpublished paper, copy on file with author) 22–3 (challenges the rule of recognition as justifying the legality of international law on the grounds that international treaties do not resolve conflicts between competing standards and the interpretation of international law is unclear).

[24] See Katharine Young, 'Securing Health through Rights' in Thomas Pogge, Matthew Rimmer and Kim Rubenstein (eds), *Incentives for Global Public Health: Parent Law and Access to Essential Medicines* (CUP, 2010) 357, 357.

[25] See also Mervyn Frost, *Ethics in International Relations: A Constitutive Theory* (CUP, 1996) 104–11, cited in Jack Donnelly, *Universal Human Rights in Theory and Practice* (2nd edn, Cornell University Press, 2003) 38. See also Beitz (n 6) 8 (stresses that the human rights enterprise is a global practice); Samuel Moyn, *The Last Utopia* (Harvard University Press, 2010) 213, 222 (argues that the 'collapse of alternative institutionalisms' such as communism and 'the crisis of other utopias' provided the opportunity for human rights to fill the void and provide the dominant vision for addressing global wrongs).

[26] See, eg, Griffin (n 4) 28 (argues that a 'legal functional account [of human rights] is short of explanatory power'); Jeremy Waldron, 'Socioeconomic Rights and Theories of Justice' (Colloquium on Law, Economics and Politics, NYU Law School, 28 September 2010) 3 (argues that a defence of economic and social rights on the grounds that they address urgent interests and command a high place in the order of moral priorities does not address the question of what kind of priority should be accorded to such rights relative to other priorities within moral and political life).

[27] Rorty (n 19) 122.

[28] For a discussion of this danger see David Kennedy, 'The International Human Rights Movement: Part of the Problem?' (2002) 15 Harv Hu251 Rts J 101; Martii Koskenniemi, 'Human Rights Mainstreaming as a Project of Power' (unpublished paper, copy on file with author, 5 February 2006).

pressing. Indeed, rather than undermine the right to health, as Henkin and Rorty might suggest, such an inquiry seeks to advance its status by offering the most 'intellectually compelling' case to justify its inclusion within the lexicon of international human rights.[29] The hope is that such an account will convince at least some of the sceptics as to the merits of an *international human right to health* while grounding but also constraining the enthusiasm of those for whom such a right is already self-evident.

III The conceptual foundations of the right to health

A Looking for foundations in incompletely theorized agreements

The international legal instruments which recognize the right to health are all examples of what can be described as incompletely theorized agreements. This term, first coined by Cass Sunstein, describes the process by which a common agreement is reached by consensus with respect to an issue in circumstances where there was disagreement as to the reasons or principles that justify the agreement.[30] The concept of incompletely theorized agreements is well-suited to capture the nature of international human rights instruments, which are generated by processes that must accommodate 'a moral universe that is diverse and pluralistic', and allow for agreement between states without the need to adhere to a particular theory of general principles.[31]

In practice this has meant that states have been able to agree on the inclusion of the right to health within international treaties without formal agreement on the *specific* principles or theory that justifies such an approach. In other words, despite the fact that states may have differing theories with respect to the justification of human rights generally, or the right to health more specifically, they have put aside these differences for the sake of achieving consensus on the need to include a right to health in international law.[32] Moreover, these same differences have militated against the prospect of achieving detailed agreement among states as to the *precise* measures required by them for the implementation of the right to health. As a consequence, international treaties recognizing the right to health reflect what Sunstein would describe as mid-level, principled, agreement. In other words, the existence of a right

---

[29] Griffin (n 4) 204. See also Amartya Sen, 'Elements of a Theory of Human Rights' (2004) 32 Phil & Pub Aff 315, 317 (argues that 'the conceptual doubts must also be satisfactorily addressed if the idea of human rights is to command reasoned loyalty and to establish a secure intellectual standing'); Michael Freeman, 'The Philosophical Foundations of Human Rights' (1994) 16 Hum Rts Q 491, 493 (argues that to evade the task of finding the best grounding for human rights is to demonstrate a lack of intellectual responsibility); Allen Buchanan, 'The Egalitarianism of Human Rights' (2010) 120 Ethics 679, 679–80 (notes that the 'nature of the justification for claims about the existence of human rights remains obscure').

[30] Cass Sunstein, 'Incompletely Theorized Agreements' (1995) 108 Harv L Rev 1733.

[31] ibid 1748.

[32] See Jacques Martin, 'Introduction' in UNESCO (ed), *Human Rights Comments and Interpretations* (Allan Wingate, 1949) 9, 10 (recounts the remark of a colleague from the UNESCO Committee on the Theoretical Bases of Human Rights that 'we agree about rights on condition that no one asks why').

to health is accepted but there is disagreement as to the specific theory that accounts for the existence of such a right and about the specific measures required to fulfil this right.[33]

Of course such an approach might be thought to produce a rather tenuous outcome for those seeking to justify a right to health. Indeed, it is 'customary to lament an outcome on the ground that it has been inadequately justified'.[34] For some, like Charles Beitz, the response is simply to abandon attempts to 'discover and describe the deeper order of values' from which human rights derive their authority and focus on the actual practice of international human rights which is said to exist 'as a political doctrine constructed to play a certain role in global political life'.[35] But such an approach risks swinging the pendulum too far. Human rights instruments may represent incompletely theorized agreements, but this does not mean that such agreements are completely barren in the sense of being devoid of *any* theoretical content or underlying values. This then invites the question as to what theoretical account of the right to health is reflected in the nature of the agreement arrived at by state parties under international law?

A simple answer to this question is that the text of the relevant international treaties reflects a moral commitment to the idea that health, and more precisely the highest attainable standard of health, is an interest worthy of recognition as an international human right. Moreover, the scope of this right is broad and extends beyond the mere protection of health or the delivery of health care services, to an obligation to take measures to realize the highest attainable standard of health. It therefore demands that states do more than simply refrain from interfering with an individual's health or providing protection against threats to health from non-state sources. But these observations do not answer the deeper question of what theory of rights, incomplete though it may be, or what moral values underlie these propositions and whether they can be justified. I intend to answer this question by examining the constitutive elements of this right and then addressing the various grounds of scepticism that characterize the status of this right within the philosophical literature.

B The idea of a human right to health

Countless pages have been written on the ideas of rights and human rights. These discussions need not be repeated here and it is sufficient to address briefly the following fundamental questions: what is a right; what is a human right; who is entitled to rights and human rights; and what is the basis or justification for a right such as the right to health? In terms of the first question, in its most basic form, a right is as an entitlement of X that gives rise to duties or obligations that can be claimed against Y.[36] A human right is a species of the genus *rights* that is granted to,

---

[33] Sunstein, 'Incompletely Theorized Agreements' (n 30) 1739.
[34] ibid 1738.
[35] Beitz (n 6) 7, 48–9. See also Rorty (n 19) 116.
[36] Joseph Raz, *The Morality of Freedom* (Clarendon Press, 1986) 166; Merritt (n 3) 277–8. It is important to note that commentators have argued that a right can either be socially recognized or exist as a

or recognized for, a person by virtue of being a human being where, in the case of international law, the duty bearer is the state.[37] In terms of who is entitled to rights, various theories take differing positions. For example, under a will or choice theory of rights, the capacity to exercise and enjoy rights is a prerequisite to the entitlement to rights. Therefore, individuals who lack autonomy, capacity, and competency such as children and adults with a severe mental illness would not be entitled to rights.[38] Under international law, however, the will theory of rights has been rejected in favour of an approach that couples the capacity to hold rights with the mere status of being human. Thus, the only prerequisite to being entitled to the human rights recognized in international law is that the claimant be human.[39]

The justification for a right or a human right remains deeply contested. Historically appeals were made to natural law and the inherent dignity of man (sic) as the foundation of all rights. Traces of this approach can be detected in the text of the international human rights instruments that protect the right to health. For example, the preamble to the Universal Declaration of Human Rights (UDHR) and the International Covenant on Economic, Social and Cultural Rights (ICESCR) speak of the 'inalienable rights of all members of the human family'.[40] But ever since Bentham's attack on natural rights as nonsense upon stilts, these metaphysical foundations have been widely considered to be inadequate as a theoretical justification for human rights.[41] At the same time, the persistent reference to these origins in the text and preamble of international human rights instruments cannot be ignored.

---

claim that it *should* be socially recognized: John Eekelaar, *Family Law and Private Life* (OUP, 2006) 134–5. The view taken in this chapter is that a claim to a right that has not yet been recognized by the relevant duty bearer as a right, is not a right that can be said to be justified. It may have a justification under a particular theory of rights based on a particular moral vision of the world. For example, Amartya Sen's theory of rights is derived from ethics and his capabilities approach: Sen (n 29) 320. But the view taken here and discussed below is that the justification for a human right rests in the social process that leads to the production and recognition of a human right.

[37] Commentators who seek to justify a theory of rights in ethics or moral values independent of their legal exposition are less proscriptive in the identification of the duty bearer when defining a human right. For example, Amartya Sen defines human rights to be ethical demands that give rise to claims that impose duties *on all members of society*. Sen (n 29) 338–41.

[38] Neil MacCormick, 'Children's Rights: A Test Case for Theories of Rights' in Neil MacCormick, *Legal Right and Social Democracy* (Clarendon Press, 1982) ch 8 (argues that a will theory must be rejected in favour of an interest theory of rights otherwise children would be precluded from enjoying rights).

[39] There is a debate as to whether the unborn child is a human for the purposes of international law. See, eg, Rita Joseph, *The Human Rights of the Unborn Child* (Kluwer, 2010); Philip Alston, 'The Unborn Child and Abortion under the Draft Convention on the Rights of the Child' (1990) 12 Hum Rts Q 156. The dominant view and the view that is consistent with a proper application of the principles of treaty interpretation under international law, is that international law allows states to determine how they will resolve this issue.

[40] cf Beitz (n 6) 20 (argues that the UDHR does not seek to locate human dignity in further considerations of human nature or as a divine gift but offers no account as to the relevance of the reference to the inalienability of human rights).

[41] Jeremy Bentham, 'Anarchical Fallacies; Being an Examination of the Declarations of Rights Issued during the French Revolution' in John Bowring (ed), *The Works of Jeremy Bentham* (William Tait 1843) vol II, 501. See also Beitz (n 6) 49–59; Sen (n 29) 316. cf Pope John Paul XXIII, *Pacem in Terris: Encyclical on Establishing Universal Peace, Justice, Charity, and Liberty* (11 April 1963).

There are two potential ways to respond to this dilemma. First, such references could be taken to reflect the personal values and preferences of individuals involved in drafting the UDHR. John Humphrey, who headed the United Nations body tasked with drafting the UDHR, has recounted his concern at the discussion and inclusion of philosophical concepts in the UDHR at the behest of the French member of the drafting team, Rene Cassin. With respect to article 1 of the UDHR, Humphrey reflected that, '[a]part from the fact that at least part of this statement is of questionable truth, it is purely hortatory and adds nothing to the authority of the Universal Declaration of Human Rights'.[42] Given the diverse moral and cultural perspectives of the states involved in the drafting of the UDHR, it is likely that the representatives of many states may have assumed that such references would have no substantive impact on the nature of the obligations to be assumed under the UDHR.

A second way to view the references to the inherent nature of rights within international instruments is to focus on the strategic purpose of such statements rather than treat them as an exposition of the theoretical foundations of human rights.[43] Under this approach, it is the political attraction of the idea of an inalienable right to health that becomes significant. Thus, in the wake of the appalling tragedy of World War II, overtures to the idea of inalienable rights can be interpreted as a political strategy to raise the status of human rights and facilitate agreement among diverse nations.

C Grounding rights in interests

Despite the political attraction of inalienable rights, most philosophers have lost interest in appealing to metaphysical justifications for human rights, and have instead turned to theories that ground rights in certain interests. However, there is all too little agreement as to the basis upon which these interests should be determined. For example, Joseph Raz argues that only those interests that are of 'ultimate value' to the well-being of an individual are sufficient to base a right.[44] James Griffin's theory of human rights contends that an interest is only sufficient to be recognized as a human right if it can be established as a component of normative agency.[45] For Amartya Sen, the interests which ground a human right are those freedoms that enhance the capabilities of an individual.[46] Allen Buchanan and

---

[42] Humphrey (n 18) 44.
[43] Peter Rosenblum, 'Teaching Human Rights: Ambivalent Activism, Multiple Discourses and Lingering Dilemmas' (2002) 15 Har Hum Rts J 301, 305.
[44] Raz, *The Morality of Freedom* (n 36) 176–83 ('Being of ultimate, ie, non-derivative value is being intrinsically valuable, ie, being valuable independently of one's instrumental value. Something is instrumentally valuable to the extent that it derives its value from the value of its consequences, or the value of the consequences it is likely to have or . . . can be used to produce': 177).
[45] Griffin (n 4) 179–87.
[46] Sen (n 29) 320–5. See also Ruger, *Health and Social Justice* (n 3) 118 (extends Sen's work to the idea of the right to health to argue that a health capability paradigm offers a philosophical justification for a right to health).

Kristen Hessler understand human rights as 'moral claims grounded in basic human interests',[47] while Charles Beitz argues that only 'urgent individual interests' against certain predictable dangers qualify for protection of human rights,[48] and in the context of children, John Eekelaar suggests that three types of interest—basic, developmental, and autonomy—justify children's rights.[49] The theme that unites the work of these theorists is that they all attempt to offer a vision of rights that is linked with those interests that are considered to be essential to achieving a particular vision which is variously described as a good life, human flourishing, personhood, and autonomy or normative agency—all ideas about what it means to be a human being and the role of rights in securing that vision.

This is not the place to undertake a critical analysis of each of these theories.[50] Instead the focus of this inquiry is to determine whether a persuasive account can be offered to justify the recognition of the interest an individual has in his or her health, as a human right in international law. The first point to make is that given the incompletely theorized nature of international agreements that protect the right to health, and the contested nature of those theories that seek to offer comprehensive accounts as to the proper nature and content of human rights, there is a need to ensure that the search for the perfect does not become the enemy of the good. Moreover, to return to the point stressed above, an incompletely theorized agreement does not equate to one that is fatally flawed.

With this in mind it is argued that in order to justify using a person's health to ground a human right it is not necessary to identify a comprehensive moral theory (the 'perfect' justification which in any event is incapable of implementation given the inevitability of incompletely theorized agreements in international law).[51] But Griffin's concern goes further than this when he concludes that there is *no* agreement

---

[47] Buchanan and Hessler (n 1) 213 (defined as interests universally shared by all human beings as kinds of interests that justify assigning obligations to others or society to protect those interests).

[48] Beitz (n 6) 109, 122 (urgent interests are said to be those interests which would be recognizable as important in a range of typical lives that occur in contemporary societies and do not necessarily include an interest possessed by everyone or desired by everyone: 110).

[49] John Eekelaar, 'The Emergence of Children's Rights' (1986) 6 OJLS 161.

[50] It is worth noting that James Griffin's work, which is generally recognized as being the most comprehensive attempt to provide a theoretical justification of human rights, has been the subject of a recent symposium and significant commentary. Thus, for a critique of his work see: Buchanan, 'The Egalitarianism of Human Rights' (n 29); Rainer Forst, 'The Justification of Human Rights and the Basic Right to Justification: A Reflexive Approach' (2010) 120 Ethics 711; Joseph Raz, 'Human Rights without Foundations' in Samantha Besson and John Tasioulas (eds), *The Philosophy of International Law* (OUP, 2010) 321, 322–8.

[51] This is not to say that such endeavours are completely futile and should be dismissed. On the contrary, the close attention given to the conceptual foundations of human rights provides significant cause to reflect on the nature of the human rights enterprise. It reveals its limitations and it also has the potential to shape the understanding of how it is to be developed in the future. For example, one of Griffin's criteria for assessing the justification for a human right is whether its obligations are 'socially manageable': Griffin (n 4) 37–9. Even if his account of human rights is rejected, this requirement of social manageability can still be accommodated within the interpretation of a state's obligations under the right to health. Indeed, in Chapter 3, I will propose an interpretative methodology that includes the requirement that any interpretation of the right to health be practical, which to borrow Griffin's phrase, means that it must be 'socially manageable'.

as to the criteria by which rights are derived from the idea of what it means to be human.[52] Although he is anxious to provide human rights with a substantive conceptual foundation, the question is whether the underlying assumption on which he bases his quest is sound. Is there really *no agreement* as to the foundations of human rights?

D A social interest theory of rights

The argument made here is that, although not completely theorized, a level of moral agreement—not merely legal or political—still exists and is reflected in the social process that leads to the recognition of a particular interest, such as the highest attainable standard of health, as a human right. The theoretical basis for this agreement may remain incomplete, but this should not preclude it from providing a 'good' or persuasive justification. Under such an approach the interests that ground and justify a human right will never be inherent, essential, urgent, or capable of determination by reference to a single test or moral theory. Instead, they will always be contested, negotiated, historically contingent, and produced by particular social processes. Thus, those interests that form the basis of a claim for a human right will only be transformed into a right if such a claim, and its attendant obligations, are accepted by the duty bearer. Under this model '[r]ights are not moral fruits that spring up from bare earth fully ripened without cultivation.'[53] But nor is it the case that 'we may claim a right to health *only* if it can be harvested from an acceptable general theory of distributive justice or from a more particular theory of justice for health and health care.'[54] A more nuanced approach is required because recourse to high level or comprehensive theories to justify human rights risks placing the bar too high given the reality of incompletely theorized agreements on matters such as a right to health.[55]

This nuanced approach requires an understanding that the recognition of a claim to a right must involve an appeal to, and awareness of, interests other than those of the beneficiary of the right.[56] The statement that 'a right gives rise to a duty' has become axiomatic in human rights discourse. But while extensive attention has been given by philosophers to the question of which interests deserve recognition as a human right, they have tended to overlook two considerations. First, it is not simply the interest that must be justified but also the *actual* content of the obligation or duty

---

[52] Griffin (n 4) 16.
[53] Daniels, *Just Health: Meeting Health Needs Fairly* (n 3) 15.
[54] ibid (emphasis added).
[55] Beauchamp and Faden (n 1) 127 (argue that 'the idea that a general theory of justice can be applied with consistency to the formulation of public policies has, for the most part been a failure').
[56] See O'Neill (n 5) 439 (argues that by shifting from an exclusive focus on the individual beneficiary of a right to the nature of the duties imposed upon states, it becomes possible to elevate the human rights enterprise from an aspirational enterprise to a normative one).

with respect to the realization of the interest that has been elevated to the status of a right.[57]

Second, they also tend to overlook both the role that rights play in the regulation of power and the deliberative nature of how human rights are produced. As John Eekelaar explains, '[a] claim to a right is a claim to a distribution of power as a matter of entitlement'.[58] Moreover, as the history of the right to health outlined in Chapter 1 demonstrates, the idea of the right to health does not possess metaphysical properties and nor was it discovered like some jewel buried in the ground. It was the need to respond to human suffering and experiences of perceived injustice within states, which inspired the idea of human rights, including the right to health. Human rights were forged as a tool to regulate the relationship between the governed and the governing within a state—to respond to the perceived failings and excesses of particular approaches to governance and power distribution.[59]

The original conception of human rights was therefore deeply political but it was not bereft of moral or ethical underpinnings and was heavily inspired by humanitarian sentiments. Indeed, the preamble of the UDHR proclaims that 'disregard and contempt for human rights have resulted in barbarous acts which have outraged the conscience of mankind'; and it determines to 'promote social progress and better standards of life in larger freedom'. It adds that the UDHR is a 'common standard of achievement for all peoples and all Nations' for which every individual and organ in society will strive to promote respect and achieve universal recognition and observance. The preamble also appeals to the 'inherent dignity' of all members of the human family and article 1 proclaims that:

All human beings are born free and equal in dignity and rights. They are endowed with reason and conscience and should act towards one another in a spirit of brotherhood.

These concepts are not morally vacuous. Indeed, they bear a close resemblance to many of the concepts, such as human flourishing, personhood, capabilities, and normative agency, that provide foundations for the theories of human rights advanced by many philosophers. It is true that they remain incompletely theorized—a feature that is vividly illustrated by the treatment of dignity within those instruments that protect the right to health.

---

[57] This is not to say that philosophers ignore the issue of duties. Griffin, for example, gives it considerable treatment: Griffin (n 4) esp 96–110. Onora O'Neill also argues that for the human rights enterprise to be taken seriously it is 'preferable to offer a serious account of the allocation of obligations that correspond to all human rights': O'Neill (n 5) 431. But as will be detailed below, in the case of Griffin's criticism of the right to health, there is a tendency to make assumptions rather than undertake careful analysis of the nature of these duties attendant upon a right such as health.

[58] Eekelaar, *Family Law and Private Life* (n 36) 137.

[59] See Cass Sunstein, *The Second Bill of Rights: Franklin Delano Roosevelt's Unfinished Revolution and Why We Need It More Than Ever* (Basic Books, 2006) 1 (rights are 'a product of wrongs'). See also Rawls (n 2) 27, 79 (perceives human rights as a mechanism 'to provide a suitable definition of and limits on a government's internal sovereignty' but his focus is on the role of human rights in informing the 'justifying reasons for war and its conduct').

E Dignity as both coterminous and foundational

The idea of the inherent dignity of every human being occupies a revered place within human rights law, but its role remains conflicted and problematic. In the case of the UDHR and Convention on the Rights of the Child (CRC), human rights and dignity are stated to be coterminous (UDHR: 'Whereas recognition of the inherent dignity and of the equal and inalienable rights...'; CRC: 'recognition of the inherent dignity and of the equal and inalienable rights of all members of the human family'). In contrast, the idea of inherent dignity is treated as the foundation of human rights in the preamble to the ICESCR ('Recognizing that these rights derive from the inherent dignity of the human person...'). It is hard to conceive of a more striking example of incomplete theorization as to the foundation of human rights—both coterminous and derived from dignity at the one time.

Moreover, the idea of *inherent* dignity within human rights instruments is also incomplete. It is generally taken to reflect the Kantian notion of dignity, which posits that dignity is the inviolable property of all human beings.[60] But this is problematic for two reasons. First, it is unaccompanied by a moral justification.[61] Second, if dignity is inalienable, it can never be lost. For Killmister, this presents the risk that human rights will offer 'little in the way of guidelines for action' because 'there is nothing to fear from those acts which are sometimes said to threaten us and human rights would provide'.[62] Thus, dignity, at least in the Kantian sense, may only offer a 'thin' philosophical justification for human rights.[63] Indeed, Schroder has suggested that it may be more advisable to 'achieve contractual agreement on specific human rights and dispense with a reference to dignity in constitutions' altogether.[64] It is a confronting argument given the special status of *inherent* dignity within human rights discourse.

A dilemma therefore exists with respect to the role of dignity in the search to secure a justification for the right to health. One way to address this dilemma is to acknowledge that, just as the notion of inherent rights played an important political role in transcending philosophical differences during the drafting of the UDHR, so too did the idea of *inherent* dignity. The widespread use of this concept in national constitutions, philosophical writings, religious beliefs, and contemporary social movements turned it into a rallying cry for the international human rights movement.[65] The appeal to the idea of dignity, therefore, arose because of its capacity to be 'used as a linguistic-symbol' that could represent 'different outlooks

---

[60] Doris Schroeder, 'Dignity: One, Two, Three, Four, Five, Still Counting' (2010) 19 Cam Q Health Ethics 1, 4 (also outlines five concepts of dignity: (i) Kantian; (ii) aristocratic; (iii) meritorious; (iv) comportment; (v) and divine/religious).

[61] ibid.

[62] Suzy Killmister, 'Dignity: Not Such a Useless Concept' (2009) 36 J Med Ethics 160, 162.

[63] ibid.

[64] Schroder (n 60) 6.

[65] See Christopher McCrudden, 'Human Dignity and the Judicial Interpretation of Human Rights' (2008) 19 EJIL 655 677–8.

thereby justifying a concrete political agreement on a seemingly shared ground.'[66] But as McCrudden has explained, '[u]nlike in linguistics...where a placeholder carries no semantic information, dignity carried an *enormous amount of content, but different content for different people*'.[67] Thus, while commentators have labelled dignity as a 'useless concept'[68] that is 'deeply obscure',[69] McCrudden has distilled an overlapping consensus within the differing conceptions of dignity which consists of three broad elements. First, that 'every human being possesses an intrinsic worth merely by being human'; second that this 'worth should be recognised and respected by others' and third, that 'the State should be seen to exist for the sake of the individual human being and not vice versa.'[70]

When viewed within this framework, the fact that dignity is stated to be coterminous or foundational in international human rights instruments that protect the right to health is largely irrelevant. Its inconsistent treatment merely reflects the incompletely theorized nature of these agreements. What matters is that an overlapping consensus can be said to exist with respect to the values that underlie its inclusion—the worth of the individual, the need to respect this worth, and the role of the state in securing the worth of individuals. Within this context, international human rights that are agreed upon by states, including the right to the highest attainable standard of health, are not only moral entitlements, albeit incompletely theorized, but also the means by which to respect, protect, and fulfil the moral value of every person.

F Beyond individualism

However, the conceptual foundations of human rights in international law are not based solely on individualistic values. As detailed in Chapter 1, their recognition was also ushered in by instrumentalist concerns and a belief that the enjoyment of human rights, and especially the right to health, would deliver peace, justice, and stability both for individual states and the global political order.[71] The coupling of this teleological (ends or goal based) dimension of human rights with its deontological (duty based) dimension is reflected in the first line of the preamble of the

---

[66] D Shultziner, 'Human Dignity—Function and Meanings' (2003) 3 Global Jurist Topics 5, 5.
[67] McCrudden (n 65) 678 (emphasis added).
[68] Ruth Macklin, 'Dignity is a Useless Concept' (2003) 327 BMJ 1419.
[69] Griffin (n 4) 203.   [70] ibid.
[71] cf Beitz (n 6) 132 (rejects a justification of human rights on the basis of a generalized concern to protect international stability because he considers that the empirical evidence to support this view is 'notably insecure' in that there is little evidence that governments that abuse the human rights of their own citizens pose a greater threat than other governments to international order). However, Beitz's criticism overlooks three factors: first, human rights are not only concerned with international stability and also offer a vision of justice within states and not just between states; second, the experiences of the Second World War provided the empirical basis upon which states determined the existence of a nexus between human rights and global stability, and third, in the context of health it has been recognized since the 1850s with the beginning of the international sanitation movement, that a failure to attend to global health issues has potentially serious consequences for global stability.

UDHR—'whereas recognition of the inherent dignity and of the equal and inalienable rights of all members of the human family *is the foundation of freedom, justice and peace in the world.*'[72] It is also manifest in the qualified nature of the obligation imposed on states to secure the right to health under the ICESCR—an obligation that remains progressive and subject to the availability of resources (article 2) and to limitation where this is necessary to promote the general welfare in a democratic society (article 4). Indeed, the drafting history of article 4 of the ICESCR notes that '[t]here was, it was said, an absolute necessity for harmonising the rights of the individual on the one hand and the requirements of the community on the other'.[73] It is thus misleading to suggest, as some commentators have, that human rights are not contingent on the outcomes arrived at by their application.[74] Consequentialism is very much a relevant consideration in the human rights enterprise given the need to balance the potentially competing rights of individuals within the context of scarce resources. But the measurement of these consequences is to be made against human rights standards rather than, for example, a simple utilitarian model.

Thus, far from being a 'vacuous concept'[75] that is 'nearly criterionless'[76] and whose intention is 'so especially thin',[77] an examination of the factors and values that led to the elevation of an individual's health to a human right in international law and its attendant duties, reveals a far more complex theory of human rights than commentators have been prepared to concede or acknowledge. The fundamental feature of this theory is that the identification of the interests that ground a human right is the result of negotiation and compromise. It is the overlapping consensus between states that enables the elevation of interests, such as health, to an international human right that provides the source of their moral authority. Moreover, it is not only the interests of a beneficiary that ground a right—it is also the interests of the duty bearer that determine the scope and content of the obligation. The recognition of a right to health and its attendant duties is not simply to benefit individuals but is also intended to bolster the interests of the broader community. Thus, far from 'espousing radical ethical individualism', the right to health must be seen 'as essential for the promotion of the common good'.[78] This idea is captured in the comments of Dr Bustos, the Chilean delegate to the International Health Conference in 1946 at which the Constitution of the World Health Organization was adopted. After affirming the inclusion of the fundamental right to health in the preamble of the WHO Constitution, he declared that:

---

[72] UDHR, preamble (emphasis added).
[73] *Annotations on the Text of the Draft International Covenants on Human Rights*, UN Doc A/2929 (1 July 1955) 25.
[74] Dan Seymour and Jonathan Pincus, 'Human Rights and Economics: The Conceptual Basis for their Complementarity' (2008) 26 Dev Pol'y Rev 387, 397.
[75] Guess (n 10) 144.
[76] Griffin (n 4) 15.   [77] ibid 16.
[78] McCrudden (n 66) 10.

The adoption of the Constitution would signify that, in the future, health would be no longer a matter of private interest to the individual and to the State, but a matter of social interest and worldwide implications.[79]

This account of the conceptual foundations of human rights is described as a social interest theory of rights. It asserts that none of the interests that ground a right and inform the nature and scope of the duties attendant upon that right will ever be fixed or determined by reference to a particular test or moral theory. On the contrary, they will always remain contested, historically contingent, and be constantly evolving. Under this theory of human rights, the justification in elevating an interest such as health to the status of a human right rests in the deliberative and collaborative process by which states (subject to lobbying and advocacy from civil society and institutional bodies) identify and elevate a particular interest to the status of a human right. This is not merely a political account of human rights although the production of international instruments is deeply embedded in systems of power.[80] It also asserts that the overlapping consensus that enables agreement on the acceptance of a particular interest, such as health, also reflects an acceptance of the moral values and theory, albeit incompletely theorized, that underpin the justification for such a right.

G Dynamic but not arbitrary

Ultimately, a social interest theory of rights reflects the idea expressed by Sally Merry that human rights is primarily a cultural system—fluid and contentious[81]—that produces and constructs rather than discovers a particular vision of what it means to 'promote social progress and better standards of life' and 'enjoy freedom from fear or want'—the aspirations identified in the preamble to the UDHR. Thus, the preamble to instruments such as the ICESCR may assert that the right to health, like all human rights, is derived from the 'inherent dignity of the human person', but this instrument cannot be taken to reflect a comprehensive theory of human dignity or 'the existence of a universal human nature'.[82] Instead, it reflects a historically contingent and contested understanding of the rights agreed to by states, albeit under an incompletely theorized agreement, that will shift and change over time. This is reflected by the fact that within a few years of the ICESCR's adoption, new international instruments such as the CRC, the Convention on the Rights of Persons with Disabilities (CRPD), and the

---

[79] WHO, *Official Records of the World Health Organization No 2: Proceedings and Final Acts of the International Health Conference Held in New York from 19 June to 22 July 1946* (UN WHO Interim Commission June 1948) 66–7.

[80] By highlighting the political nature of how human rights are produced, a social interest theory of rights does not risk overlooking how 'rights holder's interests are constructed, and by whom'—something that other interests formulations of rights 'are notably reticent' to do: Eekelaar, *Family Law and Private Life* (n 36) 136.

[81] Sally Merry, *Human Rights and Gender Violence: Translating International Law into Local Justice* (University of Chicago Press 2006) 16. See also Rorty (n 19) 115–16 (notes that although in his mind human rights culture may be morally superior to others, he does not think that 'this superiority counts in favour of the existence of a universal human nature').

[82] Rorty (n 19) 116.

Convention on the Elimination of All Forms of Discrimination against Women (CEDAW) recognized novel or modified duties with respect to the right to health that were not envisioned at the time when the ICESCR was drafted. This dynamism does not, however, produce an arbitrary theory of human rights, just one that is contingent on the 'anthropological realities' and 'contemporary political conditions' that characterize the environment in which an international human rights treaty is negotiated.[83] Significantly, in the case of the right to health, these cultural realities and political conditions reflect a long-standing acceptance, as detailed in Chapter 1, of the need for those in positions of power to take measures to advance the health of individuals both in their own interests and in the interests of the individuals concerned.

IV Dealing with the detractors: a defence of the right to health

The conceptual foundations of the right to health continue to be subject to significant challenges from a range of perspectives. The most significant critiques for our purposes are the libertarian objection, the status objection, the formulation objection, the cultural relativist challenge, and the resource allocation dilemma. As noted earlier, many of these concerns are grounded in theories or understandings of rights that do not accurately reflect the realities of international human rights law, or are based on assumptions as to the nature and scope of the right to health that are unsupported by a proper understanding of the text of the relevant instruments. These concerns can be dispatched as reflecting ignorance or misunderstanding. In contrast, concerns that arise out of theories of rights that are essentially incompatible with the approach adopted by states under international law are, by definition, going to be irreconcilable. This is especially true of those theories that reject in their entirety the liberal-egalitarian values and commitments to some form of redistributive justice that underpin the social interest theory of rights reflected in international law.[84] We turn now to examine the principal challenges.

A The libertarian objection

The duty upon states to protect the right to health in international law requires the allocation of resources to achieve the progressive realization of the highest attainable standard of health.[85] This obligation to allocate resources anticipates that states must create a tax system in order to facilitate the transfer of resources to achieve the highest attainable standard of health for every individual within the jurisdiction of a state.[86]

---

[83] Freeman (n 29) 513–14.

[84] Space does not permit a detailed account as to the basis for such a claim. However, it is generally accepted that these values characterize the rights recognized in international law. For a recent account see Buchanan, 'The Egalitarianism of Human Rights' (n 29).

[85] ICESCR, art 2.

[86] Henry Steiner, Philip Alston, and Ryan Goodman, *International Human Rights in Context: Law, Politics and Morals* (3rd edn, OUP, 2008) 305–7. See also WHO, *The World Health Report 2010: Health Systems Financing—The Path to Universal Health Coverage* (WHO 2010) ch 2.

This duty is based on beneficence and reflects a theory of redistributive justice that is hostile to the strict libertarian vision of the world with its emphasis on the autonomy of the individual.[87] Under libertarian theory, liberty is the fundamental value and states must not undertake any measures that would unreasonably interfere with the liberty of an individual.[88] The taxation of an individual for the purpose of redistributing resources to secure the right to the highest attainable standard of health of other individuals is considered by libertarians to represent an example of an unreasonable interference.[89]

Importantly, libertarian theory would not necessarily reject the idea of a right to health per se. It would advocate for the imposition of a negative duty on states to refrain from interfering with the health of an individual but it would confine the positive duty of a state to an obligation to provide protection against threats to the health of an individual that were beyond his or her capacity to control.[90] Thus, for example, vaccination programs to protect against communicable diseases, environmental regulations, and occupational health and safety laws to protect against external threats to an individual's health would generally be considered tolerable within libertarian theory, provided they remained optional.[91] Variations of this theory would also concede that education programs to raise awareness about threats to health such as sexually transmitted diseases, alcohol consumption, and drug use would also be justified.[92] Significantly all these measures are included in the obligation of states under the right to health in international law. But a libertarian would argue that if a state is required to provide medical care to all persons, or if individuals are compelled against their will to insure themselves against ill health, this would not be justified within a libertarian vision of justice and rights.[93] Moreover, it would create a perverse incentive because individuals would not be motivated to take responsibility for their own health if they knew that the state would ensure their care should they become ill.[94]

This raises a question as to whether the libertarian approach to the right to health should be preferred over the liberal-egalitarian model that characterizes the right to health in international law. The potential for the creation of perverse disincentives

---

[87] Engelhardt, 'Rights to Health Care' (n 1) 336.
[88] See Robert Nozick, *Anarchy, State and Utopia* (Blackwell 1974) 169–72. See Drane (n 1) 568–70 (discusses implications of libertarian theory for health care delivery).
[89] ibid. cf Griffin (n 4) 179 (makes the point that 'not every interference with what one wants to do is a violation of liberty' and taxation for the purposes of redistribution does not 'stop that person from pursuing or even living a valuable life' and thus does not destroy an individual's liberty); Tom Beauchamp, 'The Right to Health Care in a Capitalistic Democracy' in Thomas J Bole and William Bonderson (eds), *Rights to Health Care* (Kluwer, 1991) 77 (notes that liberty is not absolute and the reallocation of resources for purpose of achieving a minimum level of health care would not have a severe impact on liberty).
[90] See Engelhardt, *Foundations of Bioethics* (n 2) 357 in Drane (n 1) 569.
[91] Beauchamp (n 89) 73. See also Beauchamp and Faden (n 1) 122, 124.
[92] Drane (n 1) 568 (notes that state involvement in health education is more acceptable to a libertarian than state supported health care).
[93] Some libertarians might concede the need for a two tiered system in which at least some basic care is provided for those without means to obtain additional health care. See Drane (n 1) 569.
[94] Hans Martin Sass, 'My Right to Care for My Health—And What About the Needy and the Elderly?' in Thomas J Bole and William Bonderson (eds), *Rights to Health Care* (Kluwer, 1991) 243.

should never be discounted, although it may be questioned whether there is any empirical basis to support this assumption in the context of health. Moreover, as will be discussed in Chapters 4, 5, and 6 of this book, the right to health in international law does not necessarily demand that health care be provided free of charge. The real issue therefore is whether it is possible to justify the libertarian distinction between health threats that are within the control of an individual and those that are caused by social factors.[95] The epidemiological causes of disease are complex and there is a growing awareness that external social factors are, if not dispositive, then certainly contributory to many instances of ill health.[96] As such, a fundamental tenet of libertarian theory—that individuals control their own health—would appear to be on shaky ground.[97]

There is also the dilemma of how to deal with those instances of ill health— whether physical or mental—which are entirely biological and have in no way been caused by the actions of either the individual or external factors. The limited conception of the right to health advanced under a libertarian theory of justice would exclude an obligation to prevent or provide medical care for natural lottery conditions such as cystic fibrosis and haemophilia. The libertarian might argue that the market, if allowed to operate properly, would provide an opportunity for individuals to mitigate these health risks by purchasing appropriate health insurance. And when forced to concede that not all individuals may have the resources to purchase appropriate health insurance, the libertarian might further argue that beneficence and charity would accommodate their needs.[98] However, unlike human rights, beneficence and charity are subject to discretion and provide no entitlement to make a claim against the duty of a state to take measures to address the health needs of an individual. It may be the case that these health needs are beyond the capacity of a state to satisfy, but at least the individual can demand justification as to why his or her health needs were not met.[99]

Ultimately, the libertarian position rests on certain assumptions about the causes of ill health, the capacity of markets, and the role of charity and beneficence in addressing health needs. The empirical record of societies whose policies have reflected libertarian approaches does not, however, warrant great confidence in this regard. As outlined in Chapter 1, the history of public health is replete with situations in which free markets that failed to provide an adequate system of health care were not accompanied by sufficient outpourings of beneficence and charity as to make up for the shortfall. Indeed, it was these failings that gave rise to support for the notion of a right to health as a way of overcoming the limitations of existing arrangements. Importantly, the right to health does not abandon the value of

---

[95] Beauchamp and Faden (n 1) 125.
[96] ibid; Ruddick (n 1) 163.
[97] Beauchamp (n 89) 75 (argues that the libertarian argument is 'unconvincing'); Ruddick (n 1) 163 (argues that 'the distinction between deserving and undeserving ill is morally dubious').
[98] Engelhardt, *Foundations of Bioethics* (n 2) 357 (argues that 'charity can at least blunt severe losses at natural and social lotteries').
[99] See the discussion of the progressive obligation to secure the right to health in Chapter 6.

individual responsibility for health.[100] Nor does it necessarily seek to displace the role of markets or the values of beneficence and charity in addressing health needs.[101] It simply reflects the idea that free markets will never be sufficient to guarantee the health needs of all individuals.

B The status objection

Much of the theoretical opposition to the right to health is grounded in the general opposition to the entire class of economic and social rights. As Maurice Cranston famously argued, 'economic and social rights cannot logically be considered universal human rights and...the attempt to do so has vitiated the whole enterprise of protecting human rights through the United Nations.'[102] For Cranston, economic and social rights such as the right to health cannot be 'correctly seen as human rights' and only serve to muddle, obscure, and debilitate the idea of human rights.[103] Many scholars have taken issue with these sentiments and advanced a compelling case for economic and social rights.[104] These accounts need not be repeated here and it is sufficient to note that the views of Cranston and his followers can be rejected on two grounds.

First, they assert a particular theory of human rights as if it were a comprehensive and determinate theory of what constitutes a legitimate human right. No such theory exists or perhaps more accurately, there is no universal agreement as to the existence of such a theory. Cranston and his allies are of course entitled to their own theories of human rights and many more such theories will no doubt be propounded in the future. But if international human rights law is to be attacked on its own merits it is essential that its characteristics be accurately portrayed, and Cranston's theory fails to do this.

---

[100] The preamble to the UDHR actually anticipates a role for every individual in ensuring the enjoyment of human rights and article 29(1) provides that 'everyone has duties to the community in which alone the free and full development of his (sic) personality is possible'. These duties would extend to an obligation to take reasonable measures to care for one's own health. But looking beyond the text of international law, there is an incentive for individuals to take responsibility for their own health based on a version of the reciprocity thesis and the principle of risk aversion. In the context of the right to health, the reciprocity thesis posits that it is in the interests of each individual to do all that is reasonably possible to protect his or her health in order to reduce the burden on the health system and ensure availability of resources necessary to address health needs as they arise. The idea that risk aversion would encourage individual responsibility for health is based on the premise that given the reality of resource constraints and the progressive nature of the obligation to protect health, an individual can never be certain that a state will have an obligation to address his or her health needs. In order to avoid this risk of unmet medical care, an individual should take all reasonable steps to maintain his or her health.

[101] See the discussion of the role of privatization in securing the right to health in Chapter 5.

[102] Maurice Cranston, *What Are Human Rights?* (Bodley Head, 1973) 54. See also Aryeh Neier, 'Social and Economic Rights: A Critique' (2006) 12 Hum Rts Brief 1.

[103] Cranston, *What Are Human Rights?* (n 102) 65.

[104] See, eg, Buchanan and Hessler (n 1) 203, 206–8; Sen (n 29) 345–8; Sunstein, *The Second Bill of Rights* (n 60); Sandra Fredman, *Human Rights Transformed: Positive Rights and Positive Duties* (OUP, 2008); Lanse Minkler, 'Economic Rights and Political Decision Making' (2009) 31 Hum Rts Q 368.

Second, Cranston and his followers apply their theory in ways that make misplaced assumptions about the status and value of civil and political rights relative to economic social and cultural rights. Civil and political rights are said to be practical, resource neutral, readily secured by legislation, determinate, enforceable in courts, and of paramount moral importance.[105] In contrast economic and social rights are said to be impractical, resource dependent, aspirational, indeterminate, and unenforceable.[106] A detailed critique of these claims is not required here and it is sufficient to note it has been repeatedly argued that they are misplaced and unpersuasive.[107] For example, in international law, civil and political rights are not merely negative rights that require states to refrain from interfering with the liberty and autonomy rights of an individual.[108] On the contrary, they require the allocation of significant resources to ensure their effective enjoyment.[109] Take, for example, the right to life, which requires the creation of a criminal justice system to protect individuals against threats to life and hold perpetrators accountable where they violate this right.[110] Moreover, even the boundaries of rights such as the prohibition against torture and other ill treatment are constantly moving and cannot be said to be determinate.[111] In any event, the interpretation offered of the right to health in Chapters 3 to 9 of this book, will demonstrate that this right is amenable to a practical interpretation that states can implement. It will also show that elements of the right are in fact justiciable.[112] Thus, Cranston's crisis of confidence in economic and social rights is misplaced and his claim that logic precludes the inclusion of economic and social rights alongside civil and political rights within the legitimate corpus of international human rights law is unconvincing.

---

[105] Cranston, *What Are Human Rights?* (n 102) 65–71.   [106] ibid.

[107] See, eg, Malcolm Langford (eds), *Social Rights Jurisprudence: Emerging Trends in International and Comparative Law* (CUP, 2008); Asbjørn Eide and Allan Rosas, 'Economic Social and Cultural Rights: A Universal Challenge' in Asbjørn Eide, Catarina Krause and Allan Rosas (eds), *Economic Social and Cultural Rights: A Textbook* (Martinus Nijhoff, 1995) 22; Matthew Craven, *The International Covenant on Economic Social and Cultural Rights: A Perspective on its Development* (Clarendon Press, 1995); Philip Alston and Gerard Quinn, 'The Nature and Scope of States Parties Obligations under the International Covenant on Economic, Social and Cultural Rights' (1987) 9 Hum Rts Q 156; Cass Sunstein, 'Social and Economic Rights? Lessons from South Africa' (2000) 11 Constitutional Forum 123; Sandra Liebenberg, *Socio-Economic Rights—Adjudication under a Transformative Constitution* (Juta 2010).

[108] See Fredman (n 104); Tasioulas, 'The Moral Reality of Human Rights' (n 6) 89–90 (discussing scepticism of the distinction between negative liberty rights and positive welfare rights).

[109] See Stephen Holmes and Cass R Sunstein, *The Cost of Rights: Why Liberty Depends on Taxes* (WW Norton & Co 1999).

[110] See HRC, *General Comment No 6: The Right to Life*, UN Doc CCPR/C/21/Add/1 (30 April 1982) 128; Walter Kalin and Jorg Kunzli, *The Law of International Human Rights Protection* (OUP, 2009) 273–98.

[111] See, eg, *Selmouni v France* (2000) 29 EHRR 403 [110] (ECtHR) (noting that 'certain acts which were classified in the past as "inhuman and degrading treatment" as opposed to "torture" could be classified differently in future').

[112] This assertion should not be taken to imply, as commentators such as Cranston suggest, that the capacity for enforceability is a necessary condition for the justification of a human right. See Chapter 5, Part III D 2.

C The formulation objection

Although a strong case can be made to augment the legitimate place of economic and social rights within international law, the formulation of the right to health remains the subject of intense criticism. This formulation does not merely provide a right to health in the negative sense that states have a duty to prevent threats to the health of individuals. Nor is it confined to a right to receive medical care or indeed a right to receive a minimum level of medical care. Instead, it entitles every human being to the highest attainable standard of health. This formulation has aroused considerable angst among philosophers mainly because health is not seen as an appropriate interest in which to ground a right. James Griffin is the strongest proponent of this criticism. He considers the right to the highest attainable standard of health to be inconsistent with his account of the criteria for determining whether an interest should ground a human right.

Under his theory, an interest can ground a right only if it can be considered a component of normative agency necessary to realize his vision of personhood.[113] He concedes that the capacity for the exercise of normative agency requires more than the bare minimum of protection for a relevant interest but insists that such protection must not be 'lavish'.[114] The right to health as formulated in international law does not qualify under his theory of justifiable rights because it is 'particularly lavish'.[115] This is because it does not 'specify, at least roughly, the level of health we have a right to' and is therefore considered to be indeterminate.[116] Indeed, in his view 'it is not even a reasonable social aim, let alone a right'.[117] Moreover, he argues that it 'does not appear to set limits on what is required of states and does not acknowledge that states often regard themselves as free to decide when they have spent enough on health...and may devote their inevitably limited resources to education, preservation of the environment and other important social goods.'[118] For Griffin, neither the interest in which the right is grounded, nor the duties attendant upon the right, can be justified.

There are, however, at least three grounds on which to challenge Griffin's concerns. First, his theory of normative agency and personhood is not the only basis on which to determine the criteria against which to assess whether a right is grounded in a particular interest.[119] His arguments may be persuasive but they cannot be considered determinative. For example, Part III of this chapter outlined a social interest theory of rights that sought to justify the treatment of health as a human right in international law. Others have also arrived at a similar conclusion, albeit by different routes. For example, Jennifer Ruger has extended Sen's capability thesis to offer a theoretical justification of the right to health. According to Ruger, rights serve a critical role in identifying the nature and scope of the obligations necessary to

---
[113] Griffin (n 4) 33–7.
[114] ibid 183.   [115] ibid.
[116] ibid 100.   [117] ibid 99.   [118] ibid 208.
[119] John Tasioulas, 'Taking Rights out of Human Rights' (2010) 120 Ethics 647, 678 (recommends the embrace of a pluralist account of the grounds of human rights).

realize the capabilities necessary for all individuals to lead what she describes as a flourishing life.[120] For her the right to the highest attainable standard of health is intimately connected with the realization of health capabilities, and is thus justified.

Second, under Griffin's theory, the idea of 'normative agency' and the concept of 'lavishness', as the standard to preclude an interest being recognized as a human right, are both imprecise and dependent on subjective interpretation. Griffin may well perceive the right to the highest attainable standard of health to be 'particularly lavish' and an unreasonable social aim but the drafters and parties to the WHO Constitution, the ICESCR, and CRC did not take this view and nor do commentators such as Ruger. The application of his theory is therefore driven by his own subjective preferences, which may be shared by some, but cannot be considered determinative for the purpose of assessing the justification of a human right.[121]

Ultimately the most fundamental weakness in Griffin's argument for the demotion of the right to health in the list of international human rights is his reliance on an impression as opposed to an analysis of the nature of the obligations imposed on states. He argues that the 'particularly lavish' quality of the right to the highest attainable standard of health arises because it does not '*appear*' to set limits of what is required of states. But appearances are not an appropriate basis upon which to assess the legitimacy of any concept, let alone a human right. A more substantive inquiry is required—something Griffin himself proclaimed was necessary to bring credibility to the idea of human rights.[122] When such an inquiry is directed to the substantive, rather than apparent, meaning of the right to health in international law (which will be done in the remaining chapters of this book) it becomes clear that this right does set limits, as all rights do. Griffin's critique of the right to health is thus informed by impressions and assumptions rather than a careful consideration of the text that provides the basis for the right to health in international law and its attendant duties.

The other arguments he uses to challenge justifications of the right to health are also problematic. His suggestion that it does not specify the level of health to which individuals are entitled overlooks the fact that it does provide for such a specification, namely the highest attainable standard of health. To suggest that this standard is 'too indeterminate' overlooks the fact that indeterminancy is a quality that characterizes all human rights and that a persuasive account of the right to health can still be offered (such an account being the basis of the remaining chapters in this book). Moreover, his criticism that states 'often regard themselves as free to decide when they have spent enough on health',[123] is a passing comment on the practice of states that remains uninformed by any consideration as to how international human rights law actually views the obligations of states and the issue of resource allocation. Indeed, if anything it tends to mimic the standard criticism routinely directed at all international human rights that states ignore their obligations and simply do as they choose. This allegation may well have merit, but it is a concern that is relevant to

---

[120] Ruger, *Health and Social Justice* (n 3) 118.
[121] ibid 118.
[122] Griffin (n 4) 192.
[123] ibid 208.

the effectiveness of the entire international human rights system—a discrete topic—and not whether the right to health occupies a legitimate place within this system.

Beyond Griffin's concerns with the formulation, philosophers within the justice and health context have tended to shy away from a right to health in favour of a *right to medical care*. This anxiety has arisen due to an assumption that health is an inappropriate basis to ground a right because states cannot guarantee the health of an individual.[124] In contrast, medical care has been perceived as a tangible service or good that can be delivered and guaranteed by a state. Claims have been made as to the special moral importance of health, which warrants the provision of at least a minimum level of medical care by the state.[125] Under this approach the legitimacy of the right to health has been grounded in theories of justice or particular theories as to those interests that ground human rights.[126]

It is not necessary to revisit these discussions here. Rather the present focus is to assess whether the reservation about grounding a right in a standard of health as opposed to mere medical care is warranted. The view taken is that such scepticism does not threaten the legitimacy of the right to health in international law because it is founded on a false premise, namely that a right to health necessarily imposes a duty that health must be guaranteed. On the contrary, as will be detailed in Chapter 4, the right to the highest attainable standard of health in international law does not guarantee a right to be healthy. Instead, it imposes an obligation on states to progressively undertake all reasonable measures in light of available resources to create the conditions, which will prevent threats to health, remedy ill health, and facilitate the highest attainable standard of health for an individual. Although still onerous, the nature of this obligation should alleviate the concerns of those who worry that a right to health necessarily implies a right to have the health of an individual guaranteed.

D The relativist challenge

Having noted the weaknesses inherent in the libertarian, status, and formulation objections to the right to health, we are still left with the relativist challenge as an obstacle to efforts to justify the right to health. This challenge has a theoretical and a practical dimension. Although international human rights law claims to be a common standard of achievement for all peoples, it is often argued that it reflects Western values and preferences.[127] Moreover, from a practical perspective the

---

[124] See Buchanan and Hessler (n 1) 203, 205–6.
[125] See, eg, Daniels, *Just Health Care* (n 1); Daniels, *Just Health: Meeting Health Needs Fairly* (n 3).
[126] See, eg, Daniels, *Just Health Care* (n 1) 4–9; Daniels, *Just Health: Meeting Health Needs Fairly* (n 3) 144–7 (accepts that the right to health can extend beyond health care to the 'socially controllable actions that affect population health'); Buchanan and Hessler (n 1) 203, 213–14 (justification for the right to health care is said to be found in the idea that human rights are moral claims grounded in basic human interests, health care being one such interest because being healthy is a universal interest common to all people).
[127] For an overview of this debate see Steiner, Alston and Goodman (n 86) 517–39; Donnelly (n 25) 57–126. See also William Twinning (ed), *Human Rights and Southern Voices* (CUP, 2009); Griffin (n 4) 133–45.

formulation of the right to health is often considered to be so ambitious that it is simply incapable of universal implementation in a world characterized by diversity in terms of both cultural practices and available resources. The universal/relativist debate has been canvassed in detail elsewhere and need not be repeated here. Rather it is sufficient to make three observations.

First, it is generally accepted that Western states dominated the drafting of the international human rights instruments that protect the right to health. But the inclusion of the right to health was not simply a product of this influence. On the contrary, as demonstrated in Chapter 1, Latin American states, NGOs, and the Communist bloc were all instrumental in securing the inclusion of economic and social rights, such as health, within the UDHR and subsequent instruments. Indeed, if anything, it was Western states, most notably the USA and UK, which expressed some reluctance with respect to this approach. Ultimately, however, these anxieties were overcome and agreement was reached on the inclusion of both sets of rights within international law.

Second, the identification of health as an appropriate interest in which to ground a right is arguably less vulnerable to allegations that it reflects Western concerns and priorities relative to rights, such as paid holidays, or even freedom of religion. The history of the right to health suggests that the idea that people should enjoy health and that the state should have a role to play in protecting individuals against threats to health or providing health care, is one that has strong appeal and relevance irrespective of culture. As such, it does not succumb easily to allegations of cultural relativism.

This is not to say that culture is irrelevant to an understanding of the meaning of the right to health or that the implementation of this right must, should, or could be secured in identical terms in every state. In Chapter 3, I will advocate a model for the interpretation of the right to health that seeks to accommodate, and indeed respect, cultural diversity with respect to the identification of the measures necessary to secure the right to health via the concept of sensitivity to the local context and respect for the margin of appreciation.[128] Under a social interest theory of human rights, just as the grounds for such rights are contingent and evolving, so too is their meaning. This malleability demands that the interpretation of a right, such as health, is not beholden to a particular cultural perspective or set of values.[129] At the same time, the capacity for the meaning of the right to health to accommodate cultural differences does not allow for an entirely relativist approach to the right's implementation.[130]

---

[128] Buchanan and Hessler (n 1) 216 (critical of the attempt by other commentators to provide a comprehensive definition of the right to health which ignores the circumstances of individual states).

[129] I recognize, as Griffin points out, that the malleability of human rights is a cause for deep cynicism among many persons: Griffin (n 4) 16. I will argue in Chapter 3 that although this malleability is inescapable, a persuasive account of the meaning of a human right, such as health, means that the interpretative process is constrained by several factors.

[130] cf ibid 216 (argues that states should have power to interpret their obligations under the right to health because they are better suited to protecting their own citizens and have 'little impetus to violate the human rights of their own citizens'). Such an approach fails to appreciate the basis on which the international human rights enterprise was founded, namely the failure of states to protect their citizens.

Indeed, article 24(3) of the CRC demands of states that they must abolish traditional practices that are harmful to the health of a child. The real issues, however, relate to the process and criteria by which such practices are identified as harmful and the means by which they must be abolished. Chapter 8 addresses these issues in detail.

E The resource allocation dilemma

Scepticism of the right to health often reaches fever pitch when it comes to the issue of resource allocation. Concern arises on three fronts, which I label: relative resource scarcity; the risk of distorted resource allocation; and the macro/micro resource allocation dilemma.

1 Relative resource scarcity

The notion that there is a relative scarcity of resources is implicit in the view expressed by commentators such as Cranston that the idea of economic and social rights, including the right to health, is meaningless for developing countries because they lack the resources of developed states.[131] The attempt to elevate health to the status of a right is considered to 'violate the logical principle "ought implies can"',[132] and 'mocks' the moral and practical significance of civil and political rights, which are considered to be capable of universal implementation irrespective of the availability of resources.[133] However, this criticism of economic and social rights is founded on two misconceptions.

First, as noted above, the effective enjoyment of civil and political rights is not without cost and requires the allocation of significant resources. Second, international law is sensitive to, and seeks to accommodate, the reality of disparities in the resources available to states. It does not impose an obligation that each state must provide the same level of health care. On the contrary, the progressive obligation of a state to use available resources anticipates a relative approach to the realization of the right to health among states. Moreover, the obligation of international co-operation, which is made explicit with respect to the right to health under article 24(4) of the CRC, anticipates that developed states will assist developing states in securing the effective enjoyment of the right to health—an obligation that is explored more fully in Chapter 8.

2 Risk of distorted resource allocation

It is frequently said that recognition of the right to health risks distorting resource allocation decisions. The concern is that recourse to the discourse of rights, in the context of health, is 'a rhetorical device' used to 'increase health care's share of available resources'.[134] Viewed from this perspective, the right to health is

---

[131] Maurice Cranston, 'Human Rights: Real and Supposed' in DD Raphel (ed), *Political Theory and the Rights of Man* (Macmillan, 1967) 50–1.
[132] Waldron (n 26) 9.
[133] Cranston, 'Human Rights: Real and Supposed' (n 131) 50–1.
[134] Thomas Halper, 'Rights, Reforms and the Health Care Crisis: Problems and Prospects' in Thomas J Bole and William Bonderson (eds), *Rights to Health Care* (Kluwer, 1991) 141.

dangerous because it can distort the allocation of scarce resources away from appropriate targets and towards the health sector generally, or in favour of individuals who are able to invoke the language of rights in support of their particular interests.[135] This fear, however, is based on a misunderstanding as to the nature of the right to health. As will be detailed in Chapter 6, the obligation to progressively secure the right to health imposes a demand on the allocation of resources within a state and indeed, between states. But the interpretation of the scope of these demands remains subject to what I describe in Chapter 3 as the principle of system coherence. In simple terms, this means that the right to health is not to be interpreted in isolation from those other interests that are also the subject of rights in international law, such as education, housing, and the protection against threats to life which all demand the allocation of resources by states to secure their implementation. As a consequence, it does not follow that grounding a human right in the health interests of an individual will lead to an inappropriate or disproportionate allocation of resources to the health sector in a given state.

Moreover, just as the health sector in a state must compete with other sectors for its share of available resources, so too must an individual seeking to have his or her right to health satisfied. The right to health is not an absolute right and the obligation of states remains progressive and subject to the availability of resources. It also remains subject to the capacity of states to limit the right to health, like any other economic and social rights (or indeed nearly all civil and political rights), where it is necessary to do so in order to promote the general welfare in a democratic society.[136] In international law, the justification for the limitation on a person's rights must be grounded in the need to protect the right or rights of another individual or group of individuals. Thus, contrary to the individualized stereotype that is often used to characterize human rights, in international law, the human rights of an individual are very much located within a communitarian paradigm. They are not, as has been suggested by Jeremy Waldron, 'a sort of line item, presenting each individual's case peremptorily, as though it brooked no denial, no balancing, no compromise.'[137] On the contrary, any claim that makes recourse to the right to health is contingent, rather than absolute. It may be a presumptively valid claim, but it may also be overridden by more competing claims that are also grounded in human rights.[138] Thus, fears that an individual with access to effective tools to advocate his or her case will be able to use the human right to health as a trump, fail to recognize the right's heavily contingent nature.

---

[135] William Easterly, 'Human Rights Are the Wrong Basis for Healthcare', *The Financial Times* (London, 12 October 2009) <http://www.ft.com/intl/cms/s/0/89bbbda2-b763-11de-9812-00144feab49a.html> accessed 16 June 2011.

[136] ICESCR, art 4:

The States Parties to the present Covenant recognize that, in the enjoyment of those rights provided by the State in conformity with the present Covenant, the State may subject such rights only to such limitations as are determined by law only in so far as this may be compatible with the nature of these rights and solely for the purpose of promoting the general welfare in a democratic society.

[137] Waldron (n 26) 29.
[138] Beauchamp and Faden (n 1) 122.

3 The macro/micro resource allocation dilemma

The need to prioritize the allocation of scarce resources in the context of measures to secure the right to health is unavoidable. This dilemma arises at the macro level with respect to the allocation of scarce resources between health and other legitimate sectors within a state such as education, housing, and law and order, which can all be reasonably linked to the realization of other human rights. It also arises at the micro level with respect to the allocation of scarce resources from within a health budget to realize the competing health claims of individuals. For philosophers, such as Griffin and O'Neill, the failure of international human rights law to resolve these dilemmas militates against the justification of the right to health.[139] For Norman Daniels, this is the primary reason for his aversion to grounding the issue of just health within a human rights paradigm.[140] Indeed, for Jeremy Waldron, the perceived impotency of international law in relation to the issue of resource prioritization is so great that we should 'postpone talking about socioeconomic rights' such as the right to health.[141] Moreover, practitioners, not just philosophers, have expressed similar concerns.[142]

The reality is that international law does not provide any explicit formula by which to determine the appropriate level of resources to be allocated to the realization of the right to health relative to other human rights or between individuals.[143] Thus, what might be considered a 'noble ideal' that 'elicits the appeal of all those who are generous', can also serve to 'chill the enthusiasm of those in the realistic business of macroallocation'.[144] However, an examination of the duty assumed by states suggests that the buoyant hopes of the generous can be moderated and the fears of the economist allayed. In the first instance, the progressive nature of the obligation is constrained by the availability of resources *and* the capacity to limit the right to health in the face of competing interests that impact on the welfare of a society. Such a model does not predict the precise amount of funding to be allocated to the right to health—but it is questionable whether any model of distributive justice could. Instead, it demands the adoption of a *process* in which a state must give genuine consideration to the various obligations it has assumed under international human rights law and make a determination as to how to allocate its scarce resources to secure these rights. Further details as to the nature of this process are provided in

---

[139] Griffin (n 4) 208. See also O'Neill (n 5) 429.
[140] Daniels, *Just Health: Meeting Health Needs Fairly* (n 3) 315.
[141] Waldron (n 26) 29.
[142] See, eg, Lauchlan Munro, '"The Human Rights-Based Approach to Programming": A Contradiction in Terms?' in Sam Hickey and Diana Mitlin (eds), *Rights-Based Approaches to Development: Exploring the Potential and Pitfalls* (Kumarian Press 2009) 187, 200–1.
[143] It is important to note that this limitation extends to both economic and social rights and civil and political rights given that positive duties are imposed on states with respect to both sets of rights. Despite the commentary and case law to support this position, some commentators still default to the position that only economic and social rights are plagued by resource allocation issues. See, eg, Waldron (n 26) 28–9 (bases his critique of economic and social rights on the ground that such rights represent a claim to a share of scarce resources and in the absence of a sophisticated model to address conflict between such rights we should postpone further talk about them).
[144] Beauchampy and Faden (n 1) 128.

Chapter 6. In summary, it is essentially a test of reasonableness. A macro/micro resource allocation process will be deemed reasonable where it is principled (the list of principles are set out in Chapter 6); evidence based, consultative, and participatory (to the extent that this is reasonably practicable); transparent (in the sense that there is an awareness and understanding of the allocative process); and evaluative (in the sense that whatever decisions are made, they remain subject to review and monitoring).[145] Ultimately, this process demands the adoption of an allocative principle whereby (a) the right to health, to which all individuals are entitled, must be given genuine consideration in light of all other competing demands on a state's resources that can be grounded in rights, and (b) if unable to honour the right, a state must provide a reasonable justification for its failure to do so.[146]

International human rights law is not silent with respect to the macro/micro resource allocation dilemma and does not vacate the field to, for example, any of the variations of utilitarian principles that inform neoclassical economic theory,[147] or the allocative principle of each according to his or her needs,[148] or to other theories of justice, such as just desert or luck egalitarianism.[149] At the same time, it does not preclude a cost benefit analysis. Indeed, the reality of potentially conflicting rights, and the capacity under article 4 of the ICESCR to limit the right to health, where this is necessary to promote the welfare of a society, will invariably require such an analysis. This is because a state will require cogent and persuasive evidence to justify any limitations on a right, such as health, and resolve conflicting rights claims.[150]

---

[145] See Chapter 6. See also Sofia Gruskin and Norman Daniels, 'Justice and Human Rights: Priority Setting and Fair Deliberative Process' (2008) 9 A J Pub Health 1753 (illustrate a process called 'accountability for reasonableness' which has four conditions: (i) publicity; (ii) relevance; (iiii) revision; and (iv) appeals and regulation).

[146] Frost (n 21) 712 (argues that one common claim that underlies all human rights is the claim to be respected as autonomous agents who have the right not to be subjected to certain actions that cannot be adequately justified to them).

[147] See Seymour and Pincus (n 74) 391 (provide a good overview of these principles).

[148] See Waldron (n 26) 13–14 (discusses allocative theories of distributive justice within the context of socioeconomic rights but does actually engage with the idea that economic and social rights such as the right to health exist not in isolation but as part of a system of human rights protection in which certain interests are elevated to the status of a right).

[149] This theory of distributive justice requires 'correcting disadvantages for which individuals cannot be held responsible': Shlomi Segall, *Health, Luck and Justice* (Princeton University Press, 2010) 1 (provides an account of how luck egalitarianism can be applied to the allocation of resources in health care).

[150] This requirement for evidence represents an extension of the accepted principle regarding limitations on civil and political rights which has been largely overlooked in the context of economic and social rights despite the fact that the ICESCR, like the ICCPR, allows for reasonable limits to be imposed on economic and social rights. See *Siracusa Principles of the Limitation and Derogation Provisions in the International Covenant on Civil and Political Rights*, UN Doc E/CN4/1985/4 (1985) para 10 (explains that a state carries the onus to demonstrate, by reference to objective evidence and on the balance of probabilities, that any interference with a human right was necessary and proportionate on order to protect the rights of another individual or indeed the broader community). The requirement that the evidence be cogent and persuasive is a phrase that has been adopted by domestic courts when assessing the reasonableness of a limitation on a civil and political right. See, eg, *R v Oakes* [1986] 1 SCR 103 (SC, Canada); *DAS v Victorian Human Rights and Equal Opportunity Commission* (2009) 24 VR 415 [231] (Warren CJ) (VSC, Aust). Affirmed by the Court of Appeal in *R v Momcilovic* (2010) 25 VR 436 [144] (VSCA, Aust).

Moreover, the resolution of these dilemmas will often be informed by medical science and the concepts of medical necessity and medical appropriateness within medical ethics. Thus, the reasonableness of the allocation of resources to secure the implementation of the right to health will often be dependent on the knowledge and insights that other disciplines, such as economics and medicine, can offer.[151] It remains important to stress, however, that the role played by these disciplines in the assessment of reasonableness is complementary rather than determinative.

V Conclusion—an imperfect but good justification

Amartya Sen has expressed his anxiety about what he perceives as the 'softness' of human rights and the need for its 'conceptual doubts... [to] be satisfactorily addressed if the idea of human rights is to command reasoned loyalty and to establish a secure intellectual standing'.[152] This chapter has addressed these doubts in the context of the right to health. It resisted the tendency to default to Aristotle's decree from the fourth century BC that 'If we believe men have any personal rights at all as human beings, they have an absolute right to such measure of good health as society and society alone is able to give them.'[153] And it rejected the suggestion that the idea of inalienable rights and the inherent dignity of every human being were a sufficient foundation for the right to health.

It accepted the idea that interests ground rights but made no attempt to offer a comprehensive theory by which to determine what interests will be deemed suitable for grounding a right. On the contrary, it placed significant emphasis on the deliberative process by which states elevate an interest, such as the highest attainable standard of health, to the status of a human right. The idea of a 'social interest' theory of rights was adopted to recognize that the identification of the interest in which a human right, such as the right to health is grounded in international law, is not considered to be essential, basic, natural, or determinate, but the product of a social process. The agreement required to achieve this outcome in international treaties will always be incompletely theorized but this does not mean that these instruments are theoretically unconvincing. On the contrary, they reflect an overlapping consensus as to the moral value of a human being to be treated as an end, not a means, and an acceptance that the highest attainable standard of health for an

---

[151] For a discussion of these synergies see Seymour and Pincus (n 74); Malcolm Langford, 'Social Security and Children: Testing the Boundaries of Human Rights and Economics' in Stephen Marks, Bård Anders Andrassen and Arjun Sengupta, *Freedom from Poverty as a Human Right: Economic Perspectives* (UNESCO Publishing, 2009) 193; Ruger, *Health and Social Justice* (n 3) ch 8 ('Allocating Resources: A Joint Scientific and Deliberative Approach'); Edward Anderson and Marta Foresti, 'Assessing Compliance: The Challenges for Economic and Social Rights' (2009) 1 J Hum Rts Practice 469; *Report of the Special Rapporteur on the Right to Health to the General Assembly 2007*, UN Doc A/62/214 (8 August 2007) para 19 (stressing that 'prioritisation demands close collaboration between human rights specialists and health specialists, including epidemiologists and health economists').

[152] Sen (n 29) 317.

[153] Ruth Boemer, 'The Right to Health Care' in PAHO, *The Right to Health Care in the Americas: A Comparative Constitutional Study* (PAHO, 1989) 17, 17.

individual is an appropriate interest upon which to ground a human right. It is this is this consensus that provides a good, albeit not perfect, justification for the right to health.

Ultimately this justification will be insufficient to address the concerns of some who challenge the legitimacy of the right to health. For example, libertarian concerns cannot be accommodated if they are founded on a vision of justice and a theory of rights, which is antithetical to the role anticipated for the state with respect to the health of an individual under the international human rights paradigm.[154] In contrast, the status objection can be dismissed relatively easily on the basis that it makes assumptions as to the nature of economic and social rights relative to civil and political rights that are without foundation.

The other concerns—the formulation objection, the cultural relativist challenge, and the resource allocation dilemma—all suffer from a common shortcoming, namely a failure to undertake a careful inquiry into the nature of the obligations imposed upon states under the right to health in international law. Indeed, despite Griffin's otherwise 'powerful' and 'well elaborated' contribution to understanding the philosophical foundations of human rights,[155] the limitations of his approach are revealed in his treatment of the right to health in international law. He is distracted from his commitment to provide a substantive account of human rights by the impressions he forms in relation to the *idea* of the right to the highest attainable standard of health. This is a common trap for advocates and critics alike, when engaging with the discourse of human rights. But to pass judgment on the status of the right to health based upon subjective impressions and appearances is to adopt a dangerous course. It remains blind to the possibility that an alternative interpretation might exist—an interpretation that might allay the sceptic's concern or moderate the advocate's hopes. It is for this reason that I have insisted that Griffin's concerns, like those of many others who have been critical of the right to health, could be taken care of through the elaboration of a substantive and persuasive account of the meaning of the right to health. We turn now to that very task.

---

[154] Competing visions of justice will produce competing visions of rights. This is not to suggest that rights are a necessary component of every vision of justice. Indeed I am wary of Griffin's warning not 'to make everything especially important in morality into a right': Griffin (n 4) 199. Indeed, as Griffin has rightly observed, the domains of human rights and justice are not identical: Griffin (n 4) 199. At the same time I also reject the argument that human rights are neutral, benign, or adverse to the question of justice. cf Upendra Baxi, 'The Place of the Human Right to Health and Contemporary Approaches to Global Justice' in John Harrington and Maria Stuttaford (eds), *Global Health and Human Rights: Legal and Philosophical Perspectives* (Routledge, 2010) 12, 15. The view taken here is rather that international human rights law is deeply concerned with questions of justice and its norms reflect a particular, albeit imperfect, vision of justice: Roger Normand and Sarah Zaidi, *Human Rights at the UN: The Political History of Universal Justice* (Indiana University Press, 2008) esp 6–10. This vision, however, is neither comprehensive nor completely theorized and remains partial, contested, and contingent.

[155] Tasioulas, 'Taking the Rights out of Human Rights' (n 119) 678.

3
A Methodology to Produce a Meaning for the Right to Health

I Introduction

The human rights protected in international treaties are invariably vague and ambiguous. This feature is seen to be most acute with respect to economic, social, and cultural rights, especially the right to health.[1] As Jennifer Ruger has observed, 'one would be hard pressed to find a more controversial or nebulous human right'.[2] Indeed, as was demonstrated in Chapter 2, the porous nature of its boundaries is of such concern to philosophers, like James Griffin and Onora O'Neil, that neither of them considers it worthy of a place within the lexicon of international human rights law. Thus, the need to offer a substantive meaning of the right to health in international law presents a significant challenge: a challenge which is heightened by the absence of an authoritative adjudicative body to bind states parties with respect to a particular interpretation as to the nature of the right to health.[3]

---

[1] See generally Henry Steiner, Philip Alston, and Ryan Goodman, *International Human Rights in Context: Law, Politics and Morals* (3rd edn, OUP, 2008) 280–94. Importantly this ambiguity is not confined to economic and social rights and also extends to civil and political rights. For example, the precise scope of the prohibition against torture is consistently shifting: see *Selmouni v France* (2000) 29 EHRR 403 [101] (ECtHR) (noting that 'certain acts which were classified in the past as "inhuman and degrading treatment" as opposed to "torture" could be classified differently in future'). The parameters of the right to a fair trial also remain contentious: see George Letsas, 'The Truth in Autonomous Concepts: How to Interpret the ECHR' (2004) EJIL 15, 279, 292–3 (noting that there are eight possible interpretations of the right to a fair trial under the European Convention for the Protection of Human Rights and Fundamental Freedoms (ECHR)).

[2] Jennifer Ruger, 'Toward a Theory of a Right to Health: Capability and Incompletely Theorized Agreements' 18 Yale JL & Human 273, 273. The formulation of the right to health in international law gives rise to a multitude of interpretative dilemmas including what is the meaning of the highest attainable standard of health; what is the meaning of health; does it extend to the social determinants of health; what obligations flow from the requirement that states recognize the right to health; are the measures required to fulfil these obligations universal or do they differ between states; what is the minimum core of the right to health; to what extent should states be responsible for ensuring the health of an individual in the home, workplace, and general community; to what extent must states prevent threats to an individual's health from non-state actors; is privatization of health care services compatible with the right to health; is the right to health justiciable; and to what extent must intellectual property rules be designed to maximize access to medicine and medical services.

[3] Ian Johnstone, 'Treaty Interpretation: The Authority of Interpretative Communities' (1991) 12 Mich J Intl L 371, 375 (noting that the problem of authoritative decision making in international society relates to its decentralized character).

In practice other actors—academics, NGOs, treaty monitoring bodies, special rapporteurs, and states—attempt to fill this interpretative void. All too often, however, the process of defining the content of a human right, such as the right to health, is unaccompanied by any explanation, or at best a scant explanation, as to the methodology used to generate the interpretation offered.[4] Indeed, in the case of all human rights standards, not just the right to health, academics and advocates alike can be quick to adopt an autonomous style of reasoning in which the interpretation offered reflects personal preferences as to the nature of the protection which the advocate thinks the right in question does or should accord.[5] The work of the Committee bodies established to monitor implementation of human rights treaties has, at times, also been accused of such an approach.[6] Such 'result driven jurisprudence'[7] may well be persuasive among those who share similar expectations with respect to the right to health but its impact is likely to be limited especially on those who prefer to focus on what they perceive the law to be, *lex lata*, as opposed to what it should be, *lex ferenda*. Moreover, this approach encourages criticisms like that of David Kennedy that 'the human rights movement degrades the legal profession by encouraging a combination of overly formal reliance on textual articulations that are anything but clear or binding and sloppy humanitarian argument'.[8] Simply clothing an assertion as to the content of a human right, such as health, with the apparel of humanity or dignity may satisfy a moral or political urge but it does not necessarily accord with the nature of the *legal* obligations actually assumed by a state under the relevant human rights treaties.

Those who do seek to engage with this 'legal' question typically arm themselves, albeit to varying degrees,[9] with the general rule of treaty interpretation under article 31(1) of the Vienna Convention on the Law of Treaties (VCLT):

---

[4] See, with respect to the right to health: Asbjørn Eide and Wenche Barth Eide, 'Article 24: The Right to Health' in A Alen and others (eds), *A Commentary on the United Nations Convention on the Rights of the Child* (Martinus Nijhoff, 2006) (dedicating three paragraphs to the issue of methodology); Sharon Detrick, *A Commentary on the United Nations Convention on the Rights of the Child* (Martinus Nijhoff, 1999) 5–7 (taking three pages to outline her methodology); UNICEF, *Implementation Handbook for the Convention on the Rights of the Child* (2nd edn, UNICEF, 2002) xv–xvi (allocating two pages to the methodology adopted); Geraldine Van Bueren, *The International Law on the Rights of the Child* (Martinus Nijhoff Publishers, 1995) 297–312 (failing to expressly address the issue of methodology); Brigit Toebes, *The Right to Health as a Human Right in International Law* (Intersentia, 1998). Those philosophers who have addressed the right to health in international law have not offered any explanation as to the methodology they have adopted when forming their view as to the scope and meaning of the right: Jennifer Ruger, *Health and Social Justice* (OUP, 2010) 122–3; James Griffin, *On Human Rights* (OUP, 2008) 99–100, 183, 208.

[5] Jeremy Waldron, 'Judges as Moral Reasoners' (2009) 7 Int J Constitutional Law 2, 6.

[6] See Conway Blake, 'Normative Instruments in International Human Rights Law: Locating the General Comment' (NYU Law School, Center for Human Rights and Global Justice, Working Paper No 17, 2008) 12; Stephen Tully, 'A Human Right to Access Water? A Critique of General Comment No 15' (2005) 23 NQHR 35; cf Malcolm Langford, 'Ambition that Overleaps Itself? A Response to Stephen Tully's Critique of the General Comment on the Right to Water' (2005) 24 NQHR 433.

[7] Waldron (n 5) 17.

[8] David Kennedy, 'The International Human Rights Movement: Part of the Problem?' (2001) 14 Harv Hum Rts J 101, 120.

[9] See, eg, James Hathaway, *The Rights of Refugees under International Law* (CUP, 2005) 48–73; Matthew Craven, *The International Covenant on Economic, Social and Cultural Rights: A Perspective on*

A treaty shall be interpreted in good faith in accordance with the ordinary meaning to be given to the terms of the treaty in their context and in light of its object and purpose.

For good measure the provisions of the VCLT also allow recourse to subsequent practice among states, other relevant rules, and the *travaux preparatoires* of a treaty as additional tools by which to resolve the interpretative dilemma.[10] But it is necessary to consider whether such an approach is sufficient given that there is almost universal consensus, acknowledged even at the time of its adoption, that the inherent elasticity associated with an application of the general rule under the VCLT is incapable of producing *the* determinate meaning of a treaty.[11] The VCLT rule may act as a constraint on the interpretative process, but any faith in its capacity to discover *the* meaning of a text must surely be tested given the inherent indeterminacy of language. The failure to acknowledge this reality has meant, as Joseph Weiler explains, that 'article 31 has turned into a straightjacket' for conceptual thinking about the process of treaty interpretation.[12] It may frame the interpretative process, but it is ultimately unable to resolve in every instance the question of how to choose *a* meaning with respect to the right to health in international law from among the range of potential meanings that will inevitably arise.

A question therefore arises as to the features required of an interpretative methodology that is able to acknowledge the limitations associated with an application of the VCLT general rule and identify those additional factors that will inform the selection of *a* meaning from within a suite of meanings. This chapter provides an answer to this question with respect to the right to health in international law. It seeks to move beyond the straightjacket of article 31 of the VCLT and avoid excessive reliance on imprecise rules of interpretation and the use of sloppy humanitarian argument by offering a more reflective, strategic, and transparent methodology for the interpretation of the right to health.

In Part II it will be argued that the act of legal interpretation is not simply the process of attributing *a* meaning to the right to health but ultimately an act of persuasion—an attempt to persuade the relevant interpretative community that a particular interpretation of the right to health is the most appropriate meaning to adopt. Part III will explore the nature of the interpretative community relevant to the interpretation of the right to health in international law. This community will be shown to have moved beyond states and their agents towards a more communitarian model in which the interests and expertise of a much wider range of parties and actors must be taken into account in the interpretative exercise—a process that is

---

its Development (OUP, 1995) 7–8; Alexander Orakhelashvili, 'Restrictive Interpretation of Human Rights Treaties in the Recent Jurisprudence of the European Court of Human Rights' (2003)14 EJIL 529, 535–8.

[10] Vienna Convention on the Law of Treaties (VCLT) (Vienna, 23 May 1969, entered into force 27 January 1980, 1155 UNTS 331) arts 31(2)–(3), 32.

[11] Joseph Weiler, 'Prolegomena to a Meso-Theory of Treaty Interpretation at the Turn of the Century' (IILJ International Legal Theory Colloquium: Interpretation and Judgment in International Law, NYU School of Law, 14 February 2008) 5–6.

[12] ibid 5.

described as constructive engagement. Part IV will outline the features considered apposite for the performance of this task. More specifically, it will be argued that the persuasive appeal of an interpretation offered for the right to health will be enhanced if it is able to satisfy four criteria—it must be principled, clear and practical, demonstrate coherence both in its reasoning and within the system of international law, and be sensitive to the nature of the socio-political context within individual states and the international legal order.

II The act of interpretation: from intentionalism to persuasion

Legal interpretation is generally understood as an act, or some may say art, of attributing and then communicating meaning in relation to a word or collection of words within a legal text.[13] With respect to international treaties this act has long been recognized as a task of considerable difficulty given the form that such instruments invariably take. As Dr Lushington observed in 1844 in *Maltass v Maltass*:

> Now in the construction of treaties...we cannot expect to find the same nicety of strict definition as in modern documents such as deeds or Acts of Parliament; it has never been the habit of those engaged in diplomacy to use legal accuracy but rather to adopt more liberal terms.[14]

It is thus not surprising that Lord McNair in his 1961 treatise *The Law of Treaties* wrote that 'There is no part of the law of treaties which the text writer approaches with more trepidation that the question of interpretation.'[15]

Despite his misgivings McNair still thought it prudent to assert that the task of interpretation could be reduced to a single sentence: 'it can be described as the duty of giving effect to the expressed intention of the parties, that is, their intention as expressed in the words used by them in light of the surrounding circumstances.'[16] Such a comment reflects a time when the meaning of a term was considered to be transparent and readily discernible from the text of a legal instrument. In subsequent years, commentators have challenged, and for the most part, dispelled this perception. It is now widely accepted that the '[m]eaning is not present in the expression itself'.[17] Instead, the interpretative exercise is very much an active process of

---

[13] See Mark Toufayan, 'Human Rights Treaty Interpretation: A Postmodern Account of Its Claim to "Speciality"' (NYU School of Law, Center for Human Rights and Global Justice, Working Paper No 3, 2005) 23–4; Myres S McDougal, Harold D Lasswell and James C Miller, *The Interpretation of International Agreements and World Public Order: Principles of Content and Procedure* (Martinus Nijhoff, 1994) xvi (emphasizing the significance of communication in the interpretative process); Martin Bos, 'Theory and Practice of Treaty Interpretation' (1980) 27 NILR 135 (examining the debate as to the definition of interpretation within international law).
[14] As cited in Arnold McNair, *The Law of Treaties* (Clarendon Press, 1961) 392.
[15] ibid 364.   [16] ibid 365.
[17] Martti Koskenniemi, *From Apology to Utopia: The Structure of International Legal Argument* (CUP, 2005) 8.

constructing *a* meaning rather than finding *the* meaning which lies latent with the text.[18]

This change in approach, however, presents real concerns for any legal order—including international law—that prizes attributes such as objectivity, certainty, and stability. For some the prospect of a 'menu' of potential meanings for the right to health, one of which will be selected by the person undertaking the interpretative function, is more than unsettling. It carries with it the risk that the interpretative function will be transferred into one of law making.[19] The legal interpretative community—a concept that will be fully explored in Part IV—therefore accepts that rules and principles of interpretation must be created to constrain the range of potential meanings so as to protect against an unwarranted inflation of the interpretation function.[20] Owen Fiss describes this as 'bounded objectivity'.[21]

It is important to acknowledge that, as with domestic law, the interpretation of international treaties, which protect the right to health, has never been free from the strictures of principles or rules. McNair's insistence on maintaining the fidelity of the parties' intentions is an attempt to impose a constraint on the interpretative process.[22] Beyond this subjective or intentionalist approach to treaty interpretation, numerous other approaches have been advocated, each with a different point of emphasis:[23] a literal or formalist approach will focus on the text itself; an historical approach will extend its consideration to the drafting history; a systematic approach will locate the interpretation of a phrase with its broader system of meaning; a teleological approach is concerned with securing an interpretation consistent with the object and purpose of the instruments; and a sociological approach is prepared to adopt an interpretation that accords with social and political objectives even if this creates a discordance with the text.[24]

In practice the lines of demarcation between the approaches are often difficult, if not impossible to draw,[25] and the interpretative exercise invariably resembles an 'eclectic mix' of approaches which consider the text, purpose, public policy, and the history of an instrument, rather than the application of a precise mathematical

---

[18] Rosalyn Higgins, *Problems and Process: International Law and How We Use It* (Clarendon Press, 1994) 3 (quoting Sir Hersch Lauterpacht's view that judges do not 'find rules' but 'make choices').

[19] See, eg, the views of Justices Fitzmaurice and Spender in the *South-West Africa Cases (Ethiopia v South Africa; Liberia v South Africa) (Joint Dissenting Opinion of Sir Percy Spender and Sir Gerald Fitzmaurice* [1962] ICJ Rep 465, 466 (ICJ), where they explained that:

We are not unmindful of, nor are we insensible to, the various considerations of a non-judicial character, social, humanitarian and other . . . but these are matters for the political rather than the legal arena.

[20] See, eg, Koskenniemi, *From Apology to Utopia* (n 17) 7 who views 'all legal argument both in theory and doctrine as a movement between a limited set of available argumentative positions'.

[21] Owen M Fiss, 'Objectivity and Interpretation' (1982) 34 Stan L Rev 739.

[22] See McNair (n 14) 345–431 (outlining many other well-established principles).

[23] For a discussion of these approaches see Francis G Jacobs, 'Varieties of Approach to Treaty Interpretation: With Special Reference to the Draft Convention on the Law of Treaties Before the Vienna Diplomatic Conference' (1969) 18 ICLQ 318; Bos (n 13) 364–70.

[24] Bos (n 13) 364–70.

[25] Jacobs (n 23) 298 (recognizing that in practice approaches inevitably overlap and are often combined).

formula.[26] The development of such approaches has two important features. First, there is an expectation, at least within the legal interpretative community, that the interpretation exercise must be constrained in some way and that rules of interpretation are required in order to establish the nature of these constraints.[27] Second, in practice there is rarely if ever universal agreement as to where these boundaries should be placed. Instead of offering what has been described as a form of 'bounded objectivity', the rules themselves remain constantly in need of interpretation.[28]

Controversy is therefore a constant feature of the interpretative enterprise.[29] This does mean that the meaning of the right to health in international law is conditioned to being radically indeterminate in the sense of never being capable of holding *a* meaning. Instead, the accepted meaning of this right at a particular point in time will be that which attracts and achieves dominance over all other alternative understandings within the relevant interpretative community.[30] When seen from this perspective the act of interpretation is more than simply the attribution or communication of *a* meaning. It is ultimately an act of persuasion[31]—an attempt to convince the relevant interpretative community that a particular meaning from within a suite of potential meanings is the most appropriate interpretation to adopt.[32] This in turn gives rise to two questions of central relevance to this chapter: who is the relevant interpretative community for the purposes of the right to health in international law and what factors should be considered or used to inform the selection of a particular meaning of this right from within a range of possible meanings so as to enhance its persuasiveness?

The next section addresses the first of these questions. It examines the notion of an interpretative community and then offers a discussion as to the identity of this community with respect to the right to health and the challenges involved in accommodating the dissonant voices within this community. After addressing these issues this chapter proceeds in Part IV to the second question by providing a detailed discussion of those factors which should inform the selection of a meaning.

---

[26] Michael P Van Alstine, 'Dynamic Treaty Interpretation' (1998) 146 U Pa L Rev 687, 794.

[27] Detlev F Vagts, 'Treaty Interpretation and the New American Ways of Law Reading' (1993) 4 EJIL 472, 480. See also Derek C Smith, 'Beyond Indeterminacy and Self-Contradiction in Law: Transnational Abductions in Treaty Interpretation in *US v Alvarez-Machain*' (1995) 6 EJIL 1, 8–9.

[28] Johnstone (n 3) 377.

[29] See Martti Koskenniemi, 'Letter to the Editors of the Symposium' (2004) 36 J Transnat'l L &Pol'y 109, 114 (who upon reflecting that 'competent lawyers routinely drew contradictory conclusions from the same norms' determined that 'the law's indeterminancy was a property internal to law itself').

[30] Johnstone (n 3) 378.

[31] Other commentators have discussed the importance of legal argument to be 'justified' or 'valid'. See, eg, Koskenneimi, *From Apology to Utopia* (n 17) 7; Van Alstine (n 26) 714; Higgins (n 18) 7. Justification or validity however refers to the identification of the basis upon which an argument is formed. It does not however mean that such an argument will be persuasive in the sense of its acceptance or adoption within the relevant interpretative community.

[32] See Ryan Goodman, 'Sociological Theory Insights into International Human Rights Law' (IILJ International Legal Theory Colloquium: Interpretation and Judgment in International Law, NYU Law School, 3 April 2008) 5–7 (discusses definition and relevance of persuasion as mechanism for social influence within the international human rights law and notes that 'persuasion occurs when actors actively assess the content of a particular message...and change their minds').

III Defining the interpretative community—moving beyond states towards a communitarian model

The idea of interpretative communities is drawn from the work of the literary theorist, Stanley Fish.[33] Fish claims that interpretative authority does not lie in the text or the reader but in the community of individuals who share internal 'categories of understandings and stipulations of relevance and irrelevance' which constrain and inform the interpretative process thereby generating meaning.[34] Fish himself concedes that such a model would not necessarily produce universal agreement with respect to the meaning of a text. Indeed, he accepts that if the act of interpretation were performed by another community of individuals with a different set of expectations and assumptions, a different interpretation would emerge.[35] Commentators have expressed mixed views concerning Fish's work.[36] The aim of this chapter is not defend Fish or his detractors, but rather to borrow Fish's label of 'interpretative communities' to facilitate the interpretative exercise. While Fish was concerned with how meaning was produced within a particular interpretative community, the aim here is to consider how to influence the relevant interpretative community to accept a particular meaning.

For the purposes of this analysis the idea of an interpretative community is therefore used to identify those persons or entities and their agents that have an interest either direct or implied in the meaning of the right to health in international law. This interest will arise for a variety of reasons including the potential for the right to health to impose legal obligations or create benefits for certain persons or entities or for its implementation to carry practical consequences for certain persons or entities. First and foremost this community will be populated by states, which remain the central subject within the international legal system. Only they can enter treaties and be bound by their terms. As a consequence states and their agents have a direct interest in the interpretation of the right to health and must be seen to form a core part of the relevant international interpretative community. However, scholars have increasingly recognized the emergence of a communitarian paradigm within international law that 'vindicates values and pursues interests which cannot be said to be strictly an aggregation of distinct national interests'.[37] This shift from 'bilateralism to community interest'[38] has a significant impact on the composition of the

---

[33] See Stanley Fish, *Is There a Text in This Class? The Authority of Interpretive Communities* (Harvard University Press, 1980).

[34] Stanley Fish, *Doing What Comes Naturally: Change, Rhetoric, and the Practice of Theory in Literary and Legal Studies* (Duke University Press, 1989) 141–2.

[35] ibid.

[36] See, eg, Ronald Dworkin, *Law's Empire* (Hart Publishing, 1998) 425–6 n 23 (describing Fish's concept of internal conventions as somewhat 'mysterious' and 'lame'); cf Johnstone (n 3) (embracing Fish's theory to interpret international treaties).

[37] Weiler (n 11) 16. For a more detailed discussion of this paradigm see Bruno Simma, 'Bilateralism and Community Interest Confronted' (2004) 250 RCADI 229.

[38] Simma (n 37).

interpretative community when seeking to interpret the right to health. Far from being the exclusive concern of states and their officials, the meaning of the right to health will invariably be of interest to and concern a broad range of non-state actors who have an interest in the implications associated with the implementation of this right.[39] As a consequence, a narrow interpretative community, which is confined to the interests of states, will be inadequate to address this broader understanding of international law and those actors considered to be relevant to securing the implementation of the right to health.

Let us consider now the interpretative community relevant to the right to health. It is perhaps difficult to identify those actors who would *not* be relevant for inclusion within this community. Of course, health professionals will have an interest in the meaning of the right to health as will international organizations and NGOs that invoke the language of the right to health to address health needs. Given that the right to health also requires the navigation of issues such as resource allocation, community practices, cultural diversity, and international co-operation the interpretation of this right will often carry significant consequences in relation to a much broader range of actors. These actors include members of the general community who may be affected by the reallocation of resources to realize the right to health, religious groups whose traditional practices may conflict with aspects of an individual's right to health, and multinational corporations whose interests and investments may be compromised if rules regulating intellectual property were adjusted to improve access to medicines.[40]

The Committee on Economic Social and Cultural Rights (ESC Committee) recognized this multitude of actors declaring the following in its General Comment on the Right to Health:

While only States are parties to the Covenant and thus ultimately accountable for compliance with it, all members of society—individuals, including health professionals, families, local communities, intergovernmental and non-governmental organizations, civil society organizations, as well as the private business sector—have responsibilities regarding the realization of the right to health.[41]

---

[39] See *Report of the Special Rapporteur on the Right to Health to the Human Rights Council 2007*, UN Doc A/HRC/4/28 (2007) 12–17 (detailing role and relevance of civil society in implementing the right to health). It is important to recognize that a state is not a homogenous body in the sense of sharing a unified interest or common commitment to the meaning of a human right. It may represent a common position to the international community but this position will invariably represent the outcome of complex and contentious negotiations between the various agents and bodies that comprise the state.

[40] Lawrence Gostin, 'Global Health Law: Health in a Global Community' (Georgetown University, O'Neil Institute for National and Global Health Law, Scholarship Research Paper No 15, September 2008) 230 <http://ssrn.com/abstract=1272391> accessed 30 June 2011 (noting that a broad range of stakeholders exert considerable power over events that influence health and that such stakeholders may act alone, in partnership, separately or together).

[41] ESC Committee, *General Comment No 14: The Right to the Highest Attainable Standard of Health*, UN Doc E/C.12/2000/4 (11 August 2000) para 42.

The Committee on the Rights of the Child (CRC Committee) concurred with this approach in its General Comment on the measures required for implementation of a state's obligations under the Convention on the Rights of the Child (CRC).[42]

Such comments lend support to a vision of an interpretative community which is comprised of actors with diverse, overlapping, and potentially conflicting interests. This, in turn, presents a challenge to the interpretation of a standard such as the right to health. It requires recognition that 'the "clients" of international interpreters are no longer only the Governments of the States which signed the treaties'[43] and that there is a '[w]orldwide social consensus at work today that communalizes and publicizes international relations far beyond the traditional rules of governmental interaction'.[44] It has therefore been suggested, under such a model, the broader interests of non-state actors must now be taken into account when interpreting a treaty provision such as the right to health.[45]

It is possible to envisage how such a requirement could be accommodated in proceedings before a court or tribunal where the views of the relevant parties and their potentially dissonant voices could be directly represented. However, it presents a practical dilemma with respect to the interpretation of the right to health in international law, which lacks a coercive adjudicative body able to hear competing views and insist on the adoption of a particular meaning. Yet even without such bodies, it remains appropriate to be cognizant of the diverse and potentially conflicting interests within the relevant interpretative community when attributing a meaning to the right to health. Indeed it will be suggested below that the requirement to offer an interpretation that is coherent in its reasoning places a demand upon interpreters to identify, engage with, and consider such views when offering a meaning for the right to health.

This does not mean that these views must always be accommodated or reconciled before offering an interpretation. However, a careful consideration of such views, to the extent that they can be identified, contributes to a deeper and more rigorous form of analysis thus strengthening the coherence in the reasoning used to support an interpretative exercise. Such a model demands robust dialogue and engagement in the interpretative exercise as opposed to disengagement and dismissal of competing interpretations without explanation.[46] It creates an evolutionary interpretative process in the sense that a shared understanding or commitment to a particular meaning

---

[42] CRC Committee, *General Comment No 5: General Measures of Implementation for the Convention on the Rights of the Child*, UN Doc CRC/GC/2003/5 (27 November 2003) paras 1, 56 (noting that '[w]hile it is the State which takes on obligations under the Convention, its task of implementation—of making reality of the human rights of children—needs to engage all sectors of society and, of course, children themselves': para 1).

[43] Weiler (n 11) 22.

[44] Simma (n 37) 234.

[45] Weiler (n 11) 22. See also Anand Grover, 'The Power of Community in Advancing the Right to Health: A Conversation with Anand Grover' (2009) 11 Health &Hum Rts 1 (stressing the '[n]eed to pay more attention to the content of the right to health as it is experienced by communities' and shift from a top down interpretative approach to 'an ongoing process of dialogue').

[46] Weiler (n 11) 22.

will emerge over time.[47] This does not preclude the possibility of offering a robust defence of a particular meaning with respect to various aspects of the right to health. However, it does create a need to identify the most effective way to ensure that such offerings are able to persuade the interpretative community so as to generate a shared, rather than idiosyncratic, understanding as to its meaning.

Before examining this question of how to generate a persuasive interpretation it is important to acknowledge the consequences that flow from such a broad vision of the relevant interpretative community. There is a real prospect that there will be some aspects of the right to health where a shared meaning will prove to be elusive or even unachievable. If all the dissonant voices within the relevant interpretative community cannot always be heard and persuaded, who should be the primary target when seeking to generate a persuasive account as to the content of a the right to health?

With respect to this issue, states still remain the central actors to be persuaded by the interpretive exercise, as they hold the primary legal responsibility for the implementation of obligations under international treaties in which the right to health is protected.[48] From a practical perspective, however, the greater the level of support within the broader interpretative community for a particular interpretation, the greater the prospect that a state will be persuaded to adopt that particular interpretation relative to a situation in which there is a lack of support.[49] Thus, for example, in identifying those measures necessary to secure the right to health, the actions of states will be influenced by, among other actors, the views of health professionals, patient preferences and demands, the private health sector, and the competing demands within a government for the allocation of resources to secure other public objectives. An attempt to articulate a vision of the right to health that does not remain aware of these potential interests and the influence of such actors on state behaviour is unlikely to succeed.[50] For example, there is little to be gained from arguing that the obligation

---

[47] Johnstone (n 3) 407 (explaining this process as a form of intersubjective interpretation in which parties expect disagreements over the meaning of terms but assume that such disagreements will not indicate a desire to withdraw from or terminate a treaty).

[48] Simma (n 37) 224, 247 ('[d]espite development of community interest in international law, the statal paradigm remains dominant').

[49] This position is consistent with process of what has been referred to as 'acculturation' whereby actors including states adopt the beliefs and behavioural patterns and practices of the culture in which they operate. See Goodman (n 33). See also Beth Simmons, 'Explaining Variation in State Commitment to and Compliance with International Human Rights Treaties' (IILJ International Legal Theory Colloquium: Interpretation and Judgment in International Law, NYU Law School, 31 January 2008) 26–30 <http://www.iilj.org/courses/documents/2008Colloquium.Session3.Simmons.pdf> accessed 23 June 2011 (discussing the impact of human rights treaties on social mobilization and although not addressed in her work it is suggested here that the greater the shared understanding as to the content of a right within a particular society the more effective a social mobilization effort is likely to be).

[50] It is important to note that even in circumstances where there is a strong sense of a shared understanding as to the meaning of a right, this will not necessarily persuade a state to adopt such an interpretation. Thus for example, condemnation of the detention of refugees in Australia was recognized universally as being in violation of Australia's obligations under the International Covenant on Civil and Political Rights (ICCPR). The Australian Government at the time however refused to accept this interpretation.

under article 12(2)(d) of the ICESCR, which requires states to assure medical attention in the event of sickness, requires the provision of kidney dialysis *on demand*. While patients with a kidney condition would undoubtedly prefer such an interpretation, public health policy makers and medical professionals with limited resources may determine on reasonable grounds that priority should be given to other legitimate public health objectives.[51] Focusing attention on the balancing of such interests may help produce workable interpretations.

Even in those circumstances where a state and a large section of the broader interpretative community accept and agree to implement a particular interpretation with respect to an aspect of a human right, such measures are unlikely to be effective in practice unless *all* the non-state actors whose assistance is required for the implementation of the right are persuaded by the interpretation that has been adopted. For example, a large part of the relevant interpretative community including states, NGOs, academics, and UN bodies, now considers it necessary and appropriate to criminalize female genital cutting as a means of fulfilling a state's obligation under article 24(3) of the Convention on the Rights of the Child (CRC) to protect children against traditional practices prejudicial to their health.[52] However, powerful individuals remain within communities who sanction the practice, are not always persuaded as to its harmful impact, and continue to undertake clandestine measures to ensure its existence.[53] So, while there may be an agreed meaning within certain elements of the interpretative community as to the nature of a state's obligation under article 24(3) of the CRC, the failure to persuade the entire community as to the harmful nature of this practice undermines the capacity to protect children from female genital cutting. This scenario highlights the importance of ensuring that the interpretative exercise must be conscious of the need to persuade not only states of the interpretation being offered but also those other actors who have the capacity to secure or impede the realization of the right to health. The question remains, however, as to the most appropriate method by which to ensure such an outcome.

---

[51] This issue arose under the South African Constitution in the case of *Soobramoney v Minister for Health* [1998] 1 SA 765 (CC, Sth Afr). It was argued by the appellant that the right to emergency medical treatment, which is not subject to progressive implementation under the South African Constitution, extended to kidney dialysis on demand. However, the South African Constitutional Court rejected this argument and held that a right to kidney dialysis fell within the scope of the general right of access to health services, which was subject to progressive realization. Although the Court was sympathetic to the appellant's condition, it held that it would 'be slow to interfere with rational decisions taken in good faith by the political organs and medical authorities whose responsibility it is to deal with such matters': [29].

[52] See John Tobin, 'The International Obligation to Abolish Traditional Practices Harmful to Children's Health: What Does It Mean and Require of States?' (2009) 9 HRL Rev 373, 389–90 (discussing those actors and instruments that favour criminalization of female genital cutting).

[53] WHO, *Female Genital Mutilation: Programmes to Date: What Works and What Doesn't—A Review*, WHO Doc WHO/CHS/WMH/99.5 (1999); UNICEF Innocenti Research Centre, *Changing a Harmful Social Convention: Female Genital Mutilation/Cutting* (United Nations Publishing, 2008) 11.

IV Seeking to persuade by constructive engagement

A Providing a transparent account of the interpretative process

Thus far I have argued that interpretation is a process that seeks to persuade the relevant interpretative community to adopt a particular meaning in relation to the right to health in international law. This notion of interpretation as persuasion is considered to be particularly apt with respect to international human rights because they possess no mechanism by which to secure coercive compliance with a particular interpretation of a state's obligations under such instruments.[54] As a consequence, if there is a perceived controversy or uncertainty with respect to the meaning of the right to health, as is nearly always the case, there will be a need to persuade states and the broader interpretative community to adopt a particular meaning in relation to this right. The alternative is to allow states to adopt a form of auto-interpretation in which the meaning of the right to health will effectively remain dependent upon, and largely captive to, state interests. Such an outcome is inconsistent with the emergence of the communitarian model of international law discussed above, and the principle that 'the view of a state cannot be the last word on the international lawfulness of its activities...'[55] As Weiler has observed states may be 'the "masters of the treaty" but they are not masters without normative limits'.[56] To prevent state control, the international community must reject the position advanced by many states, including the United States in its 2006 dialogue with the Human Rights Committee, that 'only the parties to a treaty were empowered to give a binding interpretation of its provisions'.[57]

To conceive of interpretation as the choice of *a* meaning which is designed to persuade an interpretative community requires an interpretative methodology that will enhance the persuasiveness of the interpretation to be offered. This part of the chapter will suggest that the features of such a model require that the proposed

---

[54] It is important to recognize that a complex system has been created at the international level to achieve this end. For a discussion of this system, see Andreas Zimmermann, 'Dispute Resolution, Compliance Control and Enforcement in Human Rights Law' in Geir Ulfstein (ed), *Making Treaties Work: Human Rights, Environment and Arms Control* (CUP, 2007) 15.

[55] ILC, *Fragmentation of International Law: Difficulties Arising from the Diversification and Expansion of International Law—Report of the Study Group of the International Law Commission*, UN Doc A/CN.4/L.682 (13 April 2006) para 487 (*ILC Fragmentation Study*). See also Simma (n 38) 224, 233, 296–301. This view reflects by implication the limitations associated with art 31(3)(b) of the VCLT which allows for recourse to any subsequent practice in the application of a treaty which establishes the agreement of the parties regarding its interpretation. This rule may be relevant to the interpretation of bilateral treaties but it is extremely problematic in relation to human rights treaties where its application would create a 'very real risk that state auto-determination' as to the scope of their obligations would 'trump' the existence of any obligations under such a treaty: see Hathaway (n 9) 71.

[56] Weiler (n 11) 21. The nature of these normative limits, which are primarily located in the provisions of the VCLT, are discussed below in Part IV(B)(1). They are also found in the provisions of human rights treaties to which states are party that create systems for monitoring a state's compliance with its obligations under the respective treaties.

[57] HRC, *Consideration of Reports under Article 40 of the Covenant*, UN Doc CCPR/C/SR.2380 (27 July 2006) para 8.

meaning of right to health must: be principled; be clear and practical; demonstrate coherence in both its reasoning *and* within the system of international law; and be sensitive to the nature of the socio-political context within both individual states and the international legal order.

The identification of each of these features is an attempt to recognize what Martti Koskenneimi would term the 'rules' that govern the production of the arguments used to justify the interpretation of a human right.[58] Their cumulative impact is directed towards an interpretative technique that relies on the interpreter being engaged with the relevant interpretative community in an ongoing dialogue. This focus on engaging the interpretative community, and thus the social and political context, contrasts with the traditional view, in which 'reflection on the "political foundations" of international law...ha[s] had only marginal—if any—consequences on the doctrinal elaborations of different areas of international law'.[59] This is not to say that consideration of the VCLT's rules of interpretation is not a necessary feature of an interpretative methodology; it is. But it is not sufficient. This is because the assumption that the application of the accepted doctrine concerning treaty interpretation produces a cohesive interpretation denies the controversial nature of both the doctrines themselves and the outcomes produced by their application.[60] While the traditional doctrine may constrain the range of potential meanings, it will not deliver *the* meaning of the right to health.

It is therefore important to heed Koskenniemi's warning that to retreat to formal doctrine and ignore social theory and political practice is to become 'trapped in a prison house of irrelevance'.[61] Indeed, the danger of excessive formalism is harmful on a number of fronts. Not only do excessively formal approaches fail to take account of the political context in which states assume their obligations under international human rights law, but they also risk being disregarded by the broader interpretative community. Thus, for example, the Millennium Taskforce on Child and Maternal Health may have accepted the need for human rights to achieve the Millennium Development Goals,[62] but it also warned that 'human rights initiatives fixated on and bound by chapter and verse of human rights treaties often miss the mark'.[63]

Despite this deflation in the capacity of doctrine to produce a fixed and determinate meaning of a text, there is still a need to be cognizant of the observation that those who interpret human rights treaties tend to infuse their understanding with 'beliefs, biases, blind spots and prejudices about what it means to be a "human being"'.[64] Such subjectivity is an inescapable aspect of the interpretative process and the task is not to mask this reality but adopt a methodology that seeks to mitigate the potential for the subjective preferences of an interpreter. As an interpretative

---

[58] Koskenniemi, *From Apology to Utopia* (n 17) 8.
[59] ibid 1.   [60] ibid 3.   [61] ibid 4.
[62] Lynne P Freedman and others, UN Millennium Project Task Force on Child Health and Maternal Health, *Who's Got the Power? Transforming Health Systems for Women and Children* (Earthscan, 2005) 31.
[63] ibid 34.
[64] Toufayan (n 13) 10–11.

methodology, the requirements that an interpretation be principled, practical, coherent, and context-sensitive attempt to perform this task in a way that seeks to provide transparency to the process of how one particular meaning of the right to health is to be selected from within a suite of potential meanings.

B The features required for constructive engagement

1 Principled interpretation

(a) Overview

Lord McNair insisted in 1961 that 'Treaties must be applied and interpreted against the backdrop of the general principles of international law'.[65] Despite the misgivings about doctrine aired in the previous section, no attempt is made here to deviate from McNair's directive. Indeed, if an interpretative outcome is to have any persuasive force within an interpretative community, it must be constructed in light of the principles that have been agreed upon by that community to guide the interpretative exercise.[66] In this case, states, which are the central actors in the interpretative community, have accepted the principles of the VCLT.

Where this chapter departs from McNair's approach is in arguing that, although such principles remain insufficient, a more holistic approach is required to overcome the limitations of the VCLT.[67] McNair's work is useful for identifying those general principles that are relevant to the interpretative exercise. He declared that treaties' 'very existence and validity rest on one of the earliest and most fundamental of those principles—*pacta sunt servanda*'[68]—a principle that is now codified in article 26 of the VCLT: '[e]very treaty in force is binding upon the parties to it and must be performed by them in good faith'.

The obligation to 'perform' anticipates that the ratification of a human rights treaty will carry practical consequences in terms of measures required by states to fulfill their obligations. Moreover when this obligation is combined with the obligation of 'good faith' the result is that states may not adopt a passive response to the implementation of the right to health on the basis that its meaning is unclear or ambiguous. On the contrary, it demands that states actively engage with the formulation of this right in international law to produce an understanding as to the nature of its content so that the right is capable of effective implementation.[69]

---

[65] McNair (n 14) 466.

[66] Bos (n 13) 37 (suggests that rules of interpretation represent important tools which 'are not only steering aids for the normative concept but also instrumental in making the interpreter conscious of his (*sic*) own normative concept').

[67] Toufayan (n 13) 2.

[68] McNair (n 14) 466.

[69] Richard Gardiner, *Treaty Interpretation* (OUP, 2008) (noting that '[a]lthough it is difficult to give precise content to the concept generally, it does include one principle that applies to interpretation of specific terms used in a treaty. This is commonly described as the principle of "effectiveness"').

(b) The Vienna Convention on the Law of Treaties 1969

As to how this task is to be undertaken, article 31 of the VCLT outlines the general rule of interpretation providing in paragraph 1 that '[a] treaty shall be interpreted in good faith in accordance with the ordinary meaning to be given to the terms of the treaty in their context and in the light of its object and purpose'. Paragraph 2 explains that 'context' extends beyond the text of the treaty to include its preamble and annexes, any agreement made in connection with the treaty between all the parties, and any instrument made by one or more parties and accepted by the other parties as an instrument related to the treaty. Paragraph 3 adds that any subsequent agreement between the parties regarding the interpretation of the treaty, any subsequent practice in relation to the application of the treaty which establishes the agreement of parties regarding its application, and any relevant rules of international law, must also be taken into account.

Article 32 of the VCLT further provides that:

Recourse may be had to supplementary means of interpretation, including the preparatory work of the treaty and the circumstances of its conclusion, in order to confirm the meaning resulting from the application of article 31, or to determine the meaning when the interpretation according to article 31:
(a) leaves the meaning ambiguous or obscure; or
(b) leads to a result which is manifestly absurd or unreasonable.

As these provisions have already been the subject of significant commentary, it is unnecessary to provide a detailed analysis of their content here.[70] Instead, it is sufficient to make some observations, first, with respect to their general application and then in relation to their application to human rights treaties. Turning to the question of their application, it is important to note that they embrace a range of interpretative approaches—textual, contextual, teleological, and historical.[71] Vagts has suggested that article 31 offers a hierarchy with primary emphasis to be placed on a textual approach to treaty interpretation followed by a contextual, teleological, and historical approach in descending order.[72] In contrast, Toufayan maintains that '[n]o one single means dominates the others' and that the 'order chosen in article 31 is that of logic, proceeding from the intrinsic to the extrinsic, from the immediate to the remote, the ordinary meaning being merely a natural starting point'.[73] The *Report of the Study Group of the International Law Commission on the Fragmentation*

---

[70] See ibid; Ian Sinclair, *The Vienna Convention on the Law of Treaties* (Manchester University Press, 1984); Hathaway (n 9) 48–73.
[71] See Koskenniemi, *From Apology to Utopia* (n 17) 292 ('[i]t refers to virtually all thinkable interpretative methods'); Toufayan (n 13) 30 (suggesting that they do not extend to a restrictive interpretative approach); Bos (n 13) 145 (suggesting that provision requires 'concurrent use of no less than three methods').
[72] Vagts (n 27) 484.
[73] Toufayan (n 13) 9.

of *International Law* (*ILC Fragmentation Study*) took the similar view that '[t]here is no reason to separate these techniques too sharply from each other'.[74]

Such an approach is consistent with the role envisioned for article 31(1) of the VCLT by the International Law Commission (ILC) Commentaries on the Draft Articles provisionally adopted at the Vienna Conference in 1966:

> [T]he application of the means of interpretation in the article would be a single combined operation. All the various elements as they were present in any given case would be thrown in the crucible and their interaction would give *the* legally relevant interpretation.[75]

In practice, however, the act of interpretation is more complex and far less precise in its capacity to yield '*the*' relevant interpretation than such a comment is willing to concede. First, the comment assumes an understanding of the 'ordinary meaning' of a term will invariably be contentious. And second, the requirement of 'good faith', although unclear,[76] may have been 'intended to restrain an excessive literalism' even within the textual approach.[77]

It is true that the VCLT recognizes the limitations of a formal textual approach by including a requirement to consider the 'context'; this acknowledges that the ordinary meaning of a word cannot be ascribed in isolation.[78] But the inclusion of a requirement to consider context raises a question as to how widely 'context' is to be understood.[79] To a certain extent, the 'objects and purpose' of a treaty will assist in the resolution of this dilemma by contributing to an understanding of the 'context'. But the teleological approach is not without its own problems. As Francis Jacobs points out there are problems of priority ('what significance is to be attached to the [the object and purpose of a treaty]?') as well as problems of methodology ('are [objects and purposes] to be ascertained only by intrinsic means, ie: by reference to the text and related documents, or also by extrinsic means?').[80]

The International Court of Justice has indicated that the preamble of a treaty may assist with respect to this second question.[81] But an examination of the preamble of

---

[74] ILC, *ILC Fragmentation Study* (n 55) para 428. See also Anthony Aust, *Modern Treaty Law and Practice* (1st edn, CUP, 2000) 187.

[75] ILC, *Report of the International Law Commission on the Work of Its Eighteenth Session*, UN Doc A/CN.4/191 (4 May – 19 July 1966) 217, 219–20 para 8 (emphasis added).

[76] Jacobs (n 23) 334.

[77] ibid 334. This position is consistent with the International Law Commission Commentary on the Draft Articles which provides that, 'when a treaty is open to two interpretations one of which does and the other does not enable the treaty to have appropriate effects, good faith and the objects and purposes of the treaty demand that the former interpretation should be adopted': ILC, *Report of the International Law Commission on the work of its Eighteenth Session* (n 75) 219, para 6.

[78] See separate opinion of Judge Bernardez in *Land, Island and Maritime Frontier Case (El Salvador/Honduras, Nicaragua Intervening)* [1992] ICJ Rep 351, 719 (ICJ).

[79] Jacobs (n 23) 334.

[80] ibid 337. See also Myres S McDougal, 'The International Law Commission's Draft Articles upon Interpretation: Textuality *Redivivus*' (1967) 61 AJIL 992, 993. ('Lest it be thought that the references to "context" and to "object and purpose" are intended to remedy the blindness and arbitrariness of "ordinary meaning", context is immediately defined as including mere text').

[81] *Rights of Nationals of the United States of America in Morocco (France v United States of America)* [1952] ICJ Rep 176, 196 ('The purposes and objects of this Convention were stated in its Preamble in the

those instruments in which the right to health is protected will generally yield an answer which is expressed at such a high level of abstraction that it is unlikely to narrow the interpretative inquiry. Moreover a consideration of any subsequent agreements or practice between parties—as is permitted under article 31(3) of the VCLT—will rarely prove helpful with respect to an international human rights treaty because all too often states fail to treat their obligations under such treaties with the respect that international law demands. To be fair article 32 of the VCLT does allow for recourse to the drafting history of a treaty to resolve any interpretative dilemmas but, as will be discussed below, most commentators have recognized the limits of this source as a means of resolving such disputes.

The cumulative impact of these limitations caused Myres MacDougal to comment in his assessment of the draft VCLT provisions in 1967 that 'the Commission's formulations are so vague and imprecise and so impossible of effective application that a sophisticated decision maker can easily escape their putative limits'.[82] His concerns are not without foundation. With respect to the right to health, a requirement that states recognize the right to the highest attainable standard of health is hardly a phrase that renders itself amenable to an orderly and consistent application of the provisions of the VCLT. But as with all norms, the legal interpretative community has developed expectations and accepted practices as to the use and application of the interpretative principles under the VCLT which operate to constrain the extent to which a decision maker will be prepared to step outside these bounds.[83] Some of these accepted practices with respect to human rights treaties are outlined below.

At this point, however, it is important to acknowledge that the process of treaty interpretation, 'far from being the accounting of raw interpretative data or the prioritization of certain interpretive means over others is in reality a holistic construct'.[84] Although the principles under the VCLT do not offer a formulation that will necessarily *give* the meaning of a provision within a treaty, they still remain tools to guide this task.[85] Moreover, as there is strong expectation, at least within the legal elements of the interpretative community, that they will be used to 'frame' the

---

following words: "the necessity of establishing, on fixed and uniform bases, the exercise of the right of protection in Morocco and of settling certain questions connected therewith..." In these circumstances, the Court cannot adopt a construction by implication of the provisions of the Madrid Convention which would go beyond the scope of its declared purposes and objects. Further, this contention would involve radical changes and additions to the provision of the Convention. The Court, in its Opinion—[*Interpretation of Peace Treaties with Bulgaria, Hungary and Romania (Second Phase) (Advisory Opinion)* [1950] ICJ 229 (1CJ)]—stated: "It is the duty of the Court to interpret the Treaties, not to revise them."'). See also *Asylum Case (Colombia v Peru)* [1950] ICJ Rep 266, 282.

[82] McDougal (n 80) 998.

[83] Bruno Simma and Andreas Paulus, 'The Responsibility of Individuals for Human Rights Abuses in Internal Conflicts: A Positivist View' (1999) 93 AJIL 23, 46 (noting that in the interpretative process 'it is standards derived from legal sources deemed to be representative of the attitude of the community that provide the yardsticks for finding *a*—not *the*—correct solution to a legal problem') (emphasis in original).

[84] Toufayan (n 13) 10.

[85] *ILC Fragmentation Study* (n 55) 250 (noting that the VCLT provides a 'tool box for dealing with fragmentation').

interpretation exercise, engagement with the VCLT principles of interpretation is considered to be an essential feature of a persuasive interpretation.[86] As Ryan Goodman has explained, 'the persuasive appeal of a counter attitudinal message increases if the issue is structured to resonate with already accepted norms'.[87] The principles under the VCLT constitute those norms that have been accepted for the interpretation of international human rights. The requirement for system coherence, which is discussed in more detail below, demands that an interpretation of the right to health in international law must be informed by the provisions of the VCLT as the international instrument adopted by states to guide the interpretation of treaties. Article 31(1) of the VCLT is itself an example of a general rule of international law that, according to para (3)(c) of article 31, must be taken into account in the interpretation of any treaty.

(c) Human rights treaties and the VCLT

There is a widespread, albeit contested, view that human rights treaties, as a form of special regime, warrant a special interpretative methodology.[88] This view is essentially grounded in the non-reciprocal nature of human rights treaties as a key point of distinction from other treaties.[89] It is not necessary to examine or resolve this debate here. Rather, its significance lies in the extent to which it has led to the development of interpretative practices by human rights bodies with respect to the application of the interpretative principles under the VCLT. It is these practices that will have relevance to the interpretation of the right to health in international law.

The first point to note is that the bodies responsible for monitoring implementation of such treaties, the various treaty monitoring committees, have not as yet given any explicit or detailed consideration to the interpretative methodology they adopt when performing their role.[90] The work of regional bodies, however, is more

---

[86] *ILC Fragmentation Study* (n 55) 250 (noting that the VCLT provides a 'tool box for dealing with fragmentation').

[87] See Goodman (n 32) 6 (discusses 'framing' as the process by which an argument is structured and suggests that 'the persuasive appeal of a counterattitudinal message increases if the issue is structured to resonate with already accepted norms').

[88] See Toufayan (n 13); John Graham Merrills, *The Development of International Law by the European Court of Human Rights* (2nd edn, Manchester United Press, 1993) chs 4–5 (detailing methods of interpretation and principle of effectiveness); R Bernhardt, 'Thoughts on the Interpretation of Human Rights Treaties' in Franz Matscher and Herbert Petzold (eds), *Protecting Human Rights: The European Dimension: Studies in Honour of Gérard J Wiarda* (1st edn, Heymanns, 1988) 65.

[89] Matthew Craven, 'Legal Differentiation and the Concept of the Human Rights Treaty in International Law' (2000) 11 EJIL 489, 497, 504–13; René Provost, 'Reciprocity in Human Rights and Humanitarian Law' (1994) 65 BYBIL 383, 383–5; *Ireland v United Kingdom* (1978) Series A no 25 (ECrtHR) [239] ('unlike international treaties of the classic kind, the [European] Convention comprises more than merely reciprocal engagements between Contracting States. It creates over and above a network of mutual, bilateral relationships, objective obligations'). See also *Effect of Reservations on the Entry into Force of the American Convention on Human Rights (Arts 74 and 75)*, Advisory Opinion O-C 2/82 of 24 September 1982, Inter-Am Ct HR (Ser A) No 2 (1982) 14–16, [29]–[33]; *Restrictions to the Death Penalty (Arts 4(2) and 4(4) of the American Convention on Human Rights)*, Advisory Opinion OC 8/83 of September 1983, Inter-Am Ct HR (Ser A) No 3 (1983) 76–7 [50] (8 September 1983).

[90] This observation is based on an assessment of general comments and recommendations variously adopted by the Committee bodies in which there is no explicit reference to the general rule of

insightful on this topic. Of principal significance is the work of the European Court of Human Rights (ECtHR),[91] which has been the most sophisticated of the human rights bodies with respect to this issue. It has advocated that an interpretation of the rights under the European Convention on Human Rights and Fundamental Freedoms (ECHR) must be one which:

- 'is most appropriate in order to realize the aim and achieve the objective of the treaty not that which would restrict to the greatest possible degree the obligations undertaken by States';[92]
- will 'make its safeguards practical and effective';[93] and
- adopts a dynamic interpretation that responds to evolving standards.[94]

A similar approach has been adopted by the Inter American Court of Human Rights.[95] To a lesser extent the United Nations human rights treaty monitoring committees seem to be in agreement.[96]

---

interpretation under art 31 of the VCLT. It remains possible that the concluding observations of the Committee bodies might make some reference but given the general nature of such documents it is considered to be unlikely. Some Committees have made reference to various provisions of the VCLT such as arts 26 and 27, but art 31 has not been the subject of any direct or detailed consideration. Where it has, it has been used in the context of demanding that states avoid a form of auto-interpretation in favour of the rule under art 31. See, eg, CO HRC USA, UN Doc A/61/40 (Vol 1) (27 July 2006) 60.

[91] See generally François Ost, 'The Original Canons of Interpretation of the European Court of Human Rights' in Mireille Delmas-Marty (ed), *The European Convention for the Protection of Human Rights: International Protection Versus National Restrictions* (Martinus Nijhoff, 1991) 283–318, 285; H Mosler, 'Problems of Interpretation in the Case Law of the European Convention of Human Rights' in Fritz Kalshoven, Pieter J Kuyper, and Johan G Lammers (eds), *Essays on the Development of the International Legal Order: In Memory of Haro F van Panhuys* (Sitjhoff &Noordhoff, 1980).

[92] See, eg, *Wemhoff v Germany* (1968) Series A no 7 (ECtHR) 55 [8].

[93] See, eg, *Loizidou v Turkey (Merits)* ECHR 1996–VI 2220.

[94] See, eg, *Tyrer v United Kingdom* (1978) Series A no 26 (ECtHR).

[95] *The Right to Information on Consular Assistance in the Framework of the Guarantees of the Due Process of Law*, Advisory Opinion OC-16/99 of R1 October 1999, Inter-Am Ct HR (Ser A) No 16 (1999) [114]–[115]:

114 This guidance is particularly relevant in the case of international human rights law, which has made great headway thanks to an evolutive interpretation of international instruments of protection. That evolutive interpretation is consistent with the general rules of treaty interpretation established in the 1969 Vienna Convention. Both this Court, in the Advisory Opinion on the Interpretation of the American Declaration of the Rights and Duties of Man (1989), and the European Court of Human Rights, in *Tyrer v United Kingdom* (1978), *Marckx v Belgium* (1979), *Loizidou v Turkey* (1995), among others, have held that human rights treaties are living instruments whose interpretation must consider the changes over time and present-day conditions.

115 The *corpus juris* of international human rights law comprises a set of international instruments of varied content and juridical effects (treaties, conventions, resolutions and declarations). Its dynamic evolution has had a positive impact on international law in affirming and building up the latter's faculty for regulating relations between States and the human beings within their respective jurisdictions. This Court, therefore, must adopt the proper approach to consider this question in the context of the evolution of the fundamental rights of the human person in contemporary international law.

[96] See, eg, HRC, *General Comment No 6: The Right to Life*, UN Doc CCPR/C/21/Add/1 (30 April 1982) paras 4–5, in which the HRC stressed the obligations of state to take 'effective measures to prevent the disappearance of individuals... [and] establish effective facilities and procedures to investigate thoroughly cases of missing and disappeared persons in circumstances which may involve a violation of the

Some commentators see the adoption of such an approach as a deviation from the interpretative principles of the VCLT. For example, Vagts has suggested that human rights treaties have 'attracted a style of interpretation that has drawn away from traditional treaty reading' whereby '[t]hese courts also feel that they have tacit permission from the parties to the agreement to develop a body of jurisprudence that sacrifices fidelity to a text ... in order to develop internal consistency and to keep pace with the perceived necessities of changing times'.[97] An alternative explanation is to conceive of the approach adopted by the ECtHR as the development of practices to implement the principles under the VCLT, especially the requirements of good faith and the object and purpose test. In other words, the principles of non-restrictive interpretation, effectiveness, and dynamic interpretation do not operate to restrict states' obligations to the greatest extent possible. Rather they ensure that the states are required to take active measures to ensure the effective protection of human rights. Thus far from being deviation from the VCLT, these principles simply provide evidence of a practical application and understanding of how the general rule of interpretation under the VCLT can be applied to achieve the object and purpose of a human rights treaty. As a consequence, interpreters should use the principles of non-restrictive interpretation, effectiveness, and dynamic interpretation to assist in the interpretation of the right to health. The extent to which they should be employed, however, must be tempered by the other factors which are considered essential to ensure a constructive approach to interpretation. Thus they should be used to enable *an* interpretation but cannot be used to justify *any* interpretation.

(d) The relevance of the parties' intentions

It will be recalled that McNair's understanding as to the aim of the interpretative exercise was reduced to the simple question of identifying the intention of the parties to a treaty. Such a requirement is notably absent from the VCLT and it was the subject of criticism by commentators at the time of drafting.[98] However, the justification given in the ILC Commentaries to the draft VCLT was that 'the text [of a treaty] must be presumed to be the authentic expression of the intentions of the parties' and hence that 'the starting point of interpretation is the elucidation of the meaning of the text not an investigation *ab initio* into the intentions of

---

right to life' and 'noted that the right to life has been too often narrowly interpreted. The expression "inherent right to life" cannot properly be understood in a restrictive manner, and the protection of this right requires that States adopt positive measures'. See also CEDAW Committee, *General Recommendation No 25: Article 4, Paragraph 1, of the Convention (Temporary Special Measures)* (2004) in *Compilation of General Comments and General Recommendations Adopted by Human Rights Bodies*, UN Doc HRI/GEN/1/Rev.7 (12 May 2004) 282, para 3, in which the Committee stated that '[t]he Convention is a dynamic instrument'. See also HRC, *General Comment No 24: Issues relating to Reservations*, UN Doc CCPR/21/Rev.1/Add.6 (11 November 1994).

[97] Vagts (n 27) 499.

[98] See, eg, McDougal (n 80) 992 (damning of the explicit rejection of a quest for the 'intention of the parties as a subjective element distinct from the text' in preference for a 'basic approach which demands merely the ascription of a meaning to a text').

the parties'.⁹⁹ Thus the intention of the parties was to remain a relevant and underlying consideration, albeit in the background, that was to be given effect through an application of the principles under articles 31 and 32.

An intentionalist approach, however, comes into conflict with the principle of dynamic interpretation, that anticipates that the meaning of a term within a treaty may take on an understanding different to that which was accepted at the time of drafting. This is a well-known tension, and domestic jurisdictions have invariably given preference to the dynamic approach.¹⁰⁰ At the international level, the parties' intention also carries significant weight, given the degree to which the system is based upon the consent of sovereign states. However, the notion that the intention of the parties to a treaty can be distilled with any precision from either the text or drafting history of a treaty is problematic. As Judge Pescatore explained in 1963:

> It is not, in actual fact, on the intentions of the contracting parties that agreement is reached but only on the written formulas of the treaties and only on that. It is by no means certain that agreement on a text in any way implies agreement as to intentions. On the contrary divergent even conflicting intentions may perfectly well underlie a given text.¹⁰¹

Moreover in the construction of the multilateral treaties in which the right to health is protected 'a wide variety of different human individuals acting for a variety of constituencies participate in the negotiating drafting, signing and ratification of the document.'¹⁰² This makes it difficult to elucidate with any clarity the precise intentions of the states party to the drafting process and reflects the idea, discussed in Chapter 2, that such treaties represent incompletely theorized agreements.

This does not mean that it is impossible to identify the common intentions of the states responsible for the drafting of a human rights treaty that includes the right to health. At the most general level it is reasonable to infer from the text of the ICESCR and the CRC that it was the intention of the parties that drafted these instruments that states parties would have a progressive as opposed to an immediate obligation to secure the right to health. Moreover recourse to the drafting history of such treaties is invariably used as a tool to assist in the identification of any general themes that may emerge as to the common intentions of the parties.¹⁰³ Such a practice, however, is problematic.

(e) The need to handle with care: making recourse to the drafting history
Commentators have expressed considerable anxiety with respect to interpretative endeavours that rely upon the drafting history. Reuter, for example, has warned that 'recourse to preparatory work means treading uncertain ground: its content is not precisely defined nor rigorously certified, ... [m]oreover preparatory work is not

---

⁹⁹ ILC, *Report of the International Law Commission on the Work of Its Eighteenth Session* (n 75) 220 para 11.
¹⁰⁰ See Richard Clayton and Hugh Tomlinson, *The Law of Human Rights* (OUP, 2000) 110–18.
¹⁰¹ Lecture of 1963, cited in Vagts (n 27) 507.
¹⁰² ibid.
¹⁰³ See Hathaway (n 9) 55–6.

always published'.[104] A dilemma is also created by having recourse to the historical documents underlying the adoption of an instrument that is supposed to be given a dynamic interpretation and adapt to evolving standards. Although reliance upon *travaux preparatoires* in the interpretation of treaties is problematic, the practice remains widespread.[105]

In defence of this practice, and after a careful examination of the literature, Hathaway formed the view that:

> [T]here appears to be neither theory nor practice to justify the view that the designation of a treaty's preparatory work as a supplementary means of interpretation requires that it be relegated to an inherently subordinate or inferior place in a comprehensive, interactive process of treaty interpretation.[106]

As such, the better view would appear to be that recourse to be drafting history should be viewed as a 'as a means by which to achieve the interpretative goal set by Art 31'.[107] In other words, it should be used, albeit with due caution, to assist in providing guidance and insight as to the object and purpose of a treaty and the broad underlying intentions of the parties to the drafting process.[108] In light of Judge Pescatore's comments, such intentions should not be considered determinative or representative of the intentions of *all* the parties to the drafting process. The drafting history may play a role in contributing to an understanding of the various terms within the enumeration of the right to health, but there is no realistic process by which to identify the precise intentions of the parties in the sense anticipated by Lord McNair with respect to the full enumeration as to the meaning of this right.

Such an approach is consistent with the first condition under article 32 of the VCLT with respect to the use of a treaty's drafting history; that it can be used to *confirm* an interpretation arising from the application of article 31. It is also consistent with the condition that recourse to the *travaux preparatoires* is reasonable where an application of article 31 leaves the text of a treaty '*ambiguous or obscure*' or '*absurd and unreasonable*'. Given the limited capacity of the general rule of interpretation under article 31 to produce a determinate meaning for any treaty provision, it must follow that the threshold for making use of the drafting history will be quite low.[109] Thus if ambiguity is a feature of all treaty provisions, a consideration of the drafting history will be necessary to examine whether it has the capacity to assist in constraining the range of potential meanings for the text of such a provision. In such circumstances recourse to the drafting history of an international human rights treaty protecting the right to health actually becomes a legitimate feature of a principled interpretative approach. It will not, however, produce a single meaning for the right

---

[104] Paul Reuter, *Introduction to the Law of Treaties* (Pinter Publishers, 1989) 97–8; See also Jacobs (n 23) 339 ('Recourse to the *travaux préparatoires* as a means of establishing the intentions of the parties is fraught with practical difficulties' and thus 'should not be considered a primary means of interpretation').

[105] Hathaway (n 9) 56–7.

[106] ibid 59.   [107] ibid.

[108] Vagts (n 27) 486 (suggesting that although the use of drafting history remains contentious and will not always clarify the parties' intentions, at times it does seem helpful).

[109] See Hathaway (n 9) 60.

to health and it remains to consider what other factors beyond those identified as being relevant under the VCLT should guide the selection of a meaning from within a suite of potential meanings. First among those considerations is a requirement that the interpretation adopted is clear and practical.

2 Clear and practical

Given the high level of abstraction that characterizes human rights treaties, the interpretative process must be directed to achieving what might be described as descending levels of abstraction or increasing levels of clarity as to the content of a human right. As Maarten Bos has emphasized, the interpretative process must not only be 'an activity ... designed to clarify the text of a written manifestation of law, it must also be cognizant of the need to ensure that the interpretation offered is capable of application to the realities of daily life and practice'.[110] The interpretation of the right to health must be 'action guiding'[111] or 'socially manageable'.[112] Clarity and practicality are therefore essential attributes of an interpretative process that seeks to persuade the interpretative community as to the suitability of the interpretation offered.

The requirement that an interpretation of a human right be clear and practical is so obvious that its identification as a specific element of a persuasive interpretation could be considered unwarranted. Should not every act of interpretation instinctively be guided by these features? In practice, however, reliance on instinct raises the risk that the subjective preferences of an interpreter will be insufficiently attentive to the need to ensure that the interpretation offered is clear and practical. Take for example, the concept of minimum core obligations that was developed by the Committee on Economic Social and Cultural Rights (ESC Committee) and will be discussed in detail in Chapter 4.[113] Although intended as a tool to assist in securing the implementation of the rights under ICESCR, it still lacks a clear and practical understanding of its application.[114] In its General Comment on the right to health,

---

[110] Bos (n 13) 15.
[111] Charles R Beitz, *The Idea of Human Rights* (OUP, 2009) 46.
[112] Griffin (n 4).
[113] For the original exposition of this concept see: ESC Committee, *General Comment No 3: The Nature of States' Parties Obligations*, UN Doc E/1991/23 (14 December 1990) annex III, 86 para 10.
[114] Attempts have been made to clarify the practical meaning of this principle. See, eg, Danie Brand and Sage Russell (eds), *Exploring the Core Content of Economic and Social Rights: South African and International Perspectives* (Protea Book House, 2002). But significant work remains to be done on this project. See Katharine Young, 'The Minimum Core of Economic and Social Rights: A Concept in Search of Content' (2008) 33 Yale J Intl L 113 (providing the most comprehensive critique of this concept to date and concluding that the concept is so problematic that it ought to be stripped of any normative status and restricted to advocacy in its use). The South African Constitutional Court has also sought to grapple with the concept of the minimum core but ultimately resolved to leave it within the more general scope of the reasonableness review with respect to the implementation of the rights to health and housing: *Government of the Republic of South Africa v Grootboom* [2001] 1 SA 46 [33] (CC, Sth Afr) (declining to decide on the question of the minimum core with respect to the right to housing because of a perceived lack of information before the court to make such a finding); *Minister of Health v Treatment Action Campaign (No 2)* [2002] 5 SA 721 (CC, Sth Afr) (refusing to define a minimum core standard for the right to health largely by virtue of its perceived institutional capacity). cf Justice Goldstone, 'Foreword' in Varun Gauri

the ESC Committee embarked upon an expansion of the scope of this concept so as to include a non-derogable minimum core obligation to secure the immediate implementation of a long list of measures.[115] For many, if not all, states in both the developing and developed world, the capacity to ensure the content of the minimum core obligation required by the ESC Committee will remain as distant as the prospect of the full realization of the right to health itself. As such, this aspect of the vision of the right to health offered by the ESC is simply not practical because it cannot be achieved even when states act with the best of intentions. Human rights advocates, other treaty monitoring bodies, and even some commentators may find it be compelling and convincing,[116] but to suggest that states must secure such a vision immediately, irrespective of their available resources, is to ignore the realities that confront states when seeking to implement the right to health.

An explicit awareness of the need to pursue a clear and practical interpretation encourages a certain level of reflection in the interpretative process. Importantly the requirements of clarity and practicality do not demand that the interpretative exercise must always resolve these issues in the first instance. This may be possible where there is a rich jurisprudence and sophisticated debate within the interpretative community from which to draw and develop the interpretation offered—features which often characterize the understanding of civil and political rights. But with respect to the right to health, whose boundaries are relatively porous and uncharted, greater emphasis will need to be placed on the collaborative process necessary to identify the practical measures required for the effective implementation of this right. It would be rare indeed that an individual could claim to be the sole repository of all that is necessary to provide a comprehensive account of what is required to provide a clear and practical interpretation of every aspect of the right to health. Thus as Vagts has explained, the focus must be on the practical with 'less attention given to finding "the" right way of interpreting... than on identifying techniques that clarify, that help achieve the target of the drafters and that further a fruitful interaction between the writers and the readers of documents'.[117] The aim in such circumstances is to contribute to a dialogue with the interpretative community whereby an understanding as to the practical implementation of the right to health will be developed through consultation and negotiation.

---

and Daniel M Brinks (eds), *Courting Social Justice: Judicial Enforcement of Social and Economic Rights in the Developing World* (CUP, 2008) xii (arguing that the comments of the court should not be taken as a call to abandon any future reliance on the minimum core approach).

[115] ESR Committee, *General Comment No 14* (n 41) 43, 47.

[116] See, eg, David Bilchitz, *Poverty and Fundamental Rights: The Justification and Enforcement of Socio-Economic Rights* (OUP, 2007) 223; Audrey Chapman, 'Core Obligations related to the Right to Health' in Audrey Chapman and Sage Russell (eds), *Core Obligations: Building a Framework for Economic, Social and Cultural Rights* (Intersentia, 2002) 185 (tending to embrace the work of the ESC Committee without any critical reflection as to its legitimacy); *Report of the Special Rapporteur on the Right to Health to the Human Rights Council 2008*, UN Doc A/HRC/7/11 (31 January 2008) paras 51–3 (also embracing the approach of the ESC Committee).

[117] Vagts (n 27) 473.

An adaptation of the techniques offered by democratic experimentalism provides an example of this approach to the interpretative project, more flexible and participatory than that traditionally associated with legal scholarship.[118] Such an approach commences the interpretative process by accepting the articulation of a human right such as health at a reasonably high level of abstraction and offering an incomplete specification of a right's meaning in a particular context.[119] Thus, the obligation of a state to recognize the right to the highest attainable standard of health could be interpreted as requiring a state to ensure that its health system progressively meets the health needs of all persons within its jurisdiction without discrimination. The specific details with respect to the implementation of this directive are then left to the state subject to compliance with various procedural requirements such as effective participation in the relevant interpretative community. The interpretive exercise remains engaged with the process via a requirement to examine and monitor the results of the implementation measures. An ongoing dialogue is thus facilitated with additional directions provided to states when considered necessary to achieve the effective enjoyment of the right to health.

The decision of the South African Constitutional Court in the *Treatment Action Campaign* case,[120] which concerned access to an antiretroviral drug to prevent transmission of HIV/AIDS from mothers to their children, reflects elements of the experimentalist project. As Katharine Young has explained, the remedies adopted by the Court were directed at solving the problem 'rather than upholding a substantive and final content of the right of access to health care' as formulated under the South African Constitution.[121] Moreover, the Court provided for the ongoing revisability of the measures required to secure the right to health 'in light of better information and improved developments in scientific and professional communities'.[122]

Under this model, the interpretative process may be evolutionary and partially indeterminate but it remains clear to the extent that the measures determined to be appropriate at each stage are capable of guiding states in their attempts to transform an abstract concept, such as the right to health, into reality. Importantly the determination of whether a measure is considered to be practical is not the sole province of the interpreter and must be evaluated in light of the socio-political context within a particular state; the fourth feature of the interpretative methodology required for a constructive approach to interpretation, which is discussed below. The

---

[118] On democratic experimentalism generally see Michael C Dorf and Charles F Sabel, 'A Constitution of Democratic Experimentalism' (1998) 98 Colum L Rev 267; Michael Dorf, 'Legal Indeterminacy and Institutional Design' (2003) 78 NYU L Rev 875. See also A Bryce Hoflund and Marybeth Farquhar, 'Challenges of Democratic Experimentalism: A Case Study of the National Quality Forum in Health Care' (2008) 2 Reg &Governance 121, 123 (examining the democratic experimentalist approach to health care regulation and noting that the three core mechanisms of this approach are: benchmarking; learning by monitoring; and participation by diverse organizations in deliberative decision making).

[119] Mark Tushnet, 'New Forms of Judicial Review and the Persistence of Rights- and Democracy-Based Worries' (2003) 38 Wake Forest L Rev 813, 822.

[120] *Minister of Health v Treatment Action Campaign (No 2)* [2002] 5 SA 721 (CC, Sth Afr).

[121] Katharine Young, 'Movements in Constitutionalism: Beyond Jurisgenesis and Experiment' 49 (unpublished paper, copy on file with author).

[122] ibid.

requirement of practicality also does not mean a level of pragmatism that would leave the content of the right to health subject to those measures which states were prepared to undertake by way of implementation. On the contrary an interpretation that is clear and practical must still be principled, which demands that it must be consistent with a vision that seeks to ensure the effective realization of the object and purpose underlying the right to health, namely the highest attainable standard of health.

It is important to note that emphasis on the process required to generate a practical meaning does not mean that the modes of construction advanced under the VCLT can be abandoned. The interpretative exercise must first seek to engage with the VCLT in order to consider the extent to which the general rule is able to guide and constrain the range of potential meanings of the right to health. Recourse to a more process-orientated approach occurs after the capacity of the VCLT has been exhausted. In other words, attention to process and the particular modes of construction are considered to be an interdependent and non-severable feature of a persuasive interpretative methodology.

3 Coherence

The requirements that an interpretation of the right to health be principled, clear, and practical are necessary but not sufficient to enhance the persuasiveness of the interpretation offered. The interpretation must also demonstrate coherence both in its reasoning and coherence within the international legal system.[123] Although the two are interconnected, as Soriano explains, '[t]heories of coherence in legal reasoning focus on the arguments and on how the given arguments are connected' whereas 'coherence in the legal system focuses on fitting a decision into the legal system and on the fitting together of all components of the legal system'.[124]

(a) Coherence in reasoning

With respect to the first form of coherence, Soriano's 'modest notion of coherence in legal reasoning'[125] provides a useful insight into the process required for coherence in the articulation as to the content of the right to health. It accepts that a plurality of values forms the backdrop against which interpretative acts take place and that a fixed or definitive answer will always remain elusive. As such, the focus must shift towards an examination of the extent to which a particular interpretation can be justified. For Soriano, justification is the activity of giving arguments to support premises. The coherence of these arguments must be assessed by reference to the connectedness of their underlying reasons—what he calls their 'supportive structures'.[126]

Under such a model, interpretation essentially becomes an act of persuasion, the effectiveness of which is influenced by the depth and rigour of its analysis. Critical to this process are the properties of the supportive structures used to construct an

---

[123] Leonor Moral Soriano, 'A Modest Notion of Coherence in Legal Reasoning. A Model for the European Court of Justice' (2003) 16 Ratio Juris 296, 296.
[124] ibid 296–7.   [125] ibid.   [126] ibid 310–20.

interpretation of a particular provision and support its reasoning, that is, the link between the reasons and a decision or view. According to Soriano, the number of supportive relations, the length of the supportive structure, the strength of the support, and the capacity for what is termed 'netting' of reasons are particularly important.[127] In seeking to generate the appropriate supportive structures necessary to justify the interpretation of the right to health, it is necessary to first identify and then assess the quality of the views of those sources that have either sought to contribute to the understanding of the right or possess the capacity and expertise to do so.

Such an approach is a common feature of attempts to interpret all human rights standards. The body or person interpreting a right will almost invariably enlist the work of a human rights treaty body, a relevant special rapporteur, courts, commentators, and/or other experts to support their interpretation. In relation to the right to the highest attainable standard of health, the work of the ESC Committee and CRC Committee is deserving of close attention as these bodies have a mandate to monitor the implementation of states' obligations under their respective treaties and both have issued general comments in relation to the right to health.[128] The qualities of mandate and expertise also mean that consideration must also be given to the work of the Special Rapporteur on the Right to Health,[129] whose mandate requires that he or she prepare reports[130] which contribute to the understanding of the normative contours of the right to health.[131] Other sources to which reference should be made include the work of commentators who have contributed to the literature on the right to health and the jurisprudence of regional and domestic courts which have

---

[127] ibid 311–19. The idea of netting reasons is used in contrast to the idea of chained reasons. It is preferred because it is considered to better reflect the need to pursue the interconnectedness and reciprocal nature of reasons as opposed to the simple cummulation of independent chains of reasons: 310–11.

[128] The ESC Committee produced *General Comment No 14: The Right to the Highest Attainable Standard of Health* (n 42), and the CRC Committee adopted the following General Comments: *General Comment No 3: HIV/AIDS and the Rights of the Child*, UN Doc CRC/GC/2003/3 (17 March 2003); *General Comment No 4: Adolescent Health and Development in the Context of the Convention on the Rights of the Child*, UN Doc CRC/GC/2003/4 (1 July 2003); and *General Comment No 9: The Rights of Children with Disabilities*, UN Doc CRC/GC/2006/9 (27 February 2007). The concluding observations of each Committee also address matters in relation to the implementation by states parties of the right to health.

[129] See Commission on Human Rights, *The Right of Everyone to the Enjoyment of the Highest Attainable Standard of Physical and Mental Health*, Res 2002/31, UN Doc E/CN.4/RES/2002/31 (22 April 2002), which established the mandate of the Special Rapporteur. See also Commission on Human Rights, *The Right of Everyone to the Enjoyment of the Highest Attainable Standard of Physical and Mental Health*, Res 2005/24, UN Doc E/CN.4/RES/2005/24 (15 April 2005) and Human Rights Council, *The Right of Everyone to the Enjoyment of the Highest Attainable Standard of Physical and Mental Health*, Res 6/29, UN Doc HRC/RES/2007/6/29 (14 December 2007), which both renewed the mandate for a further three years.

[130] These reports include annual reports to the now abolished Commission on Human Rights (UN Doc E/CN.4/2003/58; UN Doc E/CN.4/2004/49; UN Doc E/CN.4/2005/51; UN Doc E/CN.4.2006/48); the Human Rights Council (UN Doc A/HRC/7/11; UN Doc A/HRC/4/28); and the UN General Assembly (UN Doc A/58/427; UN Doc A/59/422; UN Doc A/60/348; UN Doc A/61/338; UN Doc A/62/214).

[131] See, eg, *Report of the Special Rapporteur on the Right to Health to the General Assembly 2003*, UN Doc A/58/427 (10 October 2003) (attempting to develop some of the conceptual issues relevant to the right to health such as the use of indicators and benchmarks and criteria for the identification of 'good practices').

begun to recognize not only the health dimensions of civil and political rights such as the right to life but also the justiciability of the right to health as a separate norm in its own right.[132]

However, the reasons underlying recourse to the interpretative work of other actors are seldom if ever acknowledged. Perhaps it is considered to be so self-evident that no explanation is warranted. The view taken here, however, is that it remains important to expressly acknowledge why such an approach is necessary; namely, to enhance and defend the coherence of the interpretation offered. Moreover, an active awareness of the reason for 'netting' the views of other actors guards against a tendency to simply import such views into the meaning of the right subject to interpretation. Instead, careful consideration must be given to critically assessing whether the reasoning underlying such views is convincing in light of the requirements that it be principled, practical, coherent, and context sensitive.

The pursuit of coherence in reasoning must not be developed simply by reference to the views of the legal interpretative community with respect to the right to health. As noted above, the Millennium Taskforce on Child and Maternal Health accepted the need for human rights to achieve the Millennium Development Goals[133] but it also warned that 'human rights initiatives fixated on and bound by chapter and verse of human rights treaties often miss the mark'.[134] As a consequence the broader notion of interpretative community outlined in Part III anticipates that knowledge and expertise with respect to the practical and effective understanding of the right to health will rest in a much broader range of actors. With respect to the right to health there is evidence of an increasing dialogue in which an understanding with respect to the nexus between public health and human rights generally is being forged.[135] For

---

[132] See generally Toebes (n 4) 167–242 (providing a comprehensive examination of case law on the right to health until the late 1990s); *Report of the Special Rapporteur on the Right to Health to the Human Rights Council 2007* (n 40) paras 55–99 (examining cases on the right to health). See for example the case law of South African Constitutional Court including *Soobramoney v Minister for Health* [1998] 1 SA 765 (CC, Sth Afr) (determining the nature of the distinction between emergency medical treatment and access to health care); *Minister for Health v Treatment Action Campaign (No 2)* [2002] 5 SA 721 (CC, Sth Afr) (finding that a failure to provide access to anti-retrovirals to children and their mothers in all public hospitals was a violation of Constitution). See also African Commission on Human and People's Rights, *Social and Economic Rights Action Center for Economic and Social Rights v Nigeria*, Communication No 155/96 (27 October 2001) (where the Federal Republic of Nigeria was found to be in violation of the right to health for failing to regulate activities undertaken by oil companies in the Niger Delta).

[133] Freedman and others (n 62) 31.

[134] ibid 34.

[135] See generally Alicia Yamin, 'Will We Take Suffering Seriously? Reflections on What Applying a Human Rights Framework to Health Means and Why We Should Care' (2008) 10 Health & Hum Rts 45; Freedman and others (n 63) 29–35; Jonathan Mann and others (eds), *Health and Human Rights: A Reader* (Routledge, 1998); Sofia Gruskin and Daniel Tarantola, 'Health and Human Rights' in Roger Detels and others (eds) *The Oxford Textbook of Public Health* (OUP, 2004); Paul Hunt, 'The Right to Health: From the Margins to the Mainstream' (2002) 360 The Lancet 1878; Daniel Tarantola, 'Building on the Synergy between Health and Human Rights: A Global Perspective' (François-Xavier Bagnoud Center for Health and Human Rights, Working Paper Series No 8, 2000); Lynne Freedman, 'Reflections on Emerging Frameworks of Health and Human Rights' (1995) 1 Health &Hum Rts 314.

example, the World Health Organization (WHO) has developed guidelines in areas such as maternal health, children's health, and mental health that draw upon human rights principles.[136] The Millennium Development Project Task Force on Child Health and Maternal Health has stressed the importance of human rights in contributing to child and maternal health[137] and commentators have emphasized the links between human rights and health on matters such as child maltreatment[138] and public health programming.[139]

At the same time it remains important not to overstate the role that human rights discourse has come to play in public health policy. Indeed, there remains a great deal of caution and skepticism within the area of public health as to the merits of international human rights law as a strategy to secure health outcomes and 'equity' remains the preferred and dominant paradigm.[140] However, the recognition by key actors within the area of public health such as the WHO, the Millennium Development Project Taskforce on Child Health and Maternal Health, and UNICEF[141] that human rights have a significant role to play in securing public health objectives, provides an opportunity to examine the measures required for the practical implementation of the right to health. Thus while the literature emerging from public health and general medical discourse may not be directly concerned with addressing the normative content of the right to health, its capacity to contribute to an understanding as to the most effective measures by which to secure its realization warrants attention.

---

[136] See, eg, Rebecca J Cook and others, *Advancing Safe Motherhood through Human Rights*, WHO Doc WHO/RHR/01.5 (2001); WHO, *Towards a Better Tomorrow: Child Rights and Health* (WHO); *Guidelines for the Promotion of Human Rights of Persons with Mental Disorders* (WHO, 1996): <www.who.int/hhr/information/guidelines_publications/en/index.html> accessed 13 June 2011. See also WHO, *The World Health Report 2005: Make Every Mother and Child Count* (WHO, 2005), <http://www.who.int/child-adolescent-health/right.htm> accessed 13 June 2011.

[137] Freedman and others (n 62) 3.

[138] Richard Reading and others, 'Promotion of Children's Rights and Prevention of Child Maltreatment' (2009) 373 The Lancet 332.

[139] Armando De Negri Filho, 'A Human Rights Approach to Quality of Life and Health: Applications to Public Health Programming' (2008)10 Health & Hum Rts 93.

[140] See, eg, Editorial, 'Moving Forward with Maternal Health and Human Rights' (2009) 373 The Lancet 2172 (noting that health community often perceives human rights as solely about whistleblowing, lawyers, and litigation); Alexis Palmer and others, 'Does Ratification for Human Rights Treaties have Effects on Population Health?' (2009) 373 The Lancet 1987 (finding that there is no consistent association between ratification of human rights treaties and health or social outcomes). With respect to the preference for equity see Cesar G Victoria and others, 'Applying an Equity Lens to Child Health and Mortality: More of the Same is Not Enough' (2003) 362 The Lancet 233; Margaret Whitehead, 'The Concepts and Principles of Equity and Health' (1992) 22 Intl J Health Services 429; Timothy Evans and others (eds), *Challenging Inequities in Health: From Ethics to Action* (OUP, 2001). cf Paul Braveman and Sofia Gruskin, 'Defining Equity in Health' (2003) 57 J Epidemiology & Comm Health 254 (tracing congruence between equity and human rights); Freedman and others (n 62) 29–31 (recognizing the relevance and importance of human rights but as a tool for informing and understanding equity).

[141] Memorandum from Carol Bellamy, Executive Director, UNICEF, 'A Human Rights Based Approach to UNICEF Programming for Children and Women' (21 April 1998) (copy on file with author); UNICEF, *Human Rights for Children and Women: How UNICEF Helps Make Them a Reality* (UNICEF 1999). See also UNICEF, 'Realizing Rights, Getting Results' <http://www.unicef.org/rightsresults/index.html> accessed 3 June 2011.

Engagement with material generated outside the legal interpretative community represents a departure from the historical tendency of international legal scholarship to rely almost exclusively on what could be broadly labeled legal sources. It is a reflection of the dominant perception, often pervasive within domestic legal scholarship, that law is a complete system of logic and that reliance on non-legal sources will compromise the integrity of the legal analysis. This approach is rejected for two reasons. First, law is not a complete discipline and is dependent upon insights to be offered from other disciplines when attempting to map out the content of a human right such as the right to health. As a consequence, the coherence in the reasoning used to advance a particular view or vision in relation to the meaning of the right to health, will often be strengthened by the insights of other discourses. Second, as explained in Part III, the interpretative community that the interpretative act must persuade cannot be restricted to the legal fraternity. On the contrary, it must extend to those who work within fields that intersect either directly or indirectly with the implementation of the right to health. A coherence in reasoning that satisfies the expectations of only the legal interpretative community will be of little benefit if it is unable to appeal to those persons who actually develop the policies and undertake actions that affect the health of individuals.[142]

(b) System coherence

The idea of coherence within legal domestic systems has been the subject of significant commentary and according to Soriano, generally examines whether a decision coheres with a particular set of principles (Dworkin), or with the principles and norms of a branch of the legal system (Raz and Levenbook).[143] At the international level, the International Court of Justice has also held that 'an international instrument has to be interpreted and applied within the framework of the entire legal system prevailing at the time of the interpretation.'[144] Despite this directive, concern has recently emerged that the fragmentation of international law 'puts into question the coherence of international law'.[145] Although the ILC Fragmentation Study

---

[142] This is essentially an extension of the observation made by Justice Higgins that 'The making of legal choices will not even contribute to justice if it purports totally to ignore political and social contexts'. Higgins (n 18) 9.

[143] Soriano (n 123) 305. See Dworkin (n 36) 225 ('According to law as integrity propositions of law are true if they figure in or follow from the principles of justice, fairness and procedural due process that provide the best constructive interpretation of the community's legal practice'). See Joseph Raz, 'The Relevance of Coherence' in Josheph Raz (ed), *Ethics in the Public Domain: Essays on the Morality of Law and Politics* (Clarendon Press, 1994) 277, 277–325; Barbara Baum Levenbook, 'The Role of Coherence in Legal Reasoning' (1984) 3 Law & Phil 355.

[144] *Legal Consequences for States of the Continued Presence of South Africa in Namibia (South West Africa) Notwithstanding Security Council Resolution 276 (Advisory Opinion)* [1971] ICJ Rep 16, 19. See also Campbell McLachlan, 'The Principle of Systematic Integration and Article 31(3)(c) of the Vienna Convention' (2005) 54 ICLQ 279, 280 (arguing that art 31(3)(c) of the VCLT, which requires that any relevant rules of international law must be taken into account in the interpretative process, 'expresses a more general principle of treaty interpretation, namely that of systemic integration within the international legal system').

[145] *ILC Fragmentation Study* (n 55) 491.

conceded that 'coherence is . . . a formal and abstract value', it still acknowledged that '[c]oherence is valued positively owing to the connection it has with predictability and legal security'.[146] It therefore took the view that 'coherence should be understood as a constitutive value of the system'.[147] Such a position indicates that the interpretation of the right to health in international law must pursue coherence with the system of international law as a means by which to satisfy the expectations of the interpretative community and thus enhance its persuasiveness. System coherence requires that an interpretation be coherent within both (a) the entire system of international law—termed here as 'external system coherence'—and (b) the context of the other provisions of the international human rights treaty in which the right to health appears—termed here as 'internal system coherence'.[148]

External system coherence The ILC Fragmentation Study gives significant attention to external system coherence and guidance on how to achieve it. The Study explains the nature of the problem created by fragmentation in this way:

It is a preliminary step to any act of applying the law that a prima facie view of the matter is formed. This includes, among other things, an initial assessment of what might be the applicable rules and principles. The result will be that a number of standards may seem prima facie relevant. A choice is needed and a justification for having recourse to one instead of another.[149]

However, the preliminary step to which the study refers is in fact preceded by an earlier step: the development of an understanding as to the content and meaning of the potentially relevant rules. A question thus remains as to how this interpretative exercise must be undertaken.

In relation to this issue, the ILC Fragmentation Study outlined some principles that offer assistance. First, '[i]n international law there is strong presumption against normative conflict'.[150] Applying this presumption supports a preference for harmonization. Such an approach works well in resolving any apparent conflicts that may arise between the provisions of treaties that have broadly similar objects and purposes. Thus for example, harmonization offers an appropriate interpretative guideline with respect to the resolution of apparent conflicts between the formulation of the right to health under the CRC and the ICESCR. It cannot, however, resolve genuine conflicts between norms under international law.[151]

In such circumstances, the principle of *lex specialis* (that special law derogates from general law) becomes relevant as a 'widely accepted maxim of legal interpretation and

---

[146] ibid.   [147] ibid.
[148] This concept of external system coherence seeks to accommodate and exceed the requirement under art 31(3)(c) of the VCLT that the application of the general rule under art 31(1) take into account any relevant rules of international law applicable in the relations between the parties. The requirement of external system coherence requires a consideration of not just these rules but the entire system of international law especially the provisions of other human rights treaties but also other multilateral treaties and regimes within international law.
[149] *ILC Fragmentation Study* (n 55) 36.
[150] ibid para 37.   [151] ibid para 42.

technique for the resolution of normative conflicts'.[152] In the case of the interpretation of the right to health, *lex specialis* suggests that where there is a *special rule* that is relevant to the potential scope of the right to health, that special rule should inform the interpretation.[153] The principle of *lex specialis* can thus be used to perform a type of harmonization function. Such a technique also indicates that there are limits with respect to the extent to which the interpretative process can expand the meaning and content of the right to health. This is because the coherence of the legal system will be undermined if the interpretative process seeks to extend the boundaries of a provision beyond another special rule with a more precisely delimited scope of application.[154] Care must therefore be taken to maintain the distinction between *lex lata* and *lex ferenda*—the law as it is and the law as it might be.[155]

To take one example with respect to the right to health, the ESC Committee in its General Comment on the Right to Health declared that 'censoring, withholding or intentionally misrepresenting health related information including sexual education and information' would be a violation of a state's obligations.[156] Such an interpretation is problematic because it fails to recognize the existence and scope of the right to freedom of access to information—a specific rule within the ICCPR which is of relevance to the issue of censorship.[157] To censor or withhold health information *may* constitute an interference with both the right to health and freedom of access to information, but contrary to the views of the ESC Committee, it does not *necessarily* constitute a violation of either right. Ultimately this question must be resolved after considering whether the interference could be justified under the terms of article 19 of the ICCPR as being in accordance with the law and necessary to achieve a legitimate objective.[158] Thus, while the expansive approach adopted by the ESC Committee may carry a superficial allure for those seeking to advance the scope of the right to health, it carries with it a real risk of compromising the need for system coherence and perpetuating a reductionist rather than substantive

---

[152] *ILC Fragmentation Study* (n 55) para 56.
[153] ibid para 60 ('*lex specialis* may also seem useful as it may provide better access to what the parties have willed').
[154] ibid para 57.
[155] Higgins (n 18) 10.
[156] ESC Committee, *General Comment No 14* (n 41) 34.
[157] ICCPR, art 19 provides that:

(2) Everyone shall have the right to freedom of expression; this right shall include freedom to seek, receive and impart information and ideas of all kinds, regardless of frontiers, either orally, in writing or in print, in the form of art, or through any other media of his choice.
(3) The exercise of the rights provided for in paragraph 2 of this article carries with it special duties and responsibilities. It may therefore be subject to certain restrictions, but these shall only be such as are provided by law and are necessary:
  (a) For respect of the rights or reputations of others;
  (b) For the protection of national security or of public order (ordre public), or of public health or morals.

[158] HRC, *General Comment No 10: Freedom of Expression*, UN Doc HR1/GEN/1/Rev.1 (1 July 2003) para 3.

approach[159] to the question of whether a state has fulfilled its obligation to respect the right to health.

The rationale underlying *lex specialis* further demands that the interpretation of a specific provision expressed in general or broad terms such as the right to health must remain cognizant of any *special regimes*[160] that intersect or overlap with matters that could fall within the potential scope of the right to health. Failure to recognize such overlap risks further fragmentation of the international system by inflating a specific right to extend beyond matters which are already the subject of an entire, separate, special regime. This is not to suggest that a special provision such as the right to health must always yield to the provisions of another special regime or special rule.[161] Rather, the interpretation of the right to health must not take place in isolation from those other aspects of the international legal system that may overlap with and inform the potential scope of this right.

For example, the use and testing of weapons and the pollution of the environment are both matters which are subject to significant international regulation and ongoing discussions. However, the ESC Committee in its General Comment on the Right to Health explained that the scope of the right to health included an obligation to refrain from testing weapons harmful to human health and unlawful pollution. It did so without any acknowledgment as to the complexity of these issues and the level of sophistication of the measures already undertaken by states.[162] As such, the ESC Committee view appears to have been adopted without any consideration of the need to ensure external system coherence. It might be possible to offer a principled, practical, and context-sensitive defence for the inclusion of such obligations within the scope of the right to health. Such a defence, however, would need to take account of the regimes that already exist under international law with respect to the regulation of these issues.

Finally, it is also important to recognize that the application of *lex specialis* as an interpretative technique is not without its limitations and difficulties. As the ILC Fragmentation Study explains 'it is often hard to distinguish what is 'general' and what is "particular"'.[163] '[T]he principle (of *lex specialis*) also has an unclear relationship with other maxims of interpretation...such as...the principle *lex posterior deogat legi priori* (later law overrides prior law) and may be offset by normative hierarchies or informal views about "relevance" or "importance" such that a more general treaty overrides a more specific one.'[164] Notwithstanding these limitations it is suggested that the application of the principle of *lex specialis* is prima facie an

---

[159] John Tobin, 'Seeking Clarity in Relation to the Principle of Complementarity: Reflections on the Recent Contributions of Some International Bodies' (2007) 8 MJIL 356.
[160] *ILC Fragmentation Study* (n 55) 123–37.
[161] See *Gabčíkovo-Nagymaros Project (Hungary/Slovakia)(Judgment)* [1997] ICJ Rep 7, paras 114–15 ('Treaties that affect human rights cannot be applied in such a manner as to constitute a denial of human rights as understood at the time of their application'.)
[162] ESC Committee, *General Comment No 14* (n 41) 34.
[163] *ILC Fragmentation Study* (n 55) 58, 116–18.
[164] ibid 58.

essential feature of an interpretative process that seeks to maintain coherence within the international legal system.

Internal system coherence The enumeration of the right to health within an international treaty may constitute a special rule within that treaty but it is not a self-contained rule. When this occurs, there will be potential for cross-fertilization and overlap between the content of the right to health and other provisions of the treaty in which it is protected. In such circumstances, the interpretative process should seek to produce a meaning for a right that is informed by and consistent with the other provisions within the treaty. Such an outcome is described as internal system coherence and is consistent with the requirement under article 31(2) of the VCLT that the context in which a treaty is to be interpreted extend to a consideration of the text of the treaty itself.

The treatment of the right to health by the ESC Committee provides an opportunity to examine the application of this requirement for internal system coherence. In its General Comment on the right to health under article 12 of the ICESCR the ESC Committee declared that the right to the highest attainable standard of health is:

> [N]ot confined to the right to health care. On the contrary the drafting history and express wording of article 12.2 acknowledge that the right to health embraces a wide range of socio-economic factors that promote conditions in which people can lead a healthy life, and extends to the underlying determinants of health, such as food and nutrition, housing, access to safe and potable water and adequate sanitation, safe and healthy working conditions, and a healthy environment.[165]

The ESC Committee has also added that, '[t]he right to health is not to be understood as a right to be *healthy*'.[166] As a consequence the right to the highest attainable health must take 'into account both the individual's biological and socio-economic preconditions and a State's available resources'.[167] Moreover, the ESC Committee has acknowledged that '[t]here are a number of aspects which cannot be addressed solely within the relationship between States and individuals: in particular, good health cannot be ensured by a State, nor can States provide protection against every possible cause of ill health'.[168] Such an approach is practical given that no state is capable of guaranteeing the health of any individual. It also draws upon the drafting history to clarify the nature and scope of this term, which is a legitimate process in seeking to offer a principled interpretation.

An issue remains, however, as to whether the very expansive definition of health adopted by the ESC Committee can be said to satisfy the requirement of internal system coherence. With the exception of environmental and industrial hygiene, the text of article 12 of the ICESCR makes no express mention of the other socio-economic determinants of health listed in the definition of health advanced by the ESC Committee. Moreover, the ESC Committee's inclusion of these determinants arguably encroaches upon the normative territory of other rights within the ICESCR

---

[165] ESC Committee, *General Comment No 14* (n 41) 4.
[166] ibid 8.   [167] ibid 9.   [168] ibid.

which specifically address such issues including the right to an adequate standard of living.[169] It may have been more appropriate for the ESC Committee to recognize the interdependence of such rights with the right to health rather than to conflate the meaning of health where there is no explicit textual basis for this approach.

Internal system coherence prevents the conception of the right to health as a repository for everything that affects the health of an individual.[170] It is entirely appropriate to identify the overlap between one right and the other rights within a treaty; an approach which is consistent with the principle of interdependence and indivisibility. But it is also necessary to ensure internal system coherence and delineate to the extent possible the discrete domain of the right under examination. Care must be taken to ensure that the right to health is not conflated to such an extent that the rights relevant to those matters that have an effect on the health of a person—housing, working conditions, and the like—are subsumed within the right to health and thereby denied their *lex specialis* status and capacity for a content independent of the right to health.[171] Although the importance of *lex specialis* has been identified in the context of achieving external system coherence, it is important to stress that it also operates within a single instrument[172] such as the ESCR or the CRC.

The final point to emphasize with respect to the issue of internal system coherence is that the human rights treaties in which the right to health appears possess what are described in this paper as 'general principle rights'. Such rights are not confined to a particular subject area and have the potential to be of relevance to the interpretation of all the rights under a particular treaty. For example, in the case of the CRC, the CRC Committee,[173] and UNICEF[174] have identified four such rights: the prohibition against discrimination (article 2); the requirement that the best interests of the child shall be a primary consideration in all matters affecting a child (article 3); the right to survival and development (article 6); and the right to participation (article 12). In a similar vein the right to health under the ICESCR is informed by the principle of non-discrimination and an obligation to take steps to secure the progressive implementation of this right subject to available resources (article 2). The United Nations Convention on the Rights of Persons with Disabilities (CRPD) also sets out in articles 3 and 4 the general principles and general obligations of states that are to guide the interpretation and implementation the right to health under the CRPD.[175]

---

[169] ICESCR, art 11(1).
[170] Toebes (n 4) 259–60; Steven Jamar, 'The International Human Right to Health' (1994) 22 SUL Rev 2 28; Ruger, 'Toward a Theory of a Right to Health' (n 2) 312–13.
[171] Toebes (n 4) 260 (identifying four general areas which overlap with the right to health but still retain a dimension that is autonomous or independent of the right to health: (i) life; (ii) physical integrity and privacy; (iii) housing, food and work; and (iv) education and information).
[172] ibid para 68.
[173] CRC Committee, *General Comment No 5* (n 42).
[174] UNICEF, *Human Rights for Children and Women* (n 141) 8.
[175] Convention on the Rights of Persons with Disabilities (CRPD) (New York, 30 March 2007, entered into force 3 May 2008, UN Doc A/;RES/61/106) arts 3–4.

Internal system coherence demands that the process of interpreting the right to health is alert to these 'general principles' and ensures that the interpretation offered with respect to this right is consistent with and informed by these provisions. It is important to recognize, however, that a requirement to ensure system coherence, whether internal or external, focuses on the text of a treaty. As such it makes no attempt to locate the interpretative exercise within the broader socio-political context in which the purported meaning of the right to health is to be operationalized. Thus, the final factor which must inform the selection of a meaning for the right to health from within a suite of potential meanings is the need for context sensitivity.

4 Context sensitivity

It is now widely accepted that, rather than being natural and immutable, the content of international law is always contextualized.[176] Thus, for a pragmatist such as Justice Higgins, former President of the International Court of Justice, '[a] refusal to acknowledge political and social factors cannot keep law "neutral,", for even such a refusal is not without political and social consequence. There is no avoiding the essential relationship between law and politics.'[177] It follows therefore that 'the assessment of so-called extralegal considerations is part of the legal process'.[178] And for a theorist such as Martti Koskenneimi, 'it is neither useful nor ultimately possible to work with international law in abstraction from descriptive theories about the character of social life among States and normative views about the principles of justice which should govern international conduct'.[179] These observations reveal that the interpretative process does not occur within a sterile vacuum, and that attempts to fabricate or insist upon such an interpretative environment will condemn the interpretative exercise to irrelevance. Interpretation involves the process of choosing *a* meaning from a range of potential meanings, and, in order to have any persuasive capacity, that choice must also be undertaken with awareness as to the context in which it is made.

The integration of such a feature into the interpretative process is not without its difficulties. The identification of the relevant context will itself be a subjective inquiry and a matter of 'interpretation'. It may be easy to agree on the need to take account of the social and political context in which international law operates, but these broad and general exhortations conceal complex and highly contentious debates as to how these contexts are constituted. This is not the place to resolve these debates. Rather, as a minimum, the interpretative exercise must demonstrate sensitivity to context at two levels: local and global.

---

[176] See, eg, Simma and Paulus (n 83) 29; Siegfried Wiessner and Andrew R Willard, 'Policy-Oriented Jurisprudence and Human Rights Abuses in Internal Conflict: Toward a World Public Order of Human Dignity' in Stephen Ratner and Anne Marie Slaughter, *The Methods of International Law Studies* (Studies in Transnational Legal Policy No 36, ASIL, 2004) 47, 48.
[177] Higgins (n 18) 5.
[178] ibid.
[179] Koskenniemi, *From Apology to Utopia* (n 17) 1.

(a) Local context sensitivity

The accepted doctrine within international human rights law is that human rights are universal. This position is invariably subject to the criticism that such instruments impose universal standards that reflect and prioritize Western values at the expense of non-Western values.[180] Those who stir the cultural relativist cauldron remind us that rights discourse can be used in a hegemonic way to displace, devalue, and colonize all other competing agendas.[181] But it is important to remember that these qualities are not inherent features of human rights. Indeed the requirement of participation mandates that the implementation of a rights-based approach must be sensitive to, informed by, and reflect the needs and interests of local populations. Such an approach not only has intuitive appeal but is also supported by research in the area of public health for example which indicates that 'selection of effective interventions to be implemented at the level of community and health facilities, should be based on the local epidemiological profile and other locally defined key criteria'.[182] The relevance of this insight to the interpretative process is significant. It demands that the specific measures required for the implementation and operationalization of the right to health will not be universal.[183] Rather, an understanding of the required measures must be developed in consultation with states and their citizens as they attempt to accommodate the diverse needs and practices which are peculiar to each state.

Such an approach disapproves of the automatic transferability of Western expectations with respect to the measures required for the realization of the right to health in favour of models which are tailored to meet local demand and respond to local needs.[184] It therefore requires sensitivity to the social, cultural, and political practices within a particular state and allows for a degree of flexibility in the implementation of measures to secure the right to health. At the same time this does not allow for cultural or traditional practices within a state to be invoked as a defence to violations

---

[180] See generally Steiner, Alston, and Goodman (n 1) 517–40.

[181] See, eg, Kennedy (n 8).

[182] Jennifer Bryce and others, 'Reducing Child Mortality: Can Public Health Deliver?' (2003) 362 The Lancet 159, 163.

[183] See Norman Daniels, *Just Health: Meeting Health Needs Fairly* (CUP, 2008) 316–19 (expressing anxiety about the right to health in international law and defending what he believes to be a narrower understanding of the right to health that has a specific content relative to the conditions in a specific society. However, Daniels does not connect this vision with the idea that the right to health in international law does accommodate local conditions).

[184] ibid. See also Diamond, 'An Analysis of Child Protection and Protecting Children from Rights and Public Health Perspectives' (International Symposium on Human Rights in Public Health: Research, Policy and Practice, University of Melbourne, 3–5 November 2004) (warning against the 'transplant' of child protection models developed in the USA into emerging democracies and other developing nations); Beth Verhey, 'Child Soldiers: Preventing, Demobilizing and Reintegrating' (World Bank, Africa Region Working Paper Series No 23, November 2001) 17 (examining research that suggests that Western-style trauma assistance and its focus on the individual may not necessarily be as effective as psycho-social approaches which emphasize the role of family and the community in the context of the demobilization of child soldiers in Africa).

of the right to health. As Philip Alston has explained, '[j]ust as culture is not a factor which must be excluded from the human rights equation so too must it not be accorded the status of a metanorm which trumps human rights'.[185] Thus, in the context of a child's right to health, article 24(3) of the CRC demands that 'States parties shall take all effective and appropriate measures with a view to abolishing traditional practices prejudicial to the health of children'. At the same time, the measures required for the elimination of such practices are not to be imposed or defined exclusively by reference to Western values and expectations. On the contrary, a context-sensitive approach favours collaboration and consultation at the local level rather than the imposition of hegemonic visions as to the content and scope of the right to health.

Understanding this need to demonstrate local context sensitivity in the interpretative process is assisted by an examination of the margin of appreciation doctrine developed under the ECHR.[186] This principle, which is not expressly provided for within international human rights treaties and has been the subject of significant criticism, was developed by the European Court in an attempt to allow states a margin of discretion in the measures required to comply with their obligations under the ECHR in light of the particular circumstances within the state party. Although it initially applied the principle largely in the context of assessing the reasonableness of state-imposed limitations on rights, the Court now uses it to inform determinations as to the scope of a right.[187] This development indicates the potential to apply the doctrine to the task of mapping out the scope of the right to health.

One of the justifications for the margin of appreciation is the perceived need to accommodate cultural diversity within the states parties to the ECHR.[188] Following a careful analysis of the case law of the Court, Arai-Takahashi concluded that 'The doctrine's only defensible rationale... is to enable the Strasbourg Court to provide endorsement of the maintenance of cultural diversity, ensuring to the citizens of Europe the means to articulate and practice their preferred values within a multicultural democracy.'[189] Such an observation is significant in the context of this chapter and its attempt to articulate an interpretative approach to the right to health in

---

[185] Philip Alston, 'The Best Interests Principle: Towards a Reconciliation of Culture and Human Rights' in Philip Alston (ed), *The Best Interests of the Child: Reconciling Culture and Human Rights* (Clarendon Press, 1994) 20.

[186] ibid (also advocating this approach). See also Craven, *The International Covenant on Economic Social and Cultural Rights* (n 9) 115–16 (advocating this position with respect to the obligations of states under the ICESCR). The literature with respect to the principle is extensive. However the work of Howard Charles Yourow, *The Margin of Appreciation Doctrine in the Dynamics of European Human Rights Jurisprudence* (Kluwer Law International, 1996) provides one of the more comprehensive insights into the operation of this doctrine. See also Alastair Mowbray, *Cases and Materials on the European Convention on Human Rights* (2nd edn, OUP, 2007) 629–34.

[187] See Yourow (n 186).

[188] ibid 195–6; Humphrey Waldock, 'The Effectiveness of the System Set Up by the European Convention on Human Rights' (1980) 1 HRLJ 1, 1 (arguing that the margin of appreciation doctrine was designed to 'reconcile the effective operation of the Convention with the sovereign powers and responsibilities of governments in a democracy').

[189] Yutaka Arai-Takahashi, *The Margin of Appreciation Doctrine and the Principle of Proportionality in the Jurisprudence of the ECHR* (Intersentia, 2002) 49.

international law that remains sensitive to the socio-political context within a state. Despite the fact that the margin of appreciation has its dissenters,[190] it remains a necessary interpretative technique.[191] As a general rule, the scope of a state's margin will generally be wider when there is less agreement within the relevant interpretative community as to the measures required to secure the enjoyment of a particular right. This discretion accorded to states, however, is not without limits and there is an overarching requirement that whatever measures are adopted they must be directed towards the effective realization of the object and purpose of the right to health. In other words, context-sensitive interpretation must still be principled. For example, with respect to the right to health, as will be detailed in Chapter 4 there is a general obligation on states to provide appropriate sexual education for adolescents so as to minimize the threats to their health associated with issues such as teenage pregnancies and the transmission of STDs and HIV/AIDS.[192] States have a wide margin of appreciation with respect to the measures they adopt to provide such education. An abstinence-only approach, however, would not be consistent with the obligations of a state under the right to health as the evidence indicates that such a model is ineffective in securing the sexual health of adolescents.[193]

(b) **Global context sensitivity**
Context awareness also requires an understanding of the tension that marks both the origins and implementation of international human rights standards such as the right to health. Although international human rights treaties may act as a legal constraint on the exercise of state sovereignty, their implementation is still constrained by the reality of state sovereignty. Unlike domestic law, where a state cannot, as a general rule, unilaterally disengage from domestic adjudicative processes or dismiss their directives, this is a permanent and accepted feature of the international legal system. In the absence of effective coercive measures, dialogue and communication are the tools by which international human rights standards like the right to health are secured. This means that there is an ever–present risk that states will disengage from

---

[190] See, eg, Timothy Jones, 'The Devaluation of Human Rights under the European Convention' (1995) 6 PL 430; Ronald MacDonald, 'The Margin of Appreciation' in Ronald MacDonald, Franz Matscher, and Herbert Petzold (eds), *The European System for the Protection of Human Rights* (Martinus Nijhoff, 1993) 124 (expressing concern that the doctrine obscures the reasons for a court's decisions).

[191] See Jeroen Schokkenbroek, 'The Basis, Nature and Application of the Margin of Appreciation Doctrine in the Case Law of the European Court of Human Rights' (1998) 19 HRLJ 30; Paul Mahoney, 'Marvellous Richness of Diversity or Invidious Cultural Relativism?' (1998) 19 HRLJ 1 (detailing those factors which should influence and inform the scope of the margin of appreciation: (1) existence of common ground among states regarding the right; (2) the nature of the right; (3) the nature of the duty incumbent on the state (whether it is positive or negative); (4) the nature of the aim pursued by a state when interfering with the right; (5) the nature of the activity being affected including its importance for the individual and society; (6) the circumstances of the case; and (7) the actual wording of the right).

[192] See generally CRC Committee, *General Comment No 4, Adolescent Health and Development in the Context of the Convention on the Rights of the Child*, UN Doc CRC/GC/2003/4 (1 July 2003).

[193] See, eg, Mathematica Policy Research Inc, 'Impacts of Four Title V, Section 510 Abstinence Education Programs' 59–61 (2007) (noting research that confirmed the ineffectiveness of abstinence-only programs as a way of reducing teen pregnancies and the transmission of STDs).

the interpretative dialogue if they perceive that the interpretation is discordant with their expectations.

The challenge, therefore, is to develop an interpretative methodology that is sensitive to this political reality. Although a restrictive approach to interpretation is unlikely to antagonize states, such interpretative appeasement creates the risk that the object and purpose of a treaty will be subverted. In such circumstances the interpretative act risks becoming, to borrow the words of Koskenniemi, nothing more than an 'apology'.[194] It may be pragmatic, but it will not be principled.

Moreover, such an approach, even if it were adopted, would still be unable to address what are termed here as 'effectiveness gaps' in a treaty. These 'gaps' include what Dixon has labeled as 'blind spots' and 'burdens of inertia' to explain deficiencies within the domestic legislative process that occur for various reasons and require a judicial response to remedy the subsequent weaknesses in the legislation.[195] These terms are appropriated in this chapter to describe deficiencies within the drafting process of an international treaty. 'Blind spots' are taken to refer to those specific issues which were overlooked or unanticipated in the drafting process but that are essential to the effective operation of the right to health and thus require the development of an appropriate interpretative response. For example, although article 12 of the ICESCR does not address sexual health explicitly, it forms an integral element of an individual's health. As such the ESC Committee has declared that the right to control one's health and body must extend to sexual and reproductive freedom.[196]

'Burdens of inertia' refer to those matters that may have been discussed during the drafting process but which were not specifically included because factors such as time and political intransience on the part of some states prevented consensus with respect to an appropriate formulation. In such circumstances, a gap may be left within the text of a treaty protecting the right to health, which, unless addressed, may undermine its effective implementation. Thus the phrase 'effectiveness gaps' is used to illustrate the areas in which the interpretative exercise will need to develop an appropriate understanding of the right to health with respect to matters unanticipated or unresolved between states but necessary for its effective implementation. For example, although the right to health does not expressly impose an obligation on states to provide appropriate *social* and *human* resources for the realization of this right, the failure to imply such an obligation would create a serious 'effectiveness gap'. As a consequence, states must, as a matter of legal obligation, look beyond the mere accumulation of financial resources to consider the measures required to provide the social resources required for effective implementation of the right to health.

This need to remedy gaps within the human rights treaties protecting the right to health indicates that a restrictive interpretative approach is incompatible with the

---

[194] Koskenniemi, *From Apology to Utopia* (n 17).
[195] Rosalyn Dixon, 'Creating Dialogue about Socio-Economic Rights: Strong-Form Versus Weak-Form Judicial Review Revisited' (2007) 5 Int J Constitutional Law 391.
[196] ESC Committee, *General Comment No 14* (n 41) 8.

effectiveness principle. It requires the adoption of an active and creative approach to interpretation which it not without dangers. As such there is a need to exercise caution and self reflection in relation to the identification of gaps which will be a function of the subjective perceptions of an interpreter rather than an objective reality. Toufayan explores this danger in his examination of Roland Barthes' Eiffel Tower essay in which the interpretative enterprise is supposed to reveal certain landmarks.[197] When these are not visible, the interpreter fills in the gaps created by his or her experience. Under such a model the gaps are not 'real' but perceptions which have been created in light of the subjective expectations or values of an individual as to what a human rights treaty should achieve.[198] This bias is invariably unrecognized by the interpreter or even interpretative community and only '[w]hen enough time has passed and society has changed' does it become 'easier to recognize the biases'.[199]

It is conceded that this bias can never be eliminated. However, as suggested by Toufayan 'there is...a better chance to uncover biases and blind spots when a variety of alternative narratives are competing to tell the stories of international human rights law as opposed to a narrow range of "official" stories which are received without questioning and perceived as authoritative doctrine'.[200] The interpretative methodology outlined in this chapter seeks to achieve this end by a consideration of the views expressed from a variety of sources in order to enhance the coherence of the reasoning that underlines an interpretation of the right to health.

However, even where consensus exists with respect to the identification of a gap within a treaty, dissention remains as to how this should be addressed as illustrated in the following quote adopted by Justice Scalia in a 1989 United States Supreme Court opinion:

[T]o alter, amend or add to any treaty by inserting any clause whether small or great, important or trivial would be on our part an usurpation of power and not an exercise of judicial functions. It would be to make and not to construe a treaty. Neither can this court supply a casus omissus in a treaty any more than in a law. We are to find out the intention of the parties by just rules of interpretation applied to the subject matter; and having found that our duty is to follow it as far as it goes and to stop where that stops—whatever may be the imperfections or difficulties which it leaves behind.[201]

Lord McNair offered a more balanced perspective when he explained that: '[c]onditions should only be implied with great circumspection; for if they are implied too readily they would become a serious threat to the sanctity of a treaty'.[202] Importantly, however, he is still prepared to concede that 'it is reasonable to expect that circumstances should arise...in which it is necessary to imply a condition in order to give effect to this intention'.[203]

---

[197] Toufayan (n 13) 12.
[198] ibid.   [199] ibid 13.   [200] ibid.
[201] *Chan v Korean Airlines Ltd*, 490 US 122, 135 (1989) (Justice Scalia) (SC, USA), quoting *The Amiable Isabella*, 19 US (6 Wheat) 1, 71 (1821) (SC, USA).
[202] McNair (n 14) 436.
[203] ibid.

This acceptance of the need to imply conditions within a treaty to ensure its effectiveness indicates that the interpretative function is ultimately one of actively constructing meaning. At the same time, the need to offer an interpretation that makes the right to health real rather than illusory does not provide an unfettered license for conflating the terms of this right in such a way that the intentions and expectations of states are ignored. A more balanced approach is required.

In order to add more depth and flexibility in the application of such an approach, an adaptation of Tushnet's model of weak and strong forms of judicial review may prove helpful.[204] The origins and focus of this model are different to the issues required to accommodate the context in which the international human rights system operates.[205] However, the terms 'weak' and 'strong' are more appropriate in an international interpretative context than the traditional dichotomy of restraint and activism for two reasons. First, as outlined above, the idea of a restrictive approach to human rights interpretation has been discounted as a principle of interpretation in favour of a dynamic interpretation, which ensures effective implementation. Secondly, the premise underlying this chapter is that interpretation is ultimately an active process whereby meaning is created. Activism is thus a fundamental element of interpretation and the real issue is how this process should be performed.

In response to this question, the preceding discussion has indicated that a constructive approach to interpretation of the right to health is one that is principled, practical, coherent, and sensitive to local contextual considerations. Each of these features operates as a constraint on the interpretative exercise; however, their application is far from precise and there remains additional scope for the exercise of discretion in the interpretative process. The exercise of this discretion must remain balanced if it is to manage the potential conflict between the need for the interpretative exercise to remain engaged with the interpretative community and the need to construct a meaning of a right that will render it effective. But this does not address the question of how to balance these interests.

Use of the terms 'strong' and 'weak' may be of assistance. A strong approach to interpretation could be said to describe an outcome that is more demanding of states as to the nature of their obligations, and, as a consequence would offer greater protection for an individual. However, a weak approach would not mean restrictive in the sense of excessive deference to the interests of states. On the contrary, it would still pursue an interpretation that secures the effective protection of an individual's rights, but it would be less inclined to expand or conflate the nature and scope of that protection.

The adoption of a strong approach would be justified in two circumstances: first, when the interpretative inquiry relates to the scope of a state's negative obligation

---

[204] Tushnet, 'New Forms of Judicial Review' (n 119); Mark Tushnet, *Weak Courts: Strong Rights—Judicial Review and Social Welfare Rights in Comparative Constitutional Law* (Princeton University Press, 2007).
[205] Tushnet's work is primarily concerned with the methods available for judicial enforcement of rights rather than their interpretation.

A Meaning for the Right to Health 117

with respect to the right to health and second, when the strength of the supportive structures within the relevant interpretative community for the adoption of a particular interpretation are strong. In the first instance, because negative obligations are less demanding, there is less reason for states to be antagonized by a strong approach. In the second scenario, the strength of the supportive structures would act as a disincentive for states to disengage with the interpretative process. In contrast, a weak approach to interpretation would be considered more appropriate in matters that concern the scope of a state's positive obligations given the additional burden to be imposed on a state. This would be especially true when the supportive structures for a strong approach are weak.[206]

The minimum core obligation of the right to health as advanced by the ESC Committee in its General Comments No 3 and 14 provides an illustration of this weak/strong dichotomy. The original conception of this core obligation was confined to a rebuttable presumption that all states must secure the essential elements of primary health.[207] In contrast, the later exposition extended to a long list of minimum core obligations and 'obligations of comparable priority', which were said to be absolute and non-derogable irrespective of available resources. Both visions of the minimum core impose a significant burden on states. However, the former could be described as a weak interpretative approach to the extent that it was relatively modest in the list of demands imposed on states. In contrast the vision offered in General Comment 14 represents a strong interpretative approach. As to which vision should be preferred, an application of the interpretative methodology advanced in this chapter favours the original vision of the minimum core because, as argued above, the vision of the minimum core of the right to health under General Comment No 14 is unprincipled and impractical. The long list of measures required of states is so onerous that few, if any, states are likely to be persuaded to adopt such an approach.

The weak/strong dichotomy is clearly an imperfect, imprecise, and unstable classification scheme. But it is not intended to fix and direct the interpretative process to a certain outcome. Rather it provides a potential tool to guide the interpretative approach in accordance with the nature and context of the matter under consideration. It accepts that if the potential elasticity inherent in the meaning of the right to health is stretched too far, the resultant discordance with states expectations is likely to result in disengagement and a lack of implementation. On the other hand, an excessively restrictive approach that is focused on appeasement of states will jeopardize the effective implementation of the right to health. Thus, the interpretation of this right must be constantly directed towards achieving a balance somewhere between appeasement and disengagement if it is to have any capacity

---

[206] See Tushnet, 'New Forms of Judicial Review' (n 119) 823 (suggesting that weak form judicial review may be 'particularly attractive in light of widespread misgivings...about judicial enforcement of social-welfare rights'). See also Dixon (n 195) 408–15 (adapting Tushnet's analysis by using the terms 'intermediate' and 'weak' approaches to inform the respective interpretation of the negative and positive dimension of economic and social rights).

[207] ESC Committee, *General Comment No 3* (n 113) para 10.

to persuade states and the broader interpretative community to adopt the interpretation offered.

V Conclusion—towards a common understanding

In Vattel's chapter on the interpretation of treaties in *Les droit des gens,* he declared '[I]t is not permissible to interpret what has no need of interpretation. When a deed is worded in clear and precise terms, when its meaning is evident and leads to no absurdity, there is no ground for refusing to accept that meaning which the deed naturally presents.'[208] What would Vattel have made of the formulation of the right to health in international law, bought, as all human rights are, 'with the coinage of textual obfuscation'?[209] Doubtless he would have offered the series of general principles and presumptions which he had identified as tools by which to overcome such abstraction. But as Lauterpacht has observed the 'rich choice of weapons in Vattel's armoury of rules of interpretation' was such that any party to a dispute could have drawn some advantage from their application.[210] This is precisely the dilemma that confronts the interpretation of the right to health in international law. The VCLT offers a general rule for the interpretation of this right. However, this rule is fraught with so many internal inconsistencies and such ambiguity itself that commentators have largely accepted that its application is incapable of producing *the* meaning of a text. Controversy with respect to the meaning of a human right such as health is therefore a constant feature of the interpretative landscape.

Such controversy is particularly acute given the lack of an authoritative body with the coercive powers necessary to insist upon the adoption of a particular interpretation of the right to health. For some, the limitations of the VCLT may represent a form of liberation allowing the pursuit of a meaning for the right to health which accords with their own personal preferences and expectations. Such an approach might even be welcomed when the relevant interpretative community shares such preferences and expectations. The reality, however, is that this is often not the case. While a treaty body, NGO, or special rapporteur may share a common vision as to the meaning of the right to health, those other actors who are responsible for its implementation such as states may take an entirely different view. As a consequence, the absence of a common understanding with respect to the meaning of the right to health will always compromise its effective implementation. The task of interpretation must therefore be seen not simply as the attribution of meaning to a legal text but an attempt to persuade the relevant interpretative community that *a* particular meaning from within a suite of potential meanings should be adopted.

---

[208] Emer de Vattel, *Le Droit des Gens* (1758) vol I, ch XVII, para 263.
[209] Weiler (n 11) 2.
[210] Hersch Lauterpacht, 'Restrictive Interpretation and the Principle of Effectiveness in the Interpretation of Treaties' (1949) BYBIL 48, 48.

This chapter has sought to articulate an interpretative methodology apposite for this purpose. Such a methodology consists of four factors. First, given the expectations within the legal interpretative community, an application of the general rule of interpretation under the VCLT is considered to be a necessary part of any strategy to frame an interpretative exercise. This process may constrain the range of potential meanings but it will not yield *the* meaning of the right to health. As Weiler has explained, 'article 31 of the VCLT too often operates as a "straightjacket" on discussions concerning interpretation and represents an "unreal" signpost of contemporary treaty interpretation'.[211] In an attempt to move beyond this constraint, three other factors were identified as being relevant: the requirement that the interpretation offered be clear and practical, coherent, and context sensitive. It is important to stress that none of these features are considered to be mutually exclusive and nor are they capable of being applied in a precise way so as to produce some determinate and uncontested vision as to the meaning of the right to health. Rather, they are intended to act as benchmarks by which to guide the inevitable exercise of discretion that accompanies the interpretative enterprise and provide a more reflective and transparent account of the process by which the meaning of the right to health is produced. Importantly they are not considered to be severable and as such cannot be applied in a selective way.

The underlying objective of these factors is to generate *a* meaning for the right to health, which is capable of bridging the impasse that all too often characterizes the understanding of this right within the relevant interpretative community. It is accepted that these 'diverging interpretations [are] more difficult to reconcile through consultation and negotiation' than in the case of bilateral treaties.[212] But as Ian Johnstone explains, unity and an agreed meaning can be achieved when the 'participants in the enterprise share an interest in preserving the overall relationship'.[213] This last point is especially critical. It warns against the autonomous style of reasoning with respect to the meaning of the right to health in preference for an approach that accepts the need to entertain a certain level of deference to the varied and often potentially conflicting interests within the relevant interpretative community.

The requirement of a principled interpretation seeks to accommodate the *legal* nature of the right to health in international law. The requirement of a practical interpretation addresses Griffin's concern that human rights must be 'socially manageable',[214] and accepts Sen's warning that a theory of human rights cannot be sensibly confined within the juridical model within which it is frequently incarcerated.[215] The requirement of coherence in reasoning demands that the views and voices of those with relevant expertise must be considered and assessed in order to develop a common understanding as to the meaning of the right to health. The requirement of system coherence recognizes that there is a broader system of law within which the understanding of the right to health must be located. And finally,

---

[211] Weiller (n 11) 15. [212] Johnstone (n 3) 407. [213] ibid. [214] Griffin (n 4) 37–9.
[215] Amartya Sen, 'Elements of a Theory of Human Rights' (2004) 32 Phil & Pub Aff 315, 319–20.

the requirement for a context-sensitive interpretation accepts the reality that the successful implementation of a human right must occur within both a local and global socio-political context in which the power of states and their legitimate interests cannot be dismissed. The cumulative impact of these requirements is designed to generate an interpretation of the right to health that will make a persuasive and constructive contribution to what must be seen as an ongoing process by which the abstract formulations of the right to health as captured in the text of international human rights treaties is transformed into a common understanding of the measures required to secure its effective implementation.

4
The Meaning of the Highest Attainable Standard of Health

I Introduction

This chapter begins the task of using the interpretative methodology outlined in Chapter 3 to offer a persuasive account as to the meaning of the right to health in international law. A total of five chapters will be dedicated to this task and will address the following elements of the right to health:

- The meaning and scope of the interest in which the right to health is grounded in international law.
- The general obligation imposed on states to 'recognize' the right to health in international law.
- The specific steps to be taken by states to achieve the full realization of the right to health in international law.
- The obligation to abolish traditional/cultural practices that are prejudicial to the health of an individual.
- The obligation of states to co-operate with, and assist, other states to secure the full realization of the right to health in international law.

The focus of this chapter is the meaning and scope of the interest in which the right to health is grounded, namely 'the highest attainable standard of physical and mental health'. It consists of three parts. Part II examines the scope of this formulation and reveals that, despite the suggestion by some commentators that it implies a right to be healthy,[1] it does not, and was never intended, to provide individuals with a guarantee of health. On the contrary, the qualification of the right to health by the phrase, 'highest attainable standard', recognizes that the level of health enjoyed by an individual, whether physical or mental, will be dependent on factors peculiar to an individual *and* the resources available to a state. Thus, although the right to health is a universal standard its implementation and level of enjoyment will remain relative.[2]

---

[1] See, eg, Kristen Hessler and Allen Buchanan, 'Specifying the Content of the Human Right to Health Care' in Allen Buchanan (ed), *Justice and Health Care: Selected Essays* (OUP, 2009) 203, 205.

[2] See Norman Daniels, *Just Health: Meeting Health Needs Fairly* (CUP, 2008) 145–6 (stressing the need for a system-relative understanding of the right to health, which accommodates resources and relative understandings of health priorities within states).

With respect to the meaning of the term *health*, the human rights treaty monitoring bodies have overlooked this issue in preference for a focus on the entitlements of individuals under the right to health. However, a definition of health remains necessary in order to set limits on the scope of this term. It will be argued that the inclusion of the concept of social well being with the definition of health under the World Health Organization (WHO) Constitution is too broad. However, the traditional biomedical definition of health, as the absence of disease, is too narrow. In contrast the approach adopted by Norman Daniels, which defines health as the absence of a deviation from the normal range of biological functioning, although still contested captures more accurately the range of health conditions experienced by individuals and provides greater guidance in setting limits on claims that can be made under the guise of the right to health. At the same time, Daniel's emphasis on normalcy remains problematic with respect to the understanding of health conditions of persons with disabilities. Thus, it will be argued that a biopsychosocial understanding of health is the most appropriate approach to the definition of health in international law because it recognizes the potential for social factors, and not merely a pathological condition, to limit the functioning of an individual within society. This approach provides better guidance for states in identifying the measures necessary to secure the enjoyment of the right to health.

It will also be shown that the scope of the right to health is not limited to preventing, remedying, or mitigating the impact of ill health on the functioning of an individual. According to the Committee on Economic, Social and Cultural Rights (ESC Committee), it also extends to freedoms including the freedom to enjoy health including an individual's sexual and reproductive health, freedom from medical experimentation, and freedom from non-consensual medical treatment. These freedoms are also included within traditional civil and political rights such as the right to respect for private life (which includes physical integrity) and the prohibition against inhuman and degrading treatment. Thus there is an issue as to whether a persuasive account can be made to justify the inclusion of these freedoms within the scope of the right to health. Part III will examine this question and conclude that the principle of effectiveness and the obligation to respect and protect the right to health, provide justification for the approach adopted by the ESC Committee. However, the ESC Committee's treatment of these freedoms will be shown to be inadequate in providing guidance on how to address the complex issues that arise when seeking to protect these freedoms in practice. Thus, a detailed discussion will be offered as to how international law should deal with these issues in three contexts: sexual autonomy for adolescents; non-consensual medical treatment of children and adolescents; and non-consensual sterilization of women and girls with intellectual disabilities.

Part IV of this Chapter examines the four qualitative elements of the right to health that have been advanced by the human rights treaty monitoring bodies to assist in understanding the nature and scope of the right to health, namely that services and facilities to secure the right to health are available, accessible, acceptable, and of appropriate quality. Although these elements have been accepted within the human rights community, they are yet to achieve widespread acceptance among the broader interpretative community relevant to the implementation of the right to health. This would appear to be due to a lack of awareness, rather than any deep-seated objections based on ideological or pragmatic grounds. Indeed, it will be argued that the four elements serve a useful role in identifying in a clear and practical way the measures required of states to ensure the effective protection of the right to health. As such, they address the concerns of some commentators that the legitimacy of economic and social rights, such as the right to health, depends on their capacity to be 'action guiding'[3] or 'socially manageable'[4] for states.

II The scope of the interest in which the right to health is grounded

A The distinct nature of the international formulation

The formulation of the right to health adopted in international law is the right to '*the highest attainable standard of health*'. This standard appears in the preamble of the WHO Constitution, article 12(1) of the International Covenant on Economic, Social and Cultural Rights (ICESCR),[5] article 24(1) of the Convention on the Rights of the Child (CRC),[6] and article 25 of the Convention on the Rights of Persons with Disabilities (CRPD).[7] In contrast, the African Charter on Human and Peoples' Rights refers to the right to enjoy the best attainable state of physical and mental health (article 16); the African Charter on the Rights and Welfare of the Child protects the 'best attainable state of physical, mental and spiritual health' (article 14(1)); the Protocol of San Salvador protects the right to 'the enjoyment of the highest level of physical, mental and social well-being' (article 10(1)); and the European Social Charter lists specific measures that are required by states to ensure the 'effective exercise of the right to protection of health' (article 11).

As detailed in Chapter 1, the history of the formulation adopted in international law indicates that there was never any intention on the part of the drafters of the WHO Constitution to *guarantee* an individual's health. There was, however, an acceptance, as reflected in the preamble to the WHO Constitution, that:

Governments have a responsibility for the health of their peoples, which can be fulfilled only by the provision of adequate health and social measures.[8]

This responsibility was grounded in normative and instrumental considerations, which were derived from an agreement as to the central importance that health

---

[3] Charles Beitz, *The Idea of Human Rights* (OUP, 2009) 163.
[4] James Griffin, *On Human Rights* (OUP, 2008) 37–8.
[5] International Covenant on Economic, Social and Cultural Rights (ICESCR) (New York, 16 December 1966, entered into force 3 January 1976, 993 UNTS 3).
[6] Convention on the Rights of the Child (CRC) (New York, 20 November 1989, entered into force 2 September 1990, 1577 UNTS 3).
[7] Convention on the Rights of Persons with Disabilities (CRPD) (New York, 13 December 2006, entered into force 3 May 2008, UN Doc A/RES/61/106).
[8] Constitution of the World Health Organization (New York, 22 July 1946, entered into force 7 April 1948, 14 UNTS 185).

played in allowing an individual to lead a life of dignity *and* the value of a healthy individual to the broader community. As President Roosevelt declared in 1939, '[t]he ill health of the people is a public concern; ill health is a major cause of suffering, economic loss and dependency; good health is essential to the security and progress of the Nation'.[9] This same sentiment is reflected in the preambular paragraphs of the WHO Constitution which provide that, '[t]he health of all peoples is fundamental to the attainment of peace and security and is dependent upon the fullest co-operation of individuals and States' and '[t]he achievement of any State in the promotion and protection of health is of value to all'. Importantly, however, states were motivated by more than these instrumentalist considerations and accepted that the highest attainable standard of health was in and of itself a sufficient interest in which to ground a fundamental human right.

The inclusion of this standard within subsequent international instruments such as the ICESCR, the CRC, and the CRPD is very much attributable to the idea of ensuring external system coherence. In other words, the drafting history of the ICESCR, for example, indicates that the formulation originally proposed and ultimately accepted by the drafters in relation to the right to health was largely based on the formulation adopted in the WHO Constitution.[10] Significantly, the ESC Committee has stressed that, '[t]he right to health is not to be understood as a right to be *healthy*'[11]—a statement that should quell the anxieties of those who have taken the view that the right to health implies otherwise. From a practical perspective, the right to the highest attainable health requires that consideration must be given to 'both the individual's biological and socio-economic preconditions and a State's available resources' in determining the highest level of health which is attainable by an individual.[12] This reflects the reality, as recognized by the ESC Committee, that '[t]here are a number of aspects which cannot be addressed solely within the relationship between States and individuals: in particular, good health cannot be ensured by a State, nor can States provide protection against every possible cause of ill health'.[13] Thus, the right to health does not provide an individual with an entitlement to be healthy. Nor does it provide an entitlement that the highest attainable standard of health must be the same in every state—the assessment of what is attainable is relative and dependent on the availability of resources within a state.

---

[9] As cited in WHO, *Official Records of the World Health Organization No 2: Proceedings and Final Acts of the International Health Conference Held in New York from 19 June to 22 July 1946* (UN WHO Interim Commission June 1948) 31.

[10] *Annotations on the Text of the Draft International Covenants on Human Rights*, UN Doc A/2929 (1 July 1955) ch VIII, 111–12, paras 33–5; UN General Assembly Official Records, Agenda Item 31, Annexes, Eleventh Session, New York (1956–57) 19–20, paras 145–57.

[11] ESC Committee, *General Comment No 14: The Right to the Highest Attainable Standard of Health*, UN Doc E/C/12/2000/4 (11 August 2000) para 8.

[12] ibid para 9.   [13] ibid.

B The meaning of health

An attempt to capture the ordinary meaning of the term 'health' will inevitably prove contentious given the range of possible meanings attributable to this term. For example, the classic biomedical conception of health suggests that health is the absence of disease whether physical or mental. But as Norman Daniels explains, such a definition excludes 'injuries from trauma or from environmental hazards or toxins, none of which are diseases'.[14] It also excludes a range of birth defects, whether developmental or genetic, and functional deficits such as blindness of deafness.[15] At the same time, for many the idea of a functional deficit or disability is not the absence of health but merely a social construct.[16] Thus, the idea of what constitutes good health or the absence of ill health is problematic.

International law offers two approaches to the definition of health. The first is the approach adopted under the WHO Constitution, which defines health in its preamble as 'a state of complete physical, mental and social well-being and not merely the absence of disease or infirmity'. This approach, however, has not been embraced by the interpretative community relevant to securing the realization of the right to health.[17] In the first instance, states rejected this definition when they were drafting the ICESCR. It is true that the rejection was not universal. Some states 'held that it was useful since it would remove the obscurity, which surrounded the term "health", and was consistent with the "well recognised relationship between disease and social environment"'.[18] However, the position on which consensus was ultimately achieved was that: (a) a definition of 'health' was unnecessary (as no other terms had been defined in the ICESCR), and (b) the term 'social health' should be excluded because its meaning was unclear.[19]

This rejection by states of the broad definition of health adopted under the WHO Constitution is consistent with the views of commentators. Jennifer Ruger, for example, has argued that the focus on 'well being' is 'so broad as to constitute an unreasonable standard for human rights, policy and law'.[20] Similarly, Norman Daniels has warned that the inclusion of social well being in '[t]he WHO definition risks turning all of social philosophy and social policy into health care'.[21] Thus, there would appear to be a general consensus that the WHO definition of health fails to satisfy the requirements of clarity and practicality.

---

[14] Daniels (n 2) 36.   [15] ibid.
[16] See n 30 ff.
[17] Earlier scholars such as Henry Sigerist, a leading medical historian, favoured the view that health was 'not simply the absence of disease' but 'something positive, a joyful attitude toward life, a cheerful acceptance of the responsibilities that life puts on the individual': cited in Brigit Toebes, *The Right to Health as a Human Right in International Law* (Intersentia, 1999) 22.
[18] *Annotations on the Text of the Draft International Covenants on Human Rights* (n 10) 20 para 151.
[19] ibid paras 151–2.
[20] Jennifer Ruger, 'Toward a Theory of a Right to Health: Capability and Incompletely Theorized Agreements' (2006) 18 Yale JL & Human 273, 312.
[21] Daniels (n 2) 37.

However, there remains a preliminary question as to whether a definition of the right to health is actually necessary. Brigit Toebes suggests not and would prefer that an understanding as to the meaning of the health in international law should evolve via the application of this right before international and national tribunals.[22] The idea of an evolutionary understanding of the meaning of health is actually consistent with elements of the interpretative methodology adopted in this book. But Toebes' approach remains problematic for two reasons. First, the right to health in international law is rarely enforceable before judicial bodies and there is limited jurisprudence from which to draw and guide the development of an understanding as to the meaning of 'health' in international law. As a consequence it will be some time before courts and tribunals are able to produce a detailed understanding of the meaning of health. Second, even if the development of the meaning of health is to occur via practice, this will not occur without arguments from the relevant parties as to where the boundaries of the meaning of health should be drawn. It is therefore inappropriate to defer a discussion as to the meaning of health in international law and it is necessary to offer some insight into the scope of this term in order to get a sense of its limits.

C Moving beyond a biomedical definition of health

For its part, the ESC Committee, in its General Comment on the right to health under article 12 of the ICESCR, has noted that the right to the highest attainable standard of health is:

[N]ot confined to the right to health care. On the contrary the drafting history and express wording of article 12.2 acknowledge that the right to health embraces a wide range of socio-economic factors that promote conditions in which people can lead a healthy life, and extends to the underlying determinants of health, such as food and nutrition, housing, access to safe and potable water and adequate sanitation, safe and healthy working conditions, and a healthy environment.[23]

But this approach does not actually offer a definition of health and focuses on the entitlements of an individual under the right to health, namely, 'the enjoyment of a variety of facilities, goods, services and conditions necessary for the realization of the highest attainable standard of health'.[24] This is helpful to the extent that it offers a clear and practical insight into the nature of an individual's entitlement under the right to health. But it fails to identify the scope of the right to health and offers no insight into the nature of the actual interest to which such services, facilities, and goods are to be directed. For example, is health to be confined to the absence of disease or does it extend to functional deficits; is it confined to variations from a biomedical model of normal species functioning, or does it extend to unwanted

---

[22] Toebes (n 17) 24.
[23] ESC Committee, *General Comment No 14* (n 11) para 4.
[24] ibid para 9.

medical conditions, the sort of conditions that might, for example, be classified as cosmetic surgery for social rather than functional reasons?

Norman Daniels has sought to resolve these dilemmas by defining health as the absence of pathology, by which he means, 'any deviation from the natural functional organisation of a typical member of a species'.[25] Such an approach is conceptually narrower than the definition of health adopted in the WHO Constitution and seeks to limit health to 'a departure from normal functioning'.[26] According to Daniels, this standard can be objectively assessed using scientific methods as well as social epidemiology. It therefore excludes the many unwanted conditions for which people seek medical attention, but which cannot be classified as diseases or pathology. Daniels lists as examples, requests by individuals to reshape a nose, breast, or buttock by a plastic surgeon where the relevant part of the anatomy is not dysfunctional. As he explains, deviations in anatomy from individual or social conceptions of beauty do not constitute disease[27] and thus, would not fall within the scope of right to health (at least in sense of imposing a positive obligation on a state to provide such treatment). Such an approach is appealing because it allows for limits to be placed on the scope of claims for medical care that could potentially be made under the right to the highest attainable standard of health.[28]

The emphasis on normal functioning under this biomedical model will, as Daniels concedes, lead to heated disputes.[29] But controversy alone is not a sufficient reason to abandon Daniel's emphasis on normalcy. Indeed, a fundamental principle of this analysis is that the meaning of right to health will always remain contentious and the real challenge is to offer a persuasive account of its meaning. The same principle applies with respect to the distinction between medical conditions that are unwanted and those that represent a deviation from normal biomedical functioning. However, Daniel's emphasis on normalcy is particularly problematic in the context of persons with disabilities[30] who, as Barton explains, experience a 'struggle to capture the

---

[25] Daniels (n 2) 37.
[26] ibid.   [27] ibid 41.
[28] By way of example, and in response to the concern of an anonymous reviewer, a request for access to Viagra would fall within the scope of the right to health in circumstances where a male's capacity to achieve an erection was outside the range of normal functioning. But a request for a penis enlargement for purely social reasons, where a man's penis was within the range of normal functioning, would fall outside the scope of the right to health. It is important to stress, however, that any attempt to enlist the right to health to justify a right to Viagra would remain subject to the progressive nature of this obligation and the availability of resources, which a state would need to prioritize for other more urgent health needs.
[29] Daniels (n 2) 42.
[30] The phrases 'disabled person' or 'disabled child' are considered to be highly problematic because of their potential to imply that the ability of the individual person or child to function as a person or child has been disabled. As such, the Committee on Economic, Social and Cultural Rights has expressed its preference for the phrase 'persons with disabilities': ESC Committee, *General Comment No 5: Persons with Disabilities*, UN Doc E/1995/22 (9 December 1994) annex IV, 110, reprinted in *Compilation of General Comments and General Recommendations Adopted by Human Rights Treaty Bodies*, UN Doc HRI/GEN/1/Rev.6 (12 May 2003) 24, para 4. The Committee on the Rights of the Child has adopted the same approach in the consideration of such children in its concluding observations. For example, in its report on Moldova it recommended that the state '[a]void terminology such as "invalid" and use the internationally accepted terminology such as "children with disabilities"': CO CRC Moldova, UN Doc CRC/C/15/Add192, para 38(g). At the same time, it is important to be aware that some disability advocates have

power of naming difference itself[31] in a world where the 'ideology of normalcy' dominates.[32] Commentators such as Engel, for example, have suggested that the idea of normal functioning is problematic. He argues that functional limitations experienced by persons with disabilities 'are perceived and understood in terms of prevailing cultural conceptions of normal physique and physical function and of the significance of any deviation from that norm'.[33] By way of illustration he makes the point that in a society where all door and ceiling heights were designed for people who use wheelchairs, so-called 'able-bodied' persons would in fact be disabled or functionally impaired. Such an approach challenges the dominant social notion of normalcy and its concomitant construction of disability in favour of 'an ideology of difference that rejects defining a natural and thus desired state on the basis of a set of physical and cognitive characteristics'.[34]

Under this model, disability is primarily a social construction not a biological fact. As Hahn has argued:

[T]he deprivations experienced by disabled citizens are produced primarily by the stigma or prejudice bestowed upon them by society rather than by their functional limitations. Persons with disabilities are not devalued because their impediments deprive them of characteristics which are essential to human worth. Instead, the origin of their disadvantage is to found in the inordinate importance that others attach to these characteristics.[35]

So whereas Daniels might see a functional limitation as a deviation from a scientific standard of normalcy, Hahn would challenge the idea that there is ever an objective basis on which to assess normalcy.

The reality is that irrespective of the extent to which the notions of disability and normal functioning are social constructs, individuals with certain health conditions experience, within their society, functional limitations which are directly attributable to the interaction between their health condition and other contextual factors

---

reclaimed the term 'disabled persons' in order to stress that it is the person who is disabled by his or her social and physical environment: UNICEF, *Children and Disability in Transition in CEE/CIS and Baltic States* (Innocenti Research Centre, UNICEF, 2005) xvii. The limits of Daniel's approach are also apparent in his treatment of non-therapeutic abortions. According to Daniels, an unwanted pregnancy is not a disease or pathological condition and is the result of normal as opposed to abnormal functioning. As such, a non-therapeutic abortion should be omitted from the definition of a medical necessity: Daniels (n 2) 41. But such an approach does not acknowledge the health consequences associated with a woman or girl being forced to choose between carrying an unwanted pregnancy to full term, or having a clandestine abortion. These health consequences and their significance in the context of the right to health are discussed below in the context of availability of abortions under international law.

[31] L Barton, 'Disability, Difference and the Politics of Definition' (1994) 3 Aus Dis Rev 8, 18.
[32] See T Koch, 'The Ideology of Normalcy: The Ethics of Difference' (2005) 16 J Dis Pol'y Studies 123. See also Peter Singer, 'Ethics and Disability: A Response to Koch' (2005) 16 J Dis Pol'y Studies 130.
[33] DM Engel, 'Law, Culture, and Children with Disabilities: Educational Rights and the Construction of Difference' (1991) Duke LJ 166, 183.
[34] Koch (n 32) 128; cf Singer (n 32) 130 (warning of the danger in embracing disability and difference because it would be a mistake to believe that a serious disability will not make a child's life worse).
[35] H Hahn, 'Public Policy and Disabled Infants: A Sociopolitical Perspective' (1987) 3 Issues L & Med 3, 11. See also C Liachowitz, *Disability as a Social Construct* (University of Pennsylvania Press, 1988).

whether it be the physical environment, social prejudice and stereotypes, or factors particular to the individual. The definition of health in international law must accommodate, understand, and evaluate the complex interplay of these factors to identify both who has a functional limitation and the measures necessary to ameliorate the impact of his or her health condition in society. Under such an approach, Daniels' emphasis on pathology and the idea of normal functioning should not always be reduced to an assessment of whether the health condition of an individual represents a deviation from the biomedical norm. This may be appropriate with respect to many diseases and illnesses where medical treatment of the individual will be the most appropriate (and uncontested) way to prevent, restore, or mitigate ill health. But such a model will be inadequate in the context of those pathological conditions where the functional limitation experienced by a person is a consequence, not simply of the condition itself, but the failure of external factors to accommodate or mitigate the impact of the condition. In such circumstances, reliance on a narrow biomedical model will prove to be inadequate in developing an understanding of the measures required to accommodate or at least mitigate the impact of a person's health condition.

This need to move beyond a narrow biomedical approach to health is reflected in the *International Classification of Functioning, Disability and Health* (ICF), which was adopted by the World Health Assembly in 2001.[36] It severs the traditional link with notions of normalcy in preference for 'an umbrella term for impairments, activity limitation and participation restrictions'.[37] Impairments are defined as 'problems in body function or structure such as a significant deviation or loss'; 'activity limitations are difficulties an individual may have in executing activities'; while 'participation restrictions are problems an individual may experience in involvement in life situations'.[38] Significantly, this model has been adopted by the 191 member states of the World Health Organization as the basis for the scientific standardization of data on disability worldwide.[39] It therefore has strong support within the interpretative community. Importantly, the current classification system pays much greater attention to environmental and social factors. This is in contrast to the original version of the ICF guidelines published in 1980, which were heavily criticized for locating the problem of disability with an individual, being too medical, and paying insufficient attention to societal factors,[40] particularly the exclusionary and prejudicial social attitudes that often created the functional limitations experienced by persons with certain health conditions.

The WHO in its report *Towards a Common Language for Functioning, Disability and Health*, explains that the ICF offers a 'biopsychosocial model' of disability which

---

[36] World Health Assembly, *International Classification of Functioning, Disability and Health*, WHA Res 54.21, WHO Doc A/54/VR/9 (22 May 2001).
[37] WHO, *Towards a Common Language for Functioning, Disability and Health: ICF*, WHO Doc WHO/EIP/GPE/CAS/01.3 (2002) 2.
[38] ibid 10.
[39] ibid 5.
[40] *Standard Rules on the Equalization of Opportunities for Persons with Disabilities*, GA Res 48/96, UN Doc A/RES/48/96 (20 December 1993) para 20.

is based on an integration of traditional medical and social models.[41] It therefore expands, rather than rejects, a narrow biomedical model in an attempt to recognize that 'disability is a complex phenomena that is both a problem at the level of the person's body and a complex and primarily social phenomena'.[42] It acknowledges that 'disability is always an interaction between features of the person and features of the overall context in which the person lives'.[43] But at the same time, it concedes and allows for the reality that 'some aspects of disability are almost entirely internal to the person, while another aspect is almost entirely external. In other words, both medical and social responses are appropriate to the problems associated with disability.'[44]

This broader understanding of disability is also of benefit in understanding the meaning of health in international law for two reasons. First, it avoids the potential stigma that is created when a person's health condition is reduced to a deviation from normal functioning. Second, it forces a broadening of the inquiry to determine what goods, services, facilities, and conditions are to be provided by states to enable, not just an individual with a pathological condition to maximize his or her functioning in society, but for a society to accommodate or at least mitigate the functional limitations experienced by an individual because of his or her condition.

D The danger associated with inflating the right to health

An issue that arises with respect to the approach adopted by the ESC Committee concerning the scope of the right to health, is whether the inclusion of several determinants of health such as food, nutrition, and housing is justified. With the exception of environmental and industrial hygiene, the text of article 12 of the ICESCR makes no express mention of the other socio-economic determinants of health listed in the scope of the right to health advanced by the ESC Committee. The drafting history of the ICESCR indicates that the original formulation of the right to health included a requirement that states take steps to improve nutrition, housing, sanitation, recreation, economic and working conditions, and other aspects of environmental hygiene.[45] However, this formulation was subsequently rejected and replaced with the formulation that is now found in article 12(2)(b) of the

---

[41] WHO, *Towards a Common Language for Functioning, Disability and Health* (n 37) 9. The report (at 8–9) explains that:

[t]he *medical model* views disability as a feature of the person directly caused by disease, trauma or other health condition, which requires medical care provided in the form of individual treatment by professionals. Disability on this model, calls for medical or other treatment or intervention, to 'correct' the problem with the individual.

The *social model* of disability on the other hand, sees disability as a socially-created problem and not at all an attribute of an individual. On the social model, disability demands a political response, since the problem is created by an unaccommodating physical environment brought about by attitudes and other features of the social environment.

[42] WHO, *Towards a Common Language for Functioning, Disability and Health* (n 37) 9.
[43] ibid.
[44] ibid.
[45] *Annotations on the Text of the Draft International Covenants on Human Rights* (n 10) ch VIII, 111.

ICESCR namely, 'the improvement of all aspects of environmental and industrial hygiene'.[46] There is no indication in the drafting history as to the reasons for this amendment. However, the most plausible explanation is that the drafters considered the broader formulation inappropriate as the rights to food, clothing, and housing, which were originally the subject of a separate article, were consolidated with the right to an adequate standard of living.[47] Thus, the inclusion of such rights within the scope of the right to health arguably encroaches upon the normative territory of these rights, which enjoy separate protection under the ICESCR. It therefore appears that there may have been a lack of consideration given to the drafting history of the ICESCR and the requirement of internal system coherence. This gives rise to a question as to whether the recognition of the *interdependence* of other rights with the right to health would have been more appropriate than the inflation in the scope of the right to health adopted the ESC Committee.

This dilemma, however, is less of a concern with respect to the meaning of the right to health under the CRC for two reasons. First, the text of para 2 of article 24 makes reference to several underlying determinants of a child's health including food, water, sanitation, and environmental dangers. Thus, there is an explicit textual and principled basis to support the inclusion of such factors within the right to health. Moreover, the drafting history confirms that the right to health was never to be confined merely to a right to receive health care. The original Polish proposal provided that a child:

> shall be entitled to grow and develop in health; to this end, special care and protection shall be provided both to him and to his mother, including adequate pre-natal and post-natal care. The child shall have the right to adequate nutrition, housing, recreation and medical services.[48]

Instead of being rejected as too excessive in its scope, this proposal was actually criticized[49] for being too limited and the subsequent discussions throughout the drafting period only served to develop and refine those matters considered integral to the health of a child.

Thus, the drafting history of the CRC is able to confirm what the text of article 24 suggests—that there is a principled basis upon which to reject a narrow biomedical model of health, or a model which is restricted to the delivery of services that have a direct impact on the health of a child. The text of article 12 of the ICESCR, especially the list of steps to be taken by states as set out in para 2, also supports this broader notion of health. Moreover, such an approach can be justified on

---

[46] UN General Assembly, Official Records, Agenda Item 31 (n 10) 19–20, paras 147, 157.

[47] ibid 17–19, paras 120–44. Although there is no evidence in the drafting history to support this explanation, there is evidence that the drafters were alert to the issue of duplication. Thus for example, they rejected a proposal to include a right on non-consensual medical treatment on grounds which included the fact that this issue was already addressed in the limitation provision of the ICESCR as well as the prohibition against cruel and inhuman treatment under the draft ICCPR: 21, para 155.

[48] Commission on Human Rights, *Draft Convention on the Rights of the Child*, UN Doc E/CN.4/1292 (1978) annex, 124, art IV.

[49] See, eg, *Question of a Convention on the Rights of the Child: Report of the Secretary General*, UN Doc E/CN.4/1324 (27 December 1978) (comments of Sweden; Food and Agriculture Organization; WHO).

practical grounds to the extent that it reflects the reality that 'humans are biological organisms living in social environments'[50] and as a consequence there are innumerable social factors that influence and impact upon the health of individuals. Thus, as discussed in the previous section, the idea of health under international law reflects a model of health that is built upon 'a multidimensional construct that includes psychosocial as well as physical [and mental] elements'.[51]

At the same time it is important to guard against an approach whereby the right to health is conceived of as a repository for everything that impacts upon the health of an individual.[52] Although it is appropriate to identify the overlap with other rights within the other human rights treaties—an approach which is consistent with the principle of interdependence and indivisibility—it is also necessary to ensure internal and external system coherence and delineate to the extent possible the discrete domain of the right to health lest it becomes so expansive that it is without boundaries. This is not to say that it is inappropriate to identify matters relating to a person's physical integrity, education, housing, food, and the like, which impact upon the right to health. But the right to health should not be inflated to such an extent that the rights relevant to these matters are subsumed within the right to health and denied their *lex specialis* status and capacity for a content which exists independently of the right to health.[53]

This analysis, therefore, proceeds on the basis that the matters which are expressly included within the formulation of the right to health in instruments such as the ICESCR and the CRC, are appropriate for examination within the context of a discussion as to the meaning of health in international law. But those other matters, such as housing, education, and like, which are addressed in other discrete provisions of international human rights instruments, are not to be automatically subsumed within the scope of the right to health despite their potential to impact on the health of an individual. The principle of the interdependence of human rights and the requirement for system coherence demands that the potentially colonizing effects of the right to health must be avoided.

III The freedoms associated with health

The plea in the preceding paragraph to exercise caution when expanding the contours of the right to health, is challenged by the observation of the ESC Committee that the scope of the right to health includes not only entitlements, but freedoms including 'the right to control one's health and body, including sexual and

---

[50] Ruger (n 20) 316.
[51] ibid.
[52] Toebes (n 17) 259–60; S Jamar, 'The International Human Right to Health' (1994) 22 SUL Rev 2, 28; Ruger (n 20) 312–13.
[53] Toebes (n 17) 260 (identifying four general areas which overlap with the right to health but still retain a dimension that is autonomous or independent of the right to health: (i) life; (ii) physical integrity and privacy; (iii) housing, food and work; and (iv) education and information).

reproductive freedom and the right to be free from interference such as th⟨ be free from torture, non consensual medical treatment and experimentatic protection of these entitlements, which concern the physical integrity of individuals, has traditionally been located within civil and political rights such as the right to respect for private life and the prohibition against torture and cruel, inhuman, and degrading treatment. Moreover, a sophisticated and well-developed literature has been developed within these contexts as to the meaning of these rights. As a consequence, there is a *prima facie* issue as to whether an additional discussion of these issues is appropriate within the context of the meaning of the right to health.

Before undertaking a detailed examination of these freedoms, it is important to note that there is no explicit textual basis to support their inclusion in the meaning of health in international law. Thus, if a persuasive account is to be made for their inclusion, it must be derived from an argument that they are necessary to ensure the effective enjoyment of the right to health. In other words, they must to fill an 'effectiveness gap' in the implementation of the right to health or address a 'blind spot' that was overlooked or unresolved during the drafting process.

A The right to sexual and reproductive freedom—an adolescent perspective

1 A controversial but justifiable element of the right to health

An application of the effectiveness principle provides a strong case for the inclusion of sexual and reproductive freedom, as part of the right to health. There is nothing in the drafting history of the ICESCR that would indicate an intention on the part of states to exclude such autonomy or indeed sexual and reproductive health from the meaning of health. Moreover, an effectiveness gap in the implementation of the right to health would be created if this autonomy were not recognized, given its impact on the sexual health of an individual.

The ESC Committee's vision, that the right to control one's health and body extends to sexual and reproductive freedom,[55] has been increasingly accepted among the broader interpretative community in the context of adults.[56] Indeed, article 16(1) (e) of the Convention on the Elimination of All Forms of Discrimination against

---

[54] ESC Committee, *General Comment No 14* (n 11) para 8. See also *Report of the Special Rapporteur on the Right to Health to the General Assembly 2009*, UN Doc A/64/272 (10 August 2009) (examining the relationship between the right to health and informed consent).

[55] ESC Committee, *General Comment No 14* (n 11) para 8.

[56] See generally *Report of the Special Rapporteur on the Right to Health to the Commission on Human Rights 2004*, UN Doc E/CN.4/2004/49 (16 February 2004) paras 7–56. The International Conference on Population and Development (ICPD) held in Cairo in 1994 and the Fourth World Conference on Women held in Beijing in 1995 affirmed the reproductive rights of men and women: *Report of the International Conference on Population and Development*, UN Doc A/CONF.171/13 (18 October 1994) 40–1, para 7.3; *Report of the Fourth World Conference on Women*, UN Doc A/CONF.177/20/Rev.1 (1996) ch I, 36, para 96; WHO, *Reproductive Health Strategy* (WHO, 2004) 21; Jane Cottingham and others, 'Using Human Rights for Sexual and Reproductive Health: Improving Legal and Regulatory Frameworks' (2010) 88 Bull WHO 551, 551; cf Catholic Family and Human Rights Institute, *Submission to the ESC Committee Day of General Discussion on the Formulation of a General Comment on 'The Right to Sexual and Reproductive Health'* (15 November 2010) (challenging the legitimacy of the ESC Committee to make a

Women (CEDAW) provides that states must ensure equality between men and women with respect to their rights 'to decide freely and responsibly on the number and spacing of their children'.[57] But the idea of sexual autonomy is far more contentious in the context of children. This is to be expected given that reproductive health has been taken to consist of at least three elements: first, an entitlement 'to have a safe and satisfying sex life and...the capability to reproduce and the freedom to decide if, when and how often to do so'; second, the right 'of men and women to be informed and to have access to safe, effective and affordable and acceptable methods of family planning of their choice'; and third, 'sexual health, the purpose of which is the enhancement of life and personal relations and not merely counseling and care related to reproduction and sexually transmitted diseases'.[58]

The degree of sexual autonomy affirmed in this definition is not easy to reconcile with traditional constructions of adolescent sexuality. The emphasis on 'the rights of men and women' in the passage quoted above reflects a tendency, even within international human rights law, to overlook, avoid, or marginalize the issue of reproductive health and sexual autonomy for children. It is suggested, however, that the right to health, when used in conjunction with several other articles under the CRC, provides a principled justification for challenging this neglect, and demands that appropriate measures be taken by states to minimize the risks to children's health which arise in the exercise of their sexual autonomy.

In order to invoke the right to health in this way it is necessary to first establish a clear and practical nexus between children's sexual and reproductive autonomy and their health. This is precisely what the CRC Committee did in its General Comment No 4 on Adolescent Health and Development, when it acknowledged

---

general comment on the right to reproductive health due to the absence of an express reference to a right to reproductive health in the ICESCR).

[57] Convention on the Elimination of All Forms of Discrimination against Women (CEDAW) (New York, 18 December 1979, entered into force 3 September 1981) 1249 UNTS 13). See also Protocol to the African Charter on Human and Peoples' Rights on the Rights of Women in Africa (Maputo, 13 September 2000, entered into force 25 November 2005, OAU Doc CAB/LEG/66.6) art 14(1) which provides that: States Parties shall ensure that the right to health of women, including sexual and reproductive health is respected and promoted. This includes:

(a) the right to control their fertility;
(b) the right to decide whether to have children, the number of children and the spacing of children;
(c) the right to choose any method of contraception;
(d) the right to self protection and to be protected against sexually transmitted infections, including HIV/AIDS;
(e) the right to be informed on one's health status and on the health status of one's partner, particularly if affected with sexually transmitted infections, including HIV/AIDS, in accordance with internationally recognised standards and best practices.

[58] *Programme of Action of the International Conference on Population and Development*, UN Doc A/CONF.171/13 (18 October 2004) ch I, res 1, annex, ch VII, 43, para 7.2. For a comprehensive discussion of the relationship between reproductive health and human rights, see Rebecca Cook, Bernard Dickens, and Mahmoud Fathalla, *Reproductive Health and Human Rights: Integrating Medicine, Ethics, and Law* (OUP, 2006).

that '[a]dolescence is a period characterised by rapid physical, cognitive and social changes, including sexual and reproductive maturation'.[59] The CRC Committee further recognized that this transition to 'adolescence also poses new challenges to health' owing to the relative vulnerability experienced during this period and 'pressure from society, including peers, to adopt risky behaviour'.[60] Principal among these challenges are the risks of contracting sexually transmitted diseases, especially HIV/AIDS, and experiencing unwanted pregnancies.

Such risks are real and are reflected in the attention given by the CRC Committee in its concluding observations for states with respect to the high incidence of STDs and HIV/AIDS among adolescents and the rate of teenage pregnancies.[61] Beyond the health risks associated with being pregnant for a young girl[62] the CRC Committee has also identified the related issue of abortions,[63] which are often used as a method of birth control,[64] and especially illegal abortions[65] given the associated medical complications.[66] (The ESC Committee and CEDAW Committee have also identified these concerns in relation to women.)[67] The reality of these consequences demonstrates that an unbridled freedom to enjoy sexual and reproductive autonomy, as implied by the comments of the ESC Committee, actually presents a genuine threat to the realization of a child's right to health. This in turn gives rise to a question as to how to empower children to navigate the vagaries associated with the exercise of their evolving sexuality.

---

[59] CRC Committee, *General Comment No 4: Adolescent Health and Development in the Context of the Convention on the Rights of the Child*, UN Doc CRC/GC/2003/4 (1 July 2003) para 2.

[60] ibid.

[61] See especially ibid para 31. See also CO CRC Russian Federation, UN Doc CRC/C/15/Add110, para 48; CO CRC Angola, UN Doc CRC/C/15/Add246, para 45; CO CRC Morocco, UN Doc CRC/C/15/Add211, para 46; CO CRC Italy, UN Doc CRC/C/15/Add198, para 42; CO CRC UK and Northern Ireland, UN Doc CRC/C/15/Add, para 43.

[62] See generally CRC Committee, *General Comment No 4* (n 59) para 31 (recognizing that 'young mothers, especially where support is lacking, may be prone to depression and anxiety compromising their ability to care for their child'). See also WHO, *Contraception: Issues in Adolescent Health and Development* (WHO, 2004) 4–5.

[63] See, eg, CO CRC Kazakhstan, UN Doc CRC/C/15/Add213, para 58; CO CRC Czech Republic, UN Doc CRC/C/15/Add201, para 50; CO CRC Romania, UN Doc CRC/C/15/Add199, para 47(b); CO CRC Mozambique, UN Doc CRC/C/15/Add172, paras 50(a)–(b).

[64] See, eg, CO CRC Albania, UN Doc CRC/C/15/Add249, para 56; CO CRC Armenia, UN Doc CRC/C/15/Add119, para 36; CO CRC Greece, UN Doc CRC/C/15/Add170, para 60(b); CO CRC Latvia, UN Doc CRC/C/15/Add142, para 39; CO CRC Kyrgyzstan, UN Doc CRC/C/15/Add127, para 44; CO CRC Slovakia, UN Doc CRC/C/15/Add140, para 38.

[65] See, eg, CO CRC Seychelles, UN Doc CRC/C/15/Add189, para 46(b); CO CRC Kyrgyzstan, UN Doc CRC/C/15/Add127, para 45.

[66] See, eg, CO CRC Columbia, UN Doc CRC/C/15/Add137, para 48.

[67] See, eg, CO ESC Mauritus, UN Doc E/C.12/MUS/CO/4, para 25; CO ESC Poland, UN Doc E/C.12/POL/CO/5, para 28; CO ESC Brazil, UN Doc E/C.12/BRA/CO/2, para 29; CO ESC Philippines, UN Doc E/C.12/PHL/CO/4, para 31; CO CEDAW Romania, UN Doc A/55/38, pt II, 77, para 134; CO CEDAW Uzbekistan, UN Doc A/56/38, pt I, 18, para 185; CO CEDAW Paraguay, UN Doc A/60/38 part I, para 287.

2 The features of the model advanced under international law

The model advanced under the CRC to secure the sexual and reproductive health of children consists of five elements. First, the sexuality of children (and adolescents) is recognized as a legitimate and integral aspect of their identity. Moreover, given the capacity for the exercise of their sexual autonomy to impact on their physical and mental health, sexual health must form a part of a child's right to health in international law. Second, the CRC does not allow for children to be abandoned to discover and exercise their sexual autonomy in isolation in a manner that would compromise their sexual health. The best interests principle under article 3, when combined with the obligation of parents or guardians under article 5 to provide guidance and assistance with respect to the enjoyment of a child's rights under the CRC, indicates that sexual autonomy for children is to be treated as neither an invisible nor absolute concept but an evolving one. It is within this context that the CRC Committee has stressed the need to create a safe and supportive environment in which this development takes place.[68]

According to the CRC Committee, critical to this environment is the role and obligation of an adolescent's parents and family to 'fulfill with care their right and responsibility to provide direction and guidance to their adolescent child' in a manner which respects the adolescent's views'[69]—a position which is consistent with the literature.[70] Moreover, states are under an obligation to assist parents in developing this environment by 'providing adequate information and parental support to facilitate the development of a relationship of trust and confidence in which issues regarding... sexuality and sexual behaviour and risky lifestyles can be openly discussed and acceptable solutions found that respect the adolescent's rights'.[71]

The third limb of the model under the CRC relates to the obligation to provide *information* to children themselves in a manner that is consistent with their evolving capacities. Thus, for example, the CRC Committee has recommended that:

State parties should provide adolescents with access to sexual and reproductive information, including on family planning and contraceptives, the dangers of early pregnancy, the prevention of HIV/AIDS and the prevention of sexually transmitted diseases (STDs)... *regardless of marital status, and prior consent from parents or guardians.*[72]

---

[68] CRC Committee, *General Comment No 4* (n 59) pt II, paras 14–25.
[69] ibid para 7.
[70] See, eg, R Jones and H Boonstra, 'Confidential Reproductive Health Services for Minors: The Potential Impact of Mandated Parental Involvement for Contraception' (2004) 36 PSRH 182; L Hock-Long and others, 'Access to Adolescent Reproductive Health Services: Financial and Structural Barriers to Care' (2003) 35 PSRH 144 (noting that the UK and most Western European countries which allow for confidential family planning services still encourage adolescents to discuss their reproductive health needs with their parents).
[71] CRC Committee, *General Comment No 4* (n 59) para 16.
[72] ibid para 28 (emphasis added).

Such comments, which have also been made by the CESCR Committee[73] and CEDAW Committee,[74] have a principled basis in that article 13 of the CRC actually provides children with a right to receive information while the effective implementation of the right to health demands the provision of such information in a manner that is consistent with their evolving capacities.[75]

The CRC Committee has also recognized that the dissemination and content of such information must accommodate and be sensitive to the reality of the world which adolescent boys and girls experience. It has therefore recommended that states 'ensure that adolescents are actively involved in the design and dissemination of information through a variety of channels beyond the school, including youth organisations, religious, community and other groups and the media'.[76] This approach, which is actually required by article 12 of the CRC,[77] is also consistent with the view expressed in the Programme of Action adopted at the United Nations Conference on Population and Development in 1994 where it was observed that 'programmes for adolescents have been shown to be most effective when they secure the full involvement of adolescents in identifying their reproductive and sexual

---

[73] ESC Committee, *General Comment No 14* (n 11) para 23 ('the realisation of the right to health of adolescents is dependent on the development of youth friendly health care, which ... includes appropriate sexual and reproductive health services'); CO ESC Benin, UN Doc E/C.12/1/Add78, para 42; CO ESC Bolivia, UN Doc E/C.12/1/Add.60, para 43; CO ESC Jamaica, UN Doc E/C.12/1/Add.75, para 30.

[74] See CEDAW Committee, *General Recommendation No 24: Article 12 of the Convention on the Elimination of All Forms of Discrimination against Women—Women and Health*, UN Doc A/54/38/Rev.1 (1999) ch 1, para 18 (recommending that states 'ensure the rights of female and male adolescents to sexual and reproductive health education [which eliminates all forms of gender stereotyping] by properly trained personnel in specially designed programmes that respect their rights to privacy and confidentiality'). See also CEDAW, art 16(e), which provides that states must ensure for women '[t]he same rights to decide freely and responsibly on the number and spacing of their children and to have access to the information, education and means to enable them to exercise these rights'; CO CEDAW Slovakia, UN Doc CEDAW/C/SVK/CO/4, para 19.

[75] Article 13 of the CRC states that:

1 The child shall have the right to freedom of expression; this right shall include freedom to seek, receive and impart information and ideas of all kinds, regardless of frontiers, either orally, in writing or in print, in the form of art, or through any other media of the child's choice.
2 The exercise of this right may be subject to certain restrictions, but these shall only be such as are provided by law and are necessary:
   (a) For respect of the rights or reputations of others; or
   (b) For the protection of national security or of public order (ordre public), or of public health or morals.

[76] CRC Committee, *General Comment No 4* (n 59) para 28.
[77] Article 12 provides that:

1 States Parties shall assure to the child who is capable of forming his or her own views the right to express those views freely in all matters affecting the child, the views of the child being given due weight in accordance with the age and maturity of the child.
2 For this purpose, the child shall in particular be provided the opportunity to be heard in any judicial and administrative proceedings affecting the child, either directly, or through a representative or an appropriate body, in a manner consistent with the procedural rules of national law.

health needs and in designing programmes that respond to those needs'.[78] As a consequence the participation of adolescents is not only a principled, but a practical, requirement for creating effective information and awareness-raising strategies in relation to children's sexual and reproductive health.

The fourth feature of the model to secure a child's right to sexual health requires that, beyond the provision of information, states must 'ensure that appropriate goods [and] services . . . for the prevention and treatment of STDs including HIV/AIDS are available and accessible'.[79] In this context, it has urged states to:

(a) develop effective prevention programmes, including measures aimed at changing cultural views about adolescents' need for contraception and STD prevention and addressing cultural and other taboos surrounding adolescent sexuality;
(b) to adopt legislation to combat practices that either increase adolescents' risk of infection or contribute to the marginalization of adolescents who are already infected with STDs including HIV/AIDS;
(c) to take measures to remove all barriers hindering the access of adolescents to information, preventive measures such as condoms, and care.[80]

Indeed, in its General Comment No 3 on HIV/AIDS and the rights of the child, the CRC Committee stressed the need for states to provide 'free or at cost contraceptive methods and services'[81] and ensure 'the accessibility of voluntary, confidential HIV counseling and testing services with due attention to the evolving capacities of the child'.[82]

Moreover, in an attempt to prevent unwanted pregnancies the CRC Committee has urged states parties:

(a) to develop and implement programmes that provide access to sexual and reproductive health services, including family planning, contraception and safe abortion services where abortion is not against the law, adequate and comprehensive obstetric care and counseling;

---

[78] *Programme of Action of the International Conference on Population and Development* (n 58) 49–50, para 7.43. See also *Further Actions and Initiatives to Implement the Beijing Declaration and Platform for Action*, GA Res S-23/3, UN Doc A/RES/S-23/3 (16 November 2000) annex, para 79(f). On the general design and effectiveness of reproductive health strategies for adolescents including their participation see *Report of the Round Table on Adolescent Sexual and Reproductive Health and Rights: Key Future Actions* (UNFPA, 1998).

[79] CRC Committee, *General Comment No 4* (n 59) para 30. See also CO CRC Antigua and Barbuda, UN Doc CRC/C/15/Add247, para 54(a); CO CRC Zambia, UN Doc CRC/C/15/Add206, para 51(a); CO CRC Republic of Moldova, UN Doc CRC/C/15/Add192, paras 35, 36(c); CO CRC Niger, UN Doc CRC/C/15/Add179, para 49(a); CO CRC Gabon, UN Doc CRC/C/15/Add171, para 45; CO CRC Chile, UN Doc CRC/C/15/Add173, para 42(b).

[80] CRC Committee, *General Comment No 4* (n 59) para 30. See also CO CRC Indonesia, UN Doc CRC/C/15/Add233, para 57(c) (recommending that the states party 'make condoms and other contraceptives available throughout the country'); CO CRC Eritrea, UN Doc CRC/C/15/Add204, para 42 (recommending the 'availability of condoms'); CO CRC Spain, UN Doc CRC/C/15/Add185, para 39(c) ('Take steps to address adolescent health concerns, including teenage pregnancy and sexually transmitted diseases, through, inter alia, sex education, including birth control measures such as the use of condoms').

[81] CRC Committee, *General Comment No 3: HIV/AIDS and the Rights of the Child*, UN Doc CRC/GC/2003/3 (17 March 2003) para 20.

[82] ibid para 22.

(b) to foster positive and supportive attitudes towards adolescent parenthood for their mothers and fathers; and

(c) to develop policies that will allow adolescent mothers to continue their education.[83]

The fifth and final feature of the model advanced under the CRC to secure the sexual and reproductive health of children deals with the questions of privacy, confidentiality, and the related issue of informed consent. With respect to these matters, the CRC Committee has stressed 'that States parties should (a) enact laws or regulations to ensure that confidential advice concerning treatment is provided to adolescents so that they can give their informed consent'. It has added that, '[s]uch laws or regulations should stipulate an age for this process or refer to the evolving capacity of the child; and (b) provide training for health personnel on the rights of adolescents to privacy and confidentiality, to be informed about planned treatment and to give their informed consent to treatment'.[84]

The need for confidentiality remains contentious within the interpretative community. Those who oppose such a position argue that it undermines parental authority;[85] condones a culture of deception by children with respect to dealings with their parents,[86] and destabilizes the family unit.[87] In contrast, other commentators and groups have warned of the dangers associated with parental consent;[88] acknowledged the importance attached to confidentiality by adolescents themselves; the significance of confidentiality in the ethical framework of the doctor/patient relationship; and the need not to trivialize or dismiss the reality or fear of parental retribution which may be harboured by some adolescents.[89]

---

[83] CRC Committee, *General Comment No 4* (n 59) para 31. See also CEDAW Committee, *General Recommendation No 24* (n 74) ch I, para 23.

[84] CRC Committee, *General Comment No 4* (n 59) para 33. With respect to the issue of access to abortions, many jurisdictions have recognized this right. Indeed the House of Lords in the United Kingdom, in a landmark case, *Gillick v West Norfolk and Wisbech Area Health Authority (Gillick)* [1986] 1 AC 112 (HL, UK), which preceded the CRC, held that a young girl with sufficient understanding and maturity could receive information about contraception without her mother's consent. The US Supreme Court enunciated a similar principle in *Planned Parenthood v Danforth*, 428 US 52 (1976) (SC, USA). However, even in jurisdictions where the courts and legislators have secured such a right for adolescents, its legitimacy remains highly contested. See, eg, L Ross, 'Adolescent Sexuality and Public Policy: A Liberal Response' (1996) 15 Pol & Life Sci 13 (outlining several arguments in opposition to confidential contraceptive access for adolescents) and L Ross, 'Adolescent Sexuality and Public Policy: An Unrepentant Liberal Approach' (1996) 15 Pol & Life Sci 323.

[85] See, eg, Ross, 'Adolescent Sexuality and Public Policy: A Liberal Response' (n 84); US Conference of Catholic Bishops, 'Parental Notification Needed in Title X Program' <http://www.usccb.org/prolife/issues/abortion/factistook-2> accessed 13 June 2011.

[86] See, eg, Ross, 'Adolescent Sexuality and Public Policy: A Liberal Response' (n 84).

[87] See, eg, J Merrick, 'Kids, Sex and Contraceptives: Dilemmas in a Liberal Society' (1996) 15 Pol & Life Sci 281.

[88] See Jones and Boonstra (n 70) 182 (evaluates the likely impact of mandated parental involvement for contraception and suggests potential negative effects such as refusal to access prescription contraceptives, use of least effective methods, or use of no method at all).

[89] A Middleman, 'Public Policy regarding Adolescent Sexuality in a Truly Liberal State' (1996) 15 Pol & Life Sci 305.

3 Offering a defence for the model

Despite the divergence of opinion within the broader interpretative community, the position of the CRC Committee in relation to the realization of the sexual and reproductive health of children rests on a principled and practical foundation. The effective enjoyment of the right to health requires that states take appropriate measures to secure this entitlement. The evidence demonstrates that the provision of effective and developmentally appropriate sexual education for children (and their parents) is likely to decrease the prospect that girls will become pregnant and that children will contract sexually transmitted diseases.[90] A failure to act on such evidence would also be inconsistent with the general obligation under para 1 or the specific obligation under article 24(2)(f) of the CRC to develop family planning education and services. Moreover, when combined with the right to privacy under article 16, the CRC demands that states are required to ensure that adolescents have access[91] to affordable family planning services including contraceptive devices and, in those circumstances where they possess sufficient maturity and understanding, prescription contraception and abortion where it is lawful within the state.[92]

Article 5 of the CRC may require that the interpretation of article 24 must be informed by, and remain sensitive to, the views and wishes of parental and community groups—an approach required to ensure internal system coherence.[93] However, such views cannot compromise a child's right to the highest attainable standard of health. They also remain subject to the caveat that article 5 is still informed by a child's evolving capacities. Local context sensitivity will allow states a margin of appreciation in the measures they adopt to implement the recommendations of the

---

[90] See, eg, Alan Guttmacher Institute, *Sex Education: Needs, Programs, and Policies* (Alan Guttmacher Institute, 2005); S Alford, *Science and Success: Sex Education and Other Programs that Work to Prevent Teen Pregnancy, HIV, and Sexually Transmitted Infections* (Advocates for Youth, 2003); Jennifer Manlove and others, *Not Yet: Programs to Delay First Sex among Teens* (National Campaign to Prevent Teenage Pregnancy, 2004).

[91] See L Hock-Long and others (n 70) (notes that the financial considerations and structural factors such as fear of parental notification and non-youth-friendly service environments can restrict access to reproductive health services).

[92] See generally Center for Reproductive Rights, 'Implementing Adolescent Reproductive Rights through the Convention on the Rights of the Child' (CRR Briefing Paper, September 1999) 10–12; H Abbing, 'Adolescent Sexuality and Public Policy: A Human Rights Response' (1996) 15 Pol & Life Sci 314; *Beijing Platform for Action 2005*, UN Doc A/CONF.177/20/Rev.1 (2006) ch I, res 1, annex II, para 95 (notes the need for privacy and confidentiality in the context of counselling and access to sexual and reproductive health information and services) and 108(e) (recommends that Governments in co-operation with civil society '[p]repare and disseminate accessible information, . . . designed to ensure that women and men, particularly young people, can acquire knowledge about their health, especially information on sexuality and reproduction, taking into account the rights of the child to access to information, privacy, confidentiality, respect and informed consent . . . ').

[93] Article 5 of the CRC provides that:

States Parties shall respect the responsibilities, rights and duties of parents or, where applicable, the members of the extended family or community as provided for by local custom, legal guardians or other persons legally responsible for the child, to provide, in a manner consistent with the evolving capacities of the child, appropriate direction and guidance in the exercise by the child of the rights recognized in the present Convention.

CRC Committee. But this discretion cannot be extended so that the object and purpose of the right to health with respect to the sexual and reproductive health of children is defeated. Thus, the position of the CRC Committee is galvanized by the reality that inadequate information, support, services, and recognition of adolescent sexuality has real consequences for adolescent health. As such, the model advanced by the CRC Committee can be justified on the basis that it is necessary to ensure the effective implementation of article 24 and must be considered to be both principled and practical.

It is important to acknowledge that an issue with respect to external system coherence is created under this model by virtue of the fact that parents will, and indeed have, invoked their rights under other human rights instruments to resist attempts by states to provide their children with information and services relating to children's sexual health. For example, article 18(4) of the ICCPR requires states parties to respect the right of parents 'to ensure the religious and moral education of their children in conformity with their own convictions'.[94] The Human Rights Committee has not yet expressed a view as to whether compulsory family planning education would violate this provision. However, it explained in its General Comment on article 18 that if information is provided in a 'neutral and objective way' no violation will arise.[95] The CESCR Committee has expressed a similar view,[96] and the European Court of Human Rights has also applied this test to uphold the validity of compulsory sex education programs for children within the European context.[97]

However, the test adopted by the human rights treaty monitoring bodies and European Court of Human Rights still leaves several issues unresolved. First, with respect to information concerning sexual and reproductive health, it is questionable whether such information can ever be provided in a 'neutral and objective' way. Second, even if this were possible, it is unclear whether a state is still *compelled* to provide adolescents with school-based information irrespective of the wishes of a parent, or indeed the child, or whether the parent or child could seek an exemption from attendance at such classes.

Although the Human Rights Committee[98] and to a lesser extent the European Court of Human Rights[99] have entertained a high level of deference to parents on

---

[94] See also *Declaration on the Elimination of All Forms of Intolerance and of Discrimination Based on Religion or Belief*, GA Res 36/55, UN doc A/RES/36/55 (25 November 1981) art 5(2); Protocol to the Convention for the Protection of Human Rights and Fundamental Freedoms (Paris, 20 March 1952, entered into force 18 May 1954, 213 UNTS 262) art 2.

[95] HRC, *General Comment No 22: The Right to Freedom of Thought, Conscience and Religion*, UN Doc CCPR/C/21/Rev.1/Add.4 (27 September 1993) para 6.

[96] With respect to the work of the ESC Committee see, eg, CO ESC Kazakhstan, UN Doc E/C.12/KAZ/CO/1, para 33 (recommending comprehensive sexual and reproductive health education programmes for girls and boys in national school curricula that provide objective information in accordance with medical and education standards); CO ESC Republic of Korea, UN Doc E/C.12/KOR/CO/3, para 31; CO ESC Poland, UN Doc E/C.12/POL/CO/5, para 31.

[97] See n 102.

[98] Human Rights Committee, *General Comment No 22* (n 95) para 6.

[99] See n 102.

matters relating to sexual education, the comments of the CRC Committee appear to be less accommodating. For example, in its General Comment on Adolescent Health it declared that:

It is the obligation of States Parties to ensure that all adolescent boys and girls, both in and out of school, *are provided with and <u>not denied</u>, accurate and appropriate information* on how to protect their health and development and practice healthy behaviours...[and]...this should include information on...safe and respectful social and sexual behaviours.[100] (emphasis added).

Such a robust position leaves little scope for a state to defer complete responsibility for the sexual education of a child to his or her parents.

However, if parents are denied the right to claim an exemption from their child's attendance at sexual education classes within a public school, it remains unclear whether the child could be home schooled or attend a private school where no information on sexual and reproductive health was provided. This option has been contemplated as a legitimate approach by the Human Rights Committee,[101] and to a lesser extent, the European Court of Human Rights.[102] There is also an argument that article 29(2) of the CRC, which allows individuals and bodies to establish and direct educational institutions, entertains this prospect. Such a position, however, is difficult to reconcile with the notion that the provision of such education is a necessary element of a child's right to the highest attainable standard of health given the serious health implications associated with a failure to have access to such information and services. Thus, there is a strong argument that it is incumbent on states to insist that the curricula of all schools—public and private—ensure that children are provided with appropriate information regarding family planning and reproductive health. Anything less raises the prospect that a child's right to enjoy sexual and reproductive health will be compromised.

It is also important to stress that, despite its appearances, this approach is actually best described as being a weak rather than a strong model. In the first instance, the recommendations of the CRC Committee are not motivated by a desire to actively promote adolescent sexuality or the right to a safe and healthy sex life for children as being a derivate of either the right to health or the right to respect for private life under article 13. Rather, its comments are driven by a genuine and well-grounded concern that a failure to recognize the reality of adolescent sexual behaviour and

---

[100] CRC Committee, *General Comment No 4* (n 59) para 26 (emphasis added).
[101] HR Committee, *General Comment No 22* (n 95) para 6.
[102] See *Kjeldsen Busk Madsen and Pedersen v Denmark* (1976) Series A no 23 (ECrtHR) (holding that parents always had the option of home schooling their children or sending them to a private school), cf *Konrad v Germany* ECHR 2006–XIII (ECrtHR) (holding that a prohibition on home schooling was not a violation of Protocol I, article 2 of the European Convention on Human Rights and parents remained free to educate their children in conformity with their own beliefs after school and on weekends). Although these decisions appear to be irreconcilable it may assist to view the divergence in opinion more as a reflection of the Court's application of the margin of appreciation in *Konrad* than a reversal of its opinion in *Kjeldsen*.

provide an appropriate supportive environment will jeopardize the health of children.

Secondly, on no occasion has the CRC Committee advocated the right of an adolescent girl to become pregnant and undertake an abortion as being an entitlement under the right to the highest attainable standard of health or indeed any other right under the CRC. Such an approach is consistent with the approach adopted under other international instruments,[103] and the reality is that the CRC provides no mandate to express such views and the regulation of abortion is a matter left to the discretion of individual states.[104] The concern of the CRC Committee with abortions, therefore, stems from the use of abortion as a tool to deal with unwanted pregnancies and the attendant health risks to young girls.[105]

Third, the model advanced by the CRC Committee is not seeking to usurp the role of parents or undermine the family structure in the provision of family planning education. Instead, it defers to parents in the first instance to perform this role and requires states to provide assistance to parents in this regard. The CRC does not however, tolerate the absolute authority of parents over the sexuality of an adolescent and demands that states must ensure the provision of access to reproductive health information and confidential medical care for the purpose of receiving contraceptive advice and if requested services, to a young person of sufficient maturity and understanding. To do otherwise is to deny adolescents access to the information necessary for them to develop their understanding of how to prevent unwanted pregnancies and the transmission of sexually transmitted diseases.[106] Although the approach required under the CRC will unsettle the values or beliefs of certain elements of the interpretative community, especially some religious groups, this is not a sufficient basis on which to refrain from measures which are necessary to ensure the effective implementation of the right to health.

---

[103] See, eg, HRC, *KNLH v Peru*, UN Doc CCPR/C/85/D/1153/2003/Rev.1 (14 August 2006) 3 (decision of the Human Rights Committee in which it was held that the refusal to allow a 17-year-old girl an abortion in circumstances where the foetus was anencephalic and the pregnancy seriously threatened the physical and mental health of the mother and would thus have been lawful under domestic law, was a violation of the mother's rights to non-discrimination, respect for private life, and protection against inhuman and degrading treatment under arts 2, 17 and 7 respectively of the ICCPR).

[104] See Philip Alston, 'The Unborn Child and Abortion under the Draft Convention on the Rights of the Child' (1990) 12 Hum Rts Q 156, 178. The availability of abortion under international law is discussed in more detail below.

[105] CRC Committee, *General Comment No 4* (n 59) para 31; CO CRC Romania, UN Doc CRC/C/15/Add199, para 47(b).

[106] Under the CRC, the fact that adolescents may not choose to act on this information or indeed use this information to engage in sexual relations because they are aware of how to prevent its unintended consequences is irrelevant. The primary concern is to ensure that adolescents have sufficient information in relation to their sexuality. See G McGee and F Burg, 'When Paternalism Runs Amok' (1996) 15 Pol & Life Sci 308 (discussing the notion of adolescent sexuality as power and the need for the provision of information to ensure the responsible exercise of that power and the consequent irresponsibility of parents who refuse to provide such information).

B Freedom from medical experimentation

With respect to the issue of medical experimentation, there is nothing in the drafting history of the ICESCR to suggest that this issue was given any consideration within the context of the right to health. In contrast, it was the subject of discussion during the later stages of the drafting of the CRC, but a proposal to include a provision on medical experimentation as part of the right to health was ultimately rejected due to a lack of consensus on an appropriate formulation. Moreover, it was acknowledged at the time that this issue would be addressed, albeit by way of implication, in several other provisions of the CRC.[107] And the CRC Committee has also noted that where children are involved in research then:

> In line with the child's evolving capacities, consent of the child should be sought and consent may be sought from parents or guardians if necessary, but in all cases consent must be based on full disclosure of the risks and benefits of research to the child.[108]

Such an approach tends to support the view that it is unnecessary and arguably inappropriate to include freedom from medical experimentation as an element of the right to health. The drafters of the CRC gave consideration to this issue and decided that other rights under the CRC offered more appropriate normative standards, such as the right to respect for private life and the prohibition against inhuman and degrading treatment, by which to resolve the issue of when medical experimentation involving children would be permissible. Thus, for the purposes of this analysis, it is not considered necessary to examine what international law has to say with respect to the issue of medical experimentation in the context of the right to health beyond the requirement that it must be consensual.

C Freedom from non-consensual medical treatment

1 A problematic inclusion

The inclusion of freedom from non-consensual medical treatment by the ESC Committee within the meaning of the right to health is also problematic. This issue was discussed during the drafting of the ICESCR in the context of a proposal to provide safeguards against compulsory medical treatment. But it was ultimately rejected on the grounds that: (a) it did not deal adequately with the complex question of consent to medical treatment, and (b) this issue was addressed by the limitation provision under article 5 of the ICESCR and the prohibition against inhuman and degrading treatment under article 7 of the ICCPR.[109] Thus, it is arguable that the issue of non-consensual medical treatment should be addressed within the context of

---

[107] *Report of the Working Group on a Draft Convention on the Rights of the Child*, UN Doc E/CN.4/1989/48 (2 March 1989) paras 416–31. These provisions would include art 3 (the best interests principle); art 36 (protection against exploitation); and art 37 (the prohibition against torture and cruel, inhuman, and degrading treatment).
[108] CRC Committee, *General Comment No 3* (n 81) para 29.
[109] UN General Assembly, Official Records, Agenda Item 31 (n 10) 21 para 155.

Meaning of the Highest Attainable Standard of Health 145

these articles as opposed to the right to health. Indeed, this position is more consistent with the interpretative methodology adopted in this analysis which seeks to avoid the unnecessary inflation of the right to health.

At the same time, it would be odd if a text on the right to health were to completely exclude any discussion of the issue of consent. Given that the right to health in international law includes a right to receive medical care, a clear and practical understanding of this right demands that international law must also offer a process to ensure that the rights of an individual are respected in the provision of such care. Moreover, it is arguable that the obligations to respect and protect the right to health—which are discussed in detail in Chapter 5 and require that states protect individuals against threats to health from state actors or non-state actors— imposes an obligation to protect an individual against non-consensual medical treatment (or experimentation). Thus, an examination of the issue of consent in this chapter is deemed appropriate.[110]

2 A complex issue

The first point to make in this discussion is that the blanket prohibition on non-consensual medical treatment adopted by the ESC Committee, does not capture the complex issues associated with the provision of medical care and consent. Such a blanket approach lacks clarity, practicality, and coherence in its reasoning. Indeed, it was actually noted during the drafting of the right to health, there will be many occasions in which medical treatment should be given *without* a patient's consent, such as, for example, when a patient is unconscious or incapable of giving consent for some other reason.[111] Domestic legal systems have developed a sophisticated body of law to deal with this issue, whether in the context of rights such as privacy or laws relating to assault, which need not be repeated here. International guidelines and regulations have also stressed the importance of informed consent in medical contexts[112] and more recently the Special Rapporteur on the Right to Health has

---

[110] See World Medical Association *Declaration of Helsinki: Ethical Principles for Research Dealing with Human Subjects* (18th WMA General Assembly, Helsinki, Finland, June 1964), as amended most recently by the 59th WMA General Assembly, Seoul, October 2008; *Report of the Special Rapporteur on the Right to Health to the General Assembly 2009* (n 54) paras 35–42 (discussing the implications of a rights-based approach to medical research).

[111] ibid. Such circumstances would extend to compulsory treatment orders for persons who are deemed to be medically incompetent due to a mental illness and thus unable to consent to, or refuse, medical treatment. This is a complex area of law and beyond the scope of this chapter. Thus is it sufficient to make three observations. First, a compulsory treatment order is an interference with not only the right to health but also the right to privacy (and potentially the prohibition against cruel, inhuman, and degrading treatment). Second, the state bears the burden of establishing on the balance of probabilities that this interference was necessary to a legitimate aim (for example, protecting the health of the individual subject to the order or the general public). Third, the measures undertaken to achieve this aim were necessary and proportionate. This will require evidence to support the need for the order (the rational connection test). The state will also be required to prove that there was no other measure reasonably available that could have achieved the purpose for which the compulsory treatment order was made (the minimal impairment test). See Chapter 5.

[112] See, eg, OHCHR and UNAIDS, *International Guidelines on HIV/AIDS and Human Rights* (UNAIDS, 2006).

examined the consequences of a rights-based approach to the issue of consent in which he stressed the need to:

- address structural inequalities that impact on a person's relationship with a health care provider;
- provide services to support adequate comprehension and decision making;
- ensure that health information is of the highest quality, freely available, and accessible in light of differing physical, mental, social, or cultural needs.[113]

The focus of this discussion, however, will be on two areas that have been the subject of significant attention in international law—non-consensual medical treatment of children and non-consensual sterilization of women and girls with intellectual disabilities.

(a) Non-consensual medical treatment of children

Developing an appropriate test The idea that the right to health incorporates a freedom from non-consensual medical treatment, is a derivative of the well-established principle that the right to respect for private life, which includes bodily integrity, requires informed consent before any medical procedure can be performed lawfully. Consent must be provided by a person who is competent and authorized to do so, a test for which has been described as 'the search for the holy grail'[114]—an elusive test for adults made even more complex in the case of children because of their evolving capacities.[115] In formulating a response to this dilemma with respect to children, the requirement of internal system coherence requires recourse to those other provisions of the CRC, which are able to assist in the development of a model by which to address this issue.

In the first instance, article 18 of the CRC entrusts a child's parents or legal guardians with the primary responsibility for the care of a child. As a corollary, parents or guardians will *prima facie* have the authority and capacity to provide informed consent albeit by way of proxy,[116] for any medical procedures necessary to ensure the health of a child in their care. This authority to consent on behalf of a

---

[113] *Report of the Special Rapporteur on the Right to Health to the General Assembly 2009* (n 54) para 23. See also *Report of the Special Rapporteur on the Right to Health to the General Assembly 2010*, UN Doc A/65/255 (6 August 2010) para 32 (stressing that 'requirements of informed consent must be observed in administering any treatment for drug dependence—including the right to refuse drug dependence').

[114] L Roth, A Meisel and C Lidz, 'Tests of Competency to Consent to Treatment' (1977) 134 Am J Psych 279, 283.

[115] The literature with respect to this issue is vast. See, eg, Michael Freeman, *Children, Medicine and the Law* (Ashgate Publishing, 2005) (containing a comprehensive collection of essays that examine issues related to competency, participation, autonomy, and best interests in the context of the provision of medical care); E Didcock, 'Issues of Consent and Competency in Children and Young People' (2006) 16 Current Paediatrics 91 (examining studies on competency and clinical issues encountered in the determination of consent in paediatric matters); Jane Fortin, *Children's Rights and the Developing Law* (3rd edn, CUP, 2009) ch 5.

[116] See American Academy of Pediatrics, Committee on Bioethics, 'Informed Consent, Parental Permission and Assent in Pediatric Practice' (1995) 95 Pediatrics 314, 315 (considers the notion of proxy consent to be problematic with respect to children because it implies a personal decision that is not in fact being exercised by a child and prefers to use the phrase informed permission).

child is subject to two overriding qualifications. First, the principle of the evolving capacities of the child under article 5 of the CRC, when combined with the right to have a child's views given due weight in accordance with the child's age and level of maturity under article 12, envisions the possibility that a certain point, a child will be competent to consent to medical treatment irrespective of the views of his or her parents. Thus, as the Special Rapporteur has argued, 'health care providers should strive to postpone non-emergency invasive and irreversible interventions until the child is sufficiently mature to provide informed consent' such as intersex genital surgery.[117] Second, in those circumstances where a child has not attained this capacity and the procedure cannot be deferred, the parents acting on behalf of the child must ensure that, consistent with article 18, the child's best interests are their basic concern.

It is important to note that even in circumstances where a child cannot consent to a medical procedure for lack of competency, commentators have stressed the need to ensure that the child is still adequately informed about the treatment 'out of respect for the child, to answer questions and help the child know what to expect, reduce anxiety, warn about risks, prevent misunderstanding or resentment, promote confidence and courage, increase compliance and generally help the child make sense of the experience'.[118] This requirement to provide information and involve a child in the decision-making process related to his or her health care, which is consistent with articles 13 and 12 of the CRC, seeks to empower children to the extent of their capacity and competency. It aims to encourage the child to understand and accept the proposed care to the extent that he or she is capable, a process sometimes referred to as 'assent'.[119]

Thus, the model advanced under the CRC for decision making in medical proceedings involving children is characterized by three distinct concepts:

1. Informed consent by parents in circumstances where a child lacks competency (and it is inappropriate to defer the intervention until a child is competent).
2. Assent by a child consistent with the level of his or her evolving capacities.
3. Informed consent by a child who is determined to be competent.[120]

These three concepts are reflected in the CRC Committee's General Comment No 4 on Adolescent Health, which provides that, with respect to adolescents:

---

[117] *Report of the Special Rapporteur on the Right to Health to the General Assembly 2009* (n 54) para 49. See also Columbian Constitutional Court Judgment No SU-337/99 (1999) and Judgment No T-551/99 (1999) (ruling that parental consent was invalid and developed new rules after careful consideration of the CRC to ensure that children's best interests rather than parental anxiety informed intersex surgery).

[118] Priscilla Alderson, *Children's Consent to Surgery* (Open University Press, 1993), cited in Didcock (n 115) 92. See also L Schlam and J Wood, 'Informed Consent to the Medical Treatment of Minors: Law and Practice' (2000) 10 Health Matrix 141, 171–2 (stressing the need to involve children in the decision-making process even if incapable of providing informed consent).

[119] American Academy of Pediatrics, Committee on Bioethics, 'Informed Consent' (n 116) 316.

[120] These are also the central features of the model advanced by the American Academy of Pediatrics, Committee on Bioethics: ibid 317.

Before parents give their consent, adolescents need to have a chance to express their views freely and their views should be given due weight, in accordance with article 12 of the Convention. However, if the adolescent is of sufficient maturity, informed consent shall be obtained from the adolescent her/himself, while informing the parents if that is in the 'best interests of the child'.[121]

Assessing the capacity of children to consent It is important to note that the CRC Committee's comment does not outline a test to determine whether a child is of 'sufficient maturity' to provide informed consent. A review of the empirical data tends to suggest that children around the age of 14 or older may have 'as well-developed decisional skills as adults for making information health care decisions'[122] and that social context also influences a child's capacity to consent.[123] However, such generalized findings do not address the question of whether an individual child has acquired this level of understanding in the circumstances of a particular case.

National courts have sought to devise appropriate tests to determine the competency of children. In the USA, for example, the Supreme Court has held that persons under 18 have a right to consent to an abortion independent of their parent's wishes where they are 'mature enough and well enough informed' to make such a decision.[124] In the landmark decision of the House of Lords in *Gillick*,[125] which concerned access to contraceptive advice for a girl under the age of 16 without parental consent, it was held by Lord Scarman that where a child has 'a sufficient understanding and intelligence to enable...her to understand fully what is proposed',[126] the consent of her parents is unnecessary. This test, which has been adopted in other jurisdictions,[127] is, as Melinda Jones notes, 'functional rather than status based. It is not determined by the specific age of the child, but by the competency of the particular individual at the time of asserting the right'.[128] Such a

---

[121] CRC Committee, *General Comment No 4* (n 59) para 32.
[122] American Academy of Pediatrics, Committee on Bioethics, 'Informed Consent' (n 116) 317. See also L Weithorn and S Campbell, 'The Competency of Children and Adolescents to Make Informed Treatment Decisions' (1982) 53 Child Dev 1589; Priscilla Alderson, 'Everyday and Medical Life Choices: Decision Making among 8 to 15 Year Old School Students' (1992) 18 Child 81.
[123] See, eg, Priscilla Alderson, 'In the Genes or in the Stars? Children's Competence to Consent' (1992) 18 J Med Ethics 119.
[124] *Bellotti v Baird*, 443 US 622, 643 (1979) (SC, USA). See also *City of Akron v Akron Center for Reproductive Health Inc*, 462 US 416, 239–40 (1983) (SC, USA) (holding that children under 15 could be sufficiently mature to consent to an abortion). Although the Supreme Court confined its decision to young pregnant women because of 'the unique nature of the abortion decision' (642), the mature minor doctrine has been extended to other forms of medical procedure by US State Supreme Court. See Schlam and Wood (n 118); J Costello, 'The Trouble is They're Growing, the Trouble is They're Grown: Therapeutic Jurisprudence and Adolescents' Participation in Mental Health Care Decisions' (2003) 29 Ohio NUL Rev 607.
[125] *Gillick* (n 84).
[126] ibid 189 (Lord Scarman). Lord Fraser proposed that '[p]rovided the patient, whether a boy or a girl, is capable of understanding what is proposed and of expressing his or her own wishes, [there is] no good reason for holding that he or she lacks the capacity to express them validly and effectively and to authorise the medical man to make the examination or give the treatment which he advises': ibid 169.
[127] See, eg, the decision of the High Court of Australia in *Secretary, Department of Health and Community Services v JWB and SMB (Marion's Case)* (1992) 175 CLR 218 (HC, Aust).
[128] Melinda Jones, 'Adolescent Gender Identity and the Courts' (2005) 13 Intl J Child Rts 121, 121.

model, which is consistent with the notion of evolving capacities under the CRC,[129] requires a medical practitioner to assess the competency of a child and where satisfied that competency exists, maintain appropriate standards of confidentiality and privacy as required in any doctor–client relationship.

Significantly, in cases that involve major, invasive, non-therapeutic, and non-reversible medical interventions, such as gender reassignment procedures,[130] domestic courts have indicated that the decision with respect to competency should be made by a court rather than a medical practitioner. Such a requirement recognizes the potential conflict of interest that may arise between a child and his or her parents and ensures that an independent third party is able to assess the evidence to determine whether a particular procedure is in the best interests of a child. At the same time courts have recognized the limits of the therapeutic/non-therapeutic distinction[131] and commentators have criticized its use as a vague standard by which to assess whether a court should intervene in a potential medical procedure for a child or the parents and medical professionals should have sole responsibility for this decision.[132] It appears to be accepted, however, that there are occasions when the immediate health of the child is so threatened that a requirement to seek Court authorization for medical treatment is not appropriate.

Ultimately, the question that tends to underlie these judicial tests 'is whether the young person is able to understand and appreciate the proposed treatment and the medical consequences of undergoing or not undergoing treatment'.[133] Such an approach is problematic because of its focus on a child's understanding of medicine and the medicalization of a child's best interests to the extent that it prioritizes a child's physical health over his or her emotional health. It therefore encourages the 'treatment of the physical to the possible detriment of the emotional and psychological'.[134] Moreover, it is inconsistent with the best interests model advanced under the CRC, which requires consideration of the evolving capacities of children and their right to participate in all decisions that affect them—a model which anticipates that, at a certain point, 'a child's decisions should be immutably determinative of the treatment they receive'.[135] Brazier and Bridge have therefore suggested that 'the law

---

[129] It is important to note that the CRC Committee in its *General Comment No 4* on adolescent health suggested that states adopt laws or regulations with respect to the issue of informed consent which 'should stipulate an age for this process or refer to the evolving capacity of the child': CRC Committee, *General Comment No 4* (n 59) para 33. Such an approach, however, is arguably inconsistent with the provisions of the CRC, which favours a capacity-based rather than status-based approach to this issue.

[130] See, eg, *Re Alex* (2004) 180 FLR 89 (Nicholson CJ) (FamCt, Aust) (court authorization required before treatment for gender reassignment could commence); K Haas, 'Who Will Make Room for the Intersexed?' (2004) 30 AJLM 41 (examining decisions of the Columbian Constitutional Court to demand the consent of a child to any gender reconstruction surgery).

[131] See, eg, *Marion's Case* (n 127) 250 ('We hesitate to use the expression . . . because of its uncertainty. But it is necessary to make the distinction, however unclear the dividing line may be').

[132] Jones (n 128) 133–4 (conceding the utility of such a test with respect to the potential sterilization of children with intellectual disabilities but arguing that it is of limited relevance in other cases such as gender reassignment).

[133] Jamie Potter, 'Rewriting the Competency Rules for Children: Full Recognition of the Young Person as Rights Bearer' (2006) 14 JLM 64, 72.

[134] ibid.   [135] ibid 69.

should not pretend to apply a "functional test" of autonomy to every patient when younger patients are in fact subjected to an "outcome" test'.[136] The test of *Gillick* competency has also been criticized because of its insistence that children demonstrate a higher standard of understanding—*full understanding* as opposed to *understanding*—with respect to medical procedures than adults.[137] Indeed, it has been suggested that such a test is 'virtually impossible to fulfill'.[138] Moreover, the requirement of the CRC Committee that an adolescent demonstrate 'sufficient maturity' suggests that full understanding is an unnecessarily high threshold.

Importantly, professional bodies have developed tests and guidelines by which to assess competency of adolescents, which tend to mitigate some of the limitations associated with existing judicial models. The British Medical Association and Law Society, for example, have recommended that medical practitioners consider a young person's:

- ability to understand there is a choice and that choices have consequences;
- willingness and ability to make a choice (including the option that someone else makes treatment decisions);
- understanding of the nature and purpose of the proposed procedure;
- understanding of the alternatives to the procedure and risks attached to them and the consequences of no treatment; and
- freedom from pressure.[139]

Such an approach tends to reduce the emphasis placed on the medicalization of a child's best interests by placing greater emphasis on a child's understanding of not just the procedure and its attendant consequences, but also the nature of his or her choice and its implications. It also obviates the need for a 'full' understanding in preference for an understanding as to nature of process and procedure—an additional feature, which is not only practical, but tends to offer an approach that is more compatible with the principles of the CRC.

Neither the CRC nor CRC Committee have sought to dictate the model by which a state must determine whether a child possesses sufficient maturity to consent to a medical procedure. This consideration is ultimately a matter within the margin of appreciation accorded to states. However, the preceding discussion does illustrate some of the underlying features that states should seek to include *and* omit from their preferred model. Moreover, it is important to stress that even in those circumstances where an adolescent is found to be competent to consent to a medical procedure irrespective of his or parent's wishes, commentators have stressed that it remains

---

[136] M Brazier and C Bridge, 'Coercion or Caring: Analysing Adolescent Autonomy' (1996) 16 LS 84, 109.
[137] See, eg, A Grubb, 'Refusal of Treatment (Child): Competence' (1999) 7 Med L Rev 58, 60; M Enright, '"Mature" Minors and the Medical Law; Safety First?' [2003] VII Cork OL Rev 1.
[138] Potter (n 133) 69.
[139] British Medical Association and The Law Society, *Assessment of Mental Capacity* (1st edn, BMA, 1995).

good practice to encourage competent children to involve their parents in decision making unless this is contrary to the child's best interests.[140]

The right of a child to refuse life saving medical treatment One of the more contentious issues within the broader interpretative community concerning children's competency and medical procedures is the question of whether they have the right to refuse medical treatment. At the domestic level, commentators have highlighted, and in many cases criticized, the tendency of courts to deny the competency of a child in any circumstances which involve an attempt to refuse life saving medical treatment.[141] From the perspective of the CRC and the obligations of states under international law, although the CRC Committee has not commented on this issue in detail, it was addressed in its concluding observations for the Netherlands, a state which extends the possibility of voluntary euthanasia to children aged 12 or older provided parental consent is obtained where the child is under 16. Importantly the CRC Committee did not condemn this regime as being inconsistent with the right to heath under article 24 or the right to life under article 6. Instead, it expressed concern 'about the monitoring of such requests because controls are exercised after the request has been fulfilled and because some cases are not reported by doctors'.[142] It therefore recommended that the state party:

(a) Frequently evaluate, and if necessary revise, the regulations and procedures in the Netherlands with respect to the termination of life on request in order to ensure that children, including newborn infants with severe abnormalities, enjoy special protection and that the regulations and procedures are in conformity with article 6 of the Convention;
(b) Take all necessary measures to strengthen control of the practice and prevent non-reporting and to ensure that the mental and psychological status of the child and parents or guardians requesting termination are taken into consideration when determining whether to grant the request; . . . [143]

Such comments are significant to the extent that they indicate that the right to the highest attainable standard of health, when combined with the right to life and best interests principle, do not mandate that a state must take all necessary measures to prolong and maintain a child's life and secure his or her highest attainable standard of health, when this is inconsistent with the wishes of that child. Moreover, if a child

---

[140] See Didcock (n 115) 92; L Ross, 'Health Care Decision Making by Children: Is It in Their Best Interests?' (1997) 27 Hastings Center Report 41 (arguing that the empowerment of competent adolescents to consent and refuse medical treatment in consultation with health professionals is misguided because inter alia it undermines the role of the family as the locus of decision making).
[141] See, eg, Michael Freeman, 'Rethinking *Gillick*' (2005) 13 Intl J Child Rts 201; M Derish and K Heuvel, 'Mature Minors Should Have the Right to Refuse Life Sustaining Medical Treatment' (2000) 28 JL Med & Ethics 109; American Academy of Pediatrics, Committee on Bioethics, 'Guidelines on Forgoing Life Sustaining Medical Treatment' (1994) 93 Pediatrics 532, 535; S Leiken, 'A Proposal concerning Decisions to Forgo Life Sustaining Treatment for Young People' (1989) 115 J Pediatrics 17, 18.
[142] CO CRC The Netherlands, UN Doc CRC/C/15/Add227, para 33.
[143] ibid para 34 (a) and (b). See also the recommendations of the Human Rights Committee in HRC, *Consideration of Reports Submitted by States Parties under Article 40 of the Covenant: Concluding Observations of the Human Rights Committee*, UN Doc CCPR/CO/72/NET (27 August 2001) para 5.

can consent to active euthanasia it follows that a refusal to accept life saving treatment from a competent adolescent is compatible with the provisions of the CRC. At the same time, it is premature to invoke the comments and recommendations of the CRC Committee in its concluding observations for the Netherlands to assert that the right to health, in conjunction with other articles under the CRC, demands that a child be given not only a right to refuse medical treatment but also a right to active euthanasia. (A similar argument would apply with respect to adults.) On the contrary, it is more appropriate that, given the complex and controversial nature of this issue within the interpretative community, the resolution of this issue should rest within the margin of appreciation granted to states.

This position is also supported by the divergence of opinion within the broader interpretative community. Jane Fortin, for example has argued that the courts 'can legitimately argue that society has an interest in protecting underage minors, irrespective of competence, from their own dangerous mistakes until they attain the age of majority'.[144] In contrast Lewis has suggested that where an adolescent is able to make a competent choice to refuse life saving treatment, 'respecting such a choice will be difficult but it is preferable to arbitrary discrimination on the basis of age alone'.[145] Brazier and Bridge, however, have suggested that 'society might well adopt a skeptical approach to autonomy' when dealing with children and thus accept the capacity of courts to vitiate their decisions when they are deemed imprudent, albeit by reference to the standards of adults.[146] Each of these approaches could arguably find support within the text of the CRC—which perhaps serves to illustrate the point that with respect to certain issues, there is no absolute normative guidance under international law.

At the same time, there are clear principles that must inform the *process* by which these decisions are taken. This is the point that is emphasized by the CRC Committee in its recommendations for the Netherlands regarding the procedure by which a child requests euthanasia. Moreover, if a state is ultimately going to deny the autonomy of a child and insist upon life saving treatment because it decides to strike the balance in favour of a child's right to life and take measures to secure his or her physical health, it must not be deceptive or misleading in raising an expectation that knowledge and understanding will determine competency and thus provide a right to refuse life saving medical treatment. Such a process only serves to demean and disempower a child who, despite having a significant understanding of his or her condition and the consequences of refusing treatment, must be labeled 'incompetent' and in the process infantilized if the decision to refuse treatment is dishonoured. Thus rather than create the impression that the autonomy of a child is to be respected

---

[144] Fortin (n 115) 134. See also ibid 157 (arguing that the distinction between consent and refusal of treatment is sustainable because doctors only recommend treatment which is necessary and in a child's best interests especially in a context where refusal would lead to death or permanent damage).

[145] P Lewis, 'The Medical Treatment of Children' in J Fionda (ed), *Legal Concepts of Childhood* (Hart Publishing 2001) 151.

[146] Brazier and Bridge (n 136) 109.

and honoured in the decision making process, if a state's preference is to favour the protection of a child's life over respect for determinative individual autonomy, such an approach should be transparent and clearly communicated to a child.

(b) **The involuntary sterilization of women and girls**
The issue of whether, and when, a girl or woman with an intellectual disability should undergo involuntary sterilization for non-life-threatening reasons has been the subject of detailed consideration in domestic courts[147] and the literature.[148] The principal contemporary argument advanced to justify such a procedure is the prevention of an unwanted pregnancy. However, other arguments include: the need to address the inconvenience, or in some cases distress, associated with menstrual bleeding; the distress of a caregiver over expressions of a young person's sexuality; and the need to protect young girls against sexual exploitation and abuse.[149] With young boys, a request for sterilization is usually made for the purpose of decreasing sexual aggressiveness.

---

[147] See, eg, *Marion's Case* (n 127) (holding that non-therapeutic sterilization of children is only lawful where authorized by court and necessary to secure child's best interests); *Re Marion (No 2)* (1992) 17 FamLR 336 (FamCt, Aust) (listing factors to be considered when determining whether to authorize sterilization); *P v P* (1994) 181 CLR 583 (HC, Aust) (holding that sterilization of a child can be authorized by courts in certain circumstances); *Re Eve* [1986] 2 SCR 388 (SC, Canada) (holding that non-therapeutic sterilization should never be authorized under the *parens patriae* jurisdiction of the court); *Re B (a Minor)* [1988] 1 AC 199 (HL, UK) (rejecting *Eve* and prepared to authorize the sterilization of a child where necessary to secure the child's best interests).

[148] See, eg, American Academy of Pediatrics, Committee on Bioethics, 'Sterilization of Minors with Developmental Disabilities' (1999) 104 Pediatrics 337; K Savell, 'Sex and the Sacred: Sterilization and Bodily Integrity in English and Canadian Law' (2004) 49 McGill LJ 1093; D Diekema, 'Involuntary Sterilisation of Persons with Mental Retardation: An Ethical Analysis' (2003) 9 Ment Retard Dev Disabil Res Rev 21; L Dowse and C Frohmader, *Moving Forward: Sterilisation and Reproductive Health of Women and Girls with Disabilities* (Women with Disabilities Australia 2001); D Newman, 'An Examination of Saskatchewan Law on the Sterilisation of Persons with Mental Disabilities' (1999) 62 Sask L Rev 329; A Giami, 'Sterilisation and Sexuality in the Mentally Handicapped' (1998) 13 Eur Psych 113; A George, 'Sterilisation and Intellectually Disabled Children: *In the Matter of P & P*' (1996) 18 Syd LR 218; Melinda Jones and LeeAnn Marks, 'The Dynamic Developmental Model of the Rights of the Child: A Feminist Approach to Rights and Sterilisation' (1994) 2 Intl J Child Rts 265; G Applebaum and G Roberts, 'Sterilization and a Mentally Handicapped Minor: Providing Consent for One Who Cannot' (1994) 3 Cam QH Ethics 209; Western Australia Law Reform Commission, 'Report on Consent to the Sterilisation of Minors' (Project No 77 Part II, October 1994); Australian Family Law Council, *Sterilisation and Other Medical Procedures on Children—A Report to the Attorney General* (Australian Government Publishing Service 1994); K Petersen, 'The Family v the Family Court: Sterilisation Issues' (1992) 16 Aus J Pub Health 196.

[149] Historically, eugenics were used to legally sanction and justify the involuntary sterilization of a range of women and girls including those with intellectual difficulties on the basis that this was necessary to improve the 'quality' of the human species. See, eg, *Buck v Bell*, 274 US 200 (1927) (SC, USA); S Hyatt, 'A Shared History of Shame: Sweden's Four Decade Policy of Forced Sterilisation and the Eugenics Movement in the United States' (1998) 8 Ind Intl & Com LR 475. Such an approach is no longer favoured within contemporary medical or social discourse and has been struck down by domestic courts (see, eg, *Skinner v Oklahoma*, 316 US 535 (1942) (SC, USA)) and in any event would have no place under international law.

International law adopts a strong position with respect to the non-consensual sterilization of a child or adult with an intellectual disability.[150] Article 23(1)(c) of the CRPD, which is the right to respect for home and family, provides that '[p]ersons with disabilities, including children, retain their fertility on an equal basis with others'.[151] The CEDAW Committee, in its recommendation on the right to health and violence against women, recommended that states parties 'should not permit forms of coercion, such as non-consensual sterilization'[152] because it 'adversely affects women's physical and mental health and infringes the right of women to decide the number and spacing of their children'.[153] The ESC and the CERD Committees have also condemned this practice.[154] So too has the CRC Committee as reflected in its concluding observations for Australia, where it recommended that Australia:

Prohibit the sterilisation of children, with or without disabilities and promote and implement other measures or prevention of unwanted pregnancies eg: injection of contraceptives where appropriate.[155]

In none of these recommendations, however, have the human rights treaty monitoring bodies indicated whether they favour an absolution prohibition on non-consensual sterilization or merely a presumption against this practice. The tenor of their comments tends to imply a preference for an absolute prohibition, but it is unclear whether international law is prepared to accommodate non-consensual sterilization in certain circumstances.

The views with respect to this issue among members of the relevant interpretative community vary. The American Academy of Pediatrics, for example, certainly condemns the practice and has suggested that 'difficulties with menstrual hygiene

---

[150] It also prohibits the non-consensual sterilization of a woman *without* an intellectual disability. See CEDAW Committee, *Szijjarto v Hungary*, Communication No 4/2004, UN Doc CEDAW/C/36/D/4/2004 (14 August 2006) (CEDAW committee held that the procedure whereby a pregnant woman on an operating table was requested to give consent to sterilization in a language she did not understand was a violation of her right to appropriate health care services as well as her right to decide freely on the number and spacing of her children).

[151] For a general discussion of involuntary and forced treatment of persons with a disability see *Progress of Efforts to Ensure the Full Recognition and Enjoyment of the Human Rights of Persons with Disabilities: Report of the Secretary General*, UN Doc A/58/181 (24 July 2003) paras 34–42; *Principles for the Protection of Persons with Mental Illness and for the Improvement of Mental Health Care*, UN GA Res 46/119, UN Doc A/Res/46/119 (17 December 1991) annex. However, neither of these documents address this issue of involuntary sterilization directly.

[152] CEDAW Committee, *General Recommendation No 24* (n 74) ch 1, para 22.

[153] CEDAW Committee, *General Recommendation No 19: Violence against Women*, UN Doc A/47/38 (1992) 1, para 22.

[154] ESC Committee, *General Comment No 5* (n 30) para 31; CO CERD, UN Doc A/59/18, 70, para 389. See also CEDAW Committee, *General Recommendation 19* (n 153) 1, para 22 ('States Parties should not permit forms of coercion, such as non-consensual sterilization...'). Interestingly and perhaps curiously, the CEDAW Committee makes no reference to the involuntary sterilization of women (including girls) with disabilities in its recommendations regarding women with disabilities: CEDAW Committee, *Recommendation No 18: Disabled Women*, UN Doc A/46/38 (1991), contained in *Compilation of General Comments and General Recommendations adopted by Human Rights Treaty Bodies*, UN Doc HR1/GEN/1/Rev.1 (12 May 2004) 233.

[155] CO CRC Australia, UN Doc CRC/C/15/Add268, para 46(e).

frequently, but not always, improve with developmentally appropriate educational programs'; that the 'distress of a caregiver over expressions of sexuality do not justify consideration of sterilisation'; that sterilization will not protect young girls against sexual exploitation or the transmission of sexually transmitted diseases; and that there is 'little valid evidence that surgical castration' will decrease sexual aggressiveness in males.[156] Even with respect to the prevention of pregnancy, less permanent means may be available including 'barrier methods, pills, injections, intrauterine devices or subdermal implants'.[157] Moreover, the Academy suggests that 'as methods of contraception that provide alternatives to sterilisation increase the available options, permanent sterilisation becomes increasingly difficult to justify'.[158]

However, the Academy refrains from recommending an absolute prohibition on this practice and concedes that the appropriateness of alternatives will depend 'on the functional abilities of the person with [the] developmental disability and the reactions of the patient and the caregivers to nonsurgical methods to prevent pregnancy'.[159] As such, it adopts a more flexible and arguably more practical approach than the absolutist position implied in the work of the human rights treaty monitoring bodies. The Academy's approach also suggests that 'third parties have rightful interests in these matters when it is clear that the persons with disabilities who are involved can assume little or no responsibility for their own care during pregnancy or for their children after birth.'[160] Thus, while the Academy favours a presumption against non-consensual sterilization, it does not discount the possibility that it may be appropriate in exceptional circumstances where other preventative measures are not available, or appropriate, and the procedure is necessary to secure the best interests of the child.

Other commentators have adopted a similar approach to the issue[161] as have some domestic courts. In Australia, for example, the High Court held in *Marion's Case*[162] that involuntary non-therapeutic sterilization[163] of a child with an intellectual disability, as a measure of last resort, would only be lawful if authorization was provided by an independent court or tribunal and was necessary to secure the best interests of the child in circumstances where alternative and less invasive measures had failed or it was certain that no other procedure would work.[164] In this context,

---

[156] American Academy of Pediatrics Committee on Bioethics, 'Sterilization of Minors' (n 148) 339.
[157] ibid.   [158] ibid 338.   [159] ibid 339.   [160] ibid 338.
[161] See, eg, Diekema (n 148) (conceding that the interests of other persons may be important but only when they correspond to the interests of the person with the intellectual disability); Western Australia Law Reform Commission (n 148); Australian Family Law Council (n 148); S Brady, J Briton, and S Grover, *The Sterilisation of Girls and Young Women in Australia: Issues and Progress* (Australian Human Rights and Equal Opportunity Commission, 2001).
[162] *Marion's Case* (n 127).
[163] For a critique of the therapeutic/non-therapeutic distinction see Brady, Briton, and Grover (n 161); Western Australia Law Reform Commission (n 148) 93–4; Australian Family Law Council (n 148) 44–5.
[164] When the matter was remitted to the Family Court of Australia for an application of the principles to the facts of the case, the Family Court articulated the following set of factors to guide the determination of a child's best interests: the particular condition of the child who requires the treatment; the nature of the proposed treatment; the reasons for the proposed treatment; the available alternative treatments; the desirability and effect of authorizing the proposed treatment rather than the available alternatives; the

the involuntary sterilization of a girl (or woman) is considered to be 'an act done for her, rather than to her; an act of protection rather than violation'.[165] The non-consensual procedure is seen as a humane solution to a complex problem that relieves a child (or adult woman) from the 'discomforts, traumas and intrusions' that she would experience if she were to become pregnant.[166]

In contrast, the Canadian Supreme Court in *Re Eve*[167] refused to invoke its *parens patriae* jurisdiction to authorize a non-therapeutic involuntary sterilization of a young woman with an intellectual disability. The Court noted evidence that '[s]ex and parenthood hold the same significance for [learning disabled people] as for other people and ... that the removal of an individual's procreative powers is a matter of major importance and that no amount of reforming zeal can remove the significance of sterilisation and its effect on the individual psyche.'[168] Moreover, it added that '[s]tudies conclude that mentally incompetent parents show as much fondness and concern for their children as other people' and while such parents 'may have difficulty coping with the financial burdens involved ... it is a social problem ... that is not limited to incompetents'.[169]

The Canadian Supreme Court was also unswayed by claims that such a procedure could ever be necessary to secure the best interests of a person with an intellectual disability:

The grave intrusion on a person's rights and the certain physical damage that ensues from non-therapeutic sterilisation without consent, when compared to the highly questionable advantages that can result from it, have persuaded me that it can never safely be determined that such a procedure is for the benefit of that person.[170]

The decision of the Canadian Supreme Court has been described as a rejection of 'welfarist discourses that declared Eve to be better off sterilised in favour of a rights based approach that prohibited non-consensual surgical sterilisation as an infringement of Eve's bodily integrity'.[171] From the perspective of this analysis, the careful consideration of the issues allowed the Canadian Supreme Court to achieve a coherence in its reasoning that the recommendations of the human rights treaty monitoring bodies lack. It is based on an examination of the available evidence to determine how best to ensure the effective enjoyment of the rights of a girl or woman with an intellectual disability. Such an approach enhances its persuasiveness and

---

physical effects on the child and the psychological and social implications for the child of both authorizing the proposed treatment and not authorizing the treatment; the nature and degree of any risk to the child of either authorizing or not authorizing the proposed treatment; and any views expressed by the parents, other carers, or the child about the proposed treatment and the alternative: *Re Marion (No 2)* (n 147) (ironically the sterilization of Marion was ultimately justified on therapeutic grounds, namely that the procedure was necessary to minimize the potential for further neurological damage resulting from epilepsy).

[165] Savell (n 148) 1140.   [166] ibid.   [167] *Re Eve* (n 147).
[168] ibid para 80.   [169] ibid para 84.   [170] ibid para 86.   [171] Savell (n 148) 1109.

offers a strong justification for an absolute ban on non-therapeutic involuntary sterilizations.[172]

Although the reasoning adopted by the Canadian Supreme Court was concerned with the scope of the right to physical integrity, it is also relevant to the right to sexual autonomy, which is part of the right to health. Importantly, the Court's approach was also cognizant of, and responsive to, the preferences of disability advocates and the need to ensure that their rights are not compromised by 'speculative judgments about the medical and social benefits of sterilisation'[173] or assumptions about the capacity and sexuality of persons with disabilities,[174] which historically have been labelled as 'abnormal', a 'problem', and 'dangerous'.[175]

It is recognized that there will be resistance to this model among members of the interpretative community, especially some of those parents who care for their daughters within intellectual disabilities. These concerns cannot be dismissed. As noted above by the American Academy of Pediatrics, 'third parties have rightful interests in these matters when it is clear that the persons with disabilities who are involved can assume little or no responsibility for their own care during pregnancy or for their children after birth'.[176] The involuntary sterilization of children and women with intellectual disabilities may offer a practical way to address the concerns of their carers, but it is not principled. Not only does the evidence suggest that many of the concerns held by carers can be addressed by preventive measures, there is also an also an obligation for states to provide additional assistance to parents caring for such children[177]—a point which has been stressed by commentators as significantly

---

[172] The human rights committee bodies have not made a distinction between therapeutic and non-therapeutic sterilization. However, it would be impractical and contrary to the effective enjoyment of the right to health for international law to prohibit non-consensual sterilization of a child or woman where this procedure was necessary to save the life of a woman, or child, or prevent permanent bodily damage in circumstances where the women or child was suffering from, for example, cancer of the uterus or ovaries. It is recognized that this distinction is hotly contested and has been rejected by some domestic courts (see, eg, *Re B (a Minor)* (n 147)) and commentators (see, eg, Family Law Council of Australia (n 148) 44–5; Western Australia Law Reform Commission (n 148) 93–4). However, other commentators such as Brady and Grover have suggested that 'indisputably therapeutic sterilisations are readily identifiable by a simple test which asks for no more than good faith and ordinary prudence: would sterilisation be recommended but for the girl's intellectual disability?': Susan M Brady and Sonia Grover, 'The Sterilisation of Girls and Young Women in Australia: A Legal, Medical and Social Context' (Australian Human Rights and Equal Opportunity Commission December 1997) pt 2 ('The Legal Context of Sterilisation of Children').

[173] Savell (n 148) 1109.

[174] ibid 1141.

[175] See generally ibid 1129–34; Giami (n 148) (examining the social construction of the sexuality of persons with intellectual disabilities and arguing that even the contemporary use of sterilization represents a form of external control on the sexuality of such persons which is still influenced by eugenic thinking).

[176] ibid 338.

[177] See CRC, art 23(2), which provides that 'States Parties recognize the right of the disabled child to special care and shall encourage and ensure the extension, subject to available resources, to the eligible child and those responsible for his or her care, of assistance for which application is made and which is appropriate to the child's condition and to the circumstances of the parents or others caring for the child'. See also ICESCR, art 10 and ICCPR, art 24, which provide that '[t]he widest possible protection and assistance should be accorded to the family', and CRPD, art 23(2), which provides that 'States Parties shall render appropriate assistance to persons with disabilities in the performance of their child-rearing responsibilities'.

mitigating the need for parents to seek sterilization of their children.[178] Thus, on balance a persuasive case can be made to require the prohibition of non-consensual sterilization of girls and women with intellectual disabilities as an element of the right to health in international law.

IV The qualitative nature of the entitlements under the right to health

The preceding discussion sought to assess the legitimacy and meaning of a range of freedoms that the ESC Committee has included within the scope of the right to health in international law. The discussion in this section moves to an examination of the merits and value of the framework adopted by the ESC Committee for mapping out the essential elements of the right to health. This framework is based upon the principles of availability, accessibility, acceptability, and quality.[179] The ESC Committee has not offered a principled basis on which to justify the imputation of these elements into the text of the right to health. However, the justification for this framework is derived from its role as an interpretative tool that contributes to an understanding of the measures required to secure the effective implementation of the right to health and ensure its enjoyment is not illusory. By distilling the nature of the entitlements under the right to health into four essential elements, the ESC Committee is able to assist the interpretative community in understanding the practical measures required to transform an abstract concept such as the right to health into tangible elements which can be claimed by or on behalf of individuals and operationalized by states.[180] Importantly, the ESC Committee has recognized that the precise application of the elements 'will depend on the conditions prevailing in a particular State party'[181] thereby demonstrating a high level of local context sensitivity.

A question remains, however, as to the content and meaning of each of these elements. In answering this question, an emphasis has been placed on the work of the human rights treaty monitoring bodies to provide an illustration, as opposed to a comprehensive account, of what is required to satisfy these elements. It is important to stress that much of their work still remains at a fairly high level of abstraction and states remain free to exercise their margin of appreciation with respect to the

---

[178] See, eg, Brady, Briton, and Grover (n 161) 59.
[179] ESC Committee, *General Comment No 14* (n 11) para 12.
[180] The text of art 24 of the CRC actually includes a requirement that states recognize the right of a child 'to facilities for the treatment of illness and rehabilitation of health' and includes an obligation that states must 'strive to ensure that no child is deprived of his or her right of *access* to such health care services'. Thus art 24 provides an explicit textual affirmation of two of the four elements identified as being essential to the right to health by the ESC Committee. Moreover, the CRC Committee has adopted and endorsed the entire essential elements framework in its *General Comment No 4 on Adolescent Health and Development*: CRC Committee, *General Comment No 4* (n 59) para 41.
[181] ibid.

measures required to satisfy the recommendations of the human rights treaty monitoring bodies. Moreover, an understanding of the measures required for the effective realization of the essential elements of the right to health will be an evolving process that integrates and responds to the interpretative community's understanding of what is required to ensure that the entitlements under the right to health are available, accessible, acceptable, and of appropriate quality.

A Availability

With respect to 'availability', the ESC Committee has explained that this requires a state to take measures to make available '[f]unctioning public health and health care facilities, goods and services, as well as programmes'.[182] Although the precise nature of these services will differ between states, the ESC Committee has indicated that 'they will include...the underlying determinants of health, such as safe and potable drinking water and adequate sanitation facilities, hospitals, clinics and other health-related buildings, trained medical and professional personnel receiving domestically competitive salaries and essential drugs as defined by the WHO Action Programme on Essential Drugs'.[183] This is an expansive and demanding list of services, which remains subject to the progressive nature of a state's obligation to recognize the right to health—the meaning of which is discussed in Chapter 5.

1 Availability of specialist health services

With respect to the issue of availability, article 24(1) of the CRC specifically requires that states must ensure the provision of adequate facilities for the treatment and rehabilitation of children. Moreover, the CRC Committee has drawn attention to the fact that this obligation also requires the provision of specialist health facilities.

---

[182] ESC Committee, *General Comment No 14* (n 11) para 12(a).
[183] ibid. It is important to note that various initiatives have been undertaken to develop an understanding as to the nature and scope of the underlying determinants of health. For example, the World Health Assembly has established the Commission on Social Determinants of Health (CSDH) to examine the social dimensions of health: Commission on Social Determinants of Health <www.who.int/social_determinants/en/> accessed 12 June 2011. See CSDH, *Towards a Conceptual Framework for Analysis and Action on the Social Determinants of Health* (CSDH Discussion Paper No 1, July 2005); CSDH, *Action on the Social Determinants of Health: Learning from Previous Experiences* (CSDH, March 2005). See also R Wilkinson and M Marmot (eds), *Social Determinants of Health: The Solid Facts* (2nd edn, WHO, 2003) (examining the impact and relationship between various factors on health including: social status; stress; experience in early life; social exclusion; work; unemployment; social support; addiction; food; and transport). With respect to children and the social determinants of health care see, eg, S Maggi and others, *Analytic and Strategic Review Paper: International Perspectives on Early Child Development* (HELP, University of British Columbia, December 2005) (prepared for the WHO Commission on the Social Determinants of Health); N Spencer, 'Social, Economic and Political Determinants of Health of Child Health' (2003) 112 Pediatrics 704. See also *Report of the Special Rapporteur on the Right to Health to the General Assembly 2010* (n 113) paras 40–7 (stressing need to ensure availability of essential medicines which is often hampered by restrictive drug regulations). The issue of global access to medicines is discussed in Chapter 9 in the context of the international obligation to cooperate with respect to the realization of the right to health.

In its report for Yemen, for example, it recommended 'that the State party strengthen its efforts in the provision of user-friendly health-care facilities for women (antenatal, maternal and perinatal care)',[184] and 'establish health facilities and programmes for the care of children infected or affected by HIV/AIDS'.[185] And in its report for Croatia, the CRC Committee expressed concern at 'the apparent inadequacy of treatment facilities to deal with drug additions'[186] and recommended that steps be taken to 'enhance the quality of the treatment facilities'.[187]

Similarly, in its concluding observations for Mauritus, the ESC Committee, in response to concerns at the existence of a serious drug problem, recommended that the state party 'improve the availability, accessibility and quality of harm reduction services in particular needle and syringe and opioid substitution therapy with methadone'.[188] It further recommended that Mauritus implement pilot prison needle and syringe exchanges and opioid substitution therapy programmes; remove age barriers to accessing such programmes; develop youth friendly harm reduction services; make hepatitis C treatment freely available to all injecting drug users and consider decriminalization of addicted persons in favour of public-health-based measures such as prescription of buprenorphine.[189] These recommendations, which have been affirmed by the Special Rapporteur on Health,[190] focus on the health of individuals who suffer from drug dependency as opposed to law and order initiatives. But this rights-based approach challenges the dominant approach taken with respect to drug use in many states and is likely to be resisted by many actors within the interpretative community. As such, there is an issue as to whether the ESC Committee and Special Rapporteur have strayed beyond the level of local context sensitivity required for a persuasive account as to the meaning of the right to health. At the same time, their recommendations are evidence based and consistent with the approach advocated by the World Health Organization.[191] Moreover, the implementation of such measures is required to ensure the effective enjoyment of the right to health and as the Special Rapporteur has noted, the goal of the international drug control regime is protection of health. Thus the approach advocated by the ESC Committee and Special Rapporteur with respect to the availability of services for individuals with drug dependency, are both principled and practical.

---

[184] CO CRC Yemen, UN Doc CRC/C/15/Add102, para 25.
[185] ibid.
[186] CO CRC Croatia, UN Doc CRC/C/15/Add243, para 53.
[187] ibid para 54(d).
[188] CO ESC Mauritus, UN Doc E/C.12/MUS/CO/4, para 28.
[189] ibid.
[190] *Report of the Special Rapporteur on the Right to Health to the General Assembly 2010* (n 113) (examining the relationship between the right to health and international drug control and arguing that a rights-based approach must focus on measures to secure the right to health of persons suffering from drug dependency rather than a law and order response).
[191] WHO, *How to Develop and Implement a National Drug Policy* (2nd edn, WHO, 2001).

It is therefore incumbent upon states, subject to available resources, to determine the nature of the health care needs of various cohorts within their jurisdiction—whether they be children, women, indigenous people,[192] non-citizens,[193] persons with disabilities (including persons with mental health issues),[194] homeless persons,[195] or persons with a drug dependency[196]—and make available appropriate facilities to address such needs. Thus, for example, persons with mental illnesses must not be confined to institutional settings if non-institutional settings provide a more effective setting in which to address their health concerns.[197] Importantly, the process of identification, design, construction, and delivery of services to address the health needs of various groups within a state must be based on a collaborative process which engages not just health care providers and medical practitioners but also the intended beneficiaries themselves (or their advocates) to determine both the nature and form that specialist facilities should take.[198]

2 Availability of abortion services

The availability of abortion services is a regular subject of concern in the concluding observations of the human rights treaty monitoring bodies.[199] This has usually arisen in the context of those states where the high level of maternal mortality is linked with

---

[192] See, eg, CO CERD Costa Rica, UN Doc CERD A/57/18 (2002) 21, para 74 (expressing concern at the lack of health care available for indigenous people living in remote communities); CO CERD New Zealand, UN Doc A/57/18 (2002) para 416 (welcoming initiatives in the area of health designed to address the specific needs of Maori, Pacific Island People, and persons from other groups); CO CERD Suriname, UN Doc A/59/18 (2004) 36, para 198 (expressing concern at the lack of health services available to indigenous and tribal peoples).

[193] See, eg, CO CERD Slovenia, UN Doc A/58/18 (2003) 45, para 241 (expressing concern at lack of health care for non-citizens).

[194] See, eg, CO ESC Poland, UN Doc E/C.12/POL/CO/5, para 24 (expressing concern at the lack of mental health services available especially in rural areas); CO ESC Kazakhstan, UN Doc E/C.12/KAZ/CO/1, para 32 (noting the neglect of mental health patients).

[195] See, e.g, CO ESC United Kingdom of Great Britain and Northern Ireland, UN Doc E/2003/22 (2002) 39 para 241 (recommending that the state party ensure homeless persons receive adequate health care).

[196] *Report of the Special Rapporteur on the Right to Health to the General Assembly 2010* (n 113) paras 19–21 (warning that a 'war on drugs' agenda can deter those with drug dependency from accessing services and treatment because of the fear of criminal sanctions and social stigma). See also *International Guidelines on HIV/AIDS and Human Rights* (n 112) 30–1.

[197] See, eg, CO ESC Ireland, UN Doc ICESCR E/2003/22 (2002) 29, para 135.

[198] See, eg, CO ESC Mauritius, UN Doc E/C.12/MUS/CO/4, para 28 (recommending involvement of drug addicts in the design of measures to address their health concerns). See also CRC Committee, *General Comment No 12: The Right of the Child to Be Heard*, UN Doc CRC/C/GC/12 (1 July 2009) (dealing with the nature of the obligation to assure children's right to be heard in relation to all matters that affect them); ESC Committee, *General Comment No 14* (n 11) para 11 (noting that an 'important aspect' of the right to health 'is the participation of the population in all health-related decision-making at the community, national and international levels'); CRPD, art 3(c), which includes the '[f]ull and effective participation and inclusion in society' as one of the general principles of the CRPD.

[199] It has also been a concern of states. See *Report of the International Conference on Population and Development* (n 56) para 8.25 ('major public health concern'); *Report of the Fourth World Conference on Women* (n 56) paras 97, 106 ('grave' and 'major' public health concern').

the criminalization of abortion[200] or a lack of effective measures to ensure women have access to abortion services where they are lawfully available.[201] The treaty bodies have not imposed a demand on states to provide abortion services for all women and girls on request. Such an approach would have no principled basis and would lack both local and global context sensitivity. The drafting history of international instruments, such as the CRC, indicates that a consensus position was never going to be reached on the nature of the obligation of states to make abortions available under international law. As a consequence it was decided that this matter should be left to the discretion of states.[202] The divergence of opinion that created this impasse still persists and there is no prospect of agreement between the pro-life and pro-choice movements.

Despite this dilemma, the human rights treaty monitoring bodies have continued to engage states on the issue of abortion by adopting a strategy that focuses on the grave, and often fatal, health consequences of clandestine abortions, as opposed to the sexual autonomy of women and girls.[203] For example, in its concluding observations for Brazil, the ESC Committee recommended that the state party 'review' its legislation to ensure the protection of women 'from the effects of clandestine and unsafe abortions'[204] and in its observations for the Philippines it recommended that the state party 'consider reviewing' legislation criminalizing abortion in all circumstances.[205] This approach remains principled to the extent that it does not demand

---

[200] See, eg, CO ESC Committee Mauritus, UN Doc E/C.12/MUS/CO/4, para 25; CO ESC Brazil, UN Doc E/C.12/BRA/CO/2, para 29; CO ESC Philippines, UN Doc E/C.12/PHL/CO/4, para 31; CO ESC Mexico, UN Doc E/2000/22 (1999) para 391; CO ESC Kuwait, UN Doc E/C.12/1/Add.98, para 43; CO CEDAW Andorra, UN Doc A/56/38 (2001) para 48; CO CEDAW Suriname, UN Doc CEDAW/C/SUR/CO/3, para 30; CO CRC Chad, UN Doc CRC/C/15/Add.107, para 30; CO CRC Palau, UN Doc CRC/C/15/Add149, para 30. It is also a concern of the HRC because of the potential for clandestine abortions to lead to suffering that reaches the threshold of inhuman and degrading treatment under article 7 of the ICCPR. See, eg, CO HRC Columbia, UN Doc A/59/40 Vol. I (2004) 35, para 67 (13); CO HRC Poland, UN Doc A/60/40 Vol. I (2004) 40, para 85(8); CO HRC Kenya, UN Doc A/60/40 Vol. I (2005) 44, para 86(14).

[201] See, eg, CO ESC Poland, UN Doc E/C.12/POL/CO/5, para 28; CO HRC Argentina, UN Doc A/56/40 Vol I (2001) 38, para 74. See generally Cook, Dickens, and Fathalla (n 58) 164–5 (explaining that punitive context of law deters women from seeking abortion and doctors from providing this service because neither party is aware that the prohibition on abortion has exceptions where, for example, an abortion is necessary to secure the health or life of the mother). See also WHO, *Safe Abortion: Technical and Policy Guidance for Health Systems* (WHO, 2003) 12 (estimating that each year 20 million unsafe abortions are performed, 97% of which are in developing countries and that 13% of maternal mortality can be attributed to unsafe abortions).

[202] Alston (n 104). cf Rita Joseph, *The Human Rights of the Unborn Child* (Martinus Nijhoff, 2009) (arguing that international law prohibits abortions in all contexts including when pregnancy is the result of rape or incest but her interpretative methodology is deeply problematic). For a review and critique of Joseph's approach see Tania Penovic, 'Human Rights and the Unborn Child' (2011) 33 Hum Rts Q 229, which reviews Joseph's book).

[203] For a discussion of the health effects of restrictive regulation of abortion see Ronli Sifris, 'Restrictive Regulation of Abortion and the Right to Health' (2010) 18 Med L Rev 185, 196–207.

[204] CO ESC Brazil, UN Doc E/C.12/BRA/CO/2, para 29.

[205] CO ESC Philippines, UN Doc E/C.12/PHL/CO/4, para 31. See also CO CEDAW Cameron, UN Doc A/55/38 (Part II) (2000) 53, para 60. See also CO HRC Ecuador, UN Doc. CCPR/C/79/Add.92, para 11 ('The Committee expresses its concern about the very high number of suicides of young females

that states make abortion services available. It is also consistent with the views expressed by states in forums such as Fourth World Conference on Women held in Beijing in 1995 and the United Nations review in 1999 of implementation of the plan of action adopted at the International Conference on Population and Development in 1994.[206] Thus, it satisfies the requirement of global context sensitivity. Moreover, the onus placed on states to develop measures to protect the right to health for women and girls, is consistent with the principle that states must ensure the effective enjoyment of the right to health.

In this regard, the most effective measure to protect women and girls from unwanted pregnancies is to prevent such pregnancies. It is for this reason that the human rights treaty monitoring bodies have repeatedly recommended that states make family planning services, including contraception, widely available[207] and ensure the provision of sexual and reproductive health education, including the use of contraceptive methods, in schools.[208] These recommendations will be, and indeed are, resisted by elements of the interpretative community especially certain religious groups. However, as detailed above in the discussion on adolescent sexual autonomy, a persuasive account can be made to justify their inclusion as part of the right to health.[209]

A further measure to minimize the health consequences associated with a clandestine abortion is to ensure effective access to this service where it is lawfully available but physicians and clinics refuse to provide access. This can occur when a doctor has a conscientious objection to this practice *or* is unclear as to the circumstances when it is lawfully available and so declines to offer the service for fear of being prosecuted. Under either scenario, the failure by a state to ensure that a woman or girl has access to an abortion, in circumstances where it would be lawfully available, is a violation of

---

referred to in the report, which appear in part to be related to the prohibition of abortion. In this regard, the Committee regrets the State party's failure to address the resulting problems faced by adolescent girls, in particular rape victims, who suffer the consequences of such acts for the rest of their lives. Such situations are, from both the legal and practical standpoints, incompatible with articles 3, 6 and 7 of the Covenant, and with article 24 when female minors are involved. The Committee recommends that the State party adopt all necessary legislative and other measures to assist women, and particularly adolescent girls, faced with the problem of unwanted pregnancies to obtain access to adequate health and education facilities').

[206] *Report of the Fourth World Conference on Women* (n 56) para 106 (calling for a review of the criminalization of abortion).

[207] See, eg, CO ESC Mauritis, UN Doc E/C.12/MUS/CO/4, para 25; CO ESC Kazakhstan, UN Doc E/C.12/KAZ/CO/1, para 33; CO ESC Republic of Korea, UN Doc E/C.12/KOR/CO/3, para 31; CO CEDAW Uzbekistan, UN Doc A/56/38 (Part I) (2001) 18, para 186.

[208] See, eg, CO ESC Mauritis, UN Doc E/C.12/MUS/CO/4, para 25; CO ESC Kazakhstan, UN Doc E/C.12/KAZ/CO/1, para 33; CO ESC Republic of Korea UN Doc E/C.12/KOR/CO/3, para 31; CO ESC Cameron, UN Doc E/2000/22 (1999) 56, para 359. See also CEDAW Committee, *Szijjarto v Hungary* (n 150) 15, para 11.2 (noting that informed decision making about effective and safe contraception requires 'information about contraceptive measures and their use, and guaranteed access to sex education and family planning services'); *Report of the Committee on the Elimination of Discrimination against Women: Thirteenth Session*, UN Doc A/49/38 (1994).

[209] See pages 133–143.

her right to health. It may also amount to violation of several rights under the ICCPR.[210] For example, in *KNLH v Peru*, the HRC held that the failure to ensure access to what would have been a lawful abortion for a 17-year-old girl, amounted to a violation of her rights to privacy, non-discrimination and protection against inhuman and degrading treatment.[211] On the facts of the case, the young girl, who was forced to carry an anencephalic pregnancy to term, experienced deep depression after her daughter died four days after birth.

One measure to avert such scenarios is to ensure that all relevant actors are aware of the circumstances when an abortion is lawful within a particular state.[212] Indeed, the United Nations review in 1999 of the implementation of the plan of action from the International Conference on Population and Development in 1994 recommended that 'in circumstances where abortion is not against the law, health systems should train and equip health-service providers and should take other measures to ensure that such abortion is safe and accessible'.[213] The WHO has also recommended that states promote and review their relevant laws among physicians, law and order officials, and the general public; design and implement policies to ensure effective access to abortion to the extent that the law allows; and remove unnecessary regulative and administrative barriers to access.[214]

However, an obstacle to the creation of this enabling environment is the potential for doctors to refuse to perform what would otherwise be a lawful abortion, on the basis of their conscientious objection. In such circumstances, the WHO has recommended that states mandate that doctors refer a woman or girl to another easily accessible doctor who is willing to perform an abortion.[215] Similarly, the ESC Committee has recommended, in its concluding observations for Poland, that the state enforce the legislation on abortion and implement 'a mechanism of timely and systematic referral in the event of conscientious objection'.[216] The motivation for

---

[210] See Radhika Coomraswamy, *Report of the Special Rapporteur on Violence against Women*, UN Doc E/CN.4/1999/Add.4 (21 January 1999) (describing restrictions on abortion as a form of violence against women and a violation of the right to life, non-discrimination, and protection against inhuman and degrading treatment); Sifris (n 203) 187–90.

[211] HRC, *KNLH v Peru*, Communication No 1153/2003, UN Doc CCPR/C/85/1153/2003 (22 November 2005) (the complaint also alleged a violation of the right to life but the HRC declined to determine this claim as it had already determined that the facts supported the allegation of inhuman and degrading treatment).

[212] The grounds for when an abortion will be lawful within a state vary and include for example, when the life of a woman or girl is threatened; when the health (physical or mental) of a woman or girl is threatened; when the pregnancy is the result of rape or incest; when there is a foetal impairment; for economic and social reasons or on request by a woman or girl: WHO, *Safe Abortion: Technical and Policy Guidance for Health Systems* (n 201) 86–7.

[213] *Key Actions for the Further Implementation of the Programme of Action of the International Conference on Population and Development*, GA Res S-21/2, UN Doc A/RES/S-21/2 (8 November 1999) annex, para 63(iii).

[214] WHO, *Safe Abortion: Technical and Policy Guidance for Health Systems* (n 201) 86.

[215] ibid 93.

[216] CO ESC Poland, UN Doc E/C.12/POL/CO/5, para 28. See also CO CEDAW Croatia, UN Doc A/53/38, para 109; CO CEDAW Poland, UN Doc CEDAW/C/POL/CO/6, para 25; CO CEDAW Italy, UN Doc A/52/38 Rev.1, pt II, para 353; CO HRC Poland, UN Doc CCPR/CO/82/POL, para 8.

this approach is to ensure the effective enjoyment of the right to health by women and girls by facilitating effective access to abortion services that are lawfully available.

However, the WHO and human rights treaty monitoring bodies have neglected the need to ensure external system coherence by overlooking the potential for a conflict of rights to occur when doctors who oppose abortion are mandated to refer a woman or girl to an alternative service provider. This is a complex debate and it is sufficient to note here that a regime, which requires mandatory referrals, will interfere with the right of some doctors to enjoy their right to freedom of religion and belief under article 18 of the ICCPR. In such circumstances, the state carries the burden to demonstrate on the balance of probabilities that this inference is necessary and reasonable to achieve a legitimate aim.[217] The aim of any limitation on a physician's freedom of religion is legitimate, namely the health of a woman or girl. However, whether a mandatory referral system is a necessary and reasonable measure to secure the health of women and girls with unwanted pregnancies is a matter that must be assessed against the available evidence. More specifically, a state would have to demonstrate that there was a reasonable risk that women or girls would not be aware of the availability of abortion services in the absence of a mandatory referral system. If this risk were found to be present, then the potential consequences for the right to health of a woman or girl associated with a clandestine abortion would outweigh, and thus justify, any limitation on a physician's right to freedom of religion or belief. As to whether such evidence exists, will be a matter to be determined on the facts of each case.

The final feature of the approach adopted by the Committee bodies with respect to the availability of abortion is their recommendation that states allow for therapeutic abortions (when the life or health of a woman or girl is threatened) and in cases where the pregnancy is the result of rape or incest.[218] The basis for this position is the potential impact on the physical and mental health of a woman, or girl, if she were forced to have the child or resort to a clandestine abortion. It is therefore consistent with the principle that the enjoyment of the right to health must be effective not illusory. It is also consistent with the fact that a substantial number of states allow for abortions in such circumstances (97 per cent to preserve life; 67 per cent and 64 per cent respectively to preserve physical or mental health; 48 per cent where pregnancy is the result of rape or incest; 45 per cent for fetal impairment; 34 per cent for social and economic reasons; but only 28 per cent on request).[219]

---

[217] *Siracusa Principles of the Limitation and Derogation Provisions in the International Covenant on Civil and Political Rights*, UN Doc E/CN4/1985/4 (1985), para 10.

[218] See, eg, CO ESC Mauritis, UN Doc E/C.12/MUS/CO/4, para 25; CO ESC Costa Rica, UN Doc E/C.12/CRI/CO/4, paras 25, 46; CO HRC Mauritius, UN Doc A/60/40 Vol I (2005) 52 para 88(9); CO CEDAW Sri Lanka, UN Doc A/57/38 Part I (2002) para 283; CO CRC Chile, UN Doc CRC/C/CHL/CO/3 (2007) para 56.

[219] UN Population Division, Department of Economic and Social Affairs, 'World Abortion Policies 2007' <http://www.un.org/esa/population/publications/2007_Abortion_Policies_Chart/2007_WallChart.pdf> accessed 26 June 2011. These figures indicate a slight increase in the availability of abortion since 1999 when the comparable figures were 98% to preserve life; 63% and 62% respectively to preserve the physical or mental health; 43% where pregnancy is the result of rape or incest; 39% for fetal impairment;

However, these recommendations to allow abortion in a range of circumstances still remain problematic given the staunchly maintained differences among states as to the regulation of abortion. At the same time, the human rights treaty monitoring bodies have generally tended to avoid couching their observations in language that imposes a mandatory obligation on states to allow abortions. Instead, phrases such as 'should'[220] amend the law, and 'recommend'[221] amendment of the law, have been used by the committee bodies. From the perspective of this analysis, these calls to review the criminalization of abortion illustrate the way in which the contours of the right to health in international law remain subject to change.

For example, the Protocol to the African Charter on Human and Peoples' Rights on the Rights of Women in Africa, which was adopted in 2003, requires under article 14(2)(c), that states must take all appropriate measures to:

protect the reproductive rights of women by authorising medical abortion in cases of sexual assault, rape, incest, and where the continued pregnancy endangers the mental and physical health of the mother or the life of the mother or the foetus.

It may be premature, however, to claim that the right to health *in international law* imposes the same obligation on states.[222] One region of the world has accepted this broad obligation, nearly all states have accepted the legitimacy of an abortion when the life of a pregnant woman or girl is threatened, and nearly 50 per cent of states allow abortion where the pregnancy was the result of rape or incest. But to suggest that that international law demands that states provide abortions in these circumstances is arguably too strong an approach given that a persuasive account of the right to health must satisfy the requirements of local and global context sensitivity. Unsafe abortions unquestionably threaten the health of women and girls and do so in a way that is disproportionate to men and boys, who can never face the physical prospect of an unwanted pregnancy.[223] But this does not mean that restrictions on abortion are necessarily a violation of the right to health. Ultimately it depends on the nature and scope of the obligation imposed on states to protect the health of women and girls.

The reality is that many states have actively resisted the development of a broad obligation under international law to make abortion available. Many states still prohibit abortion in most circumstances, even where the health of a woman of

---

33% for social and economic reasons but only 27% on request: UN Population Division, Department of Economic and Social Affairs, *Abortion Policies: A Global Review* (UN, 2001).

[220] CO HRC Argentina UN Doc A/56/40 Vol I (2000) 38, para 74.

[221] CO ESC Mauritus, UN Doc E/C.12/MUS/CO/4, para 25.

[222] See Alison Duxbury and Christopher Ward, 'The International Law Implications of Australian Abortion Law' (2000) 23 UNSWLJ 1, 26, 34; Center for Reproductive Rights, 'Background Paper to Support the Development of a General Comment on the Right to Sexual and Reproductive Health by the Committee on Economic Social and Cultural Rights' (October 2010) 20 (advocating the ESC Committee to recommend that safe abortions 'must be available in at least certain circumstances' but not advocating abortion on request); cf Sifris (n 203) (arguing that the denial of abortion constitutes a violation of the non-discrimination component of the right to health but does not consider the drafting history of instruments such as the CRC or the current state of controversy among states; thus her analysis could be taken to express a vision of what the law should be as opposed to what the law is).

[223] Sifris (n 203) 207–11.

child is threatened or the pregnancy is the result of rape, and continue to actively resist attempts to impose an obligation on them to do otherwise.[224] This reality tends to undermine claims that the approach adopted under the African Women's Protocol reflects the current state of the law under international law generally. At the same time, this issue remains contested within the interpretative community and in time, a broad acceptance of the approach advocated by the human rights treaty monitoring bodies and adopted by the African Women's Protocol may become increasingly accepted by those states and other actors within the interpretative community that currently resist this approach.

B Accessibility

1 A multidimensional concept

According to the ESC Committee, the principle of 'accessibility' has four overlapping dimensions: non-discrimination; physical accessibility both of health services and the underlying determinants of health such as safe and potable water and adequate sanitation facilities; economic accessibility or affordability such that payment for health care services and the underlying determinants of health are based on the principle of equity and poorer households are not disproportionately burdened with health expenses compared with richer households; and information accessibility which 'includes the right to seek, receive and impart information and ideas concerning health issues'.[225]

(a) Non-discrimination

With respect to the issue of non-discrimination, this is also a specific right under article 2 of the ICESCR and article 2 of the CRC which provides protection against discrimination on the basis of a person's 'race, colour, sex, language, religion, political or other opinion, national or social origin, property, birth or other status'. Importantly, this list of protected attributes is illustrative only and the inclusion of the phrase 'other status' provides a basis for the ESC Committee and CRC Committee to express their concern that groups such as prisoners, asylum seekers in detention,[226] and persons with HIV/AIDS and mental health issues have experienced unjustifiable limitations on their ability to access health care services because of their

---

[224] For example, at the Fourth World Conference on Women in 1994, many states opposed any suggestion that restrictions on availability of abortion was a human rights violation: UN Department for Policy Coordination and Sustainable Development, *Report of the Fourth World Conference on Women*, UN Doc A/CONF.177/20 (17 October 1995) ch V.
[225] ESC Committee, *General Comment No 14* (n 11) para 12(b).
[226] See, eg, CO ESC Australia, UN Doc E/C.12/AUS/CO/4, para 30. See also *Report of the Special Rapporteur on the Right to Health to the General Assembly 2010* (n 113) para 59 (stressing the obligation to respect the right to health for prisoners and detainees and encouraging the need to adopt harm reduction initiatives, such as needle and exchange programmes). See also WHO, *The Madrid Recommendation: Health Protection in Prisons as an Essential Part of Public Health* (WHO 2009) 3 (noting that evidence demonstrates that health protection measures, including harm reduction measures, in prisons are effective).

status. In addition, the CRPD, CERD, CMWF, CEDAW, and the Standard Minimum Rules for the Treatment of Prisoners and Rules for the Treatment of Women Prisoners, all have specific provisions that are dedicated to protecting the beneficiaries of these treaties—persons with disabilities, persons from racial groups, migrant workers and their families, women, refugees, and prisoners—from discrimination in accessing health services and facilities.[227]

It is important to stress that the prohibition against discrimination in the provision of health care services does not impose an absolute prohibition on all forms of differential treatment based on the status of an individual. On the contrary, such treatment will be justified if it (a) pursues a legitimate aim (which must be consistent with international law) and (b) adopts measures that are necessary (that is, reasonable and proportionate), for the purposes of achieving the aim.[228] A state will bear the onus of satisfying this standard where it seeks to justify differential treatment.[229]

(b) Physical accessibility

In terms of physical accessibility, the human rights treaty monitoring bodies regularly express their concern that rural communities do not have reasonable access to acceptable and quality health care services. For example, in its concluding observations for Bangladesh the CRC expressed its concern 'at the lack of infrastructure for access to health facilities, notably in rural areas'.[230] And in response to its concern that 'people living in rural areas face considerable difficulties in accessing health care', the ESC Committee, in its concluding observations for Algeria, recommended that the state party 'take urgent measures to ensure universal and physical and economic access to primary health care'.[231] The same concerns regularly feature in the concluding observations of the CRC Committee. Thus, for example, in its observations for Guinea Bissau, it expressed concern at 'the limited access to, capacity and quality of health-care services, including in terms of distance between people's homes and health facilities, cost and the insufficient number of hospital beds and the limited availability of affordable and appropriate medication'.[232] It therefore recommended

---

[227] CRPD, arts 25(f) (state parties must '[p]revent discriminatory denial of health care or health services or food and fluids on the basis of disability'), 25(a)–(e), 26(1); CEDAW, arts 12(1)–(2), 14(b); International Convention on the Elimination of All Forms of Racial Discrimination (CERD) (New York, 7 March 1966, entered into force 4 January 1969, 660 UNTS 195) art 5(e)(iv); International Convention on the Protection of the Rights of All Migrant Workers and Members of their Families (CMWF) (New York, 18 December 1990, entered into force 1 July 2003, 2220 UNTS 3) art 25(1); *UN Standard Minimum Rules for the Treatment of Prisoners 1955*, adopted by the First UN Congress on Prevention of Crime and the Treatment of Offenders and approved by ECOSOC by Res 663 C (XXIV) rule 22 (prison medical services should correspond to the health facilities available to the general community); *United Nations Rules for the Treatment of Women Prisoners and Non Custodial Measures for Women Offenders (Bangkok Rules)*, UN Doc A/C.3/65/L.5 (6 October 2010) rule 10 ('gender specific health care services at least equivalent to those available in the community shall be provided to women prisoners').
[228] *Siracusa Principles* (n 217) paras 10, 11.
[229] ibid.
[230] CO CRC Bangladesh, UN Doc CRC/C/15/Add221, para 51(f).
[231] CO ESC Algeria, UN Doc E/C.12/DZA/CO/4, para 20. See also CO ESC Poland, UN Doc E/C.12/POl/CO/5, para 24.
[232] CO CRC Guinea Bissau, UN Doc CRC/C/15/Add177, para 34(a).

that the state party 'significantly improve children's access to health services and to medication including by strengthening the quality and capacity of health infrastructure'.[233] Importantly, in its report for Albania it added that the relevant state party must develop 'care and rehabilitation facilities that are accessible also *without parental consent when this is in the best interests of the child*'[234] in recognition of the potential for conflict between the wishes of parents and the health care needs of children.

The issue of physical accessibility is also the subject of consideration in article 25 of the CRPD which requires that states parties must not only provide health services needed by persons with disabilities because of their disability but also ensure that such persons receive 'the same range, quality and standard of free or affordable health care and programmes as provided to other persons, including in the area of sexual and reproductive health and population-based public health programmes' and that services should be provided as close as possible to people's own communities, including in rural areas.[235]

(c) **Financial accessibility**

Financial accessibility is an enduring concern for the human rights treaty monitoring bodies. A health system that is beyond the financial means of people cannot be said to promote the effective enjoyment of the right to health. It is on this basis, that the CRC Committee in its concluding observations for the Republic of Korea, recommended 'that the state party, increase to a significant level the funding allocated to health and establish a system of public care facilities so that low-income families may have access to health systems at no cost'.[236] Similarly in response to its concerns that 'disadvantaged and marginalised individuals do not have access to medical services'

---

[233] ibid para 35(b). See also CO CRC Sierra Leone, UN Doc CRC/C/15/Add116, para 55.
[234] CO CRC Albania, UN Doc CRC/C/15/Add249, para 57(b).
[235] CRPD, art 25 provides that:
States Parties shall take all appropriate measures to ensure access for persons with disabilities to health services that are gender-sensitive, including health-related rehabilitation. In particular, States Parties shall:

(a) Provide persons with disabilities with the same range, quality and standard of free or affordable health care and programmes as provided to other persons, including in the area of sexual and reproductive health and population-based public health programmes;
(b) Provide those health services needed by persons with disabilities specifically because of their disabilities, including early identification and intervention as appropriate, and services designed to minimize and prevent further disabilities, including among children and older persons;
(c) Provide these health services as close as possible to people's own communities, including in rural areas;
(d) Require health professionals to provide care of the same quality to persons with disabilities as to others, including on the basis of free and informed consent by, inter alia, raising awareness of the human rights, dignity, autonomy and needs of persons with disabilities through training and the promulgation of ethical standards for public and private health care;
(e) Prohibit discrimination against persons with disabilities in the provision of health insurance, and life insurance where such insurance is permitted by national law, which shall be provided in a fair and reasonable manner;
(f) Prevent discriminatory denial of health care or health services or food and fluids on the basis of disability.

[236] CO CRC Republic of Korea, UN Doc CRC/C/15/Add197, paras 48, 49(a).

in the Republic of Korea, the ESC Committee urged 'the State party to increase expenditure for health care and to take all appropriate measures to ensure universal access to health care at prices affordable to everyone'.[237] And its concluding observations for Brazil, it recommended that the state party 'increase health care funding for disadvantaged populations' and 'ensure that the people living in poverty have access to free primary health care'.[238] However, there is a level of slippage in the recommendations of the human rights treaty monitoring bodies which shift between making health care 'affordable' and making certain forms of health care available for 'free'. The precise nature of the obligation imposed upon states with respect to making health services financially accessible is discussed more fully in Chapter 5.

In the context of this current discussion, which focuses on accessibility, article 24 of the CRC requires that states shall '*strive to ensure*' that no child is deprived of his or her *right of access* to health care services. The obligation to 'strive to ensure' was the outcome of a compromise during the drafting of article 24 that resisted the imposition of an obligation on states to provide children with access to health care services free of charge. Early formulations in relation to the issue of accessibility included phrases such as 'with a gradual transition towards free medical care'[239] and 'free of charge'.[240] However, there was a concern among the drafters that to impose such an obligation 'in all circumstances... might lead to a misappropriation of resources'.[241] A compromise was therefore agreed upon whereby state parties were to strive to ensure that no child was deprived for financial reasons of his or her right of access to health care services.[242] It appears that the reference to 'financial reasons' was only removed from the final text on the basis that, because this phrase did not appear in any other human rights treaties, its meaning was not entirely clear.[243]

Despite this omission, the drafting history does indicate a strong intention that states must take steps in light of their available resources to ensure that a child's financial situation does not preclude access to health services. The obligation to 'strive' is therefore far from vacuous and its linkage with the objective to 'ensure' indicates that the nature of the obligation imposed on states under article 24 is actually quite onerous. It may fall short of an obligation to guarantee free access to health services for all children (subject to the obligation to guarantee minimum core health services, which is discussed in Chapter 5) but it still imposes a heavy burden

---

[237] CO CRC Republic of Korea, UN Doc E/C.12/KOR/CO/3, para 30.

[238] CO ESC Brazil, UN Doc E/C.12/BRA/CO/2, paras 28(b), (c). See also CO ESC Columbia, UN Doc E/2002/22 (2001) 110, para 775 (urging the state party to allocate a higher percentage of its GDP to the health system); CO ESC Benin, UN Doc E/2003/22 (2002) 34, para 197 (recommending the creation of a health policy to enable the poorest sectors to have access to free high quality heath care).

[239] Commission on Human Rights, *Question of a Convention on the Rights of the Child: Report of the Secretary-General—Addendum*, UN Doc E/CN.4/1324/Add.1 (1 February 1979).

[240] Commission on Human Rights, *Question of a Convention on the Rights of the Child: Report of the Working Group on a Draft Convention on the Rights of the Child*, UN Doc E/CN.4/1985/64 (3 April 1985) para 12.

[241] ibid para 14.   [242] ibid para 18.

[243] Commission on Human Rights, *Technical Review of the Text of the Draft Convention on the Rights of the Child*, E/CN.4/1989/WG.1/CRP.1 (1989) 30.

on states to justify that every reasonable measure has been taken in good faith to ensure accessibility to health care services for children lacking the requisite financial means.

It is within this context that the repeated preference of the CRC Committee for the provision of free health care for children and their mothers is able to find a principled basis. Thus, for example, it has commended Algeria 'for providing free medical care for all citizens';[244] and variously welcomed initiatives such as the adoption of a 'basic health insurance scheme (SUMI) that provides free medical care for children up to 5 years of age and their mothers'[245] in Bolivia; the provision of 'universal and free [HIV/AIDS] testing and treatment with antiretroviral drugs' for mothers'[246] in The Bahamas; noted 'the initiative taken by the state party to make baby products, including medicine, tax free' and 'the high level of immunization coverage and that health services are free and cover all areas of the country' in Antigua and Barbuda;[247] the provision of 'free of charge mental health care for 0–19 year olds' in the Netherlands Antilles;[248] and the 'provision of free health care to children under the age of six years and to pregnant and lactating women' in South Africa.[249] Similarly, the ESC Committee has lauded initiatives by states to ensure financial accessibility to health services and commended, for example, France on its creation of a universal health care system that provides 100 per cent coverage to persons on low incomes.[250]

The CRC Committee has also expressed concern in a range of circumstances where financial considerations have impeded the realization of various aspects of a child's right to health.[251] It is important to recognize, however, that there is no principled basis upon which the CRC Committee, or indeed any other human rights committee, can mandate that states provide such measures free of charge (subject to those services that arguably fall within the minimum core of the right to health which is discussed in Chapter 5). This is because the implementation of the right to health is ultimately dependent upon a state's available resources. At the same time, it remains legitimate for the human rights treaty monitoring bodies to demand that states must actively seek, as a progressive measure, to 'define sustainable financing mechanisms for the primary health-care system and an effective utilization of resources, including adequate salaries for child health-care professionals, in order to ensure that all children, in particular children from the most marginalized vulnerable groups, have access to free basic health care of good quality'.[252] Moreover,

---

[244] CO CRC Algeria, UN Doc CRC/C/15/Add269, para 56.
[245] CO CRC Bolivia, UN Doc CRC/C/15/Add256, para 47.
[246] CO CRC The Bahamas, UN Doc CRC/C/15/Add, para 51.
[247] CO CRC Antigua and Barbuda, UN Doc CRC/C/15/Add247, para 51.
[248] CO CRC Netherlands Antilles, UN Doc CRC/C/15/Add186, para 44.
[249] CO CRC South Africa, UN Doc CRC/C/15/Add122, para 29.
[250] CO ESC France, UN Doc E/2002/22 (2001) 121, para 860.
[251] See, eg, CO CRC Croatia, UN Doc CRC/C/15/Add243, para 51; CO CRC Kyrgyzstan, UN Doc CRC/C/15/Add244, para 49; CO CRC India, UN Doc CRC/C/15/Add228, para 52; CO CRC Bangladesh, UN Doc CRC/C/15/Add221, para 52(b); CO CRC Zambia, UN Doc CRC/C/15/Add206, para 49(b); CO CRC Malawi, UN Doc CRC/C/15/Add174, para 44(b); CO CRC Greece, UN Doc CRC/C/15/Add170, para 61(b); CO CRC Central African Republic, UN Doc CRC/C/15/Add138, para 55.
[252] CO CRC Czech Republic, UN Doc CRC/C/15/Add201, para 47(a).

there is also a principled basis on which to demand that where states have the capacity to provide free access to health care, no child is to be deprived of this entitlement on the basis of his or her status. Thus, for example, in its report for Monaco, the CRC Committee expressed concern 'that while Monegasque children have a right to free health care, domestic legislation and practice do not expressly guarantee the same right to all children in the state party, in particular children from disadvantaged backgrounds and who are neither nationals nor residents of the State party'.[253] The principle of non-discrimination in international law does not tolerate such distinctions in relation to the provision of health care services.

(d) Acceptability and quality

In relation to *acceptability* the ESC Committee has explained that 'all health facilities, good and services must be respectful of medical ethics and culturally appropriate... as well as being designed to respect confidentiality'.[254] The requirement to respect medical ethics and be culturally appropriate is consistent with the interpretative methodology adopted in this analysis to the extent that it seeks to incorporate the views and values of key actors within the relevant interpretative community, namely, the medical profession and cultural groups that access health services. But the formulation adopted by the ESC Committee is too narrow if the health services made available within a state are to be considered acceptable by those persons who provide such services *and* benefit from their delivery. In addition to being culturally appropriate they must also be gender sensitive, age appropriate (whether young or old),[255] sensitive to religious beliefs, and sensitive to status of persons with disabilities.[256] A failure to ensure that the provision of health care services and the associated determinants of health are acceptable to the beneficiaries of such services will undermine the capacity of a state to secure the effective enjoyment of the right to health.

With respect to children, for example, as the CRC Committee noted in its General Comment on the Rights of Children and HIV/AIDS, 'children are more likely to use services that are friendly and supportive, provide a wide range of services and information, are geared to their needs, give them the opportunity to participate in decisions affecting their health, are accessible, affordable, confidential and non-judgemental, do not require parental consent and are not discriminatory'.[257] This obligation to provide what the CRC Committee has described as 'child and adolescent sensitive health services'[258] is drawn from the requirement that any health

---

[253] CO CRC Monaco, UN Doc CRC/C/15/Add158, para 34.
[254] ESC Committee, *General Comment No 14* (n 11) para 12(c).
[255] See, eg, CO ESC Luxembourg, UN Doc E/1998/22 (1997) 69, para 397 (expressing concern at the absence of specialized geriatric doctors and facilities to address the problems of the large aging population).
[256] CRPD, art 4(1) requires that 'States Parties undertake to ensure and promote the full realization of all human rights and fundamental freedoms for all persons with disabilities without discrimination of any kind on the basis of disability. To this end, States Parties undertake...(c) To take into account the protection and promotion of the human rights of persons with disabilities in all policies and programmes'.
[257] CRC Committee, *General Comment No 3* (n 81) para 20.
[258] ibid pt C.

services made available by states must also be acceptable to children in a manner which is consistent with the model advanced earlier in this chapter concerning children's consent to medical treatment especially in the context of their sexual and reproductive health.

Finally, according to the CRC Committee in its General Comment on Adolescent Health, the principle of *quality* requires that 'Health services and goods should be scientifically and medically appropriate, which requires personnel trained to care for adolescents, adequate facilities and scientifically accepted methods.'[259] Thus the entitlements under the right to health have a substantive element. It is not sufficient for a state to make health care services available, accessible, and age appropriate, if the quality of such services is such that it cannot contribute in a real and effective way to the realization of the highest attainable standard of health. Moreover, the content of this qualitative element of the right to health is not to be determined exclusively by states but by medical and scientific evidence. Thus for example, if a state determines to make abortion available to women and girls, it must ensure that such a service is consistent with the recognized standards such as those in the WHO's technical guidelines on safe abortions.[260]

V Conclusion—a socially manageable meaning of health

The aim of this chapter was to examine the scope and nature of the interest in which the right to health in international law is grounded. It offered four central arguments. First, the right to health is not a right to be healthy but an entitlement to receive and enjoy the services, facilities, and conditions that are necessary to prevent, remedy, and mitigate ill health. An assessment of what is the 'highest attainable standard of health' will be a relative rather than universal assessment against the level of health which is attainable given the health condition of an individual and the resources available to a state.

Second, although the human rights treaty monitoring bodies have avoided any discussion as to the meaning of 'health', such a discussion is necessary in order to place limits on the scope of claims that can be made under the right to health. A definition of health as pathology, that is, a deviation from the normal range of species functioning, does allow limits to be placed on the scope of health. However, the focus on normalcy under this model is problematic given the capacity for social factors to contribute to, or indeed cause, the ill-functioning experienced by a person with a pathological condition. As a consequence, a biopsychosocial model of health was advocated in order to avoid the potential for stigmatization which is associated with a pathological model and ensure that states broaden their inquiry beyond the condition of an individual to consider the external factors that must be addressed in

---

[259] CRC Committee, *General Comment No 4* (n 59) para 41(d). See also ESC Committee, *General Comment No 14* (n 11) para 12(d).
[260] WHO, *Safe Abortion: Technical and Policy Guidance for Health Systems* (n 201).

developing appropriate services, facilities, and conditions to secure the health of an individual.

Third, caution must be exercised against conflating the scope of the right to health to include everything that has an impact on the health of an individual. Despite this warning, a principled and practical basis was shown to justify the inclusion of sexual autonomy and non-consensual medical treatment, within the scope of the right to health. Moreover, an examination of these freedoms in the context of adolescents revealed a persuasive case for a complex and sophisticated model in which the rights of children must be accommodated in ways that are likely to challenge dominant social and cultural expectations within elements of the interpretative community concerning children's sexual health and their capacity to not only consent to, but also refuse medical treatment.

Finally, the adoption of the essential elements framework by the human rights treaty monitoring bodies, namely that health services be available, accessible, acceptable, and of appropriate quality, is an appropriate interpretative tool for identifying those elements that constitute the right to health. It assists in transforming the abstract notion of the highest attainable standard of health into concepts that can be used by members of the interpretative community to inform and guide the development and delivery of policies, services, and facilities to secure the enjoyment of the right to health. But while this framework satisfies the requirement of commentators that human rights must be 'action guiding' and 'socially manageable', it focuses on the entitlement of an individual and therefore represents only one dimension of the right to health. An understanding of this right cannot be confined to the scope of the entitlements which it confers upon individuals, and must be accompanied by an examination as to the nature and scope of the obligation imposed upon states to respond to claims that are grounded in such entitlements. It is this dimension of the right to health that forms of the basis of the discussion in Chapter 5.

5
The Obligation to Recognize the Right to Health by All Appropriate Means

I Introduction

An adequate normative account of a human right requires that it must have a well-specified counterpart obligation.[1] For many commentators, such an account is lacking with respect to the right to health in international law. For example, for James Griffin, it offers no limit on what a state must spend to secure the right to health[2] and for Onora O'Neill, its obligations are 'muddled', 'vague', and 'insufficiently specified', thus rendering it a mere aspiration as opposed to a normative standard.[3] However, neither Griffin nor O'Neill undertake a close examination of the actual obligation specified by international law with respect to the right to health. This obligation requires that a state must *recognize* the right to health. Admittedly, this is hardly a phrase for which there is a precise and readily apparent meaning. At the same time, the drafting history of the International Covenant on Economic, Social and Cultural Rights (ICESCR)[4] indicates that, rather than being muddled, the obligation to *recognize* the right to health was actually a carefully considered and pragmatic response to the dilemmas associated with implementation of economic and social rights, such as the right to health.

During drafting, three options were considered when contemplating the obligation to be imposed on states.[5] The first view was that each article of the ICESCR should specify in detail the obligation with respect to each particular right.[6] The second view was that, because all human rights were of equal importance, the obligation under article 2 of the International Covenant on Civil and Political Rights (ICCPR), which imposes an 'obligation to take the necessary steps . . . to give effect to the rights in the covenant', should also be included in the ICESCR. The third option

---

[1] Onora O'Neill, 'The Dark Side of Human Rights' (2005) 81 Intl Affairs 427, 431. See also Maria Montero, 'Global Poverty, Human Rights and Correlative Duties' (2009) 22 CJLJ 79, 80 (argues that 'only when there is an infringement of some duty correlative to a human right can we can conclude that a human rights violation has taken place').
[2] James Griffin, *On Human Rights* (OUP, 2008) 208.
[3] O'Neill (n 1) 427, 428–9.
[4] International Covenant on Economic, Social and Cultural Rights (ICESCR) (New York, 16 December 1966, entered into force 3 January 1976, 993 UNTS 3).
[5] *Annotations on the Text of the Draft International Covenants on Human Rights*, UN Doc A/2929 (1955) 19–20, paras 18–22.
[6] ibid 19 para 19.

was to 'limit the terms of each individual article to a recognition of the particular right by the state and to add an "umbrella" article imposing a general obligation of states which would be applicable to all the rights recognized in the covenant'.[7] However, because of the nexus between the implementation of economic and social rights and the economic and social conditions in a country, it was considered to be unrealistic to require states parties 'to do more than "undertake to take steps"' to progressively achieve the full realization of the rights in the ICESCR.[8]

Ultimately, it was option three that prevailed.[9] As a consequence, the principle of internal system coherence demands that the obligation to 'recognize' the right to health under article 12 of the ICESCR, and article 24 of the Convention on the Rights of the Child (CRC),[10] must be informed by the general obligation imposed on states with respect to economic and social rights under both these treaties.[11] In this respect, article 2(1) of the ICESCR provides that:

Each State Party to the present Covenant undertakes to take steps, individually and through international assistance and co-operation, especially economic and technical, to the maximum of its available resources, with a view to achieving progressively the full realization of the rights *recognized* in the present Covenant by all appropriate means, including particularly the adoption of legislative measures.[12]

The drafting history of the ICESCR, therefore, allays the immediate interpretative concerns surrounding the meaning of the obligation to 'recognize' the right to health

---

[7] *Annotations on the Text of the Draft International Covenants on Human Rights*, UN Doc A/2929 (1955) 19–20 para 20.

[8] ibid 20 para 21.

[9] In addition to the right to health under art 12, the ICESCR uses the verb 'recognize' in relation to the rights under arts 6, 7, 9, 10, 11(1), 11(2), 12(1), 13(1) and 16(1) and the CRC uses the verb 'recognize' in relation to the rights under arts 5, 15(1), 17, 23, 24, 25, 26, 27, 28, 31, 32 and 40. It is important to note that the general obligation under arts 2 and 4 of the ICESCR and Convention on the Rights of the Child (CRC) is not confined to those rights that are 'recognized' under these instruments. On the contrary the effective implementation of the ICESCR and CRC requires that this general obligation must extend to all rights. See Matthew Craven, *The International Covenant on Economic Social and Cultural Rights: A Perspective on its Development* (Clarendon Press, 1995) 135–6.

[10] Convention on the Rights of the Child (CRC) (New York, 20 November 1989, entered into force 2 September 1990, 1577 UNTS 3).

[11] The drafting history for art 24 of the CRC indicates that there was some support for the inclusion of an obligation that States 'shall ensure' a child's right to health: *Status of a Draft Convention on the Rights of the Child: Document Submitted by Poland*, UN Doc A/C.3/36/6 (7 October 1981) pt II, 5; *Question of a Convention on the Rights of the Child: Report of the Working Group on a Draft Convention on the Rights of the Child*, UN Doc E/CN.4/1985/64 (3 April 1985) para 15. Despite this, it was ultimately 'agreed to retain the . . . word "recognize" in order to conform to the language of the International Covenant on Economic, Social and Cultural Rights': *Question of a Convention on the Rights of the Child: Report of the Working Group on a Draft Convention on the Rights of the Child*, UN Doc E/CN.4/1985/64 (3 April 1985) para 15. The need to pursue external system coherence therefore formed the basis upon which to include the requirement that states party to the CRC 'recognize' a child's right to health.

[12] (emphasis added). In a similar vein, article 4(1) of the CRC provides that 'States Parties shall undertake all appropriate legislative, administrative, and other measures for the implementation of the rights recognized in the present Convention. With regard to economic, social and cultural rights, States Parties shall undertake such measures to the maximum extent of their available resources and, where needed, within the framework of international co-operation'.

by creating a nexus with the general/umbrella obligation of states with respect to all economic and social rights. However, this nexus generates an entirely new set of interpretative concerns, which require the development of an understanding as to the meaning of a state's obligation to: (a) take steps; (b) individually and through international assistance and co-operation; (c) subject to its available resources; to (d) progressively realize the right to health by; (e) all appropriate (legislative, administrative and other) means.

The aim of this chapter is to identify the meaning of two of these phrases—the obligation to 'take steps' to realize the right to health by 'all appropriate means'. (The progressive nature of the obligation to realize the right to health subject to available resources will be discussed in Chapter 6 and the international obligation to co-operate will be discussed in Chapter 9.)[13] It will be shown that the work of the human rights treaty monitoring bodies offers considerable insights into the nature of the 'appropriate...means' required of states to secure the right to health. However, these contributions, particularly those of the Committee on Economic, Social and Cultural Rights (ESC Committee), have tended to conflate the scope of the measures required of states in a way that fails to pay sufficient attention to the need for both internal and external system coherence. A more modest vision with respect to the scope of a state's obligation will therefore be offered.

II The obligation to 'take steps'

When article 2(1) of the ICESCR was being drafted, concern was expressed that the formulation 'provided too many loop holes for states parties wishing to evade their obligations'.[14] Among the potential loop holes identified, was the obligation to 'take steps' towards the 'progressive realization' of rights such as the right to health.[15] Despite this concern, it was accepted that the reality of resource constraints meant that states were unable to guarantee such rights and the adoption of a progressive obligation was therefore appropriate.[16] However, the obligation to 'take steps' is not dependent on resources and, according to the ESC Committee, 'is not qualified or limited by other considerations'.[17] Thus, it reflects the general obligation under international law that a state party to a treaty must take measures to perform the obligations assumed under that treaty in good faith.[18] Having ratified a treaty, a state

---

[13] The obligation of international co-operation and assistance will not be discussed in this chapter, as it is the subject of a separate discussion in Chapter 9 because of its inclusion as a specific element of the right to health under art 24(4) of the CRC.
[14] *Annotations on the Text of the Draft International Covenants on Human Rights* (n 5) 20, para 23.
[15] ibid.   [16] ibid.
[17] ESC Committee, *General Comment No 3: The Nature of States Parties' Obligations*, UN Doc E/1991/23 (14 December 1990) annex III, para 2. Manisuli Ssenyonjo, *Economic, Social and Cultural Rights in International Law* (Hart Publishing, 2009) para 2.08; Craven (n 9) 114.
[18] Vienna Convention on the Law of Treaties (the Vienna Convention) (Vienna, 23 May 1969, 1155 UNTS 331 (entered into force 27 January 1980)) art 26. See also Craven (n 9) 114 (making a similar observation but relying on the decision of the PCIJ on *Exchange of Greek and Turkish Populations under the Lausanne Convention VI* [1925] PCIJ (ser B) No 10, 20, in which the PCIJ held that 'a State which has

cannot sit idle and do nothing. Indeed, as the ESC Committee, in its General Comment No 3 on 'The Nature of States Parties Obligations' under the ICESCR explained, 'the full meaning of the phrase ["to take steps"] can also be gauged by noting some of the different language versions...in French it is "to act" ("s'engage a agir") and in Spanish it is "to adopt measures" ("a adopter medidas")'.[19] It continued, 'while the full realization of the relevant rights may be achieved progressively, steps must be taken within a reasonably short time after the Covenant's entry into force for the states concerned'.[20] Moreover, '[s]uch steps should be deliberate, concrete and targeted as clearly as possible towards meeting the obligations under the Covenant'.[21]

These directives by the ESC Committee are justified to the extent that they are directed to ensuring that states must begin to take steps immediately—even if these initial steps merely involve planning as to how a state will ensure the progressive and effective enjoyment of economic and social rights such as the right to health. The ESC Committee's recommendations are therefore principled. They are also consistent with the view expressed during drafting of the ICESCR, that the obligation assumed by states under this treaty must be practical yet resistant to loop holes that would undermine the enjoyment of economic and social rights. The obligation to 'take steps', therefore, represents what is often described as an 'obligation of conduct', that is, an obligation to take actions with a view to achieving an 'obligation of result', namely the full realization of a right such as the highest attainable standard of heath.[22]

III The meaning of 'all appropriate means'

A A margin of discretion

States are required to take 'all appropriate means' (or 'measures' under the Convention on the Rights of the Child (CRC)) to progressively realize the right to health. This phrase, when viewed in isolation is particularly amorphous and its ordinary meaning is not readily apparent. The challenge, therefore, is use the interpretative methodology outlined in Chapter 3 to shape the boundaries of this obligation. In undertaking this exercise, the first point to note is that the principle of internal

---

contracted valid international obligations is bound to make in its legislation such modifications as may be necessary to ensure the fulfilment of the obligations undertaken').

[19] ESC Committee, *General Comment No 3* (n 17) para 2.

[20] ibid. The *Limburg Principles*, which were adopted by a group of distinguished experts in international law, provide that '[a]ll parties have an obligation to begin immediately to take steps towards the full realisation of the rights contained in the Covenant': *Limburg Principles on the Implementation of the International Covenant on Economic Social and Cultural Rights*, UN Doc E/CN.4/1987/17 (1987) annex para 16. The ESC Committee also stated in its General Comment No 3 that the obligation to 'take steps' was of immediate effect: ESC Committee, *General Comment No 3* (n 17) para 1.

[21] ibid.
[22] ibid para 1.

system coherence means that the scope of the *means* required of states is informed, in part at least, by the operative provisions of the right to health under instruments such as article 12 of the ICESCR and article 24 of the CRC which both identify a suite of specific measures that states must undertake ranging from providing and ensuring access to health care services to the abolition of harmful traditional practices. The meaning and scope of these specific measures are addressed in detail in Chapters 7, 8, and 9.

The second point to stress when identifying the measures required of states to protect the right to health, is that the principle of local context sensitivity demands that states must enjoy a significant margin of appreciation in determining what measures are appropriate to ensure the effective enjoyment of the right to health within their jurisdiction.[23] However, this discretion is not without limits and the ESC Committee has explained that:

While each State party must decide for itself which means are the most appropriate...with respect to each of the rights, the 'appropriateness' of the means chosen will not always be self-evident. It is therefore desirable that States parties...should indicate not only the measures that have been taken but also the basis on which they are considered to be the most 'appropriate' under the circumstances.[24]

Thus, the onus is on a state to justify, on the basis of a careful consideration of the available evidence, why the means or measures it has adopted are appropriate for the purpose of contributing to the progressive realization of the right to health. The determination of whether this burden has been satisfied is a matter for the human rights treaty monitoring bodies.[25]

B Legislative measures

1 The need for broad and diverse measures

The ICECR and CRC expressly require the adoption of legislative measures to secure the right to health. According to the ESC Committee, this does not mean that states must incorporate the right to health in international law into their domestic law.[26] Thus, legislation is not the only measure by which to secure the enjoyment of a right such as health.[27] Indeed, it may well prove to be counterproductive in some contexts—a point that is discussed in Chapter 8 in relation to the

---

[23] See *Optional Protocol to the International Covenant on Economic, Social and Cultural Rights*, GA Res 63/177, UN Doc A/RES/63/117 (10 December 2008) annex, art 8(4), which provides that when assessing the reasonableness of steps taken by a State to protect the rights under the Covenant, the ESC Committee 'shall bear in mind that the State Party may adopt a range of possible policy measures for the implementation of the rights set forth in the Covenant'.

[24] ESC Committee, *General Comment No 3* (n 17) para 4. See also ESC Committee, *General Comment No 14: The Right to the Highest Attainable Standard of Health*, UN Doc E/C.12/2000/4 (11 August 2000) para 53.

[25] ibid para 4.

[26] ESC Committee, *Draft General Comment No 9: The Domestic Application of the Covenant*, UN Doc E/C.12/1998/24 (3 December 1998) para 8.

[27] See Craven (n 9) 125–6.

impact of criminalizing female genital cutting. But legislation will often be 'highly desirable' and sometimes 'indispensable' to ensure the effective protection of a right, such as the right to health.[28]

The most common context in which legislation will be necessary to secure the right to health, is to ensure protection against discrimination in relation to access to health services for groups such as indigenous peoples,[29] persons suffering from HIV/AIDS, women, children, ethnic minorities, prisoners, people living in rural communities, refugees, and non-citizens.[30] However, legislative measures will also be required in the context of occupational health and safety;[31] regulation of tobacco use;[32] the review of legislation that criminalizes or restricts abortion;[33] the regulation of child labour to protect health;[34] the rights of patients;[35] regulation of alcohol and substance use by children and adolescents;[36] and the need to review the impact of laws on the availability of health care to disadvantaged groups.[37] The ESC Committee has also recommended that 'States *should* consider adopting a framework law to operationalise their right to health national strategy'.[38] This rather eclectic list demonstrates that the identification of when legislative measures will be deemed 'appropriate' will depend on the extent to which they are necessary to secure the effective enjoyment of the right to health within a particular state.

2 The need to justify legislation that interferes with other human rights

The recommendations of the human rights treaty monitoring bodies with respect to legislative initiatives tend to be made without any acknowledgement that such initiatives will invariably be contentious and may often interfere with other human rights. Take, for example, initiatives such as food labeling; regulation of food, alcohol, and tobacco advertising; regulations to determine which medicines can be sold over the counter and those which require a prescription; and public health regulations such as quarantining of persons with infectious diseases or compulsory immunization programmes. The human rights treaty monitoring bodies have tended to overlook the potential for conflicting rights to exist in such contexts and, as a consequence, have failed to provide states with any substantive guidance as to how to

---

[28] ESC Committee, *General Comment No 3* (n 17) para 3.
[29] See, eg, ESC CO Australia E/C.12/AUS/CO/4 para 24.
[30] See also Chapter 4 Part IV B 1 (a).
[31] See, eg, ESC CO Kazakhstan, UN Doc E/C.12/KAZ/CO/1, para 21.
[32] See, eg, ESC CO Poland, UN Doc E/C.12/POL/CO/5, para 25.
[33] See, eg, ESC CO Philippines, UN Doc E/C.12/PHL/CO/4, para 31; CO CEDAW Cameroon, UN Doc A/55/38 Part II (2000) 53, para 60; CO CEDAW Burkina Faso, UN Doc A/55/38 Part I (2000) 25, para 276; CO ICCPR Kenya, UN Doc A/60/40 Vol I (2005) 44, para 86(14).
[34] See, eg, CO ESC Poland, UN Doc E/2003/22 (2002) 54, para 386.
[35] See, eg, CO ESC Russian Federation, UN Doc E/2004/22, 64, para 474; CO CERD Slovakia, UN Doc A/59/18 (2004) 70, para 389.
[36] See, eg, CO CRC Nepal, UN Doc CRC/C/150 (2005) 66, para 364.
[37] See, eg, CO ESC Croatia, UN Doc E/2002/22 (2001) 125, para 914.
[38] ESC Committee, *General Comment No 14* (n 24) para 56 (emphasis added).

resolve such conflicts.[39] They have also failed to offer a rigorous defence of such initiatives in the face of accusations that legislation for public health purposes reflects a paternalistic or 'nanny state' mentality in which the legitimate mandate of the state is exceeded.[40] This is not the place to undertake a detailed analysis with respect to the legitimacy of legislative regulation in any of the areas where these accusations are made. It is sufficient to note that the principle of system coherence demands that legislative measures designed to protect health must not impose an unreasonable limitation on other rights to which individuals are entitled under international law.[41]

---

[39] The ESC Committee has however drawn attention to the need to justify any limitations on an individual's right to health in its *General Comment No 14* (n 24) para 28, where it explained that a state party that:

restricts the movement of, or incarcerates, persons with transmissible diseases such as HIV/AIDS, refuses to allow doctors to treat persons believed to be opposed to a government, or fails to provide immunization against the community's major infectious diseases, on grounds such as national security or the preservation of public order, has the burden of justifying such measures in relation to each of the elements identified in article 4 [of the ICESCR].

[40] See Matthew Thomas and Luke Buckmaster, 'Paternalism in Social Policy—When is it Justifiable?' (Parliament of Australia, Department of Parliamentary Services Research Paper No 8, 15 December 2010) (lists the principles to justify paternalist policy initiatives, that is measures by government which impact upon the liberty and freedom of individuals, as being non-discrimination, proportionality, accountability, and efficacy but makes no mention of the fact that human rights law provides a methodology by which to assess when limitations imposed upon rights by government in the course of pursuing a pressing social need such as public health are justified).

[41] The issue of limitations on civil and political rights in international law tends to be addressed by what are sometimes referred to as 'claw back clauses' or internal limitation provisions within rights. Typically, under the ICCPR these provisions allow for a limitation of a right where it is prescribed by law and is necessary to protect public safety, order, health, or morals or the fundamental rights and freedoms of others. See Commission on Human Rights, *Siracusa Principles on the Limitation and Derogation Provisions in the International Covenant on Civil and Political Rights*, UN Doc E/CN.4/1985/4 (28 September 1984) annex. The test of reasonableness is used in this analysis as an umbrella phrase to capture the considerations relevant when assessing the legitimacy of an interference with a civil and political right. The issue of limitations on economic and social rights is addressed under art 4 of the ICESCR which provides that:

The States Parties to the present Covenant recognize that, in the enjoyment of those rights provided by the State in conformity with the present Covenant, the State may subject such rights only to such limitations as are determined by law only in so far as this may be compatible with the nature of these rights and solely for the purpose of *promoting the general welfare in a democratic society* [emphasis added].

This particular formulation, which differs from the approach used under the ICCPR, is based on art 29(2) of the *Universal Declaration of Human Rights* (UDHR). See generally Amrei Müller, 'Limitations to and Derogations from Economic, Social and Cultural Rights' (2009) 9 HRL Rev 557, 569–84; Philip Alston and Gerard Quinn, 'The Nature and Scope of States Parties' Obligations under the International Covenant on Economic, Social and Cultural Rights' (1987) 9 Hum Rts Q 156, 192–204. The key difference between the treatment of limitations under the ICCPR and ICESCR is that, whereas non-derogable civil and political rights can be restricted for reasons of public order, the rights of others, and morals, economic and social rights can only be limited where this is necessary for the promotion of the general welfare of a democratic state. It has been suggested that general welfare refers to 'the economic and social well being of the people and its community': Müller 573. This is considered to be a slightly more restrictive basis for the limitation of rights relative to the approach adopted under the ICCPR: Alston and Quinn (n 41) 2001–2. However, it remains a very broad phrase capable of accommodating a vast range of measures that might be taken by a state to promote the general welfare. Thus, the key issue when assessing the legitimacy of an interference with a economic and social right will be whether the interference is proportional: ESC Committee, *General Comment 14: The Right to the Highest Attainable Standard of*

Thus, when contemplating legislation as a measure to contribute to the realization of the right to health, a state must first determine whether the legislation will interfere with the normative content of another human right. If so, the state must assess whether this interference is reasonable. In assessing the reasonableness of the interference there are two broad considerations: did the interference respond to a pressing social need, pursue a legitimate aim, or promote the general welfare of a state (such as a public health objective) and were the measures used to achieve that aim proportionate or justified?[42] Increasingly, these broad considerations are being informed by the following more specific considerations:[43]

(i) the nature of the right which is the subject of interference;[44]
(ii) the specific health benefit which the legislation is intended to achieve;
(iii) the nature and the extent of the limitation on any rights;
(iv) whether there is a rational connection between the measure to be taken and the intended health benefit, which will generally require evidence; and
(v) whether there are any less restrictive measures to achieve the health benefit, which are reasonably available to the state.[45]

Health, UN Doc E/C.12/2000/4 (11 August 2000) para 29; Müller 583–4. Thus, for the purposes of this analysis, the test of reasonableness is used to refer to an assessment as to whether the interference is caused by a measure designed to promote the general welfare of a State and an assessment as to the proportionality of such measures. See Brian Griffey, 'The "Reasonableness" Test: Assessing Violations of State Obligations under the International Covenant on Economic, Social and Cultural Rights' (2011) 11 HRL Rev 275, 286.

[42] *Siracusa Principles* (n 41) para 10; ESC Committee, *General Comment 14* (n 24) para 29.

[43] This list of considerations reflects the test used in numerous domestic jurisdictions when assessing the reasonableness of a limitation on a human right. See, eg, *R v Oakes* [1986] 1 SCR 103, 137 (SC, Canada); Constitution of South Africa 1996, s 26; Charter of Human Rights and Responsibilities Act 2006 (Victoria) s 7(2). It is also consistent with the *Siracusa Principles* (n 41) pt I. In the case of South Africa these considerations extend to an assessment of the reasonableness of a limitation on civil and political rights *and* economic, social, or cultural rights—an approach which affirms the interdependence and indivisibility of human rights: Sandra Liebenberg, *Socio-Economic Rights—Adjudication under a Transformative Constitution* (Juta, 2009) 93–7. This model has also been endorsed in reports about the treatment of economic and social rights in other jurisdictions. See, eg, *Towards an ACT Human Rights Act: Report of the ACT Bill of Rights Consultative Committee* (ACT Government, 2003) 5.46; Andrew Byrnes and others, 'Australian Capital Territory Economic, Social and Cultural Rights Research Project: Report' (University of New South Wales, Faculty of Law Research Series Paper No 71, September 2010) para 9.12.

[44] The relevance of this consideration is sometimes questioned given that human rights under international law are said to be interdependent and indivisible. If this is the case, an assessment as to the nature of the right subject to interference would be meaningless. However, some rights, such as the right to life and the prohibition against torture and cruel, inhuman, and degrading treatment are non-derogable. Thus, if a legislative initiative that is designed to achieve a health objective interferes with a non-derogable right, it will never be reasonable under international law. Moreover, the scope for limiting economic and social rights under international law is limited to measures that are for the purpose of promoting the 'general welfare' of a State. This is considered to be a more restrictive basis for limiting a human rights relative to considerations such as public order and morality (phrases which appear in the UDHR and ICCPR): Alston and Quinn (n 41) 201–2. Thus, when identifying the nature of the right, there is an argument that if the right subject to interference is a economic and social right, there will be a greater burden on the state to justify any interference with that right.

[45] Although the ESC Committee has not explicitly embraced this approach it did state in General Comment No 14 on the Right to Health that 'limitations must be proportional, ie the least restrictive

These considerations, which have many parallels with the emerging principles of public health ethics,[46] represent a proportionality test, whereby the burden is placed on a state to prove, on the balance of probabilities, that any legislative measures intended to realize the right to health that interfere with other human rights can be reasonably justified.[47]

With respect to the requirement for evidence, sometimes referred to as the rational connection test in human rights law, and which is similar to the effectiveness principle in public health ethics, the *Siracusa Principles* require that 'any assessment as to the necessity of a limitation shall be made on objective considerations'.[48] Similarly, courts in domestic jurisdictions have tended to stress the need for 'cogent and persuasive evidence'.[49] These domestic courts have stopped short of saying that evidence must always exist to justify any interference with a human right, but they have explained that 'this will generally be the case'.[50] Thus, a heavy onus will rest on a state to justify an interference with a human right where there is an absence of cogent and persuasive evidence.

Such a scenario is likely to arise where there is a lack of data to establish a clear causal nexus between the interference with a right and the legitimate health aim, which the interference is intended to achieve. This absence of an empirically validated connection is not necessarily fatal to the reasonableness of an interference. It will depend on the nature and scope of any interference with a right, the nature of the evidence that is available, and the extent to which it indicates a reasonable causal connection between the measures being proposed and the likely health benefit. A sliding scale would also apply to the extent that the greater and more serious the interference with a human right, the greater the burden imposed on a state to justify the proportionality and reasonableness of its measures that are intended to contribute to the realization of the right to health.

The precautionary principle has a role to play in circumstances where the evidence is unclear. For example, the 1997 *Declaration of the Environmental Leaders of the Eight on Children's Environmental Health*[51] advocated the use of the precautionary

---

alternative must be adopted where several types of limitations are available': ESC Committee, *General Comment No 14* (n 24) para 29. It failed however to recognize that this obligation to adopt the least restrictive measures is itself subject to a test of reasonableness, that is, a State is not under an obligation to adopt the least restrictive measure just the least restrictive measure that is reasonably available.

[46] Solomon Benatar, 'Facing Ethical Challenges in Rolling out Antiretroviral Treatment in Resource Poor Countries: Comment on "They Call It 'Patient Selection' in Khayelitsah"' (2006) 15 Cam QH Ethics 322, 326–7 (lists the principles of public health ethics to include: the effectiveness principle, the proportionality principle, the necessity principle, the harm principle, the least restrictive principle, the reciprocity principle, and the transparency principle).

[47] *Siracusa Principles* (n 41) para 10; Müller (n 41) 573–84. For a general discussion of the concept of proportionality in human rights law see Richard Clayton and Hugh Tomlinson, *The Law of Human Rights* (OUP, 2000) paras 6.62–6.85.

[48] *Siracusa Principles* (n 41) para 10.

[49] See, eg, *R v Oakes* (n 43) 138 (Dickson CJ) (SC, Canada); followed by *DAS v Victorian Human Rights and Equal Opportunity Commission* (2009) 24 VR 415 [147] (Warren CJ) (VSC, Aust); *R v Momcilovic* (2010) 25 VR 436 [146] (VSCA, Aust).

[50] See, eg, *R v Oakes* (n 43) 138 (Dickson CJ) (SC, Canada).

[51] Environment Leader's Summit of the Eight, Miami, Florida, May 5–6, 1997.

principle when dealing with scientific uncertainty in relation to the causal link between children's health and potential environmental factors.[52] In summary, this concept which was included in the 1992 Rio Declaration on Environment and Development as Principle 15, can be adapted with respect to the right to health to require 'that where there are threats of serious or irreversible damage [to the health of an individual] lack of full scientific certainty shall not be used as a reason for postponing cost effective measures to prevent'[53] harm to health.

3 *The need for effective legislative measures*

It remains important to recognize that the adoption of legislative measures will not necessarily be appropriate if such measures fail to contribute to the enjoyment of the right to health. In the context of national constitutions, for example, it has been found that 67.5 per cent of states include a provision addressing health or health care.[54] But many of the countries with the most 'resounding constitutional commitments to health' are countries with a relatively poor commitment to health in terms of their resource allocation.[55] In contrast, a majority of those countries who have the highest per capita government health expenditures have no or a relatively modest constitutional commitment to health care.[56] This should not be taken to mean that a constitutional commitment to health is an inappropriate measure to secure the right to health.[57] Indeed, it may serve a significant symbolic role in demonstrating a state's commitment to the right to health. But symbolism that is unaccompanied by practical measures to implement such a commitment will be insufficient to satisfy a state's obligation to secure the realization of the right to health in international law.

Ultimately, as the ESC Committee has observed, the obligation to undertake appropriate legislative measures is 'by no means exhaustive of the obligations of States parties'.[58] The crucial question, therefore, is what *other measures* will be considered *appropriate* to ensure the effective implementation of the right to health? An application of the ordinary rules of interpretation to such abstract phrases does little to assist in setting their parameters. However, an examination of the work already undertaken within the interpretative community as to the meaning of human rights generally, and more specifically the right to health, is more instructive. Of particular assistance in this regard are two developments. First, an application of what is known as the 'tripartite typology' of obligations can be used as a tool to

---

[52] For a discussion of the application of the precautionary principle in the context of children's health, see G Tamburlini and others, *Children's Health and Environment: A Review of the Evidence* (Joint Report of the European Environment Agency and the WHO Regional Office for Europe, 2002) 202–5; WHO, *The Precautionary Principle: Public Health, Protection of Children and Sustainability* (Background Document, Fourth Ministerial Conference on Environment and Health, Budapest, Hungary, 23–25 June 2004).

[53] *Rio Declaration on Environment and Development*, UN Doc A/CONF.151/26 (Vol I) (12 August 1992) annex I.

[54] Eleanor Kinney and Brian Clark, 'Provisions for Health and Health Care in the Constitutions of the Countries of the World' (2004) 37 Cornell Intl LJ 285, 291 (including the text of the relevant provisions in appendix 1).

[55] ibid 294.   [56] ibid 295.   [57] ibid 304.

[58] ESC Committee, *General Comment No 3* (n 17) para 4.

classify the types of *other measures* that states must undertake. Secondly, the work of the human rights treaty monitoring bodies in their General Comments when combined with their concluding observations concerning the obligations of states under the right to health provides significant guidance as to the measures states must take to ensure that their efforts are *appropriate*.

C Using the tripartite typology to identify 'other appropriate measures'

The obligation of states to respect, protect, and fulfil human rights has become an increasingly accepted typology of duties, especially with respect to economic, social, and cultural rights. It origins can be traced to the work of Henry Shue in 1980,[59] which was formally adopted, albeit in a modified way, by the ESC Committee in its General Comment No 12 on the Right to Adequate Food.[60] The ESC Committee has subsequently extended this typology to other rights, including the right to health in its General Comment No 14 where the ESC Committee extended the obligation to fulfil to contain 'obligations to facilitate, provide and promote'.[61] Importantly this typology has generally been embraced as a practical tool by which to generate an understanding as to the nature of states' obligations under a right.[62] This absence of disagreement within the interpretative community provides evidence of the strong supportive structure necessary to justify its use as a tool by which to classify the types of *other measures* required to secure the effective implementation of the right to health. Although the tripartite typology does not appear in the text of human rights treaties, its implication is consistent with the requirement that a principled approach to treaty interpretation demands an approach that will render the enjoyment of rights to be practical and effective. The tripartite typology is able to contribute to this objective by providing a system to classify the sorts of measures required of states.

At its most abstract level, the ESC Committee has explained that:

the obligation to *respect* requires States to refrain from interfering directly or indirectly with the enjoyment of the right to health. The obligation to *protect* requires States to take measures to prevent third parties from interfering with article 12 guarantees. Finally, the obligation to *fulfil* requires States to adopt appropriate legislative, administrative, budgetary, judicial, promotional and other measures towards the full realization of the right to health.[63]

---

[59] Henry Shue, *Basic Rights, Subsistence, Affluence and US Foreign Policy* (Princeton University Press, 1980) (referred to the duty to avoid depriving, to protect from deprivation, and to aid the deprived).
[60] ESC Committee, *General Comment No 12: The Right to Adequate Food*, UN Doc E/C.12/1999/5 (12 May 1999) para 15. See also 'Maastricht Guidelines on Violations of Economic, Social and Cultural Rights' (1998) 20 Hum Rts Q 691 (also available at UN Doc E/C.12/2000/13 (2 October 2000) 16, para 6); African Commission on Human and Peoples' Rights, *Social and Economic Rights Action Centre and the Centre for Economic and Social Rights v Nigeria*, Communication No 155/96 (27 October 2001) paras 44–8.
[61] ESC Committee, *General Comment No 14* (n 24) para 33. It has also been embraced by the CEDAW Committee in the context of women's right to health: CEDAW Committee, *General Recommendation No 24: Article 12 of the Convention on the Elimination of All Forms of Discrimination against Women—Women and Health*, UN Doc A/54/38/Rev.1 (1999) ch I, paras 14–17.
[62] See, eg, Maastricht Guidelines (n 60) para 6.
[63] ESC Committee, *General Comment No 14* (n 24) para 33.

Although these obligations remain relatively general, they still operate to focus attention on the types of measures that will be necessary to secure the effective realization of the right to health. However, their use carries the significant caveat that they cannot be employed in a way that ignores the requirements for a principled, practical, coherent, and context sensitive interpretation. Thus, the tripartite typology must be used to assist, *not displace,* these objectives, and it will be suggested that the human rights treaty monitoring bodies, particularly the ESC Committee, have paid insufficient attention to these requirements, especially the need for internal and external system coherence.

1 The obligation to respect—the need to avoid conflation

In terms of measures to *respect* the right to health, General Comment No 14 of the ESC Committee indicates that states must 'refrain from denying or limiting equal access' for all adults and children 'including prisoners or detainees, minorities, asylum seekers and illegal immigrants to preventive, curative and palliative health services; abstaining from enforcing discriminatory practices as a state policy; and abstaining from imposing discriminatory practices relating' to the health needs of girls.[64] This directive is consistent with the general principle of non-discrimination in international law that an individual must not be subject to discrimination on the basis of any status. Moreover, the list of protected categories offered by the ESC Committee is not necessarily reflective of the basis on which many children experience discrimination. Thus, to this list should be added the prohibition of discriminatory practices against children on the basis of any status including but not limited to the status of their parent(s), carer(s), or other family member(s)—which is a specific requirement under article 2(2) of the CRC.

According to the ESC Committee, the obligation to respect also prohibits states from:

- restraining or 'impeding the delivery of traditional preventive care, healing practices and medicines';
- 'marketing unsafe drugs';
- 'applying coercive medical treatments unless on an exceptional basis for the treatment of mental illness or the prevention and control of communicable diseases';
- 'limiting access to contraceptives and other means of maintaining sexual and reproductive health';
- 'censoring, withholding or intentionally misrepresenting health related information including sexual education and information';
- 'unlawfully polluting air, water and soil eg: through industrial State owned facilities';
- 'using or testing nuclear, biological or chemical weapons if such testing results in the release of substances harmful to human health'; and

---

[64] ESC Committee, *General Comment No 14* (n 24) para 34.

- 'limiting access to health care services as a punitive measure eg during armed conflicts in violation of international humanitarian law'.[65]

This list of prohibited activities invites two observations. First, each of these obligations is equally applicable to the situation and experience of adults and children subject to the caveat that, with respect to children, such practices must be consistent with the principles that are particular to the CRC, especially the best interests principle under article 3; the right to participate in all decisions affecting the child under article 12; and the protection against traditional practices prejudicial to the health of a child under paragraph 3 of article 24. Thus for example, a state may be obligated to impede the delivery of traditional preventive care, healing practices, and medicines if such practices are considered prejudicial to the health of a child.[66]

Second, the list represents a significant extension beyond the specific measures agreed to by states in the final formulation of the right to health in article 12 of the ICESCR and article 24 of the CRC. It is true that the text of both instruments imposes an expansive obligation on states to secure the realization of the right to health by taking 'all appropriate means'.[67] Thus, there are arguably grounds to support such a 'strong' interpretative approach with respect the 'means' or 'measures' required of states. But it remains problematic in that it assesses the scope of the obligation to take appropriate measures, by reference to the simple question of whether there is a nexus between an act or omission by a state and the health of an individual. As such, it demonstrates a reluctance to consider any of the factors identified in Chapter 3 as being critical to the interpretative exercise.

Given the broad definition of health outlined in Chapter 4, it may be artificial to insist upon any real limitations as to the scope of the measures states must take to secure the right to health. The work of the Indian Supreme Court with respect to the scope of the right to life provides a precedent for such a strong and expansive interpretative approach. In several cases the Court has pushed the boundaries of the right to life beyond what would be considered reasonable in many jurisdictions such that it extends to a right to protection against preventive detention,[68] a right to livelihood,[69] and a right to a healthy workplace.[70] But there are at least three reasons why caution should be exercised when considering the adoption of such an approach with respect to the right to health in international law.

---

[65] ibid.
[66] The CRC Committee has on occasions expressed concern at the potential harm to a child's health caused by recourse to traditional medical practices. For example, in its concluding observations for Nepal it expressed concern at the 'prevalence of traditional practices which could be harmful to the health of children, such as that of consulting witchdoctors instead of modern medical facilities and not giving water to children suffering from diarrhoea': CO CRC Nepal, UN Doc CRC/C/15/Add261, para 61(e). See also CO CRC Madagascar, UN Doc CRC/C/15/Add218, para 47.
[67] ICESCR, art 2(1) provides that '[e]ach State party... undertakes to take steps... to the maximum of its available resources with a view to achieving progressively the full realisation of the rights *recognized* in the... Covenant by all appropriate means...'
[68] *Francis Mullin v Administrator, Union of Delhi* (1981) 2 SCR 516 (SC, India).
[69] *Olga Tellis v Bombay Municipal Corporation* (1986) AIR SC 180 (India).
[70] *Consumer Education and Research Centre v Union of India* (1995) 1 SCR 626 (SC, India).

First, the creative jurisprudential skills of Indian jurists were a response to the demarcation between civil and political rights and economic and social rights under the Indian Constitution with only the former being justiciable.[71] Thus the Court, which views itself as having a mandate to facilitate and deliver social justice,[72] has been prepared to use the right to life as a vessel by which to import the directive principles which largely contained economic and social rights into the enforceable jurisdiction of the Court. If the human rights treaty monitoring bodies were to assume a similar role and advocate the most progressive interpretation of a right wherever the opportunity arose, this would demonstrate a serious lack of global context sensitivity. Their legitimacy would be potentially compromised and states would be unlikely to be persuaded by the interpretative efforts of the human rights treaty monitoring bodies.

Second, a move to expand the parameters of the right to health in the way suggested by the ESC Committee, tends to overlook the reality that international law consists of discrete rights and regimes, the implementation of which will often have an impact on the health of an individual. The adoption of the expansive approach advocated by the ESC Committee with respect to the content of the right to health, therefore, creates the risk of a colonizing effect, whereby the right to health subsumes the content of other independent rights. So, for example, censoring of health information is viewed by the ESC Committee as a violation of the right to health rather than an interference with the right to receive information under article 19(2) of the International Covenant on Civil and Political Rights (ICCPR) or article 13 of the CRC. But such an approach does not pay sufficient attention to the need to pursue internal and external system coherence.

This is not to say that the principle of the interdependence of human rights might be able to provide a justification for finding that the censoring of health information constitutes a violation of both rights. However, care must be taken when adopting such an approach because of the potential for the general aspects of the right to health to be used to replace and potentially displace a more specific rule such as freedom of access to information. To censor or withhold health information may *prima facie* constitute an interference with both the right to health and freedom of access to information. But contrary to the views of the ESC Committee, it does not *necessarily* constitute a violation of either right. Ultimately this question must be resolved after a consideration as to whether the interference could be justified as being in accordance with the law and necessary to achieve a legitimate objective.[73] Thus, while the

---

[71] The Constitution of India 1949, s 37.
[72] See, eg, *Education and Research Centre v Union of India* (n 70).
[73] Article 13 of the CRC states:

1 The child shall have the right to freedom of expression; this right shall include freedom to seek, receive and impart information and ideas of all kinds, regardless of frontiers, either orally, in writing or in print, in the form of art, or through any other media of the child's choice.
2 The exercise of this right may be subject to certain restrictions, but these shall only be such as are provided by law and are necessary:
   (a) For respect of the rights or reputations of others; or
   (b) For the protection of national security or of public order (ordre public), or of public health or morals.

expansive approach adopted by the ESC Committee may carry a superficial allure for those seeking to advance the health of individuals, it carries with it a real risk of compromising the need for system coherence and perpetuating a reductionist rather than substantive approach[74] to the question of whether a state has fulfilled its obligation to respect the right to health.

Related to this concern is the prospect that the simplistic nexus-based approach advanced by the ESC Committee, will obscure or overlook the significance of entire regimes that have been developed under international law to address specific issues that may by implication have an impact on the health of individuals. For example, the use and testing of weapons and the pollution of the environment are both matters which are subject to significant international regulation and ongoing discussions. To simply include within the scope of the right to health an obligation to refrain from testing weapons harmful to human health and unlawful pollution fails to acknowledge the complexity of these issues and the level of sophistication in relation to the measures already undertaken by states. As such, the ESC Committee's views appear to have been adopted without any consideration for the need to ensure external system coherence. It might be possible to offer a principled, practical, and context sensitive defence for the inclusion of such obligations within the scope of the right to health. Such a defence, however, would need to take account of the regimes that already exist under international law with respect to the regulation of these issues and no concession is even made by the ESC Committee that such regimes exist.

The third and final point that suggests the need for caution when mapping out the contours of the right to health is the nature of the debate during the drafting process as to the need to include a provision that would protect children against medical or scientific experimentation or treatment in the absence of free and informed consent.[75] Ultimately a lack of consensus as to an appropriate formulation precluded the inclusion of such a provision within article 24 of the CRC. This outcome is significant for two reasons. First, the absence of consensus among states suggests the need for a degree of caution when interpreting the scope of the obligation to respect the right to the highest attainable standard of health. If states were unprepared to include an obligation on which consensus could not be achieved, it becomes problematic if the human rights treaty monitoring bodies subsequently adopt a strong interpretative approach which imposes wide sweeping and general obligations on states. Such an approach does not demonstrate sufficient sensitivity to the nature of the international legal order and as such is likely to compromise the persuasiveness of the interpretation advanced.

Second, upon the failure to include a provision on medical and scientific experimentation, the Australian delegation explained that the absence of such a provision

---

[74] John Tobin, 'Seeking Clarity in relation to the Principle of Complementarity: Reflections on the Recent Contributions of Some International Bodies' (2007) 8 MJIL 356.

[75] See UN Doc E/CN.4/1989/WG.1.46; Commission on Human Rights, *Question of a Convention on the Rights of the Child: Report of the Working Group on a Draft Convention on the Rights of the Child*, UN Doc E/CN.4/1989/48 (2 March 1989) paras 416–31.

would not 'leave children unprotected' as other articles under the CRC 'clearly prohibited medical experimentation not in the best interests of the child'.[76]

This comment confirms the need to avoid the inflation of the right to health to the extent that it displaces other more applicable rights and thus compromises internal system coherence. It also indicates that the drafters of the CRC anticipated boundaries in relation to the scope of their obligations with respect to the right to health. To overlook this reality, which forms part of the context in which the right to health must to be interpreted, is to create the risk of an interpretative approach that is so discordant with the expectations of states that it is readily dismissed as being without foundation.

2 The obligation to protect

(a) The need for a more persuasive account of its content

The second level of obligation concerning to the right to health, which can assist in developing an understanding as to the types of *appropriate measures* required of states, is the obligation to 'protect'. This obligation requires states to regulate the behaviour of non-state actors so that they do not violate an individual's right to health. In terms of the specific measures required of states to ensure they comply with this obligation, the General Comment of the ESC Committee on the Right to Health indicates that states must:

- '[a]dopt legislation or to take other measures ensuring equal access to health care and health related services provided by third parties';
- 'ensure that privatisation of the health sector does not constitute a threat to the availability, accessibility, acceptability and quality of health facilities, goods and services';
- 'control the marketing of medical equipment and medicines by third parties';
- 'ensure that medical practitioners and other health professionals meet appropriate standards of education, skill and ethical codes of conduct';
- 'ensure that harmful social or traditional practices do not interfere with access to pre- and post-natal care and family planning';
- prevent third parties from coercing girls to undergo traditional practices such as female circumcision;
- 'take measures to protect all vulnerable or marginalised groups within society'; and
- 'ensure that third parties do not limit access to health related information and services'.[77]

This list demonstrates an awareness of the areas in which non-state actors could directly impact upon the health of an individual or the accessibility and quality of health care services provided to an individual. However, it tends to raise issues of a complex nature without any substantive discussion as to the measures required for

---

[76] Commission on Human Rights, *Question of a Convention on the Rights of the Child* (n 75) para 431.
[77] ESC Committee, *General Comment No 14* (n 24) para 35.

their operationalization. For example, the absolute prohibition on access to health-related information is raised again without any concession as to the qualified nature of the right to information under the ICCPR generally and the reality that the CRC concedes that constraints can be placed on access to health-related information and services for children in certain circumstances. Privatization is also flagged as a potential threat to the enjoyment of the right to health but there is no accompanying discussion as to how this threat is to be managed beyond some broad generalizations.[78]

Such an approach may be seen as a form of issue spotting rather than sophisticated and coherent legal analysis that is practical and principled. It could be argued that it is defensible on the basis that an exceedingly proscriptive approach would undermine the margin of appreciation afforded to states in their implementation of the obligations under the right to health. The greater risk, however, is that it will only serve to further undermine the credibility of this right. Instead of addressing its ambiguity and providing a clear and practical account of the measures required to secure the implementation of this provision, the further unravelling of its content by the ESC Committee into even more broad and generalized terms only serves to compound the perspective that this right is indeterminate.

The work of the CRC Committee does not necessarily unsettle this trend. Its General Comment on adolescent health[79] expands the list of measures against which states must protect adolescents to include:

- All forms of labour which may jeopardize the enjoyment of their rights, notably by abolishing all forms of child labour and by regulating the working environment and conditions in accordance with international standards.[80]
- All forms of intentional and unintentional injuries including those resulting from violence and road traffic accidents.[81]
- All harmful traditional practices such as early marriages, honour killings, and female genital mutilation.[82]

In fairness to the CRC Committee, its General Comment was not directed specifically at the right to health and represents a more general articulation of the matters of concern to the health of adolescents. Thus, it was not intended to provide the sort of directive as to the content of the right to health that was attempted by the ESC Committee. As a consequence, the identification of linkages between the health of an adolescent and matters such as child labour, injuries, and harmful traditional practices is not unreasonable. However, it is important to stress that only one of these matters is expressly included within article 24—harmful traditional practices, which

---

[78] See pages 222–3.
[79] CRC Committee, *General Comment No 4: Adolescent Health and Development in the Context of the Convention on the Rights of the Child*, UN Doc CRC/GC/2003/4 (1 July 2003).
[80] ibid para 39(e).   [81] ibid para 39(f).   [82] ibid para 39(g).

is dealt with under para 3—and the remainder are dealt with in specific articles of the CRC, namely article 32 which deals with exploitative child labour and article 19 which deals with violence against children. The requirement to pursue internal system coherence demands that the right to health need not be inflated so as to impose obligations on states with respect to child labour and violence given that these matters are specifically addressed in other provisions of the CRC.

The problematic nature of the approach taken by the human rights treaty monitoring bodies in articulating the content of the obligation to protect the right to health does not mean that this interpretative tool should be abandoned. Instead, greater consideration must be given to the test to be used to determine how the obligation to protect can be used in a clear and practical way to guide states in their attempts to secure the right to health. Such a test should consist of two parts: first, an examination as to whether the acts or omissions of a non-state actor have an impact, whether directly or indirectly, on the health of an individual; and if so, an examination, in light of any other relevant international legal standards, to determine whether the interference is reasonably justified. If not justifiable, there must be an assessment of those measures which can reasonably to taken by a state, in light of available resources, to ameliorate the interference.[83]

(b) The obligations of non-state actors

Any discussion of the 'obligation to protect' also gives rise to a consideration of the responsibilities of non-state actors with respect to the realization of the right to health in international law. This issue has been the subject of significant discussion in the literature[84] and more recently in the work of the UN Special Representative on Business and Human Rights.[85] It is not the place to engage in an analysis of this material and it is sufficient to make the following observations in relation to the right to health. First, as discussed in Chapter 3, the role of non-state actors in contributing to the realization or potential violation of the right to health is significant. This is especially the case with multinational corporations, such as private health companies

---

[83] This represents an adaptation of the test adopted by the European Court of Human Rights in *Osman v United Kingdom* 1998–VIII 3124 (ECtHR), in which the Court had to determine the nature of the obligation imposed on state authorities with respect to the potential threat to an individual's right to life from non-state actors. The Court held (para 116) that:

bearing in mind the difficulties involved in policing modern societies, the unpredictability of human conduct and the operational choices which must be made in terms of priorities and resources, such an obligation must be interpreted in a way which does not impose an impossible or disproportionate burden on the authorities... [and adopted the following test]:

... must be established that the authorities knew or ought to have known at the time of the existence of a real and immediate risk to the life of an identified individual from the criminal acts of a third party and that they failed to take measures within the scope of their powers which judged reasonably might have been expected to avoid that risk.

[84] See, eg, Andrew Clapham, *Human Rights Obligations of Non-State Actors* (OUP, 2006); David Kinley (ed), *Human Rights and Corporations* (Ashgate Publishing, 2009); Olivier De Schutter, *Transnational Corporations and Human Rights* (Hart Publishing, 2006).

[85] See generally Business & Human Rights Resource Centre <http://www.business-humanrights.org/Home> accessed 13 June 2011.

and pharmaceutical companies, which often possess greater capacity to influence the realization of the right to health than some states.

Second, this reality has fuelled an urge within elements of the interpretative community to impose human rights obligations on multinational corporations. Thus, for example, the Special Rapporteur has argued that 'it would be inconceivable that some human rights do not place legal obligations on business enterprises'[86] and the ESC Committee has declared that the private business sector has responsibilities regarding realization of the right to health.[87] The Special Rapporteur has also prepared *Human Rights Guidelines for Pharmaceutical Companies in Relation to Access to Medicines*, which state, in the preamble, that, '[p]harmaceutical companies, including innovator, generic and biotechnology companies, have human rights responsibilities in relation to access to medicines'.[88]

But these assertions are unaccompanied by any explanation as to the basis upon which companies are bound by human rights obligations. Thus, the intensions given for such obligations are not merely thin, but non-existent.[89] There well may be a moral justification for such obligations and there may even be a political justification.[90] But there is no legal basis upon which to transpose the obligations assumed by states under international law to multinational corporations. A principled interpretation of international law precludes such an approach. This is because the duty bearers under international human rights law are states and not non-state actors. The Special Rapporteur's justification for circumventing this fundamental principle is that it 'is inconceivable' that human rights do not impose obligations on businesses. But inconceivability is not a recognized principle that justifies a deviation from an established principled of international law.

Thus, when examining the obligations of non-state actors in international law there is a need to distinguish between what the law is (*lex lata*) and what it ought to be (*lex ferenda*). This does not mean that non-state actors will be immune from the consequences of those actions that are required to ensure a state is able to progressively realize the right to health. On the contrary, states will inevitably adopt measures to secure the right to health which impose obligations on non-state actors. The limitations of this approach are acknowledged given that in many cases, a single state will lack the capacity to control the actions of powerful multinational corporations. Indeed, this is one of the factors that generate such enthusiasm for imposing

---

[86] *Report of the Special Rapporteur on the Right to Health to the General Assembly 2006*, UN Doc A/61/338 (13 September 2006) para 93.
[87] ESC Committee, *General Comment No 14* (n 24) para 42.
[88] *Report of the Special Rapporteur on the Promotion and Protection of Human Rights and Fundamental Freedoms while Countering Terrorism*, UN Doc A/62/263 (15 August 2007) annex, preambular para (i). See also Rajat Khosla and Paul Hunt, *Human Rights Guidelines for Pharmaceutical Companies in relation to Access to Medicines: The Sexual and Reproductive Health Context* (Human Rights Centre, University of Essex, 2009).
[89] Griffin (n 2) 17.
[90] See, eg, *Report of the Special Rapporteur on the Right to Health to the General Assembly 2008*, UN Doc A/63/263 (11 August 2008) para 44 (alluding to MDG 8, a global partnership for development, which includes among its targets to, '[i]n cooperation with pharmaceutical companies, provide access to affordable essential drugs in developing countries').

human rights obligations directly on non-state actors. But this concern cannot be resolved by distorting the principles of international law. Moreover, such an approach ignores the prospect that the text of those treaties, in which the right to health is protected, actually provide a mechanism by which to address the relative lack of influence a state may experience in its relationship with non-state actors. Namely, the obligation of international co-operation—an obligation that requires states to act collaboratively to design appropriate regulatory systems and structures which will contribute to the realization of the right to health. The scope and meaning of this obligation is examined in detail in Chapter 8.

3 The obligation to *fulfil*—the need to mainstream the right to health

The final type of obligation that can be used to inform the nature of the measures required of states to secure the right to health is the obligation to *fulfil*. According to the ESC Committee in its General Comment No 14:

> The obligation to *fulfil* requires States parties, *inter alia*, to give sufficient recognition to the right to health in national political and legal systems, preferably by way of legislative implementation, and to adopt a national health policy with a detailed plan for realizing the right to health.[91]

This duty to 'give sufficient recognition' to the right to health is of profound significance in understanding the types of measures that states must take under both article 12 of ICESCR and article 24 of the CRC.

Commentators such as Jennifer Ruger have explained that the operationalization of any right including the right to health requires an internalization among the population of a state that the right itself is 'worthy of social recognition, investment and regulation'.[92] This in turn provides the political mandate at the domestic level by which a state can undertake the social organization necessary to secure the implementation of the right 'in the form of a redistribution of resources and related legislation and regulation'.[93] States must, therefore, stimulate and inspire the political, ethical, and moral commitment among their populations to accept that concern for the health of individuals is motivated not simply by beneficence or utilitarian considerations, but the idea that health is a right and entitlement.[94] It is within this context that the ESC Committee, in its concluding observations for Great Britain and Northern Ireland, recommended:

---

[91] ESC Committee, *General Comment No 14* (n 24) para 36. See also: paras 53–6.
[92] Jennifer Ruger, 'Toward a Theory of a Right to Health: Capability and Incompletely Theorized Agreements' (2006) 18 Yale JL &Hum Rts, 273.
[93] ibid 318.
[94] ibid. The transformative consequences of this approach cannot be underestimated. Indeed for Jonathan Mann, who pioneered the use of a rights based approach in addressing HIV/AIDS, his motivation was because of the revolutionary influence of human rights which 'must be understood as a challenge to the political and societal status quo': Jonathan Mann 'Health and human rights: if not now, then when?' (1997) 2 HHR 113, 117.

that the State party take effective measures to increase awareness of economic, social and cultural rights among the public at large as well as among judges, public officials, police and law enforcement officials, medical practitioners and other health-care related professionals...[95]

Importantly from the perspective of discrete groups—such as women, children, racial minorities, refugees, migrant workers, the elderly, or persons with disabilities—the promotion and recognition of the right to health within a state's legal and political system, and the development of its national health policy, must be sensitive to and respond to the special needs and experiences of discrete cohorts. Anything less would fail to satisfy the requirement to ensure the effective implementation of the right to health. In practice, this requires that the health needs of discrete groups must be mainstreamed into public health debates to ensure they remain visible and integrated rather than marginalized, isolated, or ignored in the development of national health policies.[96] At present many discussions tend to adopt the latter approach with respect to certain groups. For example, with respect to children, the Special Rapporteur on the right to health indicated at one point that he would address as part of his mandate the impact of stigma and discrimination in relation to women, racial and ethnic minorities, people with disabilities, and people living with HIV/AIDS, but omitted children.[97] This was despite repeated calls from the now abolished Commission on Human Rights that all special rapporteurs integrate a consideration of children's rights into their mandate[98] and the fact that over 26,000 children die each day from largely preventable diseases[99] while 40 million are subjected to abuse within their homes each year.[100]

Moreover, discussions about HIV/AIDS sometimes fail to make any mention at all of children,[101] notwithstanding the burden borne by those children infected and affected by this pandemic,[102] and the view expressed by the CRC Committee 'that, unfortunately, children are at the heart of the problem'.[103] Similarly discussions

---

[95] CO ESC Great Britain and Northern Ireland, UN Doc E/C.12/GBR/CO/5, para 15.

[96] See, eg, CEDAW Committee, *General Recommendation No 24* (n 61) para 31(a) (recommending that states 'place a gender perspective at the centre of all policies and programmes affecting women's health').

[97] *Report of the Special Rapporteur on the Right to Health to the Commission on Human Rights 2003*, UN Doc E/CN.4/2003/58 (13 February 2003) paras 65–8. cf ESC Committee, *General Comment 14* (n 41) paras 22–4.

[98] See, eg, Commission on Human Rights, *Rights of the Child*, Res 1995/79, UN Doc E/CN.4/RES/1995/79 (8 March 1995) para 13; Commission on Human Rights, *Rights of the Child*, Res 1997/78, UN Doc E/CN.4/RES/1997/78 (18 April 1997) preambular text.

[99] UNICEF, *The State of the World's Children 2008: Child Survival* (UNICEF 2007) 1.

[100] Submission from the World Health Organization to the Committee for its Day of General Discussion on 28 September 2001: WHO, *Prevention of Child Abuse and Neglect: Making the Link between Human Rights and Public Health* (28 September 2001) <http://www.who.int/hhr/information/treaty-body_information/en/index.html> accessed 10 January 2011.

[101] Michael Kirby, 'HIV/AIDS: The Dialogue Heats Up' (International Symposium on Human Rights in Public Health: Research, Policy and Practice, University of Melbourne 3–5 November 2004).

[102] See, eg, UNICEF and UNAIDS, *The Framework for the Protection and Care of Orphans and Vulnerable Children Living in a World with HIV/AIDS* (UNAIDS July 2004) 7–11; UNAIDS, *2004 Report on the Global Aids Epidemic* (UNAIDS 2004) 61–6, 93–8.

[103] CRC Committee, *General Comment No 3: HIV/AIDS and the Rights of the Child*, UN Doc CRC/GC/2003/3 (17 March 2003) para 2.

about inter-sectoral discrimination with respect to health policies manage to list race, gender, and class but omit any reference to children.[104] Such approaches remain blind to the disproportionate impact of disease and discriminatory practices against children because of their age and increased vulnerability relative to adults and in doing so serve to render invisible and compound the negative impact of these diseases and practices on children's health.

The mainstreaming of children's right to health, and indeed the right to health of other marginalized and vulnerable groups, into the development and implementation of national public health policies and strategies, contributes to the practical realization of their right to health. Importantly, a consideration of the rights of discrete groups whether they be women, children, or persons with disabilities, is not intended to displace the right of all other groups. Indeed, a slogan such as 'children's first', is highly problematic and does not reflect a rights-based approach.[105] As Nigel Cantwell has explained, it places children 'on a kind of "more equal than others" pedestal', which reflects a 'charity based approach to children, where sentimentality over children's vulnerability leads to facile "separate" responses: never mind human rights let's help children'.[106] In contrast, the mainstreaming of the right to health for different groups recognizes that these groups have special health needs by virtue of their social status which must be given special attention, lest they remain invisible and marginalized. But it also requires that the realization of the right to health for these groups must be addressed in conjunction with the right to health of other groups within a society via the visible integration of these groups in policy making,[107] rather than in isolation, competition, or as an 'add on'.[108]

Ultimately, the obligation to take all appropriate measures to *fulfil* the right to health in international law is concerned with the need to allocate the resources available within a state that are necessary to achieve the progressive realization of this right. The content of this obligation and the question of resource allocation will be dealt with below. However, at the core of the obligation to 'fulfil' the right to health, is a requirement that states take appropriate measures to secure the effective enjoyment of this right. This is a deeply political project. As the Task Force for the Millennium Project on Child Health and Maternal Health has observed:

Power comes in many guises. Among them is the power to set the terms of the debate, to structure the patterns of thought and language, the fundamental taken-for-granted

---

[104] Dianne Otto, 'Linking Health and Human Rights: What are the Possibilities?' (International Symposium on Human Rights in Public Health: Research, Policy and Practice, University of Melbourne, 3–5 November 2004).
[105] For a general discussion of a human rights based approach see *Report of the Special Rapporteur on the Right to Health to the Commission on Human Rights 2006*, UN Doc E/CN.4/2006/48 (3 March 2006) paras 25–8.
[106] Nigel Cantwell, 'Is the Rights Based Approach the Right Approach?' (Defence for Children International: International Symposium, Geneva, 22 November 2004).
[107] CRC Committee, *General Comment No 5: General Measures of Implementation of the Convention on the Rights of the Child*, UN Doc CRC/GC/2003/5 (27 November 2003) para 47.
[108] E Williams, 'Small Hands, Big Voices? Children's Participation in Policy Change in India' (2005) 36.1 IDS Bull 82, 83.

assumptions that shape our approaches to problems and solutions. If the current situation is indeed untenable, if the dominant categories no longer address the dominant problems, then these terms must be challenged and opened to new debate and directions.[109]

This is precisely what the internalization and mainstreaming of the right to health requires of states. It requires them to assess and challenge the impact of exiting power structures and relationships on the health of individuals within their jurisdiction and, if necessary, dismantle and reconfigure such relationships and structures.[110] It is an ambitious task and not easily achieved but it attempts to do this by first reorientating the terms of the debate towards the right to health in international law.

D Using the work of the human rights treaty monitoring bodies to develop an understanding as to the nature of 'appropriate measures'

The preceding discussion sought to demonstrate that the obligations to respect, protect, and fulfil can operate as a tool by which to identify and classify the types of measures required of states to secure their effective implementation of the right to health. The use of this typology revealed that an understanding of appropriate measures cannot be confined to prohibitions on those actions undertaken by states which may impact on an individual's health. On the contrary, it requires proactive measures that regulate the impact of non-state actors on the health of individuals and an obligation to take steps to actively facilitate the realization of the right to the highest attainable standard of health. But the discussion also revealed a tendency on the part of the ESC Committee to use the tripartite typology to generate an understanding as the nature of a state's obligation that was often oblivious to the need to ensure internal and external system coherence. This is not an inevitable result, but it does illustrate the need for caution when using the tripartite typology to assist in the interpretative process. It may be able to play a role in identifying the types of measures required of states, but the articulation of the nature and scope of these measures must remain cognizant of the need to ensure system coherence and remain context sensitive. A failure to heed these warnings will lead to a vision of the right to health that is potentially inconsistent with what states have accepted in other regimes and human rights treaties.

But even when the tripartite typology is used properly, it remains an incomplete tool by which to generate an understanding as to the nature of the *appropriate measures* that states must undertake if they are to fulfil the obligations that arise as a consequence of their *recognition* of the right to health. Ultimately, the determination of whether a *measure* is to be deemed *appropriate* will depend on the extent to which it is able to make an effective contribution to securing an individual's right to health. States must enjoy a significant margin of appreciation in determining which *other measures* they consider appropriate beyond the specific measures that are listed

---

[109] L Freedman and others, UN Millennium Project Task Force on Child Health and Maternal Health, *Who's Got the Power? Transforming Health Systems for Women and Children* (Earthscan, 2005) 19.
[110] A Hughes, J Wheeler, and R Eyben, 'Rights and Power: The Challenge for International Development Agencies' (2005) 36.1 IDS Bull 63, 63.

in the text of article 12 of the ICESCR and article 24 of the CRC.[111] However, the requirement that such measures must be *appropriate* acts as a significant textual and practical constraint on the exercise of this discretion. Moreover, a considerable body of knowledge has been accumulated within the interpretative community as to the kinds of measures that are likely to make a positive contribution to the state of an individual's health and thus satisfy the requirement of appropriateness.

It is beyond the scope of this analysis to examine every aspect of this accumulated knowledge. Instead, the focus here will be on the work of the human rights treaty monitoring bodies for two reasons. First, these bodies have been entrusted with the task of monitoring the compliance of states with their obligations under the right to health in international law and providing states with guidance as to how to satisfy these obligations. As the ESC Committee explained with respect to the phrase 'all appropriate means'—which is the equivalent of 'appropriate measures' under the CRC:

While each State party must decide for itself which means are the most appropriate in the circumstances... the ultimate determination as to whether all appropriate measures have been taken remains one for the Committee to make.[112]

It therefore follows that the human rights treaty monitoring bodies have a legal mandate to develop an understanding as to the nature of the measures considered appropriate to secure the right to health.

Secondly, the performance of this task involves, in the words of the CRC Committee itself, an 'ongoing dialogue with Governments and with the United Nations and United Nations related agencies, NGOs and other competent bodies'.[113] As outlined in Chapter 3, such a collaborative approach is an essential feature of an interpretative process that seeks to generate a common understanding as to the meaning of a concept such as the right to health. As such, the jurisprudence of the human rights treaty monitoring bodies warrants careful attention to the extent that it is able to identify those *measures* that are considered to be *appropriate* for the purpose of ensuring the effective realization of the right to health. It is important to stress, however, that the work of the human rights treaty monitoring bodies, while significant, is not beyond reproach. Thus, to the extent that their contributions to developing an understanding as to the meaning of the right to health can be said to be principled, practical, coherent, and context sensitive, their work will be embraced. Where, however, they fail to satisfy any of these criteria, the persuasiveness of the work undertaken by human rights treaty monitoring bodies will be questioned.

---

[111] See ESC Committee, *An Evaluation of the Obligation to Take Steps to the 'Maximum of Available Resources' under an Optional Protocol to the Covenant*, UN Doc E/C.12/2007/1 (10 May 2007) para 11 ('in accordance with the practice of judicial and other quasi-judicial human rights treaty bodies, the Committee always respects the margin of appreciation of States to take steps and adopt measures most suited to their specific circumstances').
[112] ESC Committee, *General Comment No 3* (n 17) 86 para 4.
[113] CRC Committee, *General Comment No 5* (n 107) para 26.

1 National plans, programs, and policies

The Guidelines prepared by the ESC Committee to assist states in preparing their reports under the ICESCR require states to indicate whether they have 'adopted a national health policy and whether a national health system... is in place'.[114] General Comment 14 of the ESC Committee affirms this requirement that states adopt a national strategy to ensure the enjoyment of the right to health, which identifies the resources available to achieve this objective.[115] Similarly, the CRC Committee has repeatedly emphasized the need for states to adopt a national health policy. Thus, for example, it has called on states, as it did in its concluding observations for Algeria, to 'develop and implement comprehensive policies and programmes for improving the health situation of children'.[116] Such a demand satisfies the criteria of being clear and practical to the extent that it is designed to provide states with guidance as to processes they should adopt in fulfilling their obligations under article 24.

Importantly, the adoption of a National Plan must be both comprehensive and responsive to the diverse health needs of various groups within a state's jurisdiction if it is to be effective. It is in this context that the CRC Committee has welcomed the adoption by states of initiatives including a National Programme for the reduction of newborn and maternal mortality rates;[117] National Reproductive Programme on Student and Adolescent Health;[118] National Program on Immunization Agency;[119] National Program for Mental Health;[120] National Water Supply and Sanitation Policy;[121] National Strategic Plan on HIV/AIDS;[122] National Action Plan for Healthcare Development;[123] National Breastfeeding Policy;[124] National Health Strategic Plan;[125] National Nutrition Strategy;[126] national programmes relating to child survival;[127] National Drug Plan;[128] National Policy for Adolescent Health;[129] and a National Policy on Early Childhood Development.[130]

---

[114] *Guidelines on Treaty-Specific Documents to be Submitted by States Parties under Articles 16 and 17 of the International Covenant on Economic, Social and Cultural Rights*, UN Doc E/C.12/2008/2 (24 March 2009) annex, para 55.

[115] ESC Committee, *General Comment No 14* (n 24) para 53.

[116] CO CRC Algeria, UN Doc CRC/C/15/Add269, para 57(a). See also CO CRC Philippines, UN Doc CRC/C/15/Add259, para 59(b); CO CRC Pakistan, UN Doc CRC/C/15/Add217, para 53(a); CO CRC Bangladesh, UN Doc CRC/C/15/Add221, para 52(a); CO CRC Haiti, UN Doc CRC/C/15/Add202, para 45(a).

[117] See, eg, CO CRC Algeria, UN Doc CRC/C/15/Add269, para 56. See also CO CRC Nicaragua, UN Doc CRC/C/15/Add, para 48.

[118] See, eg, CO CRC Mongolia, UN Doc CRC/C/15/Add264, para 45.

[119] See, eg, CO CRC Nigeria, UN Doc CRC/C/15/Add257, para 48.

[120] See, eg, CO CRC Algeria, UN Doc CRC/C/15/Add269, para 58.

[121] See, eg, CO CRC Nigeria, UN Doc CRC/C/15/Add257, para 48.

[122] See, eg, CO CRC Algeria, UN Doc CRC/C/15/Add269, para 58

[123] See, eg, CO CRC Sweden, UN Doc CRC/C/15/Add248, para 31.

[124] See, eg, CO CRC Belize, UN Doc CRC/C/15/Add252, para 53(e).

[125] See, eg, CO CRC Zambia, UN Doc CRC/C/15/Add206, para 48.

[126] See, eg, CO CRC Vietnam, UN Doc CRC/C/15/Add200, para 40(a).

[127] See, eg, CO CRC Burkina Faso, UN Doc CRC/C/15/Add193, para 38.

[128] See, eg, CO CRC Spain, UN Doc CRC/C/15/Add185, para 39(a).

[129] See, eg, CO CRC Chile, UN Doc CRC/C/15/Add173, para 41.

[130] See, eg, CO CRC Malawi, UN Doc CRC/C/15/Add174, para 43.

This long list invites three observations. First, the vast range of matters canvassed in the various policies reflects an awareness by the CRC Committee, and the states which have actually undertaken such measures, as to the nature of the *other measures* required to implement the right to health. Moreover, each of the matters has a significantly proximate relationship with children's health as opposed to another right which warrants their inclusion within the scope of the right to health. Second, a closer examination of the concluding observations of the CRC Committee reveals that, as a general rule, it has not sought to interrogate the specific process by which states prepare these plans or to comment upon the specific measures required for their implementation. Its preference is simply to advocate and commend their adoption with the details being a matter left to the discretion of states. It is an important observation with respect to the content of the right to health as it reflects a high level of local contextual sensitivity and deference to states in relation to the determination of the specific measures required to secure their obligations. Context thus plays a significant role in determining the precise content of the *measures* which will be considered to be *appropriate* in each state for the purposes of their obligations under the right to health. The obligation to adopt plans and policies by which to secure the right to health may be universal to all states, but the human rights treaty monitoring bodies are prepared to accommodate a reasonable margin of appreciation to states with respect to the implementation of this obligation.

The margin afforded to states is not, however, without boundaries. First, the principle of internal coherence, for example, requires that plans and policies must be developed in a way that ensures consistency with other articles under the relevant human rights treaties. Second, the mere adoption of a national plan or policy is insufficient and the CRC Committee, for example, has often expressed concern at the ineffective implementation of such plans[131] and recommended, as it did in its concluding observations for Algeria, that states must adopt the necessary legislative, administrative, and budgetary measures to ensure that this is not the case.[132] The ESC Committee has provided further guidance on the measures required to ensure effective implementation of a national health plan and stressed the need for states to ensure that their national health strategy is 'based on the principles of accountability, transparency and independence of the judiciary'[133] and to consider the adoption of 'a framework law to operationalise their right to health strategy' with appropriate mechanisms to monitor the implementation of the strategy.[134] Such comments reflect an attempt to strike an appropriate balance between the need to accommodate the specific socio-political context within individual states and at the same time the need to insist on effective implementation of international obligations. The key

---

[131] See, eg, CO CRC Croatia, UN Doc CRC/C/15/Add243, para 51 ('concerned about the effective implementation of breastfeeding programmes'); CO China, UN Doc CHN/CO2, para 68 ('concerned that the implementation of these policies and programmes [HIV/AIDS] is insufficient'); CO CRC Equatorial Guinea, UN Doc CRC/C/15/Add245, para 47(b) ('Strengthen the implementation and coordination of existing health policies and programmes...').
[132] CO CRC Algeria, UN Doc CRC/C/15/Add269, para 57(b).
[133] ESC Committee, *General Comment No 14* (n 24) para 55.
[134] ibid para 56.

point to stress is that institutional systems and structures must accompany the adoption of national strategies and plans if a state is to secure the effective implementation of the obligations that flow from its recognition of the right to health.

2 Accountability mechanisms

(a) **General accountability measures**

According to the ESC Committee, the provision of a system to ensure accountability and provide a remedy is considered to be an integral measure in securing the right to health. Thus, it has declared:

> Any person or group victim of a violation of the right to health should have access to effective judicial or other appropriate remedies at both national and international levels.[135]

Moreover, it has added that states should consider the incorporation of the right to health into their domestic legal system[136] and must ensure adequate reparation in circumstances where a person's right to health has been violated.[137] The CRC Committee has endorsed the notion that the effective enjoyment of human rights including children's rights requires access to a remedy and that economic and social rights are justiciable.[138]

This emphasis on the obligation of states to develop systems of accountability is a fundamental feature of human rights.[139] The recognition of a right to health creates an entitlement for an individual that there must be a system in place to hold a state accountable for fulfilling its obligation with respect to this entitlement. The precise system of accountability is a matter within the discretion of states subject to the caveat that whatever system is adopted it must be effective. In this respect, states may create systems of accountability at the domestic level or accede to regional and/or international accountability mechanisms.

With respect to the international mechanisms, the submission of timely and comprehensive reports to the human rights treaty monitoring bodies as required under the various human rights treaties, or a preparedness to allow individuals to lodge complaints with the human rights treaty monitoring bodies or accepts visits from the Special Rapporteur, represent forms of accountability. At the regional level, states may be prepared to allow individuals to take complaints with respect to the right to health to bodies such as the European Committee of Social Rights,[140] the

---

[135] ibid para 59.
[136] ibid para 60.
[137] ibid para 59.
[138] CRC Committee, *General Comment No 5* (n 107) paras 25–6; CRC Committee, *Report on the Forty-Sixth Session*, UN Doc CRC/C/46/3 (22 April 2008) ch VII, paras 84–5 (Day of General Discussion on 'Resources for the Rights of the Child—Responsibility of States', 5 October 2007).
[139] *Report of the Special Rapporteur on the Right to Health to the General Assembly 2008* (n 90) para 8; Philip Alston, 'Ships Passing in the Night: The Current State of the Human Rights and Development Debate Seen through the Lens of the Millennium Development Goals' (2005) 37 Hum Rts Q 755 (describing accountability as the *sine qua non* of human rights).
[140] See, eg, European Committee of Social Rights, *International Centre for the Legal Protection of Human Rights 'Interights' v Croatia*, Decision No 45/2007 (30 March 2009) (holding that a long term failure to provide a comprehensive and objective evidence-based sexual and reproductive health education

Inter American Commission or Court of Human Rights,[141] or the African Commission of Human Rights.[142] Finally, at the domestic level, there are several options that states can adopt to allow for a form of accountability with respect to their obligations under the right to health in international law including: the capacity of national human rights institutions and health commissioners to hear complaints or conduct inquiries in relation to the measures adopted by a state to secure the right to health, or the adoption of human rights impact assessments that scrutinize the proposed impact of legislation or policy on the right to health.[143] However, it is the capacity for a domestic judicial remedy for a violation of the right to health that is emphasized in the comments of the human rights treaty monitoring bodies.

(b) Judicial remedies
The role of civil and political rights The justiciability of economic, social, and cultural rights remains a contested issue among commentators and in the jurisdictions of most states. The debate was outlined in Chapter 2 and need not be repeated here.[144] Instead, it is sufficient to offer the following observations in relation to the right to health. First, the plea of the human rights treaty monitoring bodies for domestic incorporation of the right to health tends to display a lack of sensitivity with respect to the complex legal and hostile political obstacles that operate against the prospect of judicial scrutiny being exercised over the right to health in most domestic courts. Although, as noted above, 67.5 per cent of states provide for some kind of constitutional recognition of the right to health or a right to health care,[145] very few states have adopted the formulation of the right to health in international law and very few provide individuals with an entitlement to enforce their right to health in the courts.

---

programme was in violation of Article 11(2) of the European Social Charter which requires states to provide 'advisory and educational facilities for the promotion of health and the encouragement of individual responsibility in matters of health').

[141] See, eg, Inter-american Commission on Human Rights, *Yanomami v Brazil*, Resolution No 10/85, Case No 7615 (1985) (allegation that construction work caused displacement of indigenous people from their ancestral lands and caused many people to die from influenza, measles, and other diseases; the Inter American Commission held that the failure of the Government to provide an alternative site was a violation of the rights to life, liberty, and personal security and recommended that the Government 'take preventive and curative health measures to protect the lives and health of Indians exposed to infectious or contagious diseases').

[142] See, eg, African Commission on Human and People's Rights, *Social and Economic Rights Action Center and Center for Economic and Social Rights v Nigeria* (n 60) (holding that the failure of the Government to prevent the contamination of the environment by petroleum companies, which led to significant health problems among the Ogoni people, was a violation of several rights including their right to health).

[143] See generally *Report of Special Rapporteur on the Right to Health to the General Assembly 2007*, UN Doc A/62/214 (8 August 2007) s III; Saskia Bakker and others, 'Human Rights Impact Assessment in Practice: The Case of the Health Rights of Women Assessment Instrument' (2009) 1 J Hum Rts Practice 436.

[144] See generally Henry Steiner, Philip Alston and R Goodman, *International Human Rights in Context: Law Politics and Morals* (3rd edn, OUP, 2008) 313–57. With respect to the right to health see: Brigit Toebes, *The Right to Health as a Human Right in International Law* (Hart Publishing, 1999) 167–240; Ssenyonjo (n 17) 343–8.

[145] Kinney and Clark (n 54) 291.

Second, much of the litigation that concerns the health of individuals[146] is grounded in civil and political rights such as the right to life, protection against cruel and inhuman treatment, and the right to physical integrity. For example, in India the right to life has been held to incorporate a fundamental right to health[147] which, in turn, has formed the basis for decisions that require access to emergency medical treatment irrespective of available resources;[148] the provision of compulsory health insurance to workers exposed to asbestos;[149] and a review of drugs and medicines being marketed in India.[150] Similarly in Nepal and Pakistan, the courts have imported the right to health into the right to life and held that the right to clean water is an integral element of public health.[151] In Bangladesh, the Supreme Court has held that imported milk powder which contained radioactive material threatened the right to life which included protection of health.[152] And in Brazil the Supreme Court has held that the right to health derives from the right to life, which includes a right to medicine for the underprivileged and individuals with HIV/AIDS or other severe illnesses.[153] Similarly, the Columbian Constitutional Court has also held that the right to health is enforceable for any individual when (a) there is an inextricable relationship with a fundamental right such as the right to life such that this right would be compromised if the state failed to provide health care; (b) the claimant is in especially vulnerable circumstances; and (c) the good or service being sought is part of the minimum core of the right to health as defined by the Court.[154] And in a recent landmark decision, T-760/2008, the Columbian

---

[146] See generally Toebes, *The Right to Health as a Human Right* (n 144) 144, 170–240 (provides an examination of the jurisprudence generated by international, regional and domestic bodies with respect to the right to health as at the end of 1998); *Report of the Special Rapporteur on the Right to Health to the Human Rights Council 2007*, UN Doc A/HRC/4/28 (17 January 2007) paras 55–89; Paul Hunt and Sheldon Leader, 'Developing and Applying the Right to the Highest Attainable Standard of Health: The Role of the Special Rapporteur (2002–2008)' in John Harrington and Maria Stuttaford (eds), *Global Health and Human Rights: Legal and Philosophical Perspectives* (Routledge 2010) 39–44; Iain Byrne, 'Enforcing the Right to Health: Innovative Lessons from Domestic Courts' in Andrew Clapham and Mary Robinson (eds), *Realising the Right to Health* (Rüffer &Rub, 2009) 525.

[147] *Francis Mullin v Administrator, Union of Delhi* (n 68). Under the Indian Constitution there are fundamental rights including the right to life, which are enforceable, and directive principles such as the right to health, which are non-enforceable. The Court has overcome this limitation by importing directive principles such as the right to health into the meaning of fundamental rights such as the right to life.

[148] *Paschim Banga Khet Majoor Samity v State of West Bengal* (1996) 4 SCC 37 (SC, India).

[149] *Consumer Education and Research Centre v Union of India* (n 70).

[150] *Vincent Panikulangura v Union of India* (1987) 2 SCC 165 (SC, India); *Drug Action Forum v Union of India* (1997) 6 SCC 609 (SC, India).

[151] See *Maharjan v His Majesty of Government NKP*, 2053, vol 8, 627 (SC, Nepal); *General Secretary West Pakistan Salt Miners Labour Union, Khewra, Jhelum v Director Industries and Mineral Development, Punjab Lahore* [1994] SCMR 2061 (SC, Pakistan). See Iain Byrne and Sara Hossain, 'Economic and Social Rights Case Law of Bangladesh, Nepal, Pakistan and Sri Lanka' in Malcolm Langford (ed), *Social Rights Jurisprudence: Emerging Trends in International and Comparative Law* (CUP, 2008) 136–7.

[152] *Mohiuddin Farooque v Bangladesh* (1996) 48 DLR 438 (HC, Bangladesh).

[153] See Flavia Piovesan, 'Impact and Challenges of Social Rights in the Courts' in Malcolm Langford (ed), *Social Rights Jurisprudence: Emerging Trends in International and Comparative Law* (CUP, 2008) 185–8.

[154] Alicia Yamin and Oscar Parra-vera, 'How Do Courts Set Health Policy? The Case of the Columbian Constitutional Court' (2009) 6 PLoS Med 147, 147.

Constitutional Court ordered the Government to restructure its health system to ensure the provision of health services in accordance with these principles.[155]

With respect to the prohibition against inhuman and degrading treatment as a vehicle to protect health, the suffering required for treatment to violate this prohibition has been held to occur in circumstances where the deportation of a man suffering with HIV/AIDS to his country of origin would lead to the withdrawal of treatment and a painful death;[156] and a girl, who was forced to carry a child with anencephalia to term, in circumstances where an abortion was lawfully available, suffered significant mental harm.[157]

The justiciability dilemma Commentators tend to enlist such cases in support of the proposition that the right to health is justiciable.[158] But the automatic transferability of comparative case law is problematic and these cases arguably reveal more about the scope of civil and political rights *within a particular jurisdiction*, than the justiciability of the right to health in international law. Thus, it is premature to conclude, for example, as the Special Rapporteur has done, that 'Samity [an Indian case concerning access to emergency medical treatment] confirms that there are health related rights that give rise to some immediate obligations that are not subject to resource availability'.[159] This decision involved an interpretation by a *domestic court* of the right to life under a *national constitution*. It is inappropriate to rely upon such a case as evidence that an element of the right to health *in international law* is not subject to available resources when the formulation of this right in the ICESCR and the CRC makes no reference to emergency medical care *and* specifically states that the right to health is subject to progressive realization.

With respect to those domestic cases that directly engage the right to health, there is a stronger justification for enlisting such cases as evidence of the justiciability of the right to health in international law. At the same time this approach remains problematic as the formulation of the right to health in domestic jurisdictions is rarely the same as the formulation adopted in international law. For example, article 27(3) of the South African Constitution provides that, 'No one may be refused emergency medical treatment'—an entitlement that is arguably not subject to the availability of resources. A state is certainly free to adopt such a formulation, but the right to health in international law does not contain such an entitlement.

---

[155] For a discussion of the case see: ibid.

[156] *D v United Kingdom* 1997–III (ECtHR). cf *Henao v The Netherlands* App No 13669/03 (ECtHR, 24 June 2003) (held that a violation of the prohibition against inhuman treatment will not occur if the illness has not reached an advanced stage).

[157] HRC, *KNLH v Peru*, Communication No 1153/2003, UN Doc CCPR/C/85/1153/2003 (22 November 2005) (the complaint also alleged a violation of the right to life but the HRC declined to determine this claim as it had already determined that the facts supported the allegation of inhuman and degrading treatment).

[158] See, eg, *Report of the Special Rapporteur on the Right on the Right to Health to the Human Rights Council 2007* (n 146) paras 55–89.

[159] ibid para 67.

The Columbian Constitutional Court has also been active in giving meaning to the right to health especially in the context of children. For example, it has ordered authorities to provide a free vaccination programme for children;[160] ordered a private health provider to supply an ear implant to a 10-year-boy suffering from deafness;[161] and ordered the social security system to pay for treatment for children in specialist clinics overseas when the treatment is not available in Columbia.[162] However, unlike the right to health in international law, which remains progressive and subject to available resources for adults and children alike, article 44 of the Columbian Constitution, provides that children's health is a basic right which is directly enforceable in the courts. Thus, there is a need for caution when assessing the justiciability of the right to health in international law by reference to its treatment in regional and domestic forums.

The justiciability dilemma resolved At the same time, the comparative exercise can be used to demonstrate the justiciability of the right to health in international law and in this respect two cases arising under the South African Constitution are particular revealing.[163] Article 27 of the South African Constitution provides that:

1. Everyone has the right to have access to
   a health care services, including reproductive health care; . . .
2. The state must take reasonable legislative and other measures, within its available resources, to achieve the progressive realisation of each of these rights.

This formulation of the right to health, with its focus on access to health care services, is narrower than the formulation adopted in international law. But accessibility is still a core element of the right to health in international law and the progressive nature of the obligation under the South African Constitution is consistent with the obligation in international law.

On two occasions the South Constitutional Court has declared that the justiciability of the right to health is beyond question. The first case, *Soobramoney v Minister of Health (Kwazulu-Natal)*,[164] concerned a claim by a man in need of dialysis that he was entitled to emergency medical treatment. The court rejected this claim because it formed the view that chronic renal failure was not an emergency medical condition but an ongoing, albeit incurable, condition.[165] It then went on to consider whether the state had complied with its progressive obligation to provide access to health care

---

[160] Judgment No SU-225/98, 10.3.1998 (CC, Colombia).
[161] Judgment No T-236/98, 16.3.1998 (CC, Colombia).
[162] Judgment No T-165/95, 18.9.1995 (CC, Colombia). For a discussion of the Columbian case law see: Magdalena Sepulveda, 'The Constitutional Court's Role in Addressing Social Injustice' in Malcolm Langford (ed), *Social Rights Jurisprudence: Emerging Trends in International and Comparative Law* (CUP, 2008) 144, 152–5.
[163] See Sandra Liebenberg, *Socio-Economic Rights under a Transformative Constitution* (n 43) ch 4; Jennifer Sellin, 'Justiciability of the Right to Health—Access to Medicines: The South African and Indian Experience' (2009) 2 Erasmus L Rev 445.
[164] *Soobramoney v Minister of Health* [1998] 1 SA 765 (CC, Sth Afr).
[165] ibid para 21.

services subject to available resources. It determined that there had been no violation of the Constitution as the relevant authorities had given careful consideration to the allocation of scarce resources within South Africa and the court would be 'slow to interfere with rational decisions taken in good faith by the political organs and medical authorities whose responsibility it is to deal with such matters'.[166]

The adoption of this deferential rationality test by the South African Constitutional Court was the subject of criticism among commentators.[167] However, it has been abandoned by the Court in subsequent cases in favour of a model of reasonableness review, where the Court asks 'whether the means chosen [by the relevant state authority] are reasonably capable of facilitating the realization of the socioeconomic rights in question'.[168] For example, in the case of *Minister of Health and Others v Treatment Action Campaign and Ors (1)* 2002 (10) BCLR 1033 (CC) the Court had to review the reasonableness of a policy adopted by South African authorities in good faith with respect to the measures adopted to prevent mother-to-child transmission of HIV. The authorities had confined access to an antiretroviral drug, Nevirapine (which had been made freely available by the manufacturer) to a limited number of public clinics. It did so because it wanted to trial the drug and argued there was a lack of trained staff to administer and provide counselling to women who received the drug. The Constitutional Court rejected these arguments. It held that there was evidence that the drug was effective. It also held that the additional resources required to train the heath care staff to administer the drug was negligible relative to the benefit that would be obtained if transmission of HIV from mothers to children were reduced. The Court therefore found that the policy adopted by the relevant authorities was not consistent with the obligation to take reasonable measures to provide access to health care services.

This decision has been lauded as an effective illustration as to the justiciability of the right to health. It certainly illustrates an effective form of accountability with respect to access to health care services. But, again, caution must be exercised against inflating the significance of this decision. It only dealt with the issue of accessibility and the South African Constitutional Court is yet to deal with an allegation concerning the failure of the state to make a particular health service available—an entitlement that exists under the right to health in international law. However, there is no reason to preclude an application of the principle of 'reasonableness review' to such a claim. In other words, provided a state can demonstrate that the failure to provide a specific health service is reasonable in light of the resources available to a state *and* the other obligations it is required to satisfy, there will be no violation of the right to health. (The application of this test is discussed in more detail below in

---

[166] *Soobramoney v Minister of Health* [1998] 1 SA 765 (CC, Sth Afr) para 29.
[167] See, eg, Craig Scott and Philip Alston, 'Adjudicating Constitutional Priorities in a Transnational Context: A Comment on *Soobramoney*'s Legacy and *Grootboom*'s Promise' (2000) 16 SAJ Hum Rts 206.
[168] Sandra Liebenberg, 'Adjudicating Social Rights under a Transformative Constitution' in Malcolm Langford (ed), *Social Rights Jurisprudence: Emerging Trends in International and Comparative Law* (CUP, 2008) 75, 83.

the context of the meaning of the progressive obligation of states to realize the right to health.)

At the same time it would appear to be premature and counterproductive to demand that the right to health in international law imposes an unqualified obligation on states to provide a judicial remedy in relation to every element of the right to health. Certainly, as the ESC Committee has recognized, there are certain components of the right to health which are legally enforceable and it has noted that the 'principle of non-discrimination in relation to health facilities, goods and services is legally enforceable in numerous national jurisdictions'.[169] As a consequence, the effectiveness principle demands that states should adopt measures to enable individuals to enforce their right to non-discrimination in relation to the right to health. But the need to remain constructively engaged with states in the interpretative process suggests that a weak rather than strong approach is warranted with respect to those other aspects of the right to health which should be rendered justiciable.

The limits of litigation Moreover, the need for an accountability mechanism should not be confined to the existence of a traditional court based remedy that is based on 'strong' forms of judicial review. Indeed, the experience of South Africa suggests that weak forms of judicial review, which allow the courts to engage in a collaborative dialogue with states as to the measures required to comply with economic rights such as the right to health, may be more effective than the coercive approach associated with strong forms of review.[170] The obligation to develop an appropriate accountability mechanism therefore invites states to consider whether weak forms of judicial review may provide an effective judicial model for the enforcement of those aspects of the right to health which are considered justiciable. The requirement that the adoption of such mechanisms be effective also demands that they recognize and accommodate the difficulties that vulnerable groups such as children have 'in pursing remedies for breaches of their rights'.[171]

But when considering the issue of accountability it is important to recognize that while litigation remains an important strategy to secure aspects of the right to health, it will always remain limited in what it can achieve.[172] It tends to be reactive rather than preventative, adversarial rather than conciliatory, excessively legalistic and

---

[169] ESC Committee, *General Comment No 14* (n 24) para 1.

[170] Rosalyn Dixon, 'Creating Dialogue about Socio-Economic Rights: Strong-Form versus Weak-Form Judicial Review Revisited' (2007) 5 Int J Const Law 391, 408–15; Mark Tushnet, 'New Forms of Judicial Review and the Persistence of Rights- and Democracy-Based Worries' (2003) 38 Wake Forest L Rev 813, 823. See also ESC Committee, *An Evaluation of the Obligation to Take Steps to the 'Maximum of Available Resources' under an Optional Protocol to the Covenant* (n 111) para 13 (outlining several measures that the ESC Committee could recommend to states found to be in violation of their obligations under the ICESCR).

[171] CRC Committee, *General Comment No 5* (n 107) para 25 (it is in this context that the Committee has recommended that 'States need to give particular attention to ensuring that there are effective, child-sensitive procedures available to children and their representatives. These should include the provision of child-friendly information, advice, advocacy, including support for self-advocacy, and access to independent complaints procedures and to the courts with necessary legal and other assistance').

[172] See Liebenberg, *Socio-Economic Rights Adjudication under a Transformative Constitution* (n 43) 36–42.

invariably resource intensive. It can also be counterproductive. Indeed, it has been suggested that right to health litigation in Brazil has led to a worsening in the country's health inequities.[173] Under Brazil's Constitution, article 196 provides that 'health is the right of all and the duty of the state and shall be guaranteed by social and economic policies aimed at reducing the risk of illness and other maladies and by universal and equal access to all activities and services for its promotion, protection and recovery'. This right has been interpreted by the courts as 'an individual entitlement to the satisfaction of one's health needs with the most advanced treatment, *irrespective of costs*'.[174] Such an approach is not only unsustainable because of its drain on Brazil's limited resources, but it also skews the benefits of the right to health to those who have access to the courts.[175] Moreover, empirical studies indicate that this model has actually exacerbated health inequities.[176] For example, in the state of Sao Paulo in 2008, approximately US$200 million was spent, mostly on expensive drugs, to comply with court orders benefiting 35,000 claimants.[177] According to Ferraz, this is roughly the same level of resources that the federal Ministry of Health intended to invest in a vaccination program against pneumococcal bacteria for 3.2 million children. But the implementation of this program had to be deferred for two years because of a lack of resources.[178]

International law does not favour the Brazilian model of accountability for the right to health. It does not conceive of the right to health as a trump card. Instead its implementation must be secured within the context of limited resources and the competing rights of other individuals. But even if courts were to narrow their focus to an assessment of the conduct of a state in the context of these factors, litigation remains a limited mechanism for achieving effective accountability. This is because a range of factors invariably compromise access to the courts and appropriate legal services. In the case of Brazil, for example, research indicates that access to the courts 'is significantly easier for those with resources and social attributes [such as education] that are more predominant in higher socioeconomic groups'.[179] This does not mean that judicial remedies are inappropriate as a form of accountability, merely that they are limited and must be accompanied by other measures. The precise form of the measures adopted by a state will ultimately be determined in light of the prevailing socio-political factors within a state. But this deference to local context sensitivity remains subject to the caveat that whatever measures are adopted by a state, the cumulative effect is to create an effective and accessible system of accountability.

---

[173] Octavio Ferraz, 'The Right to Health in the Courts of Brazil: Worsening Health Inequities?' (2009) 11 Health &Hum Rts 33.
[174] ibid 34.   [175] ibid 34.   [176] ibid.
[177] ibid 41.   [178] ibid.   [179] ibid 39.

3 Data collection and the use of indicators and benchmarks

(a) Data collection—necessary but problematic

It is accepted within the field of public health that an effective health policy must be evidence-based.[180] The broad acceptance of this position within the interpretative community supports the call by the CRC Committee for states to collect epidemiological data regarding children's health so as to enable states to devise an effective national plan to respond to the diverse health needs of children within their jurisdiction.[181] Similarly, the other human rights treaty monitoring bodies have called on states to collect disaggregated data to enable states to develop targeted policies to secure the realization of the right to health generally[182] and for discrete groups such as women,[183] persons with disabilities,[184] indigenous people,[185] and people with mental health issues.[186] These recommendations represent a clear and practical measure, which is directed towards facilitating an understanding of those groups that require specific measures to secure the implementation of their right to health. It is for this reason that the CRC Committee, for example, has repeatedly expressed its concern and emphasized the need for states to undertake systematic data collection in order to monitor the health and development of children.[187] In order to be effective, such qualitative and quantitative data should be timely and reliable in relation to important national health indicators[188] including mental health indicators.[189] It should also be disaggregated according to sex, age, origin, and socio-economic status and include an analysis of the experience of specific groups

---

[180] Lynn Freedman and others, (n 109), 2–3; UNICEF, *Joint Health and Nutrition Strategy for 2006–2015*, UN Doc E/ICEF/2006/8 (15 November 2005) para 24; Solomon Benetar (n 326) (identifies the effectiveness principle as a core principle of public health ethics which requires 'evidence of the effectiveness of a measure in improving public health').

[181] See, eg, CO CRC Nigeria, UN Doc CRC/C/15/Add257, para 49(d); CO CRC Antigua and Barbuda, UN Doc CRC/C/15/Add247 para 52(b). See generally CRC Committee, *General Comment No 5* (n 107) para 48 ('Collection of sufficient and reliable data on children, disaggregated to enable identification of discrimination and/or disparities in the realization of rights, is an essential part of implementation').

[182] See, eg, CO CRC Brazil, UN Doc E/C.12/BRA/CO/2, para 28(g).

[183] See, eg, CEDAW Committee, *General Recommendation No 24* (n 61) para 9; ESC Committee, *General Comment No 14* (n 24) para 29 (calling for data about maternal mortality and abortion).

[184] See, eg, CO ESC Kazakhstan, UN Doc E/C.12/KAZ/CO/1, para 32

[185] See, eg, CO CERD Suriname, UN Doc A/59/18 (2004) 36, para 198.

[186] See, eg, CO ESC Poland, UN Doc E/C.12/POL/CO/5, para 24; CO ESC Croatia, UN Doc E/2002/22 (2001) 125, paras 914.

[187] See CRC Committee, *General Comment No 4* (n 79) para 13; CO CRC Nigeria, UN Doc CRC/C/15/Add257, para 49(d); CO CRC Antigua and Barbuda, UN Doc CRC/C/15/Add247, para 52(b); CO CRC Mongolia, UN Doc CRC/C/15/Add264, para 45; CO CRC Croatia, UN Doc CRC/C/15/Add243, para 51; CO CRC Greece, UN Doc CRC/C/15/Add170, para 56(a).

[188] CO CRC Nigeria, UN Doc CRC/C/15/Add257, para 49(d); CO CRC Antigua and Barbuda, CRC/C/15/Add247, para 52(b).

[189] See, eg, CO CRC China, UN Doc CRC/C/15/CHN/CO/2, para 66 ('concerned about the lack of data and information on mental health services available for children'); CO CRC Palau, UN Doc CRC/C/15/Add149 para 48; CO CRC Suriname, UN Doc CRC/C/15/Add130, para 45; CO CRC South Africa, UN Doc CRC/C/15/Add122, para 31.

within a state such as religious groups, ethnic and/or indigenous minorities, migrants or refugees, and persons with disabilities.[190]

With respect to each of these categories, the CRC Committee, for example, has dedicated significant attention to particular age groups, especially the health of adolescents, and has repeatedly urged states to undertake a comprehensive and multidisciplinary study with respect to this cohort and collect data on suicide rates among adolescents,[191] the incidence of sexually transmitted diseases,[192] early marriages,[193] pregnancy rates,[194] abortion rates,[195] violence,[196] substance abuse,[197] alcohol consumption,[198] and tobacco use[199] among adolescents and the incidence of HIV/AIDS.[200]

The CRC Committee's insistence upon the accumulation of such information can be defended to the extent that it is directed towards identifying those groups of children for whom *appropriate measures* must be adopted to secure their right to health. However, this approach suffers from two deficits. First, the comments of the CRC Committee generally fail to acknowledge the significant resources, both financial and human, required by states to acquire such data.[201] The other human rights treaty monitoring bodies have also failed to address this reality. The issue of resource allocation and the progressive nature of the obligation to secure the right to

---

[190] CRC Committee, *General Comment No 4* (n 79) para 13.
[191] See, eg, CO CRC Albania, UN Doc CRC/C/15/Add249, para 56; CO CRC Japan, UN Doc CRC/C/15/Add231, paras 47(b), 48; CO CRC Eritrea, UN Doc CRC/C/15/Add204, para 41; CO CRC Lesotho, UN Doc CRC/C/15/Add147, para 45; CO CRC Suriname, UN Doc CRC/C/15/Add130, para 45; CO CRC South Africa, UN Doc CRC/C/15/Add122, para 31.
[192] See, eg, CO CRC Tanzania, UN Doc CRC/C/25/Add156, para 48; CO CRC United Kingdom and Northern Ireland—Overseas Territories, UN Doc CRC/Caaaa/15/Add135, para 37; CO CRC Suriname, UN Doc CRC/C/15/Add130, para 45.
[193] See, eg, CO CRC Tanzania, UN Doc CRC/C/15/Add156, para 48; CO CRC South Africa, UN Doc CRC/C/15/Add122, para 31.
[194] See, eg, CO CRC Tanzania, UN Doc CRC/C/15/Add156, para 48; CO CRC United Kingdom and Northern Ireland—Overseas Territories, UN Doc CRC/C/15/Add135, para 37; CO CRC Suriname, UN Doc CRC/C/15/Add130, para 45; CO CRC Georgia, UN Doc CRC/C/15/Add124, para 46; CO CRC South Africa, UN Doc CRC/C/15/Add122, para 31.
[195] See, eg, CO CRC Tanzania, UN Doc CRC/C/15/Add156, para 48; CO CRC United Kingdom and Northern Ireland—Overseas Territories, UN Doc CRC/C/15/Add135, para 37; CO CRC Suriname, UN Doc CRC/C/15/Add130, para 45; CO CRC Georgia, UN Doc CRC/C/15/Add124, para 46; CO CEC South Africa, UN Doc CRC/C/15/Add122, para 31.
[196] See, eg, CO CRC Vanautu, UN Doc CRC/C/15/Add111, para 20.
[197] See, eg, CO CRC Belize, UN Doc CRC/C/15/Add252, para 55; CO CRC Palau, UN Doc CRC/C/15/Add149, para 48; CO CRC United Kingdom and Northern Ireland—Overseas Territories, UN Doc CRC/C/15/Add135, para 37; CO CRC Georgia, UN Doc CRC/C/15/Add124, para 46; CO CRC South Africa, UN Doc CRC/C/15/Add122, para 31.
[198] See, eg, CO CRC Lesotho, UN Doc CRC/C/15/Add147, para 45; CO CRC South Africa, UN Doc CRC/C/15/Add122, para 31.
[199] See, eg, CO CRC Eritrea, UN Doc CRC/C/15/Add204, para 41; CO CRC Lesotho, UN Doc CRC/C/15/Add147, para 45; CO CRC Palau, UN Doc CRC/C/15/Add149, para 48; CO CRC Georgia, UN Doc CRC/C/15/Add124, para 46; CO CRC South Africa, UN Doc CRC/C/15/Add122 para 31.
[200] See, eg, CRC Committee, *General Comment No 3* (n 103).
[201] This observation is also consistent with the discussion of data collection and indicators in the CRC Committee's General Comment No 5 where no mention is made of the resources required for data collection: CRC Committee, *General Comment No 5* (n 107) paras 48–50.

health are discussed below. However, it is important to stress here that the obligation of states with respect to data collection is also resource dependent and thus progressive. In light of this constraint, and the need to advance an understanding of the right to health that is sufficiently context sensitive, the recommendations of the human rights treaty monitoring bodies should include a directive to states to prioritize the types of information they should collect in light of the issues that are of particular concern in their jurisdiction. With respect to the identification of such issues states would enjoy significant discretion subject to the caveat that their decisions are based on consultations with all relevant actors including medical professionals, NGOs, and community leaders and remain subject to oversight by the human rights treaty monitoring bodies.

In relation to the prioritization of data collection, the Special Rapporteur has identified, as a minimum, the following grounds for disaggregation in relation to the health status of individuals: sex, race, ethnicity, rural/urban, and economic and social.[202] Curiously he failed to include age in this minimum list. An approach to the interpretation of the right to health that satisfies the requirement of system coherence demands not only the inclusion of children as a general cohort, but also those categories of childhood which have been adopted by the CRC Committee and are discussed below: early childhood, middle childhood, and adolescence.

The second deficiency of the human rights treaty monitoring bodies in their calls for the collection of data, is their reluctance to call on states to collect data to explain why individuals experience gaps in the four qualitative elements of the right to health (availability, accessibility, acceptability, and quality) and the actual cost of measures to address these gaps. There is little practical benefit, for example, in gathering statistics on the number of women or children who are denied access to health care if a state does not also collect information on the factors that are causing this denial *and* the cost of the measures to ensure effective access. In this respect, commentators are now calling on states to embrace econometric analysis to identify those factors that limit access to health care goods and services *and* undertake costing measures to establish the level of resources required by a state to address any inhibiting factors.[203] The use of such quantitative methods and economic analysis tends to fuel anxieties among human rights advocates because of the fear of reducing rights to a cost–benefit analysis. But a dose of pragmatism demands the need to collect such data as it provides the evidence required to assess (a) what measures must be taken, and (b) the resources required for this purpose. This is not a case of social science methods usurping or compromising the right to health, rather an acknowledgement that the effective implementation of this right relies upon interdisciplinary engagement and dialogue.[204]

---

[202] *Report of the Special Rapporteur on the Right to Health to the Commission on Human Rights 2006* (n 105) para 49(b).
[203] See, eg, Edward Anderson and Marta Foresti, 'Assessing Compliance: The Challenges for Economic and Social Rights' (2009) 3 J Hum Rts Practice 469; Eitan Felner, 'Closing the "Escape Hatch": A Toolkit to Monitor the Progressive Realisation of Economic, Social and Cultural Rights' (2009) 3 J Hum Rts Practice 402.
[204] Anderson and Foresti (n 203) 475.

(b) Indicators and benchmarks—the need for caution and collaboration

In addition to the need to *collect* data, the ESC and CRC committees have stressed the need to *develop* appropriate indicators and benchmarks as measures by which to assess a state's progress towards the full implementation of the right to health.[205] The Special Rapporteur on the Right to Health,[206] the OHCHR,[207] the WHO, and numerous commentators[208] have also advocated this approach with respect to the right to health. No such obligation arises directly from the text of the right to health. However, when read in conjunction with the general obligation under article 2 of the ICESCR and article 4 of the CRC to adopt all 'appropriate measures', it is arguable that indicators and benchmarks provide examples of such measures to the extent that they are able to provide practical and context sensitive mechanisms by which to monitor a state's progress with respect to the effective and progressive realization of the right to health. The recommendation by the human rights treaty monitoring bodies that states adopt these measures is therefore considered to have a principled basis to the extent that they are able to provide a tool by which to hold states accountable for their obligations under a treaty such as the CRC.[209]

Although the human rights treaty monitoring bodies have approved the use of indicators in general, they are yet to actively embrace their use in their concluding observations for states. Nor have they formally adopted or approved any of the draft indicators recently prepared such as the inter-agency consultative process which prepared indicators with respect to a child's right to survival,[210] the OHCHR draft indicators on the right to health,[211] the 'Lancet Health Indicators',[212] or the 'Human Rights Based Approach to Indicators in Relation to the Reproductive

---

[205] ESC Committee, *General Comment No 14* (n 24) paras 56–8. The CRC Committee has simply stated that '[e]valuation requires the development of indicators related to all rights guaranteed by the Convention': CRC Committee, *General Comment No 5* (n 107) para 48; CRC Committee, *Report on the Forty-Sixth Session*, UN Doc CRC/C/46/3 (n 107) paras 79–80.

[206] See, eg, *Report of the Special Rapporteur on the Right to Health to the General Assembly 2003*, UN Doc A/58/427 (10 October 2003) paras 5–37; *Report of the Special Rapporteur on the Right to Health to the Commission on Human Rights 2006* (n 105) paras 22–61.

[207] *Report on Indicators for Promoting and Monitoring the Implementation of Human Rights*, UN Doc HRI/MC/2008/3 (6 June 2008) annex 1, 25 para 8,

[208] See, eg, Gunilla Backman and others, 'Health Systems and the Right to Health: An Assessment of 194 Countries' (2008) 372 The Lancet 2047.

[209] See CRC Committee, *Report on the Forty-Sixth Session* (n 205) para 79; UNDP, *Human Development Report 2000: Human Rights and Human Development* (UNDP, 2000) 89. Although beyond the scope of this book, it is important to note that there is a lack of common approach to their classification. For a discussion of this issue see the following Reports of the Special Rapporteur: UN Doc A/58/427 (10 October 2003) paras 14–29; UN Doc A/59/422, paras 81–3; UN Doc E/CN.4/2006/48 (3 March 2006) para 26.

[210] See for example the draft child survival indicators developed as part of an inter-agency consultative process as outlined in the *Report of the Special Rapporteur on the Right to Health to the General Assembly 2004*, UN Doc A/59/422 (8 October 2004) paras 62–8.

[211] *Report on Indicators* (n 207) annex, Table 4.

[212] Backman and others (n 208) 11–12.

Health Strategy' endorsed by the World Health Assembly in May 2004.[213] Instead the approach of the human rights treaty monitoring bodies has been more rudimentary and reflects a general concern at the lack of general and disaggregated data with respect to the right to health.[214] This leaves open a question as to what indicators and benchmarks should be adopted by a state.

No attempt is made to provide a comprehensive list here. Instead the following observations are made. First, within the interpretative community, there is wide discrepancy in the type and number of indicators and benchmarks that have been proposed for the right to health.[215] For example, the 'Lancet Indicators' list 72 different indicators across 14 categories.[216] In contrast, the OHCHR indicators for the right to health are arranged under five categories, with a general requirement that all indicators must be disaggregated by the prohibited grounds of discrimination in international law.[217] Ultimately, states must enjoy a margin of appreciation in the determination of what indicators and benchmarks will be relevant to the realization of the right to health in their jurisdiction. The difficulty of this task should not be underestimated and commentators have expressed concern as to 'how to determine what would be a realistic and reasonable pace of progress in light of available resources'.[218] At the same, there should be no expectation that indicators or benchmarks are precise tools by which to measure implementation of the right to health. They will only ever be, at best, a guide and their identification will always be relative and contested. Ultimately their legitimacy will be determined by two factors. First, the process by which they are determined. This process must be collaborative and involve the various actors within the relevant interpretative community of a particular jurisdiction, especially health professionals, researchers, policy makers, and NGOs. Second, their capacity to guide states in the identification of the extent to which they are complying with their progressive realization of the right to health *and* their utility as tools by which the relevant human rights treaty monitoring bodies and the broader interpretative

---

[213] See *Report of the Special Rapporteur on the Right to Health to the Commission on Human Rights 2005* (n 105) annex ('A Human Rights-Based Approach to Indicators in relation to the Reproductive Health Strategy Endorsed by the World Health Assembly in May 2004').

[214] This may, however, change in light of its recent recommendation that UNICEF 'develop child specific indicators with a view to assisting States in improving their policy formulation, monitoring and evaluation for the implementation of child rights': CRC Committee, *Report on the Forty-Sixth Session* (n 138) para 80.

[215] *Report of the Special Rapporteur on the Right to Health to the General Assembly 2003* (n 206) para 14.

[216] Backman and others (n 208) 11–12 ('recognition of the right to health'; non-discrimination; health information; national health plan; participation; underlying determinants of health; access to health services; medicines; health promotion; health workers; national financing; international assistance and co-operation; additional safeguards; awareness raising and monitoring; accountability and redress).

[217] *Report on Indicators* (n 207) (sexual and reproductive health; child mortality and health care; natural and occupational environment; prevention, treatment and control of diseases, and accessibility to health facilities and essential medicines).

[218] SR Osmani, 'Human Rights to Food, Health and Education' (2000) 1 J Hum Dev 273, 291.

community can hold states accountable.[219] From the perspective of this analysis they should therefore be seen as an example of *measures* which are *appropriate* in virtue of their capacity to contribute to the effective implementation of the right to health.[220] Their articulation, however, must still satisfy the requirements of being practical, coherent, and context sensitive.

4 Effective participation

(a) Instrumental and normative foundations

It is increasingly recognized that 'effective provision of health services can only be assured if people's participation is secured by States'.[221] This is an inevitable requirement when it is accepted that the realization of the right to health will require efforts from, and impact upon, the interests of numerous actors within a state. For example, an effective assessment of the measures required to make health care and the underlying determinants of heath *acceptable* from a gender, children's, religious, cultural, or disability perspective, will depend on the participation of individuals or representatives from such groups. Similarly, a determination of how to secure *quality* services will require the contribution of medical practitioners and researchers whereas a determination of the measures required to ensure that appropriate services are *available and accessible* will require consultation with a vast range of groups including service users and potential providers. The principle of effectiveness therefore justifies the imposition of an obligation on states to facilitate the participation of all relevant actors in order to realize the right to health.

Beyond the instrumental value of participation, the principle of system coherence also demands that the appropriate measures adopted by states to realize the right to health are developed in consultation with the beneficiaries of this right. With respect to children, for example, article 12 of the CRC demands that states must assure that children's views are taken into consideration in relation to all matters affecting them. It is in this context that the CRC Committee has stressed, for example, that 'where appropriate adolescents should participate in the analysis [of data] to ensure that the

---

[219] Deteriorating indicators or a failure to achieve benchmarks does not necessarily provide evidence of a violation of a state's obligations. It remains necessary to assess the context in which the deterioration takes place, especially the availability of resources, before making such a determination: *Report of the Special Rapporteur on the Right to Health to the Commission on Human Rights 2006* (n 105) para 35.

[220] This is not to overstate their significance. As the Special Rapporteur has explained, 'it would be foolhardy to expect too much from right to health indicators' which can never provide a complete picture of the enjoyment of the right to health in a specific jurisdiction: *Report of the Special Rapporteur on the Right to Health to Health to the General Assembly 2003* (n 206) para 37.

[221] ESC Committee, *General Comment No 14* (n 24) 54. See also Hunt and Leader (n 146) 36; *Declaration of Alma Ata* (International Conference on Primary Health Care, Alma-Ata, USSR, 6–12 September 1978); *Ottowa Charter for Health Promotion* (First International Conference on Health Promotion, Ottawa, 21 November 1986, WHO Doc WHO/HPR/HEP/95.1); *Jakarta Declaration on Leading Health Promotion into the 21st Century* (Fourth International Conference on Health Promotion: New Players for a New Era—Leading Health Promotion into the 21st Century, Jakarta, 21–25 July 1997); Helen Potts, *Participation and the Right to the Highest Attainable Standard of Health* (Human Rights Centre, University of Essex, 2009); Anand Grover and Alec Irwin, 'The Power of Community In Advancing The Right to Health: A Conversation with Anand Grover' (2009) 11 Health &Hum Rts 1.

information is understood and utilized in an adolescent sensitive way'.[222] Moreover, the effectiveness principle requires that the participation of children must extend beyond the analysis of data collection to the opportunity to participate actively in the identification of priorities, development, implementation, monitoring, and evaluation of any policies to fulfil their right to health[223] in a manner consistent with article 12 of the CRC.

The ICESCR does not contain an explicit provision with respect to the participation of adults in the design and delivery of appropriate measures to realize the right to health.[224] However, the text of the ICCPR does provide a normative foundation for the requirement of participation, principally article 25 which declares that every individual has a right and opportunity to take part in the conduct of public affairs directly or through freely chosen representatives. This right of participation is complemented by the right to freedom of expression, which includes a right to receive information (article 19); freedom of association (article 22); and freedom of peaceful assembly (article 22). Moreover, the CRPD lists, in article 1, as one of its general principles the full and effective participation and inclusion of persons with disabilities in society. Thus, the principle of external system coherence demands that the implementation of a state's obligation under the right to health under the ICESCR must be informed by the participation of the intended beneficiaries of this right.

Such an approach demands a participatory and collaborative approach to the identification, creation, implementation, prioritization, and evaluation of health programs and policies, which challenges traditional practices that invariably discount the need for the involvement of the intended beneficiaries of such measures and devalue their capacity to make a useful contribution. As disarming as this may appear, it is important to recall, as noted by the CRC Committee in its General Comment on HIV/AIDS and the Rights of the Child, that:

Interventions have been found to benefit children most when they are actively involved in assessing needs, devising solutions, shaping strategies and carrying them out rather than being seen as objects for whom decisions are made.[225]

As such, the requirement of states to facilitate the effective participation of children and all other relevant beneficiaries in matters relating to their right to health, serves both an instrumental and normative role.

---

[222] CRC Committee, *General Comment No 4* (n 79) para 13.
[223] ibid para 39(d). See also ESC Committee, *General Comment No 14* (n 24) para 54.
[224] See ESC Committee, *General Comment No 14* (n 24) para 54; *The Limburg Principles* (n 20) para 10 (stressing the need to the full participation of all sectors of society in achieving progress in realizing economic, social and cultural rights); *Report of the Special Rapporteur on the Right to Health to the General Assembly 2007* (n 143) para 84 (noting that '[t]he active and informed participation of individuals and communities in health policy making that affects them is an important feature of the right' to health); *Report of the Special Rapporteur on the Right to Health to the Commission on Human Rights 2005*, UN Doc E/CN.4/2005/51 (11 February 2005) paras 59–61.
[225] CRC Committee, *General Comment No 3* (n 103) para 12.

(b) The scope and limits of participation

Three further comments must be stressed in relation to the requirement of participation. First, states enjoy a margin of appreciation in relation to the measures they adopt to facilitate participation. However, this discretion remains subject to the overriding caveat that whatever measures are adopted they must be 'meaningful and effective' rather than tokenistic and manipulative.[226] In this respect, states will be required to consider the development of new systems to facilitate the effective participation of the multitude of discrete groups who are entitled to the right to health such as children, women, persons with disabilities, indigenous persons, and religious groups.[227]

Second, the views expressed by such groups are informative and not necessarily determinative as to the measures that a state must adopt to ensure the effective enjoyment of the right to health. For example, in the context of children, article 12 of the CRC provides that the states need only take into account the views of children in accordance with their age and level of maturity. But even in the case of adults, states must also balance the views, demands, and expectations of one group, or individual, with respect to the right to health, against other individuals who are also entitled to the right to health. (How a state must undertake this balancing process is discussed below.)

Third, as Upendra Baxi has warned, the 'ritualistic invocation of the mantra of "participation" simply bypasses some further hard problems'.[228] It fails to address how the idea of 'deliberative democratic accountability' extends to non-state actors and the way in which, for example, a private health company or pharmaceutical company determines its priorities with respect to the provision of health care services and medicines.[229] The short answer to this dilemma is that international human rights law binds states rather than non-state actors. The advocate might be tempted to claim that the obligation to protect the right to health could be invoked to impose a due process requirement on non-state actors to adopt participatory practices when determining their health care priorities. But this would be to distort the underlying rationale of the private sector, which is driven by profit rather than an overriding commitment to realize the right to health. Thus, a more pragmatic response is that international human rights law requires states to fill those gaps where the private

---

[226] See OHCHR, *Principles and Guidelines for a Human Rights Approach to Poverty Reductions Strategies* (OHCHR, 2006) 15 (identify four phases of participation: preference revelation; policy choice; implementation; and monitoring and assessment); Roger Hart, *Children's Participation: From Tokenism to Citizenship* (Innocenti Essays No 4, UNICEF 1992) 8–11; Potts (n 221) 19 (lists four elements for effective participation in the development of health policy: an accessible and inclusive method; a fair and transparent process; indicators for monitoring and evaluating the process; and an independent accountability mechanism).

[227] Nigel Thomas, 'Towards a Theory of Children's Participation' (2007) 15 Intl J Child Rts 199, 211 (discusses the need to modify existing systems of participation and consultation to accommodate new groups with different perspectives *and* different ways of expressing themselves).

[228] Upendra Baxi, 'The Place of the Human Right to Health and Contemporary Approaches to Global Justice' in John Harrington and Maria Stuttaford (eds), *Global Health and Human Rights: Legal and Philosophical Perspectives* (Routledge, 2010) 12, 18.

[229] ibid.

sector fails to provide the services necessary to realize the right to health. States can elect to provide incentives or directly contract private entities, to consult with the beneficiaries of the right to health about the measures to secure their right, or states can undertake such consultation directly. International law expresses no preference for the model to be adopted. It simply demands that whatever approach is adopted, it contributes to the progressive realization of the right to health.

Another 'hard problem' associated with participation that commentators, such as Baxi and the human rights treaty monitoring bodies, have tended to overlook, is the reality that genuine and effective participation will not always be practical or possible with respect to decisions about how best to secure the right to health. Effective participation requires both time and resources both of which will invariably be limited. Thus, for example, it would be logistically impossible to facilitate the participation of every child, women, person with a disability, or indigenous person who will be affected by the adoption of a state's health policy. As such, the claim made by the Special Rapporteur on the Right to Health, that 'the prioritization process must include the active and informed participation of *all* stakeholders, including marginalized groups, in agenda setting, decision making and monitoring and accountability arrangements'[230] is simply unworkable. International law creates a presumption in favour of such an approach but this presumption is rebuttable.

A practical understanding of the obligation for states to facilitate effective participation must be subject to a test of reasonableness. In other words, states must make reasonable efforts in light of available resources and time constraints to facilitate collaborative and transparent participatory processes with all relevant actors in relation to the adoption of appropriate measures to secure the right to health. Moreover, where participation is possible states must (a) explain the relevant process including how the views of participants are to be integrated into the policy making process; and (b) give genuine consideration, by integrating to the extent possible, to the views and preferences expressed by participants in the formulation of health policies.[231] If these views and preferences cannot be accommodated, a state must provide the reasons for its failure to do so. In those circumstances where time or resources reasonably preclude effective participation, the process for the development and adoption of appropriate measures by the relevant representatives of a state must remain alert to, and endeavour to take into account, the discrete needs and interests of the various cohorts who will be affected by the adoption of such policies.[232]

---

[230] *Report of the Special Rapporteur on the Right to Health to the General Assembly 2007* (n 143) para 25 (emphasis added).

[231] These principles are adapted from the work of: Glenda MacNaughton and Kylie Smith, 'Engaging Ethically with Young Children: Principles and Practices for Listening and Responding with Care' in Glenda Macnaughton, P Hughes, and Kylie Smith (eds), *Young Children as Active Citizens: Principles, Policies and Pedagogies* (Cambridge Scholars Publishing, 2008) 32–45.

[232] This is linked to the idea of mainstreaming the right to health into the development of health policy. See John Tobin, 'Beyond the Supermarket Shelf: Using a Rights Based Approach to Address Children's Health Needs' (2006) 14 Intl J Child Rts 275.

5 The need for multisectoral and interdisciplinary initiatives

According to the CRC Committee, measures adopted by a state to fulfill children's right to health 'should, where feasible, adopt a multisectoral approach to the promotion and protection of adolescent health and development by facilitating effective and sustainable linkages and partnerships among all relevant actors'.[233] Although a multisectoral approach to the implementation of a rights-based approach is necessary, it is insufficient to ensure the effective enjoyment of the right to health. It must also be interdisciplinary, which requires co-ordination, collaboration, and consultation not only across a discipline, but between those disciplines that impact on health such as health, law, economics, education, and social work. Indeed, the ESC Committee has stressed that 'the realisation of the right to health may be pursued through numerous complementary approaches, such as the formulation of health policies, or the implementation of health programmes developed by the World Health Organization, or the adoption of specific legal instruments'.[234]

The requirement of an interdisciplinary approach is also significant in countering concerns about the excessive legalism of human rights. It requires that the right to health must not be invoked by lawyers and courts to displace the knowledge and experience of other professionals whose work impacts on the health of individuals. Indeed, when the South African Constitutional Court had to deal with the content of the right to health in the *Soobramoney* case, which is discussed above, it declared that 'A court will be slow to interfere with rational decisions taken in good faith by the... medical authorities whose responsibility it is to deal with such matters.'[235] This judicial deference to policy makers is a common feature of the treatment of economic and social rights, such as health, in domestic courts.[236] At the same time, in the *Treatment Action Campaign* case, which is also discussed above, the Court was prepared to direct the South African Government to ensure that antiretroviral medication was made available to all children in the public health system.[237] These decisions serve not only to allay concerns about the excessive legality of rights but also to indicate that the human right to health has the potential to act as a tool and not an impediment for public health practitioners when advocating on behalf of their patients.

6 Targeted health policies

Despite the universal nature of the right to health, international instruments require that states take targeted measures in order to realize the right to health of discrete groups such as women, children, persons with disabilities, indigenous peoples,

---

[233] CRC Committee, *General Comment No 4* (n 79) para 42.
[234] ESC Committee, *General Comment No 14* (n 24) para 1.
[235] *Soobramoney v Minister of Health* (n 164) [29].
[236] See Malcolm Langford, 'The Justiciability of Social Rights: From Practice to Theory' in Malcolm Langford (ed), *Social Rights Jurisprudence: Emerging Trends in International and Comparative Law* (CUP 2008) 33.
[237] *Minister for Health v Treatment Action Campaign (No 2)* [2002] 5 SA 721 (CC, Sth Afr).

refugees, and migrant workers.[238] The ESC Committee has also confirmed that such an obligation arises under the general right to health and has identified older persons as another group to whom states must give special consideration.[239] It remains important to recognize that the health needs of individuals within such groups are not homogenous. Thus, states must undertake additional measures to tailor the measures they adopt if they are to secure the effective enjoyment of the right to health for all persons within their jurisdiction. By way of example, the CRC Committee has recommended that appropriate measures to realize children's right to health take be undertaken in the context of two broad classifications—adolescence, middle childhood, and early childhood *and* especially vulnerable children.

(a) **Adolescence, middle childhood, and early childhood**
Both the law and society invariably see children as a discrete cohort and childhood as merely a period that proceeds adulthood. The CRC itself adopts the same approach and applies to every human being who is yet to attain the age of majority.[240] As a consequence the distinctive health needs that individuals experience as they proceed through childhood are not recognized within either the text of the CRC generally or the right to health under article 24. In contrast, the work of the CRC Committee recognizes that a national health policy must not treat children as a homogenous group. Despite the absence of any textual basis to support the position by the CRC Committee, it is considered to be a practical approach which is necessary to secure the effective implementation of the object and purpose of article 24, namely the realization of each child's right to health. Such an objective requires an approach to the delivery of health care services that is cognizant of and able to accommodate the diverse health needs of a cohort that ranges in age from a newborn child to a young person on the verge of adulthood.

As a consequence, the obligation that states must adopt *appropriate measures* to secure the right to health, demands that they must develop targeted policies which are designed to respond to the particular and divergent health needs of specific groups of children. Thus, for example, when the CRC Committee adopted its General Comment No 4 on Adolescent Health and Development, it observed that 'adolescents also pose new challenges to health and development owing to their relative vulnerability and pressure from society including peers to adopt risky health behaviour'.[241] As such, the health policies adopted by states must be tailored to the needs of children within this period in a way that responds to the challenges associated with the development of an adolescent's identity including his or her sexuality.[242]

---

[238] See CEDAW Committee, *General Recommendation No 24* (n 61) para 12 (stressing the need for States to accommodate the biological, socio-economic, and psychological factors that will impact on the types of services required to realize the right to health for women).
[239] ESC Committee, *General Comment No 14* (n 24) para 25.
[240] CRC, art 1 ('For the purposes of the present Convention, a child means every human being below the age of eighteen years unless under the law applicable to the child, majority is attained earlier').
[241] CRC Committee, *General Comment No 4* (n 79) para 2.
[242] ibid.

The CRC Committee's General Comment No 7 on Implementing Child Rights in Early Childhood[243] also indicates that the specific health needs of children within this group[244] must also be taken into account in the development of public health policies. Thus, greater attention must be given to areas such as pre- and post-natal care, immunization, the advantages of breastfeeding, and the development of healthy lifestyle practices in relation to nutrition, hygiene, and sanitation.[245] The CRC Committee has also drawn attention to the need to take all necessary steps to prevent the transmission of HIV/AIDS from mothers to their children, provide appropriate treatment where transmission has taken place, and ensure effective support and care for children who have lost their parents or primary caregivers due to HIV/AIDS.[246]

The third general classification adopted by the CRC Committee with respect to the definition of children is 'middle childhood'.[247] This classification, which covers the period from when a child has made the transition to school to the time when he or she reaches adolescence, is yet to be the subject of a general comment by the CRC Committee. However, it too is a period associated with special health needs which must be addressed in the *measures* adopted to secure a child's right to health if such measures are considered to be *appropriate*.

(b) Especially vulnerable children

Beyond the broad categories of early childhood, middle childhood, and adolescence, states must further ensure that if *other measures* designed to fulfill children's right to health are to be *appropriate,* they must take into account and contain targeted interventions that respond to the diverse needs of children who are especially vulnerable within these groups.[248] Such a demand is considered to be principled and practical given that the failure to take account of the needs of vulnerable children would compromise the effective implementation of the right to health with respect to such children. As the Special Rapporteur has observed, 'vulnerability and disadvantage are among the reasonable and objective criteria that must be applied when setting [health] priorities'.[249] Such groups of children have been identified by the CRC Committee to include children affected by armed conflict,[250] children subject to social exclusion,[251] children

---

[243] CRC Committee, *General Comment No 7: Implementing Child Rights in Early Childhood*, UN Doc CRC/C/GC/7/Rev.1 (1 November 2005).

[244] ibid paras 1–4 ('[t]he Committee's working definition of "early childhood" is all young children: at birth and throughout infancy; during the preschool years; as well as during the transition to school'. The CRC Committee has recognized that: 'Definitions of early childhood vary in different countries and regions... In some countries the transition from preschool to school occurs soon after 4 years old. In other countries this transition takes place around 7 years old'. Thus the Committee 'proposes as an appropriate working definition of early childhood the period from birth to the age of 8 years').

[245] ibid paras 27(a)–(b).

[246] ibid para 27(c).   [247] ibid para 8.

[248] See, eg, CRC Committee, *General Comment No 5* (n 107) para 39(h).

[249] *Report of the Special Rapporteur on the Right to Health to the General Assembly 2007* (n 143) para 26.

[250] CRC Committee, *General Comment No 5* (n 107) para 34.

[251] ibid.

Obligation to Recognize the Right to Health 221

with disabilities,[252] and children without families,[253] or children within and outside families especially girl children employed as domestic workers,[254] children subject to trafficking, sale, and abduction,[255] children who are victims of abuse and neglect,[256] refugees,[257] children who are subject harmful work,[258] children born with fetal alcohol or drug abuse syndrome,[259] homeless children,[260] children who are sexually exploited including in prostitution and pornography,[261] children living in poverty, and children subject to family breakdown, political, social and economic instability, and all types of migration.[262] To this list must be added children living in rural communities,[263] who are repeatedly the subject of concern in the CRC Committee's concluding observations,[264] children belonging to indigenous or minority groups,[265] especially Roma children,[266] girls[267] and children infected or affected by HIV/AIDS,[268] homosexual and transsexual children,[269] children in psychiatric hospitals,[270] and children subject to the juvenile justice system.

These categories are not mutually exclusive and children will often be characterized as falling within two or more of the categories listed above. Importantly, the identification of a child as falling within such categories provides recognition of their increased level of vulnerability with respect to their prospects for enjoyment of the right to health. It therefore demands that states avoid the imposition of a 'one size fits all model' and take the necessary and appropriate measures, which must be context sensitive, to address the special needs of certain children and the obstacles that confront their ability to enjoy his or her right to health.

---

[252] ibid para 35; CRC Committee, *General Comment No 7* (n 243) para 36(d).
[253] ibid para 36(b). [254] ibid para 36(g).
[255] ibid para 36(h). [256] ibid para 36(a).
[257] ibid para 36(c). [258] ibid para 36(e). [259] ibid para 36(f).
[260] CRC Committee, *General Comment No 4* (n 79) para 36.
[261] ibid para 37.
[262] ibid para 38.
[263] CRC Committee, *General Comment No 3* (n 103) para 21.
[264] See, eg, CO CRC Australia, UN Doc CRC/C/15/Add268, para 47; CO China UN Doc CHN/CO/2, para 62.
[265] See, eg, CO CRC Australia, UN Doc CRC/C/15/Add268, paras 47–8; CO CRC Bolivia, UN Doc CRC/C/15/Add256, para 47; CO CRC Canada, UN Doc CRC/C/15/Add215, para 35. See also: *Special Rapporteur on the Right to Health to the General Assembly 2004* (n 210) paras 55–8.
[266] See, eg, CO CRC Greece, UN Doc CRC/C/15/Add170, para 56(e); CO CRC Slovakia, UN Doc CRC/C/15/Add140, para 35.
[267] See, eg, CO CRC Liberia, UN Doc CRC/C/15/Add236, para 48; CO CRC Madagascar, UN Doc CRC/C/15/Add218, para 50(a); CO CRC Eritrea, UN Doc CRC/C/15/Add204, para 45; CO CRC Lesotho, UN Doc CRC/C/15/Add147, para 46.
[268] See generally CRC Committee, *General Comment No 3* (n 103) para 30.
[269] See CO CRC United Kingdom and Northern Ireland, UN Doc CRC/C/15/Add188, para 43.
[270] See, eg, CO CRC Finland, UN Doc CRC/C/15/Add132, para 45; CO CRC Denmark, UN Doc CRC/C/DNK/CO/3, para 42.

7 The compatibility of privatization with a state's obligation to take appropriate measures to secure children's right to health

(a) A neutral position

At the Discussion Day of the CRC on 'The Private Sector as Service Provider and its Role in Implementing Child Rights' in 2002, it was noted by the Chairperson of the CRC Committee at the time, Jap Doek, that there was increasing concern 'at the growing trend of privatisation including in the provision of services addressing basic needs including health...'.[271] Similarly, the ESC Committee in its concluding observations has expressed concern 'that the gradual privatisation of health care risks making it less accessible and affordable'[272] and 'that the quality and the availability of the health services provided... have been adversely affected by the large scale privatisation of the health service.'[273] Such concerns are well founded given research which suggests that privatization of health care 'can have a negative effect on health outcomes and on the accessibility of health care services for poor and disadvantaged people, especially children'.[274] However, as the ESC Committee has explained, the ICESCR is neutral with respect to the economic system adopted by a state to secure its obligations under the covenant including the right to health.[275] Thus, privatization of services is neither prohibited nor preferred as a measure to realize the right to health, and states are entitled to adopt whatever public/private funding mix they determine to be appropriate subject to the following caveats.

(b) The requirement for safeguards

First, a state cannot abdicate or defer the obligations that arise as a consequence of its recognition of the right to health in international law through the process of privatization. To adopt such an approach would be inconsistent with the obligation of good faith assumed by states with respect to the effective implementation of their treaty obligations. As the CRC Committee has remarked, 'in any decentralization or privatization process, the Government retains clear responsibility and capacity for ensuring respect of its obligations under the Convention'.[276] A state remains bound to ensure that any third party that assumes responsibility for the delivery of services

---

[271] CRC Committee, *Report on the Thirty-First Session*, UN Doc CRC/C/121 (11 December 2002) ch VI, 155 (Day of General Discussion on 'The Private Sector as Service Provider and Its Role in Implementing Child Rights', 20 September 2002).

[272] CO ESC Poland, UN Doc E/C.12/POL/CO/5, para 28.

[273] CO ESC India, UN Doc E/C.12/IND/CO/5, para 38.

[274] Brigit Toebes, 'The Right to Health and the Privatization of National Health Systems: A Case Study of the Netherlands', 9 Health &Hum Rts 103 (2006) 106 (citing relevant studies).

[275] See ESC Committee, *General Comment No 3* (n 17) para 8 (notes that the ICESCR is neutral with respect to the economic system adopted by a state to secure its obligations). See also: *Alyne de Silva Pimental v Brazil* CEDAW/C/49/D/17/2008 (10 August 2011) para 7.5 (noting that 'the State party is directly responsible for action of private institutions where is outsources its medical services and that... the State always maintains the duty to regulate and monitor private health care institutions... [and]... the State party has a due diligence obligation to take measures to ensure that the activities of private actors in regard to health policies are appropriate').

[276] CRC Committee, *Report on the Thirty-First Session* (n 271) para 15.

which are within the scope of a state's obligations under the right to health, secures that entitlement. The ESC Committee originally explained in its General Comment on Health, and the CRC Committee has subsequently affirmed, that a state must 'ensure that privatisation of the health sector does not constitute a threat to the availability, accessibility, acceptability and quality of health facilities, goods and services'.[277] Privatization may be a means to achieve the highest attainable standard of health. Moreover, a context-sensitive approach to the interpretation of a state's obligations under the right to health must accept the reality that a state will rely upon the actions of non-state actors to contribute to the realization of this right. However, this deference to non-state actors cannot be a means to avoid the obligations of a state.

Second, where a state determines that privatization is to play a role in securing the right to health, the CRC Committee has recommended that this decision must be preceded by a 'comprehensive and transparent assessment of the political, financial and economic implications and the possible limitation[s]'[278] of this process on the right to health—sometimes referred to as a 'right to health impact assessment'[279]. Such a directive represents a practical measure by which to ensure that a state takes appropriate measures to ensure privatization will not compromise the effective enjoyment of children's right to health. The CRC Committee has not specified the form in which such an assessment must take place and a significant margin of appreciation will be accorded to states with respect to this issue. However, this discretion afforded to states remains subject to the caveat that the measures taken to assess the impact of privatization are 'comprehensive' and 'transparent'.

Finally, beyond the decision to privatize, the actual delivery of health care services under a system of privatization must be consistent with international human rights standards 'at all stages including policy formulation, monitoring and accountability arrangements'[280] to ensure that such a system is contributing to the realization of the right of all children to the highest attainable standard of health. Anything less would threaten the object and purpose of the right to health. According to the CRC Committee, in practice this requires that states create some institutional or regulatory framework to 'ensure independent monitoring of implementation as well as transparency of the entire process so as to contribute to the process of accountability'.[281] Thus, while privatization is not incompatible with the requirement that states must take appropriate measures to secure the right to health, this practice must be subject to significant conditions in order to ensure that it contributes to the progressive realization of this right.

---

[277] ESC Committee, *General Comment No 14* (n 24) para 35. See also CRC Committee, *Report on the Thirty-First Session* (n 271) para 8.
[278] ibid para 11.
[279] Toebes, 'The Right to Health and the Privatization of National Health Systems' (n 274) 112. For a more detailed discussion of health impact assessments more generally see: *Report of the Special Rapporteur on the Right to Health to the General Assembly 2007* (n 143) paras 33–44; Bakker (n 143) 436.
[280] CRC Committee, *Report on the Thirty-First Session* (n 271) para 8 (Japp Doek).
[281] ibid para 14.

IV Conclusion—moving towards a sufficiently specified account of the measures required to secure the right to health

O'Neill's concern that economic and social rights, such as the right to health, have insufficiently specified counterpart obligations may well be justified if the assessment of a state's obligations were confined to the phrase 'all appropriate means including particularly the adoption of legislative measures'. However, the meaning of this phrase is not be interpreted in isolation and remains highly contextualized. In the first instance it is informed by the specific measures listed in the sub-paragraphs of article 12 of the ICESCR and article 24 of the CRC. However, an application of the interpretative methodology advanced in Chapter 3 enables the exposition of a series of quite distinct and specific obligations that states have with respect to realization of the right to health.

Of particular significance in this regard is the work of the human rights treaty monitoring bodies. Although unreasonably inflated at times, it still indicates that the effective enjoyment of the right to health requires states to adopt national health plans, effective accountability measures, collect appropriate data and develop appropriate benchmarks, facilitate effective participatory strategies, encourage multisectoral and interdisciplinary initiatives, and develop targeted health policies for especially vulnerable groups. All of these measures, however, remain subject to the caveat that their implementation is to be progressive and subject to the resources available to a state. The question that remains unanswered in this discussion, however, is the meaning to be attributed to the progressive nature of this obligation. It is to this central question, which has been described as the 'lynchpin' of economic and social rights that I now turn.[282]

---

[282] Alston and Quinn (n 41) 172.

6

The Progressive Obligation to Realize the Right to Health

I Introduction

The preceding chapter outlined a range of *means* and *measures* that are considered *appropriate* for states to undertake on the grounds that they can be justified as being principled, practical, and capable of a context-sensitive application for the purpose of contributing to the effective realization of the right to health. But each of these measures, even protection against non-discrimination, requires the allocation of resources. This reality weighed heavily on the minds of states when they were drafting the International Covenant on Economic, Social and Cultural Rights (ICESCR). Although there was a determination to impose the 'firmest commitment' possible on states to realize the rights in the Covenant, there was also an acceptance that this commitment had to be reasonable.[1] The result was the adoption of the obligation for states to take steps to progressively realize economic and social rights, such as the right to health, subject to the maximum resources available to a state.

At the time of drafting, concerns were expressed that these caveats provided states with loopholes to evade their obligations.[2] However, it was ultimately accepted that 'the enjoyment of economic, social and cultural rights depended in part upon available resources and upon domestic and international economic and social conditions over which a state exercised only incomplete control'.[3] It was also recognized 'that countries could not progress faster than such resources and conditions would allow', which justified the inclusion of the progressive obligation.[4] The challenge, however, is to develop an understanding of how these concessions must be operationalized in practice—made 'action guiding'[5] and 'socially manageable'[6]—by a state to ensure the realization of the right to health.

Considerable literature on the progressive and resource dependent nature of economic social and cultural rights already exists and need not be repeated

---

[1] *Annotations on the Text of the Draft International Covenants on Human Rights*, UN Doc A/2929 (1955) 19–20 para 22.
[2] ibid para 23.
[3] ibid para 24.
[4] ibid.
[5] Charles Beitz, *The Idea of Human Rights* (OUP, 2009) 46.
[6] James Griffin, *On Human Rights* (OUP, 2008) 37–9.

here.[7] Instead, this discussion will focus on the meaning of the phrase 'maximum available resources' and the obligation of progressive obligation *in the context of the right to health*. The discussion will then shift to an examination of the extent to which the contentious concept of minimum core obligations is able to provide a persuasive tool to guide states in the implementation of their obligation to secure the right to health.

It will be argued that despite the apparently amorphous nature of this obligation, it remains possible to articulate a persuasive account of how states can implement this obligation in a way that is principled, practical, coherent, and context sensitive. A process will also be outlined by which to guide states in the resolution of the macro/micro resource allocation dilemma, outlined in Chapter 2. It will be shown that international law accommodates the reality of the need for states to prioritize the allocation of scarce resources, provided a state is able to demonstrate that the process for allocating these resources can be shown to be reasonable. This standard will be satisfied where the decision making process is shown to be principled, evidence based, consultative, transparent, and evaluative. The chapter will conclude with an analysis of the controversial concept of minimum core obligations. From relatively humble beginnings, it will be shown that the Committee on Economic, Social and Cultural Rights (ESC Committee) has expanded this concept as it applies to the right to health in a way that fails to satisfy any of the requirements outlined in the interpretative methodology to be used in this analysis. But rather than abandon this concept, it will be argued that a principled and practical defence can be advanced to justify its use as a tool to assist in understanding the nature of a state's obligation to secure the right to health within the context of limited resources.

II The meaning of 'maximum available resources'

A Towards a dynamic understanding of available resources

When the Committee on the Rights of the Child (CRC Committee) dedicated its annual Day of General Discussion to the issue of 'Resources for the Rights of the Child' in 2007, it declared that 'resources must be understood as encompassing not only financial resources but also other types of resources relevant for the realisation of economic, social and cultural rights such as human, technological, organisational,

---

[7] See, eg, Philip Alston and Gerard Quinn, 'The Nature and Scope of States Parties' Obligations under the International Covenant on Economic, Social and Cultural Rights' (1987) 9 Hum Rts Q 156; Matthew Craven, *The International Covenant on Economic, Social and Cultural Rights: A Perspective on Its Development* (OUP, 1995) 129–34; Robert Robertson, 'Measuring State Compliance with the Obligation to Devote the "Maximum Available Resources" to Realising Economic Social and Cultural Rights' (1994) 16 Hum Rts Q 693; Magdalena Sepulveda, *The Nature of the Obligations under the International Covenant on Economic, Social and Cultural Rights* (Intersentia, 2003); Manisuli Ssenyonjo, *Economic, Social and Cultural Rights in International Law* (Hart Publishing, 2009) paras 2.22–2.33.

natural and information resources'.[8] When this comment is examined in light of the general rule of interpretation under s 31 of the Vienna Convention on the Law of Treaties (VCLT), there is a persuasive argument that this understanding as to the meaning of the term 'resources' is principled and practical. Although the ordinary meaning of the term 'resources' is not necessarily apparent, it tends to refer to the means or facilities which enable the performance of a certain function. With respect to the right to health, the practical means by which a state will realize an individual's highest attainable standard of health will require, not simply financial resources, but the range of resources identified by the CRC Committee.

The work of the CRC Committee also indicates a willingness to adopt an open-ended vision as to the scope of the phrase 'resources' which will allow for a context sensitive understanding as to meaning of this term. Within the context of the right to health, the CRC Committee has variously called upon states to '[e]nsure that *appropriate* resources are allocated for the health sector and develop and implement comprehensive policies and programmes for improving the health situation of children';[9] '[e]nsure the provision of *adequate* financial and human resources for the effective implementation of the health programmes';[10] '[i]ncrease efforts to allocate *appropriate* resources and develop and implement comprehensive policies and programmes to improve the health situation of children';[11] '[a]llocate *appropriate* resources for health and develop and implement comprehensive policies and programmes to improve the health situation of children';[12] and '[d]efine sustainable financing mechanisms for the primary health-care system and an effective utilization of resources [including adequate salaries for child health-care professionals], in order to ensure that all children, in particular children from the most marginalized vulnerable groups, have access to free basic health care of good quality'.[13]

In a similar vein the ESC Committee has recommended that states 'increase public spending on health';[14] 'train and recruit... medical staff, in particular midwives, nurses, obstetricians and gynaecologists';[15] 'increase expenditure for health care and to take all appropriate measures to ensure universal access to health care at prices affordable to everyone';[16] ensure the commitment 'to primary health care is

---

[8] CRC Committee, *Report on the Forty-Sixth Session*, UN Doc CRC/C/46/3 (22 April 2008) ch VII, para 65 (Day of General Discussion on 'Resources for the Rights of the Child—Responsibility of States', 5 October 2007).
[9] CO CRC Philippines, UN Doc CRC/C/15/Add.259, para 59(b).
[10] CO CRC Equatorial Guinea, UN Doc CRC/C/15/Add.245, para 47(d).
[11] CO CRC Liberia, UN Doc CRC/C/15/Add.236, para 47(a).
[12] CO CRC Pakistan, UN Doc CRC/C/15/Add.217, para 53(a).
[13] CO CRC Czech Republic, UN Doc CRC/C/15/Add.201, para 47(a). See also CO CRC Romania, UN Doc CRC/C/15/Add.199, para 45(a).
[14] CO ESC Kazakhstan, UN Doc E/C.12/KAZ/CO/1, para 40. See also CO ESC Brazil, UN Doc E/C.12/BRA/CO/2, para 28(b); CO ESC Iceland, UN Doc E/2000/22 (1999) 26, para 86.
[15] CO ESC Kazakhstan, UN Doc E/C.12/KAZ/CO/1, para 40.
[16] CO ESC Republic of Korea, UN Doc E/C.12/KOR/CO/3, para 30.

met by adequate allocation of resources';[17] and 'increase its budget allocation for health'.[18]

The themes which underlie such comments, are that states must ensure the allocation of 'adequate' and 'appropriate' resources that are 'effective' and 'sustainable' in securing the implementation of the right to health. Although they reflect a significant degree of deference to states, and thus offer a context-sensitive understanding of the term resources, other comments of the treaty bodies indicate that this margin is not without constraints.[19] For example, the CRC Committee has urged states to ensure that expenditure on children's health remains a priority in state budgets at all times.[20] The ESC Committee has also expressed its concern with respect to the distribution of resources to purchase weapons as opposed to investing in areas such as primary or preventive health services[21] and expressed its concern that 'health allocations are consistently diminishing',[22] and, 'in spite of high GDP growth rate, the national spending on social services such as ... health ... remains low'.[23]

Moreover, far from being empty and aspirational pleas, the treaty bodies have been prepared to hold states to account where they have failed to reach this standard. Thus, for example, the CRC Committee expressed its concern in its report for Costa Rica 'at the cuts in social expenditure in the national budget, as a result of the recent economic reforms, and at their negative impact on health, education and other traditional welfare areas for children'.[24] It therefore recommended 'that the state party take effective measures to allocate the maximum extent of available resources for social services and programmes for children, and that particular attention be paid to the protection of children belonging to vulnerable and marginalized groups'.[25] Such comments are considered to have a principled basis given that they are directed to ensuring that states take effective measures to secure the realization of children's right to health. If states were granted unfettered discretion with respect to the allocation of their available resources—a form of auto-interpretation—the object and purpose of the right to health would be completely compromised.

In terms of further constraining the way in which states allocate their resources, the CRC Committee has also highlighted the need for states to adopt political, institutional, and administrative structures and processes that ensure the transparent, equitable, efficient, and effective use of available resources.[26] Thus, for example in its

---

[17] CO ESC Ukraine, UN Doc E/2002/22 (2001) 78, para 512.
[18] CO ESC Poland, UN Doc E/C.12/POL/CO/5, para 29. See also CO ESC Philippines, UN Doc E/1996/22 (1996) 30, para 123 (consider increasing the proportion of the national budget devoted to health programmes).
[19] See Craven (n 7) 136–7 (makes a similar observation with respect to the ICESCR).
[20] See, eg, CO CRC Togo, UN Doc CRC/C/15/Add.83, para 34. See also CRC Committee, *Report on the Forty-Sixth Session* (n 8) para 71(a).
[21] See, eg, CO ESC Philippines, UN Doc E/C.12/1995/7, para 21.
[22] CO ESC Nigeria, UN Doc E/1999v22 (1998) 27, para 124. See also CO ESC Mongolia, UN Doc E/2001/22 (2000) 53, para 273; CO ESC Kenya, UN Doc E/C.12/1/Add.59, para 9.
[23] CO ESC Philippines, UN Doc E/C.12/PHL/CO/4, para 17.
[24] CO CRC Costa Rica, UN Doc CRC/C/15/Add.117, para 14.
[25] ibid.
[26] CRC Committee, *Report on the Forty-Sixth Session* (n 8) paras 73–5.

concluding observations for Togo, the CRC Committee expressed its concern at 'reports of widespread corruption, which has a negative impact on the level of resources available for the implementation of the Convention'[27] and in its report for Bosnia and Herzegovina it expressed concern at the 'significance difference in public expenditure between the two Entities in the areas of social security, education and healthcare and that the complex structure of the state party is not conducive to an optimal realization of the limited resources available'.[28] It therefore recommended 'that the State party pay particular attention to the full implementation of article 4 of the Convention, by prioritizing budgetary allocations to ensure implementation of the economic, social and cultural rights of children, in particular those belonging to economically disadvantaged groups, "to the maximum extent of...available resources and, where needed, within the framework of international cooperation"'.[29] Moreover, it further recommended 'that the State party harmonize the expenses for the purpose of children's rights protection between the Entities so that a minimum level of social and health protection for all children throughout the country is guaranteed'.[30]

Such observations tend to demonstrate a significant degree of local context sensitivity to the extent that the treaty bodies are acutely aware of the reality that many states, especially developing states, will often lack the necessary financial and human resources to secure the enjoyment of even the essential elements of a child's right to health. At the same time they are not prepared to allow a lack of resources to justify inertia on the part of states. Thus, the CRC Committee has recommended that states encourage public dialogue on state budgets, develop effective resource tracking systems, and provide statistical information on the allocation of resources towards the realization of children's rights.[31] Implicit in these comments of the CRC Committee that states must address matters such as corruption, discriminatory expenditures and budgetary allocations, is a requirement that states must actively seek to develop internal systems of fiscal management (including a review of the taxation system) and governance that will generate the resources necessary to enable effective implementation of economic and social rights such as the right to health.[32] Such demands are considered to be clear and practical and must be seen to have a principled basis to the extent that they generate an understanding of the obligations of states that is directed towards securing the object and purpose of the right to health.

Importantly, the position advanced by the treaty bodies reflects a dynamic understanding as to the meaning of phrase 'maximum available resources'. It rejects

---

[27] CO CRC Togo, UN Doc CRC/C/15/Add.255, para 17.
[28] CO CRC Bosnia and Herzegovina, UN Doc CRC/C/15/Add.260, para 16.
[29] ibid para 17.
[30] ibid.
[31] CRC Committee, *Report on the Forty-Sixth Session* (n 8) para 75.
[32] Henry Steiner, Philip Alston, and Ryan Goodman, *International Human Rights in Context: Law, Politics and Morals* (3rd edn, OUP, 2008) 305–7 (notes that the fiscal dimension of determining available resources has traditionally been neglected with human rights scholarship and advocacy and provides brief discussion of what this might mean).

the blunt assertion often made by states that they simply lack the resources necessary to undertake the various measures required to secure the right to health.[33] It attempts to pierce this veil and demands an inquiry as to the way in which existing resources within a jurisdiction are *distributed* including how they can be *redistributed* so as to secure the right to health. This is not to say that the right to health must be accorded priority over all other considerations in decisions concerning the distribution of resources within a state. The requirement for system coherence demands that the other obligations a state has assumed under international law must also be considered (as to how these competing obligations must be reconciled is discussed below). A burden is, however, imposed on states to demonstrate that they are actively seised of ways in which they can increase the resources required to implement the right to health through the adoption of appropriate policies with respect to fiscal and general governance matters.

B Developing social resources

Strengthening the capacity of a health system to deliver appropriate health services requires more than the creation and allocation of adequate financial resources to construct the necessary institutional structure. It also requires the development of appropriate social resources. In the first instance this includes the family unit—a point which is reflected in the statement of the CRC Committee as to 'the importance of systematically supporting parents and families who are among the most important available resources for children'[34] and the requirement under subparagraphs (e) and (f) of article 24(2) of the CRC that states provide information and guidance to parents in relation to children's health needs. Beyond the family unit, however, the provision, training, and funding of adequately trained health professionals is also critical.[35] Indeed a lack of such social resources has been repeatedly identified by the CRC Committee especially in developing states where it is now acknowledged that not only is there a significant shortage of health workers[36] but a migration of such personnel from developing states to developed states—the so-called skills or brain drain.[37]

Such a practice seriously undermines the capacity of a state to secure its obligations under the right to health and demands that measures be taken to both arrest this

---

[33] See WHO, 'Spending on Health 2007—A Global Update' (WHO Fact Sheet, 2010) <http://www.who.int/nha/use/global_fact_sheet_2007-Jun_2010.pdf> accessed 8 June 2011 (noting that in 2007 there were 40 WHO member states where health spending by government, households and the private sector, and funds provided for by external donors was lower than USD$43 per person per year, the WHO estimate of minimum spending to provide basic life saving services).

[34] CRC Committee, *Report on the Forty-Sixth Session* (n 8) para 66.

[35] Lynn P Freedman and others, UN Millennium Project Task Force on Child Health and Maternal Health, *Who's Got the Power: Transforming Health Systems for Women and Children* (Earthscan, 2005) 9.

[36] *Report of the Special Rapporteur on the Right to Health to the General Assembly 2005*, UN Doc A/60/348 (12 September 2005) paras 27–8.

[37] ibid paras 29–90 (examines scope of problem, reasons for its existence, human rights implications, and possible strategies to address the issue). See also World Health Assembly, Res WHA57.19 (adopted 22 May 2004); World Health Assembly, Res WHA58.17 (adopted 25 May 2005).

trend[38] and ensure the development of the local capacities required to respond to the health needs of individuals within a state's jurisdiction. Thus, while the right to health in international law does not expressly impose an obligation on states to provide appropriate social and human resources to realize the right to health, the failure to imply such an obligation would leave a serious 'effectiveness gap' in the implementation of the right to health. States must, therefore, as a matter of legal obligation look beyond the mere accumulation of financial resources to consider the measures required to provide the social resources required for the effective implementation of the right to health.

Moreover, the personnel that represent such resources must be provided with adequate training and education in relation to human rights generally and the right to health specifically.[39] Such information and skills are necessary to ensure not only awareness of human rights but also to ensure that such personnel deliver their services in a manner consistent with human rights—a form of system coherence—and are in a position to document and identify when an individual's right to health has been violated.

Finally, the social resources available to a state are not confined to those resources over which the state has direct control. As commentators have recognized, 'available resources refers to resources available within the society as a whole, from the private sector as well as the public'.[40] Thus the obligation of states is to 'mobilise these resources', to the extent that it is reasonably practicable to do so, for the purpose of securing the realization of the right to health.[41]

C Seeking international co-operation as a source of resources

The ESC Committee has also explained that the resources available to a state refer 'to both the resources existing within a State and those available from the international community through international cooperation and assistance'.[42] Such an approach has a principled basis given the inclusion of the obligation referring to international co-operation in articles 2 of the ICESCR and articles 4 and 24(4) of the CRC. Moreover, during drafting it was noted that 'the reference to "available resources" contemplated not only the national resources of a country but also the resources

---

[38] See *Report of the Special Rapporteur on the Right to Health to the General Assembly 2005* (n 36) paras 61–89; Eric A Friedman, *Action Plan to Prevent Brain Drain: Building Equitable Health Systems in Africa* (Physicians for Human Rights 2004); WHO, *International Recruitment of Health Personnel: Draft Global Code of Practice*, WHO Doc EB124/13 (4 December 2008); World Health Assembly, Res WHA57.19 (adopted 22 May 2004).
[39] With respect to human rights training for health professionals generally see: *Report of the Special Rapporteur 2005* (n 36) paras 8–17.
[40] Ssenyonjo (n 7) 62, citing Audrey Chapman and Sage Russell, 'Introduction' in Audrey Chapman and Sage Russell (eds), *Core Obligations: Building a Framework for Economic, Social and Cultural Rights* (Intersentia 2002) 1, 11.
[41] ibid.
[42] ESC Committee, *General Comment No 3: The Nature of States Parties' Obligations*, UN Doc E/1991/23 (14 December 1990) annex III, para 13; CRC Committee, *Report on the Forty-Sixth Session* (n 8) para 65.

which it might receive from abroad'.[43] The nature of this obligation is dealt with in detail in Chapter 9. At this point, it is sufficient to note that, with respect to the question of maximum available resources, the CRC Committee has encouraged states to seek international assistance in this regard[44] and suggested that resources, 'whether from State allocations or from direct international assistance, are... distributed evenly among the population according to need'.[45] Importantly, in relation to the provision of assistance by organizations such as the international financial institutions, the CRC Committee, which is mindful of the potential negative impact of structural adjustment policies on social service expenditure, has also recommended, as it did in its report for Sri Lanka, that states parties '[p]rioritize the provision of services to children in loan and structural adjustment negotiations with international donors'.[46] Such comments represent practical yet balanced directives to states and are consistent with the underlying objectives of an interpretative approach that seeks to facilitate a constructive engagement between states and the bodies responsible for monitoring their efforts to secure the progressive realization of the right to health.

In light of the preceding discussion, the policy maker and rights sceptic might be persuaded to acknowledge that the work of the treaty bodies is able to provide guidance with respect to the meaning of the phrase 'available resources'. They might also concede that the call to increase expenditure on health, or prioritize health expenditure in budgets, will contribute to the realization of the right to health. But they would be entitled to respond that this obligation is progressive and James Griffin would undoubtedly retort, that the question of 'what level of resources must be allocated by a State?' still remains unanswered. As a consequence, glib calls by the treaty bodies or advocates to increase expenditure on health are meaningless unless they are accompanied by an understanding of what international law has to say with respect to the reality that states must prioritize and ration scarce resources both within health budgets and across competing areas such as education, defence, and law and order. It is to these issues that this discussion now turns.

III The progressive nature of a state's obligations and the process for prioritization

A The need for a dialogue

In its General Comment No 3, the ESC Committee declared, with respect to the obligation of progressive realization, that it '... constitutes a recognition of the fact that full realisation of all economic, social and cultural rights will generally not be able to be achieved in a short period of time'.[47] This approach is consistent with the

---

[43] *Annotations on the Text of the Draft International Covenants on Human Rights* (n 1) 20 para 24.
[44] See, eg, CO CRC The Bahamas, UN Doc CRC/C/15/Add.253, para 19.
[45] CO CRC Burundi, UN Doc CRC/C/15/Add.133, para 18.
[46] CO CRC Sri Lanka, UN Doc CRC/C/15/Add.207, para 18(b).
[47] ESC Committee, *General Comment No 3* (n 42) para 9.

intention of the drafters of the ICESCR who, despite concerns that a progressive obligation could be used as a loophole by some states, recognized that such an obligation was inevitable.[48] Indeed, the drafting history records that it was claimed that, 'the use of the term "progressively" in fact placed upon signatories a duty to achieve ever higher and higher levels of fulfilment of rights'.[49] In fact it is within this context that the ESC Committee has explained that the progressive obligation 'imposes an obligation to move as expeditiously and effectively as possible towards' full realization of the right to health.[50] Moreover, according to the ESC Committee, 'any deliberate retrogressive measures in that regard would require the most careful consideration and would need to be fully justified by reference to the totality of rights provided for in the Covenant'.[51]

Such an approach seeks to inform the obligation of progressive implementation with an appropriate blend of pragmatism and local context sensitivity. In terms of operationalization, it imposes a substantial onus on states to justify the measures they have taken to secure the right to health in light of their available resources. As the ESC Committee in its General Comment on the Right to Health declared:

If resource constraints render it impossible for a State party to comply fully with its Covenant obligations, it has the burden of justifying that every effort has nevertheless been made to use all available resources at its disposal in order to satisfy as a matter of priority, the obligations [imposed on States under the right to health].[52]

In light of this comment, an assessment as to whether a state has complied with the progressive nature of its obligation will always remain relative to the circumstances prevailing within a state.[53] This obligation does not seek to mandate that certain levels of the right to health must be secured (obligations of result), or that certain measures must be taken by states (obligations of conduct), at certain levels of resource availability. Instead it operates to facilitate and frame a dialogue within the relevant interpretative community with respect to the direction and speed at which a state should pursue measures to secure the implementation of the right to health.

---

[48] *Annotations on the Text of the Draft International Covenants on Human Rights* (n 1) 20 paras 23–4.
[49] ibid para 24.
[50] ibid.
[51] ibid. The CRC Committee has done little to develop an understanding as to the nature of the progressive obligation beyond affirming its significance (CRC Committee, *General Comment No 5: General Measures of Implementation for the Convention on the Rights of the Child*, UN Doc CRC/GC/2003 (27 November 2000) para 7) and adopting the earlier work of the ESC Committee (CRC Committee, *Report on the Forty-Sixth Session* (n 8) paras 87–8).
[52] ESC Committee, *General Comment No 14: The Right to the Highest Attainable Standard of Health*, UN Doc E/C/12/2000/4 (11 August 2000) para 47.
[53] ESC Committee, *An Evaluation of the Obligation to Take Steps to the 'Maximum of Available Resources' under an Optional Protocol to the Covenant*, UN Doc E/C.12/2007/1 (10 May 2007) para 10 (noting that the ESC Committee will take into account (a) the country's level of development; (b) the severity of the alleged breach; (c) the country's current economic situation; (d) the existence of other serious claims on the state party's limited resources such as a recent natural disaster or armed conflict; (e) whether the state party has sought to identify low cost options; and (f) whether the state party has sought co-operation from the international community).

The nature of this dialogue is likely to be influenced by the approach foreshadowed by the ESC Committee with respect to the process it intends to adopt with respect to communications under the Optional Protocol to the ICESCR, which was adopted by the Human Rights Council in June 2008.[54] In a Statement on how it intends to evaluate the extent to which states have complied with their progressive obligation under the ICESCR, the ESC Committee indicated that it would consider factors such as:

(a) the extent to which the measures taken were deliberate, concrete, and targeted towards the fulfilment of economic, social, and cultural rights;
(b) whether the State party exercised its discretion in a non-discriminatory and non-arbitrary manner;
(c) whether the State party's decision (not) to allocate available resources is in accordance with international human rights standards;
(d) where several policy options are available, whether the State party adopts the option that least restricts Covenant rights;
(e) the time frame in which the steps were taken; and
(f) whether the steps had taken into account the precarious situation of disadvantaged and marginalized individuals or groups, and whether they were non-discriminatory, and whether they prioritized grave situations or situations of risk.[55]

Significantly, this model has been endorsed by the CRC Committee,[56] as an appropriate methodology by which to assess compliance with the progressive nature of a state's obligation to secure the right to health.

Moreover, it would appear to be principled, practical, coherent, and context sensitive. The ESC Committee has acknowledged that when applying this model it will always respect 'the margin of appreciation of States to take steps and adopt measures most suited to their specific circumstances'.[57] But this deference is qualified by normative standards such as non-discrimination and the requirement to take appropriate measures to promote substantive equality with respect to the right to health, which demands prioritization of measures to address the rights of the most vulnerable groups.[58] It is further qualified by the requirement to adopt the least restrictive measure (which is reasonably available) where there is a range of alternative

---

[54] Human Rights Council, *Optional Protocol to the International Covenant on Economic, Social and Cultural Rights*, UN Doc A/63/435 (28 November 2008) annex; Optional Protocol to the International Covenant on Economic, Social and Cultural Rights (Optional Protocol to the ICESCR) (New York, 24 September 2009, C.N.869.2009.TREATIES-34) (not yet in force).

[55] ESC Committee, *An Evaluation of the Obligation to Take Steps to the 'Maximum of Available Resources' under an Optional Protocol to the Covenant* (n 53) para 8.

[56] CRC Committee, *Report on the Forty-Sixth Session* (n 8) para 90.

[57] ESC Committee, *An Evaluation of the Obligation to Take Steps to the 'Maximum of Available Resources' under an Optional Protocol to the Covenant* (n 53) para 11.

[58] Brian Griffey, 'The "Reasonableness" Test: Assessing Violations of State Obligations under the Optional Protocol to the International Covenant on Economic, Social and Cultural Rights' (2011) 11 Hum Rts L Rev 275, 319 (argues that a legal standard of 'appropriateness' sets a higher bar than 'reasonableness' because it may require budgetary prioritization and optimization).

options.[59] A state party's effort must also be consistent with the interpretative principles that guide the meaning of standards such as the right to health. Thus, for example, the demand by the ESC Committee that states take deliberate, concrete, and targeted measures is consistent with the obligation of good faith and the effectiveness principle. Finally, the approach by the ESC Committee demonstrates an awareness of the need to ensure external system coherence to the extent that the measures adopted by states must be evaluated in light of international human rights generally and not simply the right to health.[60]

B Addressing the resource allocation dilemma

A question remains as to whether the methodology outlined by the ESC Committee is sufficient to address the perceived failure of international human rights law to resolve the resource allocation dilemma and the need for states to prioritize their expenditures. However, the blending of pragmatism and principle within the Statement has enabled the ESC Committee to provide a suitable methodology to scrutinize the process by which states resolve the resource allocation dilemma.[61] This methodology is essentially a test of reasonableness,[62] the assessment of which is informed by the factors outlined in the Statement by the ESC Committee (and the additional considerations outlined below).[63]

The application of this test defers primary responsibility for the resolution of the resource allocation dilemma to states and only seeks to dictate the *principles* that must inform this process. As such, it should not be seen as methodology to resolve the resource allocation dilemma in a precise and determinate way. Instead,

---

[59] The ESC Committee omits any express reference to the requirement that the adoption of the least restrictive measure must be reasonably available. However, this requirement of reasonableness is necessary to ensure a practical and context-sensitive interpretation of a state's obligations. Moreover, domestic jurisdictions have recognized this when articulating their tests to assess the reasonableness of a limitation. See Chapter 5.

[60] See ESC Committee, *General Comment No 3* (n 42) para 9 (stating that any retrogressive measures with respect to the enjoyment of a right 'would need to be fully justified by reference to the totality of the rights provided for in the Covenant and in the context of the full use of the maximum available resources'). Although the position in this general comment does not demonstrate an awareness of the need for external system coherence (ie, an acknowledgement that resources will be required to secure rights other than economic and social rights), this consideration is addressed in point (c) of the ESC Committee Statement, which refers to the need for resource allocation in accordance with international human rights generally.

[61] ibid para 8.

[62] Indeed, art 8(4) of the Optional Protocol to the ICESCR provides that, '[w]hen assessing communications under the Present Protocol, the Committee shall consider the reasonableness of the steps taken by the State party...' For a discussion of the contentious nature of this formulation during drafting of the Protocol, see Griffey (n 58) 294–304.

[63] The test of 'reasonableness' is commonly used to assess the legitimacy of a state's acts or omissions in various contexts whether it be tort or administrative law in the common law system or reasonableness review under the South African Constitution. See Griffey (n 58) 304–17; Sandra Liebenberg, *Socio-Economic Rights—Adjudication under a Transformative Constitution* (Juta, 2010). Although the standard of reasonableness under the ICESCR shares characteristics with these other tests, it remains an autonomous test.

international human rights law imposes a burden on states to adopt a *framework* to inform this process which enables an assessment of whether a state has engaged in reasonable priority setting[64]—an obligation of conduct rather than result.

The application of this model can be demonstrated in the context of the following scenario contemplated in the recent report of the National Consultation on Human Rights in Australia.[65] The legitimacy of economic and social rights were measured, in part, against the capacity of the right to health to resolve a dilemma whereby a decision had to be made as to whether a remote Aboriginal community retained a primary school or a health clinic.[66] The view taken by those who authored the report was that the right to health was unable to assist in the resolution of this dilemma.[67] However, no attempt was made to apply the test of reasonableness as outlined by the ESC Committee. Had this been done, the following inquiries would have been required. First, an assessment would have been required to determine whether the mooted closing of the health clinic was an interference with the normative content of right to health.[68] On the facts, this is patently the case as it involves an issue in relation to the availability and accessibility of health services, which are central elements of the right to health. Having established the interference with the right to health, the assessment to determine whether the closure of the clinic would be reasonably justified would be informed by the following questions:

(i) was the decision to reduce funding for the relevant community based on discriminatory grounds;
(ii) did Australia have an evidence based program to address the systemic health problems of indigenous Australians in the short, intermediate, and long term which was informed by appropriate indicators and benchmarks and developed in consultation with all relevant parties including indigenous people, health professionals, and NGOs;
(iii) on the evidence available, did Australia actually lack the resources to fund both the clinic *and* school;
(iv) if there was a genuine lack of resources, was the decision to withdraw resources from the community the result of a decision to *redistribute* resources into other initiatives that were considered necessary and appropriate, based on the available evidence, to realize the right to health for other indigenous or non-indigenous groups *or* the realization of other human rights obligations assumed by the state in international law;
(v) did the authorities consider the availability, appropriateness, and reasonableness of alternative policies that would have minimized the impact of closing the health clinic on the indigenous community, such as the provision of mobile health services or the provision of access to alternative health services in nearby communities;

---

[64] Liebenberg (n 63) 173.
[65] National Human Rights Consultation Committee, *National Human Rights Consultation Report* (Australia Government, 2009).
[66] ibid 355–6.
[67] ibid.
[68] Liebenberg (n 63) 175 (warning of the tendency to overlook the normative discussion as to the scope of the right).

(vi) did the authorities engage in genuine, effective, and transparent consultation with the local indigenous community *and* broader community, including experts on indigenous health (to the extent that this was reasonably practicable), to assess their views and preferences as to whether to retain the school or health clinic;
(vii) did the final decision of the authorities involve a genuine consideration, and reasonable integration, of the views expressed by the community;
(viii) was the community effectively advised as to the reasons for the decision of the relevant authority;
(ix) was genuine provision made to ensure that those affected by the decision were entitled to have the decision reviewed by another body if they were dissatisfied with the decision; and
(x) was an effective system put in place to monitor and evaluate the impact of the decision on the availability, accessibility, acceptability, and quality of health services available to the indigenous community.

If the relevant authority complied with the principle of non-discrimination, and answered 'yes' to each of other questions, its decision would be deemed reasonable irrespective of whether it decided to close the health clinic. The right to health does not demand that the clinic remain open. It simply demands that states undertake progressive and appropriate measures to secure the effective realization of the right to health for everyone within their jurisdiction in accordance with a process that will determine the reasonableness of its actions. The fact that a state will often struggle to secure the highest attainable standard of health will not, of itself, constitute a violation of the right to health provided the process adopted by a state to balance competing rights in the context of limited resources is reasonable.

The assessment of what constitutes reasonableness will remain subject to ongoing debate. As a minimum however, it is suggested that for a decision-making process to be considered reasonable it must be:

- *principled* (that is, consistent with the principles identified by the ESC Committee and informed by the rights under international law especially non-discrimination);
- *evidence based* as opposed to speculative (to ensure the effective enjoyment of all rights);
- *consultative* and participatory (to the extent that this is reasonably practicable);
- *transparent* (in the sense that there is an awareness and understanding of the process to be adopted); and
- *evaluative* (in the sense that whatever decisions are made they remain subject to review and monitoring).

Importantly, the requirement of reasonableness also applies to decisions made by relevant state authorities with respect to the adoption a particular strategy from among a range of potential strategies that could all contribute to the realization of the right to health.[69] The progressive realization of the right to health concedes that

---

[69] See Sofia Gruskin and Norman Daniels, 'Justice and Human Rights: Priority Setting and Fair Deliberative Process' (2008) 98 Am J Pub Health 1573 (illustrate a process called accountability for

states must make decisions that involve prioritization in the allocation of resources to secure the right to health *and* the other obligations a state may have assumed under international law. But a heavy burden is cast upon states to justify their decisions regarding the distribution of scarce resources. Added to this burden is the requirement that states must also secure the minimum core of the right to health—a controversial concept that has been embraced by some and is the subject of denigration by others. The discussion that follows examines this concept and attempts to offer a persuasive case for its role in understanding the right to health.

IV The concept of minimum core obligations

A Genesis and inflation

In contrast to the abstract and open-ended nature of a state's progressive obligation, the ESC Committee in its General Comment No 3 introduced the idea that states parties to the ICESCR were under 'a minimum core obligation to ensure the satisfaction of, at the very least, minimum essential levels of each of the rights' which in the context of health was said to extend to essential primary health care.[70] In an attempt to give further meaning to this concept, the ESC Committee in its later General Comment No 14 on the Right to Health declared that, when 'read in conjunction with more contemporary instruments such as the Programme of Action of the International Conference on Population and Development, the Alma-Ata Declaration provides compelling guidance on the core obligations arising from article 12'.[71]

It subsequently identified the following minimum core obligations of states under the right to health as the obligation:

(a) To ensure the right of access to health facilities, goods and services on a non-discriminatory basis especially for vulnerable or marginalized groups;
(b) To ensure access to the minimum essential food which is nutritionally adequate and safe, to ensure freedom from hunger to everyone;
(c) To ensure access to basic shelter, housing and sanitation and an adequate supply of safe and potable water;
(d) To provide essential drugs as from time to time defined under the WHO Action Programme on Essential Drugs;
(e) To ensure equitable distribution of all health facilities, goods and services;
(f) To adopt and implement a national public health strategy and plan of action on the basis of epidemiological evidence, addressing the health concerns of the whole population; the strategy and plan of action shall be devised and periodically reviewed, on the basis of a participatory and transparent process; they shall include methods, such as right to health

---

reasonableness, which has four conditions—publicity; relevance; revision; and appeals and regulation—to the decision of a state to adopt one of five possible strategies to improve maternal health).

[70] ESC Committee, *General Comment No 3* (n 42) para 10.
[71] ibid para 43.

indicators and benchmarks, by which progress can be closely monitored; the process by which the strategy and plan are devised as well as their content, shall give particular attention to all vulnerable and marginalized groups.[72]

Beyond this list the ESC Committee further explained that the following are 'obligations of comparable priority':

(a) To ensure reproductive, maternal (pre-natal as well as post-natal) and child health care;
(b) To provide immunization against the major infectious diseases occurring in the community;
(c) To take measures to prevent, treat and control epidemic and endemic diseases;
(d) To provide education and access to information concerning the main health problems in the community, including methods of preventing and controlling them; and
(e) To provide appropriate training for health personnel, including education on health and human rights.[73]

The ESC Committee went further again by declaring that 'a State party cannot, under any circumstances whatsoever, justify its non-compliance with the core obligations, set out above...which are non-derogable'.[74] This is in contrast to the original exposition of minimum core obligations by the ESC Committee in its General Comment No 3 where it accepted 'that any assessment as to whether a State has discharged its minimum core obligations must also take account of resource constraints applying within the country concerned'.[75] It added that 'in order for a State party to be able to attribute its failure to meet at least its minimum core obligations to a lack of available resources it must demonstrate that every effort has been made to use all resources that are at its disposition in an effort to satisfy, as a matter of priority, those minimum obligations'.[76]

This transformation and inflation as to the nature and scope of the minimum core obligations under the right to health by the ESC Committee is considered to be problematic under the terms of the interpretative approach employed in this analysis. In the first instance there is no principled justification offered by the ESC Committee for the shift from a presumptive to a non-derogable minimum core obligation. States never contemplated the notion of a minimum core when drafting the ICESCR or CRC let alone a non-derogable minimum core. On the contrary, the realization of the right to health was expressly stated to be a progressive obligation. This does not necessarily preclude the interpretative exercise from implying such a concept if it can be shown to have a principled basis or to have been embraced by subsequent state practice. But the absolute nature of the approach adopted by the ESC Committee tends to stretch the accepted principles of treaty interpretation in a way that is unaccompanied by any justification to legitimize this approach.

---

[72] ESC Committee, *General Comment No 14* (n 52) paras 43(a)–(f).
[73] ibid paras 44 (a)–(e).
[74] ibid para 47.
[75] ESC Committee, *General Comment No 3* (n 42) para 10.
[76] ibid.

A purposive approach to interpretation may, as will be argued below, justify the idea of minimum core obligations. However, the general rule of interpretation under article 31 of the VCLT does not condone an interpretative exercise that completely overlooks the actual text of a treaty—the ordinary meaning of 'progressive', especially when considered in the context of the obligations assumed by states under both the ICESCR and the ICCPR, strongly mitigates against an interpretation that imposes an absolute non-derogable minimum core set of obligations.

The introduction of the notion of obligations of 'comparable priority' is also unaccompanied by any principled justification. So too is the extraordinary conflation in the list of specific measures identified as minimum core obligations when compared to the original vision which simply referred to the provision of basic primary health care. Moreover, from a purely practical perspective, for many states the capacity to ensure the realization of these minimum core obligations will remain as distant as the prospect of the full realization of the right to health itself. To take just one example, the requirement to not only adopt but *implement* a national health strategy based on epidemiological evidence attendant with relevant benchmarks, indicators, and monitoring and review mechanisms is an objective that many developed states would struggle to achieve.

As a consequence, the vision of the minimum core obligations of states under the right to health, as advanced by the ESC Committee, is disassociated from the capacity of states to realize this vision. It simply does not offer a principled, practical, or coherent rationale which is sufficiently sensitive to the context in which the right to health must be operationalized. In light of such observations it is not difficult to see why commentators have referred to the 'meandering course of logic on what amounts to some obligations'[77] and questioned the extent to 'which they meet the actual health needs of all countries and accordingly the extent to which they warrant prioritization in all contexts'.[78] Moreover, although some courts have been prepared to engage with this concept and affirmed its relevance[79] others have found its implementation difficult and confusing.[80] This is despite attempts by other

---

[77] Katharine Young, 'The Minimum Core of Economic and Social Rights: A Concept in Search of Content' (2008) 33 Yale J Intl L 113, 154.

[78] Karrisha Pillay, 'South Africa's Commitment to Health Rights in the Spotlight: Do we Meet the International Standard?' in Sage Russell and Daniel Brand (eds), *Exploring the Core Content of Economic and Social Rights: South African and International Perspectives* (Protea Book House, 2002) 61, 66–8.

[79] Inter-American Commission on Human Rights, Press Communique No 14/93, (Washington DC, 10 August 1993), in *Annual Report of the Inter-American Commission on Human Rights 1993*, IACHR Doc OEA/SER.L/V/II.85 Doc. 9 rev (11 February 1994) 603–4 (stating that the OAS members states are 'obligated... to guarantee a minimum threshold of [ESC] rights'); African Commission on Human and Peoples' Rights, *Social and Economic Rights Action Center and the Center for Economic and Social Rights v Nigeria*, Communication No 155/96 (27 October 2001) [65]–[66] (noting that rights under the African Charter have a minimum core).

[80] The South African Constitutional Court has sought to grapple with the concept of the minimum core but ultimately resolved to leave it within the more general scope of the reasonableness review with respect to the implementation of the rights to health and housing: *Government of the Republic of South Africa v Grootboom* [2001] 1 SA 46 (CC, Sth Afr) [33] (declined to decide on the question of the minimum core with respect to the right to housing because of a perceived lack of information before the court to make such a finding); *Minister of Health v Treatment Action Campaign (No 2)* [2002] 5 SA 721

commentators to advance the merit of the concept and the means by which to secure its implementation.[81]

Indeed Katie Young, who provides the most detailed and insightful examination of the minimum core to date, concludes that the concept is so problematic that it ought to be stripped of any normative status and restricted in its use to advocacy—a political tool that can be utilized by the marginalized and disadvantaged to catalyse their claims for the realization of their rights.[82] This analysis shares Young's vision as to the political economy of the minimum core concept. But it is not prepared to abandon its interpretative potential as a principled case can be made to justify such an interpretative concept and it is also possible to offer a vision as to its content which is practical and sensitive to its context.

B In search of a principled basis for minimum core obligations

The rationale offered by the ESC Committee when it originally articulated the concept of the minimum core in its General Comment No 3 was based on what have been described as 'two fairly elusive reasons'.[83] First, that it was necessary to require such an obligation of result in light of its experience in examining states' reports[84] and second, '[i]f the Covenant were to be read in such a way as not to establish such a minimum core obligation, it would largely be deprived of its raison d'etre'.[85] As David Bilchitz has explained the 'first reason is...inadequate as it fails to explain the problems that the [ESC] Committee had experienced and why recognition of the minimum core obligation would serve to rectify such difficulties' whereas the 'second reason provided by the [ESC] Committee is incomplete' as it fails to explain why recognition of the minimum core is necessary to realize the objective of the Covenant.[86]

In his attempt to remedy these deficits, Bilchitz tends to focus his inquiry on the political and philosophical basis for a minimum core, rather than the question as to whether there is a principled basis under international law upon which to imply such an obligation.[87] In contrast, it is argued here that such a justification can be

---

(CC, Sth Afr) (refused to define a minimum core standard for the right to health largely by virtue of its perceived institutional capacity). cf Justice Goldstone, 'Foreword' in Varun Gauri and Daniel Brinks (eds), *Courting Social Justice: Judicial Enforcement of Social and Economic Rights in the Developing World* (CUP, 2008) xii (argues that comments of the court should not be taken as a call to abandon any future reliance on the minimum core approach).

[81] See, eg, Craig Scott and Philip Alston, 'Adjudicating Constitutional Priorities in a Transnational Context: A Comment on *Soobramoney's* Legacy and *Grootboom's* Promise' (2000) 16 S Afr J Hum Rts 206; David Bilchitz, *Poverty and Fundamental Rights: The Justification and Enforcement of Socio-Economic Rights* (OUP, 2007); Audrey Chapman and Sage Russell (eds), *Core Obligations: Building a Framework for Economic Social and Cultural Rights* (Intersentia, 2002); Brigit Toebes, 'Towards an Improved Understanding of the International Right to Health' (1999) 21 Hum Rts Q 661, 674–7.

[82] Young (n 77) 173.
[83] Bilchitz (n 81) 185.
[84] ESC Committee, *General Comment No 3* (n 42) para 10.
[85] ibid.
[86] Bilchitz (n 81) 185.   [87] ibid ch 6.

found in the application of the ordinary rules of treaty interpretation. A textual approach alone does not admit to the legitimacy of the minimum core as an obligation imposed on states—indeed the inclusion of a progressive obligation strongly militates against such a finding. But when used in conjunction with a purposive approach and the attendant need to give effect to the object and purpose of a treaty, there is a strong argument that the concept of a minimum core obligation is essential to guide states in their efforts to realize economic and social rights and give effect to the object and purpose of treaties such as the ICESCR and the CRC.

This argument rests on the basis that the progressive nature of rights such as health carries three consequences. First, the ordinary meaning of the term 'progressive' is associated with the idea of a gradual movement from one level to a higher level. This is consistent with the view expressed during the drafting of the ICESCR that the progressive obligation 'placed upon signatories a duty to achieve ever higher and higher levels of fulfilment of rights' as permitted by available resources.[88] Second, the assessment of the extent to which a state has complied with its progressive obligation, is an extremely inaccurate process in the absence of systems or concepts to guide its understanding. Third, the abstract nature of a progressive obligation carries the risk that states will attempt to hide behind its indeterminacy and thus thwart the effective implementation of rights such as health. Collectively these factors are suggestive of the need to develop interpretative tools that will not only guide states in their efforts to implement their progressive obligation, but also militate the potential for such an obligation to be used to undermine the effective implementation of economic and social rights.

It is within this context that the concept of the 'minimum core' represents a modest attempt at the development of such a tool by seeking to inform states that there are core obligations associated with each right that must be secured if states are to fulfil their obligation of good faith under a treaty such as the ICESCR or the CRC. The obligation to secure the right to health may be progressive but this does not entitle a state to do nothing. To adopt such an approach would render the effective implementation of the right illusory. If the obligation of good faith requires that states must be taking effective steps to secure the realization of the right to health, the idea of minimum core obligations represents an attempt to advise states of the minimum measures they are required to take as they commence their journey towards the progressive realization of the right to health.

The development of minimum core obligations is therefore an example of an interpretative tool developed by the ESC Committee to address what would otherwise have been a serious 'effectiveness' gap in the realization of economic and social rights. The ESC Committee itself hinted at this justification when it defended its original exposition of the concept as being necessary to ensure the 'raison d'etre' of the ICESCR. It just neglected to take the additional step of expressly linking this explanation to the accepted principles of interpretation under the VCLT and the need to develop the concept as a means by which to give effect to the object and

---

[88] *Annotations on the Text of the Draft International Covenants on Human Rights* (n 1) 20 para 24.

purpose of a treaty. But while a principled defence of minimum core obligations can be mounted, the real issue on which there is an absence of anything approximating consensus, is the means by which to determine the content of minimum core obligations.

C In search of a practical content for the minimum core obligations under the right to health

The list of minimum core obligations under the right to health compiled by the ESC Committee in its General Comment No 14 is said to have been informed by the cumulative assessment of states' reports by the ESC Committee[89]—a method by which matters that are commonly or routinely dealt with by states in their reports are converted into minimum core obligations. Such an approach, however, is fraught with danger. It tends to transform the references to certain matters by states in the reporting process into evidence of an accepted understanding as to the nature of core obligations irrespective of the practice of states. The reality is that states do not refer to their minimum core obligations in their reports in any uniform way. Moreover, within domestic and regional jurisdictions only a handful of judicial systems have actively embraced and applied the concept of minimum core obligations in the adjudication of a dispute.[90] State practice simply does not provide any consensus with respect to the list of minimum core obligations identified by the ESC Committee.

In light of this reality it is suggested that a more modest and practical vision of the minimum core of the right to health must be constructed—a vision which is not simply concerned with obligations of result but also obligations of conduct and which remains practical and contextually sensitive. A return to the original General Comment of the ESC Committee in which it outlined the idea of a minimum core obligation provides a useful starting point for this exercise where, in contrast to the long list that is found in General Comment No 14, the ESC Committee confined the minimum core of the right to health to '*essential* primary health care' (emphasis added).[91] Young has suggested that such an approach is suggestive of a methodology that ties an understanding of the minimum core to the basic needs required for survival and life.[92] It is therefore considered useful by some commentators 'because it focuses attention on the most urgent steps necessary for the satisfaction of those rights which are required for the exercise of all rights'.[93] But while Young's observation may be relevant with respect to the description given by the Committee as to the minimum core of other rights—'essential foodstuffs, . . . basic shelter or housing

---

[89] See Young (n 77) 117, referring to ESC Committee, *General Comment No 3* (n 42) para 10. See also ESC Commmittee, *General Comment No 14* (n 52) para 6.
[90] See nn 79, 80.
[91] ESC Committee, *General Comment No 3* (n 42) para 10. See also Toebes (n 81) 675 (also suggests that inspiration be drawn from the Primary Health Care Strategy of the WHO).
[92] Young (n 77) 127.
[93] ibid 129.

or . . . the most basic forms of education'—it is questionable whether this is the case with respect to the right to health.

The reference to essential primary health care is not the same as stipulating that states must provide the essential requirements to ensure the survival of every individual within its jurisdiction. Indeed, as Bilchitz has recognized, such an approach is unworkable with respect to the right to health as it 'would involve not only primary health care, but also the provision of expensive drugs and treatments such as dialysis and heart transplants that are necessary to preserve life'.[94] Thus, for him the detailed list offered by the ESC Committee in General Comment 14 on the right to health represents a pragmatic minimum threshold for the right to health.[95] In contrast, it has been suggested in this analysis that the list offered by the ESC Committee is neither principled nor practical and its expansive scope and lack of local context sensitivity is reflected in the failure of states and the broader interpretative community to actively engage with the vision of a state's minimum core obligations under the right to health as advanced by the ESC Committee.[96]

In light of the controversy and indeterminancy surrounding this concept, a weak rather than strong approach must be adopted with respect to the content of the minimum core obligations in relation to the right to health. Such an approach must be informed by the principle underlying the justification for the adoption of the minimum core concept. As such, the content of this principle must be reduced to the following question: what are the minimum or first steps required of states as they commence, in good faith, their obligation to progressively secure the effective realization of the highest attainable standard of health?

The answer to this question is not without difficulty and Young's critique of the various approaches used to enliven the concept of the minimum core to date, suggests that the impasse between the concept and its content may be insurmountable. One of her primary concerns is the allegation that the ESC Committee has failed to articulate a coherent, stable, and determinate vision of minimum core duties and continues to shift without explanation as to its understanding of such obligations.[97] No issue is taken in this analysis with this criticism of the ESC Committee's work. However, its failings should not be taken to signal the death knoll for the concept of minimum core obligations. On the contrary it has been argued that this concept provides an essential interpretative tool to enable navigation of the vagaries created by the progressive nature of economic and social rights such as the right to health. The question remains, however, on what basis is content to be ascribed to

---

[94] Bilchitz (n 81) 221.
[95] ibid 223.
[96] cf Audrey Chapman, 'Core Obligations related to the Right to Health' in Audrey Chapman and Sage Russell (eds), *Core Obligations: Building a Framework for Economic, Social and Cultural Rights* (Intersentia, 2002) 185 (tends to embrace the work of the ESC Committee without any critical reflection as to its legitimacy); *Report of the Special Rapporteur on the Right to Health to the Human Rights Council 2008*, UN Doc A/HRC/7/11 (31 January 2008) paras 51–3 (also embraces the approach of the ESC Committee).
[97] Young (n 77) 156.

such obligations? What follows is a tentative attempt to outline the contours of the minimum core obligations of states under the right to health.

It starts from the premise outlined above that minimum core obligations must seek to identify the minimum or first steps that states must take as they embark on their progressive obligation to secure the highest attainable standard of health for every individual within its jurisdiction. It requires that such obligations must be practical in the sense that they remain responsive to the most pressing health needs of individuals within a particular state and are sensitive to the capacity of a state to undertake the necessary measures to address such needs. It further asserts that minimum core obligations must include obligations of conduct and obligations of result if they are to have any relevance for states and indeed the broader interpretative community.

1 Minimum core obligations of conduct

In terms of obligations of conduct with respect to the right to health, they can be separated into two types. First, there is an obligation to ensure that when taking steps to secure the right to health, states remain cognisant of the interdependence of this right with other rights. Thus, for example, states must not violate the prohibition against discrimination with respect to any efforts taken to realize the right to health; states must not violate the prohibition against torture, cruel, inhuman, and degrading treatment, and punishment which would be contrary to the health of an individual, and states must not violate the right to privacy in relation to the delivery of any health services—all rights which are subject to immediate implementation and will undermine an individual's right to health if not secured. Such conduct obligations reflect not only the interdependence of human rights but also the need to ensure internal system coherence in the interpretation of a state's obligations under the right to health.

The second type of conduct obligation concerns the processes required for the direct realization of the right to health. As a minimum states must undertake reasonable efforts to develop an appropriate health strategy or plan to achieve this end. Such a plan must be a collaborative and participatory process that seeks to engage with all relevant parties—state representatives, health professionals, and representatives of the various groups for whom special measures must be taken such as women, children, persons with disabilities, indigenous, and religious groups. It must be designed in such a way as to provide a response to the health needs of individuals not only in the long term, but also the medium and short term.[98] This requires that special consideration must be given to the identification of those measures which are thought to be necessary to respond to the most urgent and pressing health needs of individuals as a cohort within a particular jurisdiction.

---

[98] This proposition represents an appropriation from the principle in the decision of the South African Constitutional Court in *Government of the Republic of South Africa v Grootboom* (n 80), where it was held that a *reasonable* housing policy required measures to address immediate, medium, and long term housing needs.

It will be recalled that the ESC Committee listed a national plan of action as part of a state's minimum core obligations. However, it required not only the adoption of such a plan, but its implementation on the basis of epidemiological evidence with appropriate benchmarks and indicators and systems of review and monitoring. Such a model is something that all states must progressively aspire to achieve. However, given the reality that even developed states continue to struggle to create such a sophisticated system, and the health systems in a vast number of countries are said to be 'on the point of collapse',[99] it should not be considered a minimum core obligation. In contrast, the starting point for states must be a commitment and evidence of reasonable and genuine efforts to at least develop an appropriate health policy.

A further minimum core conduct obligation is the obligation to make reasonable efforts to seek assistance from the international community to provide resources—both physical and financial—to assist in the development and implementation of a national strategy to realize the right to the highest attainable standard of health.[100] There are two additional dimensions to this international conduct obligation. First, a state should not refuse, without reasonable grounds, assistance which may be provided by humanitarian agencies to address the health needs of individuals within its jurisdiction.[101] Second, in any negotiations to provide financial assistance to a state with international financial institutions, such as the World Bank and IMF, a state must insist that the terms of such assistance remain cognisant of the state's obligations under the right to health in international law.[102]

2 Minimum core obligations of result

In terms of the minimum core *result* obligations the ESC Committee has provided a long list that stretches from access to health facilities, essential food, basic shelter,

---

[99] WHO, *Everybody's Business: Strengthening Health Systems to Improve Health Outcomes: WHO's Framework for Action* (WHO, 2007) 1.

[100] In *General Comment No 14*, the ESC Committee anticipated that the obligation of international assistance and co-operation under art 12 of ICESCR would operate to enable developing countries to fulfil their core obligations: *ESC General Comment No 14* (n 52) para 45. But it did not identify any obligations imposed upon developing states with respect to the actions to seek or refuse assistance.

[101] The requirement of system coherence requires that reasonable grounds to refuse assistance would have to be consistent with international legal principles. Thus, for example, a state could refuse assistance if the conditions attached to that assistance were inconsistent with the international rights and obligations of a state. A detailed discussion of this issue is beyond the scope of this analysis. However with respect to an emerging agreement as to the way in which aid should be delivered see the *Paris Declaration on Aid Effectiveness*, which were endorsed by a High Level Forum organized by the Organisation for Economic Co-operation and Development on 2 March 2005.

[102] It is recognized that the practical capacity of states to insist upon such conditions is often undermined by the inequality in negotiating power that characterizes negotiations between developing states and international financial institutions. However, a detailed analysis of this issue is beyond the scope of this analysis. Moreover, it will be argued in Chapter 9 that the nature of the international obligation imposed on states under international human rights law extends to an obligation to take reasonable measures to ensure that those international organizations over which they have control, such as the international financial institutions, act in a way that is compatible with international human rights standards in their dealings with states.

housing, and essential drugs to immunization, disease control, and training for health personnel. That few, if any, states have actually achieved all of these objectives does not appear to have hampered the ESC Committee's enthusiasm for the adoption of such a lengthy and ambitious list which are said to be non-derogable obligations. The alternative proposed here is significantly more modest in light of: (a) the underlying rationale of minimum core obligations as being minimum not optimal measures that states must take; (b) the reality that states have limited resources and any vision of minimum core obligations must be sensitive to this reality; and (c) states have not engaged with the promotion of such a list as containing their minimum core obligations.

In the first instance, the result obligations concerning access to shelter and housing, while relevant to the health of an individual, are not expressly included within the right to health, and are dealt with in other articles under the ICESCR and CRC. Thus, they should not be imported into the minimum core result obligations of states under the right to health. A more effective approach is that, given the interdependence of human rights, a state's efforts to secure its result obligations under the right to health must also be accompanied by efforts to secure the minimum core result obligations of other relevant rights.

In terms of result obligations that are particular to the right to health, it is not considered appropriate to construct a definitive or exhaustive list because the identification of those health matters which are considered to be a priority within a particular state will be influenced by local conditions—both the health needs of individuals and a state's capacity to address those needs.[103] This is not to say that the determination of minimum core result obligations must be devolved to states. On the contrary, guidance must be provided by sources other than states on this issue, but in a way that is less utopian than is currently the case. To this end it is suggested that attention be given to the development of a presumptive list of result obligations, which satisfies the elements of constructive engagement. Individual states would not be bound to comply with this list but they would be required to explain or justify their failure to achieve such outcomes. Under such a model, the minimum core places greater emphasis on the need for dialogue and is more likely to achieve its underlying objective, that is, to force states to engage in a discussion about the minimum measures they must adopt as they commence their task of progressively realizing the right to health.

Although the content of any presumptive list will be contentious, it must be remembered that the objective of such a list is to facilitate rather than finalize a discussion as the minimum core result obligations of states. A tentative offering to this discussion is to suggest that the list of minimum result obligations begin with two: the provision of selective and integrated primary health care and the provision of food and water necessary to survive.

---

[103] See *Report of the Special Rapporteur to the Human Rights Council 2008* (n 96) para 52 (notes that 'because health challenges vary widely from one state to another...the minimum "basket" may vary between countries').

(a) A minimum core obligation to provide basic food and water

With respect to the provision of food and water as a minimum core result obligation, these items are actually listed as specific measures to realize the right to the highest attainable standard of health under article 24(c) of the CRC.[104] Although a state may argue that it lacks sufficient resources to deliver such entitlements for adults and children, as outlined above, it has minimum conduct obligations to actively seek and not reasonably refuse humanitarian assistance. As such it is difficult to envisage how it could defend its failure to provide basic food and water for individuals within its jurisdiction given the apparent willingness of humanitarian agencies to supply such necessities.[105] A question remains, however, as to what amounts to '*basic*' food and water. Such an inquiry forces the discussion to travel back into the dangerous territory of what Young described as the 'essence' approach to the concept of the minimum core. For her, such an approach reduces the analysis to a scientific assessment, denies a broader and more participatory notion of survival, and transforms the notion of the minimum core into the 'more flexible arena of setting standards and devising benchmarks'.[106]

Young's concerns are significant but they are not sufficient to abandon the insistence upon *basic* food and water as being part of the minimum core for three reasons. First, the participatory model for the determination of the minimum core, which has been advanced above, demands that the issue is not simply reduced to a scientific consideration. Science can, and must, inform the assessment. But given that this process itself will be contested, broader participation among the relevant interpretative community will be required to assess what is reasonably agreed upon as *basic* food and water within a particular jurisdiction.[107] Second, the obligation to progressively pursue the right to the highest attainable standard of health, prohibits

---

[104] See also ESC Committee, *General Comment No 15: The Right to Water*, UN Doc E/C.12/2002/11 (20 January 2003) para 37(a) (states that a minimum core obligation of the right to water, which forms part of the right to an adequate standard of living under art 11 of the ICESCR includes an obligation '[t]o ensure access to the minimum essential amount of water, that is sufficient and safe for personal and domestic uses to prevent disease').

[105] This is clearly a generalization that conceals a complex debate as to the preparedness of such agencies to assist states. Space does not permit a detailed examination of this issue here and it suffices to note that the commitment of humanitarian agencies is often thwarted by reluctance on the part of states for various reasons to facilitate the provision of assistance. As evidence of the commitment on the part of humanitarian agencies to assist developing states, see for example: UNICEF, *Water Sanitation and Hygiene Strategies for 2006–2015*, UN Doc E/ICEF/2006/6 (15 November 2005) para 22 (states that the objective of UNICEF is to contribute to among things equitable and sustainable access to and safe use of water); Sphere Project, *Humanitarian Charter and Minimum Standards in Disaster Response* (Sphere Project 2004) (details the standards which humanitarian organizations aspire to achieve in assisting states in emergency situations).

[106] Young (n 77) 131.

[107] A significant amount of research has already been undertaken in this regard which should be used to inform the understanding of the minimum water and nutritional needs of children. See, eg, Sphere Project, *Humanitarian Charter and Minimum Standards in Disaster Response* (n 105) (outlines detailed minimum standards with respect to among other things water supply, nutrition, and food aid which were the result of two years of inter-agency collaboration); WHO, 'Minimum Water Quantity Needed for Domestic Use in Emergencies' (Technical Note No 9, Revised Draft, 7 January 2005).

the capacity for any assessment as to the basic needs of a child to be used, as feared by Young, to prescribe the '"inner limits" of survival'.[108] Indeed, it is a curious omission of Young's analysis that she does not locate her critique of the minimum core within the broader context of the progressive obligation given that it serves to alleviate much of her concerns. Finally, to conceive of the minimum core as a form of indicator or benchmark is not fatal to its legitimacy. On the contrary, the model advanced in this analysis to defend this concept, is ultimately based on the proposition that the minimum core serves as a tool by which to direct states as to the minimum measures they must undertake when they undertake their progressive obligation to fulfil their obligation to secure the right to health.

(b) A minimum core obligation to provide the essential elements of primary health care

The inclusion of elements of primary health care as an example of a minimum core result obligation is arguably more problematic than access to basic food and water. As will be discussed below in Chapter 6, there are disputes as to the meaning of the term 'primary health care' and the nature of its relationship with secondary and tertiary health care. Indeed, the ESC Committee in its General Comment on the Right to Health formed the view that, '[s]ince these forms of health care frequently overlap and often interact, the use of this typology does not always provide sufficient distinguishing criteria...and is therefore of limited assistance in relation to the normative understanding of article 12'.[109] Despite these concerns, its inclusion as part of states' minimum core obligations under the right to health is considered justifiable for three reasons.

First, article 24 of the CRC specifically refers to primary health care as a measure to secure a child's right to health. Article 24(2)(b) demands that the provision of necessary medical assistance and health care must take place 'with emphasis on the development of primary health care' and article 24(2)(c) requires that efforts to combat disease and malnutrition must take place 'within the framework of primary health care'. This prominence given to primary health care, in circumstances where the drafters would have been aware of its omission from the text of the ICESCR, indicates evidence of an evolving understanding of the special place of primary health care within the context of realizing the right to health.

Second, this textual support for primary health care as a minimum core result obligation is further strengthened by its status within accepted public health care strategies.[110] Of greatest significance in this respect is the Declaration of Alma Ata adopted at the International Conference on Primary Health Care in 1978[111] which embraced the primary health care approach. More recently, a Taskforce on the realization of the Millennium Development Goals to reduce infant and maternal

---

[108] Young (n 77) 132.
[109] ESC Committee, *General Comment No 14* (n 52) n 9.
[110] See UNICEF, *The State of the World's Children 2008: Child Survival* (UNICEF, 2007) 30–4.
[111] *Declaration of Alma-Ata International Conference on Primary Health Care*, Alma-Ata, USSR, 6–12 September 1978.

mortality, actually recommended that 'highest priority be given to strengthening the primary healthcare system from community based interventions to the first referral level facility at which emergency obstetric care is available'.[112] Despite the potential for such an approach to overlap with secondary and tertiary forms of health care, as its name suggests, primary health care is still recognized as the first and basic measure in the design of any effective health care system. As such there is a synergy between primary health care and the rationale underlying the concept of minimum core obligations which is designed to identify the first measures to be taken by states in their efforts to progressively secure the right to health. It is within this context that the CRC Committee, in its report for Belarus, expressed concern at 'the apparent priority given to curative health care rather than decentralized preventive health care'[113] and recommended that 'a stronger emphasis [be] placed on primary health care activities'.[114]

Finally, despite the existence of some controversy surrounding the definition of primary health care, a focus on certain core elements of the primary health care model remains consistent with the notion of minimum core obligations. The underlying principles of this approach are said to 'encompass the tenets of equity, community involvement, intersectoral collaboration, use of appropriate technology, affordability and health promotion'.[115] It therefore represents a model that is well suited to the idea of minimum core result obligations which, given their minimalist nature, imply a need to possess a low cost relative to the scope of their impact and demonstrate a strong participatory basis. Thus, the fact that a system of primary health care may vary in its specific features from one jurisdiction to the next should not be considered a reason to omit it from a list of core result obligations. Rather, provided the features of a system are reflective of its participatory design, this should be considered to be the strength of such a model.

Although the specific activities required under the primary health care model advanced under the Declaration of Alma Ata are quite extensive, it has been suggested by UNICEF that they include as a minimum the following activities:

- health education;
- promotion of adequate supplies of food and proper nutrition;
- safe water and basic sanitation;
- maternal and child care;
- immunization against the major childhood diseases;
- appropriate treatment of common diseases and injuries;
- prevention and control of locally endemic diseases; and
- provision of essential drugs.[116]

---

[112] Freedman and others (n 35) 6.
[113] CO CRC Belarus, UN Doc CRC/C/15/Add.17, para 9.
[114] ibid para 14.
[115] UNICEF, *State of the World's Children 2008* (n 110) 30.
[116] ibid.

This list reflects several of the elements which are included in the heavily criticized list of minimum core obligations advanced by the ESC Committee in its General Comment on the Right to Health. Such open-ended and resource-intensive measures are not compatible with the vision of the minimum core advanced in this analysis.

Moreover, despite the enthusiasm that accompanied the adoption of the Declaration of Alma Ata, the evidence suggests that the objectives of this Declaration were beyond the capacity of many states.[117] As a consequence, an alternative model known as 'selective primary health care' was developed to provide the 'first step towards the implementation of primary health care'.[118] The model focused on four low-cost interventions known as 'GOBI—growth monitoring for under nutrition, oral rehydration therapy to treat childhood diarrhoea, breastfeeding to ensure the health of young children and immunization against six deadly childhood diseases'.[119] It was subsequently complemented with the addition of 'three more components—food supplementation, family spacing and female education – and became known as GOBI FFF'.[120]

The features of the selective primary health care model, which place an emphasis on the provision of 'a core group of cost effective solutions in a timely way to address specific health challenges',[121] resonate strongly with the notion of minimum core obligations advanced in this analysis. However, there is a risk that its implementation in isolation from the participatory strategies that form the basis of the primary health care model could lead to a top-down expert-driven understanding of minimum core obligations. In order to avert such a risk, the dominant approach within public health discourse is to favour an integrated approach that draws on the underlying features of primary health care such as 'community participation, intersectoral collaboration and integration in the general health delivery system'.[122] Such a development is significant for this analysis in its attempt to map out, with some degree of clarity, the minimum core obligations of states under the right to health. It suggests that, from a practical perspective, the realization of the goals of primary health care are beyond the scope of the minimum core. But a selective primary health core model, when integrated with participatory processes, is widely accepted as a model that all states should be capable of adopting with appropriate assistance. As such, the minimum core obligation of states should extend to the provision of an integrated selective primary health model.

Such an approach is not that dissimilar to, and arguably offers a greater understanding of, the original vision of the minimum core offered by the ESC Committee in 1993 which it confined to 'essential primary health care'.[123] It therefore offers a

---

[117] UNICEF, *State of the World's Children 2008* (n 110) 29–30.
[118] ibid 31.   [119] ibid.   [120] ibid.   [121] ibid.   [122] ibid 32–3.
[123] ESC Committee, *General Comment No 3* (n 42) para 10. Interestingly the CRC Committee endorsed this position rather than the later visions given by the ESC Committee as to the minimum core obligations of various rights including health in its recommendations given at the Day of General Discussion on resources for the rights of the child: CRC Committee, *Report on the Forty-Sixth Session* (n 8) para 89.

sharp contrast with its later and more elaborate enumeration of a state's minimum core obligations in General Comment No 14. However, unlike each of these positions, an attempt has been made in this analysis to articulate a principled justification for the existence of the minimum core concept and a clear and practical vision as to its content, in light of the need to ensure coherence and context sensitivity. Moreover, contrary to the non-derogable nature of the minimum core, as advanced by the ESC Committee in its General Comment on the Right to Health—which has been endorsed by the CRC Committee[124]—a return to the presumptive nature of minimum core obligations, as originally envisioned by the ESC Committee and recently endorsed in its Statement on 'Evaluation of the obligation to take steps to the "maximum of available resources" under an Optional Protocol to the Covenant', is more appropriate.[125]

The availability of resources will always impact upon the ability of a state to secure any level of the right to health. The realities of armed conflict, natural disaster, economic dysfunction, and global inequality mean that there will be circumstances in which states cannot secure elements of the right to health for a child even with the best of intentions.[126] The failure to accept this reality by the ESC Committee in its General Comment on the Right to Health, and its insistence upon an absolute and fixed concept of minimum core obligations, undermines the potential for engagement with this concept by states, courts, and commentators. A more modest vision of minimum core obligations, as offered here, is intended to reignite this conversation in a way that is principled and practical, and informed by the realities of life within states.

V Conclusion—progressive as a pragmatic and principled process

The progressive nature of the obligation of states to recognize the right to health subject to available resources is both the strength and weakness of this right. It is actually a profoundly pragmatic formulation that seeks to accommodate the reality that the resources available to a state will determine the extent to which it is able to secure economic and social rights, such as the right to health. But its implementation presents real challenges. For those within the interpretative community who assess the legitimacy of human rights by reference to their capacity to impose immediate obligations on states that can be enforced in courts, a progressive obligation is indefensible. For those who must contend with the daily reality of prioritizing the distribution of scarce resources, a progressive obligation is invariably seen to be

---

[124] CRC Committee, *Report on the Forty-Sixth Session* (n 8) para 89 ('complying with obligations relating to the core of a right should not be dependent on the availability of resources').
[125] ESC Committee, *An Evaluation of the Obligation to Take Steps to the 'Maximum of Available Resources' under an Optional Protocol to the Covenant* (n 53) para 6.
[126] See ibid para 10 (lists these factors as being relevant to the determination of whether a state's alleged failure to secure economic and social rights can reasonably be attributed to a lack of available resources).

impractical and unhelpful—a promise of everything without any guidance on how to deliver anything.

But there is a need for those members of the interpretative community who challenge the legitimacy of economic and social rights, such as the right to health, to question the assumptions that inform their views. Thus, for example, the potential justiciability of the right to health is but one measure, to be contemplated from among a range of measures, that are appropriate for the purpose of realizing the right to health. Moreover, the experience of jurisdictions such as South Africa and Columbia demonstrate that the justiciability of the right to health is beyond question.

In terms of the resource allocation dilemma, contrary to popular opinion, international law does actually offer a process by which to guide states in the resolution of this dilemma. This process does not seek to impose or demand the adoption of a mathematical formula by states. Instead, the key question to be considered by, and asked of states is, was the decision to allocate (or redistribute) resources for the realization of the right to health reasonable. Debates will continue as to what constitutes reasonableness. However, the contribution offered in this chapter is that the reasonableness of any decision in relation to resource allocation will be determined by the extent to which it is shown by a state to be principled, evidence based, consultative and participatory, transparent, and evaluative.

7

Specific Measures Required to Secure the Right to Health

I Introduction

The previous two chapters sought to translate the abstract nature of the obligation to 'recognize' the right to health into a series of principled, practical, coherent, and context sensitive measures that are required of states. The formulation of the right to health in international law also lists a series of explicit measures that states must pursue in order to secure the full implementation of this right. These measures, which range from an obligation to reduce infant mortality to the development of preventive health care and family planning services, are extremely broad and open textured. As such, there is a need to interrogate the extent to which parameters can be placed around their meaning in a way that allows states and the broader interpretative community to agree on the nature of the practical steps required to secure their implementation. It is this task that Chapter 7 seeks to perform.

The central theme to emerge from this analysis is that considerable deference must be given to states' margin of appreciation to allow for a context-sensitive implementation of the specific measures required to secure the right to health in international law. However, this margin remains subject to the overriding caveat that whatever measures are adopted by states they must be undertaken in a manner that is directed towards securing the effective implementation of the right to health and pursue coherence with the other obligations imposed under the International Covenant on Economic, Social and Cultural Rights (ICESCR), the Convention on the Rights of the Child (CRC), and the broader system of international law. Moreover, the requirement that the measures be 'appropriate' demands that they must also be effective. In relation to this assessment of effectiveness, it will be shown that the work of the committee bodies provides some guidance as to the steps which states should adopt. However, traditional legal interpretative techniques, which draw on comparative jurisprudence, are of limited assistance in relation to this question as there is very little case law on the nature of the practical measures required of states under, for example, para 2 of article 12 of the ICESCR and article 24 of the CRC. As a consequence extensive recourse must be made to the research within other disciplines to assist in the resolution of this issue. Although unorthodox, such an approach is actually consistent with the interpretative methodology adopted in this book which rejects the traditional approach to legal interpretation and its tendency towards a closed circuit of legal logic in favour of a common narrative that is informed by a broad range of disciplines.

The structure of this chapter is largely based on the specific measures listed in para 2 of article 24 of the CRC. This is because there is a significant overlap between this paragraph and the measures listed in paragraph 2 of article 12 of the ICESCR. Indeed, article 24(2) of the CRC not only adopts, but expands, the specific measures required of states under article 12(2) of the ICESCR. The only area in which the text of the CRC does not affirm the approach adopted under the ICESCR is with respect to issues concerning occupational safety and the environment. In relation to this issue, article 12(2)(b) of the ICESCR requires the 'improvement of all aspects of environmental hygiene' whereas article 24(2)(c) only requires states to consider 'the dangers and risks of environmental pollution'.

Thus, this chapter will examine:

- the obligation to diminish infant and child mortality;
- the obligation to provide medical assistance and health care especially primary health care;
- the obligation to combat disease and malnutrition;
- the obligation to ensure occupational health and safety and address environmental threats to health;
- the obligation to provide pre-natal and post-natal health care;
- the obligation to raise awareness and ensure access to information concerning health; and
- the obligation to develop preventive health care including family planning education and services.

Importantly, the specific obligations with respect to the right to health under other international human rights instruments, such as the Convention on the Elimination of All Forms of Discrimination against Women (CEDAW), the Convention on the Rights of Persons with Disabilities (CRPD), and the International Convention on the Protection of the Rights of All Migrant Workers and Members of Their Families (CMWF) can all be accommodated within these obligations. Each of the regional instruments that protect the right to health also impose a series of specific obligations on states, which in some cases replicate, and in other instances advance the measures required of states. Where appropriate, attention will be drawn to these measures, but for reasons of space no detailed analysis will be offered as to their meaning.[1]

II The obligation to diminish infant and child mortality

In contemporary society it is self-evident that a critical measure in securing the right to health is an obligation on states to diminish infant and child mortality rates.

---

[1] With respect to the meaning of the right to health under art 11 of the European Social Charter see: Council of Europe, *Digest of the Case Law of the European Committee of Social Rights* (COE, 2008) 81–8.

Historically, however, infant deaths were considered as part of the 'nature of infancy'.[2] Indeed, it was not until the early decades of the twentieth century that infant mortality became thought of as 'illnesses and avoidable' and it was only then that a decrease in infant mortality became 'one of the most perceptible indicators' for measuring the progress of a country.[3] With the adoption of Millennium Development Goal No 4,[4] which aims to reduce the under-five infant mortality by two-thirds by 2015, infant mortality has become not merely a measure of a state's progress but that of the entire international community. Unfortunately in light of current trends there is some way to go given that, on 2007 figures, about 17,000 children under the age of five die every day from largely preventable diseases.[5]

It is against this backdrop that the obligation to take appropriate measures 'to diminish infant and child mortality' must be seen. Significantly it is listed as the first of the explicit measures required of states under both article 24(2)(a) of the CRC and article 12(2)(a) of the ICESCR, which also provides that states must take those steps necessary for 'the provision for the reduction of the still-birth rate and of infant mortality and for the healthy development of the child'.[6] Despite the variation in the terminology used to describe the nature of the obligation under the CRC and the ICESCR—to 'diminish' under the CRC, as opposed to 'reduction', as appears in article 12 of the ICESCR—this should not be taken to create a variation in the substantive nature of the obligation.[7] The ordinary meaning of both terms is to lower, a phrase that was actually proposed in early drafts of para 2(a),[8] but ultimately rejected in preference for the phrase 'diminish'. Such an obligation does not demand that states eradicate child or infant mortality rates in the short, medium, or even long term as this would be unrealistic.

At the same time, the obligation to diminish does not bestow upon states an exclusive power to determine the rate at which their mortality rates should decline or to cease taking measures to achieve this end once a certain mortality rate has been achieved. Rather, states are accountable to the committee bodies to demonstrate on a regular basis via the reporting process and the use of appropriate indicators and benchmarks that, subject to available resources, every reasonable measure has been

---

[2] Rosa Ballester, 'Child Mortality: Social and Medical Responses' (1999) 354 The Lancet SIV27.
[3] ibid. See also WHO, *The World Health Report 2005: Make Every Mother and Child Count* (WHO, 2005) 2–3 (links early concerns at infant mortality with military and economic calculations).
[4] *United Nations Millennium Declaration*, GA Res 55/2, UN Doc A/RES/55/2 (8 September 2000) para 19.
[5] WHO, 'Children: Reducing Infant Mortality' (WHO Fact Sheet 178, November 2009) <http://www.who.int/mediacentre/factsheets/fs178/en/> accessed 16 June 2011.
[6] See also African Charter on the Rights and Welfare of the Child (Addis Ababa, 11 July 1990, entered into force 29 November 1999, OAU Doc CAB/LEG/24.9/49) art 14(2)(a), which imposes an obligation on states to take measures 'to reduce infant and child mortality rates'.
[7] The CRC Committee has almost exclusively addressed the issue of infant mortality in terms of a State's obligation to 'reduce' this rate. See, eg, CO CRC Dominican Republic, UN Doc CRC/C/15/Add.150, para 36; CO CRC Nicaragua, UN Doc CRC/C/15/Add.263, para 47(c).
[8] UN Doc E/CN.4/1349 (Revised Polish Draft 1979) ('take measures to lower the mortality index of babies').

taken to achieve a reduction in the infant and child mortality rates.[9] It is in this context that the CRC Committee and the ICESCR Committee have regularly expressed concern at the general infant mortality rate within states.[10] The CRC Committee has also drawn attention to the mortality rate among certain groups of children such as Roma children,[11] indigenous children,[12] and children living in rural areas[13] in its concluding observations and welcomed efforts to arrest these rates.[14]

The CRC Committee has also subsequently called on states to '[c]ontinue and strengthen efforts to reduce infant mortality',[15] 'reduce the incidence of maternal, child and infant mortality'[16] and 'take all necessary measures'[17] to achieve this aim. But rather than detail what it considers to be 'all necessary measures', and consistent with the need to offer a context sensitive interpretation of a state's obligations, the CRC Committee has tended to provide general recommendations in its concluding observations on a range of matters that are related to the infant mortality rate. Thus, for example, in its report for Mali it recommended that the state party 'allocate appropriate resources and develop comprehensive policies and programmes to improve the health situation of children; facilitate access to primary health services; reduce the incidence of maternal, child and infant mortality'.[18]

Such comments are exceedingly general and it is questionable whether they provide any real insight into the actual nature of a state's obligation to diminish infant mortality. However, they should be seen as attempt by the CRC Committee to engage the relevant states in a dialogue akin to the approach advocated by proponents of democratic experimentalism. Thus, the abstract nature of their comments provides an invitation for states to respond with the details of their endeavours in a process that seeks to develop accountability through dialogue rather than directives. As the dialogue between states and the committee bodies evolves, it is characterized by more specific directions. Thus, for example, beyond the general exhortations of the CRC Committee to reduce infant mortality, its jurisprudence

---

[9] See Jay Ovsiovitch, 'Reporting Infant and Child Mortality under the United Nations Human Rights Conventions' (1998) 46 Buffalo L Rev 543 (evaluates efforts of states to provide Committee with data on infant mortality).
[10] See, eg, CO CRC Eritrea, UN Doc CRC/C/15/Add.204, para 39; CO CRC Kazakhstan, UN Doc CRC/C/15/Add.213, para 57; CO CRC New Zealand, UN Doc CRC/C/15/Add.216, para 35. With respect to the ESC Committee see: CO CRC India, UN Doc E/C.12/IND/CO5, para 33; CO CRC Kazakhstan, UN Doc E/C.12/KAZ/CO/1, para 40; CO ESC Republic of Moldova, UN Doc E/2004/22 (2003) 49, para 317; CO ESC Guatemala, UN Doc E/2004/22 (2003) 59, paras 417. The Human Rights Committee has also expressed its concern at the level of infant mortality within states in the context of the right to life. See, eg, CO HRC Albania, UN Doc A/60/40 Vol. I (2004) 25, para 82(14). As has the CEDAW Committee in the context of women's right to health. See, eg, CO CEDAW Gambia, UN Doc A/60/38 Part II (July 2005) 122, para 203.
[11] See, eg, CO CRC Slovakia, UN Doc CRC/C/15/Add.140, para 35.
[12] See, eg, CO CRC Canada, UN Doc CRC/C/15/Add.215, para 36.
[13] See, eg, CO CRC Romania UN Doc CRC/C/15/Add.199, para 44(b)
[14] See, eg, CO CRC Pakistan UN Doc CRC/C/15/Add.217, para 52; CO CRC Czech Republic, UN Doc CRC/C/15/Add.201, para 46.
[15] CO CRC St Vincent and Grenadines, UN Doc CRC/C/15/Add.184, para 35(b).
[16] CO CRC Liberia, UN Doc CRC/C/15/Add.236, para 47(b).
[17] CO CRC Belize, UN Doc CRC/C/15/Add.252, para 53(b).
[18] CO CRC Mali, UN Doc CRC/C/15/Add.113, para 26.

also contains some specific guidance as the measures expected of states including an obligation to 'establish appropriate mechanisms to assess important health indicators, inter alia the infant mortality rate';[19] '[i]mprove the effectiveness of antenatal care and maternal health education with a view to reducing the high incidence of infant mortality';[20] '[c]ontinue to expand access to health services, in particular in rural areas, and increase the skills of health personnel with a view to reducing infant mortality rates';[21] 'adopt public health education programmes which are used to lower infant mortality rates';[22] '[i]mplement the National Health Policy and enforce the Strategy on Promoting Effective Perinatal Care of the World Health Organization (WHO) in order to further reduce perinatal and infant mortality'[23] and 'undertake initiatives related to the reduction of infant mortality such as the "Integrated Management of Childhood Illnesses" (IMCI)'.[24] Although such measures still possess a relatively high level of abstraction they are concerned with specific measures required of states to diminish infant mortality. Moreover, the failure of the committee bodies to specify the precise mechanisms by which such measures are to be implemented remains compatible with the need to ensure local context sensitivity and recognize an appropriate margin of appreciation for states.

At the same time the dialogue with respect to the nature of a state's obligation to reduce infant mortality must not be restricted to a discussion between the committee bodies and states if a 'common narrative' with respect to this obligation is to be generated. On the contrary, the public health literature must also inform the understanding as to the measures required of states to ensure their efforts to reduce infant mortality are *practical* and *effective*. As this literature is vast[25] it is not possible to examine it in detail here and it is sufficient to make four observations.

First, in relation to the need for indicators, commentators have stressed the need to measure, not only infant mortality rates but also stillbirths[26] and ensure that the adoption of any preventative measures are 'based on reasonably accurate information about the causes of deaths' in order to prioritize interventions, plan for their delivery,

---

[19] CO CRC Solomon Islands, UN Doc CRC/C/15/Add.208, para 41(c).
[20] CO CRC Georgia, UN Doc CRC/C/15/Add.222, para 49(b).
[21] CO CRC Eritrea, UN Doc CRC/C/15/Add.204, para 40(a).
[22] CO CRC Ethiopia, UN Doc CRC/C/15/Add.144, para 53.
[23] CO CRC Republic of Moldova, UN Doc CRC/C/15/Add.192, para 34(a).
[24] CO CRC Dominican Republic, UN Doc CRC/C/15/Add.150, para 36. See also CO CRC Costa Rica, UN Doc CRC/C/15/Add.11, para 26; CO CRC Honduras, UN Doc CRC/C/15/Add.103, para 26. The Integrated Management of Childhood Illness (IMCI) is a WHO initiative that is designed to provide an integrated approach to child health that adopts a holistic approach. Its focus is children under five and includes both preventive and curative elements that are implemented in collaboration with families, communities, and health professionals. See WHO, 'Child and Adolescent Health and Development: Integrated Management of Childhood Illness (IMCI)' <http://www.who.int/child_adolescent_health/topics/prevention_care/child/imci/en/index.html> accessed 2 August 2011, and WHO, *Child Health in the Community: 'Community IMCI'—Briefing Package for Facilitators* (WHO, 2004).
[25] For a detailed analysis of the literature see WHO, *The World Health Report 2005* (n 3); Lynn Freedman and others, UN Millennium Task Force on Child Health and Maternal Health, *Who's Got the Power? Transferring Health Systems for Women and Children* (Earthscan, 2005).
[26] Cynthia Stanton and others, 'Stillbirth Rates: Delivering Estimates in 190 Countries' (2006) 367 The Lancet 1487.

and assess their effectiveness.[27] It is important to note that from a practical perspective, the burden imposed on states, especially developing states, to acquire such information remains significant and where necessary they should seek the assistance of organizations such as the United Nations Children's Fund (UNICEF) and the WHO to enable them to acquire the necessary information.[28] The collection of such data must also reflect local epidemiological conditions rather than simply relying on data collected for geopolitical regions, given that the causes of death differ from one country to another.[29]

Second, while improved epidemiological data is essential, 'social visibility' is also considered to be important.[30] As Lawn and others explain, 'once communities and decision makers perceive high neonatal (and maternal) deaths as an issue, public ownership of the problem and process will be more likely'.[31] This requires that states actually raise awareness of, and promote the importance of, diminishing child mortality in a way that will create a collaborative response to this issue in which all actors especially parents and other primary care givers who 'form the first line of care'[32] are aware of the important role they play.

Third, in addition to the delivery of traditional interventions such as immunization and oral rehydration therapy, attention should extend beyond causes of death to an identification and understanding of the risk factors for child mortality—whether they be structural, social, cultural, environmental, or economic—in order to develop effective strategies to prevent or mitigate the effects of various sets of risk factors.[33] Although the literature in this area is vast[34] and skewed towards the experience of

[27] Jennifer Bryce and others, 'WHO Estimates of the Causes of Death in Children' (2005) 365 The Lancet 1147.

[28] Importantly, UNICEF and the WHO have agreed upon and apply standard procedures to produce consistent estimates as to the cause of death among children younger than five and the WHO established a Child Health Epidemiology Reference Group in 2001 which has developed systematic methods to estimate deaths for the major causes of death worldwide: Bryce, 'WHO Estimates of the Causes of Death in Children' (n 27) 1147.

[29] Robert Black, Saul Morris and Jennifer Bryce, 'Where and Why are 10 Million Children Dying Every Year?' (2003) 361 The Lancet 2226.

[30] Joy Lawn, Simon Cousens, and Jelka Zupan, ' 4 Million Neonatal Deaths: When? Where? Why?' (2005) 365 The Lancet 891.

[31] ibid. See also José Martines and others, 'Neonatal Survival: A Call for Action' (2005) 365 The Lancet 1189 (also stress need for community engagement and mobilization).

[32] UNICEF, *The State of the World's Children 2008: Child Survival* (UNICEF, 2007) 45.

[33] Bryce and others, 'WHO Estimates of the Causes of Death in Children' (n 27) 2227 (note that 'unhygienic and unsafe environments place children at risk of death. Ingestion of unsafe water, inadequate availability of water for hygiene and lack of access to sanitation contribute to about 1.5 million child deaths and around 88% of deaths due to diarrhoea'; also identify other risk factors such as birth spacing and exclusive breastfeeding); N Spencer, 'The Effect of Income Inequality and Macro-Level Social Policy on Infant Mortality and Low Birthweight in Developed Countries: A Preliminary Systematic Review' (2004) 30 Child 699, 699–700 (review of literature suggests association between IMR and higher income inequality and other indicators of less redistributive social policy).

[34] See, eg, WHO, *The World Health Report 2005* (n 3); Gary Darmstadt and others, 'Evidence Based, Cost Effective Interventions: How Many Newborn Babies Can We Save?' (2005) 365 The Lancet 977 (provides comprehensive examination of the efficacy and effectiveness of a range of interventions); Freedman and others (n 25) 57–69 (discuss timing and nature of effective interventions at the antenatal, intrapartum, and post-natal stages).

developed states,[35] several common factors have been identified as reducing infant mortality[36] including increased birth intervals, higher levels of schooling among mothers, reduced prevalence of smoking during pregnancy,[37] early initiation of breastfeeding,[38] immunization, improved nutrition,[39] water supply and sanitation,[40] malaria and HIV/AIDS control, and increased levels of income.[41] Studies have also confirmed that 'improved availability of skilled care during childbirth and family/community based care through postnatal home visits will benefit mothers and their newborn babies'.[42]

Fourth, the measures required by states to reduce infant mortality are complex and require integrated multidisciplinary strategies[43] that are developed in response to local epidemiological conditions in collaboration with local populations and the international community.[44] They must be targeted, sustainable, and effective[45] and address the social, economic, and political conditions that contribute to infant mortality.[46] International human rights law concedes that their implementation is to be progressive and will remain dependent on the resources available to states. At the same time, it is important to recognize that studies repeatedly dispel the conception that highly technical care and vast quantities of money are required to

---

[35] Joy Lawn and others, '1 Year after the Lancet Neonatal Survival Series—Was the Call for Action Heard?' (2006) 367 The Lancet 1541 (notes that 'although 99% of deaths in newborn babies occur in developing countries less than 1% of published neonatal research during the past decade is relevant to deaths in low resource settings').

[36] See generally Gareth Jones and others, 'How Many Child Deaths Can We Prevent This Year?' (2003) 362 The Lancet 65 (examine effectiveness and cost of several interventions); Jennifer Bryce and others, 'Reducing Child Mortality: Can Public Health Deliver?' (2003) 362 The Lancet 159 (stresses need for targeted and accessible interventions to ensure effective reduction of child mortality); Cesar Victora and others, 'Applying an Equity Lens to Child Health and Mortality: More of the Same is Not Enough' (2003) 362 The Lancet 233.

[37] See, eg, MS Kramer, 'Determinants of Low Birth Weight: Methodological Assessment and Meta-Analysis' (1987) 65 Bull WHO 663.

[38] Karen Edmond and others, 'Delayed Breastfeeding Initiation Increases Risk of Neonatal Mortality' (2006) 117 Pediatrics 905.

[39] Freedman and others (n 25) 55–6.

[40] ibid 8.

[41] Victora and others (n 36); Freedman and others (n 25) 62–4.

[42] Martines and others (n 31) (also estimate that the cost per neonatal death averted is USD$2100). See also Freedman and others (n 25) 64–9 (stress significance of home and community based interventions); WHO, *The World Health Report 2005* (n 3) 86–90.

[43] Such an approach contrasts with the historical model adopted by organizations such as the WHO whereby a single technology was developed to respond to a single disease such as oral rehydration therapy to treat childhood diarrhoea: Davidson Gwatkin, 'Integrating the Management of Childhood Illness' (2004) 364 The Lancet 1557.

[44] Bryce and others, 'Reducing Child Mortality: Can Public Health Deliver?' (n 36) (stresses need to avoid 'global one size fits all delivery strategies'). Although the IMCI developed by WHO and UNICEF requires such an integrated health approach, it plays less attention to undertaking an examination and if necessary, alteration of the structural and social conditions that contribute to infant mortality in the first place.

[45] See generally Bryce and others, 'Reducing Child Mortality: Can Public Health Deliver?' (n 36); Victora and others (n 36); Cesar Victora and others, 'Co-Coverage of Preventive Interventions and Implications for Child Survival Strategies: Evidence from National Surveys' (2005) 366 The Lancet 1460; Darmstadt and others (n 34).

[46] Freedman and others (n 25) 9–10.

reduce infant mortality. For example, it has been suggested that 'up to 75% of such deaths could be prevented with low technology interventions at an additional cost of US$1 per head for the 75 countries with the highest mortality'.[47] The WHO has also estimated that to 'scale up child health interventions to full coverage in the 75 countries with the greatest mortality rates would require an increase in expenditure from an additional USD$0.47 in 2005 to USD$1.48 a head at full coverage by 2015 or an extra $52.4 billion in addition to what is already being spent'.[48] Such sums are not vast especially in light of UNICEF's assessment that in 2003 alone world military spending exceeded USD$950[49]—a figure which challenges the claim made by any state, and indeed the international community, that the resources necessary to tackle the issue of child mortality are lacking.

It is important to note that para (2)(a) of article 12 of the ICESCR imposes an obligation on states not merely to reduce infant mortality, but to take steps to achieve the healthy development of the child. To date the ESC Committee has offered little guidance as to the scope of this obligation other than to affirm the specific measures required of states under the CRC (the meaning of which is discussed below).[50] The ESC Committee has also stressed that 'State parties should provide a safe and supportive environment for adolescents, that ensures the opportunity to participate in decisions affecting their health...'.[51] Although this obligation is already imposed on states under article 12 of the CRC, it is significant that the ESC Committee has also recognized that children's participation is critical to the adoption of appropriate measures to secure their healthy development.

III The obligation to provide medical assistance and health care, especially primary health care

A Introduction

Article 12(2)(d) of the ICESCR requires states to take steps necessary for 'the creation of conditions which would assure to all medical service and medical

---

[47] Lawn and others, '1 Year after the Lancet Neonatal Survival Series' (n 35) (also note that newborn, child, and maternal deaths receive relatively little funding compared with the resources allocated to Global Alliance for Vaccines Initiative and the Global Fund to Fight AIDS, Tuberculosis and Malaria).

[48] Elizabeth Mason, 'Child Survival: Time to Match Commitments with Action' (2005) 365 The Lancet 1286; Jennifer Bryce and others, 'Can the World Afford to Save the Lives of 6 Million Children Each Year?' (2005) 365 The Lancet 2193 (estimate USD$5.1 billion in new resources is needed annually to save 6 million lives in 42 countries responsible for 90% of child deaths in 2000 or an average cost per child saved of $887).

[49] UNICEF, *The State of the World's Children 2005: Childhood under Threat* (UNICEF, 2005). Although more recent estimates vary, global military expenditure would appear to exceed USD$1.5 trillion per year: (USD$2.157 trillion in 2011) <http://www.globalsecurity.org/military/world/spending.htm> accessed 16 June 2011; (USD$1.6 trillion in 2010) <http://www.sipri.org/media/pressreleases/milex> accessed 16 June 2011.

[50] ESC Committee, *General Comment No 14: The Right to the Highest Attainable Standard of Health*, UN Doc E/C.12/2000/4 (2000) para 22.

[51] ibid para 23.

attention in the event of sickness'.[52] In a variation of this formulation, para 2(b) of article 24 of the CRC requires states to 'ensure the provision of necessary medical assistance and health care to all children *with an emphasis on the development of primary health care*' (emphasis added). The African Charter on the Rights and Welfare of the Child adopts the same formulation (article 14(2)(b)). It is debatable whether there is any substantive difference between the obligation to 'create conditions' to assure medical services under the ICESCR, as opposed to the obligation to 'ensure the provision of necessary medical assistance' under the CRC. Under each formulation, the object and purpose of the formulation is to ensure that a person with a medical condition has access to appropriate medical services. Moreover, each formulation remains subject to the progressive nature of the obligation under the right to health. As such, states are not required to 'assure' medical services or 'ensure' the provision of medical assistance. Instead, their obligation is to take all appropriate measures in light of available resources to satisfy the qualitative requirements as outlined by the ESC Committee and discussed in Chapter 4 to ensure that medical services are available, accessible, acceptable, and of appropriate quality to the various cohorts within their jurisdiction.

With respect to the issue of availability of medical services for women, for example, article 12 of CEDAW requires that states parties 'shall ensure to women appropriate services in connection with pregnancy, confinement and the post natal period'. It also adds that states are to provide such services for free where necessary. Moreover, the CEDAW Committee has noted that 'it is the duty of states parties to ensure women's right to safe motherhood and emergency obstetric services and they should allocate to these services the maximum extent of available resources'.[53] With respect to the provision of medical services for persons with disabilities,[54] the CRPD also includes a specific obligation for states to provide medical services tailored to the needs of such persons. Article 25(b) requires states to:

Provide those health services needed by persons with disabilities specifically because of their disabilities, including early identification and intervention as appropriate, and services designed to minimize and prevent further disabilities...

In terms of the specific obligation to assure the provision of medical services under ICESCR, the ESC Committee has further explained that it requires:

the provision of equal and timely access to basic preventive, curative, rehabilitative health services and health education; regular screening programmes; appropriate treatment of prevalent diseases, illnesses, injuries and disabilities preferably at community level; the provision of essential drugs; and appropriate mental health treatment and care.[55]

---

[52] See African Charter on Human and Peoples' Rights (African Charter) (Bunjil Charter) (Nairobi, 27 June 1981, entered into force 21 October 1986, 1520 UNTS 217) art 16(2) which provides that 'States parties... shall take the necessary measures to protect the health of their people and to ensure that they receive medical attention when sick'.
[53] ibid.
[54] Convention on the Rights of Persons with Disabilities (CRPD) (New York, 30 March 2007, entered into force 3 May 2008, UN Doc A/RES/61/106) art 25.
[55] ESC Committee, *General Comment No 14* (n 50) para 17.

The ESC Committee has also explained that:

A further important aspect is the improvement and furtherance of participation of the population in the provision of preventive and curative health services, such as the organization of the health sector, the insurance system and, in particular, participation in political decisions relating to the right to health taken at both the community and national levels.[56]

These observations are equally applicable to the nature of states' obligations under para 2(b) of article 24 of the CRC. Moreover, they would appear to offer practical insights, albeit at a reasonably high level of abstraction, as to the type of measures required of states in a context where states enjoy a sufficient margin of appreciation so as to ensure the context-sensitive implementation of such measures.

The obligation to 'ensure the provision of medical assistance' would also extend to an obligation to create 'a system of urgent medical care in cases of accidents, epidemics and similar health hazards and the provision of disaster relief and humanitarian assistance in emergency situations'.[57] Clearly such measures carry significant resource implications but, as discussed in Chapter 4, the progressive nature of the obligation to secure the right to health is designed to accommodate this reality. And although such recommendations remain at a high level of abstraction they still provide the platform for an ongoing dialogue between states, the committee bodies, and the broad interpretative community as to the precise measures required to secure the effective implementation of these recommendations.

B The emphasis on primary health care

Where para 2(b) of article 24 of the CRC differs from the general obligation to provide medical assistance under article 12(2)(d) of ICESCR, is with respect to the explicit emphasis on primary health care under the CRC. This emphasis can also be found in the formulation of the right to health in the Protocol of San Salvador (article 10(2)(a)) and the African Charter on the Rights and Welfare of the Child (article 14(2)(b)). With respect to the actual meaning of this concept, the work of the CRC Committee has tended to adopt a rather haphazard approach. Many of its comments tend to be confined to expressions of concern '[a]t the poor quality and accessibility of primary health-care services, especially in rural areas, and for poor households'[58] and 'the unavailability and/or inaccessibility of free, high quality primary health care'.[59] It has, however, hinted at the participatory and collaborative nature of primary health care in for example, its report for Botswana where it noted 'with appreciation the developments in the primary health care strategy, notably the decentralisation and mobile units as well as the dialogue conducted with traditional leaders to ensure that health care strategies are complementary'.[60] It has also

---

[56] ibid.
[57] ibid para 16 (although this comment of the ESC Committee is located under its discussion of the obligation to prevent, treat, and control diseases, it has relevance and application beyond such a context).
[58] CO CRC Romania, UN Doc CRC/C/15/Add.199, para 44(a).
[59] CO CRC India, UN Doc CRC/C/15/Add.228, para 52.
[60] CO CRC Botswana, UN Doc CRC/C/15/Add.242, para 48.

recognized the emphasis on low cost medical care generally associated with primary health care in its report for Tanzania, where it recommended that the state party, 'take all effective measures to facilitate greater access to health services by, inter alia, abolishing or rationalising user fees in primary health to reduce the burden on poor families...'.[61] However, the work of the CRC Committee reveals no recognition of the often controversial and contentious nature of this term.[62]

By way of background it is significant to note that the concept of primary health care emerged in response to the ineffectiveness of the dominant Western model of medical or institutional based health care in developing countries[63] and the shortcomings of 'traditional vertical programs concentrating on specific diseases'.[64] Its original meaning is generally linked with the Declaration of Alma Ata, adopted at an International Conference on Primary Health Care in Alma Ata in 1978 which provides in article VI that:

Primary health care is essential health care based on practical, scientifically sound and socially acceptable methods and technology made universally accessible to individuals and families in the community through their full participation and a cost that the community and country can afford to maintain at every stage of their development in the spirit of self-reliance and self-determination. It forms an integral part both of the country's health system, of which it is the central function and main focus, and of the overall social and economic development of the community. It is the first level of contact of individuals, the family and community with the national health system bringing health care as close as possible to where people live and work, and constitutes the first element of a continuing health care process.[65]

However, the precise meaning, understanding, and implementation of this holistic community-based approach to the delivery of health care has remained both challenging and somewhat elusive.[66] As a result of difficulties associated with its initial implementation, it was filtered down by the adoption of 'selective primary health care' which involved 'a package of low cost technical interventions to tackle the main disease problems of poor countries'.[67] Indeed, at one point the WHO actually

---

[61] CO CRC Tanzania, UN Doc CRC/C/15/Add.156, para 47.
[62] See generally John MacDonald, 'Primary Health Care: A Global Overview' (2006) 5(4) Prim'ry HCR & Dev 284, 286–7; Marcos Cueto, 'The Origins of Primary Health Care and Selective Primary Health Care' (2004) 94 Am J Public Health 1864.
[63] ibid 1864.
[64] ibid 1866.
[65] *Declaration of Alma Ata* (International Conference on Primary Health Care, Alma Ata, USSR, 6–12 September 1978).
[66] See WHO, 'What are the Advantages and Disadvantages of Restructuring a Health Care System to Be More Focused On Primary Care Services?'(WHO Report, January 2004) 7. See generally Cueto (n 62); Maria Dawson, 'Primary Health Care: Concept and Challenges for its Implementation' (2002) 8(1) Aus J Primary Health 30; James Frankish and others, 'Setting a Foundation: Underlying Values and Structures of Health Promotion in Primary Health Care Settings' (2006) 7(2) Prim'ry HCR & Dev 172; Glen Moulton and others, 'Building on a Foundation: Strategies, Processes and Outcomes of Health Promotion in Primary Health Care Settings' (2006) 7 Prim'ry HCR & Dev 269.
[67] Ceuto (n 62) 1868. See discussion in Chapter 2. See also Commission on Social Determinants of Health, *Action on the Social Determinants of Health: Learning from Previous Experiences* (WHO, March 2005) 16–18.

conceded that '[n]o uniform universally applicable definition of primary health care exists'.[68]

Such a position presents a challenge for the interpretative exercise being pursued in this analysis. At the same time, indeterminancy has already been recognized as a constant feature of interpretative landscape. As a consequence, the absence of consensus as to the precise boundaries of primary health care is almost immaterial. Of greater relevance is the apparent agreement as to the core principles underlying the Alma Ata declaration which, according to the WHO, are considered to be:

- universal access to care and coverage on the basis of need;
- commitment to health equity as part of development orientated towards social justice;
- community participation in defining and implementing health agendas; and
- intersectoral approaches to health.[69]

Moreover, beyond these general principles there is also a general acceptance with respect to certain core elements of the primary health model, namely selective primary health care, which is discussed in Chapter 4. Beyond these core elements, the fact that debate exists as to the peripheral boundaries of primary health care is actually consistent with and a reflection of the need for community participation to define and implement health agendas which are relevant to their health needs.

It is important to stress that the special attention given to primary health care under the CRC is not intended to dilute or diminish the reality that medical institutions and medical technology play a significant role in contributing towards the realization of the right to the highest attainable standard of health. However, it provides recognition of the reality that research increasingly indicates that community-based systems and processes that respond to and address the social determinants of health and develop links with secondary and tertiary systems for the delivery of health care services are vital.[70]

Moreover, it is also important to recognize that, although the idea of 'primary health care' emerged as an attempt by developing states to resist the imposition of Western medical practices, is not only an effective strategy[71] but also one that must be adopted by states as a matter of international law. This contrasts with the historical assumption that primary health care was 'relegated to being of relevance in "other" places, so called developing countries'.[72] This model is not to be

---

[68] WHO, *The World Health Report 2003: Shaping the Future* (WHO, 2003) 106 (provides overview of selective PHC).
[69] ibid 107. See also art 10(2)(a) of the Protocol of San Salvador, which defines primary health care as 'essential health care made available to all individuals and families in the community'.
[70] UNICEF, *The State of the World's Children 2008* (n 32); MacDonald (n 62) (asserts that 'the primary health care model is still relevant in all countries of the world'); Frankish and others (n 66) (recognizes that a number of Western jurisdictions have articulated the need for an integrated health system with increased emphasis on primary health care); WHO, 'What Are the Advantages and Disadvantages of Restructuring a Health Care System to be More Focused on Primary Care Services?' (n 66).
[71] See MacDonald (n 62).
[72] ibid 286.

considered as 'an isolated part of a health care system' or 'limited to marginal, low cost treatment for the poor'.[73] Rather, it seeks to provide 'a system of health care turned towards peoples' needs at the level of the front line (primary), but with mechanisms of referral in place to secondary and even tertiary levels when necessary'[74] and operates to challenge and mitigate an 'overemphasis on medical technical interventions to the neglect of the health enhancing or health threatening contexts in which people live out their lives'.[75]

The 2008 World Health Report for the WHO, *Primary Health Care: Now More than Ever*, indicates a resurgent commitment to primary health care.[76] This report also provides evidence-based guidance for states of the measures required to deliver primary health care.[77] However, it is important to note that the model advanced in the WHO report is underpinned by the concept of equity rather than the right to health.[78] When viewed from a rights-based perspective, equity remains a central concern, but the design and delivery of a primary health care system becomes an international legal obligation that must satisfy the qualitative indicia of availability, accessibility, acceptability, and quality.[79] In order to satisfy these requirements special measures must be taken to ensure that these criteria are satisfied with respect to the diverse health needs of individuals within the jurisdiction of a state. For example, with respect to adolescents, research suggests that young people face several barriers to receiving and accessing quality primary health care.[80] Specific concerns include lack of confidentiality, embarrassment, lack of awareness and information about available services, and difficulty in accessing them due to structural factors such as cost, opening hours, and lack of transport.[81] Gender,[82] race, and socio-economic[83] status have also been found to impact on access to primary health care for children. Moreover, even when adolescents are able to access services there is often a lack of expertise in both dealing with the issues that are particular to adolescents and communicating with this cohort.[84]

States must therefore take steps to address these issues and provide for an effective right to receive primary health care services for the various cohorts within their

---

[73] See MacDonald (n 62).   [74] ibid.   [75] ibid.
[76] WHO, *The World Health Report 2008: Primary Health Care* (WHO, 2008).
[77] ibid xvi–xvii (these measures are structured around four sets of reforms: (i) universal coverage; (ii) service delivery; (iii) leadership; and (iv) public policy.)
[78] ibid 24–5.
[79] See chapter II. See also CRC Committee, *General Comment No 4: Adolescent Health and Development in the Context of the Convention on the Rights of the Child*, UN Doc CRC/GC/2003/4 (1 July 2003) para 41.
[80] Melissa Kang and others, 'Primary Health Care for Young People' (2006) 25(2) Youth Studies Aus 49.
[81] ibid.
[82] See, eg, Cheryl Cashin, Michael Borowitz and Olga Zuess, 'The Gender Gap in Primary Health Care Resource Utilization in Central Asia' (2002) 17(3) Health Pol'y & Planning 264.
[83] See, eg, Paul Newacheck and Dana Hughes, 'Children's Access to Primary Care: Difference by Race, Income and Insurance Status' (1996) 97 Pediatrics 26.
[84] ibid.

jurisdiction such as women, the elderly, indigenous people, children, and adolescents. With respect to adolescents, for example, various initiatives have been undertaken and proven to be effective in this regard.[85] Thus, for example, in the USA, school-based health centres have been found to improve access especially for females and children from lower socio-economic backgrounds[86] and the CRC Committee has stressed the role played by schools generally in promoting a healthy lifestyle and behaviour for adolescents including the provision of relevant topics in school curricula.[87] Youth-specific services have also been shown to improve access[88] while innovative programs using art and music or the internet and phone-based services have been found to be effective in engaging 'difficult target groups such as alienated young people, homeless youth and young people with mental health issues'.[89]

Ultimately the principle of local context sensitivity means that it will remain for each state to determine in collaboration with all relevant parties, including where relevant children and adolescents themselves,[90] what is the most appropriate model or models for the delivery of primary health care services. At the same time, it is worth bearing in mind the 'principles of better practice' identified by one evaluative study of programs delivered in Australia which were found to be: access facilitation, evidence-based practice, youth participation, collaboration, professional development, sustainability, and evaluation[91]—principles which all have been emphasized by the CRC Committee in its General Comment on Adolescent Health.[92]

IV The obligation to combat disease and malnutrition

A Introduction

Article 12(2)(c) of the ICESCR requires states to take steps to prevent, treat, and control epidemic, endemic, occupational, and other diseases. Article 24(2)(c) of the CRC affirms this obligation to combat disease and extends it to an obligation to combat malnutrition.[93] It also lists examples of the various measures required to realize these obligations and provides that states must take steps:

---

[85] ibid (provides an evaluation of six different models undertaken in Australia: the youth health service model; the area-based youth co-ordinator model; the GPs in local schools model; the co-located GP-run clinic; the school-based clinic; and innovative access points model which used arts, music, the internet, and telephone as strategies to assist in meeting children's health needs).

[86] ibid (citing various studies).

[87] CRC Committee, *General Comment No 4* (n 79) para 17. See also Janis Jarvis and Sheila Stark, 'Partnership Working and the Involvement of Parents in the Health Education of 7–11 Year Olds' (2005) 6 Prim'ry HCR & Dev 208 (research indicates that 'partnership working between teachers, health professionals and parents would appear to be the ideal in effectively reinforcing health messages to children').

[88] ibid (citing studies).   [89] ibid.

[90] CRC Committee, *General Comment No 4* (n 79) para 8.

[91] ibid.   [92] ibid.

[93] See also European Social Charter (Turin, 18 October 1961, entered into force 26 February 1965, 529 UNTS 89) art 11(3), which requires States parties 'to prevent as far as possible epidemic, endemic and other diseases'; Protocol of San Salvador, art 10, which requires the 'prevention and treatment of endemic, occupational and other diseases'.

To combat disease and malnutrition, including within the framework of primary health care, through, inter alia, the application of readily available technology and through the provision of adequate nutritious foods and clean drinking-water, taking into consideration the dangers and risks of environmental pollution.

The drafting history of this provision indicates that:

> In introducing the proposal, the representative of India stated that it was aimed at covering situations which existed, in particular, in developing countries, where almost all of the 14 million cases of premature death as a consequence of disease occurred.[94]

The object and purpose of this provision is therefore relatively clear—to impose an obligation on states to address two of the factors which undermine health and contribute to preventable deaths, namely disease and malnutrition. Although there is no explicit obligation to combat malnutrition under article 12(2)(c) of the ICESCR, the ESC Committee has repeatedly expressed its concern at the incidence of malnutrition within states.[95] The effectiveness principle provides a basis for the expression of such concerns. Malnutrition renders a person more susceptible to disease. Thus, the obligation to prevent diseases under the ICESCR must include an obligation to combat malnutrition.

With respect to the practical measures by which states are to combat disease and malnutrition, article 24(2)(c) of the CRC lists three specific, albeit not exhaustive, measures:

- the application of readily available technology;
- the provision of adequate nutritious foods and clean drinking water; and
- consideration of the dangers and risks of environmental pollution.

Each of these specific measures will be addressed in detail below. In contrast to the text of the CRC, the ESC Committee has tended to adopt a rather general or circular approach to the obligation to prevent, treat, and control diseases. Thus, for example, it has stressed that it '... requires the establishment of prevention and education programmes for behaviour related concerns'[96] while '[t]he control of diseases refers to states's individual and joint efforts to *inter alia* make available relevant technologies, using and improving epidemiological surveillance and data collection on a disaggregated basis, the implementation or enhancement of immunization programmes and other strategies of infectious disease control'.[97] Public health literature concerning disease control and malnutrition is more detailed and provides an essential support system in seeking to map out with some degree of clarity the practical measures required of states to fulfill their obligation to combat diseases.

---

[94] UN Doc E/CN.4/1988/28 (1989) para 60.
[95] See, eg, CO ESC Venezuela, UN Doc E/2002/22 (2001) 29, para 85; CO ESC Senegal, UN Doc E/2002/22 (2001) 61, para 354; CO ESC Panama, UN Doc E/2002/22 (2001) 73, para 443; CO ESC Solomon Islands, UN Doc E/2003/22 (2002) 65, para 460.
[96] ESC Committee, *General Comment No 14* (n 50) para 16.   [97] ibid.

B Disease prevention

1 The definition of disease

With respect to the terms 'disease' and 'malnutrition', the committee bodies have not adopted a specific definition. Instead, the CRC Committee, for example, has tended to express concern at the rate of malnutrition within a state[98] or the incidence of preventable diseases both communicable[99] and non-communicable.[100] Such an approach appears appropriate given the absence of universal consensus as to the meaning of both terms. Although the WHO Glossary of terminology does not actually include a definition of disease,[101] the John Hopkins School of Public Health defines disease as 'a term of health status when something is wrong with bodily function'.[102] It is this idea of malfunctioning that is common to most definitions. As to the types of diseases states are required to prevent, there is no restriction, and it extends to food-related diseases, animal-related diseases, sexually transmitted diseases, water-related diseases, insect and anthropod-related diseases, diseases of the nervous system, circulatory system, digestive system, and so on.[103] There are, however, certain diseases to which certain groups such as children or the elderly are generally considered to be more susceptible[104] and states must take appropriate measures to identify and prevent such diseases.

The Special Rapporteur has also drawn attention to neglected diseases,[105] such as leprosy, Chagas disease, sleeping sickness, and river blindness,[106] which have been described by the WHO as those diseases that 'affect almost exclusively poor and

---

[98] See, eg, CO China, UN Doc CHN/CO/2 Add., para 62; CO CRC Australia, UN Doc CRC/C/15/Add.268, para 47; CO CRC Algeria, UN Doc CRC/C/15/Add.269, para 56.

[99] Typical communicable diseases identified by the CRC Committee in its reports include: measles, meningitis; diphtheria; diarrhea; mosquito borne diseases especially malaria, typhoid, cholera; intestinal infectious diseases; bacterial infections; acute respiratory diseases such as tuberculosis and pneumonia; and sexually transmitted diseases such as HIV/AIDS.

[100] The references of the CRC Committee to non-communicable diseases are less frequent but include in its report for Belarus, concern at the incidence of cancer and immunological diseases linked to the Chernobyl nuclear disaster (CO CRC Belarus, UN Doc CRC/C/15/Add.180, para 11) and in its report for Mongolia, concern 'that insufficient attention has been given to adolescent health in the context of non-communicable diseases related to lifestyle factors, such as tobacco smoking, alcohol consumption and drug abuse' (CO CRC Mongolia, UN Doc CRC/C/15/Add.264, para 45).

[101] See Health Systems Performance, 'Glossary' <www.who.int/health-systems-performance/docs/glossary.htm> accessed 15 June 2011.

[102] See <www.jhsph.edu/publichealthexperts/Glossary.htm> accessed 8 September 2008.

[103] See WHO, *International Statistical Classification of Diseases and Related Health Problems* (10th rev, 2007) <http://apps.who.int/classifications/apps/icd/icd10online/> accessed 15 June 2011.

[104] See, eg, US National Center for Infectious Diseases <http://www.cdc.gov/ncidod/diseases/children/index.htm> accessed 15 June 2011 (provides list of selected childhood diseases).

[105] *Interim Report of the Special Rapporteur on the Right to Health to the General Assembly 2003*, UN Doc A/58/427 (10 October 2003) para 76; *Report of the Special Rapporteur on the Right to Health to the Commission on Human Rights 2003*, UN Doc E/CN.4/2003/58, paras 73–81; *Report of the Special Rapporteur on the Right to Health to the Commission on Human Rights 2004*, UN Doc E/CN.4/2004/49 (16 February 2004) paras 76–80.

[106] *Report of the Special Rapporteur on the Right to Health to the Commission on Human Rights 2004* (n 105) para 76.

powerless people living in rural parts of low income countries'.[107] The 'neglect' to which the title of such diseases refers, is the lack of research and development to create appropriate drugs, vaccines, and other medical interventions to address such diseases—the so called 10/90 disequilibrium whereby only 10 per cent of health research and development spending is directed at the health problems of 90 per cent of the world's population.[108] This disequilibrium and neglect is largely considered to be a result of the lack of an effective market amongst those suffering from the disease because of their economic status, which precludes the creation of an effective incentive to undertake appropriate research and development.[109]

The right to health imposes an obligation on states to take all appropriate measures subject to available resources to prevent such diseases rather than simply abandon this issue to the commercial interests of those who engage in research and development. The reality, however, is that the states in which neglected diseases are most prevalent, are the states that are least able to counter the existing imbalance in disease prevention research and development. It is within this context that the obligation of international co-operation under the right to health—the meaning of which is discussed in Chapter 9—becomes significant.[110]

2 General measures to prevent disease

The effectiveness principle demands that the measures adopted by a state to prevent diseases must be evidence based. Thus, states must develop systems and processes to engage with and access the vast literature on preventive measures,[111] if necessary seeking international co-operation to achieve this end, in order to develop effective measures that respond to the nature of the disease risk profile among children within their jurisdiction.

---

[107] Mark Kay Kindhauser (ed), *Communicabale Diseases 2002: Global Defence against the Infectious Disease Threat* (WHO, 2002) 96.
[108] *Interim Report of the Special Rapporteur on the Right to Health to the General Assembly 2003* (n 105) para 77.
[109] ibid.
[110] In this context consider for example the UNDP/World Bank/WHO Special Programme for Research and Training in Tropical Diseases (TDR) which, as the Special Rapporteur explains, was created in 1975 largely in response to the failure of market forces to drive the development of new drugs, vaccines, and diagnostic tools for diseases causing a heavy burden in tropical countries: *Report of the Special Rapporteur on the Right to Health to the General Assembly 2003* (n 106) para 78.
[111] See generally US Center for Disease Control and Prevention <www.cdc.gov/ncidod/op/resources.htm> accessed 15 June 2011 (provides detailed information on simple preventive measures); WHO <http://www.who.int/topics/health_promotion/en/> accessed 15 June 2011 (provides detailed information on measures to promote health and prevent disease). See also Larry Pickering (ed), *Red Book: 2006 Report of the Committee on Infectious Diseases* (27th edn, American Academy of Pediatrics, 2006) (provides details on the manifestations, etiology, epidemiology, diagnosis, and treatment of more than 200 conditions). See also, eg, the literature generated by the Millennium Project Taskforce regarding preventive measures for particular diseases such as HIV/AIDS: Paul A Wilson and others, UN Millennium Project, *Combating Aids in the Developing World* (Earthscan, 2005) 27–72; and malaria: Awash Teklemaimanot and others, UN Millennium Project, *Coming to Grips with Malaria in the New Millennium* (Earthscan, 2005) 3.

Preventive measures will also invariably require the provision or scaling up of medical services and interventions. This would include, for example, a coordinated and well-resourced immunization program which is accessible to all to prevent diseases such as polio, leprosy, and whooping cough or the provision of insecticide-treated nets and effective anti-malarial medicines and diagnostics to combat malaria.[112] However, in many cases successful prevention measures will require broad-based changes in behaviour such as promoting healthy lifestyles including appropriate levels of physical activity, a balanced diet and responsible sexual activity, appropriate hand hygiene, food preparation, and care for pets. For example, and unsurprisingly, studies have confirmed that 'hand washing with soap prevents two clinical syndromes that cause the largest number of childhood deaths globally—diarrhoea and acute respiratory infections'.[113]

Importantly, while raising awareness among a community as to the merits of these measures is necessary, it does not guarantee behaviour modification and states must play a role in reshaping cultural and social practices to ensure that they are conducive to the realization of the right to the highest attainable standard of health. Dissemination of information alone will rarely, if ever, be adequate to achieve this aim. As a study on the prevention of HIV/AIDS recognized, 'the capacity of individuals to change their behaviour and to protect themselves is often very constrained by economic circumstances, by gender inequities and by cultural norms' while 'the impetus for lasting change ... must come from communities themselves'.[114] In short, the need for genuine participation of all members of a community including children in the design, implementation, and monitoring of preventive measures is not only required under international law but also essential if the measures adopted are to be sustainable and effective.[115]

Ultimately states exercise a margin of appreciation in the development of measures that are relevant and targeted to the needs of individuals and different groups within their jurisdiction in light of the particular cultural and social practices within a state.

---

[112] Teklemaimanot and others (n 112) 3.

[113] Stephen P Luby and others, 'Effect of Handwashing on Child Health: A Randomised Controlled Trial' (2005) 366 The Lancet 225. See also Guy Howard and Jamie Bartram, *Domestic Water Quantity, Service Level and Health*, WHO Doc WHO/SDE/WSH/03.02 (2003) 14–15 (examine literature on hand washing and note that some studies suggest that action of rubbing hands is more important than the agent used). It is important to note that in 2001 the Water Supply and Sanitation Collaborative Council, which was established in 1990 by the UN General Assembly to build on the achievements of the International Decade for Water Supply and Sanitation in the 1980s, launched the Water, Sanitation and Hygiene (WASH) campaign. This campaign attempts to promote access to water, sanitation, and the development of appropriate hygiene standards and practices. See Water Supply & Sanitation Collaborative Council <http://www.wash-cc.org> accessed 15 June 2011.

[114] Wilson and others (n 112) 28. See also Teklemaimanot and others (n 112) (stressing need for community participation in planning and implementation of malaria controls).

[115] Wilson and others (n 112) (identify benefits of community participation generally rather than children's participation specifically to include local information, local capacity, local ownership, local channels of communication, and local autonomy and self-determination); UNICEF, *State of the World's Children Report 2008* (n 32) 45–62 (reviews critical significance of community partnerships to children's health).

However, it is worth noting that the WHO has recognized the vital role played by schools in developing and raising awareness of preventive strategies in its Global School Health Initiative which aims to mobilize and strengthen health promotion among students, school personnel, families, and other members of the community through schools.[116] Importantly, the WHO has also recognized that many of the contemporary 'leading causes of death, disability and disease such as cardiovascular disease, cancer, chronic lung diseases, depression, violence, substance abuse, injuries, nutritional deficiencies, HIV/AIDS/STD and helminth infections can be significantly reduced by preventing six interrelated categories of behaviour that are initiated during youth and fostered by political and social policies and conditions namely: Tobacco use, behaviour that results in injury or violence; alcohol and substance abuse, dietary and hygienic practices that cause disease, sedentary lifestyle and sexual behaviour that causes unintended pregnancy and disease.'[117]

3 Specific measures to prevent disease
(a) **Application of readily available technology**
The drafting history for article 24 of the CRC does not indicate the kinds of measures anticipated to fulfill the obligation of states to apply 'readily available technology' to prevent diseases among children. Its ordinary meaning, however, within the context of subparagraph (c) would suggest that it extends beyond technical knowledge to the application of technological developments, including systems and processes that are not particularly resource intensive and thus capable of ready application even in developing states. Thus, there is no obligation to develop the appropriate technology to prevent, diagnose, and/or treat diseases for children or indeed create the necessary infrastructure and systems to take advantage of technological developments that address the broader social determinants of health.[118] Such obligations arise from the general right to the highest attainable standard of health and are very much resource-dependent and thus progressive in their realization. On the contrary, the obligation to *apply available technology* imposes on obligation on states not to refuse, omit, overlook, neglect, or ignore the potential to use *existing* technological developments to assist in the prevention of disease.

Moreover, it imposes an obligation on states to address the social, political, and cultural obstacles that impede their application. For example, it is recognized that 'a full complement of technologies is now available for the provision of safe and reliable sanitation services in almost any setting... however, sanitation planners are unable to take advantage of many of these technical options [because] they are constrained by policies, planning regulations, technical norms and standards and

---

[116] WHO, 'Global School Health Initiative' <www.who.int/school_youth_health/gshi/en/index.html> accessed 15 June 2011.
[117] ibid.
[118] In this context see, eg, Calestous Juma and Lee Yee-Cheong, UN Millennium Project Task Force on Science Technology and Innovation, *Innovation: Applying Knowledge in Development* (Earthscan, 2005) (examines means and strategies required of developing states to create the capacity to take advantage of various technological developments to increase economic growth); UNDP, *Human Development Report 2001: Making Technologies Work for Human Development* (UNDP, 2001).

conventions'.[119] A lack of community understanding and knowledge may also present an impediment to their implementation. Thus, states are required to address any social, cultural, or political obstacles that impede application of readily available technology, subject to the caveat that this process must be sensitive to and respectful of existing cultural practices and be based on community understanding and participation.

It also imposes an obligation on states to create the necessary systems and processes that allow for the implementation and adaptation of available technology to advance the health of all individuals within their jurisdiction. As the Millennium Taskforce on Science, Technology and Innovation has observed:

Technology is a knowledge system, not simply physical technology and equipment. It relies heavily on modes of learning; adaptation to new technologies; educational systems; industrial policies and policies on science, technology, and innovation; the nature and composition of the private sector; and the capabilities inherent in the private sphere.[120]

Such a system does not develop without the assistance of states in collaboration with various sectors of the community to identify, design, and implement the most effective means by which to take advantage of existing technology and enhance the local capacities to use such technology to assist in the prevention of disease.

It would be difficult if not impossible to compile a stock list of those forms of technology that could be considered 'readily available' and have a nexus with disease prevention or nutrition. Indeed, such a list, dependent as it is upon the readiness of availability, albeit if necessary with international assistance, is likely to vary from state to state. However, as mentioned above, sanitation technology is one key example. Lack of access to sanitation is a constant cause of concern for the committee bodies[121] given its potential to contribute towards the spread of numerous communicable diseases. Thus, for example, the CRC Committee has repeatedly recommended that states 'ensure universal access'[122] to sanitation services; undertake 'effective measures'[123] and 'all necessary measures'[124] to ensure adequate access to

---

[119] Roberto Lenton, Albert M Wright, and Lristen Lewis, UN Millennium Project Task Force on Water and Sanitation, *Health Dignity and Development: What Will It Take?* (Earthscan, 2005) 87.
[120] Calestous Juma and Lee Yee-Cheong (n 118) 33.
[121] With respect to the CRC Committee see, eg, CO CRC Mongolia, UN Doc CRC/C/15/Add.264, para 43; CO CRC Nepal, UN Doc CRC/C/15/Add.261, para 61(d); CO CRC Jordan, UN Doc CRC/C/15/Add.125, para 49; CO CRC Liberia, UN Doc CRC/C/15/Add.236, para 46; CO CRC Sao Tome and Principe, UN Doc CRC/C/15/Add.235, para 44; CO CRC South Africa, UN Doc CRC/C/15/Add.122, para 29. With respect to the ESC Committee see, eg, CO Solomon Islands ICESCR, E/2003/22 (2002) 65, paras 461; CO ESC Mali, UN Doc E/1995/22 (1994) 64, para 350; CO ESC Solomon Islands, UN Doc E/2000/22 (1999) 40, para 205; CO ESC Venezuela, UN Doc E/2002/22 (2001) 29, paras 85; With respect to the CDEAW Committee see, eg, CO CEDAW Israel, UN Doc A/60/38 Part II (2005) 129, para 259; With respect to the CERD Committee see, eg, CO CERD Slovakia, UN Doc A/55/18 (2000) 47, para 265. See also Anqing Shi, 'How Access to Urban Potable Water and Sewerage Connections Affects Child Mortality' (World Bank Development Research Working Paper No 2274, 2000) (examines literature which reveals that improved access to potable water and sewerage connection is associated with lower child mortality).
[122] See, eg, CO CRC Nigeria, UN Doc CRC/C/15/Add.257, para 49(e); CO CRC Belize, UN Doc CRC/C/15/Add.252, para 53(d); CO CRC Mongolia, UN Doc CRC/C/15/Add.264, para 44(f).
[123] See, eg, CO CRC Philippines, UN Doc CRC/C/15/Add.259, para 61(c).
[124] See, eg, CO CRC Dominica, UN Doc CRC/C/15/Add.238, para 39.

sanitation; 'prioritize the provision of sanitation services';[125] 'prioritize the construction and expansion' of sanitation infrastructure;[126] and if necessary obtain 'international assistance to increase access to sanitation'.[127]

The use of oral rehydration solutions (ORS) for diarrhoea, is a further example of a readily available technology and an issue on which the CRC Committee has occasionally commented.[128] For example, in its concluding observations for the Syrian Arab Republic, it expresses concern that 'only 25 per cent of mothers in the north treat their children's diarrhoea correctly with oral rehydration therapy',[129] which serves to demonstrate the point that availability of technology may be necessary but this is not sufficient in the absence of appropriate training and education.

Importantly, media and communication devices such as radio, TV, and internet have been identified as a further example of technology which is readily available in many jurisdictions and which can be used in a practical way to raise awareness and provide education to children, their parents, and the broader community about a variety of health issues ranging from alcohol abuse and smoking[130] to the harm of female genital cutting.[131]

(b) The provision of adequate nutritious foods

The obligation to address disease prevention by ensuring the provision of nutritious food especially for children reflects the reality that according to the WHO and UNICEF, '50 to 70% of the burden of diarrhoeal disease, measles, malaria and lower respiratory infections in childhood is attributable to undernutrition'.[132] In addition malnutrition is responsible for one-third of the nine million deaths annually among children under five.[133] As such, the provision of adequate nutritious food becomes a necessary condition in the struggle to prevent disease. Importantly, its relevance is not confined to the context of the starving child and extends to the healthy development of all individuals beyond mere survival.

In terms of the specific measures that states must adopt in order to fulfill their obligation to provide nutritious food, the jurisprudence of the CRC Committee provides some guidance. First, it has repeatedly stressed the need for states to adopt

---

[125] See, eg, CO CRC Togo, UN Doc CRC/C/15/Add.255, para 51(iv); CO CRC Indonesia, UN Doc CRC/C/15/Add.223, para 57(b); CO CRC Sao Tome and Principe, UN Doc CRC/C/15/Add.235, para 45(c).
[126] See, eg, CO CRC Vietnam, UN Doc CRC/C/15/Add.200, para 42.
[127] See, eg, CO CRC Kyrgyzstan, UN Doc CRC/C/15/Add.244, para 50.
[128] CO CRC Nigeria, UN Doc CRC/C/15/Add.257, para 48.
[129] CO CRC Syrian Arab Republic, UN Doc CRC/C/15/Add.212, para 40(d).
[130] See, eg, CO CRC Romania, UN Doc CRC/C/15/Add.199, para 47(d).
[131] See, eg, CO CRC Egypt, UN Doc CRC/C/15/Add.145, para 45.
[132] WHO and UNICEF, *Global Strategy for Infant and Young Child Feeding* (WHO, 2003) v. See World Bank *World Development Indicators 2011* (World Bank USA, 2011) 110–13 (provides global figures in relation to undernourishment and child malnutrition).
[133] WHO 'Children: Reducing Mortality' (WHO Fact Sheet 178, November 2009) <http://www.who.int/mediacentre/factsheets/fs178/en/> accessed 16 June 2011.

and implement a national nutritional policy[134] which remains subject to ongoing evaluation to ensure its effectiveness[135] especially with respect to the nutritional needs and status of the most vulnerable children.[136] It would appear to be a requirement that such a policy include measures to facilitate the provision of 'adequate nutritional food and supplements',[137] especially 'among mothers and children';[138] and include measures to ensure accessibility to markets and other venues which provide food and affordability of essential food stuffs.[139] The CRC Committee's expression of concern in its report for the Marshall Islands at the 'importation of food having high levels of sugar and fat'[140] and recommendation in its report for the Russian Federation that the state party 'pass the law on universal salt iodization and ensure its full implementation',[141] also reflects the need for a state to ensure not only access to and affordability of food, but also its nutritional quality.

According to the CRC Committee a national nutritional policy must also include 'education and promotion of healthy feeding practices',[142] 'including breastfeeding'[143] and 'the development of campaigns to inform parents on basic knowledge of child health and nutrition'.[144] Moreover, it must address any social or cultural taboos or customs with respect to certain foods that have a negative impact on women's and children's nutrition. It is for this reason that the CRC Committee in its report for Guinea Bissau observed 'that traditional food taboos are common and thought to be one cause of malnutrition among children and mothers'[145] and thus recommended that the state party '[t]ake steps to end the practise of harmful traditional food taboos by children and mothers'.[146] The CEDAW Committee has also highlighted the gendered dimensions of the malnutrition experienced by women and girls, which states are under an obligation to address.[147]

---

[134] See, eg, CO CRC Dominican Republic, UN Doc CRC/C/15/Add.150, para 36; CO CRC Guatemala, UN Doc CRC/C/15/Add.154, para 43; CO CRC Costa Rica, UN Doc CRC/C/15/Add.11, para 26. The World Declaration on Nutrition adopted at the International Conference in Rome in 1992 also calls upon states to adopt a national policy on nutrition.
[135] See, eg, CO CRC Marshall Islands, UN Doc CRC/C/15/Add.139, paras 47.
[136] See, eg, CO CRC Australia, UN Doc CRC/C/15/Add.268, para 47 ('the Committee remains concerned at malnutrition and undernutrition of indigenous children compared with overnutrition, overweight and obesity at the national level').
[137] CO CRC Democratic People's Republic of Korea, UN Doc CRC/C/15/Add.239, para 51(c).
[138] CO CRC Guyana, UN Doc CRC/C/15/Add.224, para 42(c).
[139] See, eg, CO CRC Israel, UN Doc CRC/C/15/Add.195, para 44 (expressing concern at 'malnutrition in children owing to the disruption of markets and the prohibitively high prices of basic foodstuffs').
[140] CO CRC Marshall Islands, UN Doc CRC/C/15/Add.139, para 46.
[141] CO CRC Russian Federation, UN Doc CRC/C/RUS/CO/3, para 53(c)
[142] CO CRC Philippines, UN Doc CRC/C/15/Add.259, para 59(e). See also CO CRC Belize, UN Doc CRC/C/15/Add.252, para 53(c); CO CRC Albania, UN Doc CRC/C/15/Add.249, para 55(b); CO CRC Democratic People's Republic of Korea, UN Doc CRC/C/15/Add.239, para 51(c).
[143] CO CRC Sao Tome and Principe, UN Doc CRC/C/15/Add.235, para 45(g).
[144] CO CRC Turkey, UN Doc CRC/C/15/Add.152, para 52.
[145] CO CRC Guinea Bissau, UN Doc CRC/C/15/Add.177, para 42(c).
[146] ibid para 43(c).
[147] See, eg, CO CEDAW Ukraine, UN Doc A/57/38 Part II (2002) 114, paras. 289; CO CEDAW Bangladesh, UN Doc A/59/38 Part II (2004) 134, paras 260; CO CEDAW Burkina Faso, UN Doc A/55/38 Part I (2000) 25, paras 274; CO CEDAW Maldives, UN Doc A/56/38 Part I (2001) 15, para 142.

The obligation of effectiveness also demands that states take account of the vast and growing body of literature in relation to nutritional needs of individuals.[148] Thus, for example, the WHO and UNICEF *Global Strategy for Infant and Young Child Feeding* 2003 places significant emphasis on the need to promote exclusive breastfeeding in the first six months of a child's life and ensure the provision of appropriate complementary feeding while breastfeeding continues for up to two years of age or beyond.[149] It also stresses the need for mothers to receive 'accurate information and skilled support from the family community and health care system' and the provision of culture-specific nutrition counselling.[150]

The UN Millennium Project Taskforce on Hunger, for example, has stressed the need for a 'targeted life cycle approach' because of the intergenerational cycle of malnutrition whereby poverty and gender invariably conspire to deny women the knowledge, capacity, and income necessary to ensure an adequate nutritional diet for themselves and their children.[151] Thus, it has been found that any effective response to child malnutrition must target women as they are generally the primary care givers for their children and that 'increasing women's income and their control over family assets is also known to improve the nutritional status of their children'.[152]

In terms of the strategies to deliver such an outcome, the Taskforce has recommended the creation or improvement of 'existing formal networks of paraprofessional nutrition extension workers and informal self help and mother to mother groups of nutrition and health volunteers at the village level' and the strengthening or creation of 'comprehensive community and school based feeding programs that offer systematic deworming, micronutrient supplementation' and education on nutrition and hygiene.[153] In order to address malnutrition among children under five it has recommended the provision of 'fortified or blended complementary foods' in addition to therapeutic care for all seriously malnourished children and stressed that all feeding programs should be sourced, where possible, from locally produced foods rather than imported food aid.[154] It has also suggested that 'vitamin and mineral intake can be improved by increasing the consumption of micronutrient rich foods, improving food fortification and increasing micronutrient supplementation

---

[148] See, eg, American Academy of Pediatrics, 'Policy Statements' <http://aappolicy.aappublications.org/policy_statement/index.dtl> accessed 15 June 2011 (the AAP Committee on Nutrition has issued several policy statements on matters related to the nutrition of infants); WHO, 'Child and Adolescent Health and Development' <http://www.who.int/child_adolescent_health/en/> accessed 15 June 2011; WHO and UNICEF, *Global Strategy for Infant and Young Child Feeding* (n 133); Pedro A Sanchez and others, *Halving Hunger: It can be done* (UN Millennium Project Taskforce on Hunger, Earthscan, 2005) 126–42 (details interventions required to address nutrition for chronically hungry and vulnerable groups such as children); Ronald E Kleinman R (ed), *Pediatric Nutrition Handbook* (5th edn, Committee on Nutrition, American Academy of Pediatrics, 2003); Kathy King and Patricia Queen Samour, *Handbook of Pediatric Nutrition* (3rd edn, Jones and Bartlett, 2003).
[149] WHO and UNICEF, *Global Strategy for Infant and Young Child Feeding* (n 133) 7–8.
[150] ibid 9.
[151] Sanchez and others (n 149) 11.
[152] ibid 12.   [153] ibid.   [154] ibid.

where necessary' and these actions 'should be promoted through village extension workers'.[155]

Importantly, the Taskforce recommendations are not made in a vacuum and acknowledge that the problem of malnutrition within a state is often a reflection of complex social, political, and economic factors not only within a state but the broader international community. Thus, its recommendations to address malnutrition are also accompanied by recommendations that seek to mobilize the international community's response to this problem more effectively,[156] reform national policies to ensure rule of law, respect for human rights, the empowerment of women and girls, and the removal of internal and regional barriers to trade in order to promote food security;[157] increase the agricultural productivity of food-insecure farmers;[158] reduce the vulnerability of the acutely hungry through productive safety nets;[159] increase incomes and make markets work for the poor;[160] and finally, restore and conserve the natural resources essential for food security.[161]

The vast nature and scope of these recommendations need not be the focus of discussion here. Their mention, however, is important as it reflects and indicates the holistic and interdisciplinary nature of the right to the highest attainable standard of health. The realization of the obligation to provide nutritional food to hungry children and adults is not simply a matter of handing out food packages in times of crisis. It requires the creation of a comprehensive national policy, with the assistance of the international community, which has clearly defined local priority interventions that are identified in collaboration with all key stakeholders.[162] It must also aim to strengthen the capacity of parents and local communities to meet the nutritional needs of children in a sustainable manner and encourage a multisectoral collaborative approach to address the root causes of malnutrition whether they be poverty, low food production, lack of education, or gender discrimination.[163] Moreover, it must be designed and tailored to meet not just the nutritional needs of infants or young children but also adolescents, a group whose nutritional needs have been traditionally overlooked.[164] Indeed, it has been observed of this cohort that, even in the absence of food scarcity, psycho-social factors such as the search for identity, concern about appearance, and vulnerability to peer pressure may influence their eating habits in a way that undermines their ability to enjoy a nutritious diet.[165] This creates an entirely different context in which states must develop appropriate measures to develop and encourage appropriate dietary patterns among adolescents that is consistent with their best interests.

---

[155] ibid.   [156] ibid 6–7.
[157] ibid 8–10.   [158] ibid 10–11.
[159] ibid 13–14.   [160] ibid 14–16.
[161] ibid 16.   [162] ibid 17.   [163] ibid.
[164] Helene Delisle, V Chandra-Mouli, and Bruno De Benoist, *Should Adolescents be Specifically Targeted for Nutrition in Developing Countries? To Address Which Problems and How?* (WHO, 2000) (provides comprehensive examination of nutritional deficiencies experienced by adolescents and measures to promote, manage, and address their nutritional needs).
[165] ibid 10.

(c) **The provision of clean drinking water**

The ESC Committee has declared that 'the human right to water is indispensable for leading a life in human dignity' and 'is a prerequisite for the realization of other human rights'.[166] Despite its significance it is estimated that at least 1.1 billion people lack access to safe water, which, when combined with the 2.6 billion people who lack access to basic sanitation, leads to the death of 3,900 children every day.[167] Indeed, disease transmission through water or human excrement is the second leading cause of death among children worldwide after respiratory diseases[168] and '88% of diarrheal disease is attributed to unsafe water supply or inadequate sanitation and hygiene'.[169] Given this reality it is hardly surprising that target 10 of the MDG, which is linked to MDG 7 and environmental sustainability, aims to halve by 2015 the proportion of people without sustainable access to safe drinking water.[170] Nor is it surprising that the Special Rapporteur on the Right to Health has focused his attention on access to water as an element of the right to health.[171] Moreover, the committee bodies, especially the CRC Committee, have regularly expressed concern in their concluding observations at the lack of access to safe drinking water, especially the discrepancy experienced by children living in rural and country areas as opposed to urban areas.[172]

The right to water, which has been recognized in various instruments,[173] is intimately linked with the realization of other rights such as the right to an adequate standard of living, housing, and food.[174] Investment in water (and sanitation) also carries significant economic benefits.[175] However, in the context of the right to health it is the importance of water to the preservation of an individual's health which is significant given that water is a necessary condition 'to prevent death from

---

[166] ESC Committee, *General Comment No 15: The Right to Water*, UN Doc C/C.12/2002/11 (20 January 2003) para 1.
[167] Lenton, Wright, and Lewis (n 120) 3.
[168] ibid 4.
[169] ibid 20–1. See also Howard and Bartram (n 114) 15–16 (discuss relationship between water hygiene and other infectious diseases).
[170] *UN Millennium Declaration* (n 4) para 19.
[171] See *Report of the Special Rapporteur on the Right of Everyone to the Highest Attainable Standard of Physical and Mental Health* (8 August 2007) A/62/214 paras 50–69.
[172] With respect to the CRC Committee see, eg, CO CRC Nigeria, UN Doc CRC/C/15/Add.257, para 48; CO CRC Nicaragua, UN Doc CRC/C/15/Add.265, para 47(g); CO CRC Mongolia, UN Doc CRC/C/15/Add.264, para 43; CO CRC Philippines, UN Doc CRC/C/15/Add.259 para 60. See also CO CERD Slovakia, UN Doc A/59/18 (2004) 70, para, 388; CO ESC Solomon Islands, UN Doc E/2003/22 (2002) 65, para 461; CO CEDAW Bangladesh, UN Doc A/59/38 Part II (2004) 134, paras 259.
[173] For a general discussion of the legal bases of the right to water and the instruments in which appears see ESC Committee, *General Comment No 15* (n 167) paras 2–6, n 5.
[174] ibid para 3.
[175] See Barbara Evans, Guy Hutton, and Laurence Haller, *Closing the Sanitation Gap: The Case for Better Public Funding of Sanitation and Hygiene* (OECD, 2004) (study suggests that investment in water and sanitation would yield an economic return of $3 to $4 for every $1 invested and avoid $7.3 billion per year in health related costs).

dehydration, to reduce the risk of water related disease and to provide for consumption, cooking, personal and domestic hygienic requirements'.[176]

In terms of the obligation to ensure the provision of clean drinking water, the CRC Committee has variously recommended that states 'ensure universal access to drinking water';[177] 'prioritize the provision of safe drinking water';[178] 'take effective measures';[179] and 'take all necessary measures'[180] to improve access to safe drinking water. Despite the general nature of such obligations, which leave states with significant discretion as to the measures they ultimately adopt, the language used by the CRC Committee still creates an onerous obligation on states to take necessary and effective measures as a matter of urgency and priority.

Beyond the general recommendations of the CRC Committee, it has been prepared to direct states with respect to the specific measures required to fulfill their obligation with respect to the provision of drinking water. In this context it has welcomed the adoption of a national policy for safe water in Bangladesh;[181] called upon Vietnam to prioritize the construction and expansion of water infrastructure;[182] suggested to Jordan that it maintain data on access to drinking water;[183] recommended to Georgia that it 'address the supply of safe drinking water by inter alia seeking support from the World Bank...';[184] and urged the Seychelles to '[e]nforce existing environmental regulations so as to ensure universal access to safe drinking water and sanitation'.[185] Such comments indicate, by implication, the need for states to develop a national drinking water policy based on reliable data[186] which should include measures to develop and maintain appropriate infrastructure to be funded if necessary with international assistance and the creation of an appropriate legislative, monitoring, and enforcement structure to regulate the provision of safe water within a state.[187]

---

[176] ibid para 2. See also Howard and Bartram (n 114) 5 (examine water required for each of these functions and note that loss of water from bodies of small children are proportionately considerably greater than for adults; 15% of fluid per day as opposed to 4%; thus a 7kg child requires 1 litre per day fluid to replace lost fluid compared to 2.9 litres for a 70kg adult male).

[177] See, eg, CO CRC Nigeria, UN Doc CRC/C/15/Add.257, para 49(e); CO CRC Belize, UN Doc CRC/C/15/Add.252, para 53(d); CO CRC Nicaragua, UN Doc CRC/C/15/Add.265, para 48(a); CO CRC Mongolia, UN Doc CRC/C/15/Add.264, para 44(f).

[178] See, eg, CO CRC Togo, UN Doc CRC/C/15/Add.255, para 51(iv).

[179] See, eg, CO CRC Philippines, UN Doc CRC/C/15/Add.259, para 61(c).

[180] See, eg, CO CRC Dominica, UN Doc CRC/C/15/Add.238, para 39.

[181] CO CRC Bangladesh, UN Doc CRC/C/15/Add.221, para 53.

[182] CO CRC Vietnam, UN Doc CRC/C/15/Add.200, para 42.

[183] CO CRC Jordan, UN Doc CRC/C/15/Add.125, para 50.

[184] CO CRC Georgia, UN Doc CRC/C/15/Add.222, para 49(c).

[185] CO CRC Seychelles, UN Doc CRC/C/15/Add.189, para 43(a).

[186] See WHO and UNICEF, Joint Monitoring Programme for Water Supply and Sanitation, which provides global data in relation to water supply and sanitation coverage: WHO, Water Sanitation Health (WASH) <www.who.int/water_sanitation_health/en> accessed 15 June 2011. WASH has produced various reports. See, eg, WHO and UNICEF, *Global Water Supply and Sanitation Assessment 2000 Report* (WHO and UNICEF, 2000), WHO and UNICEF, *Making the MDG Drinking Water and Sanitation Target: A Mid Term Assessment of Progress* (WHO and UNICEF, 2004).

[187] See also ESC Committee, *General Comment No 15* (n 167) paras 45–59 (outlines strategies and measures required for implementation of the right to water at the national level including the features required of a national water policy).

The realization of such an objective is not without difficulties and commentators have stressed that states must address the various constraints that impede the development and implementation of such a policy.[188] Such constraints often involve a lack of political will or corruption, which either prevents investment in appropriate infrastructure and development of water policies, or diverts water to those who are able to influence officials.[189] Institutional constraints, which involve either a lack of appropriate institutions, or chronic dysfunction of existing institutional arrangements, are also common and require states to provide the necessary financial, technical, managerial, and social intermediation capacity to ensure the effective and sustainable provision of safe drinking water.[190] Moreover, states must be prepared to develop appropriate accountability mechanisms and regulatory systems to ensure the effective delivery of water services.[191] Importantly this process will fail in the absence of sufficient community involvement to define and develop solutions related to water, sanitation, and disease control in collaboration with persons with appropriate expertise.[192]

The reality is that 'expanding access to water supply and sanitation requires money—whether from national and sub-national government tax revenues, user charges, cross subsidies from users who can afford to pay, private sector investment, or official development assistance'.[193] Although international law does not mandate the measures by which states should fund the delivery of water—an appropriate approach given the need to allow for a context sensitive implementation of a state's obligations—it does require that states must ensure the economic accessibility of water for all individuals within their jurisdiction irrespective of their financial position. The ESC Committee has made it clear that 'the direct and indirect costs and charges associated with securing water must be affordable and must not compromise or threaten the realization of other Covenant rights'[194] including the right to health. It has added that not only must water be available but its quantity 'should correspond to World Health Organization Guidelines';[195] and states must 'ensure access to the minimum essential amount of water that is sufficient and safe for personal and domestic uses to prevent disease'.[196] Water must be safe and 'free from micro-organisms, chemical substances and radiological hazards that constitute a

---

[188] See, eg, WHO and UNICEF, *Global Water Supply and Sanitation Assessment 2000 Report* (n 187) 15; Lenton, Wright, and Lewis (n 120) 62–70.
[189] Lenton, Wright, and Lewis (n 120) 62–3).
[190] ibid 64–5.
[191] ibid 67–8.
[192] WHO and UNICEF, *Global Water Supply and Sanitation Assessment 2000 Report* (n 187) 15 (discusses the Participatory Hygiene and Sanitation Transformation Approach (PHAST)).
[193] ibid 69–70.
[194] ESC Committee, *General Comment No 15* (n 167) para 12.
[195] See WHO, *Guidelines for Drinking-Water Quality* (3rd edn, WHO, 2006) <http://www.who.int/water_sanitation_health/dwq/guidelines/en/> accessed 15 June 2011.
[196] ibid para 37(a). See Howard and Bartram (n 114) 1 (examine available literature and estimate that 'a minimum of 7.5 litres per capita per day will meet the requirements of most people under most conditions').

threat to a person's health',[197] and 'must be within safe physical reach' and 'accessible within or in the immediate vicinity of each household, educational institution or workplace'.[198] The CRC Committee has added that children must not be 'prevented from enjoying their human rights due to the lack of adequate water in educational institutions and households or through the burden of collecting water'.[199] Moreover, the 'provision of adequate water to educational institutions without adequate drinking water should be addressed as a matter of urgency'[200]—an approach which is consistent with the identification of access to water as a minimum core obligation of states as discussed in Chapter 4.

(d) **The obligation to take into account the dangers of environmental pollution**
The link between the environment and health is now well recognized and extensively documented.[201] Indeed, in the context of children the WHO estimates that 'more than three million children under five die each year from environment related causes and conditions'.[202] It is for this reason that article 24(2)(c) of the CRC requires that, when implementing the various measures outlined above to combat disease and malnutrition, states must also take into account the dangers and risks associated with environmental pollution.[203] The right to health under the ICESCR adopts a slightly different approach with respect to the impact of the environment on health by

---

[197] ESC Committee, *General Comment No 15* (n 167) para 12.
[198] ibid.   [199] ibid para 16(b).   [200] ibid.
[201] See, eg, WHO, 'Children's Environmental Health' <www.who.int/ceh/en/> accessed 15 June 2011; WHO Regional Office for Europe <http://www.euro.who.int/en/home> accessed 15 June 2011, Children's Environment and Health Action Plan for Europe (CEHAPE), both of which have links to various publications and initiatives. See also US Environmental Protection Agency <www.epa.gov> accessed 15 June 2011, which has a section dedicated to Children's Health Protection; Bruce Gordon, Richard Mackay, and Eva Rehfuess, *Inheriting the World: The Atlas of Children's Health and the Environment* (WHO, 2004); Giorgio Tamburlini, Ondine S Von Ehrenstein, and Roberto Bertollini (eds), *Children's Health and Environment: A Review of the Evidence* (European Environment Agency, 2002) (provides a comprehensive account of the relationship between children's health and the environment which is based on existing literature); Institute for Children's Environmental Health, which has links to an extensive list of resources: <www.iceh.org> accessed 15 June 2011. There have also been several declarations adopted, including: *Declaration of the Environment Leaders of the Eight on Children's Environmental Health* (1997); WHO and UNECE, *Declaration of London on Environmental Health* (June 1999); Commission for Environmental Cooperation of North America, *Children's Health and the Environment*, Council Res No 00-01, CEC Doc C/00-00/RES/03/Rev.09 (13 June 2000); *The Berlin Commitment for Children of Europe and Central Asia* (18 May 2001).
[202] See WHO, 'The Environment and Health for Children and Their Mothers' (WHO Fact Sheet No 284, February 2005) <http://www.who.int/mediacentre/factsheets/fs284/en/index.html> accessed 15 June 2011 (major environment-related killers include diarrhoea caused mainly by unsafe water and poor sanitation; air pollution and use of biomass fuels often causing acute respiratory infections; malaria associated with poor water management and storage; unintentional injuries often associated with environmental hazards such as drowning, fires, falls, poisonings, and road traffic accidents).
[203] Note here that the focus is on environmental pollution rather than physical, household, or community environmental hazards, which may result or contribute to drowning, fires, falls, and road traffic accidents. The obligation to prevent children from these outcomes forms part of the obligation to protect children against injury under art 19 of the CRC.

requiring states to take steps to improve all aspects of environmental hygiene. The drafting history for both instruments provides no real insights as to the intended meaning and scope of these formulations. Moreover, the committee bodies have not sought to address the significance of the textual discrepancy between the two instruments.[204] The principle of external system coherence, however, supports a common interpretation. Thus, the formulation adopted in each instrument should be interpreted as an obligation on states to take all reasonable measures within the scope of their available resources to prevent and mitigate the impact of environmental factors on the health of individuals.

In terms of the measures required of states to assess, prevent, or mitigate the dangers and risks associated with environmental factors on health, the ESC Committee has provided only limited guidance. For example, it has indicated that the right to health extends to a right to a 'healthy environment'[205] and that states must take measures to prevent and reduce 'the population's exposure to harmful substances such as radiation and harmful chemicals or other detrimental environmental conditions that directly or indirectly impact upon human health'.[206] It has also called on states to take immediate steps, including through regional co-operation as appropriate, to address environmental hazards that affect the health of population, to allocate more resources to address environmental issues, and to strictly enforce environmental legislation.[207]

The CRC Committee has devoted significant attention to the impact of the environment on children's health and has called upon states to '*protect* children from the consequences of environmental pollution';[208] 'address the issue of environmental pollution *effectively*';[209] intensify '*efforts* to address environmental health concerns, particularly with regard to air pollution and solid waste management';[210] continue 'efforts to *prevent and combat* the damaging effects of environmental pollution, such as chemical defoliants, on children, including through *international cooperation*';[211] increase 'efforts to facilitate the implementation of *sustainable development programmes* to prevent environmental degradation, especially as regards air pollution';[212] '*take all appropriate measures*, including international cooperation, to

---

[204] In its General Comment on the right to health, the ESC Committee paraphrased art 12(2)(b) as the 'right to healthy natural and workplace environments': ESC Committee, *General Comment No 14* (n 50) para 15. However, its discussion as to the scope of this provision does not suggest that the ESC Committee considers that the reference to environment in art 12(2)(b) is confined to workplace environments. For example, it suggests that this provision comprises *inter alia* measures to prevent and reduce 'the population's exposure to harmful substances such as radiation and harmful chemicals or other detrimental environmental conditions that directly or indirectly impact upon human health': para 15.
[205] ESC Committee, *General Comment No 14* (n 50) para 4.
[206] ibid para 15.
[207] See, eg, Kazkhstan, UN Doc C/C.12/KAZ/CO/1, para 35.
[208] CO CRC Mongolia, UN Doc CRC/C/15/Add.264, para 44(f) (emphasis added).
[209] CO CRC India, UN Doc CRC/C/15/Add.228, para 53 (emphasis added).
[210] CO CRC Jamaica, UN Doc CRC/C/15/Add.210, para 41(b) (emphasis added). See also CO CRC Grenada, UN Doc CRC/C/15/Add.121, para 24.
[211] CO CRC Vietnam, UN Doc CRC/C/15/Add.200, para 42 (emphasis added).
[212] CO CRC South Africa, UN Doc CRC/C/15/Add.122, para 30 (emphasis added).

prevent and combat the damaging effects of environmental degradation on children, including pollution and contamination of water supplies';[213] 'effectively address the problem of pollution and environmental degradation, including by *seeking bilateral agreements* and international cooperation... [and]... strengthen its environmental health education';[214] continue and strengthen 'efforts to reduce pollution and environmental degradation by strengthening the implementation of *domestic environmental laws*... [and]... increase *children's knowledge* of environmental health issues by introducing environmental health education programmes in schools';[215] and undertake '*comprehensive research* on the possible effects of environmental pollution on the health of children with a view to effectively addressing this problem'.[216]

When synthesized these comments indicate that states are under a general obligation to take effective and appropriate measures to address environmental risks and dangers to the health of individuals. Although states have a significant margin of appreciation with respect to the measures they undertake, as a minimum they must ensure the provision of education with respect to environmental health issues and facilitate comprehensive research to enable the implementation of a sustainable development programme, which is accompanied by an appropriate regulatory regime and, where necessary, international co-operation including bilateral agreements to secure the implementation of this programme.

An examination of the literature reveals a consistency with the obligations outlined by the CRC Committee and provides greater depth in terms of detail which should inform the nature of the measures undertaken by states to prevent and mitigate environmental harm to ensure such measures are effective.[217] In the first instance, the literature confirms the need for states to allocate sufficient resources to promote, facilitate, and exchange research as to the particular exposure and sensitivities of individuals, especially specific groups such as children, to environmental hazards.[218] Such research must then be used to:

(a) raise awareness, educate, and provide appropriate training so as to enable parents, children themselves, and the broader community to better protect health; and
(b) develop policies and regulatory systems with appropriate assessment, monitoring, and evaluation systems to prevent exposure to environmental hazards.

---

[213] CO CRC Kyrgyzstan, UN Doc CRC/C/15/Add.127, para 47 (emphasis added). See also CO CRC Kazakhstan, UN Doc CRC/C/15/Add.213, para 60(g).
[214] CO CRC Ecuador, UN Doc CRC/C/15/Add.262, paras 53–54 (emphasis added).
[215] CO CRC Philippines, UN Doc CRC/C/15/Add.259, paras 60–61 (emphasis added).
[216] CO CRC Czech Republic, UN Doc CRC/C/15/Add.201, para 47(b) (emphasis added).
[217] See especially Tamburlini and others (n 202) 12–14 (provides summary of various international initiatives with respect to children's health and the environment); Canadian Institute of Child Health, *Joint Declaration from Children's Environmental Health II: A Global Forum for Action* (September 2001) <www.cehn.org> accessed 15 June 2011.
[218] See WHO and UNEP, Health and Environment Linkages Initiative (HELI), 'Scientific Assessment Tools' <http://www.who.int/heli/tools/en/> accessed 2 August 2011 (provides links to tools for collection, analysis, and reporting of health data). Such an analysis should also be informed by existing literature as to the impact of various environmental hazards on children. See, eg, Tamburlini and others (n 202).

Although many states already undertake environmental impact assessments and/or social impact assessments,[219] such assessments must integrate a consideration of the health consequences of proposed developments in a manner which recognizes the special vulnerability of specific groups like children and takes into account the 'specific exposure pathways and response characteristics of children'.[220]

In this context, it is worth noting that the 1997 *Declaration of the Environmental Leaders of the Eight on Children's Environmental Health*[221] advocated the use of the precautionary principle when dealing with scientific uncertainty in relation to the causal link between children's health and potential environmental factors.[222] In summary, this concept, which was included in the 1992 *Rio Declaration on Environment and Development* as Principle 15, can be adapted with respect to the situation of health to require 'that where there are threats of serious or irreversible damage [to the health of individuals] lack of full scientific certainty shall not be used as a reason for post-phoning cost effective measures to prevent [such harm]'.[223] Moreover, it has been suggested that the application of this principle requires not only 'explicit scientific consideration of children's characteristics and behaviour'[224] but also the involvement of all interested parties in the assessment process—'participatory risk management'[225]—which would include, in accordance with article 12 of the CRC, 'mechanisms for ensure that children's interests are taken into consideration during the assessment process'.[226]

The enormity of addressing the risks posed to the health of children and adults by environmental factors should not be understated as it will often require vast resources to address existing threats such as poor water quality and air pollution. It will also invariably require a reconciliation of the interests of a state in pursuing economic development goals, either directly or indirectly by facilitating private sector investment, and the right of all individuals to enjoy the highest attainable

---

[219] WHO and UNEP, The Health and Environment Linkages Initiative (HELI), 'Policy Brief: Impact Assessment—Bridging Science and Decisions' <www.who.int/heli/impacts/en/index.html> accessed 15 June 2011, which provides linkages to numerous articles on various types of impact assessments including health, environment, strategic environment, social impact, and integrated assessments. See also eg, Ramesh Shademani and Yasmin Von Schirnding, *Health Impact Assessment in Development Policy and Planning: Report of an Informal WHO Consultative Meeting* (WHO, 2001) (discuss integration of health impact assessment into environmental impact assessments).
[220] Tamburlini and others (n 202) 13. See also Amy D Kyle and others, 'Integrated Assessment of Environment and Health: America's Children and the Environment' (2006) 114 Enviro Health Perspectives 447.
[221] Adopted at the Environment Leader's Summit of the Eight Miami, Florida, May 5–6, 1997.
[222] For a discussion of the application of the precautionary principle in the context of children's health see: Tamburlini and others (n 202) 202–5; WHO European Centre For Environment And Health, *The Precautionary Principle: Public Health, Protection of Children and Sustainability* (Background Document, Fourth Ministerial Conference on Environment and Health Budapest, Hungary, 23–25 June 2004).
[223] UN Doc A/CONF.151/26 (Vol I) (12 August 1992) annex I.
[224] *Declaration of the Environmental Leaders of the Eight on Children's Environmental Health* (Environment Leader's Summit of the Eight Miami, Florida, May 5–6, 1997).
[225] Tamburlini and others (n 202) 204.
[226] ibid.

standard of health. To date the treaty supervisory bodies have tended to avoid the complexity of this reality. As a result their jurisprudence offers limited guidance as to how to reconcile the competing demands associated with the limited resources of a state and the goals of economic development on the one hand and the obligation to protect against environmental harm to health on the other.

With respect to the issue of a state's lack of resources, it is important to recall that international human rights law is prepared to accommodate the progressive realization of the right to the highest attainable standard of health. Thus, there is no expectation that states must eliminate all environmental threats posed to the health of individuals immediately. At the same time states must 'take steps', based on the best available evidence, to achieve this end in collaboration with all relevant actors. They should also, where necessary, call upon the international community and the various international agencies to provide assistance in the development and implementation of measures to prevent and mitigate environmental threats to the health of individuals. In this context, the WHO,[227] for example, has developed a number of measures, such as the Health and Environment Linkages Initiative,[228] and programmes with respect to issues such as water and sanitation, vector-borne diseases, indoor air pollution, chemical safety, transport, ultraviolet radiation, and the like.

In relation to what is arguably the more complex and controversial issue in terms of how states should strike a balance between the interests of development, environmental protection, and the right to health, this is a matter which is beyond the scope of this book. Suffice to say that it remains the subject of ongoing debate not only within international law generally[229] but also international environmental law and international human rights law[230] and that further discussion and research is required with respect to the place and treatment of human rights within this debate.

---

[227] WHO, 'The Environment and Health for Children and Their Mothers' (n 203).
[228] See WHO, 'Health and Environment Linkages Initiative' <www.who.int/heli/en/> accessed 15 June 2011 (program to support action by policy makers in developing countries to address environmental threats to health).
[229] See, eg, the work of UNEP <www.unep.org> accessed 15 June 2011; UN Department of Economic and Social Affairs Division for Sustainable Development <www.un.org/esa/sustdev/documents/agreed.htm> accessed 15 June 2011 and the UNDP <http://www.beta.undp.org/undp/en/home.html> accessed 15 June 2011. See also the Millennium Development Goals, which seek to reconcile objectives relating to development, environmental sustainability, and human rights; Don Melnick and others (eds), *Environment and Human Well Being: A Practical Strategy* (Earthscan, 2005) (specifically addresses need to address drivers of air and water pollution in order to reduce under five mortality and morbidity rates).
[230] It is important to note that international environmental law and international human rights law have traditionally traveled along distinctive trajectories; there is evidence of not so much a convergence but an increasing understanding that each discourse shares complementary aims in seeking to resolve the existing tensions. See, eg, Alan E Boyle and Michael R Anderson, *Human Rights Approaches to Environmental Protection* (OUP, 1996); OHCHR <http://www.ohchr.org/EN/Pages/WelcomePage.aspx> accessed 15 June 2011 'Human Rights and the Environment' (provides links to several papers which discuss link between human rights and the environment). The WHO and UNEP 'Health and Environment Linkages Initiative' also provides an example of this development.

V The obligation to ensure occupational health and safety

According to the ILO, '[e]very day, 6,300 people die as a result of occupational accidents or work-related diseases—more than 2.3 million deaths per year. Over 337 million accidents occur on the job annually; many of these resulting in extended absences from work.'[231] The economic burden associated with poor occupational health and safety standards is huge and estimated by the International Labour Organization (ILO) to be 4 per cent of global Gross Domestic Product each year.[232] From a human rights perspective however, these deaths and injuries represent potential violations of, not only the right to life under the ICCPR, but also the general obligation to protect the right to health under article 12(1) of the ICESCR and article 24(1) of the CRC. They also represent a potential violation of article 12(2)(b) of the ICESCR which requires states to take steps, subject to available resources, to improve all aspects of industrial hygiene.[233] The inclusion of this obligation serves as a reminder of the pragmatic considerations that entertained the minds of states when drafting the right to health. It also challenges the skepticism of those commentators whose critique of the right to health is unaccompanied by any consideration of the specific measures required of states to secure the effective realization of the right to health. The obligation to improve industrial hygiene is a clear and practical directive for states.

As with all other measures to secure the right to health, states enjoy a margin of appreciation when developing strategies to improve occupational health and safety. As a minimum, however, such measures must be effective. The ESC Committee has also stressed that the obligation under article 12(2)(b) of the ICESCR requires 'preventive measures in respect of occupational accidents and diseases'[234] and 'the minimization, so far as is reasonably practicable, of the causes of health hazards inherent in the working environment'.[235] Beyond such general exhortations, the recommendations of the ESC Committee in its concluding observations tend to reflect two broad themes. First, a requirement to ratify ILO Conventions which address occupational health and safety especially ILO Convention No 174 (1993) Concerning the Prevention of Major Industrial Accidents[236] and ILO Convention No 81 (1947) concerning Labour Inspection in Industry and Commerce.[237] This

---

[231] ILO, 'Safety and Health at Work' <http://www.ilo.org/global/topics/safety-and-health-at-work/lang–en/index.htm> accessed 13 January 2011.
[232] ibid.
[233] In the context of children who suffer workplace deaths and injuries there is also a potential violation of art 32 of the CRC, an obligation that would arise under the CRC by virtue of not just art 24 but also art 6 (the right to survival and development), art 19 (the obligation to prevent injuries), and art 32 (the obligation to protect children against labour harmful to their development).
[234] ESC Committee, *General Comment No 14* (n 50) para 15.
[235] ibid.
[236] See, eg, CO ESC France, UN Doc E/2002/22 (2001) 121, para 879; CO ESC Iceland, UN Doc E/2002/22 (2003) 39, para 234; CO ESC Kuwait, UN Doc E/2005/22 (2004) 29, para 208; CO ESC Malta, UN Doc E/2005/22 (2004) 45, para 363.
[237] See, eg, CO ESC China, UN Doc E/2006/22 (2005) 25, para 182; CO ESC Iceland, UN Doc E/2004/22 (2003) 39, para 234.

demand is consistent with the principle of external system coherence.[238] It also reflects an awareness on the part of the ESC Committee that the ILO Conventions, which are negotiated by relevant members of the interpretative community, namely states, employer organizations, and employee organizations, provide more detailed guidance as to the measures required to ensure a safe workplace than the provisions of the ICESCR.

However, ratification of an ILO Convention will not automatically improve industrial hygiene.[239] Thus, the second theme to emerge from the ESC Committee's concluding observations is the need to ensure not only the passage of relevant laws, but also their effective implementation.[240] In this respect, the ESC Committee has repeatedly recommended that states allocate sufficient resources to a labour inspectorate with appropriate powers to monitor working conditions in all areas of a state[241] including rural areas which are often overlooked.[242] It has also stressed the need for states to ensure the provision of appropriate education and training about occupational health and safety for both employers and employees[243] and provide 'effective sanctions with respect to violations of safety regulations'.[244] Such recommendations are considered justified to the extent that they are clear, practical, and required if states are to secure the effective enjoyment of the right to health for workers.

VI The obligation to provide pre-natal and post-natal health care for mothers

A A progressive or immediate obligation

It is estimated that in 2008 alone, there were 358,000 maternal deaths worldwide.[245] It is thus not surprising that the Human Rights Council has expressed its grave

---

[238] There are numerous ILO Conventions and Recommendations concerning occupational health and safety generally and also several which deal with the health and well being of children within the workplace specifically. See the ILO International Occupational Safety and Health Information Centre (CIS), which provides links to the text of these Conventions and recommendations: <http://www.ilo.org/public/english/protection/safework/cis/> accessed 15 June 2011.

[239] Moreover, any deference given here by human rights standards to the relevant ILO standards, should not interpreted as a concession that the ILO standards are themselves are clear, determinate, and beyond reproach. Such standards will also be the subject of interpretative dilemmas and criticism by commentators as their legitimacy and relevance.

[240] See, eg, CO ESC Poland, UN Doc E/2003/22 (2002) 54, para 384.

[241] See, eg, CO ESC Poland, UN Doc E/2003/22 (2002) 54, para 384; CO ESC Guatemala, UN Doc E/2004/22 (2003) 59, para 425; CO ESC Russian Federation, UN Doc E/2004/22 (2003) 64, para 489; CO ESC Lithuania, UN Doc E/2005/22 (2004) 18, para 102; CO ESC Kuwait, UN Doc E/2005/22 (2004) 29, para 208; CO ESC Spain, UN Doc E/2005/22 (2004) 34, para 254.

[242] CO ESC Guatemala, UN Doc E/2004/22 (2003) 59, para 407; CO ESC Ecuador, UN Doc E/2005/22 (2004) 39, para 204.

[243] See, eg, CO ESC Iceland, UN Doc E/2004/22 (2003) 39, para 234.

[244] See, eg, CO ESC Poland, UN Doc E/2003/22 (2002) 54, para 384.

[245] WHO, UNICEF, UNFPA and World Bank, *Trends in Maternal Mortality 1990 to 2008* (WHO, 2010) 1. See also WHO, *Making a Difference in Countries: Strategic Approach to Improving Maternal and Newborn Survival and Health* (WHO, 2006) 4; WHO, *The World Health Report 2005* (n 3).

concern at the unacceptably high rate of preventable maternal mortality and morbidity and called on states to 'redouble their efforts to ensure the full and effective implementation of their [relevant] human rights obligations...'.[246] Among these obligations is the requirement under under para 2(d) of article 24 of the CRC to ensure the provision of appropriate pre-natal and post-natal care for mothers. Importantly, other international instruments have also recognized the significance of such care. Thus, for example, article 10(2) of the ICESCR provides that:

Special protection should be accorded to mothers during a reasonable period before and after childbirth. During such period working mothers should be accorded paid leave or leave with adequate social security benefits.

Article 12(2) of CEDAW further elaborates on the general obligation under the ICESCR to require that:

States parties shall ensure to women appropriate services in connection with pregnancy, confinement and the post-natal period, granting free services where necessary, as well as adequate nutrition during pregnancy and lactation.

It is clear, therefore, that the right to health under international law imposes an obligation on states to provide appropriate maternal health care for women and that such care must be free where necessary. A question remains however as to when it will be 'necessary' to provide such services for free.

The argument has been made that the use of the word 'ensure' in article 12 of the CEDAW means that maternal health care should not be subject to the progressive obligation that generally accompanies economic and social rights.[247] Certainly the human rights treaty monitoring bodies have expressed their concern at the imposition of fees on maternal health care services. For example, the CRC Committee in its concluding observations for the Central African Republic expressed its concern that 'the charging of fees for basic health care, and particularly prenatal and maternal care, may limit the access of disadvantaged children and their mothers to health services'.[248] But such an observation falls short of imposing an immediate obligation on states to provide maternal health care services. Moreover, the CEDAW Committee in its General Recommendation on women and health explained:

that it is the duty of States parties to ensure women's right to safe motherhood and emergency obstetric services and they *should allocate to these services the maximum extent of available resources.*[249]

---

[246] A/HRC/RES/11/8 'Preventable maternal mortality and morbidity and human rights' adopted 17 June 2009 paras 1 and 3 in Report of the Human Rights Council 11th Session A/64/53, 134-135. See also: A/HRC/RES/15/17 'Preventable maternal mortality and morbidity and human rights: follow up to Council resolution 11/8'; Report of the Office of the United Nations High Commissioner for Human Rights on preventable maternal mortality and morbidity and human rights, 16 April 2010 A/HRC/14/39.
[247] *Alyne de Silva Pimental v Brazil* CEDAW/C/49/D/17/2008 (10 August 2011) para 3.3.
[248] CO CRC Central African Republic, UN Doc CRC/C/15/Add.138, para 54.
[249] CEDAW Committee, *General Recommendation No 24: Women and Health*, UN Doc A/54/38 (1999) para 27 (emphasis added).

Moreover, in the 2011 decision of *Alyne de Silva Pimental v Brazil*, the CEDAW Committee affirmed its earlier recommendation with respect to the progressive nature of women's right to maternal health.[250] Thus, states cannot be said to be under an immediate obligation to provide all women with free maternal health services.

But there is an explicit obligation under article 12 of CEDAW to provide such services for free '*where necessary*'. The decision of the CEDAW Committee in *Alyne de Silva Pimental v Brazil* provides some guidance with respect to this issue. The facts involved a woman whose death was linked to obstetric complications related to her pregnancy. She had presented to her health centre with severe nausea and abdominal pain but the centre had failed to perform a blood test and urine tests, which would have ascertained that her unborn child had died. There were a series of other failures to properly treat Ms Pimentel including delays in surgery and transportation by ambulance, which ultimately led to a failure to provide timely emergency obstetric care and her death. The CEDAW Committee held that 'the lack of appropriate maternal health services in the State party... clearly fails to meet the specific, distinctive health needs and interests of women' and was a violation of the right to health, protection against discrimination, and the right to life under CEDAW.[251]

Although the CEDAW Committee did not expressly consider the meaning of the phrase 'where necessary', its views tend to suggest that this threshold will be satisfied where the relevant maternal health services are reasonably necessary to prevent any genuine and real threats to the life of a mother. As to whether this can be taken to mean that the obligation on states to provide free maternal health services in such circumstances will be immediate rather than progressive still remains debatable. There is an argument to say that because of the nexus between the right to life (which is a civil and political right subject to immediate implementation) and the right to health, that the obligation to deliver maternal health services where there is a threat to the right to life should be immediate. But even the CEDAW Committee did not advance this position in *Alyne de Silva Pimental v Brazil* and opted for an affirmation of the obligation on states to allocate emergency obstetric services to 'the maximum extent of available resources'.

B The meaning of 'appropriate' pre- and post-natal care

Although states enjoy a significant margin of appreciation with respect to the specific measures they adopt to fulfill their obligation regarding the provision of pre- and post-natal care, this flexibility remains subject to the constraint that such services must be appropriate. As to what constitutes 'appropriate' pre- and post-natal care, the committee bodies have tended to avoid this discussion in preference for rather general recommendations that states 'ensure that all women receive adequate medical care during pregnancy and childbirth',[252] provide

---

[250] *Alyne de Silva Pimental v Brazil* (n 248) para 7.3.
[251] ibid para 7.6.
[252] See, eg, CO ESC Azerbaijan, UN Doc E/1998/22 (1997) 61, para 353.

'adequate prenatal care',[253] and 'improve prenatal care'.[254] The CRC Committee has, however, stressed the need to train 'birth attendants in healthy midwifery'[255] and 'local villagers in safe midwifery'[256] and in its report for Nigeria, recommended that the state party '[t]ake measures to introduce awareness-raising programmes for women, on the importance of, inter alia, prenatal and post-natal health care'.[257] Such recommendations are at least slightly more directed in guiding states as to some of the practical measures required to ensure their pre- and post-natal services are appropriate.

In order to develop a more sophisticated and rigorous understanding of what constitutes appropriate pre- and post-natal services, there must be a constructive engagement by states with bodies who have expertise in this area such as UNICEF and WHO[258] and the vast body of literature on this subject. Although a detailed engagement with this literature is not required here, it is worth noting some of the key themes to emerge with respect to the processes and general features which states should progressively endeavour to develop in order to ensure the provision of appropriate pre- and post-natal care.

First, the design, delivery, and monitoring of such care should be adequately resourced in terms of both the institutions and personnel[259] required for the delivery of such services. They must be evidence based,[260] regulated by appropriate standards,[261] and undertaken in consultation with women and, as appropriate, their families, including men.[262] They must also be accessible, affordable, and available to all women and sufficiently flexible to accommodate and respond to the personal, physical,[263] social, cultural, and religious differences among pregnant women

---

[253] CO CRC Panama, UN Doc CRC/C/15/Add.233, para 44.
[254] CO CRC Guyana, UN Doc CRC/C/15/Add.224, para 42(a).
[255] CO CRC Botswana, UN Doc CRC/C/15/Add.242, para 49.
[256] CO CRC Panama, UN Doc CRC/C/15/Add.233, para 44.
[257] CO CRC Nigeria, UN Doc CRC/C/15/Add.257, para 49(c).
[258] See generally WHO, 'Maternal and Perinatal Health: Publications' <http://www.who.int/reproductivehealth/publications/maternal_perinatal_health/en/index.html> accessed 15 June 2011. See especially WHO, UNFPA, UNICEF, and World Bank, *Pregnancy, Childbirth, and Postpartum and Newborn Care: A Guide for Essential Practice* (2nd edn, WHO, 2006) (provides comprehensive discussion of care required for pregnant women); WHO, *Standards for Maternal and Neonatal Care* (WHO, 2006) (details general standards for healthy pregnancy and childbirth and special standards for childbirth and postpartum period; post-natal care; standards for managing complications; and health service delivery standards). See generally WHO, *The World Health Report 2005* (n 3) 125–48 (examines measures to reconcile maternal and child health within health system).
[259] See WHO, *Making a Difference in Countries* (n 246) (discusses strategies to ensure skilled care at every birth). See also WHO, *Making Pregnancy Safer: The Critical Role of the Skilled Attendant—A Joint Statement by WHO, ICM and FIGO* (WHO, 2004).
[260] WHO, *Evidence-Led Obstetric Care: Strategies to Change Practice and Policy. Report of a WHO Meeting—Geneva, Switzerland, 28–30 January 2004*, WHO Doc WHO/RHR/05.14 (2005).
[261] WHO, *Standards for Maternal and Neonatal Care* (n 259).
[262] WHO, *Programming for Male Involvement in Reproductive Health* (WHO, 2002).
[263] Consider for example the needs of women with physical disabilities such as women suffering from obstetric fistula: Gwyneth Lewis and Luc De Bernis (eds), *Obstetric Fistula: Guiding Principles for Clinical Management and Programme Development* (WHO, 2006); or female circumcision/genital mutilation: WHO, *Management of Pregnancy, Childbirth and Postpartum Period in the Presence of Female Genital Mutilation* (WHO, 2001).

including the special needs of adolescent girls who become pregnant. Finally, states must not simply provide institutional care and essential medicines,[264] but also aim to empower women and their families through the provision of knowledge and education about childrearing[265] and care for their own bodies as well as facilitating the creation of effective and sustainable community supports.[266] States will retain a significant discretion as to the specific measures they adopt to achieve these objectives. However, an engagement with the relevant literature provides a means by which to identify the broad requirements necessary to ensure *appropriate* pre- and post-natal care. Such an approach also serves to demonstrate the need for collaboration within the interpretative community if a practical and effective understanding as to the meaning of an obligation such as that imposed under para 2(d) of article 24 is to be generated.

VII The obligation to raise awareness and ensure access to information concerning health

A Introduction

Paragraph 2(e) of article 24 of the CRC imposes an obligation on states:

> To ensure that all segments of society, in particular parents and children, are informed, have access to education and are supported in the use of basic knowledge of child health and nutrition, the advantages of breast-feeding, hygiene and environmental sanitation and the prevention of accidents.

This cumbersome formulation is not matched by an equivalent provision in the formulation of the right to health under article 12 of ICESCR. However, in a less expansive formulation, article 10(h) of CEDAW imposes an obligation on states to ensure 'access to specific educational information to help to ensure the health and well being of families...'.[267]

The ambiguous and ambitious scope of these obligations tends to distract from their enormous practical significance. The right to health cannot be secured by the actions of states alone. As UNICEF affirmed in its *State of the World's Children Report*

---

[264] WHO, *The Interagency List of Essential Medicines for Reproductive Health* (WHO, 2006).
[265] For example, education about breastfeeding and birth spacing: WHO, *Report from a WHO Technical Consultation on Birth Spacing: Geneva, 13–15 June 2005* (WHO, 2005) (recommends two to three years between births in order to reduce the risk of adverse maternal and child health outcomes) and the management of mastitis: WHO, *Mastitis: Causes and Management* (WHO, 2000).
[266] WHO, *Working with Individuals, Families and Communities to Improve Maternal and Newborn Health* (WHO, 2010).
[267] Article 10(h) specifically lists 'information and advice on family planning' as information that must be provided to families. However, art 24(2)(f) of the CRC actually deals with this type of information separately by imposing an obligation on States 'to develop preventive health care, guidance for parents and family planning education and services'. The nature of this obligation is discussed below. Article 11(2) of the European Social Charter requires States 'to provide advisory and educational facilities for the promotion of health and encouragement of individual responsibility in matters of health'. For a discussion of the case law of the European Committee of Social Rights concerning this provision see: Council of Europe, *Digest of the Case Law of the European Committee of Social Rights* (n 1) 84–5.

2008, 'without the participation of communities, the goal of "health care for all" will remain severely constrained'.[268] More importantly, such rhetoric is supported by the evidence. For example, research indicates 'that using a combination of community outreach programmes and family community care strategies at 90 per cent national coverage could reduce neonatal mortality by 18–37% even in the absence of improvements in facility based care services'.[269] It is within this context that the meaning and significance of para 2(e) of article 24 of the CRC and article 10(h) of CEDAW must be located. It recognizes that children, their parents, and the broader communities in which they reside, have the capacity to play a significant role in preventing harm to health if they are not only aware of but also able to take the appropriate steps to avert the relevant health risks. It also recognizes that it is states which have the capacity to facilitate this awareness-raising and capacity-building role. Thus, while the obligation to raise awareness and ensure access to information about health may be specific to the CRC and the CEDAW (and the European Social Charter and Protocol of San Salvador)[270] it should also be implied within the general obligation of states to take appropriate measures to recognize the right to health under article 12(1) of the ICESCR. Such an approach provides a principled basis for the claim of the ESC Committee that the right to health extends to 'access to health-related education and information'.[271]

In contrast to the general nature of the obligation to disseminate health information under CEDAW, and the implied nature of this obligation under the ICESCR, the obligation under article 24(2) (e) of the CRC consists of a three-pronged strategy. First, it requires the provision of information on six discrete factors that impact on children's health—child health, nutrition, breastfeeding, hygiene, environmental sanitation, and the prevention of accidents. The second aspect is the ability to *access* education and measures with respect to these factors, and third, a requirement that parents, children, and members of the community are supported in their ability to constructively apply the information and education they acquire to adopt strategies that will contribute to the realization of the right to the highest attainable standard of health.

The drafting history of the CRC does not provide any insights into the specific measures by which states should fulfill this awareness-raising and capacity-building obligation and the work of the CRC Committee is also of limited value. In any event, the requirement of local context sensitivity means that, in practice, states will enjoy a significant margin of appreciation with respect to the measures they adopt

---

[268] UNICEF, *State of the World's Children Report 2008* (n 32) 45.
[269] ibid 63.
[270] See also European Social Charter, art 11(2), which requires states parties 'to provide advisory and educational facilities for the promotion of health and the encouragement of individual responsibility in matters of health'; Protocol of San Salvador, art 10, which requires states parties to educate 'the population on the prevention and treatment of health problems'.
[271] ESC Committee, *General Comment No 14* (n 50) para 11. See also para 12(b)(iv) in which the ESC Committee explains that the qualitative requirement of accessibility in relation to the right to health extends to information accessibility which includes 'the right to seek, receive and impart information and ideas concerning health issues'.

subject to the caveat that whatever measures are adopted they remain effective—a qualitative assessment which must be undertaken in a collaborative way that reflects the particular socio-economic, political, and cultural features of each jurisdiction.

B The information about health which all segments of society are entitled to receive

Although para 2(e) of article 24 of the CRC does not list the means by which to raise awareness about children's health, it does identify the areas in which knowledge and education must be provided, namely: basic knowledge of child health and nutrition; the advantages of breastfeeding; hygiene and environmental sanitation; and the prevention of accidents. Some of these areas such as health, nutrition, and environmental sanitation have been addressed in previous sections and it is not intended to expand on these discussions here. Rather, an examination of the issues surrounding the provision of information on the advantages of breastfeeding will be offered as a means of illustrating the various considerations that should inform states when they consider the development of strategies to raise awareness and build capacity with respect to the use of information to enhance the health of children.

1 Case study: Information on the advantages of breastfeeding

The inclusion of the obligation to raise awareness as to the merits of breastfeeding was a reflection of international concern during the time of the drafting of the CRC at the efforts by multinational corporations to promote and market the advantages of formula in developing countries potentially at the expense of children's health. It was during the 1985 session of the Working Group that the representative of the United States of America presented a proposal for what was to become sub paragraph (e) which sought to 'encourage the provision of full, accurate and balanced information regarding methods of infant feeding, including the advantages of breast-feeding'.[272]

The references to full, accurate, and balanced information were all omitted from the final formulation. With respect to the reference to 'balanced' information, this was specifically withdrawn at the suggestion of the observer for UNICEF for reasons which are not explained.[273] In relation to the requirement that the information be 'full' and 'accurate', this appears to have been an inadvertent omission when the proposed text of sub paragraph (e) as adopted at first reading, was replaced with a new formulation submitted by India in 1988,[274] which became the foundation for the final text. Despite these developments, it would be inappropriate to suggest that they indicate that information about the advantages of breastfeeding (or indeed any of the areas listed in article 24(2)(e)) need not be full, accurate, and balanced. On the contrary, the principle of effectiveness demands that such information must satisfy these criteria lest it be misleading and potentially harmful to securing not only a child's health but also the health of a mother.

[272] UN Doc E/CN.4/1985/64 para 30.
[273] ibid para 31.
[274] UN Doc E/CN.4/1988/WG.1.WP.14.

In terms of the contribution of the CRC Committee to the understanding of the obligation to provide information on the advantages of breastfeeding, it has repeatedly expressed its concern at the limited or decreasing use of this practice in its concluding observations for states, and recommended that states 'encourage exclusive breastfeeding for six months after birth, with the addition of an appropriate infant diet thereafter...'.[275] Such comments are often accompanied by recommendations to regulate the marketing of infant formula via the adoption and implementation of the International Code of Marketing of Breast Milk Substitutes.[276] Thus, to a certain extent the CRC Committee's recommendations with respect to the need for an exclusive period of breastfeeding could be seen as an attempt to counter the persuasive influence of infant formula manufacturers which inspired the inclusion of the obligation in para 2(e) of article 24. Moreover, its recommendations are consistent with the literature[277] and the position advocated by the World Health Organization[278] and UNICEF[279] that infants be exclusively breastfed for the first six months of life.

---

[275] CO CRC Algeria, UN Doc CRC/C/69/Add.269, paras 56, 57(a). See also, eg, CO CRC Bolivia, UN Doc CRC/C/15/Add.256, para 48; CO CRC Belize, UN Doc CRC/C/15/Add.252, para 53(a); CO CRC Angola, UN Doc CRC/C/15/Add.246, para 43(d); CO CRC Guyuna, UN Doc CRC/C/15/Add.224, para 42(d).

[276] See, eg, CO CRC Mongolia, UN Doc CRC/C/15/Add.264, para 44(c); CO CRC Croatia, UN Doc CRC/C/15/Add.243, para 52; CO CRC Singapore, UN Doc CRC/C/15/Add.222, para 39(a); CO CRC United Kingdom and Northern Ireland, UN Doc CRC/C/15/Add.188, para 42. See World Health Assembly, *International Code of Marketing of Breast-Milk Substitutes*, WHO Doc WHA34.22 (21 May 1981) annex.

[277] See, eg, WHO, *The Optimal Duration of Exclusive Breastfeeding: Report of an Expert Consultation* (WHO, 2002) (review of literature revealed several benefits of exclusive breastfeeding for six months on infants and mothers and recommended complementary foods and breastfeeding thereafter); Michael S Kramer and Ritsuko Kakuma, *Optimal Duration of Exclusive Breastfeeding* (2002) Cochrane Database Syst Rev 1: CD003517 (also confirm less morbidity from gastrointestinal infection among infants exclusively breastfed for six months compared to three or four months); Aimin Chen and Walter J Rogan, 'Breastfeeding and the Risk of Postneonatal Death in the United States' (2005) 113 Pediatrics 435; WHO Collaborative Study Team on the Role of Breastfeeding in the Prevention of Infant Mortality, 'Effect of Breastfeeding on Infant and Child Mortality due to Infectious Diseases in Less Developed Countries: A Pooled Analysis' (2000) 355 The Lancet 451 (studies provide evidence that infant mortality is higher among infants never breastfed as compared to infants for whom breastfeeding is at least initiated); Black, Morris, and Bryce (n 29) (cite studies which suggest that 'infants aged 0–5 months who are not breastfed have seven-fold and five-fold increased risks of death from diarrhoea and pneumonia compared with infants who are exclusively breastfed'); Laurie A Nommsen-Rivers, 'Is There a Difference in the Risk of Death among Infants Predominantly Breastfed as Compared to Infants Exclusively Breastfed?' (2005) 21 J Hum Lact 477.

[278] See WHO, 'Breastfeeding' <www.who.int/topics/breastfeeding/en> accessed 16 June 2011 (also provides links to various publications and reports relating to breastfeeding); WHO, *Infant and Young Child Nutrition: Fifty-Fourth World Health Assembly, Seventh Plenary Meeting, 18 May 2001, Geneva Switzerland* (WHO, 2001) 1–4.

[279] See: UNICEF, 'Infant and Young Child Feeding' <www.unicef.org/nutrition/index_breastfeeding.html> accessed 16 June 2011 (also provides links to various publications). See also UNICEF, *Breastfeeding: Foundation for Healthy Future* (UNICEF, 1999) 1. Also consider: *Innocenti Declaration on the Promotion, Protection and Support of Breastfeeding*, adopted at the WHO/UNICEF meeting 'Breastfeeding in the 1990s: A Global Initiative', Florence, Italy, 30 July–1 August 1990 (recommended exclusive breastfeeding from birth to four to six months with complementary feeding in addition to breastfeeding up to the age of two and beyond); UNICEF, *State of the World's Children 2008* (n 32) 47.

This position, however, represents an unbalanced and incomplete perspective on this issue. In the first instance, the CRC Committee has failed to detail in full the merits of exclusive breastfeeding.[280] Of greater concern, is the dogmatic approach adopted by the CRC Committee with respect to this issue. For many women in developing and developed states alike, breastfeeding is simply not an option. Cultural and social practices may prevent or impede a mother's ability to breastfeed. Physical reasons may mean that a woman may not have the ability to breastfeed a child at all or to produce sufficient milk to satisfy her child's nutritional needs. Personal reasons may also mean that a woman may choose not to breastfeed her child—she may, for example, choose to return to work to maintain her career or indeed be forced to return to work for financial reasons. In such circumstances the edict of the CRC Committee, that a woman should breastfeed her child exclusively for six months, not only fails to accommodate both the reality and autonomy of many women's lives, but also raises the very real prospect that those women who do not breastfeed may experience guilt or stigmatization. It thus lacks awareness of the need to ensure external system coherence in its approach to breastfeeding by recognizing and accommodating the autonomy rights of women as recognized under international law.

It is for this reason that the concern expressed by the CRC Committee in a few reports at the decline in breastfeeding among working mothers[281] is problematic. In defence of the CRC Committee, it has accompanied such expressions of concern with recommendations that states encourage the practice of breastfeeding in the workplace,[282] provide adequate maternity leave,[283] and facilitate childcare opportunities within the workplace to allow mothers to breastfeed their children while at work.[284] This is consistent with the ILO Maternity Protection Convention No. 183 (2000) and Recommendation 191 (2000) to support and facilitate breastfeeding by women in employment[285] and the literature which indicates a need to provide adequate social and nutritional support to lactating women.[286]

---

[280] The literature indicates that it provides protective effects against gastrointestinal infection, prolongs the duration of lactational amenorrhea for mothers, is associated with higher post partum weight loss in mothers, and increased protection against diarrhoeal morbidity and mortality. But it also indicates the need for additional research to assess any disadvantages regarding micronutrient status and growth faltering: WHO, *The Optimal Duration of Exclusive Breastfeeding* (n 278).
[281] See, eg, CO CRC Palau, UN Doc CRC/C/15/Add.149, para 46.
[282] ibid.
[283] CO CRC Lebanon, UN Doc CRC/C/15/Add.169, para 45(a).
[284] CO CRC Barbados, UN Doc CRC/C/15/Add.113, para 26 ('The Committee encourages the State party to continue its efforts to provide sufficient numbers of child-care services and to consider the possibility of setting up child-care facilities at the workplace for public employees, thus facilitating breastfeeding practices').
[285] ILO, 'C183 Maternity Protection Convention, 2000' (ILO, 2000) art 10.1 ('A woman shall be provided with the right to one of more daily breaks or a daily reduction in hours of work to breastfeed her child'), 10.2 ('these breaks or the reduction of daily hours of work shall be counted as working time and remunerated accordingly').
[286] WHO, *The Optimal Duration of Exclusive Breastfeeding* (n 278) 2. See also: *Innocenti Declaration* (n 280) (recommends reinforcement of a 'breastfeeding culture' and efforts to increase women's confidence in their ability to breastfeed).

Thus, it is clear that the CRC Committee is not attempting to demonize working mothers who choose not to breastfeed their children and recognizes the need for states to adopt appropriate support mechanisms and policies. At the same time, the requirement that information concerning the advantages of breastfeeding be accurate and balanced demands that any recommendation made with respect to a period of exclusive breastfeeding be accompanied by comments that accept and reflect the need for women to exercise their own right to physical and bodily integrity. As an Expert Consultation convened by the WHO to examine the optimal duration of breastfeeding, observed, 'some mothers will be unable or choose not to' follow its recommendation of exclusive breastfeeding for six months and in such circumstances 'these mothers should also be supported to optimize their infant's nutrition'.[287] Moreover, there is a need for states to identify the 'biological and social constraints to exclusive breastfeeding...and develop appropriate and effective interventions to deal with these barriers'.[288] In relation to this issue, there are a number of initiatives such as the UNICEF/WHO Baby Friendly Hospital Initiative[289] and the Global Strategy for Infant and Young Child Feeding[290] on which states should draw in designing effective interventions in collaboration with health professionals, mothers, and their communities to ensure an appropriate response which remains sensitive to factors such as a mother's culture, religion, ethnicity, and physical wellbeing especially in the context of mothers with HIV/AIDS.[291]

VIII The obligation to develop preventive health care, guidance for parents, and family planning education and services

A Introduction

Paragraph 2(f) of article 24 of the CRC is a curious provision. It is concerned with three issues—preventive health care, guidance for parents, and family planning. Each of these issues has already been discussed within the context of the interpretation of other obligations under the right to health. For example, the obligation to adopt

---

[287] WHO, *The Optimal Duration of Exclusive Breastfeeding* (n 278) 2.
[288] ibid.
[289] The WHO/UNICEF Baby Friendly Hospital Initiative was launched in 1991 in an attempt to ensure that all maternities whether free standing or in a hospital became centres of breastfeeding support. The indicia of a baby friendly hospital are linked to refusal to accept low-cost or free breast milk substitutes, feeding bottles, or treats, and implementation of 10 steps to support successful breastfeeding: <http://www.unicef.org/programme/breastfeeding/baby.htm> accessed 16 June 2011. See also WHO, UNICEF, and Wellstart International, *The Baby Friendly Hospital Initiative. Monitoring and Reassessment—Tools to Sustain Progress* (WHO, 1999); WHO, *Evidence for the Ten Steps to Successful Breastfeeding* (WHO, 1998) (summarizes and evaluates maternity practices necessary to support breastfeeding).
[290] WHO and UNICEF, *Global Strategy for Infant and Young Child Feeding* (n 133). See also WHO and UNICEF, *Implementing the Global Strategy for Infant and Young Child Feeding* (WHO, 2003); WHO, *Infant and Young Child Feeding: A Tool for Assessing national Practices Policies and Programmes* (WHO, 2003).
[291] See, eg, WHO, *HIV and Infant Feeding: Framework for Priority Action* (WHO, 2003); WHO, *HIV and Infant Feeding: Guidelines for Decision Makers* (WHO, 2003).

preventive measures has been shown to underlie virtually all subparagraphs of article 24(2) of the CRC, whereas subparagraph (e) of article 24 actually imposes an express obligation to ensure that parents are empowered to make use of information in a range of areas which will prevent harm to their children's health. Even the provision of family planning, which is not expressly provided for elsewhere in article 24, has been shown in Chapter 4 to be a necessary part of the general obligation to recognize the right to health by virtue of its contribution to the sexual and reproductive health of an individual. A question therefore arises as to the extent to which para 2(f) of article 24 of the CRC can be given an independent sphere of meaning.

Although the drafting history is not particularly helpful in this respect, the fact that the provision was adopted tends to indicate an expectation that it was not intended to be redundant or superfluous to the scheme created for the realization of children's health under article 24. Moreover, a careful analysis of the text of article 24 reveals that subparagraph (f) carries significant practical consequences.

B The obligation to develop preventive health care

1 Overview

The reference to preventive health care in subparagraph 2(f) is open-ended when compared with the other preventive measures required under para 2 which are linked to specific measures or objectives. It thus operates to impose a much broader and open-ended obligation on states with respect to the range of preventive health care measures they must adopt. It is true that this same obligation could also be implied as a feature of the general obligation to recognize the right to health under article 24(1) of the CRC or indeed article 12(1) of the ICESCR. However, its express exclusion in article 24(2)(f) of the CRC leaves no doubt as to the nature of this requirement.

This expansive preventive obligation provides the principled basis upon which the CRC Committee has made recommendations with respect to a number of matters which are not expressly included within article 24. Thus, for example, it has recommended that states 'take preventive action to avoid a rise in the rates of obesity among children';[292] '[u]ndertake effective preventive and other measures to address the rise in alcohol consumption by adolescents;'[293] 'strengthen mental health programmes for children, both preventive and interventional';[294] 'take appropriate measures to reduce the suicide rates, including by improving preventive and interventional mental health services';[295] and expressed its concern 'at the lack of preventive measures, including information campaigns, regarding sexually transmitted diseases (STDs) and HIV/AIDS'.[296] Although these comments represent a significant inflation of the scope of the issues that fall within the scope of the right to health, they reflect a determination by the CRC Committee to ensure that the

---
[292] CO CRC St Vincent and Grenadines, UN Doc CRC/C/15/Add.184, para 35(b).
[293] CO CRC Dominica, UN Doc CRC/C/15/Add.238, para 41(b).
[294] CO CRC Sweden, UN Doc CRC/C/15/Add.248, para 32(e).
[295] CO CRC Albania, UN Doc CRC/C/15/Add.249, para 57(c).
[296] CO CRC Yemen, UN Doc CRC/C/15/Add.102, para 25.

implementation of this provision responds to the practical challenges confronting children's health.

2 The nature of the obligation to develop preventive health care

The obligation to *develop* is not found elsewhere in the CRC and a question remains as to its meaning. The work of the CRC Committee is not particularly helpful in this regard as it has tended to adopt a rather general approach which includes, for example, recommendations that states '[e]mphasize the role of preventive health care';[297] 'enhance preventive interventions in primary health care;'[298] '[t]ake all necessary measures to... develop preventive health care'.[299] Beyond these circular and somewhat vacuous exhortations, an application of the ordinary rules of interpretation suggests that the obligation to *develop* is a progressive one that states must undertake subject to their available resources. The burden imposed, however, remains significant. Thus, for example, the CRC Committee in its report for the Czech Republic expressed its deep concern 'that the present economic situation in the health sector does not allow for compulsory preventive medical check-ups of children, from birth to the age of 3, to be covered by public health insurance'.[300] Such comments tend to indicate that, although the availability of resources will influence the content of preventive health strategies, states still carry a heavy onus to justify circumstances where young children are denied access to preventive measures.

As to the process by which preventive health care strategies are developed, states will retain a significant margin of appreciation subject, as is always the case, to the requirement that such measures be effective. From a practical perspective this will require not only consultation and collaboration with public health professionals but all those other actors that have a capacity to impact on children's health such as educators, social workers, parents, and the broader interpretative community. Moreover such an approach is also required as a matter of principle given the general obligations of states to consult with children,[301] their parents, and the broader community in a manner which is consistent with articles 12 and 5 of the CRC respectively.

C The obligation to develop guidance for parents

The generality of subparagraph (f) to develop preventive health care is informed by the specific requirements that guidance must be provided for parents and states must develop family planning education and services. The inclusion of these additional items in a provision that is ostensibly dedicated to preventive health care is arguably clumsy in its formulation and even somewhat curious. For example, the content of

---

[297] CO CRC Pakistan, UN Doc CRC/C/15/Add.217, para 53(b).
[298] CO CRC Russian Federation, UN Doc CRC/C/RUS/CO/3/Add.110, para 53(a).
[299] CO CRC New Zealand UN Doc, CRC/C/15/Add.216, para 36(b).
[300] CO CRC Czech Republic, UN Doc CRC/C/15/Add.201, para 46.
[301] See, eg, CO CRC Zambia, UN Doc CRC/C/15/Add.206, para 53(c) ('Involve children in formulating and implementing preventive and protective policies and programmes' to address the incidence of HIV/AIDS).

the obligation to provide guidance for parents is not fully enumerated and leaves open the question, which is yet to be clearly answered by the CRC Committee[302]— guidance as to what?

In any event, an application of the ordinary rules of interpretation, which require that the various terms be considered in light of the object and purpose of subparagraph (f) and its general context, suggests first, that the obligation to provide 'guidance for parents' requires the provision of guidance with respect to preventive health care for children *and* family planning. Such an approach reflects and anticipates the reality that parents or those persons caring for a child will in practice be the primary actors in preventing harm to the health of a child.[303] Thus, they must be given the skills necessary to fulfill this objective. In this respect, subparagraph (f) is closely linked with the obligation to inform and educate parents about child health and its various determinants as listed under subparagraph (e) of article 24 of the CRC.

D The obligation to develop family planning education and services

In Chapter 4 it was argued that the right to health extended to the sexual and reproductive health of an individual, the effective protection of which required the provision of information and services with respect to reproductive health. It was recognized that this suggestion would be contentious among elements of the interpretative community within many states. However, it was suggested that this position was supported by the obligation under paragraph 2(f) of article 24 of the CRC to develop 'family planning education and services' and the obligation under article 10(h) of CEDAW to provide information and advice on family planning to families. Although the meaning of 'family planning education and services' was not the subject of debate during drafting of the CRC or the CEDAW, it is generally accepted to mean the provision of information and services in relation to birth control and reproductive health including contraception, birth spacing, and sexually transmitted diseases which aim to empower people especially women and girls to make informed choices about their sexual and reproductive health and wellbeing.[304] Thus, for example, the *Programme of Action* adopted at the United Nations International Conference on Population and Development in Cairo in 1994 asserts that:

The aim of family-planning programmes must be to enable couples and individuals to decide freely and responsibly the number and spacing of their children and to have the information

---

[302] The CRC Committee has rarely made comment on the nature of the obligation to provide guidance under subparagraph (f). In its report for New Zealand it recommended that the State Party '[t]ake all necessary measures to ensure universal immunization coverage and develop preventive health care and guidance for parents and families that effectively address the relatively high rates of infant mortality and injuries': CO CRC New Zealand, UN Doc CRC/C/15/Add.216, para 36(b). Such a comment, given its emphasis on infant mortality and injuries, both largely preventable, does tend to imply a nexus between the provision of guidance and preventive health measures.

[303] UNICEF, *State of the World's Children 2008* (n 32) 19, 45.

[304] See generally: WHO, 'Screening for syphilis prevents stillbirth and newborn deaths' <www.who.int/reproductive-health/family_planning/index.html> accessed 15 June 2011.

and means to do so and to ensure informed choices and make available a full range of safe and effective methods.[305]

The specific inclusion of an obligation to develop and deliver family planning services within para 2(f) of article 24 of the CRC and article 10(h) of CEDAW must therefore be seen in the context of the reality that a lack of knowledge about family planning often leads to unwanted pregnancies both for adult women and girls[306]—an almost universal phenomenon about which, as noted in Chapter 4, the committee bodies have repeatedly expressed their concern.[307] In many cases such pregnancies carry significant health risks for both the mother and unborn child and this is especially the case with young girls.[308] For example, inadequate birth spacing between pregnancies creates an additional health burden on both mother and child, while teenage pregnancies that are carried to full term are associated with increased health risks for both mother and child. There is also the reality that many unwanted pregnancies result in termination in circumstances that are often clandestine—also a concern for the committee bodies[309]—and which present significant health risks for the mothers that could have been avoided if there had been access to appropriate family planning services to prevent the pregnancy in the first place. As a consequence, the provision of family planning education and services should be seen as a significant element of any preventive health care strategy and its specific inclusion in the CRC and CEDAW is a strong reminder to not only states, but the broader interpretative community, of the practical nexus between the two issues.

Ultimately, states retain a significant margin of appreciation with respect to the processes and measures they adopt in order to satisfy their obligation to develop and provide family planning education and services. This broad discretion, however, as with all the obligations under the right to health, remains subject to the caveat that such measures are appropriate and effective in contributing to children's right to the

---

[305] *Programme of Action of the International Conference on Population and Development*, UN Doc A/CONF.171/13 (18 October 1994) ch I, res 1, annex, para 7.12 (adopted at the United Nations International Conference on Population and Development in Cairo, 5–13 September 1994).

[306] According to the Special Rapporteur on the Right to the Highest Attainable Standard of Health, 'about 80 million women annually experience unwanted pregnancies, some 45 million of whom have abortions. Of this number some 19 million undergo unsafe abortions resulting in 68,000 deaths... In addition 340 million new cases of largely treatable sexually transmitted bacterial infections occur annually': *Report of the Special Rapporteur on the Right to Health to the Commission on Human Rights 2004* (n 106) paras 11–12.

[307] With respect to the concerns of the CRC Committee see, eg, CRC Committee, *General Comment No 4* (n 79) para 31. See also, eg, CO CRC Russian Federation UN Doc CRC/C/15/Add.110 para 48; CO CRC Angola UN Doc CRC/C/15/Add.246 para 45; CO CRC Jamaica UN Doc CRC/C/15/Add.210 para 43(b). With respect to the concerns of the CEDAW Committee see, eg, CO CEDAW Uruguay UN Doc A/57/38 Part I (2002) para 203; CO CEDAW Russian Federation UN Doc A/57/38 Part I (2002) para 400; CO CEDAW Suriname UN Doc A/57/38 Part II (2002) 82, para 58.

[308] See generally WHO, 'Contraception: Issues in Adolescent Health and Development' (WHO, 2004) 4–5.

[309] See, eg, CO CRC Mozambique, UN Doc CRC/C/15/Add172, para 46(c); El Salvador, ICCPR, UN Doc A/58/40 Vol. I (2003) 61, para 84(14); CO ICCPR Lithuania, UN Doc A/59/40 Vol. I (2004) 52, para 71(12); CO ESC Jamaica, UN Doc E/2002/22 (2001) 130, para 941; CO CEDAW Portugal, A/57/38 Part I (2002) 35, para 345; CO CEDAW Uruguay, UN Doc A/57/38 Part I (2002) para 203.

highest attainable standard of health. As detailed in Chapter 4, the CRC Committee has identified a number of measures which it considers appropriate, which need not be repeated here. There is also a significant and developing body of literature on family planning generally and adolescent reproductive health[310] to guide states in the development of their programs which only serves to affirm the need for a collaborative approach when seeking to understand the measures required for the effective implementation of a state's obligation to provide family planning education and services.

IX Conclusion—deference with limits

The recurring theme in the analysis offered with respect to each of the specific measures required of states in the formulation of the right to health in international law is that a wide margin of appreciation must be granted to states in order to enable a locally context sensitive implementation of their obligations. However, this discretion remains subject to the overarching caveat that, whatever measures are adopted by states, they must contribute to the effective realization of the right to health. This principle of effectiveness in turn demands that the implementation process must be informed by a dialogue among members of the relevant interpretative community to identify which strategies are effective in practice. Although the work of the treaty bodies is able to make some contributions in this respect, it is the literature from within the discourse of public health that is able to offer the most significant observations with respect to the measures required for the effective implementation of the specific obligations in para 2 of article 12 of the ICESCR and article 24 of the CRC. Moreover, a constant theme to emerge from this literature is that the absence of community based partnerships and sensitivity to the health needs of discrete groups such as women, children, persons with the disabilities, and indigenous groups will prove fatal to the identification, design, and implementation of strategies to secure each of these obligations.

This is a significant observation as it indicates that it is the *process* by which states seek to fulfil their obligations under the right to health that will often be as important as the actual measures adopted. States cannot be the 'masters' of treaty interpretation and they must be encouraged to engage in a process that will generate a collaborative narrative as to the nature of the measures required for the effective implementation of their obligations within their jurisdiction. This collaboration will not always yield a precise and immediate understanding of the measures required. Indeed, much of

---

[310] See, eg, Rebecca J Cook, Bernard M Dickens, and Mahmoud F Fathalla, *Reproductive Health and Human Rights: Integrating Medicine, Ethics and Law* (OUP, 2003) 276–86; Maria Raguz, 'Adolescent Sexual and Reproductive Rights in Latin America' (2001) 5 Health & Hum Rts 30; Guttmacher Institute, an NGO which publishes the journals *Perspectives on Sexual and Reproductive Health and International Family Planning Perspectives.* <www.guttmacher.org/archive/searchPSRH.jsp> accessed 15 June 2011; Center for Reproductive Rights, *Bibliography: Adolescent Sexual Health* <www.crlp.org> accessed 15 June 2011; WHO Adolescent and Reproductive Health <www.who.int/reproductive-health/adolescent/index.htm> accessed 15 June 2011.

the commentary in this chapter remains at a relatively high level of abstraction. Over time, however, a greater understanding as to the meaning of the measures required of states will emerge as members of the interpretative community engage with each other in an attempt to develop an understanding of those measures considered to be most effective. The content of this chapter must be assessed in this context and represents an attempt to provide and encourage further contributions to this ongoing and evolving narrative. It remains important to stress, however, that the development of this narrative is not without limits and its parameters are informed by the formulations adopted in para 2 of article 12 of the ICESCR and article 24 of the CRC. The interpretation of these formulations remains constrained by the ordinary rules of interpretation and the need to ensure both internal and external system coherence. Critically, however, the capacity to create a narrative which is guided by these constraints, indicates that it is possible to translate the broad and ambitious obligations imposed on states into an evolving set of clear and practical measures that will contribute to their effective realization.

8

The Obligation to Abolish Traditional Practices Harmful to Health

I Introduction

It is now widely recognized that a person's health is not merely compromised by gaps in medical knowledge, a lack of health services, or inadequacies in the social determinants of health, such as housing and food. Many traditional cultural practices are also maintained despite their prejudicial impact on the health of individuals.[1] Although this issue is not explicitly addressed in the International Covenant on Economic, Social and Cultural Rights (ICESCR), the drafters of the Convention on the Rights of the Child (CRC) were acutely aware of this reality when formulating the nature of a child's right to health. They were also aware of the constant, and at times seemingly irresolvable, dilemma that characterizes international human rights law—the need to accommodate and respect cultural differences and at the same time protect the internationally recognized rights of individuals.[2] Indeed, the drafting history for the CRC indicates that the delegation of Senegal 'counselled prudence when dealing with issues that entailed differences in cultural values and emphasized the dangers of forcing practices into clandestinity if they were prohibited by State legislation'.[3]

The drafting history also illustrates that following this comment from Senegal, a vigorous discussion ensued as to how to reconcile the need to respect cultural values with the reality that the health of many children was being compromised by traditional practices. Significantly the resolution of this debate lay with the following proposal from Senegal which was adopted by the Working Group: 'The State parties

---

[1] See, eg, Etienne G Krug and others (eds), *World Report on Violence and Health* (WHO, 2002) 62–3, 64–5, 69–70 (examines the widespread use of culturally accepted and traditional methods of physical abuse and non-physical abuse of children and their associated health consequences); Radhika Coomraswamy, *Report of the Special Rapporteur on Violence against Women: Cultural Practices in the Family that are Violent towards Women*, UN Doc E/CN.4/2002/83 (31 January 2002) (examines the gendered nature of cultural practices that are harmful not only to women's but also girls' health).

[2] Philip Alston, 'The Best Interests Principle: Towards a Reconciliation of Culture and Human Rights' in Philip Alston (ed), *The Best Interests of the Child: Reconciling Culture and Human Rights* (Clarendon Press, 1994); Sally Merry, *Human Rights and Gender Violence: Translating International Law in Local Justice* (University of Chicago Press, 2006) 6–16.

[3] *Report of the Working Group on a Draft Convention on the Rights of the Child*, UN Doc E/CN.4/1987/25 (9 March 1987) para 29.

to the present Convention shall seek to take all effective and appropriate measures with a view to abolishing traditional practices prejudicial to the health of children.'[4]

The ultimate adoption of this formulation indicates that States were not prepared to jeopardize the health of children in order to maintain the integrity of traditional practices. At the same time the drafting history suggests that this preparedness to challenge cultural practices was never intended to act as a vehicle by which developed states could disguise their contempt for traditional practices which were peculiar to developing states. Indeed, the drafters of the CRC were aware of and sensitive to the need to ensure that the provisions of the CRC were to be applied internationally. As a consequence, the formulation adopted was not intended to explicitly denigrate or devalue a specific practice or culture per se but rather to pursue the elimination of specific traditional practices, irrespective of their origin, that were prejudicial to the health of children.

The aim of this chapter is to explore more carefully the precise way in which states are to secure these dual objectives. Three central questions will be addressed in undertaking this endeavour: first, what is the general nature of a state's obligation to abolish traditional practices that are harmful to health; second, what are the practices which states are required to abolish; and third, what are the precise measures which states are required to undertake to secure this end? The conclusions to be drawn are as follows. First, the obligation to abolish harmful traditional practices is a progressive one which requires states to take a combination of whatever measures are necessary—legislative, administrative, social, and education—to ensure the effective eradication of such practices. Second, an assessment as to the prejudice of a particular practice to the health of a child cannot be reduced to a simple biomedical assessment and the broader psycho-social impacts and significance of a practice must be taken into account. Third, an examination of the treatment of corporal punishment and male circumcision by the body responsible for monitoring implementation of the CRC, the Committee on the Rights of the Child (CRC Committee), provides evidence of both a cultural and gender bias in the identification of practices deemed harmful to the health of a child. Fourth, the practice of female genital cutting will be used to demonstrate that rather than adopt a simple legislative regime based on zero tolerance, a multifaceted approach which is generated through dialogue with the communities that tolerate harmful practices, must be adopted if the effective elimination of harmful practices is to be achieved. Finally, it is important to stress that although the right to health under the ICESCR does not include a specific obligation to abolish harmful traditional practices, it is reasonable to imply such an obligation in the general obligation of states to take measures to protect the health of individuals from the practices of non-state actors.[5]

---

[4] *Report of the Working Group on a Draft Convention on the Rights of the Child* (n 3) para 39.

[5] None of the regional treaties include a provision equivalent to art 24(3) of the CRC. Moreover, CEDAW does not include such a provision but the obligation under art 12 to 'take all appropriate measures to eliminate discrimination against women in the field of health care' would extend to an obligation to abolish traditional discriminatory practices that were harmful to women and girls.

II The nature of a state's obligation—making progress towards effective abolition

Article 24(3) of the CRC requires that states parties 'shall take all effective and appropriate measures' with a view to abolishing harmful traditional practices. The inclusion of the verb 'shall' imposes a mandatory and immediate obligation to take such measures. It is therefore an onerous obligation and was intended to be so. The original proposal for article 24(3) had merely required that states 'seek to eradicate traditional practices'[6] but it was noted by the Netherlands during the 1987 session of the Working Group that this formulation was too weak and should be replaced with the 'more forceful language'.[7] Then, during the Technical Review, the observer for UNICEF noted that '[t]he use of the verb "to seek to" is highly unusual in human rights treaties since it further dilutes the nature of an already qualified obligation'.[8] Accordingly, when the proposal for article 24(3) came before the Working Group at the Second Reading, the obligation to 'seek' was omitted and simply required that 'States Parties shall take all effective and appropriate measures...'.[9]

It is important to recognize that this obligation does not require that states immediately abolish such practices. Indeed the inclusion of the phrase 'with a view to abolishing' provides recognition of the fact that the abolition of harmful traditional practices will take time and is thus a progressive obligation.[10] Moreover, it does not necessarily require the abolition of traditional practices, customs, and rituals in their entirety—only those aspects of a traditional practice which are prejudicial to health. In this context it is important to recall the content of article 30 of the CRC which affirms the value of traditional practices and provides:

In those States in which ethnic, religious or linguistic minorities or persons of indigenous origin exist, a child belonging to such a minority or who is indigenous shall not be denied the right, in community with other members of his or her group, to enjoy his or her own culture, to profess and practise his or her own religion, or to use his or her own language.[11]

---

[6] *Report of the Working Group on a Draft Convention on the Rights of the Child* (n 3) para 50.

[7] *Report of the Working Group on a Draft Convention on the Rights of the Child* (n 3) para 32 (Netherlands).

[8] *Technical Review of the Text of the Draft Convention on the Rights of the Child*, E/CN.4/1989/WG.1/CRP.1 (15 October 1988) 30.

[9] *Convention on the Rights of the Child: Text of the Draft Convention*, E/CN.4/1989/48 (26 July 1989) para 410.

[10] During the Technical Review the observer for UNICEF also noted that eradication of traditional practices, which was the phrase used in earlier drafts of para 3, could not be assured: (n 8) 30.

[11] See also International Covenant on Civil and Political Rights (ICCPR) (New York, 16 December 1966, entered into force 23 March 1976, 999 UNTS 171) art 27, which provides that:

In those States in which ethnic, religious or linguistic minorities exist, persons belonging to such minorities shall not be denied the right, in community with the other members of their group, to enjoy their own culture, to profess and practise their own religion, or to use their own language.

At the same time, this affirmation of cultural and traditional practices is a right to be enjoyed rather than imposed on a child especially where it is prejudicial to the child's health.

Although states have a significant level of discretion with respect to the particular measures they adopt, article 24(3) imposes the qualitative requirement that they must be 'effective' and 'appropriate'. The original proposal specifically required states to take all 'necessary legislative, administrative, social and educational measures'.[12] However this listing was omitted in response to the concerns voiced by the delegation for Senegal which, as noted above, 'emphasized the dangers of forcing practices into clandestinity if they were prohibited by legislation'.[13] At the same time, this omission should not be taken to mean that legislative measures or indeed administrative, social, and educational measures will not be an appropriate way to achieve the abolition of harmful traditional practices. In fact article 4 of the CRC still operates to require states to 'undertake all appropriate legislative, administrative, and other measures for the implementation of the rights recognized in the present Convention' including the abolition of practices prejudicial to the health of a child. The same obligation arises under article 2(1) of the ICESCR. However, the comments of Senegal reflect the reality that legislation, particularly when enacted in isolation from other measures, rarely has the effect of eliminating any practice. Rather it simply forces it to go 'underground'. Thus states are not prevented from adopting legislative measures. Rather they are under an obligation to ensure that that the adoption of such an approach is likely to be effective in contributing towards the abolition of harmful traditional practices.

III The practices to be abolished: 'traditional practices prejudicial to the health of children'

A Prejudice to health as a contested concept

Article 24 of the CRC does not provide a list of those traditional practices which are deemed to be prejudicial to the health of children. Similarly the drafting history does not evidence any intention on behalf of the drafters to detail such a list. Rather the phrase 'traditional practices prejudicial to the health of a child' has been adopted as the basis for adjudging whether a practice falls within the scope of para 3. A question remains however as to the extent and way in which a traditional practice must be prejudicial to the health of a child (or an adult given that a similar obligation is implied under the right to health in the ICESCR) before a state must take steps to secure its abolition.

During drafting of the CRC there was considerable discussion about the precise formulation of this phrase. Some delegations considered that it should be limited to very harmful practices and suggested the use of the phrases 'seriously harm',[14] or

---

[12] *Report of the Working Group on a Draft Convention on the Rights of the Child* (n 3) para 50.
[13] ibid para 29.
[14] ibid paras 30, 32 (Canada).

'seriously and adversely affect'.[15] However, another delegation was of the view that the term 'affect' should be used without qualification.[16] As a compromise position, the delegation from Senegal suggested that the phrase 'prejudicial to the health of children' be used,[17] which was accepted by the Working Group.[18]

The rejection of qualifying terms such as 'seriously' or 'seriously and adversely' indicates that the Working Group did not wish to unnecessarily restrict the scope of article 24(3). It also provides some insight into the meaning of the term 'prejudicial' to the extent that this phrase does not appear to require that the harm suffered to a child's health reach a certain threshold before the obligations of a State are invoked under article 24(3). On the contrary it suggests that any aspect of a traditional practice which in any way has a negative impact on the health of a child, whether mental or physical, temporary or permanent, must be abolished. Moreover the assessment as to the prejudicial impact of such a practice is not to be based on assumptions or speculation, which are invariably informed by social and cultural values, but on medical evidence which quantifies its physiological and/or psychological impact.

However this deference to scientific evidence as being an objective measure by which to assess the harm of a practice to the health of a child obscures the complex debates as to the purported objectivity of medical knowledge. From a strategic perspective such an approach is understandable as it allowed the drafters of the CRC to avoid the explicit condemnation of cultural practices by diverting attention from their cultural significance to their health impact. In practice however it is often more difficult to maintain such a distinction as cultural and social values will invariably influence the understanding of harm, especially psychological harm. Ritual initiation ceremonies provide a good example of such a dilemma. They may involve the infliction of significant physiological harm which would *prima facie* fall within the scope of article 24(3). But, if abolished, those children who were not subject to the relevant initiation practice may experience significant social isolation and exclusion which could lead to them suffering significant psychological harm. Such a conundrum is not insurmountable and it will be suggested below in the discussion of the measures required to abolish traditional practices that it is resolvable. At this point however it is important to stress that the emphasis placed on the medical harm of a particular traditional practice must be seen within its psychosocial context rather than being merely reduced to its physiological impact.

B The identification of those practices to be abolished

1 Towards a tentative list

Despite the absence of an express list in article 24(3) detailing those practices which fall within the scope of this provision, the drafting history provides some indication as to the types of practices which the Working Group anticipated would be

---

[15] ibid para 33 (USA). [16] ibid para 33.
[17] ibid para 34. [18] ibid para 39.

considered prejudicial to children's health. Attempts were made to specifically include certain practices within paragraph 3, most notably female genital 'mutilation',[19] on the basis that this was 'the traditional practice of greatest concern' and 'would demonstrate that the practices to be abolished were those of a serious nature'.[20] However, these attempts were ultimately resisted on the basis that it would be inappropriate to make a specific reference to just one 'traditional practice', when there were many traditional practices that were prejudicial to children's health.[21] At the same time the consensus to omit a reference to any specific traditional practices was achieved on the basis of several delegations expressing their 'understanding that the term traditional practices included all those practices outlined in the 1986 report of the Working Group on Traditional Practices affecting the Health of Women and Children (E/CN.4.1986/42)'.[22]

The 1986 report therefore becomes an important document in ascertaining the practices that fall within the scope of para 3. It states that traditional practices which are prejudicial or harmful include: 'female circumcision, other forms of mutilation (facial scarification), forced feeding of women, early marriage, the various taboos or nutritional practices which prevent women from controlling their own fertility, nutritional taboos and traditional birth practices'.[23] Moreover, in the discussion preceding the preparation of the list, reference was also made to 'dowries in certain regions of the world, crimes of honour and the consequences of preferential treatment for male children'.[24]

It is important to note that the use of the phrase 'such as' demonstrates that the Report was never intended to provide a definitive list of all prejudicial practices. Thus although this list has remained fairly constant, over time new practices have been added. For example, during a 1994 UN seminar on traditional practices and subsequent Plan of Action for the Elimination of Harmful Traditional Practices Affecting the Health of Women and Children ('Plan of Action'),[25] the concept of violence against women was considered and discussed. Moreover, the practices relating to marriage thought to be harmful to women and children became broader in the 1994 Plan of Action than when first identified in 1986 report. In 1994 such practices extended to early marriage, early pregnancy, dowry, and the status of divorced women[26] whereas the 1986 report omitted early pregnancy and the status

---

[19] *Report of the Working Group on a Draft Convention on the Rights of the Child* (n 3) paras 30 (Canada), 34 (Italy), 35 (UK and USA), 38 (Netherlands).
[20] ibid para 35 (USA).
[21] ibid para 36 (International Movement for Fraternal Union among Races and Peoples). See also para 38 (Senegal resists a further attempt by the Netherlands to specifically include female circumcision).
[22] ibid para 37 (Canada is supported by Japan, Sweden, and Venezuela).
[23] ibid para 18.
[24] ibid.
[25] *Plan of Action for the Elimination of Harmful Traditional Practices affecting the Health of Women and Children*, UN Doc E/CN.4/Sub.2/1994/10/Add.1 (22 July 1994); and *Report of the Second United Nations Regional Seminar on Traditional Practices affecting the Health of Women and Children*, UN Doc E/CN.4/Sub.2/1994/10/Corr.1 (3 August 1994).
[26] ibid paras 46–63.

of divorced women.[27] As a result, although the 1986 report provides some guidance on what is covered by the term prejudicial traditional practices as it appears in article 24 of the CRC, it does not provide an exhaustive list of such practices.

The CRC Committee has largely affirmed the list of harmful traditional practices listed above. Its primary focus, like the ESC Committee[28] and the CEDAW Committee,[29] has been female genital cutting, or 'female genital mutilation'[30] as it prefers to describe this practice—a term or label which is considered to be problematic for reasons which are outlined below. However it has also expressed its concern in its concluding observations for States with respect to the practice of forced or early marriages,[31] ritual killings,[32] the caste system,[33] dowry disputes,[34] virginity testing,[35] food taboos,[36] forced feeding,[37] consanguineous marriages,[38] milk teeth extraction,[39]

---

[27] *Report of the Working Group on Traditional Practices affecting the Health of Women and Children*, UN Doc E/CN.4/1986/42 (4 February 1986) para 18.

[28] See ESC Committee, *General Comment No 14: The Right to the Highest Attainable Standard of Health*, UN Doc E/C.12/2000/4 (11 August 2000) para 22. See also, eg, CO ESC Chad, UN Doc E/C.12/TCD/CO/3, para 19; CO ESC Democratic Republic of Congo, UN Doc E/C.12/COD/CO/4, para 20; CO ESC Kenya, UN Doc E/C.12/KEN/CO/1, para 23.

[29] See CEDAW Committee, *General Recommendation No 14: Female Circumcision*, UN Doc A/45/38 (2 February 1990).

[30] See, eg, CO CRC United Kingdom and Northern Ireland, UN Doc CRC/C/15/Add.188 (9 October 2002) paras 41–2; CO CRC Sudan, UN Doc CRC/C/15/Add.190 (9 October 2002) paras 47–8; CO CRC Burkina Faso, UN Doc CRC/C/15/Add.193 (9 October 2002) paras 44–5; CO CRC Switzerland, UN Doc CRC/C/15/Add.182 (7 June 2002) paras 40–1(d); CO CRC Spain, UN Doc CRC/C/15/Add.185 (13 June 2002) paras 40–1(a); CO CRC Niger, UN Doc CRC/C/15/Add.179 (13 June 2002) paras 52–3; CO CRC Guinea-Bissau, UN Doc CRC/C/15/Add.177 (13 June 2002) para 42; CO CRC Egypt, UN Doc CRC/C/15/Add.145 (21 February 2001) paras 45–6; CO CRC Ethiopia, UN Doc CRC/C/15/Add.144 (21 February 2001) paras 64–5; CO CRC Lesotho, UN Doc CRC/C/15/Add.147 (21 February 2001) paras 47–8; CO CRC Côte d'Ivoire, UN Doc CRC/C/15/Add.155 (9 July 2001) paras 44–5; CO CRC Democratic Republic of the Congo, UN Doc CRC/C/15/Add.153 (9 July 2001) paras 56–7; CO CRC Tanzania, 9 July 2001, UN Doc CRC/C/15/Add.156 at paras. 50–1; CO CRC Central African Republic, UN Doc CRC/C/15/Add.138 (18 October 2000) paras 58–9; CO CRC Djibouti, UN Doc CRC/C/15/Add.131 (28 June 2000) paras 43–4; CO CRC South Africa, UN Doc CRC/C/15/Add.122 (23 February 2000) para 33.

[31] See, eg, CO CRC Uganda, UN Doc CRC/C/UGA/CO/2 (23 November 2005) paras 53, 55; CO CRC Niger (n 30) paras 54–5; CO CRC Sao Tome and Principe, UN Doc CRC/C/15/Add.235 (1 July 2004) paras 48–9; CO CRC Pakistan, UN Doc CRC/C/15/Add.217 (27 October 2003) paras 55–6; CO CRC Zambia, UN Doc CRC/C/15/Add.206 (2 July 2003) para 50; CO CRC Eritrea, UN Doc CRC/C/15/Add.204 (2 July 2003) paras 45–6; CO CRC Burkina Faso (n 30) para 40.

[32] See, eg, CO CRC Nigeria, UN Doc CRC/C/15/Add.257 (13 April 2005) para 56.

[33] See, eg, CO CRC Nepal, UN Doc CRC/C/15/Add.261 (21 September 2005) para 67 (and traditions such as the *Deuki, Kumari, Jhuma, Badi, Kamlari* and *Chaupadi*, causing extreme insecurity, health hazards, and cruelty to girl children).

[34] See, eg, CO CRC Togo, UN Doc CRC/C/15/Add.255 (31 March 2005) para 56.

[35] See, eg, CO CRC South Africa (n 30) para 33.

[36] See, eg, CO CRC Burkina Faso (n 30) paras 44–5; CO CRC Guinea-Bissau (n 30) paras 42(c), 43 (c); CO CRC Democratic Republic of the Congo (n 30) paras 56(b), 57(b).

[37] See, eg, CO CRC Niger (n 30) para 52.

[38] See, eg, CO CRC Lebanon, UN Doc CRC/C/15/Add.169 (21 March 2002) paras 44, 45(b).

[39] See, eg, CO CRC Ethiopia (n 30) para 64.

infanticide[40] and selective abortions,[41] traditional medical practices,[42] and traditional practitioners.[43]

Space does not permit a close examination of the prejudicial health impacts of each of these practices to verify whether their inclusion within the scope of practices to be prohibited under article 24(3) is warranted. In any event, even a rudimentary understanding as to the nature of such practices is likely to identify a nexus between each practice and the potential for it have a prejudicial impact on the health of a child. Another characteristic common to the practices on this list, but more problematic, is that their origins and continued practice lie almost exclusively within non-Western cultural traditions. Such an approach has been identified as a cause for concern by several commentators due to its tendency to condemn non-Western cultural practices and condone or overlook the deeply embedded traditional practices within Western cultures that may also be harmful to the health of children.[44] Moreover an examination of the treatment of corporal punishment by the CRC Committee, which is a deeply embedded practice in many Western states, confirms this concern.

2 Cultural bias in the identification of harmful traditional practices

The CRC Committee has devoted considerable attention to the practice of corporal punishment and in 2006 it issued a General Comment on the practice in which it recognized that the 'widespread traditional acceptance'[45] of this practice, 'may inflict serious damage to the physical, psychological and social development of children'.[46] Despite this admission it failed to link the abolition of this traditional practice with the obligations of states under article 24(3) instead preferring to examine it primarily by reference to the obligations of states under articles 19, 28(2), and 37 of the CRC.[47] Such an approach not only creates a jurisprudential anomaly but also fails to deflect criticism that the implementation of article 24(3) has become a mechanism for the

---

[40] See, eg, CO CRC Tanzania (n 30) para 51; CO CRC India, UN Doc CRC/C/15/Add.115 (23 February 2000) para 49.

[41] See, eg, CO CRC India (n 40) para 49.

[42] See, eg, CO CRC Nepal (n 33) para 61(e) (expresses concern at the 'prevalence of traditional practices which could be harmful to the health of children, such as that of consulting witchdoctors instead of modern medical facilities and not giving water to children suffering from diarrhoea').

[43] See, eg, CO CRC Madagascar, UN Doc CRC/C/15/Add.218 (27 October 2003) para 47 ('The Committee is concerned that this situation [lack of adequate resources] has led to increasing recourse to traditional practitioners, some of whom are unscrupulous charlatans').

[44] See, eg, Sonja Harris-Short, 'Listening to "the Other"? The Convention on the Rights of the Child' (2002) 2 MJIL 304. See also Merry (n 2) 12–13 (discusses the problematic use of 'tradition' as a way of understanding culture and how the term has been 'smuggled into prevailing theoretical models by maintaining the binary distinction between modernity and tradition' and that such terms operate to 'juxtapose modernity and savagery and locate culture in the domain of the latter and civilization in the former').

[45] CRC Committee, *General Comment No 8: The Right to Protection from Corporal Punishment and Other Cruel or Degrading Forms of Punishment*, UN Doc CRC/C/GC/8 (2 March 2007) para 45.

[46] ibid para 37.

[47] Articles 19, 28(2) and 37 of the Convention deal with: (i) violence against children; (ii) discipline within schools; and (iii) cruel, inhuman, and degrading treatment against children.

condemnation of non-Western traditional practices that harm the health of children and a failure to identify the harmful traditional practices that exist in the West.

From the perspective of this analysis it also demonstrates the dangers attached to an interpretative exercise that is not sufficiently reflective as to the values and assumptions that inform and shape an act of interpretation. During the drafting history there was an acute awareness and determination to ensure that article 24(3) did not become a vehicle for condemning the practices within particular cultures. Notwithstanding this commitment, a Western-centric vision of what amounts to a harmful traditional practice has emerged in the work of the CRC Committee, which must be remedied for three reasons. First, the obligation to abolish harmful traditional practices was never intended to be restricted to practices which are peculiar to non-Western states. Second, the legitimacy and status of the CRC Committee will be undermined if its works generate a perception that it will only be the cultural practises of some states that will fall within the scope of article 24(3). Third and finally, a blind spot with respect to the identification of harmful traditional practices within Western states creates the risk that the existence of such practices will be overlooked. The effective implementation of this provision therefore demands a genuine interrogation of all traditional practices within any state that may be prejudicial to the health of a child and corporal punishment is arguably one such practice.

3 Gender bias in the identification of harmful traditional practices

In contrast to its preoccupation with female genital cutting, the CRC has failed to make any substantive comments with respect to male circumcision, also a traditional practice[48] still carried out in many Western states.[49] This omission could arguably provide further evidence to support the contention of cultural bias in the identification of harmful traditional practices.[50] But rather than explore this possibility here, it is suggested that the treatment of male circumcision is more interesting as a potential example of how cultural and social values with respect to gender construction may influence the identification of traditional practices considered harmful to a child.

As a practice, male circumcision has received significantly less attention than female circumcision in the literature and the CRC Committee's failure to address this issue within the context of article 24(3) is thus consistent with broader academic

---

[48] S Hellsten, 'Rationalising Circumcision: From Tradition to Fashion, from Public Health to Individual Freedom—Critical Notes on Cultural Persistence of the Practice of Genital Mutilation' (2004) 30 J Med Ethics 248.

[49] See M Fox and M Thomson, 'Short Changed? The Law and Ethics of Male Circumcision' (2005) 13 Intl J Child Rts 161, 176 (considers male circumcision to be an initiation into masculinity which underpins the deep-rooted cultural preference for this practice in the Anglo-American world).

[50] Irrespective of the cultural relativist dimension of this debate, some commentators have suggested that the practice of male circumcision is just as objectionable as forms of female circumcision and thus that the lack of attention to this practice is anomalous: Aleeb Abu-Sahlieh, 'To Mutilate in the Name of Jehovah or Allah: Legitimization of Male and Female Circumcision' (1994) 13 Med & L 575; W E Brigman, 'Circumcision as Child Abuse: The Legal and Constitutional Issues' (1985) 23 J Fam L 337; Hellsten (n 48).

and research trends.[51] Commentators have suggested that this neglect is 'partly attributable to the way in which routine infant male circumcision... is typically characterised in opposition to female circumcision'.[52] This distinction is said to be driven by among other things a construction of male circumcision 'as a standard and benign medical practice'[53] in contrast to the violent effect of 'female circumcision' on the health and sexuality of girls. An examination of the literature tends to confirm that unlike female circumcision where the negative impact on a girl's health is virtually uncontested, the evidence with respect to male circumcision is far more equivocal at least in those circumstances where is it performed in a medical setting.[54] For example, a meta-analysis in sub-Saharan Africa has suggested that male circumcision halves the relative risk of HIV infection[55] while another study in Europe has indicated that circumcised men are less likely to have human papilloma virus and that their female partners are therefore less likely to develop cervical cancer.[56] Such studies could be taken to affirm the silence of the CRC Committee in the identification of male circumcision as a traditional practice that states must abolish.

At the same time many commentators and medical bodies are cautious as to the medical benefits of male circumcision especially when weighed against the risks associated with the procedure.[57] For example, the American Academy of Pediatrics Task Force on Circumcision, after an examination of the available evidence, concluded that potential medical benefits *may* be associated with newborn male circumcision.[58] However it added that the data was not sufficient to recommend routine neonatal circumcision. Thus, it has been suggested that the most appropriate

---

[51] This is not to say that the literature is silent, but rather that it is limited. See, eg, the symposiums on male circumcision in: *The American Journal of Bioethics* (2003) 3(2); *Journal of Medical Ethics* (2004) 30 (3). See also Fox and Thomson (n 49).

[52] Fox and Thomson (n 49) 161. This is notwithstanding that the origins of this practice can be traced to explanations that are similar to those used to justify or explain female circumcision and include religion, misheld medical beliefs about the influence of the penis on the general health of men, attempts to curb masculine sexuality, especially masturbation, hygiene, and the existence of circumcision as a signifier of social standing or distinction: 170–3.

[53] ibid 161.

[54] This however does not explain the absence of concern for the practice in non-medical settings where the performance of the procedure is associated with significant levels of pain and the risk of infection. Whether this medicalization has lead to the legitimization of the practice such that little concern is expressed for its practice in non-medical settings is an issue that requires further consideration.

[55] H Weiss and others, 'Male Circumcision and Risk of HIV Infection in Sub Saharan Africa: A Systematic Review and Meta Analysis' (2000) 14 AIDS 2361. The authors have recently published a new study on the same issue in a 2010 edition of AIDS: H Weiss and others, 'Male Circumcision for HIV Prevention: Current Research and Programmatic Issues' (2010) 24 AIDS S61.

[56] Xavier Castellsagué and others, 'Male Circumcision, Penile Human Papillomavirus Infection and Cervical Cancer in Female Partners' (2002) 346 New Eng J Med 1105.

[57] See J Hutson, 'Circumcision: A Surgeon's Perspective' (2004) 30 J Med Ethics 238 (provides a detailed assessment of the surgeon's duty to examine the costs and benefits of circumcision).

[58] American Academy of Pediatrics, Task Force on Circumcision, 'Circumcision Policy Statement' (1999) 103 Pediatrics 686. Similar views have been expressed by the following: British Medical Association, 'The Law and Ethics of Male Circumcision: Guidance for Doctors' (2004) 30 J Med Ethics 259; Canadian Pediatrics Association, Fetus and Newborn Committee, 'Neonatal Circumcision Revisited' (1996) 154 CMAJ 769; Royal Australasian College of Physicians, 'Position Statement on Circumcision' (RACP, 2002).

course is to provide accurate and unbiased information to parents to enable them to make an informed choice.[59]

Other commentators are far more sceptical about the medical rationalization for male circumcision and its purported benefits[60] and question the legitimacy of a potentially harmful non-consensual, non-therapeutic intervention on a child for which, they assert, there is no moral justification.[61] Commentators have also questioned whether parents should have the power to decide whether their son should be circumcised and instead would prefer that a boy himself have the right to determine whether he wishes to undergo such a procedure when he is capable of providing informed consent.[62] These are matters which have only just been raised within a human rights context[63] and on which neither the domestic courts, regional bodies, nor the CRC Committee are yet to make significant comment. As such the dominant consensus would appear to be that male circumcision, although a traditional practice which carries with it the normal risks associated with any medical procedure and specific risks, including inadequate sexual function,[64] is not considered to be sufficiently prejudicial to the health of boys[65] to warrant state intervention and regulation—at least when it is performed in an appropriate medical setting under anaesthetic.[66]

This position however may change as closer attention is given to the issue from the perspective of the rights of the child rather than parental preferences and there is a

---

[59] American Academy of Pediatrics, Task Force on Circumcision (n 58). See also British Medical Association, 'The Law and Ethics of Male Circumcision' (n 58); M Benetar and D Benetar, 'Between Prophylaxis and Child Abuse: The Ethics of Neonatal Male Circumcision' (2003) 3 Am J Bioethics 35 (in absence of unequivocal evidence circumcision of boys should be a matter of parental discretion).

[60] See, eg, Fox and Thomson (n 49) 167–70.

[61] Hellsten (n 48).

[62] See, eg, R Short, 'Male Circumcision: A Scientific Perspective' (2004) 30 J Med Ethics 241; Fox and Thomson (n 49) 177 (in cases of demonstrable harm such as male circumcision, the law should be motivated by child protection until the child can make his an autonomous decision); J Svoboda, R Van Howe, and J Dwyer, 'Informed Consent for Neonatal Circumcision: An Ethical and Legal Conundrum' (2000) 17 J Contemp'ry HL & Pol'y 61 (in the absence of appreciable medical benefits, parental consent is invalid and the decision must be deferred to an adult male to decide for himself); Hutson (n 57) (indicates that from a medical perspective circumcision, if warranted, is more appropriate on a young boy rather than neonate because of the way the penis develops). cf A Viens, 'Value Judgment, Harm and Religious Liberty' (2004) 30 J Med Ethics 241 (argues that parents' freedom to choose infant male circumcision is the correct policy).

[63] Viens (n 62) 244–5 (attempts to reconcile rights of child with a policy that enables parents to determine whether a boy should undergo the procedure); British Medical Association, 'The Law and Ethics of Male Circumcision' (n 58) 260 (considers but does not seek to resolve the potential for non-therapeutic male circumcision to be considered a violation of the European Convention on Human Rights and the Convention on the Rights of the Child).

[64] See Hutson (n 57) (details complications and risks associated with the procedure).

[65] Indeed during a UN seminar in 1991 'it was recommended that efforts should be made to separate, in people's minds, male circumcision, which has a hygienic function, and female circumcision, which is a grave attack on the physical integrity of women': *Report of the UN Seminar on Traditional Practices Affecting the Health of Women and Children*, UN Doc E/CN.4/Sub.2/1991/48 (12 June 1991) para 27.

[66] Hutson (n 57) (notes that in the absence of anaesthetic as is the case in many traditional communities, male circumcision is 'physically cruel and potentially dangerous and must leave major psychological scars').

reversal of what Fox and Thomson have identified as a tendency to focus on the perceived harms and risks associated with failing to have a boy circumcised as opposed to the actual harms and risks associated with such a procedure.[67] At this juncture it is important to note that the discussion of male circumcision illustrates that the notion of harm—the basis upon which article 24(3) invokes an obligation on States to take measures to abolish traditional practices—is not necessarily an objective and quantifiable consequence. On the contrary it will often remain a contested, fluid, and subjective concept that is constructed by social values and expectations. Moreover the case of male circumcision arguably provides an example whereby the construction of masculinity has created a situation in which the harm inflicted upon boys may be less visible than that inflicted on girls. As Fox and Thomson have observed, 'male bodies are typically constructed as safe, bounded and impermeable' which makes it 'more difficult to uncover harms to boys—a contention which seems to be borne out by the tendency of Anglo-American legal commentators to minimize the harms inflicted on boys by circumcision'.[68] From the perspective of this chapter such an observation is critical as it serves as a reminder of the need to be vigilant in scrutinizing the values and assumptions that inform or potentially limit the understanding of harm as it appears in article 24(3) of the CRC.

IV Measures to abolish traditional practices prejudicial to a child's health

A Case study: female genital cutting

The obligation on States Parties under article 24(3) to take measures with a view to abolishing traditional harmful practices is unaccompanied by any further direction as to the nature of the specific measures states ought adopt. This leaves states with a wide margin of appreciation to determine what measures are appropriate to meet this obligation within their own particular context. This discretion however remains subject to the caveat that such measures are effective, which in turn demands a consideration as to the general form and shape such measures might take. It is beyond the scope of this analysis to consider the nature of the measures required to abolish all those traditional practices that are considered to be harmful to the health of a child. As a consequence, the approach taken here is to consider the practice of female genital cutting as a case study in an attempt to offer some general guidance as to the measures required of states to abolish harmful traditional practices. The benefit of using this practice is that it has been the subject of significant debate in the literature and numerous measures have been adopted in an attempt to address it. Thus the effectiveness of such measures can be examined with a view to providing insights into the measures that may be considered most appropriate in relation to other harmful practices.

---

[67] Fox and Thomson (n 49) 173.   [68] ibid 176.

B The problem of classification

It is suggested that the actual term or label used to describe a practice identified as being harmful to the health of a child may of itself have an impact on the effectiveness of measures taken by a state to abolish such a practice. This suggestion rests on the proposition that effective abolition of a practice will invariably depend upon effective engagement with those persons who maintain the practice. Thus if the term or label used to describe a practice is inflammatory it is unlikely to facilitate any constructive engagement between those actors who will play a role in facilitating its abolition.

Various labels have been used to describe the practice of female genital cutting. The most common, which is adopted by the CRC Committee,[69] the ESC Committee,[70] the CEDAW Committee,[71] the World Health Organization (WHO),[72] the Office of the High Commissioner for Human Rights,[73] the United Nations Special Rapporteur on Violence Against Women,[74] the Inter-African Committee on Traditional Practices Affecting the Health of Women and Children,[75] the European Parliament,[76] and what was the Sub Commission on the Prevention of Discrimination and Protection of Minorities,[77] is 'female genital mutilation' or 'FGM' as it is commonly abbreviated. Other commentators prefer the term 'female circumcision',[78] because it is considered to be more neutral, less laden with cultural bias, and thus less inflammatory. Radical female circumcision and excision are also used. Where there is a considered preference for the phrase 'FGM', this appears to be based on the belief that terms such as 'circumcision' tend to trivialize the harm

---

[69] See, eg, the concluding observations of the CRC Committee, above, n 30.

[70] ESC Committee, *General Comment No 14* (n 28) para 22.

[71] CEDAW Committee, *General Recommendation No 24: Women and Health*, UN Doc A/54/38 (5 February 1999) para 12(b). However in 1990 the CEDAW Committee adopted a general recommendation dedicated to a discussion of the practice of female circumcision: CEDAW Committee, *General Recommendation No 14* (n 29).

[72] See, eg, H Lovel and others, *A Systematic Review of the Health Complications of Female Genital Mutilation including Sequelae in Childbirth* (WHO 2000).

[73] OHCHR, 'Harmful Traditional Practices Affecting the Health of Women and Children' (OHCHR Fact Sheet No 23) <http://www.ohchr.org/Documents/Publications/FactSheet23en.pdf> accessed 14 June 2011.

[74] *Report of the Special Rapporteur on Violence against Women: Cultural Practices in the Family that are Violent towards Women* (n 1) paras 12–20.

[75] See Inter-African Committee on Traditional Practices Affecting the Health of Women and Children, *Newsletter No 28* (December 2000) 3.

[76] *European Parliament Resolution on Female Genital Mutilation* [2002] OJ C 77 E/126.

[77] *Plan of Action for the Elimination of Harmful Traditional Practices affecting the Health of Women and Children* (n 25).

[78] This was the label adopted by the CEDAW Committee in its 1990 *General Recommendation No 14* on female circumcision: CEDAW, *General Recommendation No 14* (n 29) This approach was also maintained in its general recommendation on violence against women in 1992: CEDAW Committee, *General Recommendation No 19: Violence against Women*, UN Doc A/47/38 (1992) para 11. It has also been adopted by numerous commentators. See, eg, E Gruenbaum, *The Female Circumcision Controversy: An Anthropological Perspective* (University of Pennsylvania Press 2001); C Little, 'Female Genital Circumcision: Medical and Cultural Considerations' (2003) 10 J Cultural Div 30 (uses female circumcision interchangeably with FGM).

associated with the practice and its gendered nature by falsely implying an analogy with male circumcision.[79] Thus the more provocative and emotive term 'mutilation' is warranted.

The phrase preferred here, notwithstanding its inconsistency with the approach adopted by the CRC Committee and other UN bodies, is female genital cutting.[80] It is adopted because it is considered to be less judgemental in its description of the practice[81] and thus more useful as a basis for constructive engagement with those communities where the practice takes place. The view taken here is that to label a person—or more specifically a mother or a respected member of a girl's community—a mutilator, when they invariably believe that their actions are consistent with the best interests of the child, is not a helpful strategy if the objective is to abolish those elements of this practice which are prejudicial to a girl's health.

C The nature and health consequences of the practice

Beyond the question of labelling, the nature and elements of a practice which are harmful to the health of a child must be identified as this is the basis upon which a practice falls within the scope of article 24(3). With respect to female genital cutting, this practice is generally taken to comprise 'all procedures that involve partial or total removal of the female external genitalia and/or injury to the female genital organs for cultural or any other non-therapeutic reasons'.[82] Although the origins of the practice are uncertain,[83] it is estimated that over 130 million girls and women have undergone female genital mutilation and '2 million girls are at risk of undergoing

---

[79] See Hellsten (n 48) (recognizes the distinction between the practice as performed on male and female children but stresses the need to draw parallels due to implications of performing any potentially harmful non-therapeutic, non-consensual procedure that is performed on children for social rather than medical reasons).

[80] See, eg, R Skaine, *Female Genital Mutilation: Legal, Cultural and Medical Issues* (McFarland, 2004) (uses terms interchangeably but with a preference for female genital cutting and the more neutral circumcision when talking with those connected with the practice); R Cook, B Dickens, and M Fathalla, 'Female Genital Cutting (Mutilation/Circumcision): Ethical and Legal Dimensions' (2002) 79 Intl J Gyn & Obs 281; N Ford, 'Communication for Abandonment of Female Genital Cutting: An Approach Based on Human Rights Principles' (2005) 13 Intl J Child Rts 183.

[81] Cook, Dickens, and Fathalla (n 80) 282.

[82] Lovel and others (n 72) 11. The WHO definition of FGM contains four classifications: Type I—excision of the prepuce with or without excision of part or all of the clitoris; Type II—excision of the prepuce and clitoris together with partial or total excision of the labia minora; Type III—excision of part or all of the external genitalia and stitching/narrowing of the vaginal opening; Type IV—unclassified: including for example: pricking, piercing, or incision of the clitoris and/or labia; stretching of the clitoris and/or labia: ibid 11.

[83] See M Knight, 'Curing Cut or Ritual Mutilation? Some Remarks on the Practice of Female and Male Circumcision in Graeco-Roman Egypt' (2001) 92 Isis 317 (provides detailed examination of ancient texts and archaeological artefacts to offer a hypothesis as to the origins of the practice, suggesting a 'menu of motivations' which included medical and curative considerations on the one hand and ritual nature on the other); OHCR (n 73) (provides some discussion of the history of the practice which predates Christianity and Islam).

some form of procedure every year'.[84] Its biomedical health consequences are well documented[85] which is the reason it is examined as a harmful traditional practice under article 24.

At the same time it is important to note that despite attempts to depoliticize this practice by focusing on its health consequences, it remains a deeply political and embedded cultural practice. Sensitivity to the local context in which the practice is performed is thus an important criterion in the identification of measures to abolish those aspects of this practice deemed harmful to the health of a child and demands that the views of those communities that engage in the various forms of this practice cannot simply be 'buried' or dismissed as being 'politically unreasonable'.[86] As a consequence there is a need to ensure that the response to a harmful traditional practice such as female genital cutting is not confined to a narrow Western-centric assessment of health risk.[87] Rather it is important to develop a broader notion of a child's health that takes into account the legal, social, economic, and cultural practices that shape and maintain the structures, systems, values, and beliefs that enable the practice to exist.

This observation is also relevant in relation to the practice of female genital cutting on women as opposed to girls. To date, this discussion has proceeded on the basis that this practice is imposed on a child against her will or in circumstances where she lacks the competency to consent to such a practice in her own right. However, there are many instances where an adult woman may wish to consent to such a practice. This gives rise to complex debates as to whether the consent is genuine. It is not appropriate to canvass these debates here and it is sufficient to note that under international human rights law, an adult can consent to a medical practice notwithstanding that such a practice may be considered prejudicial to her (or his) health from a biomedical perspective or even the dominant socio-medical perspective. The situation with respect to children who possess the competency to consent to medical treatment is slightly more complex and is discussed at length in Chapter 4.

D The measures to be adopted by states

States have a significant degree of discretion with respect to the measures they adopt to abolish the harmful elements of a harmful traditional practice such as female genital cutting subject to the caveat that such measures are appropriate and effective. In addition to the vast and expanding literature on this subject,[88] there are several

---

[84] A Mohamud and others (eds), *Female Genital Mutilation: Programmes to Date: What Works and What Doesn't—A Review*, WHO Doc WHO/CHS/WMH/99.5 (1999) 3. See also OHCR (n 73).

[85] See Lovel (n 72) (provides comprehensive evaluation of the available literature); WHO Study Group on Female Genital Mutilation and Obstetric Outcome, 'Female Genital Mutilation and Obstetric Outcome: WHO Collaborative Prospective Study in Six African Countries' (2006) 367 The Lancet 1835.

[86] J Rogers, 'Making the Crimes (Female Genital Mutilation) Act 1996, Making the "Non-Mutilated" Woman' (2003) 18 A Fem LJ 93.

[87] N Toubia and E Sharief, 'Female Genital Mutilation: Have We Made Progress?' (2003) 82 Intl J Gyn & Obs 251.

[88] See, eg, T Levin, 'World Wide Web Review: Internet Based Resources on Female Genital Mutilation' (2002) 23 Feminist Collections 19; WHO, *Female Genital Mutilation: A Joint WHO/UNICEF/ UNFPA Statement* (WHO 1997) 13–15; CEDAW Committee, *General Recommendation No 14* (n 29);

themes which emerge from the work of the CRC Committee that provide some guidance and direction by which to assess the efforts of states. First, the CRC Committee has typically recommended that states adopt legislative measures with effective enforcement as the first and central plank in their strategy to abolish female circumcision.[89] Such an approach has also been advocated in numerous international instruments[90] and by various commentators[91] on the basis that it seeks to invoke the power of law as a tool by which to condemn and proscribe social practices. But it remains a contentious mechanism by which to address female genital cutting[92] for reasons which include the tendency of legislative initiatives to overlook effective consultation with affected communities[93] and the associated failure to address those factors that generate the demand for this practice which in turn raises the real potential that it will be driven underground, further threatening the health of girls.[94] Thus while the requirement to adopt legislation to prohibit harmful traditional practices such as female genital cutting may have widespread support within elements of the international community, states must ensure that such legislation is

---

Plan of Action for the Elimination of Harmful Traditional Practices affecting the Health of Women and Children (n 25); Protocol to the African Charter on Human and Peoples' Rights on the Rights of Women in Africa (Maputo, 13 September 2000, entered into force 25 November 2005, OAU Doc CAB/LEG/66.6) art 5 (outlines measures required to eliminate harmful practices including female genital mutilation); *Special Rapporteur on Violence against Women: Cultural Practices in the Family that are Violent towards Women* (n 1) paras 120–32 (makes several recommendations to address cultural violence towards women and girls); Mohamud and others (n 84) (recommendations based on comprehensive assessment of the available literature); *European Parliament Resolution on Female Genital Mutilation* (n 76) (provides detailed set of recommendations); Gruenbaum (n 78) (assesses impact of various agents for change including legislation, advocacy, and international human rights movement); A Rahman and N Toubia, *Female Genital Mutilation: A Guide to Laws and Policies Worldwide* (Zed Books, 2000); L Shaaban and S Harbison, 'Reaching the Tipping Point against Female Genital Mutilation' (2005) 366 The Lancet 347; Skaine (n 80); Toubia and Sharief (n 87) (stresses need to ensure investments in psychological and economic empowerment of women); Ford (n 80) (emphasizes need for dialogue).

[89] See, eg, CO CRC Uganda (n 31) para 56; CO CRC Nigeria (n 32) para 58; CO CRC Liberia, UN Doc CRC/C/15/Add.236 (1 July 2004) para 53; CO CRC Eritrea (n 31) para 46; CO CRC Niger (n 30) para 53; CO CRC Côte d'Ivoire (n 30) para 45; CO CRC Sierra Leone, UN Doc CRC/C/15/Add.116 (24 February 2000) para 62.

[90] See, eg, *Plan of Action for the Elimination of Harmful Traditional Practices affecting the Health of Women and Children* (n 25) para A(3); Protocol to the African Charter on Human and Peoples' Rights on the Rights of Women in Africa, art 5(b); *European Parliament Resolution on Female Genital Mutilation* (n 76) para 11; *Further Actions and Initiatives to Implement the Beijing Declaration and Platform for Action*, GA Res S-23/3, UN Doc A/RES/S-23/3 (16 November 2000) para 69(e).

[91] See, eg, *Special Rapporteur on Violence against Women: Cultural Practices in the Family that are Violent towards Women* (n 1) para 125; Mohamud and others (n 84) 14–16; A Magied and others, 'Midwives, Traditional Birth Attendants and the Perpetuation of Female Genital Mutilation in Sudan' (2003) 20 Ahfad J 38; WHO, *Female Genital Mutilation: A Joint WHO/UNICEF/UNFPA Statement* (n 88) 13.

[92] It is interesting to note that the need for legislative measures to prohibit female circumcision is conspicuously absent from *General Recommendation No 14* (n 29) of the CEDAW Committee. It is however present in its *General Recommendation No 24* (n 71) para 16(e), where the Committee also refers to female genital mutilation rather than circumcision as it did in *General Recommendation No 14*.

[93] Rogers (n 86).

[94] Mohamud and others (n 84) 14; WHO, *Female Genital Mutilation: A Joint WHO/UNICEF/UNFPA Statement* (n 88) 15 (notes that legislation against FGM in absence of community-based action is an insufficient and inappropriate strategy).

effective rather than merely tokenistic or indeed potentially harmful if criminalization operates to compound rather than alleviate the harm to girls caused by this practice.

Although the CRC Committee has not expressly acknowledged the limitations and potential dangers associated with the criminalization of female genital cutting, it has, like the CEDAW Committee in its General Recommendation on Female Circumcision,[95] recommended the adoption of several additional measures, which indicates an understanding of the need to adopt a multifaceted strategy. Included in this strategy must be awareness raising[96] and sensitization[97] campaigns that involve health professionals,[98] the media,[99] NGOs,[100] and community leaders[101] as to the nature, scope, and health consequences of female genital cutting. The ultimate aim must be to change the complex and culturally entrenched beliefs on traditional harmful practices such as this—the so-called 'mental map'[102]—that not only tolerate but ensure that communities maintain this practice. As a WHO report on the practice notes:

> strong enforcement mechanisms have been put in place by communities. These include rejection of women who have not undergone FGM as marriage partners, immediate divorce for unexcised women, derogatory songs, . . . instillation of fear of unknown through curses and evocation of ancestral wrath. On the other hand, girls who undergo FGM are provided with rewards, including public recognition and celebrations, gifts, potential for marriage, respect and the ability to participate in adult social functions.[103]

In light of these deeply embedded cultural enforcement mechanisms, legal prohibition can become a blunt and ineffective tool in addressing the phenomenon of female genital cutting. Education through awareness raising and sensitization campaigns based on dialogue, community participation,[104] and cultural respect, rather than shame and punishment are therefore seen as necessary and complementary measures by which to develop the understanding necessary to support the legitimacy of a legal prohibition with respect to the practice.[105] According to the CRC Committee, such

---

[95] CEDAW Committee, *General Recommendation No 14* (n 29).

[96] See, eg, CO CRC Uganda (n 31) para 56; CO CRC Nigeria (n 32) para 58; CO CRC Togo (n 34) para 57; CO CR Eritrea (n 31) para 46.

[97] See, eg, CO CRC Uganda (n 31) para 56; CO CRC Liberia UN Doc CRC/C/15/Add.236 (1 July 2004) para 53; CO CRC Cote d'Ivoire (n 30) para 45.

[98] CEDAW Committee, *General Recommendation No 14* (n 29) (stresses the special responsibility of health personnel to explain the harmful effects of female circumcision); American Academy of Pediatrics 'Policy Statement—Ritual Genital Cutting of Minors' (2010) 125 Pediatrics 1088.

[99] See, eg, CO CRC Togo (n 34) para 57. For a discussion of the role of the media, see Mohamud and others (n 84) 47.

[100] See, eg, CO CRC Eritrea (n 31) para 46.

[101] See, eg, ibid.

[102] Mohamud and others (n 84) 4–6.

[103] ibid 1.

[104] Ford (n 80).

[105] Mohamud and others (n 84) 14; L Bitong, 'Fighting Genital Mutilation in Sierra Leone' (2005) 83 Bull WHO 806 (details effectiveness of mass literacy and education campaigns); Toubia and Sharief (n 87) (notes that general improvement in literacy among women has been found to reduce the incidence of the practice).

education campaigns must be aimed at not only the general public but the specific audiences that are intimately connected with the performance and continuation of the practice such as the practitioners who perform the practice,[106] families, and religious leaders.[107]

Interesting is the CRC Committee's apparent failure to specifically and repeatedly recommend that states raise awareness and develop an understanding of the practice among young people themselves. This is a curious omission given that studies indicate that adolescents are more likely to disapprove of the practice than their parents and should be seen as key agents in changing beliefs and attitudes.[108] Also absent from the recommendations of the CRC Committee with respect to education, is an obligation to undertake research to determine the existence and causes of female genital cutting. The CEDAW Committee has however recommended collection and dissemination of data about the practice by universities and medical bodies.[109] Such data will vary between and within jurisdictions and although inextricably linked to gender inequality the practice is often tied to religion, rituals, marriage, social status, sexuality, socio-economic status, ethnicity, and cultural beliefs about women's bodies.[110] The research suggests that data collection with respect to these matters is critical to ensure that any response is tailored to local needs and cultural values.[111]

At the same time the CRC Committee has recognized that steps must be taken to retrain practitioners, provide them with an alternative source of income,[112] and develop alternative cultural practices that are not prejudicial to the health of a girl.[113]

---

[106] See A Magied and others, 'Midwives, Traditional Birth Attendants and the Perpetuation of Female Genital Mutilation in Sudan' (2003) 20 Ahfad J 38 (explains that early efforts to enlist midwives in the campaign to abolish practice only saw it perpetuated in a medical setting in absence of measures to educate midwifes about the health hazards of the practice and impose penalties for performing such acts).

[107] See, eg, CO CRC Uganda (n 31) para 56; CO CRC Togo (n 34) para 57(c). This approach is consistent with the literature: Mohamud and others (n 84) 40.

[108] ibid 32–3.

[109] CEDAW Committee, *General Recommendation No 14* (n 29).

[110] The causes of the practice are a subject of significant debate especially within the feminist and anthropological literature and a detailed discussion need not be repeated here. See generally Gruenbaum (n 78); Rahman and Toubia (n 88). See also Little (n 78) (examines several cultural beliefs relating to misconceptions about a female's body such as a belief that the clitoris will grow with age or that a baby will die if it touches the clitoris in childbirth); A Magied and others, 'The Impact of Socio Economic Status on the Practice, Perception and Attitudes of Secondary School Girls towards Female Genital Mutilation (FGM)' (2003) 20 Ahfad J 4 (study in Sudan found that girls with parents of lower socio-economic status and lack of education were more likely to be circumcised).

[111] See also CEDAW Committee, *General Recommendation No 14* (n 78) para (a)(i) (recommends 'the collection and dissemination by universities, medical or nursing associations, national women's organisations or other bodies of basic data about such traditional practices'); Mohamud and others (n 84) 52 (discusses need for research to inform programme design); Gruenbaum (n 78) 220–1 (change requires understanding of purpose of the practice including context, motive, and perspective of the practitioners).

[112] See, eg, CO CRC Uganda (n 31) para 56; CO CRC Djibouti (n 30) para 44; CO CRC Niger (n 30) para 53; CO CRC Togo (n 34) para 57. cf Mohamud and others (n 84) 37 (suggests that this should not be the major strategy for change); Shaaban and Harbison (n 88) (warns that such an approach in isolation is not effective as it fails to address community demand for the practice); Toubia and Sharief (n 87) (adds that only appropriate where practice associated with a ritual such as coming of age).

[113] See, eg, CO CRC Sierra Leone (n 89) para 62.

It has also stressed the need to adopt measures to provide support for girls at risk and girls who refuse to undergo this practice and rehabilitation services for those who do[114]—an obligation which is also required under article 39 of the CRC. According to a WHO study, this requires both the 'mainstreaming of FGM prevention issues into national reproductive women's [and adolescent] health and literacy development programmes' and the provision of 'trained staff who can recognise and manage the complications of FGM'.[115]

Importantly commentators[116] and organizations such as the WHO and UNICEF[117] have stressed the need to ensure that this process does not lead to the medicalization of female genital cutting, whereby the performance of the practice in a clinical setting enables the practice to be legitimized and thus thwarts efforts for its elimination. At the same time other commentators have suggested that there is insufficient evidence to support such a staunch position and 'that medicalisation, if implemented as a harm reduction strategy may be a sound and compassionate approach to improving women's health in settings where abandonment of the practice of "circumcision" is not immediately attainable'.[118]

None of the human rights treaty bodies have sought to respond to this concern. However, as a transitional approach it requires careful consideration given that to insist upon a form of zero tolerance with respect to the practice is unlikely to prove to be an effective measure in securing its abolition. Indeed such a strong form of obligation as urged by bodies such as WHO and UNICEF is difficult to reconcile with the need to an adopt an interpretation of article 24(3) which remains not only practical and effective but sensitive to the local context in which the protection against harmful traditional practices is to be achieved. Thus the progressive realization of the obligation to abolish harmful traditional practices would appear to anticipate the adoption of measures that minimize harm to a girl in circumstances where the complete abolition of the practice is not yet feasible given the reality of social and cultural constraints. It is recognized that such a concession is problematic but so too is the insistence on complete prohibition when such a call is being made from outside the community in which the practice is tolerated. The point to stress therefore is that dialogue rather than directives must inform the nature of the measures adopted with respect to the abolition of a practice such as female genital cutting if such measures are to be effective.

This emphasis on dialogue is consistent with the literature which suggests that there is a need to ensure that all stakeholders including children—both female and

---

[114] See, eg, CO CRC Nigeria (n 32) para 58.
[115] Mohamud and others (n 84) 8. See also WHO, *Female Genital Mutilation: The Prevention and the Management of the Health Complications—Policy Guidelines for Nurses and Midwives* (WHO, 2001) 13.
[116] See, eg, C Derby, 'The Case against the Medicalization of Female Genital Mutilation' (2004) 24 Canadian Woman Studies 95; British Medical Association, 'Female Genital Mutilation: Caring for Patients and Children Protection—Guidance from the Ethics Department' (BMA, 2006) para 2.5.
[117] WHO *Female Genital Mutilation: A Joint WHO/UNICEF/UNFPA Statement* (n 88) 14; WHO, *Female Genital Mutilation: The Prevention and the Management of the Health Complications* (n 115) 13.
[118] B Shell-Duncan, 'The Medicalization of Female "Circumcision": Harm Reduction or Promotion of a Dangerous Practice' (2001) 52 Soc Sci & Med 1013.

male[119]—must be included in the design, implementation, and evaluation of programmes to eliminate female genital cutting.[120] Indeed a policy that is participatory in design and implementation is critical not only for its effectiveness and sustainability but also necessary to avoid the imposition of measures in a colonial or ethnocentric manner—an issue that has long plagued responses to female genital cutting.[121] This is not to say that states should not call upon the expertise and assistance of other states and international institutions. Indeed the CRC Committee has emphasized the need for states to draw on the experience of other states in identifying effective measures to eliminate this practice;[122] and to cooperate with other states through bilateral and multilateral initiatives[123] and with organizations such as DAW, the division for the Advancement of Women, and UNICEF.[124] Rather, such engagement and dialogue must be collaborative in its exchange if it is to ensure that the behaviour modifications required to abolish the practice are not imposed but owned and internalized by local populations.[125]

Moreover the strategies developed must not simply raise awareness about the health implications of female genital cutting but also facilitate discussions as to the means by which to resist the practice.[126] Importantly, as Neil Ford, UNICEF's regional advisor for Programme Communication in Eastern and Southern Africa has argued, the objective must be to move beyond the tendency to prescribe 'expert driven solutions... to helping communities develop their own solution'.[127] According to Ford this requires a shift from the use of behaviour change communication strategies which emphasize directive communication towards the attainment of goals set by the 'experts' to a communication strategy based on human rights principles. Such an approach rests on the principles of participation, self-determination, and

---

[119] WHO, *Female Genital Mutilation: A Joint WHO/UNICEF/UNFPA Statement* (n 88) 15 (stresses the need to enlist men's participation so that as women's attitudes begin to change they find support among brothers, fathers, friends, and partners).

[120] See, eg, Mohamud and others (n 84) 29–30; Ford (n 80) (proposes a model of communication based on human rights principles of self determination, participation, and inclusion).

[121] See Ford (n 80) 187 (examines how behaviour change communication strategies remain dominant model in public health but that such a process, while allowing for participation, is directive in the sense that it does not allow participants to influence the objectives or agenda of the strategy; thus advocates a human rights communication strategy which is considered to be non-directive to the extent that participants influence and own the process and its implementation).

[122] See, eg, CO CRC Djibouti (n 30) para 44. For an evaluation of various preventive measures see Mohamud and others (n 84).

[123] See, eg, Protocol to the African Charter on Human and Peoples' Rights on the Rights of Women, art 5, which lists the obligations of State with respect to the elimination of harmful practices. See also *European Parliament Resolution on Female Genital Mutilation* (n 76).

[124] See, eg, CO CRC Togo (n 34) para 57(f).

[125] See Toubia and Sharief (n 87) 256 (highlights the need for trust between insiders and outsiders and importance of local ownership); Ford (n 80) 185 (provides discussion of the means by which outside specialists can communicate effectively with local population groups).

[126] Ford (n 80) 185 (makes the point that many awareness-raising strategies provide knowledge but fail to deliver guidance as to the means by which to act on such knowledge and resist the strong cultural preference for female circumcision).

[127] ibid 188.

inclusion and aims to facilitate the involvement of local communities in the determination of the goals to be set and the means by which achieve them.[128]

V Conclusion—the need for a culturally sensitive approach

In late 2006, an Ethiopian immigrant to the USA was sentenced to 10 years imprisonment when he was found guilty of aggravated battery and cruelty to a child after using scissors to remove his daughter's clitoris. The decision, which was the first of its kind in the USA, was hailed by a US women's rights group as a victory against female genital 'mutilation' worldwide. As the jury verdict was being read, the father wept loudly, denied the charges, and said that he found the practice to be reprehensible.[129]

The obligation to abolish harmful traditional practices is designed to capture such a practice and the prosecution of a father for inflicting such harm on his daughter is a measure anticipated as being within the scope of a state's obligations under this provision. But the tears and protestations of the father reveal the need for a broader and more nuanced approach to be taken by states if they are to ensure the effective abolition of harmful traditional practices. They raise a question as to whether a prosecutorial approach to female genital cutting, and indeed any other harmful practice, will be truly effective in the absence of a program that seeks to engage with and educate members of the relevant communities as to the harm of such a practice and the existence of alternatives. Had such an approach been adopted in this case, there is every prospect (although no guarantee) that the little girl may have avoided both the physical harm inflicted by her father and the harm caused by his imprisonment and subsequent absence from family life for 10 years. This is the type of approach which article 24(3) of the CRC demands if states are to fulfil their obligation to ensure the effective abolition of harmful traditional practices.

It requires awareness that the identification of what amounts to a harmful traditional practice will be influenced by cultural values and other subjective considerations such as the construction of gender. It requires recognition that a focus on the biomedical impact of a traditional practice to the exclusion of the cultural and social context in which that practices takes place will always be inadequate. This does not mean that states must adopt an entirely relativist notion in identifying the harm to a child's health as this would defeat the underlying purpose of the obligation to abolish harmful traditional practices. But it does carry significant consequences in terms of both the extent to which harmful traditional practices can be identified within a particular community and the measures required to ensure abolition of their harmful effects.

---

[128] ibid 188–9 (outlines three generic steps for this process: giving a voice to both the voiceless, such as girls, and the powerful, such as community leaders; facilitating community dialogue on the rights and responsibilities of all community members; and building communication channels between communities and Governments to enable support for community initiatives).

[129] 'Female Genital Mutilation: Father Jailed in United States', *CRIN List Serve* (2 November 2006).

In terms of these measures the discussion concerning female genital cutting indicates that they are often designed with an absence of sufficient cultural and social sensitivity. This is reflected in an overemphasis on legislative measures and expert driven solutions that do not take sufficient account of the need to adopt a strategy that engages with the actual communities that undertake the harmful practices. The need to facilitate a dialogue among all relevant actors therefore emerges as the critical mechanism by which to not only understand but generate the measures required to abolish harmful traditional practices. Anything less is unlikely to shift the culturally entrenched beliefs that allow for the continuation of such practices and their attendant prejudice to the health of children and adults alike.

9

The International Obligation to Secure the Right to Health

I Introduction

In international law a state has the primary responsibility for securing the realization of the right to health for the individuals within its jurisdiction.[1] But this goal cannot be achieved in the absence of international co-operation. As the WHO has declared, 'health is a shared responsibility, involving equitable access to essential care and collective defence against transnational threats'.[2] Moreover, as the Committee on Economic, Social and Cultural Rights (ESC Committee) has explained, 'formidable structural and other obstacles resulting from international and other factors beyond the control of states... impede the full realisation of' the right to health.[3] States are cognisant of these realities and at the World Summit on the MDGs in September 2005, 170 states made a commitment 'to improve health systems in developing countries and those with economies in transition with the aim of providing sufficient health workers, infrastructure, management systems and supplies to achieve the health related Millennium Development Goals by 2015'.[4] Beyond this political commitment, however, there is also an explicit legal obligation on states in international law to co-operate for the purpose of securing the right to health.

This obligation arises by virtue of article 2(1) of the International Covenant on Economic, Social and Cultural Rights (ICESCR), which provides that states parties 'undertake to take steps, individually and *through international assistance and cooperation*, especially economic and technical' to progressively realize all economic and

---

[1] See Convention on the Rights of the Child (CRC) (New York, 20 November 1989, entered into force 2 September 1990, 1577 UNTS 3) art 2(1) ('States Parties shall respect and ensure the rights set forth in the present Convention to each child within their jurisdiction...'). There is no equivalent provision under the ICESCR. However, the ICJ has held that the Covenant 'guarantees rights which are essentially territorial': *Legal Consequences of the Construction of a Wall in the Occupied Palestinian Territory (Advisory Opinion)* [2004] ICJ Rep 136 [112]. See also Sigrun Skogly, *Beyond National Borders: States' Human Rights Obligations in their International Cooperation* (Intersentia, 2006) 138.

[2] WHO, 'About WHO' <http://www.who.int/about/en/> accessed 14 April 2011. See also UN Secretary-General, *Global Strategy for Women's and Children's Health* (2010).

[3] ESC Committee, *General Comment No 14: The Right to the Highest Attainable Standard of Health*, UN Doc E/C/12/2000/4 (11 August 2000) para 5.

[4] *2005 World Summit Outcome*, GA Res 60/1, UN Doc A/RES/60/1(24 October 2005) para 57(a).

social rights including the right to health.[5] This general obligation is confirmed in article 4 of the CRC, albeit by way of a slightly different formulation, which requires states parties to take all appropriate measures to realize the rights, including health, 'within the framework of international co-operation.'[6] Within the context of the right to health, the CRC further provides under article 24(4) that:

States Parties undertake to *promote* and *encourage* international co-operation with a view to achieving progressively the full realization of the right recognized in the present article. In this regard particular account shall be taken of the needs of developing countries. (emphasis added)

The meaning of this international obligation, which is sometimes referred to as an extraterritorial obligation,[7] a third state obligation,[8] a shared responsibility,[9] or a collective obligation[10]—has remained contested and elusive. Moreover, despite its significance to the enjoyment of the right to health, it has been received limited attention within this context.[11] The aim of this chapter is to address this gap and

---

[5] International Covenant on Economic, Social and Cultural Rights (ICESCR) (New York, 16 December 1966, entered into force 3 January 1976, 993 UNTS 3).

[6] The Convention on the Rights of Persons with Disabilities (CERD) (New York, 30 March 2007, entered into force 3 May 2008, 660 UNTS 195) art 4(2) adopts the same formulation. The African Charter on Human and Peoples' Rights (African Charter) (Bunjil Charter) (Nairobi, 27 June 1981, entered into force 21 October 1986) 1520 UNTS 217) art 21(3) states that the free disposal of natural resources shall not infringe on the 'obligation of promoting international economic cooperation based on mutual respect, equitable exchanges and the principles of international law'. The American Convention on Human Rights (Pact of San José, Costa Rica) (American Convention) (San José, 22 November 1969, entered into force 18 July 1978, 1144 UNTS 123) art 26 on progressive development requires states 'to adopt measures, both internally and through international cooperation, especially those of an economic or technical nature, with a view to achieving progressively... the full realization of the rights implicit in the economic, social, economic, scientific and cultural standards'. The Additional Protocol to the American Convention on Human Rights in the Area of Economic, Social and Cultural Rights (Protocol of San Salvador) (San Salvador, 17 November 1988, entered into force 16 November 1999, OAS Treaty Series No 69 (1988), 28 ILM 156) art 1 obligates states parties to 'adopt the necessary measures, both domestically and through international cooperation, especially economic and technical, to the extent allowed by their available resources, and taking into account their degree of development, for the purpose of achieving progressively and pursuant to their internal legislations, the full observance of the rights recognized in this Protocol'; art 12(2) provides that states 'agree to promote greater international cooperation' in order to 'improve methods of production, supply and distribution of food'; art 14(4) acknowledges that states 'recognize the benefits to be derived from the encouragement and development of international cooperation and relations in the fields of science, arts and culture, and accordingly agree to foster greater international cooperation in these fields'.

[7] See, eg, Skogly (n 1).

[8] See, eg, Wouter Vandenhole, 'Economic Social and Cultural Rights in the CRC: Is there a Legal Obligation to Cooperate Internationally for Development' (2009) 17 Int'l J Child Rts 23, 25.

[9] See, eg, Margot Salomon, *Global Responsibility for Human Rights: World Poverty and the Development of International Law* (OUP, 2007).

[10] ibid 6, 182.

[11] See, eg, CRC Committee, *Report of the Forty-Sixth Session*, UN Doc CRC/C/46/3 (22 April 2008) ch VII, paras 91–3 (Day of General Discussion on 'Resources for the Rights of the Child—Responsibility of States', 5 October 2007); Brigit Toebes, *The Right to Health as a Human Right in International Law* (Hart Publishing, 1999) 138–9 (allocates four paragraphs in her examination of the obligation of international co-operation and assistance as it relates to the right to health); Geraldine Van Bueren, *The International Law on the Rights of the Child* (Martinus Nijhoff, 1995) 294–7; Sharon Detrick, *A Commentary on the United Nations Convention on the Rights of the Child* (Martinus Nijhoff, 1999)

examine the nature of a state's international obligation with respect to the realization of the right to health. The overarching conclusion to be drawn is that although the 'parameters of international assistance and cooperation are not yet fully drawn',[12] it remains possible to articulate 'a convincing account' as to the scope of the obligation 'in order to articulate its concrete implications' for states with respect to the areas and means by which co-operation should take place.[13]

Part II of this Chapter provides an examination of the nature and scope of the international obligation to co-operate and reveals that this obligation consists of three discrete obligations—an obligation to take reasonable measures subject to available resources to *respect, protect,* and *fulfil* the right to health of individuals in other states. Part III involves an application of these obligations to a case study, namely access to medicines and the TRIPS regime, to assess the legitimacy of a state's involvement in this regime. It concludes that, on balance, involvement in TRIPS does not necessarily violate the *respect* and *protect* elements of a state's international obligation to secure the right to health. But this regime is not an effective mechanism by which to facilitate access to medicines in developing states and the international obligation to *fulfil* the right to health requires that states must make bona fide efforts to develop a complementary system which is more likely to achieve this end.

II The nature and scope of the international obligation to co-operate

A A vision of qualified solidarity

The acceptance of an international obligation to co-operate for the purpose of protecting global health can be traced to the international sanitation conferences which began in the 1850s.[14] These conferences led to the creation of the *Office International d'Hygiene Publique* in 1907 and the League of Nations (LON) Health

---

419–20; Asbjørn Eide and Wenche Barth Eide, *A Commentary on the United Nations Convention on the Rights of the Child: Article 24:—the Right to Health* (Martinus Nijhoff, 2006) 48–51; Katarina Tomasevski, 'Health Rights' in Asbjørn Eide, Catarina Krause, and Allan Rosas (eds), *Economic, Social, and Cultural Rights: A Textbook* (Martinus Nijhoff, 1995) 125; Lawrence Gostin, 'Meeting Basic Survival Needs of the World's Least Healthy People: Toward a Framework Convention on Global Health' (2008) 96 Geo LJ 330, 382 (dismisses the significance of the obligation because of his perception that there is no systematic mechanism for implementation and enforcement). For a more detailed account see: Salomon (n 9) ch 2; Skogly (n 1) chs 4, 6, which both provide an examination as to nature of the obligation to co-operate generally as opposed to its relevance in the context of the right to health). See also *Report of the Special Rapporteur on the Right to Health to the General Assembly 2005*, UN Doc A/60/348 (12 September 2005) paras 59–65 (provides general overview of the obligation to co-operate in the context of health); (2010) 12 Health & Hum Rts (provides series of articles on international assistance and co-operation in the context of health).

[12] ibid para 60.

[13] Allen Buchanan and David Golove, 'The Philosophy of International Law' in Jules Coleman and Scott Shapiro (eds), *The Oxford Handbook of Jurisprudence and Philosophy of Law* (OUP, 2002) 868, 906 (posit this dilemma with respect to the scope of a non-interactionist approach to international distributive justice which seeks to require persons to refrain from violating the rights of others while also working to ensure access to institutions to protect rights).

[14] See Chapter 1.

Organization in 1920, both of which were largely designed for instrumentalist reasons, namely, to stop the spread of communicable diseases. Indeed, the mandate for the LON Health Organization was based on article 23 of the LON Covenant, which required the League to 'take steps in matters of international concern for the prevention and control of disease'.

Within the context of contemporary international human rights law, the international obligation to co-operate can be traced to the collective ideals on which the UN system is based. For example, article 1 of the UN Charter lists as one of the purposes of the UN, 'To achieve international cooperation in solving international problems of an economic, social, cultural or humanitarian character...'. Article 56 of the UN Charter also requires that all members take joint and separate action to achieve the purposes set out in article 55, which includes the promotion and respect of human rights. A similar sentiment informs the text of the UNDR. For example, article 22 provides that 'Everyone... is entitled to realization, through national effort and international cooperation... of the economic, social and cultural rights indispensable for his (sic) dignity and free development of his (sic) personality' and article 28 states that '[e]veryone is entitled to a social and international order in which the rights and freedoms set forth in this Declaration can be fully realized'.

The inclusion of the international obligation to co-operate under the UN Charter and UDHR was also motivated, in part, by instrumentalist considerations, namely the need to maintain international peace and security.[15] However, the drafting of these instruments was also underlined by a genuine moral commitment—albeit incompletely theorized[16]—to protect human rights, and international co-operation was recognized as being essential to the achievement of this objective. The international obligation to co-operate therefore reflects what Bruno Simma has described as the maturing of international law into a 'much more socially conscious legal order',[17] which seeks to meet the needs of a community that extends beyond nation states to include human beings.[18]

But the drafting history of the ICESCR indicates that this maturity had its limits. States recognized that international assistance would have to be provided to developing states if they were to realize the rights under the draft Covenant.[19] However, as Alston and Quinn have explained, this 'consensus... did not extend much, if at all, beyond' this general proposition.[20] It is true that during the drafting of the ICESCR, several states sought to convert the moral imperative underlying the need for co-operation into a binding and specific legal obligation. However, this move was

---

[15] See Chapter 1.   [16] See Chapter 2.
[17] Bruno Simma, 'From Bilateralism to Community Interest in International Law' (1994) 250 RCADI 217, 224, 234.
[18] See also David Fidler, 'Fighting the Axis of Illness: HIV/AIDS, Human Rights and Foreign Policy' (2004) 17 Harv Hum Rts J 99, 108–9 (discusses this transformation as shift to a post-Westphalian governance structure).
[19] For a detailed analysis of the drafting history see Philip Alston and Gerard Quinn, 'The Nature and Scope of States Parties' Obligations under the International Covenant on Economic, Social and Cultural Rights' (1987) 2 Hum Rts Q 156, 186–92.
[20] ibid 189.

resisted in equal measure by other states. Thus, Alston and Quinn have concluded that, 'on the basis of the preparatory work it is difficult is not impossible, to sustain the argument that the commitment to international cooperation contained in the Covenant can accurately be characterized as a legally binding obligation upon a particular state to provide *any form of assistance*'.[21]

In contrast to the drafting of the ICESCR, the discussions around the inclusion of the international obligation to co-operate during the drafting of the CRC were relatively uncontroversial.[22] One possible explanation is that, given the history of negotiations for the ICESCR, states were not burdened by any expectation that the inclusion of the international obligation in the CRC would require the provision of specific forms of assistance to other states. There was some discussion as to 'whether this idea of international co-operation should be included in the [right to health] ... or if it should be the subject of a general article of the Convention'—the approach adopted under the ICESCR.[23] Although 'widely divergent views' were held with respect to this issue, the final text of article 24 of the CRC indicates that this debate was ultimately resolved in favour of the inclusion of a specific paragraph on international co-operation within the right to health.[24] However, the drafting history of the CRC fails to offer any insights that might advance our understanding of the precise nature and scope of the obligation to co-operate beyond a requirement that states must 'promote and encourage' such co-operation. Thus, the meaning of this phrase remains an open question.

B The obligation to promote and encourage co-operation under the CRC

The obligation to 'promote and encourage' international co-operation with respect to the realization of the right to health under article 24(4) of the CRC is a curious inclusion. It also appears in relation to the right to education under article 28(3) of the CRC but is not found in any other enumeration of the obligation to co-operate under other international instruments.[25] The closest expression is that found in article 1(3) of the United Nations Charter (UNC) which lists the purposes of the United Nations (UN) to include '*promoting* and *encouraging* respect for human rights and for fundamental freedoms for all...'. In contrast, article 55 of the UNC only requires the UN to *promote*, among other things, human rights and solutions of international health problems. Similarly, para 3 of article 23 of the CRC, which deals with the rights of children with disabilities, only requires states to *promote* co-operation.

---

[21] ibid 191 (emphasis added).
[22] Skogly (n 1) 102.
[23] Article 2 of the ICESCR provides that '[e]ach state party... undertakes to take steps, individually *and through international assistance and co-operation*...' (emphasis added).
[24] Commission on Human Rights, *Question of a Convention on the Rights of the Child: Report of the Working Group on a Draft Convention on the Rights of the Child*, UN Doc E/CN.4/1985/64 (3 April 1985) para 36.
[25] See generally Salomon (n 11) ch 2 (examines the sources of co-operation for human rights in international law).

It is unclear from the drafting history of the CRC why the obligation to 'encourage' was included in the right to health and it is probably best characterized as an unintended drafting innovation. It is also unclear how the inclusion of the obligation to 'encourage' would extend or add anything to the obligation to 'promote'. There is no commentary with respect to the inclusion of the term 'encourage' in the UNC which would suggest that it has a discrete sphere of meaning relative to the obligation to 'promote'. Thus, it would seem appropriate to interpret the ordinary meaning of the obligation to 'encourage' as being largely synonymous with the obligation to 'promote', at least for the purposes of para 4 of article 24.

With respect to the content of this obligation to 'promote' there were no discussions during drafting as to its meaning. However, the drafting history reveals that the adoption of this phrase under article 23 of the CRC came as a result of objections to the suggestion that states be under an obligation to 'guarantee' international co-operation[26]—a concern that was also present during the drafting of article 2(1) of the ICESCR. Thus, it is reasonable to extend this explanation to para 4 of article 24, which suggests that the intention was that states should not be taken to have an obligation to *actually achieve* international co-operation. As such, it represents an obligation of *conduct rather than result*—an interpretation that is not only principled but practical given that a result obligation would be inappropriate due to the fact that the realization of such an objective is contingent on the actions of other states.

The drafting history concerning the inclusion of the obligation to 'promote' in the UNC is also instructive as to the scope of this term as it appears in the CRC. There was concern that an obligation to 'promote' would provide the UN with the power to interfere in the domestic affairs of member states. In order to allay this worry the Commission responsible for drafting the UN formally adopted the interpretation that the provision could not be 'construed as giving authority to the UN to intervene in the domestic affairs of member States'.[27] Thus, an application of the principle of external system coherence to the interpretation of the obligation to *promote* co-operation under article 24(4) of the CRC, suggests that this obligation should not be taken as authorizing unilateral intervention in the domestic affairs of another state.

Unfortunately, the commentary on the nature of the obligation to 'promote' under the UNC does not offer any further insights into the substantive nature of this obligation. However, far from being 'meaningless' and 'redundant'—terms which have been used to describe the obligation of states under article 56 of the UNC to co-operate with the UNC[28]—the obligation to promote and encourage co-operation under article 24(4) of the CRC is capable of being given substantive

---

[26] See Commission on Human Rights, *Question of a Convention on the Rights of the Child: Report of the Working Group on a Draft Convention on the Rights of the Child*, UN Doc E/CN.4/1983/62 (25 March 1983) paras 82–3.

[27] Rüdiger Wolfrum, 'Article 55(a) and (b)' in Bruno Simma (ed), *The Charter of the United Nations: A Commentary* (2nd edn, OUP, 2002) 897, 900.

[28] See Rüdiger Wolfrum, 'Article 56' in Bruno Simma (ed), *The Charter of the United Nations: A Commentary* (2nd edn, OUP, 2002) 941, 942.

content. At the most abstract level, an application of the ordinary rules of interpretation suggests that if the obligation to 'promote and encourage' is to be performed in good faith, it requires that states take every reasonable measure subject to their available resources and capacities to facilitate effective international co-operation with respect to the right to health.[29]

C A tripartite international obligation

The preceding statement as to the nature of the obligation to promote and encourage international co-operation is unlikely to be controversial given its high level of abstraction—the acceptance of a proposition is made easier when it does not embrace any obvious and discrete measures that states are required to undertake. At the same time, the generality of this statement permits such a wide margin of appreciation for states that it carries the real prospect that the obligation will be rendered meaningless. The challenge, therefore, is to articulate a vision of the obligation to promote and encourage international co-operation that is able to demonstrate its 'concrete implications'[30] for the behaviour of states. It is suggested that the features of the interpretative methodology used in this analysis are capable of producing such a vision. More specifically it is suggested that an interpretation of the obligation to promote and encourage international co-operation that is principled, practical, coherent, and context sensitive should be seen to consist of three obligations for states with respect to the right to health:

- an obligation to refrain, to the extent that it is reasonably practicable to do so, from measures that undermine the actual or potential enjoyment of a person's right to health in another state;
- an obligation to prevent, to the extent that it is reasonably practicable to do so, non-state actors from threatening the enjoyment of the right to health for individuals in another state; and
- an obligation to take measures, both individually and collectively, to the extent that it is reasonably practicable, to assist (directly or indirectly) another state realize the right to health for individuals in that other state.

The use of this typology represents a form of coherence with the tripartite typology to respect, protect, and fulfil the right to health *within* a state (the *internal* obligation with respect to the right to health) as a means by which to assist in understanding the discrete duties that are part of the obligation to promote and encourage international co-operation.[31] It is recognized that elements of this model

---

[29] Richard Gardiner, *Treaty Interpretation* (OUP, 2008) 151 (good faith includes the principle of effective interpretation).

[30] Buchanan and Golove (n 13) 906.

[31] See Matthew Craven, *The International Covenant on Economic Social and Cultural Rights: A Perspective on its Development* (Clarendon Press, 1995) 147 (also advocates this typology with respect to the general obligation to undertake international co-operation and assistance under the ICESCR); Manisuli Ssenyonjo, *Economic, Social and Cultural Rights in International Law* (Hart, 2009) para 2.48–2.54.

will be controversial especially with respect to the obligation to provide assistance.[32] However, the failure to extend such a model to relations *between* states would severely compromise the effective implementation of the right to health, especially in developing states.

1 The international obligation to respect the right to health

Geoffrey Warnock, in *The Object of Morality*, opined that part of the 'human predicament' is that every individual stands outside the limited scope of ethical concern of many other communities and as a consequence is vulnerable to their injurious behaviour.[33] It was on this basis that he sought to justify the extension of the liberal harm principle to international relations. In Warnock's mind, just as the actions of an autonomous individual must not cause harm to other individuals, so too must the actions of a sovereign state not cause harm to another state. In a similar vein the ESC Committee in its General Comment on the Right to Health declared that state parties must 'respect the enjoyment of the right to health in other countries'.[34] This international obligation to *respect* the right to health reflects Warnock's concern in that it imposes a legal obligation on states to take reasonable measures to ensure that the consequences of their actions are not harmful to the health of persons in jurisdictions other than their own. Put simply, it demands a cognisance among states of the consequences of their actions beyond the sphere of their own jurisdiction. As the Special Rapporteur on the Right to Health has explained, 'international assistance and cooperation require that all those [states] in a position to assist should, first, refrain from acts that make it more difficult for the poor to realise their right to health'.[35] Implicit in this assertion is an extension of the liberal version of the harm principle to states in their relationship within the international context and the impact of their acts on the right to health in jurisdictions other than their own.[36]

In terms of the precise nature of this obligation, the treaty bodies are yet to address this issue. It should not, however, be interpreted to impose an absolute obligation in the sense that any action taken by a state that has a negative impact on the health of

---

[32] See CRC Committee, *Report of the Forty-Sixth Session* (n 11) para 91.

[33] Geoffrey James Warnock, *The Object of Morality* (Methuen 1971) 87, 150.

[34] ESC Committee, *General Comment No 14* (n 3) para 39.

[35] *Report of the Special Rapporteur on the Right to Health to the General Assembly 2004*, UN Doc A/59/422 (8 October 2004) para 33.

[36] Andrew Linklater, 'The Harm Principle and Global Ethics' (2006) 20 Global Society 329 (explores the adoption of the harm principle in international conventions and although he limits the notion of harm to the infliction of serious bodily or mental harm, it is suggested in this thesis that the international duty to respect health represents a broader notion of harm). See also: *The Rainbow Warrior (New Zealand v France)* (1990) 82 ILR 449 (France–New Zealand Arbitration Tribunal) (affirms the general principle of international law that states are under an obligation not to cause harm outside their territory); *Responsibility of States for Internationally Wrongful Acts*, GA Res 56/83, UN Doc A/RES/56/83 (12 December 2001) annex, arts 30–1 (stating that any state responsible for an internationally wrongful act is under an obligation to cease the act, guarantee non-repetition, and to make full reparation for the injury caused by the act, including both material and moral damage).

an individual in another state is necessarily a violation of the international obligation to respect to the right to health.[37] This 'causal thesis'[38] is inappropriate because it imposes an excessive burden on states and is unlikely to satisfy the requirement of global context sensitivity. Instead, the test to determine whether a state has complied with its obligation should involve the following assessment—did the state, to the extent that it was reasonably practicable in light of its available resources and the totality of its obligations under international law (including the obligation to fulfil the rights of individuals within its own jurisdiction), refrain from measures that undermined the actual or potential enjoyment of a person's right to health in another state? This test is more practicable than a strict liability test and although it reduces the burden on states, they still carry the burden of demonstrating that any actions that undermine the health of individuals in another jurisdiction can be justified as being reasonable in the circumstances.[39]

There remains a question as to which measures would violate this international obligation to respect the right to health. It is beyond the scope, and indeed unnecessary for the purposes of this analysis to detail what these measures might be. However, the work of the ESC Committee suggests that states must examine both the *direct* and *indirect* consequences of their actions on the health of individuals in another jurisdiction. With respect to the impact of direct actions, for example, it has explained that 'State parties should *refrain at all times* from imposing embargoes or similar measures restricting the supply of another State with adequate medicines and medical equipment. Restrictions on such goods should never be used as instruments of political and economic pressure'.[40] But this proposition is problematic to the extent that it implies an absolute prohibition on sanctions and similar measures. A more nuanced approach should be preferred in which a state that undertakes such measures must carry the burden of demonstrating how they were reasonable in the circumstances.

The same rationale extends to the prohibition against indirect measures harmful to the health of an individual. The practical identification of such measures will invariably be more contentious. As a minimum, however, the ESC Committee has recommended that 'State parties should ensure that the right to health is given *due attention* in international agreements and... take steps to ensure that these agreements do not adversely impact upon the right to health'.[41] The ESC Committee has also stressed that states must ensure that their participation in the decision-making process of bodies such as the IMF, World Bank, and WTO must also *take into account* their obligations with respect to the realization of human rights including the

---

[37] See Ssenyonjo (n 31) 73.
[38] Julio Montero, 'Global Poverty, Human Rights and Correlative Duties' (2009) 22 CJLJ 79, 79.
[39] The assessment of reasonableness would involve a consideration of the legitimacy of the aim being pursued by the State and the extent to which the measures used to achieve this aim were necessary and proportionate. See Chapter 5.
[40] ESC Committee, *General Comment No 14* (n 3) para 41. See also ESC Committee, *General Comment No 8: The Relationship between Economic Sanctions and Respect for Economic Social and Cultural Rights*, UN Doc E/C.12/1997/8 (12 December 1997) para 4 (emphasis added).
[41] ESC Committee, *General Comment No 14* (n 3) para 39 (emphasis added).

right to health.⁴² This position is consistent with the requirement of external system coherence. Moreover, it has been affirmed by the Special Rapporteur on the Right to Health who has declared that states must 'ensure that no international agreement or policy adversely impacts upon the right to health [in other jurisdictions] and that their representatives in international organizations take due account of the right to health as well as the obligation of international assistance and co-operation in all policy making matters'.⁴³

These comments invite two observations. First, the ESC Committee and Special Rapporteur have not clarified how the obligation to *'take into account'* or *'take due account'* will be satisfied by a state. Second, their comments give rise to a question as to whether the involvement of states in the existing international financial and trade regimes is consistent with this duty. Both these issues will be explored in more detail in Part III of this Chapter. At this point it is sufficient to note that the requirement to 'take into account' or take 'due account' means that states must pursue harmonization between competing regimes within international law and where an irreconcilable conflict exists, any interference with the right to health must be justified as being reasonable in all the circumstances.⁴⁴ As to whether this duty is currently being satisfied by states three observations are offered. First, there is no compelling evidence to suggest that states have been consciously aware of and/or take seriously the nature of their obligation to take due account of the right to health when engaging with the international system on matters such as trade, investment, and intellectual property.⁴⁵ This is unsurprising given the fragmentation of international law and the reality that the purpose of the trade and human rights regimes are invariably seen as being fundamentally different. As Philip Alston has explained, 'human rights are recognised for all on the basis of the inherent dignity of all persons' whereas 'trade related rights are granted to individuals for instrumentalist reasons'.⁴⁶

---

⁴² See, eg, CO ESC Belgium, UN Doc E/C.12/1/Add.54 (1 December 2000) para 31; CO ESC Japan, UN Doc E/C.12/1/Add.67 (24 September 2001) para 37; CO ESC United Kingdom, UN Doc E/C.12/1/Add.79 (5 June 2002) para 26.

⁴³ *Report of the Special Rapporteur on the Right to Health to the Commission on Human Rights 2003*, UN Doc E/CN.4/2003/58 (13 February 2003) para 28. See also *Report of the Special Rapporteur on the Right to Health to the General Assembly 2005* (n 11) para 63; Human Rights Council, *Access to Medicine in the Context of the Right of Everyone to the Enjoyment of the Highest Attainable Standard of Physical and Mental Health*, Res 12/24, UN Doc A/HRC/RES/12/24 (12 October 2009) para 3 (calling on states to take due account of the right to health in international agreements). Such a position is also consistent with the broader work of some commentators. See, eg, Thomas Pogge, 'Recognised and Violated by International Law: The Human Rights of the Global Poor' (2005) 18 LJIJ 717, 742; Salomon (n 11) 105.

⁴⁴ See Chapter 3 (discussion of fragmentation).

⁴⁵ Robert Howse, 'Human Rights in the WTO: Whose Rights, Whose Humanity? Comment on Petersmann' (2002) 3 EJIL 651, n 7 (notes that at the World Trade Forum in Berne 2001, 'where many of the leading traditional WTO experts gathered to address the question of WTO law and human rights, several of the most eminent of them even questioned whether any human rights were sufficiently well understood or clearly embodied in international law so as to be relevant to the operation of the WTO!'). As will be discussed in Part II of this chapter, there is evidence of a growing awareness that the international IP regime under TRIPS must take into account public health concerns, but this is yet to translate into an awareness and acceptance of a state's international obligation under the right to health.

⁴⁶ Philip Alston, 'Resisting the Merger and Acquisition of Human Rights by Trade Law: A Reply to Petersmann' (2002) 4 EJIL 815, 826. See also David Kinley and Justine Nolan, 'Trading and Aiding

The existence of such a seismic gap in the underlying rationale of each regime does little to encourage attempts to develop any cohesion between human rights law and trade law especially when there is no coercive mechanism to insist upon a reconciliation of the objectives for each regime.

Second, as a consequence of this tension, commentators have identified various aspects of the international system that actually undermine the progressive realization of the right to health.[47] The impact of Trade-Related Aspects of Intellectual Property Rights (TRIPS) on the right to health which has been criticized by a host of human rights bodies, and which will be examined in Part III, is a case in point.[48] Such concerns indicate the existence of a potential disjunction between the practices of states and their obligation, described by the Special Rapporteur on Health as being '... to ensure that the trade rules they select are consistent with their legal obligations in relation to the right to health'[49]—an approach which he refers to as the 'principle of policy coherence'[50] and is described in this analysis as the requirement for external system coherence. In practice, the 'concrete implication' of such an obligation is that it requires states to undertake 'a transparent consideration of the likely impact of trade rules and policies on the enjoyment of the right to health and related human rights ... through a participatory process with concerned individuals and groups'.[51]

Finally, it is important to stress that a global institutional order that promotes the liberalization of international trade, investment, and intellectual property rights is

---

Human Rights: Corporations in the Global Economy' (University of Sydney, Legal Studies Research Paper No 08/13, January 2008) 362 (emphasizing that the interests of TNCs actually drive the international trade regime that is created by states and that human rights are incidental at best in the decisions taken by TNCs whose principal goals are growth and profit maximization); Laurence R Helfer and Graeme W Austin, *Human Rights and Intellectual Property: Mapping the Global Interface* (CUP, 2011) 33 (arguing that principal justification for IP rights 'lies not in deontological claims about the inalienable liberties of human beings but rather economic and instrumental benefits'); Sarah Joseph, *Blame It on the WTO?* (OUP, 2011).

[47] See, eg, Sandra Fredman, *Human Rights Transformed: Positive and Negative Duties* (OUP, 2008) 48–53 (discusses potential for rules of the WTO and TRIPS to undermine protection of human rights); Robert Howse and Makau Mutua, 'Protecting Human Rights in a Global Economy: Challenges for the World Trade Organization' (International Center for Human Rights and Democratic Development, Policy Paper 6, 2000) <http://www.dd-rd.ca/site/_PDF/publications/globalization/wto/protecting_human_rightsWTO.pdf> accessed 25 March 2011; Salomon (n 11) ch 3; *Report of the Special Rapporteur on the Right to Health, on his Mission to the World Trade Organization 2004*, UN Doc E/CN.4/2004/49/Add.1 (1 March 2004).

[48] See, eg, Commission on Human Rights, *Access to Medication in the Context of Pandemics such as HIV/AIDS*, Res 33, UN Doc E/CN.4/RES/2001/33 (20 April 2001); UN Sub-Commission on Promotion and Protection of Human Rights, *Intellectual Property Rights and Human Rights*, Res 21, E/CN.4/SUB.2/RES/2001/21 (16 August 2001).

[49] *Report of the Special Rapporteur on the Right to Health, on his Mission to the World Trade Organization 2004* (n 47) 2.

[50] ibid para 79.

[51] ibid para 53. In this respect the Special Rapporteur has highlighted the need to mainstream gender into trade policy (ibid paras 57–8). But this approach is insufficient with respect to the experience of children who are also at risk of being disproportionately affected by trade policies. As such they must have their experiences and entitlements accounted for in the development and implementation of all policies which impact on their right to health. Such a position is strengthened by the requirement under art 3 of the CRC that the best interests of the child must be a primary consideration in all matters affecting children.

not *necessarily* antithetical or incompatible with the realization of the right to health. Some commentators may seek to justify this position from an ethical or political perspective,[52] but from an international legal perspective the requirement for external system coherence demands harmonization between the human rights regime and those other regimes under international law that form the global institutional order.[53] Of critical concern, however, are the process, content, development, and implementation of such regimes. Thus, if a state chooses to engage in trade or financial liberalization, or any other policies that could potentially impact on the right to health, it must select 'the form, pacing and sequencing of liberalization that is the most conducive to the progressive realization of the right to health for all',[54] which means not just individuals in their own jurisdiction but also within the global context. So, for example, with respect to the General Agreement on Trade in Services, a regime which is designed to achieve the progressive liberalization of trade in services, including health, the Special Rapporteur has stressed 'the importance of a WTO member undertaking a right to health impact assessment before making a commitment to open up the health service sector to international competition'.[55] Moreover, where a policy of trade liberalization is pursued, the CRC Committee has recommended that such a commitment should be monitored as to its impact on the rights of children including their right to health.[56]

Importantly, the practical relevance of the international obligation to respect is not limited to an obligation to avoid the potentially harmful effects on the right to health associated with its participation in the global institutional order. It also extends to other areas in which the actions of a state can indirectly undermine the capacity of another state to secure the right to health in particular. Of principal concern here is the growing practice by developed states to recruit social and professional staff from developing states thereby jeopardizing the capacity of such

---

[52] See, eg, Pogge, 'Human Rights of the Global Poor' (n 43) 722 (argues that such outcomes represent the result of affluent states 'which are ruthlessly advancing their own interests and those of their corporations and their citizens'). cf Debra Satz, 'What Do We Owe the Global Poor?' (2005) 19 EIA 47 (critical of Pogge's failure to sustain an empirical defence of his position); Mathias Risse, 'Do We Owe the Global Poor Assistance or Rectification?' (2005) 19 EIA 19 (argues that far from being fundamentally unjust, the global institutional order has provided a net benefit to the global poor; concedes however that it is 'incompletely just').

[53] Such coherence would not be satisfied by a vision, as advocated by some scholars, that would effectively subsume the human rights enterprise within that of the WTO. See Alston (n 46). Rather greater efforts must be made to focus 'on the ways in which the two separate bodies of law can best be reconciled and made complementary to the greatest extent possible...': 41.

[54] *Report of the Special Rapporteur on the Right to Health, on his Mission to the World Trade Organization 2004* (n 47) para 80. See Christian Salazar Volkmann, 'Children's Rights and the MDGs: The Right to Health within Vietnam's Transition towards a Market Economy' (2006) 9 Health & Hum Rts 56 (review of experience in Vietnam suggests that trade liberalization does not necessarily lead to worse health conditions but poor children benefit less from liberalization and are at greatest risk of further marginalization relative to other groups within society).

[55] *Report of the Special Rapporteur on the Right to Health, on his Mission to the World Trade Organization 2004* (n 47) para 52.

[56] CRC Committee, *Report of the Thirty-First Session*, UN Doc CRC/C/121 (11 December 2002) ch VI, 155 para 13 (Day of General Discussion on 'The Private Sector as Service Provider and Its Role in Implementing Child Rights', 20 September 2002).

states to deliver health care services for persons within their own jurisdiction. The Special Rapporteur on Health has actually suggested that:

> If a developed country actively recruits health professionals in a developing country that is suffering from a shortage of health professionals in such a manner that the recruitment reduces the developing country's capacity to fulfill the right to health obligations that it owes its citizens, the developed country is prima facie in breach of its human rights responsibility of international assistance and co-operation in the context of the right to health.[57]

Such a view represents a particularly strong interpretation of the nature of the international obligation of co-operation and is likely to be the subject of criticism by states. A question therefore exists as to whether it represents a legitimate and defensible interpretation of a state party's obligation to co-operate under the right to health or an unjustified inflation as to the nature of this obligation.

The adoption of overseas recruitment practices will invariably be driven by a genuine and legitimate desire within a developed state to enhance its own capacity to secure the right to health of persons *within* its jurisdiction. However, the existence of an obligation to co-operate internationally represents a clear limitation on the measures that can be undertaken to achieve this purpose. The intention of those states responsible for drafting the right to health was clear—its implementation required international co-operation with the primary beneficiaries of such co-operation to be individuals in developing states. To permit measures that would undermine the realization of this objective would create an absurd result in the interpretation of the right to health. Indeed, the absence of an implied obligation to prohibit such measures would create an effectiveness gap with respect to the implementation of this right. Thus, the views of the Special Rapporteur in relation to the recruitment practices of developed states are both principled and practical and demonstrate that far from being a vague and inherently indeterminate provision, the international obligation to respect the right to health is capable of being given a discrete and operative meaning. In this respect it is also important to note that the World Health Assembly adopted the WHO Code of Practice on the International Recruitment of Health Personnel in 2010.[58] Although this code remains non-binding, it does provide evidence of a growing awareness of the need for states to take measures to refrain from recruitment practices that are harmful to the realization of health in developing countries.

2 The international obligation to protect the right to health

In addition to the obligation to respect the right to health in other states, especially developing countries, it is suggested that states are also under an international obligation to take all reasonable measures to protect the right to health in other states.[59]

---

[57] *Report of the Special Rapporteur on the Right to Health to the General Assembly 2005* (n 11) para 61.
[58] Manuel Dayrit and others, 'WHO Code of Practice on the International Recruitment of Health Personnel' (2008) 86 Bull WHO 737.
[59] Such an obligation is akin to what Cruft refers to as a precautionary duty to ensure that other people are not likely to violate rights: Rowan Cruft, 'Human Rights and Positive Duties' (2005) 19 EIA 29, 32.

According to the ESC Committee, this requires states 'to prevent third parties from violating the right in other countries, if they are able to influence these parties by way of legal or political means, in accordance with the Charter of the United Nations and applicable international law'.[60] As with the international obligation to respect, there is no explicit textual basis for the imposition of such an obligation. However, the positive nature of the obligation to 'undertake to promote and encourage international co-operation' would be rendered ineffective in the absence of such an obligation. Importantly, it is not an absolute obligation to prevent harm and the reasonableness of a state's efforts will be assessed in light of its capacity to exert influence over or control of a non-state actor whose actions impact negatively on the realization of the right to health.

It is within this context that the ESC Committee has recommended that 'State parties which are members of international financial institutions, notably the International Monetary Fund, the World Bank and regional development banks, should pay greater attention to the protection of the right to health in influencing lending policies, credit agreements and international measures of these institutions'.[61] Importantly such a comment is not intended to address the direct obligations of such institutions with respect to the protection of the right to health, an issue that goes beyond the scope of both the Committee's General Comment and the present analysis.[62] The concern here is with respect to the conduct of those states which have the capacity to influence the behaviour of these institutions. To refrain from the imposition of an international obligation to protect the right to health would allow a state to effectively avoid its obligation to promote and encourage international co-operation by deferring absolute responsibility for the harm caused to a person's right to health to non-state actors over which they had some, albeit limited, form of control.[63] Such a position is untenable as it would undermine the object and purpose of the right to health which requires that a state must demonstrate that it has taken every reasonable measure within its capacity to ensure that an international institution does not take measures that unreasonably harm the progressive realization of the right to health.

Importantly, this obligation on states to guard against the potentially detrimental impact of non-state actors on the right to health in other jurisdictions is not confined

---

[60] ESC Committee, *General Comment No 14* (n 3) para 39. *Report of the Special Rapporteur on the Right to Health to the General Assembly 2005* (n 11) para 62 ('take all reasonable measures to prevent third parties from jeopardizing the enjoyment of the right to health in other countries').

[61] ESC Committee, *General Comment No 14* (n 3) para 39. The CRC Committee has recommended that international financial institutions support the implementation of children's Rights: CRC Committee, *Report of the Forty-Sixth Session* (n 11) para 93(d). However it has failed to link this demand with the international obligations of the member states of such organizations.

[62] Although there is a significant amount of literature with respect to this issue for a detailed examination, see Mac Darrow, *Between Light and Shadow: The World Bank, the International Monetary Fund and International Human Rights Law* (Hart, 2003).

[63] See *Waite and Kennedy v Germany* App No 26083/94 (ECtHR, 18 February 1999) para 67 (held that it would be incompatible with the object and purpose of the ECHR if states which establish organizations to pursue co-operation in certain fields were absolved from all responsibility in relation to the activities of such organizations). See also Salomon (n 11) 106–8.

to those institutions in which it may have membership. It also extends to those private and commercial entities, such as multinational corporations, that are subject to the jurisdiction of state and whose activities have an impact on the right to health of persons in other jurisdictions.[64] An example would be private health recruitment agencies that recruit health professionals from developing countries. Such an act of itself will not necessarily compromise the capacity of a developing state to secure the right to health. However, as discussed above there is a significant potential for abuses to occur and it is for this reason that the Special Rapporteur on Health has emphasized the need for states to 'regulate private recruitment agencies that operate internationally with a view to ensuring that they do not recruit in a manner that reduces a developing country's human resource capacities'.[65]

It could be argued that the drafters of the right to health under the ICESCR or the CRC never anticipated its application in such contexts. Irrespective of whether this is true, drafters cannot be expected to anticipate all future contexts in which the international obligation to protect the right to health may have relevance, and thus the extension of this obligation to such contexts cannot be excluded. If a principled justification for such an approach can be offered which does not violate the ordinary rules of interpretation, then its legitimacy should be respected. And such a justification can be made. The drafters of the right to health, especially the CRC, clearly recognized the importance of international co-operation to the realization of the right to health especially in developing states and thus imposed an obligation to promote and encourage this objective. A corollary of this commitment is that states cannot subsequently remain passive in response to actions by non-state actors subject to their jurisdiction that would undermine the right to health in other jurisdictions.

---

[64] cf Human Rights Council, *Business and Human Rights: Mapping International Standards of Responsibility and Accountability for Corporate Acts*, UN Doc A/HRC/4/035 (9 February 2007) para 15 (argues that '[c]urrent guidance from the Committees suggests that the treaties do not require states to exercise extraterritorial jurisdiction over business abuse' and that 'debate continues over precisely when the protection of human rights justifies extraterritorial jurisdiction'. It is acknowledged that the debate concerning the exercise of extraterritorial jurisdiction is complex and beyond the scope of this analysis. However, the conclusions of the Special Representative appear to have been made without a consideration as to the nature of the obligations that arise under art 24(4) of the CRC. Nor does the Special Representative appear to have considered the comments of the ESC Committee in its General Comment on the right to health and the Special Rapporteur for Health concerning the obligations of states to prevent, to the extent that they are able, violations of the right to health in other countries by actors over which they have jurisdiction.)

[65] *Report of the Special Rapporteur on the Right to Health to the General Assembly 2005* (n 11) para 62. The WHO has arguably taken steps to encourage such an approach in its Draft Code of Practice on the International Recruitment of Health Personnel' which is directed towards not just WHO member States but health workers, recruiters, employers, and civil society: WHO 'Draft Code of Practice on the International Recruitment of Health Personnel' (4 December 2008) EB124/13. On 1 September 2008 the WHO Secretariat commenced web-based public hearings on the draft. It is important to note however that there is little in the draft to suggest that it was conceptualized as an illustration of the international obligation to either respect or protect the right to health. Indeed much of its focus concerns the rights of health workers.

3 The international obligation to provide assistance to developing states to fulfil the right to health

(a) A controversial duty

Andrew Linklater, in his examination of the relationship between the harm principle and global ethics, has argued that the harm principle (considered in this chapter as being equivalent to the international duty to respect) cannot be reduced to 'rules of forbearance' and must also 'require duties of assistance, steps to dismantle "coercive regimes" and efforts to create global political arrangements which can represent the voices of vulnerable people and communities'.[66] He lamented, however, that 'current expressions of the harm principle in contemporary international law are deficient because they do not require states and other actors to promote global distributive justice...'.[67] His discussion made no reference to the ICESCR or CRC and certainly not the obligation to encourage and promote international co-operation to secure the right to health. Had he done so, it is suggested that his analysis would have revealed that the third limb of the international obligation of states with respect to the right to health consists of a requirement that a state must make reasonable efforts either individually or collectively, in light of its available resources and the totality of its obligations under international law, to assist other states, especially developing states, fulfil the right to health.

The scope and nature of this obligation to provide assistance remains contested. It has a solid textual foundation under article 2(1) of the ICESCR, which requires that states undertake steps individually and through international assistance and co-operation to realize the rights under the Covenant. But as noted above, the drafting history of the ICESCR indicates an absence of consensus among states, indeed an explicit resistance by some states that this obligation would mandate a *particular* form of assistance.[68] This same resistance was evident in the drafting of the Optional Protocol to the ICESCR with several states claiming that, although the need for international co-operation and assistance reflected an 'important moral obligation', it was 'not a legal entitlement'.[69] Moreover, the text of the CRC expressly omits any reference to assistance and favours the phrase 'framework of international cooperation'. Thus, it could be argued that this reflects an emphasis on collaboration between sovereign states as opposed to the creation of a legal obligation to provide assistance by one state to another or an entitlement to claim such assistance.

However, two factors demand a more rigorous and nuanced approach with respect to the issue of international assistance. First, the fact that states did not agree on the specific meaning of this obligation during the drafting of various international instruments in which it is found does not mean that 'the relevant commitment

---

[66] Linklater (n 36) 343.
[67] ibid 338.
[68] Alston and Quinn (n 19) 191.
[69] UNCHR, 'Report of the Open Ended Working Group to Consider Options regarding the Elaboration of an Optional Protocol to the International Covenant on Economic, Social and Cultural Rights on its Second Session' (10 February 2005) UN Doc E/CN.4/2005/52 para 76.

is meaningless'.[70] It exists within the text of international treaties and cannot be ignored because of its indeterminacy. The challenge is to offer a persuasive meaning for this phrase. Second, the specific inclusion of the obligation to pay particular attention to the needs of developing states in article 24(4) of the CRC reflects an acceptance that Western states *would* be required to take measures to assist developing states in fulfilling their obligations under the right to health. The precise form of this obligation may not be clear. Indeed it is a perfect example of an 'imperfect obligation'.[71] As a corollary, there is no legal basis for a state to invoke this obligation to demand a particular form of assistance. But a principled and practical interpretation of this obligation requires that an obligation to promote and encourage assistance must form a necessary part of the obligation to co-operate—a position that other commentators have also taken with respect to the interpretation of article 2(1) of the ICESCR which imposes an obligation to realize economic and social rights through international assistance and co-operation.[72] Importantly, as noted above, this international duty of assistance is not a derivative assistance duty to be 'triggered by someone's reneging on, or threatening to renege on, more fundamental negative duties'.[73] On the contrary, it is a fundamental assistance duty which is 'entailed directly by the interests or needs that justify' the right to health under the ICESCR and the CRC.[74]

In mapping out a persuasive account of the obligation to assist, the first point to note is that it is not an unqualified obligation and, as the ESC Committee has recognized, it will depend on the availability of a state's resources.[75] At the most general level, the ESC Committee has recommended that 'States *should* facilitate access to essential health facilities, goods and services in other countries, wherever possible and provide aid when required.'[76] It has further argued that in times of humanitarian crises states parties have joint and individual responsibility in accordance with the UN Charter and other relevant instruments 'to cooperate in providing disaster relief and humanitarian assistance, ... including assistance to refugees and internally displaced persons. Each State should contribute to this task to the maximum of its capacities.'[77] Importantly, such a model of assistance is not grounded simply in moral theories of beneficence or distributive justice[78] but exists

---

[70] ibid 191.   [71] Montero (n 38) 86–91.

[72] Salomon (n 11) 78; Craven (n 31) 147. cf Vandenhole (n 8) 26 (argues that 'no general obligation exists under the CRC to cooperate internationally for development or to provide development assistance').

[73] Cruft (n 59) 37.

[74] ibid.

[75] ESC Committee, *General Comment No 14* (n 3) para 39.

[76] ibid (emphasis added). See also *Report of the Special Rapporteur on the Right to Health to the General Assembly 2005* (n 11) para 64.

[77] ESC Committee, *General Comment No 14* (n 3) para 40.

[78] See Sylvie Loriaux, 'Beneficence and Distributive Justice in a Globalising World' (2006) 20 Global Society 251 (provides discussion of competing but complementary models which are often used as the moral justification for assisting the world's poor); Alicia Yamin, 'Our place in the world: Conceptualising Obligations Beyond Borders in Human Rights Based Approaches to Health' (2010) 12 Health & Hum Rts 3, 4.

as a legal obligation, which states assumed when they ratified the ICESCR and the CRC. This legal obligation cannot compel a state to provide assistance and can only require that a state give genuine consideration to its capacity to do so in light of its available resources. Although this is a weak conduct obligation, it still remains a legal obligation for which states are accountable. In practical terms, this means that a state must justify its failure to provide assistance as being reasonable in all the circumstances.

Thus, the strength of this obligation lies in ability to require states to remain actively focused on, and accountable for, the measures by which they intend to give effect to their obligation to assist other states in light of their own resource constraints. Moreover, its legal expression creates a site of controversy within which those agitating for the provision of greater assistance by developed states to developing states to secure the right to health can locate their demands. It thus provides a context for dialogue and negotiation as to whether a state is satisfying its international obligation of assistance. It is not suggested that this is the only site in which such a conversation can take place—public health debates around global equity or philosophical discussions around distributive justice are additional discourses which invariably frame this discussion.[79] However, the international obligation to assist under the right to health does provide an additional site in which states are required as a matter of international law to be cognisant of this obligation and may be required to defend and justify their actions with respect to its fulfilment. It is within this space that the treaty bodies have, for example, urged states to meet the UN goal of allocating 0.7% of GNP to overseas development assistance[80] and criticized states when they have failed to meet this target.[81] The weak and imprecise nature of the international obligation to co-operate means that the treaty bodies do not have a

---

[79] The statistics certainly reveal an inequitable distribution of global health resources between the developed and developing states. In 2007 the world spent US$5.3 trillion on health of which 86% was spent in OECD countries representing just 18% of the world's population. In 40 WHO member states health spending by government, households, the private sector, and funds provided by donors was lower than USD$43 per person per year, the WHO minimum spending needed to provide basic life saving services. In contrast the average spending in OECD countries was USD$3881: <http://www.who.int/nha/use/global_fact_sheet_2007-Jun_2010.pdf> accessed 8 June 2011. See also World Bank, *World Development Indicators 2011* (World Bank 2011) 94–7 (provides comparative figures for states in relation to health expenditure, number of health workers and hospital beds).

[80] See, eg, CRC Committee, *General Comment No 5: General Measures on the Implementation of the Convention on the Rights of the Child*, UN Doc CRC/GC/2003/5 (27 November 2003) para 61. See also CO ESC France, UN Doc E/C.12/1/FRA/CO/3, paras 16, 30; CO ESC Finland, UN Doc E/C.12/1/Add.52 (1 December 2000) paras 13, 23; CO ESC Spain, UN Doc E/C.12/1/Add.99 (7 June 2004) paras 10, 27. Moreover this target is affirmed in *Monterrey Consensus of the International Conference on Financing for Development*, UN Doc A/CONF.198/11 (2002) ch 1, res 1, annex, para 42 ('urge developed countries that have not done so to make concrete efforts towards the target of 0.7 per cent of gross national product (GNP) as ODA to developing countries and 0.15 to 0.20 per cent of GNP of developed countries to least developed countries').

[81] See, eg, CO ESC Belgium (n 42) paras 16, 30; CO ESC Iceland, UN Doc E/C.12/1/Add.89 (23 May 2003) paras 11, 20; CO ESC Spain (n 80) paras 10, 27; CO ESC Germany, UN Doc E/C.12/1/Add.68 (24 September 2001) paras 15, 33; CO CRC Austria, UN Doc CRC/C/15/Add.251 (31 March 2005) para 14; CO CRC Germany, UN Doc CRC/C/15/Add.226 (26 February 2004) para 21; CO CRC Iceland, UN Doc CRC/C/15/Add.203 (31 January 2003) para 16, 17.

mandate to find a state to be in violation of its obligation if it fails to reach this target. But they do have a mandate to create a debate with states about the types of measures that they might be expected to take in order to contribute to securing the right to health in all states. Moreover, states parties to the relevant international treaties have an obligation to participate in this debate, which has been initiated by the bodies responsible for monitoring implementation of these treaties, and to justify on reasonable grounds any failure to meet this target.

(b) Forms of assistance

No attempt is made here to provide a comprehensive list of the potential forms of assistance that states could provide in satisfaction of their international obligation to provide assistance to other states in order to enhance their capacity to secure the right to health. It is sufficient to note that article 23 of the ICESCR provides that 'international action for the achievement of the rights recognised in the... Covenant includes such methods as the conclusion of conventions, the adoption of recommendations, the furnishing of technical assistance and the holding of regional meetings and technical meetings'. International treaties and agreements relating to health such as WHO Framework Convention on Tobacco Control,[82] the International Health Regulations,[83] the WHO International Code of Marketing of Breast-Milk Substitutes,[84] and the WHO Global Code of Practice on the International Recruitment of Health Personnel[85] provide examples of the measures anticipated under article 23 of the ICESCR. Other forms of assistance could include the provision of human resources, enabling access to research literature,[86] the development of collaborative research agendas that enable researchers in developed countries to address the health needs of developing countries,[87] educational and academic scholarships and exchanges, direct investment, and joint venture programs in the creation of various projects relating to the various determinants of the right to health ranging from infrastructure creation to production and dissemination of medicines.

---

[82] Geneva, 21 May 2003, entered into force 27 February 2005, 2302 UNTS 166.
[83] Geneva, 23 May 2005, entered into force 15 June 2007. See also: WHO, 'International Health Regulations (IHR)' <http://www.who.int/ihr/en/>; WHO, 'International Health Regulations' <http://www.who.int/ihr/elibrary/legal/en/> accessed 10 June 2011.
[84] Geneva, 21 May 1981, 20 ILM 1004.
[85] WHO 'International Recruitment of Health Personnel: Draft Global Code of Practice' (adopted 15 April 2010) UN Doc A63/8. <http://www.who.int/hrh/migration/code/practice/en/index.html> accessed 16 June 2011.
[86] See Gavin Yamey, 'Excluding the Poor from Accessing Biomedical Literature: A Rights Violation that Impedes Global Health' (2008) 10 Health & Hum Rts 1 (details denial of access to medical research caused by prohibitive subscription fees especially within developing countries and advocates alternative publishing model known as 'open access'). See also *Universal Declaration of Human Rights*, GA Res 217A (III), UN Doc A/810 (10 December 1948) art 27(1) (UDHR) which provides that everyone has the right 'to share in scientific advancement and its benefits'.
[87] Joy E Lawn and others, '1 Year after the Lancet Neonatal Survival Series—Was the Call for Action Heard?' (2006) 367 The Lancet 1541 (notes that 'although 99% of deaths in newborn babies occur in developing countries less than 1% of published neonatal research during the past decade is relevant to deaths in low resource settings').

Measures to satisfy a state's obligation to assist in the context of international co-operation should also be seen as extending to the contributions and assistance provided by a state to the various international institutional bodies and other entities including NGOs that directly undertake measures to assist developing states in their measures to realize the right to health. Especially relevant in this context are the WHO,[88] UNICEF,[89] the United Nations Population Fund (UNFPA),[90] and UNAIDS,[91] which have all been identified at various times by the CRC Committee as entities with which states should co-operate and seek assistance. Support for the Special Rapporteur on the Right to Health should also been seen within the purview of the obligation to promote international co-operation given that this mandate was designed as a mechanism to facilitate international co-operation with respect to the realization of the right to health.[92]

(c) The issue of global institutional reform
Beyond direct financial assistance and the other forms of co-operation listed above, there is an issue as whether the international obligation to assist should extend to a requirement that measures be taken to ensure not only that the global institutional structure does not harm the right to health—the obligation to respect—but to actively facilitate a regime that will contribute to the progressive realization of this right. It is suggested here that although contentious, such a positive obligation should be seen as a principled, practical, coherent, and context sensitive feature of this right.

From the perspective of a principled interpretation of the right to health, the ordinary meaning of the obligation to 'promote and encourage' international co-operation imparts a duty to take steps towards international co-operation in a manner that will contribute to the progressive realization of the right to health. It would thus lead to an absurd result if the provision could be read in such a way that

---

[88] See, eg, CO CRC Philippines, UN Doc CRC/C/15/Add.259 (21 September 2005) para 63(g); CO CRC Chad, UN Doc CRC/C/15/Add.107 (24 August 1999) para 28; CO CRC Central African Republic, UN Doc CRC/C/15/Add.138 (18 October 2000) para 55; CO CRC Togo, UN Doc CRC/C/15/Add.255 (31 March 2005) para 53(d); CO CRC Panama, UN Doc CRC/C/15/Add.233 (30 June 2004) para 48(d). It is worth noting that the preamble to the WHO Constitution notes that the adoption of this instrument by states was for the 'purpose of co-operation among themselves and with others to promote and protect the health of all peoples': Constitution of the World Health Organization (New York, 22 July 1946, entered into force 7 April 1948, 14 UNTS 185). However the WHO is not necessarily perceived as an example of states undertaking their obligation to promote and encourage international co-operation under art 24(4) of the CRC despite its functions being directed to *inter alia* the achievement of health outcomes which are consistent with art 24.
[89] See, eg, CO CRC Chad (n 88) para 28; CO CRC Central African Republic (n 88) para 55; CO CRC Togo (n 88) para 53(d); CO Belize CRC (31 March 2005) UN Doc CRC/C/15/Add.252 para 53(f).
[90] See, eg, CO CRC Philippines (n 88) para 63(g); CO CRC (n 88) para 48(d); CO CRC Guatemala, UN Doc CRC/C/15/Add.154 (9 July 2001) para 41.
[91] See, eg, CO CRC Chad (n 88) para 28; CO CRC Guinea, UN Doc CRC/C/15/Add.100 (10 May 1999) para 25; CO CRC Philippines (n 88) para 63(g); CO CRC Togo (n 88) para 53(d); CO CRC Panama (n 88) para 48(a).
[92] *Interim Report of the Special Rapporteur on the Right to Health to the General Assembly 2003*, UN Doc A/58/427 (10 October 2003) paras 38–63.

this obligation should be suspended or quarantined in relation to matters that are not directly related to the health of individuals even though they have the capacity to have a profound effect on the capacity of a state to secure the right to health.

The fragmentation of contemporary international law may explain why such outcomes occur in practice, but it does not offer a principled justification. On the contrary the ILC Study on Fragmentation has recognized the need to pursue coherence between different regimes within international law.[93] The implication of this recommendation for the obligation to promote and encourage international co-operation under the right to health requires not just the avoidance of conflict between international legal regimes, but a duty to actively pursue measures by which the capacity of a developing state to secure the right to health can be enhanced and not merely protected against the impact of the global institutional system.

Such an interpretation reveals the ambitious scope of the right to health especially in light of the observation that the WTO regime includes few clear avenues by which human rights concerns can gain entry[94] and the discouraging historical evidence which suggests that human rights-compatible improvements in the global institutional order are difficult to achieve and difficult to sustain.[95] Thus, there is a genuine need to assess whether the principled justification which has been advanced to justify this obligation can be reconciled with the requirement that it remain capable of practical implementation. Simma's work is particularly helpful in highlighting this predicament. He has identified the tension between the investment in international law of values of social accountability and community interests and fears that the still 'essentially bilateralist infrastructure upon which the new more progressive edifices rest will turn out to be too weak to come to terms with the implications of such community interest'.[96] As such, he believes that there is 'reason to be concerned about new conceptions being grafted upon universal international law without support through and serious attempts at adequate institution building'.[97] The suggestion in the present analysis that the right to health imparts a positive obligation to promote a global institutional order that contributes to the realization of this right to health would fall within Simma's suite of concerns.

Such concerns, however, highlight a real issue within international human rights law generally, not only as to the practical implementation of such standards but also the expectation deficit that is created when visions as to the content of a human right are offered in the absence of any effective mechanisms to secure their enjoyment. The suggestion being made here that the right to health must be read to include an obligation of international assistance is especially vulnerable to this criticism. Indeed, a lack of institutional capacity has been identified by other commentators as a core reason to oppose the inclusion within international law of standards concerning

---

[93] See Chapter 3.
[94] Kinley and Nolan (n 46) 364 (also provide a discussion of how human rights can be inserted, albeit minimally, into trade relations: 365–70).
[95] Pogge, 'Human Rights of the Global Poor' (n 43) 744.
[96] Simma, 'From Bilateralism to Community Interest in International Law' (n 17) 224, 249.
[97] ibid.

global distributive justice.⁹⁸ Notwithstanding these concerns it is submitted that the insistence on an international obligation to assist as a core feature of the right to health remains defensible.

Beyond the attempt to advance a principled justification for the inclusion of such an obligation above, it is recognized that the practical implementation of an international duty to assist is not without its difficulties. Indeed, Simma has warned that 'the realisation of community interests [such as international co-operation to secure the right to health] depends not only on the creation of norms positing an "international community" but also on the existence of an institutional structure providing for the promotion as well as protection of these interests'.⁹⁹ It is suggested, however, that the existing international order is not devoid of an institutional structure that necessarily lacks the capacity to contribute to the realization of the right to health. Simma himself has actually recognized that a 'complicated network of organizations and agencies have emerged to deal with almost every... issue imaginable'.¹⁰⁰ With respect to the right to health this list is long and could be seen to include the World Health Organization, UNAIDS, UNICEF, the CRC Committee, the Special Rapporteur on the Right to Health, the Office of the High Commissioner for Human Rights, the Millennium Development Project, and arguably even organizations such as the World Bank, which is increasingly concerned with the health of individuals.¹⁰¹

At the same time it must be conceded that the institutional order includes a vast number of other organizations that do not have the health of individuals as their primary or even a secondary concern—the International Monetary Fund and the World Trade Organisation being perhaps the most striking examples. Thus, as Simma explains, 'such abundance of institutions leads to the disadvantages of rendering co-ordination within the system extremely difficult and of preventing the solution of conflicts between competing community interests'.¹⁰² This concern reflects the comments made earlier in this chapter that the fragmentation of international law has contributed to a high level of system incoherence in the way in which international institutions undertake their work. The argument made here, however, is that such an outcome is not inevitable and the obligation to promote and encourage international co-operation extends to a positive duty for states to remain actively seized of ways in which the diverse and often competing interests within the international legal system can be reconciled.

It does not demand that such an enterprise in international co-operation *must* achieve an outcome which is consistent with the progressive realization of the right to health—only that every reasonable effort must be made in good faith to *promote and encourage* such a result. At the same time, this onerous requirement that the right to health must be taken into consideration in all matters affecting health is not designed

---

⁹⁸ For a discussion of institutional incapacity see Buchanan and Golove (n 13) 901–2; Gostin, 'Meeting Basic Survival Needs of the World's Least Healthy People' (n 11) 382.
⁹⁹ Simma, 'From Bilateralism to Community Interest in International Law' (n 17) 224, 285.
¹⁰⁰ ibid 283.
¹⁰¹ See Lawrence Gostin, 'Global Health Law: Health in a Global Community' (Georgetown University, O'Neil Institute for National and Global Health Law, Scholarship Research Paper No 15, September 2008) <http://scholarship.law.georgetown.edu/ois_papers/15> accessed 30 May 2011, 230–4.
¹⁰² ibid.

to displace all other legitimate considerations in international relations. States may carry a heavy burden to justify any actions or omissions that will be contrary to an individual's right to health, but this right is not the only or even the paramount consideration relevant in decision making. Importantly, however, the international obligation to co-operate for the purpose of realizing the right to health does operate to recalibrate the balancing process and make visible the right to health in contexts where it may have been overlooked, marginalized, or devalued in the behaviour of states both within and beyond their own jurisdiction.

The case to defend the imposition of an international obligation of assistance under the right to health is also considered to satisfy the requirements of local and global context sensitivity. With respect to the former, it does not seek to impose an obligation that is insensitive to the capacity of a state to contribute to international co-operative efforts. Indeed the inclusion of the need to pay special attention to the needs of developing states within article 24(4) of the CRC provides recognition of the reality that the capacity of states to promote and encourage international co-operation will be varied.

In relation to the issue of global context sensitivity, it is recognized that an international obligation of assistance that extends beyond assistance to the potential for regime change presents a challenge to the existing distribution of power within the international system. As Simma has explained, 'we must constantly be aware that in principle human rights constitute a threat—or at least a considerable nuisance—to holders of political power'.[103] Thus, it is reasonable to expect the prospect of significant political resistance from those actors within the international system that would be forced to 'bear some opportunity costs of making the international trade, lending, investment and intellectual property regimes fairer to the global poor as well some costs of compensating for harms done—for example by helping to fund basic health facilities, vaccination programmes'[104] and the like.

Such a prospect unquestionably raises the danger of disengagement by states with the vision of the right to health as offered in this chapter. However, it is submitted that despite its ostensible appearance, the obligation of assistance remains in many ways a relatively weak as opposed to a strong form of obligation. It does not demand the immediate creation of a system that will necessarily be consistent with the progressive realization of the right to health. Nor does it demand that other interests must necessarily be considered illegitimate and rendered subservient to the right to health. It certainly does demand a recalibration of the extent to which the right to health features within the dynamics of the international system and a much more active consideration of how this system can be reoriented to assist in the realization of the right to health.[105]

---

[103] Simma, 'From Bilateralism to Community Interest in International Law' (n 17) 224, 243.

[104] Pogge, 'Human Rights of the Global Poor' (n 43) 744–5 (focuses on affluent states but concerns would also extend to the interests of non-state groups within affluent states; also suggests that '[r]elatively small reforms of little consequence for the world's affluent would suffice to eliminate most of [the current] human rights deficit').

[105] In this respect, the proposal for a Framework Convention on Global Health being promoted by the Joint Action and Learning Initiative on National and Global Responsibilities for Health, warrants careful and genuine consideration by States as a potential example of how international co-operation might assist

Although some states would be challenged by these demands, they remain relatively weak. Moreover, they ultimately do nothing more than seek to hold states accountable for their own commitments made during (a) the drafting of the international obligation in the ICESCR and CRC with respect to the right to health; (b) the subsequent ratification by states parties of the ICESCR and CRC with the knowledge of its binding status; and (c) the numerous subsequent declarations in which states themselves have affirmed the need to adopt collaborative efforts to transform the right to health into a reality.[106] Thus somewhat ironically, the support systems needed to enhance the coherence and legitimacy of the claim that the right to health includes an obligation to actively promote an international institutional order conducive to the realization of this right are provided by the stated commitments of states themselves.

(d) The process by which assistance should be provided
International law not only imposes an obligation on states to assist other states in their efforts to realize the right to health, it also guides states in relation to the process by which such assistance must be provided. In the first instance, such assistance must not take place in a manner which would violate the prohibition against interference in the domestic affairs of a state under article 2(7) of the UNC. Furthermore, in light of the principle of sovereign equality[107] between states and the principle of self-determination, it is important that international co-operation to realize the right to health is not undertaken in a hegemonic or imperialistic way and remains culturally sensitive to indigenous distributive processes and conceptions of justice.[108]

Historically these principles of tolerance and respect for cultural diversity have often been lacking in efforts to secure international co-operation between developed

---

in the realization of the right to health: Joint Action And Learning Initiative (JALI), 'Towards a Framework Convention on Global Health' (Factsheet, November 2010) <http://www.section27.org.za/wp-content/uploads/2010/11/JALI-Factsheet1.pdf>; Gostin, 'Meeting Basic Survival Needs of the World's Least Healthy People' (n 11) 330.

[106] See, eg, *Millennium Declaration Resolution*, UNGA Res 55/2, UN Doc A/55/L.2 (8 September 2000); *Keeping the Promise: United to Achieve the Millennium Development Goals*, UNGA Res 65/1, UN Doc A/RES/65/1 (19 October 2010) especially paras 73–6; Resolution adopted by the Human Rights Council: *The Right of Everyone to the Highest Attainable Standard of Physical and Mental Health*, GA Res 15/11, UN Doc A/HRC/RES/15/22 (6 October 2010) para 9; *World Declaration on the Survival, Protection and Development of Children* para 17 ('These tasks [including the enhancement of children's health] require a continued and concerted effort by all nations, through national action and international co-operation') and *Plan of Action for Implementing the World Declaration on the Survival Protection and Development of Children in the 1990s* (UN Doc E/CN.4/1991/59 (12 December 1990); *A World Fit for Children*, UN GA Res S-72/2, UN Doc A/RES/S-27/2 (10 May 2002) (also affirms commitment to international co-operation to secure children's rights). For a discussion of other declarations and conferences in which international co-operation has been affirmed as a necessary mechanism to secure the objectives of the international human rights system generally, see Salomon (n 11) 83–98.

[107] See *Limburg Principles on the Implementation of the International Covenant on Economic Social and Cultural Rights*, UN Doc E/CN.4/1987/17 (1987) annex, para 33.

[108] See Buchanan and Golove (n 13) 900 (discuss theory of societal distributive autonomy which resists role of transnational distributive justice because of threat it presents to integrity of indigenous distributive processes and conclude that it is important to caution against global insensitivity in setting global standards but no reason to exclude principles of transnational distributive justice in the system of international law).

and developing states.[109] Indeed, the use of the phrase 'co-operation' has often been a misnomer to conceal the reality that inappropriate strategies and conditionalities have been imposed on assistance provided to developing states at the behest of developed states and/or the international agencies they dominate.[110] The international obligation to co-operate for the purpose of securing the right to health recognizes that developing states will need assistance, but it does not tolerate the imposition or importation of measures to address health needs of the people in these states that are based on judgements that are insensitive to, and intolerant of, of local cultural considerations and needs. Local context sensitivity is, therefore, a critical consideration in the provision of assistance by developed states to developing states.

Indeed, the requirement for participation discussed in Chapter 5 mandates that the implementation of a state's *international* obligation with respect to the right to health must also be sensitive to, informed by, and reflect the needs and interests of local populations to the extent that this is reasonably practicable to do so.[111] Such an approach not only has intuitive appeal but is supported by research in the area of general health which indicates that:

selection of effective interventions to be implemented at the level of community and health facilities, should be based on the local epidemiological profile and other locally defined key criteria.[112]

This approach therefore disapproves of the transplant of Western models for the delivery of health care and other related service in favour of models which are tailored to meet local demand and respond to local needs.[113] International co-operation, whatever form it takes, must therefore respect cultural differences and

---

[109] See, eg, Thomas W Ditcher, *Despite Good Intentions: Why Development Assistance to the Third World has Failed* (University of Massachusetts Press, 2003); William Easterly, *The White Man's Burden: Why the West's Efforts to Aid the Rest Have Done So Much Ill and So Little Good* (Penguin Press, 2006); Roger C Riddell, *Does Foreign Aid Really Work?* (OUP, 2007); Fiona Terry, *Condemned to Repeat? The Paradox of Humanitarian Action* (Cornell University Press, 2002).

[110] See CRC Committee, *Report of the Forty-Sixth Session* (n 11) para 93(f) ('Bilateral and multilateral aid should not depend on any conditions which may have a negative or harmful impact on the rights of children and other... groups'). See also, eg, Dina Bogecho and Melissa Upreti, 'The Global Gag Rule—An Antithesis to the Rights-Based Approach to Health' (2006) 9 Health & Hum Rts 17 (argue that US restrictions attached to funding for family planning are incompatible with international human rights because of the negative impact of such restrictions on the health of women).

[111] See Stamford Interagency Workshop on a Human Rights-Based Approach in the Context of UN Reform, *Statement on a Common Understanding of a Human Rights-Based Approach to Development Cooperation* (United Nations 2003), as agreed at the Stamford Workshop and endorsed by the UNDG Programme Group (2003). See UNDG, 'Human Rights-Based Approach to Development Programming (HRBA)' <http://www.undg.org/?P=221> accessed 31 May 2011.

[112] Jennifer Bryce and others, 'Reducing Child Mortality: Can Public Health Deliver?' (2003) 362 The Lancet 159, 163.

[113] ibid. See also Susan Diamond, 'An Analysis of Child Protection and Protecting Children from Rights and Public Health Perspectives' (International Symposium on Human Rights in Public Health: Research, Policy and Practice, University of Melbourne, 3–5 November 2004) (warns against the 'transplant' of child protection models developed in the USA into emerging democracies and other developing nations); Beth Verhey, *Child Soldiers: Preventing, Demobilizing and Reintegrating* (World Bank Africa Region Working Paper Series No 23, November 2001) 17 (research suggests that Western-style trauma assistance and its focus on the individual may not necessarily be as effective as psycho-social

accept the need for a degree of flexibility in the implementation of measures to secure the right to the highest attainable standard of health. While 'global one size fits all delivery strategies may have been adequate in the days of vertical programmes such as the expanded programme on immunisation or control of diarrhoeal diseases',[114] such an approach is no longer sufficient.[115] In contrast, the effective enjoyment of the right to health requires locally designed strategies to address the health needs of populations that are informed rather than determined by the co-operation that is provided by other states. These features, which must inform how the process of international co-operation takes place, such as participation, collaboration, and cultural sensitivity, are increasingly referred to as a 'rights based approach' to development—an approach that has been called for by the CRC Committee and endorsed by numerous UN bodies as well as state development agencies.[116]

This is not to say that cultural or traditional practices must always be tolerated within strategies for international co operation.[117] As detailed in Chapter 8, article 24(3) of the CRC sets a limit on the extent of this tolerance by the imposition of the requirement that 'States parties shall take all effective and appropriate measures with a view to abolishing traditional practices prejudicial to the health of children'. At the same time, the process and measures required for the elimination of such practices are not to be imposed or defined exclusively by reference to Western values, judgements, and expectations. On the contrary, an approach to international co-operation that is consistent with the values of equality and participation that underpin human rights standards,[118] favours collaboration and consultation rather than the

---

approaches which emphasize the role of family and the community in the context of the demobilization of child soldiers in Africa).

[114] Bryce and others (n 112) 163.

[115] See also UNICEF, *State of the World's Children 2008: Child Survival* (UNICEF, 2007) especially Chapter 3 (stresses importance of community-based partnerships in securing health for children); Lynn P Freedman and others, UN Millennium Project Task Force on Child Health and Maternal Health, *Who's Got the Power? Transforming Health Systems for Women and Children* (Earthscan 2005); Joseph E Stiglitz, *Making Globalisation Work* (WW Norton & Co, 2006) xii (recognizes that 'one size fits all solutions do not, can not, capture' the complexities of development assistance).

[116] See CRC Committee, *General Comment No 5* (n 80) para 61. See also *Statement on a Common Understanding of a Human Rights-Based Approach to Development Cooperation* (n 111); UNDP, *Human Development Report: Human Rights and Development* (OUP, 2000); Marta Santos-Pais, *A Human Rights Conceptual Framework for UNICEF* (Innocenti Essays No 9, UNICEF and ICDC, 1999); Andre Frankovits, 'Mainstreaming Human Rights: The Human Rights-Based Approach and the United Nations System' (Desk Study Prepared by the Human Rights Council of Australia, UNESCO 2005); United Kingdom Department for International Development (DFID), 'Realising Human Rights for Poor People' (DFID Target Strategy Paper, 1997); DFID, 'Human Rights for Poor People' (Target Strategy Paper, DFID, 2000); New Zealand Agency for International Development, 'Human Rights Policy Statement' (NZAID, 2002). See generally Mac Darrow and Amparo Tomas, 'Power, Capture and Conflict: A Call for Human Rights Accountability in Development Cooperation' (2005) 27 Hum Rts Q 471.

[117] See Buchanan and Golove (n 13) 900–1 (examines dangers in excessive deference to indigenous distributive processes).

[118] *Statement on a Common Understanding of a Human Rights-Based Approach to Development Cooperation* (n 111); Santos-Pais (n 116); UNICEF, 'Human Rights for Women and Children: How UNICEF Helps Make Them a Reality' (Programme Policy Document, UNICEF, 1999); *Report of the Special Rapporteur on the Right to Health to the Human Rights Council 2008*, UN Doc A/HRC/7/11 (31 January 2008) paras 41–2.

imposition of hegemonic or paternalistic strategies to secure the realization of the right to health.[119]

III Case study: the impact of the international obligation to co-operate on access to medicines

A The dilemma: intellectual property rights v access to medicines

The preceding section sought to outline the broad parameters of the international obligation of states with respect to the right to health. It was argued that this obligation consists of three elements—an international obligation to respect, protect, and provide assistance with respect to the realization of the right to health by individuals in other states especially developing states. The discussion in this section seeks to illustrate the impact of these obligations on a particular issue, namely access to medicines,[120] which is an element of the right to health.[121] The objective is to detail how this issue is conceptualized and informed through the prism of the *international* obligation to secure the realization of the right to health.[122] At its most general level, this obligation requires that states must: (a) refrain from unreasonable measures that undermine the right of access to medicines for individuals in other jurisdictions; (b) take reasonable measures to protect against measures by

---

[119] A practical implementation of such an approach is reflected in the work of T Kok-Chor, 'International Toleration: Rawlsian versus Cosmopolitan' (2005) 18 LJIL 685, 704 (argues that a cosmopolitan vision of justice is not necessarily interventionist in implementation and should be seen as demanding nothing more than 'open debate and constructive criticism in international fora concerning nonliberal practices'. Kok-Chor further explains that: 'By open debate I mean that liberal peoples must be prepared always to give reasons and arguments for their criticisms and to reply in good faith to the responses of those criticized').

[120] The United Nations Development Program defines access to mean 'having medicines continuously available and affordable at public or private health facilities or medicine outlets that are within one hour's walk from the homes of the population': MDG Gap Task Force, *Millennium Development Goal 8: Delivering on the Global Partnership for Achieving the Millennium Development Goals* (UN, 2008) 35, n 2.

[121] See Chapter 5; Stephen Marks, 'Access to Essential Medicines as a Component of the Right to Health' in Andrew Clapham and Mary Robinson (eds), *Realising the Right to Health* (Rüffer & Rub, 2009) 80, 86–91, 94–5 (discusses foundation of the right of access to medicines). Much of the discussion in the area focuses on access to essential medicines and the ESC Committee has stressed that 'States parties... have a duty to prevent unreasonably high costs for access to essential medicines': ESC Committee, *General Comment No 17: The Right of Everyone to Benefit from the Protection of the Moral and Material Interests Resulting from Any Scientific Literary, Artistic Production of Which He or She is the Author*, UN Doc E/C.12/GC/17 (12 January 2006) para 35. However, the realization of the right to health requires progressive access to all medicines not just those that are identified as essential. In terms of prioritization in the context of limited resources, prioritization must be given to essential medicines which are defined by the WHO as those that 'satisfy the priority health care needs of the population': WHO, 'Essential Medicines' <http://www.who.int/medicines/services/essmedicines_def/en/> accessed 31 May 2011.

[122] It is important to note that states also have an internal obligation to ensure access to medicines which consists of an obligation to respect, protect, and fulfil this dimension of the right to health (see Holger Hestermeyer, *Human Rights and the WTO: The Case of Patents and Access to Medicines* (OUP, 2007) 107–10. The focus in this section however is on the nature of the international obligation imposed on states with respect to access to medicines.

non-state actors that undermine the right; and (c) take reasonable measures, subject to available resources, individually and collectively to assist in fulfilling the right of access to medicines for individuals in other jurisdictions, especially developing states. Within contemporary debates, the most significant challenge to the realization of these obligations is generally seen as the WTO Agreement on TRIPS.[123]

TRIPS requires that WTO member states must provide protection of 20 years for valid patent claims.[124] Once granted, this protection enables a patent holder to have exclusive rights (a monopoly) in relation to the production and distribution of, for example, a patented medicine. In practice, this means that, all other things being equal, the monopoly price for a patented medicine will be higher than if the medicine were not patented because the patent holder is free to set the price and is not subject to any market competition. As a consequence, in the absence of measures being adopted by a state to subsidize the cost of patented medicines, access to such medicines will be reduced.[125] Moreover, because TRIPS is designed to protect private intellectual property rights it is often seen as creating little incentive for pharmaceutical companies to invest in the development of drugs that would address the diseases that afflict people in developing countries, the so-called 'neglected diseases' and the phenomenon of the 10/90 gap whereby 'only 10 per cent of global health research is devoted to conditions that account for 90 per cent of the global disease burden'.[126] Thus, from the perspective of some advocates and human rights

---

[123] Marrakesh Agreement Establishing the World Trade Organization (Marrakesh, 15 April 1994, entered into force 1 January 1995) 1867 UNTS 3) annex 1C (Agreement on Trade-Related Aspects of Intellectual Property Rights) (TRIPS). See, eg, Helfer and Austin (n 46) 1–169; UN Millennium Project Task Force on HIV/AIDS, Malaria, TB, and Access to Essential Medicines, *Prescription for Healthy Development: Increasing Access to Medicines* (Earthscan, 2005) (Millennium Project Task Force Report); Hestermeyer (n 122); Thomas Pogge, Matthew Rimmer and Kim Rubenstein (eds), *Incentives for Global Public Health: Patent Law and Access to Essential Medicines* (CUP, 2010); Stephen Marks (n 121); Paul O'Connell, 'The Human Right to Health in an Age of Market Hegemony' in John Harrington and Maria Stuttaford (eds), *Global Health and Human Rights: Legal and Philosophical Perspectives* (Routledge, 2010) 190, 203–6; Lisa Forman, 'Trade Rules, Intellectual Property and the Right to Health' (2007) 21 EIA 337; Chian Kee, 'Efficiency, Equity and Ethics: Examining the Policy Behind Compulsory Licensing and Access to Medicines in Developing Countries' (2007) 18 AIPJ 39; Prabhash Ranjan, 'Understanding the Conflicts between the TRIPS Agreement and Human Right to Health' (2008) 9 J World Invest & Trade 551; Audrey Chapman, 'Approaching Intellectual Property as a Human Right' (2001) 35 Copyright Bull 4; Peter K Yu, 'Reconceptualizing Intellectual Property Interests in a Human Rights Framework' (2007) 49 UC Davis L Rev 1039.

[124] TRIPS, arts 27, 33. Unlike human rights treaties TRIPS has an effective enforcement mechanism and member states that fail to provide patent protection as required under TRIPS can be brought before the dispute settlement procedure of the WTO. For a discussion of the conditions of patentability and the rights conferred, see Hestermeyer (n 122) 53–70.

[125] See, eg, Oxfam International, 'Investing for Life: Meeting Poor People's Needs for Access to Medicines through Responsible Business Practices' (Oxfam Briefing Paper No 109, November 2007) <http://www.oxfam.org/sites/www.oxfam.org/files/bp109-investing-for-life-0711.pdf> (provides examples of high cost of patented drugs relative to generic versions); Hestermeyer (n 122) 138–49 (examines both the theory and empirical studies on the interference of patents with access to medicines due to price effects).

[126] *Report of the Special Rapporteur on the Right to Health, on his Mission to the World Trade Organization 2004* (n 47); Drugs For Neglected Diseases Working Group, 'Fatal Imbalance: The Crisis in Research

bodies, TRIPS violates the right to health because it undermines *access* to medicines. This argument runs along the following lines—member states of the WTO have failed to respect, protect, and fulfil their international obligation with respect to the right to health because they have: (a) participated in the adoption of a regime that harms the health of individuals in other states; (b) have allowed non-state actors to adopt pricing strategies that undermine access to medicines; and (c) have failed to create an international regime that contributes to the fulfilment of the right to health in developing states.

These claims are galvanized by the reality that approximately two billion people are without access to essential medicines[127] and expanding access to existing medical interventions, including medicines, in areas such as maternal and child health and non-communicable diseases would, according to the WHO, save more than 10.5 million lives a year by 2015.[128] These figures sit in stark contrast to the vast profits that many of the world's pharmaceutical companies continue to enjoy and which are facilitated, at least in part, by the patent protection afforded under TRIPS.[129] However, the existence of this inequity does not necessarily mean that states are in breach of their international obligation to co-operate under the right to health. TRIPS may reduce *financial accessibility* to medicines, but this only represents an *interference* with the right to health. The real issue is whether this interference can be justified—a question that tends to be overlooked in most discussions about TRIPS and its impact on access to medicines.[130]

and Development for Drugs for Neglected Diseases' (Médecins Sans Frontières Access to Essential Medicines, Geneva 2001) 10 <http://www.msf.org/source/access/2001/fatal/fatalshort.pdf> accessed 15 August 2011.

[127] WHO, *WHO Medicines Strategy 2000–2003: Framework for Action in Essential Drugs and Medicines Policy*, WHO Doc WHO/EDM/2000.1 (2000) <http://apps.who.int/medicinedocs/en/d/Jwhozip16e/> accessed 11April 2011.

[128] WHO, *WHO Medicines Strategy 2004–2007: Countries at the Core*, WHO Doc WHO/EDM/2004.5 (2004) 3 <http://whqlibdoc.who.int/hq/2004/WHO_EDM_2004.5.pdf> accessed 27 June 2011.

[129] According to the European Commission, the annual turnover for Lipitor, the highest selling drug, was in excess of 9 billion Euros: European Commission, 'Pharmaceutical Sector Inquiry: Preliminary Report' (DG Competition, Staff Working Paper, 2008) 34 <http://ec.europa.eu/competition/sectors/pharmaceuticals/inquiry/preliminary_report.pdf> accessed 27 June 2011. It has also been suggested that in 2002 the top 10 US drug companies enjoyed 'a median profit margin of 17% compared with only 3.1% for the other industries on the Fortune 500 list': Marcia Angell, 'Excess in the Pharmaceutical Industry' (2004) 171 CMAJ 1451, 1451.

[130] A rights-based approach to this issue does not require, as has been suggested by some commentators, that public health must be placed ahead of economic claims: *Intellectual Property Rights and Human Rights* (n 48) para 3; Heinz King, 'Access to Essential Medicines—Promoting Human Rights Over Free Trade and Intellectual Property Claims' in Keith E Maskus and Jerome H Reichman (eds), *International Public Goods and Transfer of Technology under a Globalized Intellectual Property Regime* (CUP, 2005) 481, 492. Nor does it favour what Montero has described as the 'causal thesis' whereby a violation of the right to health has occurred simply because TRIPS may have reduced access to medicines: Montero (n 38) 79.

B Can TRIPS be justified?

In international law, an interference with a human right will only be justified where it is considered to be reasonable.[131] In order to assess the reasonableness of an interference, there are two broad considerations—first, is the interference designed to promote the general welfare of a state (the phrase used for economic and social rights) or pursue a pressing social need (the phrase generally associated with civil and political rights).[132] With respect to these phrases the common theme is the need to assess the legitimacy of the aim of the interference in light of the nature of the right being limited and the importance of the purpose of the limitation. Once the legitimacy of the aim has been established, the inquiry must shift to an assessment of whether the measures used to achieve the stated aim are necessary and proportionate. This involves a consideration of the nature and extent of the limitation; the relationship between the purpose and its limitation; and whether there were any less restrictive means reasonably available to achieve the purpose that the limitation seeks to achieve.[133] States must individually and collectively turn their minds to each of these considerations if their involvement in TRIPS and the TRIPS agreement itself can be justified.

1 The legitimacy of the aim being pursued under TRIPS
(a) The importance of the right to health

The right to health is a fundamental right within the corpus of international human rights law. It is not, however, a non-derogable right such as the right to life or the prohibition against torture and other forms of ill treatment. Within the context of a state's international obligation under the right to health, this means that states need not treat the right to health as a paramount consideration and it remains subject to limitations in light of resource constraints and other legitimate considerations. At the same time, a state is not free to ignore the right to health and must, as a minimum, be cognisant of the importance of this right in debates concerning protection of intellectual property rights to ensure that any inference with the right to health is justified. Indeed, the principle of external system coherence demands that harmonization between regimes of international law—such as trade and human rights—must be pursued and where interference with an element of one regime is to occur—whether it is the right to health or the intellectual property rights—this interference must be justified.[134]

Within this context, it is significant to note that the preamble to TRIPS makes no reference to human rights generally or the right to health specifically. This is hardly surprising given that TRIPS is an international trade law treaty and its primary purpose is not to protect the right to health.[135] However, the failure to identify the

---

[131] See Chapter 5 pp 180–4.
[132] ibid.   [133] ibid.   [134] See Chapter 3 pp 105–8.
[135] Helfer and Austin (n 46) 31–4 (discuss historical isolation of human rights and intellectual property regimes).

right to health as being part of the context in which TRIPS was to operate, suggests that states did not consider their international obligation with respect to the right to health when negotiating TRIPS. To be fair, article 7 does stress the need to protect intellectual property rights 'in a manner conducive to social and economic welfare' and article 8(1) provides that:

Members may... adopt measures necessary to protect public health and nutrition, and to promote the public interest in sectors of vital importance to their socio-economic and technological development, provided that such measures are consistent with the provisions of this Agreement.

Moreover, article 27 allows members to exclude from patentability inventions necessary to protect health and therapeutic methods for the treatment of humans.

However, these provisions are relatively weak concessions and are not framed in terms of the right to health and its attendant obligations on states under other international instruments. Thus, in any perceived conflict, the balance is already tilted in favour of the protection of private intellectual property rights which provide the underlying rationale for the Agreement. A blind spot exists within TRIPS to the extent that it contains no awareness of: (a) the relevance of right to health; and (b) the process required under international law to justify any limitation with this right as a consequence of the protection accorded to intellectual property rights. Irrespective of the impact of TRIPS on access to medicines, the apparent failure to consider the right to health in the drafting of this instrument represents a violation of the conduct element of the international obligation under the right to health. Put simply, states did not ensure the adoption of a procedure that would enable a reasonable balancing between any conflict that would arise between the right to health and the need to protect intellectual property rights.

In response to this disequilibrium, the Declaration on the TRIPS Agreement and Public Health, which was adopted by the WTO Ministerial at Doha in 2001 ('Doha Declaration'), represents an attempt to address the disproportionate and thus unreasonable approach adopted under TRIPS.[136] Although there is no explicit recognition of the right to health in the Doha Declaration, the preambular paragraphs are consistent with the values that underlie this right. For example, there is an acknowledgement of the need for TRIPS to 'be part of the wider national and international action' to address global public health issues, a recognition that 'intellectual property protection is important for the development of new medicines', and agreement that

---

[136] WTO, *Declaration on the TRIPS Agreement and Public Health*, WTO Doc WT/MIN(01)/DEC/2 (20 November 2001, adopted 14 November 2001) (Ministerial Declaration) (Doha Declaration). Two high profile cases concerning access to medicines also formed the background to the adoption of the Doha Declaration: *Pharmaceutical Manufacturers' Association of South Africa v President of the Republic of South Africa*, Notice of Motion, Case No 4183/98 (February 1998) (HC, Sth Afr); and *Brazil—Measures Affecting Patent Protection*, WTO Doc WT/DS199/4, G/L/454, IP/D/23/Add.1 (19 July 2001) (Notice of Mutually Agreed Solution). It has also been influenced by a concerted effort from civil society, developing nations and mid-tier nations such as Thailand, India, and Brazil: Thomas Pogge, Matthew Rimmer, and Kim Rubenstein, 'Access to Essential Medicines: Public Health and International Law' in Thomas Pogge, Matthew Rimmer, and Kim Rubenstein (eds), *Incentives for Global Public Health: Patent Law and Access to Essential Medicines* (CUP, 2010) 1, 11.

TRIPS 'can and should be interpreted and implemented in a manner supportive of WTO members' right to protect public health and, in particular, to promote access to medicines for all.'[137] This rhetoric may fall short of a conscious acknowledgement of the importance of the right to health but it is a significant advance on TRIPS.

(b) The importance of the purpose of the limitation

The preamble to TRIPS indicates that the original purpose of this instrument was confined to the protection of private intellectual property rights in a market-based system. Commentators may object to this system on moral or ethical grounds,[138] but under existing international law, which allows for market based systems, such an objective is legitimate. Indeed, intellectual property rights have been protected under international law since the adoption of the Paris Convention for the Protection of Industrial Property in 1883.[139] Moreover, article 15(1)(c) of the ICESCR actually requires 'protection of the moral and material interests resulting from any scientific, literary or artistic production.'[140] There is some debate as to the scope of this

---

[137] Doha Declaration (n 136) preamble 1–4.

[138] See, eg, Thomas Pogge, *World Poverty and Human Rights: Cosmopolitan Responsibilities and Reforms* (2nd edn, Polity Press, 2008) 222–61 (considers the international regime for the protection of intellectual property rights morally problematic); the 'Manchester Manifesto', adopted by a group of leading scientists and academics in November 2009, calls for a reassessment of the current system of patents and intellectual property regulated by national and international laws: Institute For Science Ethics And Innovation, 'Who Owns Science? The Manchester Manifesto' (University of Manchester, 2009) <http://www.isei.manchester.ac.uk/TheManchesterManifesto.pdf> accessed 27 June 2011.

[139] Paris Convention for the Protection of Industrial Property (Paris, 20 March 1883, entered into force 26 April 1970, 828 UNTS 305).

[140] This principle is also contained in art 27(2) of the UDHR (n 86) which provides that, 'Everyone has the right to the protection of the moral and material interests resulting from any scientific, literary or artistic production of which he is the author.' See also art 13(2) of the American Declaration of the Rights and Duties of Man, OAS Res XXX (Ninth International Conference of American States, 1948), reprinted in Basic Documents Pertaining to Human Rights in the Inter-American System at OEA/Ser L V/II.82 Doc 6 Rev 1 at 17 (1992), art 13(2); art 14(1)(c) of the Additional Protocol to the American Convention on Human Rights in the Area of Economic, Social and Cultural Rights (Protocol of San Salvador) (San Salvador, 17 November 1988, entered into force 16 November 1999, OAS Treaty Series No 69 (1988), 28 ILM 156), reprinted in Basic Documents Pertaining to Human Rights in the Inter-American System OEA/Ser L V/II.82 Doc 6 Rev 1 at 67 (1992); and, albeit not explicitly, in art 1 of Protocol No 1 to the Convention for the Protection of Human Rights and Fundamental Freedoms (European Convention on Human Rights, as amended) (ECHR). It is important to note that the ICESCR also demands a redistributive approach with respect to scientific advancements, the benefits of which are to be shared: see ICESCR, art 15(1)(b). The ESC Committee actually issued a Statement on Human Rights and Intellectual Property in 2001 in which it declared that 'the intellectual property rights must be balanced with the right...to enjoy the benefits of scientific progress and its applications': Economic and Social Council, *Human Rights and Intellectual Property*, UN Doc E/C.12/2001/15 (14 December 2001) para 4. There has also been some suggestion that IP rights should not enjoy the same status as human rights. The ESC Committee has tended to reflect this position. For example in its G*eneral Comment No 17* it declared that '[i]n contrast with human rights, intellectual property rights are generally of a temporary nature and can be revoked, licensed or assigned to someone else...': ESC Committee, *General Comment No 17* (n 121) para 2. But such an approach is problematic as it starts to import subjective assessments as to the legitimacy and status of certain rights under the ESC. A more appropriate approach is simply to recognize that health and IP have both been identified by States as interests worthy of the status of an international human right. The issue therefore is how to balance these rights when they come into conflict, which requires the adoption of the proportionality analysis discussed in this section.

provision, and whether it entitles an inventor of a medicine to be granted a patent, and also whether it can be invoked by pharmaceutical companies who are not human beings and thus not rights holders.[141] Hestermeyer actually argues that article 15(1)(c) 'offers very little ground to stand on as a justification for an interference with the right to access to medicine'.[142] But this conclusion fails to recognize that intellectual *property rights* and patents, although not fundamental *human rights*,[143] can represent legitimate measures by which to give effect to article 15(1)(c). It also overlooks the reality that the real issue is not the granting of the patent but whether its impact on access to medicines and the human right to health is disproportionate.

The other purported aim of TRIPS, as reflected in the preamble to the Doha Declaration, is the idea that 'intellectual property protection is important for the development of new medicines'.[144] This proposition is almost self-evident given that new medicines require significant investment in research and development—between $115 and $802 million according to some estimates—and without patent protection, pharmaceutical companies would have little incentive to allocate the vast sums required to develop new medicines.[145] Moreover, few would challenge the claim that this protection has led to an increase in the *availability* of medicines—a key element of the right to health—and has arguably satisfied the requirement under article 4 of the ICESCR that an interference with an economic and social right will be justified where its purpose is to promote the general welfare in a society. The problem with this model, however, is that an instrument which is designed to protect intellectual property (IP) rights in a market-based system, provides limited incentive to create the new medicines most needed by developing states which are in great need but have limited purchasing power.[146]

However, the fact that TRIPS and the Doha Declaration do not create the optimal conditions for the fulfilment of the right to health in developing states in terms of *availability* and *financial accessibility* of medicines, does not mean that this regime violates the right to health. It simply means that TRIPS is not a sufficient or effective mechanism to *fulfil* these elements of the international obligation with respect to the right to health. Thus, the real issue in this discussion is whether TRIPS actually represents a violation of the international obligation to respect and protect the right to health by denying individuals access to existing medicines. There are strong

---

[141] See Hestermeyer (n 122) 153–7; Helfer and Austin (n 46) ch 3.
[142] Hestermeyer (n 122) 157–8.
[143] CRC Committee, *General Comment No 17* (n 121) para 1. See also Chapman (n 123) (argues that drafting history supports idea of intellectual property rights as being instrumental in character rather than fundamental human rights).
[144] Doha Declaration (n 136) preamble para 3.
[145] Harvey E Bale Jr, 'Patents, Patients and Developing Countries: Access, Innovation and the Political Dimensions of Trade Policy' in Brigitte Granville (ed), *The Economics of Essential Medicines* (Royal Institute of International Affairs, 2002) 100, 102ff; Hestermeyer (n 122) 159. See also Joseph A DiMasi, Ronald W Hansen and Henry G Grabowski, 'The Price of Innovation: New Estimates of Drug Development Costs' (2003) 22 J Health Econ 151, 180 (suggests costs of developing a new drug and bringing it to market can be US$900 million).
[146] Consider the trickle-down effect: Doris Schroeder and Peter Singer, 'Access to Life Saving Medicines and Intellectual Property Rights: An Ethical Assessment' (2011) 20 Cam Q Health Ethics 279, 8–9.

grounds to argue that the underlying aims of TRIPS are legitimate and it is too simplistic to assert that this instrument is simply a prioritization of IP rights over the right to health.[147] A question remains as to whether the scheme created under TRIPS and the Doha Declaration is reasonable and necessary for the purpose of achieving its aims. This is essentially a proportionality assessment which requires a consideration of the nature and extent of the limitation caused by TRIPS on the right to health; the relationship between the purposes of TRIPS and the interference with the right to health (the rational connection test); and whether there are any less restrictive means reasonably available to achieve these purposes (the minimal impairment test).

2 The proportionality assessment

(a) The nature and extent of the limitation caused by TRIPS on the right to health

There is some debate as to the nature and extent of the interference with access to medicines caused by TRIPS.[148] One commentator, for example, has claimed that of the 319 drugs on the WHO Model List of Essential Medicines, few are patentable and of those that are, the patented incidence is only 1.4 per cent.[149] However, in response to this claim, the Director of Medicines Policy and Standards at the WHO has argued that these figures are misleading because a range of additional factors must be considered including the relevant geographical area and the reality that it only takes a few patented medicines in high demand areas to affect accessibility because of the cost of these medicines.[150] Moreover, the right of access to medicines, which is derived from the right to health, is not confined to essential medicines and extends progressively to a right to any medicine that will treat or mitigate the impact of ill health. Thus, as a general proposition, it remains reasonable to assert that the impact of TRIPS will be to increase the price of a drug and thus reduce access, compared to a situation in which there is less effective patent protection. Moreover, the impact on access is likely to be more acute in developing countries because of the relatively limited purchasing power of the individuals who require the patented medicine *and* the greater likelihood that a developing state will not have a national medicines policy to reduce the cost of medicines to an individual.[151]

However, this interference with access to medicines does not per se constitute a violation of the right to health. That will depend on whether the resulting restrictions on access can be justified. As a general rule, the greater the reduction in access to a medicine and the greater the impact of a medicine on the health of an individual, the greater the burden on a state to justify any interference with the right of access to medicines that would arise under TRIPS. This general rule has two consequences. First, it imposes obligations on states, such as those involved in the drafting of TRIPS,

---

[147] cf O'Connell (n 123) 203, 206.
[148] See Hestermeyer (n 122) 148–52.
[149] Amir Attaran, 'How Do Patents and Economic Policies Affect Access to Essential Medicines in Developing Countries?' (2004) 23 Health Affairs 155, 157.
[150] Hans Hogerzeil, 'WHO Model List of Essential Medicines and Patents' (Online forum post, 23 March 2005) <http://www.essentialdrugs.org/edrug/archive/200503/msg00071.php> accessed 27 June 2011.
[151] Hestermeyer (n 122) 148–9.

to provide an objective basis to justify the nature of the patent protection offered under TRIPS, and second, it demands TRIPS include a degree of flexibility to accommodate the reality that the impact of patents on access to medicine and the health of individuals will vary.

(b) **The rational connection test and minimal impairment principle**
The requirement to justify an interference with a human right on the basis of cogent and persuasive evidence is sometimes referred to as the rational connection test.[152] It means that mere assumptions or assertions by states, or the pharmaceutical industry, that the absence and duration of a patent would act as a disincentive to the development of new medicines are inadequate. The burden rests on those agitating for protection of IP rights to establish on the balance of probabilities a rational and objective connection between the legitimate aims of incentivizing and rewarding research and the actual protection being sought.

In this respect the justification for the current protection of 20 years is questionable as it rests on an historic coincidence that dates back to Belgium patent legislation adopted in 1854, rather than on cogent economic analysis.[153] Christie and Rotstein have, however, sought to assess whether 20 years' protection is within the reasonable bounds of what might be considered optimal taking into account the marginal social benefit of a patent over time and the marginal social cost.[154] Their examination of the studies done in this area indicate that, depending on the assumptions, the optimal duration of a patent is likely to lie with the range of one year to infinity. Such a finding is perhaps not surprising and indicates the difficulty in establishing cogent and persuasive evidence to support the 20-year rule. However, by examining patent renewal data from several jurisdictions, Christie and Rotstein were able to establish that approximately 50 per cent of patents lapse after eight years and only 15 per cent survive the full period of protection. Using this data, they argue that a 20-year protection period, although erring on the side of being too long, is still within the reasonable bounds of what could be considered an optimal patent system provided that: (a) renewal fees for patents increased over time; and (b) there remained the capacity to reduce the maximum duration of a patent on a case-by-case basis by use of a compulsory licence.[155]

These findings are of relevance to this inquiry in two respects. First, the fact that the 20-year period was found to err on the side of being too long raises the question of whether a shorter period would be adequate. But at least there is some research to justify the 20-year period as being within a range of reasonable alternatives. Second, and perhaps more importantly, the TRIPS regime does not preclude member states from developing a patent renewal system with fees that increase over the life of the

---

[152] See Chapter 5 p 182.
[153] ibid 159.
[154] Andrew F Christie and Fiona Rotstein, 'Duration of Patent Protection: Does One Size Fit All?' (Intellectual Property Research Institute of Australia, Working Paper No 04.07, June 2007).
[155] ibid 15.

patent.[156] It also includes mechanisms by which the duration and effect of a patent can be reduced or suspended on a case-by-case basis. The most notable flexibility mechanism is article 31 which also allows for 'other use' of a patent without the authorization of the right holder, 'including use by the government or third parties authorized by the government'.[157] In theory, this provision entitles a member state to grant a licence without the patent holder's consent ('a compulsory licence') to a pharmaceutical company within its jurisdiction to manufacture or import the patented product where certain conditions are satisfied. Amongst these conditions are the payment of remuneration and reasonable efforts to obtain authorization (a voluntary licence) from the patent holder. Significantly, a member may waive this requirement for authorization 'in the case of a national emergency or other circumstances of extreme urgency or in cases of public non-commercial use'.[158] Thus, TRIPS does provide a mechanism to minimize the extent of its interference on the right of access to medicines in certain circumstances—an approach which represents an attempt to balance protection of IP rights with protection of the right to health.

However, the exception under article 31 is illusory for those states that lack the capacity to manufacture the relevant medicines within their own jurisdiction under a compulsory licence. Although there is still a capacity to import patented medicines under a compulsory licence, this would only be a viable option if the imported product was below market price.[159] Moreover, TRIPS requires that compulsory licences are to be predominantly for the supply of the domestic market and, as Mitchell and Voon have argued, 'only a relatively small portion of pharmaceuticals manufactured pursuant to compulsory licences worldwide may be legitimately exported to countries in need and lacking manufacturing capacity'.[160]

---

[156] For example, in Australia maintenance fees are payable to IP Australia yearly after the 4th anniversary of the grant. USD$132 is payable on the fifth anniversary and this figure rises to USD$877 on the 20th anniversary: IP Australia, 'Patent Fees' (Fee Schedule, effective 1 August 2010) <http://www.ipaustralia.gov.au/patents/fees_index.shtml> accessed 30 May 2011. The EPO maintenance fees are paid annually after the second anniversary with the fee starting at USD$445 for the 3rd year and rising to USD $1195 for the tenth and each subsequent year. The fees at the USPTO are payable after 3.5 years (USD $900), 7.5 years (USD$2,300) and 11.5 years (USD$3,800): United States Patent and Trademark Office (USPTO), 'Patent Maintenance Fees' (Fee Schedule effective 2 October 2008) <http://www.uspto.gov/web/offices/ac/qs/ope/fee2009september15.htm#maintain> accessed 30 May 2011.

[157] See also TRIPS, art 30, which allows members to 'provide limited exceptions to the exclusive rights conferred by a patent, provided that such exceptions do not unreasonably conflict with a normal exploitation of the patent and do not unreasonably prejudice the legitimate interests of the patent owner, taking account of the legitimate interests of third parties'. This provision arguably provides a basis for a state to manufacture or import generic versions of patented medicines without the patent holder's consent. However, as Mitchell and Voon have observed, 'the likely outcome in the case of challenge to such a practice under the WTO dispute settlement system is uncertain': Andrew Mitchell and Tania Voon, 'Patents and Public Health in the WTO, FTAs and Beyond: Tension and Conflict in International Law' (2009) 43 J World Trade 571, 575. An interim measure provided for under TRIPS to alleviate the burden on developing states (or LDCs) was to provide for a longer transition period with respect to implementation during which such States could use cheaper versions of generic drugs to address public health crises such as HIV/AIDS: TRIPS, arts 65, 66.

[158] TRIPS, art 31.
[159] Mitchell and Voon (n 157) 576.
[160] ibid 576.

The impact of the Doha Declaration The Doha Declaration was adopted in an attempt to overcome the limitations of article 31 and increase the flexibility under TRIPS. It seeks to minimally impair the interference with the right of access to medicines by adopting two strategies. First, it extends the implementation period for least developing countries (LDCs) from 2006 to 2016 thereby giving these states more time to create an appropriate domestic legislative framework with respect to the protection of intellectual property rights.[161] But if a concession for LDCs can be made now without compromising the aims of TRIPS, this raises a question as to why this concession is subject to a temporal rather than qualitative consideration. As Hetermeyer explains, the markets in developing states are relatively insignificant in the world economy with the major drug companies achieving 80 per cent of their sales in the USA, Canada, the EU, and Japan.[162] In contrast, Africa represents just 1.1 per cent of the global market.[163] Such figures suggest there is a limited connection between the need to extend TRIPS to developing states and its aim of protecting intellectual property rights. Thus, to the extent that TRIPS does impact on the right to health in developing countries, there is an issue as to whether the expiration of the extension for LDCs in 2016 would be consistent with the requirement that TRIPS must adopt a regime that minimally impairs the right to health if the qualitative characteristics that justified the exemption for these states were to persist in 2016. The counter to this concern is the argument that TRIPS will incentivize research and development for new drugs in developing states. However, the evidence available to date simply does not support this assumption and the research priorities of pharmaceutical companies will, all other things being equal, continue to be focused on the more profitable markets in developed countries.[164] Moreover, the extended transition period does not address the issue of access to medicines in those developing states that lack both an effective manufacturing capacity and the resources to import expensive patented medicines.

The Doha Declaration seeks to provide a strategy to address these concerns and allow developing states in these circumstances to take advantage of the flexibilities created under article 31 of TRIPS. Paragraph 6 of the Declaration recognized 'that WTO Members with insufficient or no manufacturing capacities in the pharmaceutical sector could face difficulties in making effective use of compulsory licensing under the TRIPS Agreement'. It therefore instructed 'Council for TRIPS to find an expeditious solution to this problem and to report to the General Council'. The Decision of the General Council, adopted in August 2003,[165] creates the capacity to seek a waiver of article 31(f) of the TRIPS agreement so that a member state that

---

[161] LDCs are defined by the UN Committee for Development Policy based on income, human assets, and economic vulnerability: ESC Committee for Development Policy, *Report of the Eighth Session: 20–24 March 2006*, UN Doc E/2006/33(Supp) (25 April 2006) 16. As Kee explains LDCs not only lack a TRIPS compatible domestic IP regime but they also lack the resources necessary to defend a complaint before the WTO Dispute Settlement Body. Thus they are unlikely to avail themselves of any of the potential flexibilities under TRIPS for fear of litigation: Kee (n 123) 48.

[162] Hestermeyer (n 122) 161.
[163] ibid. [164] ibid 163.
[165] *Implementation of Paragraph 6 of the Doha Declaration on the TRIPS Agreement and Public Health*, WTO Doc WT/L/540 (2 September 2003) (Decision of 30 August 2003); Doha Declaration (n 136).

lacks manufacturing capacity (an 'eligible importing member') can import patented medicines from another member state under a compulsory licence provided certain conditions are satisfied.[166] When viewed from a human rights perspective, the aim of this strategy is to reduce the impact of TRIPS on access to medicines and minimally infer with the right to health.

The decision of the General Council was lauded by member states—developing and developed—as a significant breakthrough in resolving the tension between IP protection and access to medicines.[167] However, commentators take differing views as to whether this approach strikes the appropriate balance. Mitchell and Voon, for example, argue that '[t]he WTO should be applauded for having reached an interim solution to the conflict between patents and public health' and believe that the current approach enhances the opportunities for developing countries to access generic medicines when dealing with grave public health concerns.[168] Joseph is more circumspect and points to uncertainty in relation to the extent to which the waiver will apply beyond health crises and thus suggests that it 'may do little to enhance access to drugs for sufferers of cancer or heart disease'.[169] Others have described it as excessively complex[170] and ineffectual in practice[171]—a claim that is said to find support in the fact that only one state, Rwanda, has taken advantage of the flexibilities, to import cheap drugs from Canada.[172] It also remains an interim measure rather than a permanent solution because member states are yet to formally amend TRIPS to include the waiver.

However, in terms of the proportionality assessment, which is used to determine the legitimacy of any interference caused by TRIPS with the right of access to medicines, the current model would appear to be justified (subject to the absence of an objective basis to support the temporal transition period for LCDs). It reflects an awareness of the need to strike an appropriate balance between the need to protect IP rights and incentivize research and development in new medicines on the one hand, and an acknowledgement that in the absence of the extended transition time

---

[166] The importing member must make a recommendation to the Council for TRIPS providing: the names and expected quantities of the product(s) needed; confirmation that the eligible importing member has established that it has insufficient or no manufacturing capacities for the product in question; and confirmation that it has granted or intends to grant a compulsory licence if the product is patented in its territory. See *Implementation of Paragraph 6 of the Doha Declaration on the TRIPS Agreement and Public Health* (n 165) para 2(e). Once granted, the compulsory licence must contain several conditions regarding the quantity of the drug produced, its packaging, and labelling: para 2(b).

[167] See Hestermeyer (n 122) 271.

[168] Mitchell and Voon (n 157) 581, 601.

[169] Sarah Joseph, 'Trade and the Right to Health' in Andrew Clapham and Mary Robinson (eds), *Realising the Right to Health* (Rüffer & Rub, 2009) 359, 362.

[170] Ranjan (n 123) 569–70.

[171] See, eg, Brook Baker, 'Arthritric Flexibilities for Accessing Medicines: Analysis of WTO Action Regarding Paragraph 6 of the Doha Declaration on the TRIPS Agreement and Public Health' (20004) 14 Ind Int'l & Comp L Rev 613; Matthew Rimmer, 'Race against Time: The Export of Essential Medicines to Rwanda' (2008) 1 PHE 89; 'The Jean Chrétien Pledge to Africa Act: Patent Law and Humanitarian Aid' (2005) 15 Expert Op Therapeutic Patents 889; 'A Joint Submission to the Joint Standing Committee on Treaties: The Hong Kong Amendment to the TRIPS Agreement' (Submission 2, 9 May 2007). cf Hestermeyer (n 122) (identifies factors to explain limited use of scheme).

[172] See Matthew Rimmer, 'The Jean Chretien Pledge to Africa Pact: Patent Law and Humanitarian Aid' (2005) 15 Expert O Therapeutic Patents 888; Rimmer (n 171).

for LCDs and the flexibility provided by the waiver, then the measures under TRIPS would remain disproportionate. The adoption of the interim approach is not necessarily inconsistent with the right to health as it provides an opportunity to monitor and review the impact of the measures under the Doha Declaration. As discussed in Chapter 5, this capacity for review is an essential element in assessing the reasonableness of any policy that impacts on the right to health.

The effectiveness of the article 31 waiver Although the limited use of the waiver is a cause for concern, it does not necessarily mean that the process provided under the Doha Declaration is incapable of providing the flexibility required to ensure that TRIPS avoids a one size fits all approach. Consideration needs to be given as to why member states are reluctant to use this process. In this respect it is important to note that paragraph 8 of the Decision on Implementation of Paragraph 6 of the Doha Declaration requires the Council to review annually the effectiveness of the waiver.[173] If the procedures are deemed to be excessive and cumbersome then this would require a refinement of the process.[174] But if the reasons are linked to national political or strategic considerations, indifference, or anxiety about the reaction of pharmaceutical companies,[175] then member states must be reminded of both their internal and international obligation with respect to the health. A state's internal obligation demands that if it lacks the manufacturing capacity to provide effective access to medicines, it should request a waiver as an eligible importing member in order to facilitate the provision of such medicines. Indeed, it within this context that the CRC Committee has recommended, in its concluding observations for the Philippines, that the state party, 'Make use—in the negotiations of Free Trade Agreement—of all the flexibilities reaffirmed by the Doha Declaration and the mechanisms at its disposal to ensure access to affordable medicines in particular for the poor and most vulnerable children and their parents'.[176]

With respect to the *international* obligation of states to take measures to contribute to the realization of the right to health, states must give proper consideration to

---

[173] *Implementation of Paragraph 6 of the Doha Declaration on the TRIPS Agreement and Public Health* (n 165) para 8. See for example the report of the 2010 Review: WTO, 'Members Ask: Is the "Par.6" System on Intellectual Property and Health Working?' (News Item, 2 March 2010) <http://www.wto.org/english/news_e/news10_e/trip_02mar10_e.htm> accessed 14 April 2011 (2010 Review); Hestermeyer (n 122) 272; Ben Sihanya, 'Patents, Parallel Importation and Compulsory Licensing of HIV/AIDS Drugs: The Experience of Kenya' (Managing the Challenges of WTO Participation Case Study No 19) <www.wto.org/english/res_e/booksp_e/casestudies_e/case19_e.htm> accessed 12 April 2011 (suggests that local manufacturing companies are afraid to invest in compulsory licensing or parallel imports for fear of taking on pharmaceutical giants).

[174] See 2010 Review (n 173), which suggest mixed views among members. cf Professor Jayashree Watal, 'Access to Medicines and Human Rights' (Public Lecture, Melbourne Law School, 21 April 2011) (suggesting that the limited use of para 6 of the DOHA Declaration was because there was limited need for it use because, for example, in the area of HIV/AIDS drugs, a drop in price of 90% meant they had become more affordable to LDCs).

[175] Sihanya (n 173).

[176] CO CRC Philippines (n 88) para 59(f). It has also warned that states 'undertake assessments of the potential impact of global trade policies concerning liberalisation of trade in services on the enjoyment of human rights including children's rights': CRC Commitee, *Report of the Thirty-First Session* (n 56) para 13.

their capacity to provide a compulsory licence to meet the needs of an eligible importing member. Proper consideration does not mandate that a state must grant a compulsory licence but it does require that a state must be actively alert to, and give genuine consideration to, such a measure in light of its international obligation under the right to health. Moreover, a failure to grant such a licence must be justified as being reasonable in the circumstances.

In assessing reasonableness, economic considerations are appropriately taken into account. This is especially relevant given that an exporting Member must pay adequate compensation and this may act as a disincentive to granting a compulsory licence.[177] But the international obligation to co-operate reflects a legal commitment, albeit weak, to the notion of global distributive justice. Thus, developed states cannot play the resource card as a trump to refuse the grant of a compulsory licence. They must demonstrate why in light of the totality of their available resources *and* their internal and international obligations with respect to realizing all human rights (not just the right to health), that the issue of a compulsory licence would be unreasonable in the circumstances. And even if a state lacks the resources necessary to support the issue of a compulsory licence, it is still under an obligation to make reasonable efforts to promote and encourage other states or indeed non-state actors such as international institutions, pharmaceutical companies, philanthropists, and civil society to contribute the resources necessary to ensure access to medicines for persons in developing countries.

C Trade law and human rights—in search of system coherence

The final point to make in the assessment of TRIPS is that there is scope within the existing agreement to reconceptualize its provisions by shifting away from the trade perspective that has 'animated' its interpretation to an approach that grapples with the need to ensure coherence within the right to health.[178] The challenge here is twofold—first, to recalibrate the expectations of the WTO interpretative community which has historically had an aversion to the interpretative role and significance of human rights in a trade instrument[179] and second, to ensure that human rights advocates recognize that use of the right to health as an interpretative tool for TRIPS does not mean that this right must always receive priority over intellectual property rights. This is clearly not permitted under the text of TRIPS but nor is it required by the right to health. The requirement to pursue external system coherence when interpreting an international treaty has two consequences. First, harmonization

---

[177] CO CRC Philippines (n 88) para 59(f). It has also warned that states 'undertake assessments of the potential impact of global trade policies concerning liberalisation of trade in services on the enjoyment of human rights including children's rights': CRC Commitee, *Report of the Thirty-First Session* (n 56) para 272.

[178] Rochelle C Dreyfuss, 'TRIPS and Essential Medicines: Must One Size Fit All? Making the WTO Responsive to the Global Health Crisis' in Thomas Pogge, Matthew Rimmer and Kim Rubenstein (eds), *Incentives for Global Public Health: Patent Law and Access to Essential Medicines* (CUP, 2010) 35, 48–9; Hestermeyer (n 122) ch 5; Helfer and Austin (n 46) 506–22.

[179] Helfer and Austin (n 46) 31–4 (examine the historical isolation of the human rights and intellectual property regimes).

between legal regimes should be preferred over fragmentation, which means that the interpretation of the provisions under TRIPS should be informed, where relevant, by the international right to health.[180] Second, harmonization is not always possible and in the event of an irreconcilable normative conflict under international law, decision makers must, within the context of TRIPS, ensure that any interference with the right of access to medicines caused by the protection of IP rights can be justified as being reasonable, that is, necessary and proportionate, to achieve the legitimate aims under TRIPS. Moreover, the burden rests on states agitating for IP protection to demonstrate on the basis of evidence that the patent protection under TRIPS is necessary. Thus, while the Doha Declaration represents an indication that member states of the WTO are now more cognizant of the need to accommodate public health concerns, there is still limited evidence to suggest that these concerns are motivated by an explicit awareness as to the nature of the international obligation imposed on states with respect to the realization of the right to health.

This lack of awareness is manifest in the adoption of so-called 'TRIPS +' agreements which are negotiated at a bilateral level between states. These agreements often threaten or undermine the flexibilities created within TRIPS as a result of the Doha Declaration by pressuring states to provide protection for intellectual property rights which are more demanding than TRIPS. Moreover, they are unaccompanied by any evidence to justify this additional protection and appear to be driven solely by the profit demands of pharmaceutical companies. When viewed from a human rights perspective, the obligation to achieve a proportionate and justifiable form of patent protection in light of the right to health appears to be an irrelevant consideration in these agreements. This is not to say that the impact of such agreements will always be negative on the right of access to medicines.[181] But the failure to consider the relevance and impact of this right creates such a risk because of the tendency for such agreements to increase IP protection in 'areas such as the existence and duration of exclusivity or by reducing the use of flexibilities such as compulsory licensing and parallel imports'.[182] Indeed, Mitchell and Voon have gone so far as to suggest that if

---

[180] See Hestermeyer (n 122) ch 5 (examines articles under TRIPS the interpretation of which could be informed by the right to health). This same principle applies with respect to the interpretation of the GATT as incorporated into the WTO in those cases where protective trade practices are adopted for public health reasons. See Joseph (n 169) 366. A discussion of the cases in this area is beyond the scope of this chapter.
[181] Nor it is suggested that the potentially negative impact of such agreements on access to medicines will be confined to developing countries see: Thomas Faunce, Jimmy Bai, and Duy Nguyen, 'Impact of the Australia–US Free Trade Agreement on Australian Medicines Regulation and Prices' (2010) 7 J Gen Med 18, 26 (examine the impact of the US–Australia Free Trade Agreement, and conclude that despite the determination of the Australian Government to preserve access to medicines under its Pharmaceutical Benefits Scheme when negotiating the Agreement, the subsequent domestic regulatory changes made in light of the Agreement will over time 'result in higher prices for some patented drugs than would have been the case under previous pricing arrangements').
[182] Gaëlle Krikorian and Dorota Szymkowiak, 'Intellectual Property Rights in the Making: The Evolution of Intellectual Property Provisions in US Free Trade Agreements and Access to Medicine' (2007) 10 JWIP 388, 408. See also MDG Gap Task Force (n 120) 72–3.

such bilateral practices continue, then the 'flexibility to address public health purposes under the TRIPS waiver will become an "empty shell"'.[183] The international obligation to co-operate for the purpose of securing the right to health does not tolerate behaviour of states that seeks to shift the balance in favour of large pharmaceutical companies in the absence of any rational basis to justify this realignment of interests. States that facilitate and enter such agreements without a proper consideration of the impact on access to medicines are in violation of their international obligation to respect, protect, and fulfil the right to health.

D TRIPS and access to medicines—adjusting and reviewing expectations

It is important to note that the international regime for the protection of IP rights cannot and need not be seen as the sole mechanism by which international co-operation should be undertaken for the purpose of securing access to medicines in developing states. To invest an expectation in TRIPS that this agreement will secure access to medicines for all is to misunderstand its *raison d'etre*. TRIPS may play a role in contributing to this end. But even if it fails in this respect (and the evidence to date suggests that it has been of limited benefit to developing states at least in the short term),[184] from a human rights perspective, the minimum concern is to ensure that a member state's involvement in TRIPS does not violate its international obligation to *respect* and *protect* the right to health. That TRIPS does not satisfy the international obligation to *fulfil* the right to health means that states must continue to co-operate for the purposes of identifying what other measures could address this gap including further amendments to TRIPS or the development of alternative or complementary systems.[185]

This is not the place to examine in detail what these measures might be and it is sufficient to note that commentators have suggested schemes such as a Health Impact Fund to complement TRIPS,[186] prizes for medical innovation,[187] and an agreement

---

[183] Mitchell and Voon (n 157) 601. See also Hestermeyer (n 122) 289–92; Hitoshi Nasu, 'Public Law Challenges to the Regulation of Pharmaceutical Patents in the US Bilateral Free Trade Agreements' in Thomas Pogge, Matthew Rimmer and Kim Rubenstein (eds), *Incentives for Global Public Health: Patent Law and Access to Essential Medicines* (CUP, 2010) 77, 89–90 (discusses the issue of normative fragmentation in the context of bilateral free trade agreements especially the potential for conflict with the right to health).

[184] See Schroeder and Singer (n 146) 8–9 (suggest that the social utility of TRIPS for the poor is difficult to assess because although monopoly pricing reduces accessibility in the short term, it creates incentives for the development of new drugs which may benefit the poor in the future when the patents expire and prices drop).

[185] See Manchester Manifesto (n 138).

[186] Aidan Hollis and Thomas Pogge, *The Health Impact Fund: Making New Medicines Available for All* (Incentives for Global Health, 2008) <http://www.yale.edu/macmillan/igh/e-library.html#> accessed 11 April 2011. For a critique of Pogge's model see: Aidan Hollis, 'The Health Impact Fund: A Useful Supplement to the Patent System?' (2008) 1 PHE 124.

[187] See, eg, William Fischer and Talha Syed, 'Global Justice in Health Care: Developing New Drugs for the Developing World'(2007) 40 UC Davis L Rev 581; Joseph Stiglitz, 'Scrooge and Intellectual Property Rights: A Medical Prize Fund Could Improve the Financing of Drug Innovations' (2006) 333

on health technology innovation.[188] As a matter of international law, states are not bound to adopt any of these measures. As a minimum, however, the international obligation to promote and encourage assistance to other states requires a good faith consideration of these suggestions and the development of others in the spirit of collaboration. Although this is a relatively weak obligation, it still creates a site in which states must engage in a discussion of these issues, which is informed by the right to health and access to medicines rather than simply the interests of pharmaceutical companies. Moreover, it imposes an onus on states to co-operate for the purposes of developing appropriate strategies to address the failure of the international community to provide access to medicines. Significantly there are already a number of global initiatives with respect to the issue such as the Intergovernmental Working Group on Public Health, Innovation and Intellectual Property whose global strategy was adopted by the World Health Assembly in 2008,[189] the World Intellectual Property Organisation's agenda with respect to public health,[190] and efforts such as the UNDP MDG Gap Task Force to realize MDG Goal 6, which is to combat HIV/AIDS, malaria, and other diseases. The involvement of states in these initiatives should be seen as example of international co-operation.

Finally, it is important to point out that even if the international community were to develop an international system to ensure the availability and accessibility of medicines to all states, this would not guarantee access to medicines *within* a state. Internal barriers such as inadequate national commitment and inadequate human resources have been identified as key barriers to the creation of an effective internal system for the delivery of medicines.[191] States have a progressive obligation to address these obstacles as part of their *internal* obligation to provide access to medicines. However, the *international* obligation under the right to health also demands that states must not only respect and protect foreign domestic health systems, but actively and genuinely consider the measures by which they can individually and collectively assist developing states create the domestic infrastructure necessary to support access to medicines.

BMJ 1279; James Love and Tim Hubbard, 'The Big Idea: Prizes to Stimulate R&D for New Medicines' (2007) 82 Chi-Kent L Rev 1519.

[188] See Faunce, Bai, and Nguyen (n 181).

[189] World Health Assembly, Res WHA61.21 (adopted 24 May 2008). The aim of the strategy is to enhance research and development relevant to diseases which disproportionately affect developing countries: Annex para 13.

[190] See WIPO, 'Intellectual Property and Public Health' <http://www.wipo.int/patentscope/en/lifesciences/ip_health.html> accessed 11 April 2011. See also the *Geneva Declaration on the Future of the World Intellectual Property Organization* (4 March 2005) <http://www.cptech.org/ip/wipo/futureofwipodeclaration.pdf> (adopted in 2005 by a group of academics and NGOs and challenges WIPO to review the need for a uniform approach to IP laws).

[191] Millennium Project Task Force Report (n 123) 29–31. The Working Group on Access to Essential Medicines of the UN Millennium Project identified the following barriers: (i) the failure of the international community to keep its promises to developing states; (ii) a lack of co-ordination of international aid; (iii) obstacles created by TRIPS; (iv) an inadequate incentive structure for the development of medicines to address neglected diseases; as well as (v) inadequate national commitment and human resources.

IV Conclusion

The meaning of the international obligation to co-operate for the purpose of realizing the right to health is far from settled. But its ambiguity and contested nature, especially in the context of international assistance, are not sufficient grounds to relegate this obligation to the periphery in any discussions concerning the right to health. On the contrary it must occupy a more central place in such debates given that co-operation between states is critical to ensuring the effective enjoyment of the right to health. The challenge, however, is to provide a persuasive interpretation that can outline the 'concrete measures' required for its effective implementation.

The contribution of the treaty bodies has not always been helpful in this regard. For example, the CRC Committee has tended to focus on the obligations of developing states to seek assistance by recommending that states '[c]ontinue taking all appropriate measures to improve the health infrastructure, including through international cooperation';[192] '[t]ake all appropriate measures, including seeking international cooperation, to prevent and combat the damaging effects of environmental degradation on children . . .';[193] and seek 'international cooperation, in order to ensure access to basic health care and services adequately stocked with appropriate resources, including basic medicines for all children'.[194] Moreover, its conception of co-operation in the context of the right to health has been almost exclusively confined to recommendations that states seek the assistance of UN bodies[195] such as UNICEF, UNAIDS, and the WHO.[196]

Such an approach tends to marginalize and obscure the critical role that a more nuanced understanding of the role international co-operation has to play in securing the right to the highest attainable standard of health.[197] The emphasis of the CRC Committee on the need for developing states to *seek* the assistance of developed states, also means that it offers a very limited insight into the precise nature of the obligation imposed on developed states. As a consequence it does nothing to lift the veil of ignorance that often characterizes the lack of awareness within developed states as to the impact of their actions on the capacity of developing states to secure the right to health.[198] There is simply insufficient attention given by the CRC Committee as to the significance that must arise as a consequence of the deliberate and

---

[192] CO CRC Jamaica, UN Doc CRC/C/15/Add.210 (4 July 2003) para 41(a).
[193] CO CRC Kazakhstan, UN Doc CRC/C/15/Add.213 (10 July 2003) para 60(g); See also CO CRC Ecuador, UN Doc CRC/C/15/Add.262 (13 September 2005) para 54; CO CRC Vietnam, UN Doc CRC/C/15/Add.200 (18 March 2003) para 42.
[194] CO CRC Antigua and Barbuda, UN Doc CRC/C/15/Add.247 (3 November 2004) para 52(a).
[195] CRC Committee, *General Comment No 5* (n 80) para 63.
[196] See, eg, CO CRC Liberia, UN Doc CRC/C/15/Add.236 (1 July 2004) para 47(d); CO CRC India, UN Doc CRC/C/15/Add.228 (26 February 2004) para 53; CRC CO Panama (n 88) para 48(d).
[197] See Skogly (n 1) 158–61 (also critical of the failure of the CRC Committee to develop the content of the obligation to co-operate).
[198] Pogge, 'Human Rights of the Global Poor' (n 43) 741 (refers to the 'wilful indifference' and subsequent harm caused by developed states in advancing their own ends).

specific inclusion within the text of article 24(4) that international co-operation take particular account of the needs of developing countries.

Thus it is not appropriate for the CRC Committee to impishly suggest that it merely '*believes* that rights of children are a shared responsibility between developed and the developing countries'.[199] The text of the CRC specifically includes a *legal obligation* to this effect in recognition of the capacity disparities that exist between states and the subsequent need to embark upon a collaborative enterprise in order to secure children's right to health. Also implicit in this acknowledgement of the needs of developing states, is a model of international co-operation that is based on burden sharing rather than blame allocation. The challenge, however, is to offer an interpretation of such a vision that is capable of translating the normative commitment to international co-operation into a series of 'concrete measures' which can contribute to the effective realization of the right to health.

The ESC Committee has been slightly more robust in detailing the nature of the international obligation imposed on states to assist other states realize the right to health and its work supports the idea of an *international* obligation to take reasonable measures in light of available resources and other obligations under international law to respect, protect, and fulfil the right to health in other jurisdictions. Importantly, the expansion of the international obligation in this way is principled, coherent, and context sensitive. As the discussion concerning access to medicines and the TRIPS regime demonstrated, the international obligation with respect to the right to health is not the paramount consideration in relations between states or within the international legal and institutional regime. However, the principles of effectiveness and external system coherence demand that it must occupy a much more visible and integrated role than is currently the case. It is not to be a peripheral consideration that can be readily marginalized by states as they seek to manage their competing priorities. On the contrary, states are under an international legal obligation which demands that bona fide efforts must be made to reconcile these priorities and that any interference with the right to health in other jurisdictions must be justified as being reasonable. The international obligation also demands that states must actively consider measures by which they can individually and collectively assist other states *fulfil* the right to health.

Despite these implications, this interpretation of the international obligation with respect to the right to health ultimately represents a weak rather than strong model of co-operation. It does not entitle developing states to demand a specific form of assistance from developed states and nor does it provide a mandate to the treaty bodies to demand of any state the adoption of specific measures to secure the health of individuals in other states. The constraints imposed by the drafting history of the ICESCR and the text of the ICESCR and CRC—especially the CRC, which requires that states merely 'promote' and 'encourage' international

---

[199] CRC Committee, *Report of the Forty-Sixth Session* (n 11) para 92 (emphasis added). cf CRC Committee, *General Comment No 5* (n 80) para 7 ('When States ratify the Convention they take on obligations not only to implement it within their jurisdiction but to contribute through international cooperation, to global implementation').

co-operation—cannot be overlooked. At the same time, the very inclusion of such an obligation, when combined with the subsequent affirmation by states in various declarations and resolutions as to the need for and commitment to international co-operation, provides the basis upon which to demand both the construction of a dialogue and a critical assessment as to the nature and impact of the actions *between* states in which the right to health must occupy a legitimate space. Thus, states may enjoy significant discretion with respect to the measures they adopt to satisfy their international obligation to secure the right to health but they are still required to justify whatever measures they adopt as being reasonable in the circumstances.

Conclusion

The distinguished British international lawyer Sir Hersh Lauterpacht famously remarked that 'if international law is... at the vanishing point of law, the law of war is... at the vanishing point of international law'.[1] Lauterpacht was writing about the then recently adopted Geneva Conventions of 1949 and his purpose was twofold. On the one hand, he sought to highlight and to celebrate the extent to which the laws of war had been transformed from the pre-existing provisions, which had been in force during the Second World War. On the other hand, he wanted to draw attention both to the relative fragility of the new law and to the magnitude of the challenge which had been created for international lawyers and others if they were to succeed in transforming the 'stupendous positive achievement' of the Conventions into legal practice.[2] The problem was that the Conventions 'abound in gaps, compromises, obscurities and somewhat nominal provisions resulting from the inability of the parties to achieve an agreed effective solution'.[3] As a result, the challenge was to ensure '[s]ustained scientific effort directed towards the clarification and expansion' of the relevant legal provisions.[4]

There is an instructive parallel to be drawn between Lauterpacht's description of the challenge confronting those seeking to give effect to the newly emerged body of international humanitarian law (as he preferred to characterize it), and the challenge that today confronts those wanting to achieve practical implementation of the human right to health. Following Lauterpacht, it can safely be said that if economic and social rights are at the vanishing point of human rights law, as a surprising number of jurists and philosophers still seem to think, then the right to health is at the vanishing point of economic and social rights. In terms reminiscent of Lauterpacht, Matthew Craven concluded his careful critique of the ICESCR by suggesting that the major problem confronting proponents of economic and social rights in general was that the rights in the treaty 'are stated in an excessively broad and general manner'.[5] It is an observation that holds particular resonance with respect to the formulation of the right to the highest attainable standard of physical and mental

---

[1] Hersch Lauterpacht, 'The Problem of the Revision of the Law of War', 1952 *Brit YB Int'l L* 360, 382.
[2] ibid 379–80.
[3] ibid 380.   [4] ibid 381–2.
[5] Matthew Craven, *The International Covenant on Economic Social and Cultural Rights: A Perspective on its Development* (Clarendon Press, 1995) 353.

health. Since Craven's work was first published in 1995, significant work has been dedicated to the project of seeking to address the elusive meaning of the right to health. Commentators, the treaty supervisory bodies, and the Special Rapporteur on the Right to Health have all made important contributions. But this interpretative project is far from complete.

The goal of this book is to shed light upon the current state of this vitally important project by providing a thorough and balanced account of the jurisprudential development of the right that has been achieved in the course of seven decades since its recognition in the Universal Declaration of Human Rights in 1948. The book seeks to navigate a middle course between the unqualified enthusiasm of many proponents of the right to health and the deep pessimism of those who doubt the legitimacy and relevance of this right. This has required a careful review of the history of the right and of the many ways in which its broad and expansive provisions have been interpreted and applied in a wide range of settings. In genealogical terms the right was shown to have deeply pragmatic origins that reflect an alignment of humanitarian and instrumentalist considerations.

Philosophers, however, have tended to downplay the significance of these deep roots and have instead concentrated on the more tenuous nature of the conceptual foundations generally relied upon to justify the right to health. In turn, such philosophical challenges have tended to be ignored by most right to health advocates and treated as irrelevant by international lawyers who are content to invoke positive treaty and other legal provisions as providing a sufficient foundation. But the preoccupations of philosophers warrant attention not simply because their critique has the potential to undermine the perceived legitimacy of the right within the broader community, but because engagement with the concerns underlying the critique leads to a deeper and more sophisticated understanding of the rationale of the right to health and of its overall contours.

This book argues that, although not completely theorized, there is an overlapping consensus as to the conceptual foundations of the right to health in international law, which is derived from the social process that led to the recognition of a person's interest in achieving the highest attainable standard of health as the basis for a human right—described in this book as a 'social interest' theory of rights.

But advancing one theory to justify the right to health will hardly be sufficient in the absence of a systematic rebuttal of the principal arguments that have been used to critique and undermine the legitimacy of the right to health. The book thus gives careful consideration to what are described as the status objection, the formulation objection, and the resource allocation dilemma, and concludes that none of these oft-repeated objections can withstand careful scrutiny. In contrast, concerns that arise from theories of rights that are essentially incompatible with the approach adopted under international law are, by definition, going to be irreconcilable. Libertarian theory is a case in point. As a consequence, where this theory has a strong hold on the development of policy within a state, implementation of the right to health as it is understood in international law will be problematic at best.

The fundamental challenge when discussing the right to health is to offer an account of its meaning that adequately specifies both the nature of the interest in which the right is grounded *and* the obligation of states with respect to securing that interest. Far too often in discussions concerning the right to health all the emphasis is placed on the scope of the interest, which is then inflated, perhaps understandably, in an attempt to ensure that it covers urgent and serious health needs. But by overstating its content and thus pushing the purported correlative obligations beyond any point of reasonableness or even feasibility such an approach risks reducing the right to health to a mere rhetorical claim incapable of influencing policy on health and its social determinants. The challenge then is to offer an understanding of the right to health that is sensitive to the needs and interests of both its beneficiaries and its duty bearers and can actually guide policy makers, health professionals, and health economists in ways that are both viable and sensitive to the legitimate and competing demands made upon states from a range of actors. In short, there is a need to offer an understanding that is able to persuade those actors who have the capacity, whether through their acts or omissions, to secure the right of everyone to the highest attainable standard of health.

An approach to the interpretation of treaty provisions that satisfies these objectives must be principled, practical, coherent, and context sensitive. This requires an application, at least in the first instance, of the principles of interpretation reflected in the VCLT. The consequence of such an approach is significant in that it imposes a constraint on the interpretative process—a constraint that both the ESC Committee and CRC Committee have on occasions tended to overlook in their enthusiasm to develop a vision of the right to health, which may be appealing but has no textual foundation.

At the same time, the insistence that legal doctrine has a role to play in the interpretative process must be significantly tempered in light of Koskenniemi's warning that a retreat to doctrine risks condemning the process to a 'prison house of irrelevance'.[6] Indeed, the danger of excessive formalism is harmful on a number of fronts. Quite apart from the fact that such formalism fails to take account of the political context in which states assume their obligations under international human rights law, it also risks being disregarded by the broader interpretative community. Thus, for example, the Millennium Taskforce on Child and Maternal Health may have accepted the need for human rights to achieve the Millennium Development Goals,[7] but it also warned that 'human rights initiatives fixated on and bound by chapter and verse of human rights treaties often miss the mark'.[8]

Aware of these dilemmas, the interpretative methodology adopted in this book seeks to accommodate both the need to embrace the accepted principles of interpretation but also to advance a model that is simultaneously able to deal with the inherent limitations of those principles while remaining constructively engaged with the broader interpretative community. The analysis starts from the proposition that

---

[6] Martti Koskenniemi, *From Apology to Utopia: The Structure of International Legal Argument* (CUP, 2006) 4.

[7] L Freedman and others, UN Millennium Project Task Force on Child and Maternal Health, *Who's Got the Power? Transforming Health Systems for Women and Children* (Earthscan, 2005) 31.

[8] ibid 34.

the choice of *a* meaning from within a suite of potential meanings is an inevitable dimension of any interpretative enterprise. As such, it offers a transparent account of the factors to be considered in undertaking the myriad of choices that accompany the exercise of discretion in interpreting the right to health. The application of these factors is then used to generate a convincing account of the measures required for the concrete implementation of the right to health.

Importantly, no claim is made that this book offers the definitive account as to the meaning of this right. Instead, the book offers a cautious and carefully constructed approach that draws upon a diverse and eclectic set of sources in order to produce a synthesis of the current state of the art. The specific content and implications of a complex right like the right to health will always be open to divergent interpretations, and will inevitably evolve significantly over time.

One of the ironies of a relatively open-ended concept like the right to health is that its appeal to certain commentators will sometimes lie precisely in its malleability and in the potential it offers to accommodate widely diverging interpretations. It therefore remains to be seen whether a carefully constructed legal analysis of the type reflected in this book will prove attractive to many in the broader interpretative community. Equally problematic is the extent to which some of the key players seem to have opted not to engage in or with any sustained approach to interpretation of the right to health, despite its centrality to much of their professional activity. For example, whatever the rhetoric of lead international organizations in the area of children's health may be, there is often a disconcerting absence of any substantive engagement with a child's right to health in their work. Such discussions are conspicuously absent from key reports in relation to which they would seem to be of direct relevance such as UNICEF's annual report *The State of the World's Children 2008*[9] which focuses on child survival and WHO's annual *World Health Report 2008*,[10] which focuses on primary health care.

Thus, beyond the need to develop a common understanding as to the content of the right to health, the next challenge in securing the implementation of this right is to stimulate a conversation within the interpretative community about the right's relevance and the obligations it imposes upon states both individually and collectively in relation to both local and global health needs. Within this context, perhaps one of the most notable features of this book, which is essentially an act of legal interpretation, is the significant reliance on non-legal sources to assist in securing its objective. This reflects the reality that although law may establish that the principle of effectiveness is an important interpretative principle, legal discourse alone is ill-equipped to provide compelling answers to many of the questions that arise. Thus, for example, an understanding of which measures will be effective in reducing child

---

[9] UNICEF, *State of the World's Children 2008: Child Survival* (UNICEF, 2007) (dedicates just two pages on the link between human rights, community-based health care, and child survival: 90–1).

[10] WHO, *The World Health Report 2008: Primary Health Care: Now More than Ever* (WHO, 2008) (makes one passing reference to the right to the highest attainable standard of health: xii; but offers no discussion of states' obligation even in its analysis of what it describes as Governments being 'brokers for PHC (primary health care) reform': 82).

mortality, malnutrition, and disease prevention will require a creative synthesis of the relevant legal and non-legal discourses. It therefore follows that a collaborative approach must be undertaken in order to generate an effective and persuasive understanding of the evolving content of the right to health and of the practical measures required to secure its effective implementation. As Amartya Sen has rightly warned, 'a theory of human rights cannot be sensibly confined within the juridical model within which it is frequently incarcerated'.[11]

By the same token, of course, law and legal obligations are important. To take but one example of many, when 1,000 women[12] and over 17,000 infants under the age of five who die every day due to complications that could have been prevented or treated with simple medical interventions,[13] it is surely not enough merely to express sympathy and to hope that things will improve over time. The fact that the great majority of states have voluntarily accepted a legal obligation in good faith to ensure the effective implementation of the right to health must instead lead to an inquiry as to whether states acting both individually and collectively have fulfilled their legal obligations to avert such tragedies.

It requires an acceptance that the right to health need not be confined to the margins of debates around health policy and the social determinants of health. It also requires recognition that moralizing or making vague appeals to international law will not be sufficient to transform the right to health from a rhetorical weapon into a fully articulated and reasoned legal argument capable of constraining, guiding, and mobilizing governments, individuals, and other actors. Thus proponents of the right bear the burden of demonstrating that it provides a principled and pragmatic vision, albeit incompletely theorized, of the appropriate role of the state and other actors in securing health needs. There is also a need to recognize that although the obligation imposed on states may be couched in legal terms, it also has immense transformative potential and is deeply political.[14] Thus, it challenges a society to think beyond whether there are enough doctors, medicines, or hospital beds. It demands an evaluation of the cultural and social practices, systems, and structures, both local and global, which undermine the availability, accessibility, acceptability, and quality of such medical services and the social determinants of health.[15] And it demands a commitment from states to take reasonable measures to transform these practices, systems, and structures to secure the right of every individual to the highest attainable standard of physical and mental health.

---

[11] Amartya Sen, 'Elements of a Theory of Human Rights' (2004) 32 Phil &Pub Aff 315, 319–20.
[12] WHO, UNICEF, UNFPA, and World Bank, *Trends in Maternal Mortality 1990 to 2008* (WHO, 2010).
[13] WHO, *Children: Reducing Mortality* (WHO Fact Sheet 178, November 2009) ⟨http://www.who.int/mediacentre/factsheets/fs178/en/index.html⟩ accessed 14 June 2011.
[14] Jonathan Mann, 'Health and Human Rights: If Not Now, Then When?' (1997) 2 Health &Hum Rts 113, 117 (noting that the adoption of a human rights based approach to health 'must be understood as a challenge to the political and societal status quo').
[15] Report of the Special Rapporteur *Right of Everyone to the Highest Attainable Standard of Physical and Mental Health* A/HRC/17/25 (12 April 2011) paras 17–24 (provides summary of the comprehensive measures required of states under a right to health framework).

APPENDIX

International and Regional Treaties That Include A Right to Health

Convention on the Rights of the Child[1]

Article 24

(1) States Parties recognize the right of the child to the enjoyment of the highest attainable standard of health and to facilities for the treatment of illness and rehabilitation of health. States Parties shall strive to ensure that no child is deprived of his or her right of access to such health care services.
(2) States Parties shall pursue full implementation of this right and, in particular, shall take appropriate measures:
  (a) To diminish infant and child mortality;
  (b) To ensure the provision of necessary medical assistance and health care to all children with emphasis on the development of primary health care;
  (c) To combat disease and malnutrition, including within the framework of primary health care, through, inter alia, the application of readily available technology and through the provision of adequate nutritious foods and clean drinking-water, taking into consideration the dangers and risks of environmental pollution;
  (d) To ensure appropriate pre-natal and post-natal health care for mothers;
  (e) To ensure that all segments of society, in particular parents and children, are informed, have access to education and are supported in the use of basic knowledge of child health and nutrition, the advantages of breastfeeding, hygiene and environmental sanitation and the prevention of accidents;
  (f) To develop preventive health care, guidance for parents and family planning education and services.
(3) States Parties shall take all effective and appropriate measures with a view to abolishing traditional practices prejudicial to the health of children.
(4) States Parties undertake to promote and encourage international co-operation with a view to achieving progressively the full realization of the right recognized in the present article. In this regard, particular account shall be taken of the needs of developing countries.

---

[1] (CRC) (New York, 20 November 1989, entered into force 2 September 1990, 1577 UNTS 3).

Convention on the Elimination of All Forms of Discrimination against Women[2]

Article 12

(1) States Parties shall take all appropriate measures to eliminate discrimination against women in the field of health care in order to ensure, on a basis of equality of men and women, access to health care services, including those related to family planning.
(2) Notwithstanding the provisions of paragraph I of this article, States Parties shall ensure to women appropriate services in connection with pregnancy, confinement and the post-natal period, granting free services where necessary, as well as adequate nutrition during pregnancy and lactation.

Convention on the Rights of Persons with Disabilities[3]

Article 25—Health

States Parties recognize that persons with disabilities have the right to the enjoyment of the highest attainable standard of health without discrimination on the basis of disability. States Parties shall take all appropriate measures to ensure access for persons with disabilities to health services that are gender-sensitive, including health-related rehabilitation. In particular, States Parties shall:

(a) Provide persons with disabilities with the same range, quality and standard of free or affordable health care and programmes as provided to other persons, including in the area of sexual and reproductive health and population-based public health programmes;
(b) Provide those health services needed by persons with disabilities specifically because of their disabilities, including early identification and intervention as appropriate, and services designed to minimize and prevent further disabilities, including among children and older persons;
(c) Provide these health services as close as possible to people's own communities, including in rural areas;
(d) Require health professionals to provide care of the same quality to persons with disabilities as to others, including on the basis of free and informed consent by, inter alia, raising awareness of the human rights, dignity, autonomy and needs of persons with disabilities through training and the promulgation of ethical standards for public and private health care;

---

[2] (CEDAW) (New York, 18 December 1979, entered into force 3 September 1981, 1249 UNTS 13).
[3] (CRPD) (New York, 30 March 2007, entered into force 3 May 2008, UN Doc A/RES/61/106).

(e) Prohibit discrimination against persons with disabilities in the provision of health insurance, and life insurance where such insurance is permitted by national law, which shall be provided in a fair and reasonable manner;
(f) Prevent discriminatory denial of health care or health services or food and fluids on the basis of basis of disability.

International Convention on the Protection of the Rights of All Migrant Workers and Members of Their Families[4]

Article 25

(1) Migrant workers shall enjoy treatment not less favourable than that which applies to nationals of the State of employment in respect of remuneration and:
   (a) Other conditions of work, that is to say, overtime, hours of work, weekly rest, holidays with pay, safety, health, termination of the employment relationship and any other conditions of work which, according to national law and practice, are covered by these terms; . . .

Article 28

Migrant workers and members of their families shall have the right to receive any medical care that is urgently required for the preservation of their life or the avoidance of irreparable harm to their health on the basis of equality of treatment with nationals of the State concerned. Such emergency medical care shall not be refused them by reason of any irregularity with regard to stay or employment.

Article 43

(1) Migrant workers shall enjoy equality of treatment with nationals of the State of employment in relation to:
. . .
   (e) Access to social and health services, provided that the requirements for participation in the respective schemes are met; . . .

Article 45

(1) Members of the families of migrant workers shall, in the State of employment, enjoy equality of treatment with nationals of that State in relation to:
. . .
   (c) Access to social and health services, provided that requirements for participation in the respective schemes are met; . . .

---

[4] (CMWF) (New York, 18 December 1990, entered into force 14 March 2003, 2220 UNTS 3).

European Social Charter[5]

Article 11—The Right to Protection of Health

With a view to ensuring the effective exercise of the right to protection of health, the Contracting Parties undertake, either directly or in co-operation with public or private organisations, to take appropriate measures designed *inter alia:*

(1) to remove as far as possible the causes of ill-health;
(2) to provide advisory and educational facilities for the promotion of health and the encouragement of individual responsibility in matters of health;
(3) to prevent as far as possible epidemic, endemic and other diseases.

African [Banjul] Charter on Human and Peoples' Rights[6]

Article 16

(1) Every individual shall have the right to enjoy the best attainable state of physical and mental health.
(2) States Parties to the present Charter shall take the necessary measures to protect the health of their people and to ensure that they receive medical attention when they are sick.

African Charter on the Rights and Welfare of the Child[7]

Article 14—Health and Health Services

(1) Every child shall have the right to enjoy the best attainable state of physical, mental and spiritual health.
(2) States Parties to the present Charter shall undertake to pursue the full implementation of this right and in particular shall take measures:
   (a) to reduce infant and child morality rate;
   (b) to ensure the provision of necessary medical assistance and health care to all children with emphasis on the development of primary health care;
   (c) to ensure the provision of adequate nutrition and safe drinking water;
   (d) to combat disease and malnutrition within the framework of primary health care through the application of appropriate technology;
   (e) to ensure appropriate health care for expectant and nursing mothers;

---

[5] (Turin, 18 October 1961, entered into force 26 February 1965, 529 UNTS 89).
[6] (African Charter) (Nairobi, 27 June 1981, entered into force 21 October 1986, 1520 UNTS 217).
[7] (Addis Ababa, 11 July 1990, entered into force 29 November 1999, OAU Doc CAB/LEG/24.9/49).

(f) to develop preventive health care and family life education and provision of service;
(g) to integrate basic health service programmes in national development plans;
(h) to ensure that all sectors of the society, in particular, parents, children, community leaders and community workers are informed and supported in the use of basic knowledge of child health and nutrition, the advantages of breastfeeding, hygiene and environmental sanitation and the prevention of domestic and other accidents;
(i) to ensure the meaningful participation of non-governmental organizations, local communities and the beneficiary population in the planning and management of a basic service programme for children;
(j) to support through technical and financial means, the mobilization of local community resources in the development of primary health care for children.

Protocol of San Salvador[8]

Article 10—Right to Health

(1) Everyone shall have the right to health, understood to mean the enjoyment of the highest level of physical, mental and social well-being.
(2) In order to ensure the exercise of the right to health, the States Parties agree to recognize health as a public good and, particularly, to adopt the following measures to ensure that right:
   (a) Primary health care, that is, essential health care made available to all individuals and families in the community;
   (b) Extension of the benefits of health services to all individuals subject to the State's jurisdiction;
   (c) Universal immunization against the principal infectious diseases;
   (d) Prevention and treatment of endemic, occupational and other diseases;
   (e) Education of the population on the prevention and treatment of health problems, and
   (f) Satisfaction of the health needs of the highest risk groups and of those whose poverty makes them the most vulnerable.

Article 11—Right to a Healthy Environment

(1) Everyone shall have the right to live in a healthy environment and to have access to basic public services.
(2) The States Parties shall promote the protection, preservation, and improvement of the environment.

---

[8] Additional Protocol to the American Convention on Human Rights in the Area of Economic, Social and Cultural Rights (Protocol of San Salvador) (San Salvador, 17 November 1988, entered into force 16 November 1999, OAS Treaty Series No 69 (1988), (1989) 28 ILM 156).

Select Bibliography

2005 World Summit Outcome, GA Res 60/1, UN Doc A/RES/60/1 (24 October 2005).
A World Fit for Children, GA Res S-72/2, UN Doc A/RES/S-27/2 (10 May 2002).
Abbing, H, 'Adolescent Sexuality and Public Policy: A Human Rights Response' (1996) 15 Pol & Life Sci 314.
Additional Protocol to the American Convention on Human Rights in the Area of Economic, Social and Cultural Rights (Protocol of San Salvador) (San Salvador, 17 November 1988, entered into force 16 November 1999, OAS Treaty Series No 69 (1988), 28 ILM 156).
African Charter on Human and Peoples' Rights (African Charter) (Nairobi, 27 June 1981, entered into force 21 October 1986, 1520 UNTS 217).
African Charter on the Rights and Welfare of the Child (Addis Ababa, 1 July 1990, entered into force 29 November 1999, OAU Doc CAB/LEG/24.9/49).
African Commission on Human and Rights, *Social and Economic Rights Action Center and the Center for Economic and Social Rights v Nigeria*, Communication No 155/96 (27 October 2001).
Alderson, P, 'Everyday and Medical Life Choices: Decision Making among 8 to 15 Year Old School Students' (1992) 18 Child 81.
—— 'In the Genes or in the Stars? Children's Competence to Consent' (1992) 18 J Med Ethics 119.
Aleeb Abu-Sahlieh, S, 'To Mutilate in the Name of Jehovah or Allah: Legitimization of Male and Female Circumcision' (1994) 13 Med & L 575.
Alex, Re (2004) 180 FLR 89 (FamCt, Aust).
Alstine, MP Van, 'Dynamic Treaty Interpretation' (1998) 146 U Pa L Rev 687.
Alston, P, 'The Unborn Child and Abortion under the Draft Convention on the Rights of the Child' (1990) 12 Hum Rts Q 156.
—— 'The Best Interests Principle: Towards a Reconciliation of Culture and Human Rights' in P Alston (ed), *The Best Interests of the Child: Reconciling Culture and Human Rights* (Oxford: Clarendon Press, 1994).
—— 'Resisting the Merger and Acquisition of Human Rights by Trade Law: A Reply to Petersmann' (2002) 13 EJIL 815.
—— 'Ships Passing in the Night: The Current State of the Human Rights and Development Debate Seen through the Lens of the Millennium Development Goals' (2005) 27 Hum Rts Q 755.
—— and Quinn, G, 'The Nature and Scope of States Parties' Obligations under the International Covenant on Economic, Social and Cultural Rights' (1987) 9 Hum Rts Q 156.
American Academy of Pediatrics, Committee on Bioethics, 'Guidelines on Forgoing Life Sustaining Medical Treatment' (1994) 93 Pediatrics 532.
American Academy of Pediatrics, Task Force on Circumcision, 'Circumcision Policy Statement' (1999) 103 Pediatrics 686.
American Declaration of the Rights and Duties of Man, OAS Res XXX (Ninth International Conference of American States, 1948).
Angell, M, 'Excess in the Pharmaceutical Industry' (2004) 171 CMAJ 1451.

Annotations on the Text of the Draft International Covenants on Human Rights, UN Doc A/2929 (1 July 1955).
Asylum Case (Columbia/Peru) (Judgment) [1950] ICJ Rep 266 (ICJ).
Attaran, A, 'How Do Patents and Economic Policies Affect Access to Essential Medicines in Developing Countries?' (2004) 23 Health Affairs 155.
Baker, B, 'Arthritic Flexibilities for Accessing Medicines: Analysis of WTO Action Regarding Paragraph 6 of the Doha Declaration on the TRIPS Agreement and Public Health' (2004) 14 Ind Intl & Comp L Rev 613.
Bale, HE, 'Patents, Patients and Developing Countries: Access, Innovation and the Political Dimensions of Trade Policy' in B. Granville (ed), *The Economics of Essential Medicines* (London: Royal Institute of International Affairs, 2002).
Ballester, R, 'Child Mortality: Social and Medical Responses' (1999) 354 The Lancet SIV27.
Baxi, U, 'The Place of the Human Right to Health and Contemporary Approaches to Global Justice' in J Harrington and M Stuttaford (eds), *Global Health and Human Rights: Legal and Philosophical Perspectives* (Oxford: Routledge, 2010).
Bayer, R and others, 'Toward Justice in Health Care' (1988) 78 Am J Pub Health 583.
Baynes, K, 'Rights as Critique and the Critique of Rights: Karl Marx, Wendy Brown and the Social Function of Rights' (2000) 28 Pol Theory 451.
Beauchamp, T, 'The Right to Health Care in a Capitalistic Democracy' in TJ Bole and W Bonderson (eds), *Rights to Health Care* (Dordrecht: Kluwer, 1991).
—— and Faden, R, 'The Right to Health and the Right to Health Care' (1979) 4 J Med & Phil 118.
Beijing Declaration 2005, UN Doc A/CONF.177/20/Rev.1 (2006) ch 1, res 1, annex I.
Beijing Platform for Action 2005, UN Doc A/CONF.177/20/Rev.1 (2006) ch 1, res 1, annex II.
Beitz, C, *The Idea of Human Rights* (Oxford: OUP, 2009).
Bellotti v Baird, 443 US 622 (1979) (SC, USA).
Benetar, M and Benetar, D, 'Between Prophylaxis and Child Abuse: The Ethics of Neonatal Male Circumcision' (2003) 3 Am J Bioethics 35.
Bentham, J, 'Anarchical Fallacies; Being an Examination of the Declarations of Rights Issued during the French Revolution' in J Bowring (ed), *The Works of Jeremy Bentham* (Edinburgh: William Tait, 1843) vol II.
Berlin, Commitment for Children of Europe and Central Asia (18 May 2001).
Bitong, L, 'Fighting Genital Mutilation in Sierra Leone' (2005) 83 Bull WHO 806.
Black, R, Morris, S, and Bryce, J, 'Where and Why Are 10 Million Children Dying Every Year?' (2003) 361 The Lancet 2226.
Boemer, R, 'The Right to Health Care' in PAHO, *The Right to Health Care in the Americas: A Comparative Constitutional Study* (Washington DC: PAHO, 1989).
Bogecho, D and Upreti, M, 'The Global Gag Rule—An Antithesis to the Rights Based Approach to Health' (2006) 9 Health & Hum Rts 17.
Bole, T and Bonderson, W (eds), *Rights to Health Care* (Dordrecht: Kluwer, 1991).
Bos, M, 'Theory and Practice of Treaty Interpretation' (1980) 27 NILR 135.
Bourne, P, *New Directions in International Health Cooperation: A Report to the President* (Washington DC: US Government Printing Office, 1978).
Braveman, P and Gruskin, S, 'Defining Equity in Health' (2003) 57 J Epidemiology & Comm Health 254.
Brazier, M and Bridge, C, 'Coercion or Caring: Analysing Adolescent Autonomy' (1996) 16 LS 84.

Brigman, WE, 'Circumcision as Child Abuse: The Legal and Constitutional Issues' (1985) 23 J. Fam L 337.
British Medical Association, 'The Law and Ethics of Male Circumcision: Guidance for Doctors' (2004) 30 J Med Ethics 259.
—— 'Female Genital Mutilation: Caring for Patients and Children Protection—Guidance from the Ethics Department' (London: BMA, July 2006).
—— and The Law Society, *Assessment of Mental Capacity* (1st edn, London: BMA, 1995).
Brockington, CF, *A Short History of Public Health* (London: J & A Churchill, 1956).
Bryce, J and others, 'Can the World Afford to Save the Lives of 6 Million Children Each Year?' (2005) 365 The Lancet 2193.
—— and others, 'Reducing Child Mortality: Can Public Health Deliver?' (2003) 362 The Lancet 159.
—— and others, 'WHO Estimates of the Causes of Death in Children' (2005) 365 The Lancet 1147.
Buchanan, A, 'Justice: A Philosophical Review' in E Shelp (ed), *Justice and Health Care* (Dordrecht: D Reidel Publishing Co, 1981).
—— 'The Right to a Decent Minimum of Health Care' (1984) 13 Phil & Pub Aff 55.
—— 'The Egalitarianism of Human Rights' (2010) 120 Ethics 679.
—— and Golove D, 'The Philosophy of International Law' in J Coleman and S Shapiro (eds), *The Oxford Handbook of Jurisprudence and Philosophy of Law* (Oxford: OUP, 2002).
—— and Hessler, K, 'Specifying the Content of the Human Right to Health Care' in A Buchanan (ed), *Justice and Health Care: Selected Essays* (Oxford: OUP, 2009).
Buergenthal, T, 'The Normative and Institutional Evolution of International Human Rights' (1997) 19 Hum Rts Q 703.
Burke, R, *Decolonization and the Evolution of International Human Rights* (Philadelphia: University of Pennsylvania Press, 2010).
Campbell, T, *The Left and Rights: A Conceptual Analysis of the Idea of Socialist Rights* (London: Routledge and Kegan Paul, 1983).
Canadian Pediatrics Association, Fetus and Newborn Committee, 'Neonatal Circumcision Revisited' (1996) 154 CMAJ 769.
Cantwell, N, 'Is the Rights-Based Approach the Right Approach?' (Defence for Children International: International Symposium, Geneva, 22 November 2004).
Carozza, P, 'From Conquest to Constitutions: Retrieving a Latin American Tradition of the Idea of Human Rights' (2003) 25 Hum Rts Q 281.
Cashin, C and others, 'The Gender Gap in Primary Health Care Resource Utilization in Central Asia' (2002) 17 Health Pol'y & Planning 264.
Castberg, F, 'Natural Law and Human Rights' in A Eide and A Schou (eds), *International Protection of Human Rights* (Stockholm: Almquist & Wiksell, 1968).
Castellsague, X and others, 'Male Circumcision, Penile Human Papillomavirus Infection and Cervical Cancer in Female Partners' (2002) 346 New Eng J Med 1105.
CEDAW Committee, *General Recommendation No 14: Female Circumcision*, UN Doc A/45/38 (1990).
—— *General Recommendation No 19: Violence against Women*, UN Doc A/47/38 (1992).
—— *General Recommendation No 24: Women and Health*, UN Doc A/54/38 (1999).
—— *General Recommendation 24: Article 12 of the Convention on the Elimination of All Forms of Discrimination against Women—Women and Health*, UN Doc A/54/38/Rev.1 (1999).
—— *General Recommendation No 25: Article 4, Paragraph 1, of the Convention (Temporary Special Measures)* (2004), reprinted in *Compilation of General Comments and General*

Recommendations Adopted by Human Rights Bodies, UN Doc HRI/GEN/1/Rev.7 (12 May 2004) 282.

Center for Reproductive Rights, 'Implementing Adolescent Reproductive Rights through the Convention on the Rights of the Child' (Center for Reproductive Rights, Briefing Paper, September 1999).

Chan v Korean Airlines Ltd, 490 US 122 (1989) (SC, USA).

Chapman, A, 'Approaching Intellectual Property as a Human Right' (2001) 35 Copyright Bull 4.

Charter of the United Nations (San Francisco, 26 June 1945, entered into force 24 October 1945, 1 UNTS XVI).

Chen, A and Rogan, WJ, 'Breastfeeding and the Risk of Postneonatal Death in the United States' (2005) 113 Pediatrics 435.

Christie, AF and Rotstein, F, 'Duration of Patent Protection: Does One Size Fit All?' (Intellectual Property Research Institute of Australia, Working Paper No 04.07, June 2007).

City of Akron v Akron Center for Reproductive Health Inc, 462 US 416 (1983) (SC, USA).

Clayton, R and Tomlinson, H, *The Law of Human Rights* (Oxford: OUP, 2000).

Commission for Environmental Cooperation of North America, *Children's Health and the Environment*, Council Res No 00-01, CEC Doc C/00-00/RES/03/Rev.09 (13 June 2000).

Commission on Human Rights, *Question of a Convention on the Rights of the Child: Report of the Working Group on a Draft Convention on the Rights of the Child*, UN Doc E/CN.4/1983/62 (25 March 1983).

—— *Question of a Convention on the Rights of the Child: Report of the Working Group on a Draft Convention on the Rights of the Child*, UN Doc E/CN.4/1985/64 (3 April 1985).

—— *Siracusa Principles on the Limitation and Derogation Provisions in the International Covenant on Civil and Political Rights*, UN Doc E/CN4/1985/4 (1985).

—— *Plan of Action for the Elimination of Harmful Traditional Practices Affecting the Health of Women and Children*, Res 1994/30, UN Doc E/CN.4/Sub.2/1994/10/Add.1 (26 August 1994).

—— *Access to Medication in the Context of Pandemics such as HIV/AIDS*, Res 2001/33, UN Doc E/CN.4/RES/2001/33 (20 April 2001).

Commission on Social Determinants of Health, *Action on the Social Determinants of Health: Learning from Previous Experiences* (Geneva: WHO, March 2005).

—— 'Towards a Conceptual Framework for Analysis and Action on the Social Determinants of Health' (WHO Discussion Paper, 1 July 2005).

Committee of Advisors on Essential Human Rights, American Law Institute, 'Statement of Essential Human Rights' (1946) 243 Annals Am Acad Pol & Soc Sci 18.

Constitution of the World Health Organization (New York, 22 July 1946, entered into force 7 April 1948, 14 UNTS 185).

Convention on the Elimination of All Forms of Discrimination against Women (CEDAW) (New York, 18 December 1979, entered into force 3 September 1981, 1249 UNTS 13).

Convention on the Rights of Persons with Disabilities (CRPD) (New York, 13 December 2006, entered into force 3 May 2008, UN Doc A/RES/61/106).

Convention on the Rights of the Child (CRC) (New York, 20 November 1989, entered into force 2 September 1990, 1577 UNTS 3).

Cook, R, Dickens, B, and Fathalla, M, 'Female Genital Cutting (Mutilation/Circumcision): Ethical and Legal Dimensions' (2002) 79 Intl J Gyn & Obs 281.

—— *Reproductive Health and Human Rights: Integrating Medicine, Ethics, and Law* (Oxford: OUP, 2003).

Costello, J, 'The Trouble is They're Growing, the Trouble is They're Grown: Therapeutic Jurisprudence and Adolescents' Participation in Mental Health Care Decisions' (2003) 29 Ohio NU L Rev 607.
Cranston, M, 'Human Rights, Real and Supposed' in DD Raphel (ed), *Political Theory and the Rights of Man* (London: MacMillan, 1967).
—— *What Are Human Rights?* (London: Bodley Head, 1973).
Craven, M, *The International Covenant on Economic Social and Cultural Rights: A Perspective on its Development* (Oxford: Clarendon Press, 1995).
—— 'Legal Differentiation and the Concept of the Human Rights Treaty in International Law' (2000) 11 EJIL 489.
CRC Committee, *General Comment No 3: HIV/AIDS and the Rights of the Child*, UN Doc CRC/GC/2003/3 (17 March 2003).
—— *General Comment No 4: Adolescent Health and Development in the Context of the Convention on the Rights of the Child*, UN Doc CRC/GC/2003/4 (1 July 2003).
—— *General Comment No 5: General Measures on the Implementation of the Convention on the Rights of the Child*, UN Doc CRC/GC/2003/5 (27 November 2003).
—— *General Comment No 7: Implementing Child Rights in Early Childhood*, UN Doc CRC/C/GC/7 (1 November 2005).
—— *General Comment No 8: The Right to Protection from Corporal Punishment and Other Cruel or Degrading Forms of Punishment*, UN Doc CRC/C/GC/8 (21 August 2006).
—— *General Comment No 9: The Rights of Children with Disabilities*, UN Doc CRC/C/GC/2006/9 (27 February 2007).
—— *General Comment No 12: The Right of the Child to Be Heard*, UN Doc CRC/C/GC/12 (1 July 2009).
Cruft, R, 'Human Rights and Positive Duties: Response to *World Poverty and Human Rights*' (2005) 19 EIA 29.
Cueto, M, 'The Origins of Primary Health Care and Selective Health Care' (2004) 94 Am J Pub Health 1864.
Daniels, N, *Just Health Care* (Cambridge: CUP, 1985).
—— *Just Health: Meeting Health Needs Fairly* (Cambridge: CUP, 2008).
—— and Gruskin, S, 'Justice and Human Rights: Priority Setting and Fair Deliberative Process' (2008) 9 Am J Pub Health 1753.
Darmstadt, G and others, 'Evidence Based Cost Effective Interventions: How Many Newborn Babies Can We Save?' (2005) 365 The Lancet 977.
Darrow, M, *Between Light and Shadow: The World Bank, the International Monetary Fund and International Human Rights Law* (Oxford: Hart Publishing, 2003).
—— and Tomas, A, 'Power, Capture and Conflict: A Call for Human Rights Accountability in Development Cooperation' (2005) 27 Hum Rts Q 471.
Dawson, M, 'Primary Health Care: Concept and Challenges for Its Implementation' (2002) 8 Aus J Primary Health 30.
Dayrit, M and others, 'WHO Code of Practice on the International Recruitment of Health Personnel' (2008) 86 Bull WHO 737.
Declaration of Alma Ata (International Conference on Primary Health Care, Alma Ata, USSR, 6–12 September 1978).
Declaration of Independence (USA, 1776).
Declaration of the Environmental Leaders of the Eight on Children's Environmental Health (Environment Leader's Summit of the Eight, Miami, Florida, 5–6 May 1997).
Declaration of the Rights of Man and of the Citizen (France, 1789).

Declaration on the Rights of Indigenous Peoples, GA Res 61/295, UN Doc A/RES/61/295 (13 September 2007) annex.

Declaration on the TRIPS Agreement and Public Health, WTO Doc WT/MIN(01)/DEC/2 (20 November 2001, adopted 14 November 2001) (Ministerial Declaration) (Doha Declaration).

Dembour, M-B, *Who Believes in Human Rights? Reflections on the European Convention* (Cambridge: CUP, 2006).

Derby, C, 'The Case against the Medicalization of Female Genital Mutilation' (2004) 24 Canadian Woman Studies 95.

Derish, M and Heuvel, K, 'Mature Minors Should Have the Right to Refuse Life Sustaining Medical Treatment' (2000) 28 JL Med & Ethics 109.

Detrick, S, *A Commentary on the United Nations Convention on the Rights of the Child* (The Hague: Martinus Nijhoff, 1999).

Diamond, S, 'An Analysis of Child Protection and Protecting Children from Rights and Public Health Perspectives' (International Symposium on Human Rights in Public Health: Research, Policy and Practice, University of Melbourne, 3–5 November 2004).

Didcock, EA, 'Issues of Consent and Competency in Children and Young People' (2006) 16 Current Pediatrics 91.

DiMasi, JA, Hansen, RW, and Grabowski, HG, 'The Price of Innovation: New Estimates of Drug Development Costs' (2003) 22 J Health Econ 151.

Ditcher, TW, *Despite Good Intentions: Why Development Assistance to the Third World Has Failed* (Amherst: University of Massachusetts Press, 2003).

Dixon, R, 'Creating Dialogue about Socio-Economic Rights: Strong-Form versus Weak-Form Judicial Review Revisited' (2007) 5 International Journal of Constitutional Law 391.

Donnelly, J, *Universal Human Rights in Theory and Practice* (2nd edn, Ithaca: Cornell University Press, 2003).

Dorf, M and Sabel, C, 'A Constitution of Democratic Experimentalism' (1998) 98 Colum L Rev 267.

Drane, J, 'Justice Issues in Health Care Delivery' (1990) 24 Bull PAHO 566.

Dreyfuss, RC, 'TRIPS and Essential Medicines: Must One Size Fit All? Making the WTO Responsive to the Global Health Crisis' in T Pogge, M Rimmer and K Rubenstein (eds), *Incentives for Global Public Health: Patent Law and Access to Essential Medicines* (Cambridge: CUP, 2010).

Duxbury, A and Ward, C, 'The International Law Implications of Australian Abortion Law' (2000) 23 UNSWLJ 1.

Dworkin, R, 'Human Rights and International Law: Political Legitimacy' (unpublished paper, copy on file with author).

Easterly, W, *The White Man's Burden: Why the West's Efforts to Aid the Rest Have Done So Much Ill and So Little Good* (New York: Penguin Press, 2006).

Edmond, K and others, 'Delayed Breastfeeding Initiation Increases Risk of Neonatal Mortality' (2006) 117 Pediatrics 905.

Eekelaar, J, 'The Emergence of Children's Rights' (1986) 6 OJLS 161.

—— *Family Law and Private Life* (Oxford: OUP, 2006).

Effect of Reservations on the Entry into Force of the American Convention on Human Rights (Arts 74 and 75), Advisory Opinion OC-2/82 of 24 September 1982, Inter-Am Ct HR (Ser A) No 2 (1982) (Inter-Am Ct HR).

Eide, A and Eide, BW, *A Commentary on the United Nations Convention on the Rights of the Child: Article 24—The Right to Health* (Dordrecht: Martinus Nijhoff, 2006).

―― and Rosas, A, 'Economic Social and Cultural Rights: A Universal Challenge' in A Eide, C Krause, and A Rosas (eds), *Economic Social and Cultural Rights: A Textbook* (Dordrecht: Martinus Nijhoff, 1995).

Engelhardt, T, *Foundations of Bioethics* (Oxford: OUP, 1986).

Enright, M, '"Mature" Minors and the Medical Law; Safety First?' (2003) VII Cork OL Rev 1.

ESC Committee, *General Comment No 3: The Nature of States Parties' Obligations*, UN Doc E/1991/23 (14 December 1990) annex III.

―― *General Comment No 12: The Right to Adequate Food*, UN Doc E/C.12/1999/5 (12 May 1999).

―― *General Comment No 14: The Right to the Highest Attainable Standard of Health*, UN Doc E/C/12/2000/4 (11 August 2000).

―― *Human Rights and Intellectual Property*, UN Doc E/C.12/2001/15 (14 December 2001).

―― *General Comment No 15: The Right to Water*, UN Doc E/C.12/2002/11 (20 January 2003).

―― *General Comment No 17: The Right of Everyone to Benefit from the Protection of the Moral and Material Interests Resulting from any Scientific Literary, Artistic Production of which He or She is the Author*, UN Doc E/C.12/GC/17 (12 January 2006).

―― *An Evaluation of the Obligation to Take Steps to the 'Maximum of Available Resources' under an Optional Protocol to the Covenant*, UN Doc E/C.12/2007/1 (10 May 2007).

European Convention for the Protection of Human Rights and Fundamental Freedoms (European Convention on Human Rights) (Rome, 4 November 1950, entered into force 3 September 1953, 213 UNTS 221).

European Parliament Resolution on Female Genital Mutilation [2002] OJ C 77 E/126.

European Social Charter (Turin, 18 October 1961, entered into force 26 February 1965, 529 UNTS 89).

Faunce, T, Bai, J, and Nguyen, D, 'Impact of the Australia–US Free Trade Agreement on Australian Medicines Regulation and Prices' (2010) 7 J Generic Med 18.

Fee, E, 'Public Health and the State: The United States' in D Porter (ed), *The History of Public Health and the Modern State* (Amsterdam: Rodopi, 1994).

―― and Parry, P, 'Jonathan Mann, HIV/AIDS and Human Rights' (2008) 19 J Pub Health Pol'y 54.

Fidler, D, 'Fighting the Axis of Illness: HIV/AIDS, Human Rights and US Foreign Policy' (2004) 17 Harv Hum Rts J 99.

Fischer, W and Syed, T, 'Global Justice in Health Care: Developing New Drugs for the Developing World' (2007) 40 UC Davis L Rev 581.

Ford, N, 'Communication for Abandonment of Female Genital Cutting: An Approach Based on Human Rights Principles' (2005) 13 Intl J Child Rts 183.

Forst, R, 'The Justification of Human Rights and the Basic Right to Justification: A Reflexive Approach' (2010) 120 Ethics 711.

Fox, M and Thomson, M, 'Short Changed? The Law and Ethics of Male Circumcision' (2005) 13 Intl J Child Rts 161.

Frankish, C and others, 'Setting a Foundation: Underlying Values and Structures of Health Promotion in Primary Health Care Settings' (2006) 7 Prim'ry HCR & Dev 172.

Frankovits, A, 'Mainstreaming Human Rights: The Human Rights-Based Approach and the United Nations System' (Desk Study Prepared by the Human Rights Council of Australia, UNESCO 2005).

Fredman, S, *Human Rights Transformed: Positive Rights and Positive Duties* (Oxford: OUP, 2008).

Freedman, L, 'Reflections on Emerging Frameworks of Health and Human Rights' (1995) 1 Health & Hum Rts 314.
—— and others, UN Millennium Project Task Force on Child Health and Maternal Health, *Who's Got the Power? Transforming Health Systems for Women and Children* (London: Earthscan, 2005).
Freeman, M, 'The Philosophical Foundations of Human Rights' (1994) 16 Hum Rts Q 491.
—— 'Rethinking *Gillick*' (2005) 13 Intl J Child Rts 201.
French Declaration of the Rights of Man and Citizen of 1793.
Fried, C, 'Equality and Rights in Health Care' (1976) 6 Hastings Center Report 29.
Frost, M, *Ethics in International Relations: A Constitutive Theory* (Cambridge: CUP, 1996).
Fuenzalia-Puelma, H and Connor, S (eds), *The Right to Health in the Americas: A Comparative Constitutional Study* (Washington DC: PAHO, 1989).
Further Actions and Initiatives to Implement the Beijing Declaration and Platform for Action, GA Res S-23/3, UN Doc A/RES/S-23/3 (16 November 2000).
Gabčíkovo-Nagymaros Project (Hungary/Slovakia) (Judgment) [1997] ICJ Rep 7 (ICJ).
Gardiner, R, *Treaty Interpretation* (Oxford: OUP, 2008).
Gautier, G, *Morality by Agreement* (Oxford: OUP, 1986).
Gavison, R, 'On the Relationship between Civil and Political Rights and Social and Economic Rights' in J-M Coicaud, MW Doyle and AM Gardner (eds), *The Globalization of Human Rights* (Tokyo: United Nations University Press, 2003).
Geneva Declaration on the Future of the World Intellectual Property Organization (4 March 2005).
Gillick v West Norfolk and Wisbech Area Health Authority [1986] 1 AC 112 (HL, UK).
Glendon, M, 'The Forgotten Crucible: The Latin American Influence on the Universal Human Rights Idea' (2003) 16 Harv Hum Rts J 27.
Goldstone, J, 'Foreword' in V Gauri and Brinks (eds), *Courting Social Justice: Judicial Enforcement of Social and Economic Rights in the Developing World* (Cambridge: CUP, 2008).
Goodman, R, 'Sociological Insights Insights into International Human Rights Law' (IILJ International Legal Theory Colloquium: 'Interpretation and Judgment in International Law', NYU School of Law, 3 April 2008).
Gostin, L, 'Global Health Law Governance' (2008) 22 Emory Intl L Rev 35.
—— 'Global Health Law: Health in a Global Community' (Georgetown University, O'Neil Institute for National and Global Health Law, Scholarship Research Paper No 15, September 2008).
—— 'Meeting Basic Survival Needs of World's Least Healthy People' (2008) 96 Geo LJ 343.
Griffey, B, 'The "Reasonableness" Test: Assessing Violations of State Obligations under the Optional Protocol to the International Covenant on Economic, Social and Cultural Rights' (2011) 11 HRL Rev 275.
Griffin, J, *On Human Rights* (Oxford: OUP, 2008).
Grubb, A, 'Refusal of Treatment (Child): Competence' (1999) 7 Med L Rev 5.
Gruskin, S and Tarantola, D, 'Health and Human Rights' in Roger Detels and others (eds), *The Oxford Textbook of Public Health* (Oxford: OUP, 2004).
Guess, R, *History and Illusion in Politics* (Cambridge: CUP, 2001).
Gwatkin, D, 'Integrating the Management of Childhood Illness' (2004) 364 The Lancet 1557.
Haas, K, 'Who Will Make Room for the Intersexed?' (2004) 30 AJLM 41.
Halper, T, 'Rights, Reforms and the Health Care Crisis: Problems and Prospects' in TJ Bole and W Bonderson (eds), *Rights to Health Care* (Dordrecht: Kluwer, 1991).

Hamlin, C, 'State Medicine in Great Britain' in D Porter (ed), *The History of Public Health and the Modern State* (Amsterdam: Rodopi, 1994).

—— 'The History and Development of Public Health in Developed Countries' in R Detels and others (eds), *Oxford Textbook on Public Health Volume 1: The Scope of Public Health* (5th edn, Oxford: OUP, 2009).

Hannum, H, 'Human Rights in Conflict Resolution: The Role of the Office of the High Commissioner for Human Rights in Peacemaking and Peacebuilding' (2006) 28 Hum Rts Q 1.

Harrington, J and Stuttaford, M, 'Introduction' in J Harrington and M Stuttaford (eds), *Global Health and Human Rights: Legal and Philosophical Perspectives* (London: Routledge, 2010).

Harris-Short, S, 'Listening to "the Other"? The Convention on the Rights of the Child' 2 MJIL 304 (2002).

Helfer, LR and Austin, GW, *Human Rights and Intellectual Property: Mapping the Global Interface* (Cambridge: CUP, 2011).

Hellsten, S, 'Rationalising Circumcision: From Tradition to Fashion, from Public Health to Individual Freedom—Critical Notes on Cultural Persistence of the Practice of Genital Mutilation' (2004) 30 J Med Ethics 248.

Henkin, L, *The Age of Rights* (New York: Columbia University Press, 1990).

Hestermeyer, H, *Human Rights and the WTO: The Case of Patents and Access to Medicines* (Oxford: OUP, 2007).

Hock-Long, L and others, 'Access to Adolescent Health Service: Financial and Structural Barriers to Care' (2003) 35 PSRH 144.

Hollis, A, 'The Health Impact Fund: A Useful Supplement to the Patent System?' (2008) 1 PHE 124.

Holmes, S and Sunstein, CR, *The Cost of Rights: Why Liberty Depends on Taxes* (New York: WW Norton & Co, 1999).

Howse, R, 'Human Rights in the WTO: Whose Rights, Whose Humanity? Comment on Petersmann' (2002) 3 EJIL 651.

—— and Mutua, M, 'Protecting Human Rights in a Global Economy: Challenges for the World Trade Organization' (International Center for Human Rights and Democratic Development, Policy Paper No 6, 2000).

HRC, *General Comment No 6: The Right to Life*, UN Doc CCPR/C/21/Add/1 (30 April 1982).

—— *General Comment No 22: The Right to Freedom of Thought, Conscience and Religion*, UN Doc CCPR/C/21/Rev.1/Add.4 (27 September 1993).

—— *General Comment No 24: Issues relating to Reservations*, UN Doc CCPR/21/Rev.1/Add.6 (11 November 1994).

—— *General Comment No 10: Freedom of Expression*, reprinted in UN Doc HR1/GEN/1/Rev.1 (1 July 2003).

—— *KNLH v Peru*, Communication No 1153/2003, UN Doc CCPR/C/85/1153/2003 (22 November 2005).

Hughes, A, Wheeler, J, and Eyben, R, 'Rights and Power: The Challenge for International Development Agencies' (2005) 36.1 IDS Bull 63.

Human Rights Council, *Business and Human Rights: Mapping International Standards of Responsibility and Accountability for Corporate Acts*, UN Doc A/HRC/4/035 (9 February 2007).

—— *Access to Medicine in the Context of the Right of Everyone to the Enjoyment of the Highest Attainable Standard of Physical and Mental Health*, Res 12/24, UN Doc A/HRC/RES/12/24 (12 October 2009).

—— *The Right of Everyone to the Highest Attainable Standard of Physical and Mental Health*, Res 15/11, UN Doc A/HRC/RES/15/22, (6 October 2010).

Humphrey, J, *Human Rights and the United Nations: A Great Adventure* (New York: Transnational, 1984).

Hunt, L, *Observing Human Rights: A History* (New York: WW Norton & Co, 2007).

Hunt, P, 'The Right to Health: From the Margins to the Mainstream' (2002) 360 The Lancet 1878.

—— 'The Health and Human Rights Movement: Progress and Obstacles' (2008) 15 JLM 714.

Hutson, J, 'Circumcision: A Surgeon's Perspective' (2004) 30 J Med Ethics 238.

ILC, 'Draft Articles on the Law of Treaties with Commentaries' [1966] II YB Intl L Comm'n 172.

Implementation of Paragraph 6 of the Doha Declaration on the TRIPS Agreement and Public Health, WTO Doc WT/L/540 (2 September 2003) (Decision of 30 August 2003).

Inter-African Committee on Traditional Practices Affecting The Health of Women and Children, *Newsletter No 28* (December 2000).

International Commission of Jurists, 'Maastricht Guidelines on Violations of Economic Social and Cultural Rights' (26 January 1997).

International Convention on the Elimination of All Forms of Racial Discrimination (CERD) (New York, 21 December 1995, entered into force 4 January 1969, 660 UNTS 195).

International Convention on the Protection of the Rights of All Migrant Workers and Members of their Families (CMWF) (New York, 18 December 1990, entered into force 1 July 2003, 2220 UNTS 3).

International Covenant on Civil and Political Rights (ICCPR) (New York, 16 December 1966, entered into force 23 March 1976, 999 UNTS 171).

International Covenant on Economic, Social and Cultural Rights (ICESCR) (New York, 16 December 1966, entered into force 3 January 1976, 993 UNTS 3).

Ireland v United Kingdom Series (1978) Series A no 25 (ECtHR).

Ishay, M, *A History of Human Rights: From Ancient Times to the Globalization Era* (Berkeley: University of California Press, 2004).

Jacobs, F, 'Varieties of Approach to Treaty Interpretation: With Special Reference to the Draft Convention on the Law of Treaties before the Vienna Diplomatic Conference' (1969) 18 ICLQ 318.

Jamar, S, 'The International Human Right to Health' (1994) 22 SUL Rev 2.

Jarvis, J and Stark, S, 'Partnership Working and the Involvement of Parents in the Health Education of 7–11 in Year Olds' (2005) 6 Prim'ry HCR & Dev 208.

Johns, G, 'The Right to Health Care and the State' (1983) 132 Phil Q 279.

Johnson, T, 'Expertise and the State' in M Gane and T Johnson (eds), *Foucault's New Domains* (London: Routledge, 1993).

Joint Declaration from Children's Environmental Health II: A Global Forum for Action (Conference organized by Canadian Institute of Child Health, September 2001).

Jones, G and others, 'How Many Child Deaths Can We Prevent This Year?' 362 The Lancet 65.

Jones, M, 'Adolescent Gender Identity and the Courts' (2005) 13 Intl J Child Rts 121.

Jones, NH, *The Scientific Background of the International Sanitary Conferences 1851–1938* (Geneva: WHO, 1975).

Jones, R and Boonstra, H, 'Confidential Reproductive Health Services for Minors: The Potential Impact of Mandated Parental Involvement for Contraception' (2004) 36 PSRH 182.
Jones, T, 'The Devaluation of Human Rights under the European Convention' (1995) PL 430.
Joseph, R, *The Human Rights of the Unborn Child* (Leiden: Kluwer, 2010).
Joseph, S, 'Trade and the Right to Health' in A Clapham and M Robinson (eds), *Realising the Right to Health* (Zurich: Rüffer & Rub, 2009).
—— *Blame It on the WTO?* (Oxford: OUP, 2011).
Kang, M and others, 'Primary Health Care for Young People: Are There Models of Service Delivery that Improve Access and Quality?' (2006) 25 Youth Studies Aus 49.
Kaufman, C, 'The Right to Health Care: Some Cross-National Comparisons and US Trends in Policy' (1981) 15 F Soc Sci & Med 157.
Kee, C, 'Efficiency, Equity and Ethics: Examining the Policy behind Compulsory Licensing and Access to Medicines in Developing Countries' (2007) 18 AIPJ 39.
Keeping the Promise: United to Achieve the Millennium Development Goals, GA Res 65/1, UN Doc A/RES/65/1 (19 October 2010).
Kennedy, D, 'The International Human Rights Movement: Part of the Problem?' (2002) 15 Harv Hum Rts J 101.
—— *The Dark Side of Virtue: Reassessing International Humanitarianism* (Princeton: Princeton University Press, 2004).
Killmister, S, 'Dignity: Not Such a Useless Concept' (2009) 36 J Med Ethics 16.
King, H, 'Access to Essential Medicines—Promoting Human Rights Over Free Trade and Intellectual Property Claims' in KE Maskus and JH Reichman (eds), *International Public Goods and Transfer of Technology under a Globalized Intellectual Property Regime* (Cambridge: CUP, 2005).
Kinley, D and Nolan, J, 'Trading and Aiding Human Rights: Corporations in the Global Economy' (University of Sydney Law School, Legal Studies Research Paper No 08/13, January 2008).
Kirby, M, 'HIV/AIDS: The Dialogue Heats Up' (International Symposium on Human Rights in Public Health: Research, Policy and Practice, University of Melbourne, 3–5 November 2004).
Kirku, A and Evans, T, 'The Myth of Western Opposition to Economic, Social, and Cultural Rights? A Reply to Whelan and Donnelly' (2009) 31 Hum Rts Q 221.
Kjeldsen Busk Madsen and Pedersen v Denmark (1976) Series A no 23 (ECtHR).
Knight, M, 'Curing Cut or Ritual Mutilation? Some Remarks on the Practice of Female and Male Circumcision in Graeco-Roman Egypt' (2001) 92 Isis 317.
Kok-Chor, T, 'International Toleration: Rawlsian versus Cosmopolitan' (2005) 18 LJIL 685.
Konrad v Germany ECHR 2006-XIII (ECtHR).
Korey, W, *NGOs and the Universal Declaration of Human Rights: A Curious Grapevine* (New York: St Martin's Press, 1998).
Koskenniemi, M, *The Gentle Civiliser of Nations: The Rise and Fall of International Law from 1870–1960* (Cambridge: CUP, 2001).
—— 'Letter to the Editors of the Symposium' (2004) 36 J Transnat'l L & Poly 109.
—— '*From Apology to Utopia: The Structure of International Legal Argument*' (Cambridge: CUP, 2005).
—— 'Human Rights Mainstreaming as a Project of Power' (unpublished paper, copy on file with author, 5 February 2006).
Kramer, MS, 'Determinants of Low Birth Weight: Methodological Assessment and Meta-Analysis' (1987) 65 Bull WHO 663.

Krikorian, G and Szymkowiak, D, 'Intellectual Property Rights in the Making: The Evolution of Intellectual Property Provisions in US Free Trade Agreements and Access to Medicine' (2007) 10 JWIP 388.

Kyle, A and others, 'Integrated Assessment of Environment and Health: America's Children and the Environment' (2006) 114 Enviro Health Perspectives 447.

Land, Island and Maritime Frontier Dispute (El Salvador v Hondouras) (Judgment) [1992] ICJ Rep 351 (ICJ).

Langford, M (ed), *Social Rights Jurisprudence: Emerging Trends in International and Comparative Law* (Cambridge: CUP, 2008).

—— 'Social Security and Children: Testing the Boundaries of Human Rights and Economics' in S Marks, BA Andrassen and A Sengupta (eds), *Freedom from Poverty as a Human Right: Economic Perspectives* (Paris: UNESCO Publishing, 2009).

Lauren, PG, *The Evolution of International Human Rights: Visions Seen* (3rd edn, Philadelphia: University of Pennsylvania Press, 2011).

Lauterpacht, H, *An International Bill of the Rights of Man* (New York: Columbia University Press, 1945).

—— *International Law and Human Rights* (Hamden: Archon Books 1968).

Lawn, J and others, '1 Year after the Lancet Neonatal Survival Series—Was the Call for Action Heard?' (2006) 367 The Lancet 1541.

Lawn, J, Cousens, S, and Zupan, J, '4 Million Neonatal Deaths: When? Where? Why?' (2005) 365 The Lancet 891.

Legal Consequences for States of the Continued Presence of South Africa in Namibia (South West Africa) Notwithstanding Security Council Resolution 276 (Advisory Opinion) [1971] ICJ Rep 16 (ICJ).

Legal Consequences of the Construction of a Wall in the Occupied Palestinian Territory (Advisory Opinion) [2004] ICJ Rep 136 (ICJ).

Leiken, S, 'A Proposal concerning Decisions to Forgo Life Sustaining Treatment for Young People' (1989) 115 J Pediatrics 17.

Levenbook, B, 'The Role of Coherence in Legal Reasoning' (1984) 3 L & Phil 355.

Levin, T, 'World Wide Web Review: Internet Based Resources on Female Genital Mutilation' (2002) 23 Feminist Collections 19.

Lewis, P, 'The Medical Treatment of Children' in Fionda, J (ed), *Legal Concepts of Childhood* (Oxford: Hart Publishing, 2001).

Liebenberg, S, *Socio-Economic Rights—Adjudication under a Transformative Constitution* (Cape Town: Juta, 2010).

Limburg Principles on the Implementation of the International Covenant on Economic Social and Cultural Rights, UN Doc E/CN.4/1987/17 (1987) annex.

Linklater, A, 'The Harm Principle and Global Ethics' (2006) 20 Global Society 329.

Little, C, 'Female Genital Circumcision: Medical and Cultural Considerations' (2003) 10 J. Cultural Div 30.

Loizidou v Turkey (Merits) ECHR 1996–VI 2220 (ECtHR).

Loriaux, S, 'Beneficence and Distributive Justice in a Globalising World' (2006) 20 Global Society 251.

Love, J and Hubbard, T, 'The Big Idea: Prizes to Stimulate R&D for New Medicines' (2007) 82 Chi-Kent L Rev 1519.

Luby, SP and others, 'Effect of Handwashing on Child Health: A Randomised Controlled Trial' (2005) 366 The Lancet 225.

MacCormick, N, *Legal Right and Social Democracy* (Oxford: Clarendon Press, 1982).

MacDonald J, 'Primary Health Care: A Global Overview' (2004) 5 Prim'ry HCR & Dev 284.

Macklin, R, 'Dignity is a Useless Concept' (2003) 327 BMJ 1419.

Magied, A and others, 'Midwives, Traditional Birth Attendants and the Perpetuation of Female Genital Mutilation in Sudan' (2003) 20 Ahfad J 38.

—— and others, 'The Impact of Socio Economic Status on the Practice, Perception and Attitudes of Secondary School Girls towards Female Genital Mutilation (FGM)' (2003) 20 Ahfad J 4.

Mahoney, P, 'Marvellous Richness of Diversity or Invidious Cultural Relativism?' (1998) 19 HRLJ 1.

Mann, J, 'Health and Human Rights: If Not Now, Then When?' (1997) 2 Health & Hum Rts 113.

—— 'Human Rights and AIDS: The Future of the Pandemic' in J Mann and others (eds), *Health and Human Rights: A Reader* (London: Routledge 1999).

Marks, S, 'From the "Single Confused Page" to the "Decalogue for Six Billion Persons": The Roots of the Universal Declaration of Human Rights in the French Revolution' (1998) 20 Hum Rts Q 459.

—— 'Access to Essential Medicines as a Component of the Right to Health' in A Clapham and M Robinson (eds), *Realising the Right to Health* (Zurich: Rüffer & Rub 2009).

Marrakesh Agreement Establishing the World Trade Organization (Marrakesh, 1 January 1995, 1867 UNTS 3) annex 1C (Agreement on Trade-Related Aspects of Intellectual Property Rights).

Martin, J, 'Introduction' in UNESCO (ed), *Human Rights Comments and Interpretations: A Symposium* (London: Allan Wingate, 1949).

Martines, J and others, 'Neonatal Survival: A Call for Action' (2005) 365 The Lancet 1189.

Mason, E, 'Child Survival: Time to Match Commitments with Action' (2005) 365 The Lancet 1286.

McCrudden, C, 'Human Dignity and the Judicial Interpretation of Human Rights' (2008) 19 EJIL 655.

McDougal, M, 'The International Law Commission's Draft Articles upon Interpretation: Textuality *Redivivus*' (1967) 61 AJIL 992.

—— Lasswell, HD, and Miller, JC, *The Interpretation of International Agreements and World Public Order: Principles of Content and Procedure* (Dordrecht: Martinus Nijhoff, 1994).

McGee, G and Burg, F, 'When Paternalism Runs Amok' (1996) 15 Pol & Life Sci 308.

McLachlan, C, 'The Principle of Systematic Integration and Article 31(3)(c) of the Vienna Convention' 54 ICLQ 279 (2005).

MDG Gap Task Force, *Millennium Development Goal 8: Delivering on the Global Partnership for Achieving the Millennium Development Goals* (UN 2008).

Meier, B, 'Global Health Governance and the Contentious Politics of Human Rights: Mainstreaming the Right to Health for Public Health Advancement' (2010) 46 Stan, J Intl L 1.

—— 'The World Health Organization, the Evolution of Human Rights and the Failure to Achieve Health for All' in J Harrington and M Stuttaford (eds), *Global Health and Human Rights: Legal and Philosophical Perspectives* (London: Routledge, 2010).

Merrick, J, 'Kids, Sex and Contraceptives: Dilemmas in a Liberal Society' (1996) 15 Pol & Life Sci 281.

Merritt, M, 'Bioethics, Philosophy and Global Health' (2007) 7 Yale JH Pol L & Eth 273.

Merry, S, *Human Rights and Gender Violence: Translating International Law into Local Justice* (Chicago: University of Chicago Press, 2006).

Middleman, A, 'Public Policy regarding Adolescent Sexuality in a Truly Liberal State' (1996) 15 Pol & Life Sci 305.

Minister of Health v Treatment Action Campaign (No 2) [2002] 5 SA 721 (CC, Sth Afr).
Minkler, L, 'Economic Rights and Political Decision Making' (2009) 31 Hum Rts Q 368.
Mitchell, A and Tania, V, 'Patents and Public Health in the WTO, FTAs and Beyond: Tension and Conflict in International Law' (2009) 43 J World Trade 571.
Montero, Julio, 'Global Poverty, Human Rights and Correlative Duties' (2009) 22 CJLJ 79.
Monterrey Consensus of the International Conference on Financing for Development, UN Doc A/CONF.198/11 (2002) ch 1, res 1, annex.
Morsink, J, 'The Philosophy of the Universal Declaration' (1984) 6 Hum Rts Q 209.
—— *The Universal Declaration of Human Rights: Origins, Drafting and Intent* (Philadelphia: University of Pennsylvania, 1999).
Moulton, G and others, 'Building on a Foundation: Strategies, Processes and Outcomes of Health Promotion in Primary Health Care Settings' (2006) 7 Prim'ry HCR & Dev 269.
Moyn, S, 'On the Genealogy of Morals' (2007) 284 The Nation 25.
—— *The Last Utopia: Human Rights in History* (Cambridge MA: Harvard University Press, 2010).
Müller, A, 'Limitations to and Derogations from Economic Social and Cultural Rights' (2009) 9 HRL Rev 557.
Munro, L, '"The Human Rights-Based Approach to Programming": A Contradiction in Terms?' in S Hickey and D Mitlin (eds), *Rights-Based Approaches to Development: Exploring the Potential and Pitfalls* (Sterling VA: Kumarian Press, 2009).
Murphy, T and Whitty, N, 'Is Human Rights Prepared? Risk, Rights and Public Health Emergencies' (2009) 17 Med L Rev 219.
Nasu, H, 'Public Law Challenges to the Regulation of Pharmaceutical Patents in the US Bilateral Free Trade Agreements' in T Pogge, M Rimmer, and K Rubenstein (eds), *Incentives for Global Public Health: Patent Law and Access to Essential Medicines* (Cambridge: CUP, 2010).
Neier, A, 'Social and Economic Rights: A Critique' (2006) 13 Hum Rts Brief 1.
New Zealand Agency for International Development, *Human Rights Policy Statement* (NZAID, 2002).
Newacheck, P and others, 'Children's Access to Primary Care: Difference by Race, Income and Insurance Status' (1996) 97 Pediatrics 26.
Normand, R and Zaidi, S, *Human Rights at the UN: The Political History of Universal Justice* (Bloomington: Indiana University Press, 2008).
Nozick, R, *Anarchy, State and Utopia* (Oxford: Blackwell, 1974).
O'Connell, P, 'The Human Right to Health in an Age of Market Hegemony' in J Harrington and M Stuttaford (eds), *Global Health and Human Rights: Legal and Philosophical Perspectives* (London: Routledge, 2010).
O'Neill, O, 'The Dark Side of Human Rights' (2005) 81 Intl Affairs 427.
Otto, D, 'Linking Health and Human Rights: What Are the Possibilities?' (International Symposium on Human Rights in Public Health: Research, Policy and Practice, University of Melbourne, 3–5 November 2004).
Ovsiovitch, J, 'Reporting Infant and Child Mortality under the United Nations Conventions' (1998) 46 Buff L Rev 543.
Paine, T, *Rights of Man* (1791) (New York: Penguin Books, 1984).
Paris Convention for the Protection of Industrial Property (Paris, 20 March 1883, entered into force 26 April 1970, 828 UNTS 305).
Paris Declaration on Aid Effectiveness (2 March 2005).
Pellegrino, E, 'The Social Ethics of Primary Care: The Relationship between a Human Need and an Obligation of Society' (1978) 45 Mt Sinai J Med 593.

Pickering, L (ed), *Red Book: 2006 Report of the Committee on Infectious Diseases* (27th edn, Elk Grove Village, IL: American Academy of Pediatrics, 2006).
Pierkik, R and Werner, W, 'Cosmopolitism, Global Justice and International Law' (2005) 18 LJIL 679.
Planned Parenthood v Danforth (1976) 428 US 52 (SC, USA).
Pogge, T, *World Poverty and Human Rights: Cosmopolitan Responsibilities and Reforms* (2nd edn, Cambridge: Polity Press, 2008).
—— 'Recognised and Violated by International Law: The Human Rights of the Global Poor' (2005) 18 LJIL 717.
—— Rimmer, M and Rubenstein, K (eds), *Incentives for Global Public Health: Patent Law and Access to Essential Medicines* (Cambridge: CUP, 2010).
Porter, D (ed), *The History of Public Health and the Modern State* (Amsterdam: Rodopi, 1994).
—— *Health Civilisation and the State: A History of Public Health from Ancient to Modern Times* (London: Routledge, 1999).
Potter, J, 'Rewriting the Competency Rules for Children: Full Recognition of the Young Person as Rights Bearer' (2006) 14 JLM 64.
Programme of Action of the International Conference on Population and Development, UN Doc A/CONF.171/13 (18 October 1994) ch I, res 1, annex.
Protocol to the African Charter on Human and Peoples' Rights on the Rights of Women in Africa (Maputo, 13 September 2000, entered into force 25 November 2005, OAU Doc CAB/LEG/66.6).
Provost, R, 'Reciprocity in Human Rights and Humanitarian Law' (1994) 65 BYBIL 383.
Raguz, M, 'Adolescent Sexual and Reproductive Rights in Latin America' (2001) 5 Health & Hum Rts 31.
Rahman, A and Toubia, N, *Female Genital Mutilation: A Guide to Laws and Policies Worldwide* (London: Zed Books, 2000).
Ramsey, M, 'Public Health in France' in D Porter (ed), *The History of Public Health and the Modern State* (Amsterdam: Rodopi, 1994).
Ranjan, P, 'Understanding the Conflicts between the TRIPS Agreement and the Human Right to Health' (2008) 9 J World Invest & Trade 551.
Rawls, J, *The Law of Peoples* (Cambridge MA: Harvard University Press, 2002).
Raz, J, *The Morality of Freedom* (Oxford: Clarendon Press, 1986).
—— *Ethics in the Public Domain: Essays on the Morality of Law and Politics* (Oxford: Clarendon Press, 1994).
—— 'Human Rights without Foundations' in S Besson and J Tasioulas (eds), *The Philosophy of International Law* (Oxford: OUP, 2010).
Report of the Round Table on Adolescent Sexual and Reproductive Health and Rights: Key Future Actions (UNFPA, 1998).
Reports of the Special Rapporteur on the Right to Health to the Commission on Human Rights: UN Doc E/CN.4/2006/48 (2006); UN Doc E/CN.4/2005/51 (2005); UN Doc E/CN.4/2004/49 (2004); UN Doc E/CN.4/2003/58 (2003).
Reports of the Special Rapporteur on the Right to Health to the General Assembly: UN Doc A/65/255 (2010); UN Doc A/64/272 (2009); UN Doc A/63/263 (2008); UN Doc A/62/214 (2007); UN Doc A/61/338 (2006); UN Doc A/60/348 (2005); UN Doc A/59/422 (2004); UN Doc A/58/427 (2003).
Reports of the Special Rapporteur on the Right to Health to the Human Rights Council: UN Doc A/HRC/17/25 (2011) UN Doc A/HRC/14/20 (2010); UN Doc A/HRC/11/12 (2009); UN Doc A/HRC/7/11 (2008); UN Doc A/HRC/7/11 (2007); UN Doc A/HRC/4/28 (2007).

Responsibility of States for Internationally Wrongful Acts, GA Res 56/83, UN Doc A/RES/56/83 (12 December 2001) annex.
Restrictions to the Death Penalty (Arts 4(2) and 4(4) of the American Convention on Human Rights), Advisory Opinion OC-8/83 of 8 September 1983, Inter-Am Ct HR (Ser A) No 3 (1983) (Inter-Am Ct HR).
Reuter, P, *Introduction to the Law of Treaties* (London: Pinter Publishers, 1989).
Riddell, R, *Does Foreign Aid Really Work?* (Oxford: OUP, 2007).
Rights of Nationals of the United States in Morocco [1952] ICJ Rep 176 (ICJ).
Rimmer, M, 'The Jean Chrétien Pledge to Africa Pact: Patent Law and Humanitarian Aid' (2005) 15 Expert Op Therapeutic Patents 888.
—— 'Race against Time: The Export of Essential Medicines to Rwanda' (2008) 1 PHE 89.
Risse, M, 'Do We Owe the Global Poor Assistance or Rectification?' (2005) 19 EIA 19.
Roemer, R, 'The Right to Health Care' in H Fuenzalia-Puelma and S Connor (eds), *The Right to Health in the Americas: A Comparative Constitutional Study* (Washington DC: PAHO, 1989).
Rogers, J, 'Making the Crimes (Female Genital Mutilation) Act 1996, Making the "Non-Mutilated" Woman' (2003) 18 A Fem LJ 93.
Rorty, R, 'Human Rights, Rationality and Sentimentality' in S Shute and S Hurley (eds), *On Human Rights* (New York: Basic Books, 1993).
Rose, N, 'Governing "Advanced" Liberal Democracies' in A Barry, T Osborne and N Rose (eds), *Foucault and Political Reason: Liberalism, Neo-Liberalism and Rationalities of Government* (London: UCL Press, 1996).
Rosen, G, *A History of Public Health* (New York: MD Publications, 1958).
Rosenblum, P, 'Teaching Human Rights: Ambivalent Activism, Multiple Discourses and Lingering Dilemmas' (2002) 15 Harv Hum Rts J 301.
Ross, L, 'Adolescent Sexuality and Public Policy: A Liberal Response' (1996) 15 Pol & Life Sci 13.
—— 'Adolescent Sexuality and Public Policy: An Unrepentant Liberal Approach' (1996) 15 Pol & Life Sci 323.
—— 'Health Care Decision Making by Children: Is It in Their Best Interests?' (1997) 27 Hastings Center Report 41.
Roth, L, Meisel, A and Lidz, C, 'Tests of Competency to Consent to Treatment' (1977) 134 Am J Psych 279.
Ruddick, W, 'Why Not a General Right to Health Care?' (1989) 56 Mt Sinai J Med 157.
Ruger, J, 'Toward a Theory of a Right to Health: Capability and Incompletely Theorized Agreements' (2006) 18 Yale JL & Hum Rts 273.
—— *Health and Social Justice* (Oxford: OUP, 2010).
Salomon, ME, *Global Responsibility for Human Rights: World Poverty and the Development of International Law* (Oxford: OUP, 2007).
Samour, P and King, K, *Handbook of Pediatric Nutrition* (3rd edn, Sudbury MA: Jones and Bartlett, 2005).
Santos-Pais, M, *A Human Rights Conceptual Framework for UNICEF* (Innocenti Essays No 9, UNICEF and ICDC, 1999).
Sass, HM, 'My Right to Care for My Health—And What About the Needy and the Elderly?' in TJ Bole and W Bonderson (eds), *Rights to Health Care* (Dordrecht: Kluwer, 1991).
Satz, D, 'What Do We Owe the Global Poor? Response to *World Poverty and Human Rights*' 19 EIA 47 (2005).
Schlam, L and Wood, J, 'Informed Consent to the Medical Treatment of Minors: Law and Practice' (2000) 10 Health Matrix 141.

Schokkenbroek, J, 'The Basis, Nature and Application of the Margin of Appreciation Doctrine in the Case Law of the European Court of Human Rights' (1998) 19 HRLJ 30.

Schroeder, D, 'Dignity: One, Two, Three, Four, Five, Still Counting' (2010) 19 Cam Q Health Ethics 188.

——and Singer, P, 'Access to Life Saving Medicines and Intellectual Property Rights: An Ethical Assessment' (2011) 20 Cam Q Health Ethics 276.

Scott, C and Alston, P, 'Adjudicating Constitutional Priorities in a Transnational Context: A Comment on *Soobramoney*'s Legacy and *Grootboom*'s Promise' (2000) 16 SA J Hum Rts 206.

Secretary, Department of Health and Community Services v JWB & SMB (Marion's Case) (1992) 175 CLR 218 (HC, Aust).

Segall, S, *Health, Luck and Justice* (Princeton: Princeton University Press, 2010).

Selmouni v France (2000) 29 EHRR 403 (ECtHR).

Sen, A, 'Elements of a Theory of Human Rights' (2004) 32 Phil & Pub Aff 315.

Seymour, D and Pincus, J, 'Human Rights and Economics: The Conceptual Basis for their Complementarity' (2008) 26 Dev Pol'y Rev 387.

Shaaban, L and Harbison, S, 'Reaching the Tipping Point against Female Genital Mutilation' (2005) 366 The Lancet 347.

Shell-Duncan, B, 'The Medicalization of Female "Circumcision": Harm Reduction or Promotion of a Dangerous Practice?' (2001) 52 Soc Sci & Med 1013.

Short, R, 'Male Circumcision: A Scientific Perspective' (2004) 30 J Med Ethics 241.

Shue, H, *Basic Rights, Subsistence, Affluence and US Foreign Policy* (Princeton: Princeton University Press, 1980).

Shultziner, D, 'Human Dignity—Function and Meanings' (2003) 3 Global Jurist Topics 5.

Sifris, R, 'Restrictive Regulation of Abortion and the Right to Health' (2010) 18 Med L Rev 185.

Simma, B, 'From Bilateralism to Community Interest in International Law' (1994) 250 RCADI 217.

——and Paulus, A, 'The Responsibility of Individuals for Human Rights Abuses in Internal Conflicts: A Positivist View' (1999) 93 AJIL 302.

Simmons, B, 'Explaining Variation in State Commitment to and Compliance with International Human Rights Treaties' (IILJ International Legal Theory Colloquium: Interpretation and Judgment in International Law, NYU School of Law, 31 January 2008).

Sinclair, I, *The Vienna Convention on the Law of Treaties* (Manchester: Manchester University Press, 1984).

Skaine, R, *Female Genital Mutilation: Legal, Cultural and Medical Issues* (Jefferson NC: McFarland Jefferson, 2005).

Skogly, S, *Beyond National Borders: States' Human Rights Obligations in International Cooperation* (Antwerp: Intersentia, 2006).

Soobramoney v Minister for Health [1998] 1 SA 765 (CC, Sth Afr).

Soriano, L, 'A Modest Notion of Coherence in Legal Reasoning: A Model for the European Court of Justice' (2003) 16 Ratio Juris 296.

South-West Africa Cases (Ethiopia v South Africa; Liberia v South Africa) (Preliminary Objections) [1962] ICJ Rep 319 (ICJ).

Special Representative of the Secretary-General, *Business and Human Rights: Mapping International Standards of Responsibility and Accountability for Corporate Acts*, UN Doc A/HRC/4/035 (9 February 2007).

Spencer, N, 'Social, Economic and Political Determinants of Child Health' (2003) 112 Pediatrics 704.

Spencer, N, 'The Effect of Income Inequality and Macro-Level Social Policy on Infant Mortality and Low Birthweight in Developed Countries—A Preliminary Systematic Review' (2004) 30 Child 699.
Sphere Project, *Humanitarian Charter and Minimum Standards in Disaster Response* (Geneva: Sphere Project, 2004).
Ssenyonjo, M, *Economic, Social and Cultural Rights in International Law* (Oxford: Hart Publishing, 2009).
Stammers, N, 'A Critique of Social Approaches to Human Rights' (1995) 17 Hum Rts Q 488.
Stanton, C and others, 'Stillbirth Rates: Delivering Estimates in 190 Countries' (2006) 367 The Lancet 1487.
Statement on a Common Understanding of a Human Rights-Based Approach to Development Cooperation (UN Stamford Workshop, 2003).
Steiner, H, Alston P and Goodman R, *International Human Rights in Context: Law, Politics, Morals* (3rd edn, Oxford: OUP, 2008).
Stiglitz, J, 'Scrooge and Intellectual Property Rights: A Medical Prize Fund Could Improve the Financing of Drug Innovations' (2006) 333 BMJ 1279.
—— *Making Globalisation Work* (New York: WW Norton & Co, 2006).
Sunstein, C, 'Incompletely Theorized Agreements' (1995) 108 Harv L Rev 1733.
—— 'Social and Economic Rights? Lessons from South Africa' (2000) 11 Constitutional Forum 123.
—— *The Second Bill of Rights: Franklin Delano Roosevelt's Unfinished Revolution and Why We Need It More Than Ever* (New York: Basic Books, 2006).
Svoboda, J, Van Howe, R and Dwyer, J, 'Informed Consent for Neonatal Circumcision: An Ethical and Legal Conundrum' (2000) 17 J Contemp'ry HL & Pol 61.
Tarantola, D, 'Building on the Synergy between Health and Human Rights: A Global Perspective' (François-Xavier Bagnoud Center for Health and Human Rights, Working Paper Series No 8, 2000).
Tasioulas, J, 'The Moral Reality of Human Rights' in Thomas Pogge (ed), *Freedom from Poverty as a Human Right: Who Owes What to the Poor?* (Oxford: OUP, 2007).
Terry, F, *Condemned to Repeat? The Paradox of Humanitarian Action* (Ithaca: Cornell University Press, 2002).
Toebes, B, *The Right to Health as a Human Right in International Law* (Oxford, Hart Publishing, 1999).
—— 'Towards an Improved Understanding of the International Human Right to Health' (1999) 21 Hum Rts Q 661.
—— 'The Right to Health and the Privatization of National Health Systems: A Case Study of the Netherlands' (2006) 9 Health & Hum Rts 103.
Tomasevski, K, 'Health Rights' in A Eide, C Krause and A Rosas (eds), *Economic, Social, and Cultural Rights: A Textbook* (Dordrecht: Martinus Nijhoff, 1995).
Toubia, N and Sharief, E, 'Female Genital Mutilation: Have We Made Progress?' (2003) 82 Intl J Gyn & Obs 251.
Toufayan, M, 'Human Rights Treaty Interpretation: A Postmodern Account of its Claim to "Speciality"' (NYU School of Law, Center for Human Rights and Global Justice, Working Paper No 3, 2005).
Tushnet, M, 'New Forms of Judicial Review and the Persistence of Rights- and Democracy-Based Worries' (2003) 38 Wake Forest L Rev 813.
Twinning, W (ed), *Human Rights and Southern Voices* (Cambridge: CUP, 2009).
Tyrer v United Kingdom (1978) Series A no 26 (ECtHR).
UN Millennium Declaration Resolution, GA Res 55/2, UN Doc A/55/L.2 (8 September 2000).

UN Millennium Project Task Force on HIV/AIDS, Malaria, TB, and Access to Essential Medicines, *Prescription for Healthy Development: Increasing Access to Medicines* (London: Earthscan, 2005).

UN Secretary-General, *Global Strategy for Women's and Children's Health* (2010).

UN Sub-Commission on the Promotion and Protection of Human Rights, *Intellectual Property Rights and Human Rights*, Res 2001/21, UN Doc E/CN.4/SUB.2/RES/2001/21 (16 August 2001).

UNCHR, *Report of the Open-Ended Working Group to Consider Options regarding the Elaboration of an Optional Protocol to the International Covenant on Economic, Social and Cultural Rights on Its Second Session*, UN Doc E/CN.4/2005/52 (10 February 2005).

UNDP, *Human Development Report 2000: Human Rights and Human Development* (UNDP, 2000).

UNICEF, 'Human Rights for Women and Children: How UNICEF Helps Make Them a Reality' (Programme Policy Document, UNICEF 1999).

—— *Implementation Handbook for the Convention on the Rights of the Child* (2nd edn, UNICEF, 2002).

—— *Joint Health and Nutrition Strategy for 2006–2015*, UN Doc E/ICEF/2006/8 (15 November 2005).

—— *The State of the World's Children 2008: Child Survival* (UNICEF, 2007).

United Kingdom Department for International Development, 'Realising Human Rights for Poor People' (DFID Target Strategy Paper, 1997).

United Nations Millennium Declaration, GA Res 55/2, UN Doc A/RES/55/2 (18 September 2000).

Universal Declaration of Human Rights, GA Res 217A (III), UN Doc A/810 (10 December 1948).

Vagts, D, 'Treaty Interpretation and the New American Ways of Law Reading' (2003) 4 EJIL 472.

Van Bueren, G, *The International Law on the Rights of the Child* (Dordrecht: Martinus Nijhoff, 1995).

Vandenhole, W, 'Economic Social and Cultural Rights in the CRC: Is There a Legal Obligation to Cooperate' (2009) 17 Intl J Child Rts 23.

Verhey, B, 'Child Soldiers: Preventing, Demobilizing and Reintegrating' (World Bank, Africa Region Working Paper Series No 23, November 2001).

Victora, C and others, 'Applying an Equity Lens to Child Health and Mortality: More of the Same is Not Enough' (2003) 362 The Lancet 233.

—— and others, 'Co-Coverage of Preventive Interventions and Implications for Child Survival Strategies: Evidence from National Surveys' (2005) 366 The Lancet 9495.

Vienna Convention on the Law of Treaties (VCLT) (Vienna, 23 May 1969, entered into force 27 January 1980, 1155 UNTS 331).

Viens, A, 'Value Judgment, Harm and Religious Liberty' (2004) 30 J Med Ethics 241.

Volkmann, CS, 'Children's Rights and the MDGs: The Right to Health within Vietnam's Transition towards a Market Economy' (2006) 9 Health & Hum Rts 56.

Waite and Kennedy v Germany App No 26083/94 (ECtHR, 18 February 1999) (ECtHR).

Waldock, H, 'The Effectiveness of the System Set Up by the European Court of Human Rights' (1980) 1 HRLJ 1.

Waldron, J, 'Socioeconomic Rights and Theories of Justice' (Colloquium on Law, Economics and Politics, NYU Law School, 28 September 2010).

Walter, K and Kunzli, J, *The Law of International Human Rights Protection* (Oxford: OUP, 2009).

Walters, FP, *A History of the League of Nations* (Oxford: OUP, 1960).
Warnock, G, *The Object of Morality* (London: Methuen, 1971).
Weiler, J, 'Prolegomena to a Meso-Theory of Treaty Interpretation at the Turn of the Century' (IILJ International Legal Theory Colloquium: 'Interpretation and Judgment in International Law', NYU School of Law, 14 February 2008).
Weiss, H and others, 'Male Circumcision and Risk of HIV Infection in Sub-Saharan Africa: A Systematic Review and Meta-Analysis' (2002) 14 AIDS 2361.
Weithorn, L and Campbell, S, 'The Competency of Children and Adolescents to Make Informed Treatment Decisions' (1982) 53 Child Dev 1589.
Wemhoff v Germany (1968) Series A no 7 (ECtHR).
Whelan, D and Donnelly, J, 'The West, Economic and Social Rights and the Global Human Rights Regime: Setting the Record Straight' (2007) 29 Hum Rts Q 908.
—— 'Yes, a Myth: A Reply to Kirkup and Evans' (2009) 31 Hum Rts Q 239.
Whitehead, M, 'The Concepts and Principles of Equity and Health' (1992) 22 Intl J Health Services 429.
WHO, *Official Records of the World Health Organisation No 1: Minutes of the Technical Preparatory Committee for the International Health Conference Held in Paris from 18 March to 5 April 1946* (UN WHO Interim Commission October 1947).
—— *Official Records of the World Health Organization No 2: Proceedings and Final Acts of the International Health Conference Held in New York from 19 June to 22 July 1946* (UN WHO Interim Commission June 1948).
—— *The First Ten Years of the World Health Organization* (Geneva: WHO, 1958).
—— *Mastitis—Causes and Management* (Geneva: WHO, 2000).
—— *Management of Pregnancy, Childbirth and Postpartum Period in the Presence of Female Genital Mutilation* (Geneva: WHO, 2001).
—— *Prevention of Child Abuse and Neglect: Making the Link between Human Rights and Public Health* (28 September 2001).
—— *Programming for Male Involvement in Reproductive Health* (Geneva: WHO, 2002).
—— *The Optimal Duration of Exclusive Breastfeeding: Report of an Expert Consultation*, WHO Doc WHO/NHD/01.09, WHO/FCH/CAH/01.24 (2002).
—— *International Statistical Classification of Diseases and Related Health Problems* (10th rev, Geneva: WHO, 2003).
—— *Working with Individuals, Families and Communities to Improve Maternal and Newborn Health* (Geneva: WHO, 2003).
—— *The World Health Report 2003: Shaping the Future* (Geneva: WHO, 2003).
—— *Making Pregnancy Safer: The Critical Role of the Skilled Attendant—A Joint Statement by WHO, ICM and FIGO* (Geneva: WHO, 2004).
—— 'Minimum Water Quantity Needed for Domestic Use in Emergencies' (WHO Technical Note No 9, Revised Draft, 7 January 2005).
—— *The World Health Report 2005: Make Every Mother and Child Count* (Geneva: WHO, 2005).
—— *Obstetric Fistula: Guiding Principles for Clinical Management and Programme Development* (Geneva: WHO, 2006).
—— *Standards for Maternal and Neonatal Care* (Geneva: WHO, 2006).
—— *Strategic Approach to Improving Maternal and Newborn Survival and Health* (Geneva: WHO, 2006).
—— *The Interagency List of Essential Medicines for Reproductive Health* (Geneva: WHO, 2006).

―― *Everybody's Business: Strengthening Health Systems to Improve Health Outcomes* (Geneva: WHO, 2007).
―― *Draft Code of Practice on the International Recruitment of Health Personnel*, WHO Doc EB124/13 (4 December 2008).
―― 'Children: Reducing Mortality' (WHO Fact Sheet No 178, November 2009).
―― 'Spending on Health 2007—Global Update' (WHO Fact Sheet, 2010).
―― *The World Health Report 2010: Health Systems Financing—The Path to Universal Health Coverage* (Geneva: WHO, 2010).
―― *World Health Statistics 2011* (Geneva: WHO, 2011).
―― and UNICEF, *Innocenti Declaration on the Promotion, Protection and Support of Breastfeeding* (Florence, 30 July – 1 August 1990).
―― and UNECE, *Declaration of London on Environmental Health* (June 1999).
―― UNICEF, and Wellstart International, *The Baby Friendly Hospital Initiative: Monitoring and Reassessment—Tools to Sustain Progress* (Geneva: WHO, 1999).
―― and UNICEF, *Global Water Supply and Sanitation Assessment 2000 Report* (Geneva: WHO and UNICEF, 2000).
―― and UNICEF, *Meeting the MDG Drinking Water and Sanitation Target: A Mid Term Assessment of Progress* (Geneva: WHO and UNICEF, 2004).
―― UNFPA, UNICEF, and World Bank, *Pregnancy, Childbirth, Postpartum and Newborn Care: A Guide for Essential Practice* (2nd edn, Geneva: WHO, 2006).
―― UNICEF, UNFPA and World Bank, *Trends in Maternal Mortality 1990 to 2008* (Geneva: WHO, 2010).
WHO Collaborative Study Team on the Role of Breastfeeding on the Prevention of Infant Mortality, 'Effect of Breastfeeding on Infant and Child Mortality Due to Infectious Diseases in Less Developed Countries: A Pooled Analysis' (2000) 355 The Lancet 451.
WHO Study Group on Female Genital Mutilation and Obstetric Outcome, 'Female Genital Mutilation and Obstetric Outcome: WHO Collaborative Prospective Study in Six African Countries' (2006) 367 The Lancet 1835.
Wilkinson, R and Marmot, M (eds), *Social Determinants of Health: The Solid Facts* (2nd edn, Geneva: WHO, 2003).
Williams, E, 'Small Hands, Big Voices? Children's Participation in Policy Change in India' (2005) 36.1 IDS Bull 82.
Wilson, P and others, UN Millennium Project Task Force on HIV/AIDS, Malaria, TB and Access to Essential Medicines, Working Group on HIV/AIDS, *Combating Aids in the Developing World* (London: Earthscan, 2005).
Wolfrum, R, 'Article 55(a) and (b)' in B Simma (ed), *The Charter of the United Nations: A Commentary* (2nd edn, Oxford: OUP, 2002).
―― 'Article 56' in B Simma (ed), *The Charter of the United Nations: A Commentary* (2nd edn, Oxford: OUP, 2002).
Wollstonecraft, M, *A Vindication of the Rights of Women* (1792) (2nd edn, Penguin Books, 1992).
World Bank, *World Development Indicators 2011* (World Bank 2011).
World Declaration on the Survival, Protection and Development of Children and Plan of Action for Implementing the World Declaration on the Survival, Protection and Development of Children in the 1990s, UN Doc E/CN.4/1991/59 (12 December 1990).
World Health Assembly, *Infant and Young Children Nutrition*, WHA Doc WHA54.2 (18 May 2001).
―― *International Migration of Health Personnel: A Challenge for Health Systems in Developing Countries*, WHA Doc WHA58.17 (25 May 2005).

World Health Assembly, *Prevention and Control of Sexually Transmitted Infections: Global Strategy*, WHA Doc WHA59.19 (27 May 2006).
Yamey, G, 'Excluding the Poor from Accessing Biomedical Literature: A Rights Violation that Impedes Global Health' (2008) 10 Health & Hum Rts 1.
Yamin, A, 'Will We Take Suffering Seriously? Reflections on What Applying a Human Rights Framework to Health Means and Why We Should Care' (2008) 10 Health & Hum Rts 45.
——'Suffering and Powerlessness: The Significance of Participation in Rights-Based Approaches to Health' (2009) 11 Health & Hum Rts 5.
——'Our Place in the World: Conceptualising Obligations beyond Borders in Human Rights Based Approaches to Health' (2010) 12 Health & Hum Rts 3.
Young, K, 'The Minimum Core of Economic and Social Rights: A Concept in Search of Content' (2008) 33 Yale J Intl L 113.
——'Securing Health through Rights' in T Pogge, M Rimmer, and K Rubenstein (eds), *Incentives for Global Public Health: Parent Law and Access to Essential Medicines* (Cambridge: CUP, 2010).
Yourow, H, *The Margin of Appreciation Doctrine in the Dynamics of the European Human Rights Jurisprudence* (Dordrecht: Kluwer Law International, 1996).
Yu, PK, 'Reconceptualizing Intellectual Property Interests in a Human Rights Framework' (2007) 49 UC Davis L Rev 1039.
Zimmermann, A, 'Dispute Resolution, Compliance Control and Enforcement in Human Rights Law' in G Ulfstein (ed), *Making Treaties Work: Human Rights, Environment and Arms Control* (Cambridge: CUP, 2007).

Index

Abolition of harmful traditional practices
  CRC text 376
  education through technology 274
  effect on adolescent health 191
  impact of non-state actors 190
  necessary measures 12
  need for culturally sensitive approach 323–4
  overview 303–4
  practices prejudicial to health of children
    contested concept 306–7
    cultural bias in identification 310–11
    gender bias in identification 311–14
    identification by list 307–10
  progressive recognition 305–6
  specific measures
    female genital cutting 314
    margins of appreciation 317–23
    nature and consequences of particular practices 316–17
    terminology and labelling 315–16
Abortion services
  availability 161–7
  children 148
  highest attainable standard of health 300
  recognition of right 139–40
  traditional medical practices 310
Acceptable health care
  adolescent's rights 136
  effective participation 214
  family planning 134
  meaning of health 11
  primary health care 264
  qualitative nature of the entitlements
    financial accessibility 169–72
    interpretative methodology 172–4
    overview 159
    physical accessibility 168–9
Access to health care
  historical role of public health 35
  impact of IPR
    adjusting and reviewing expectations 366–7
    impact on access to medicine 350–3
    justifications for TRIPS 354–64
    need for system coherence 364–6
  migrant workers 378
  primary health care 265
  qualitative nature of entitlements
    acceptability and quality 172–3
    financial accessibility 169–72

  non-discrimination 167–8
  physical accessibility 168–9
Accountability mechanisms
  data collection
    indicators and benchmarks 212–14
    problematic necessity 209–11
  general measures 201–2
  judicial remedies
    comparative examples 205–7
    limits of litigation 207–8
    problematic transfer of case law 204–5
    role of civil and political rights 202–4
All appropriate means
  accountability mechanisms
    general measures 201–2
    judicial remedies 202–8
  African Charter Art 16 378
  CEDAW Art 12 377
  conclusions 224
  CRC text 376
  data collection
    indicators and benchmarks 212–14
    problematic necessity 209–11
  effective people participation
    instrumental and normative foundations 214–15
    scope and limits of participation 216–17
  European Social Charter Art 11 378
  interdisciplinary initiatives 218
  legislative measures
    effectiveness principle 184–5
    justifiable interferences with other rights 181–4
    need for broad and diverse approach 179–80
  margins of appreciation 178–9
  multisectoral initiatives 218
  national plans, programs and policies 199–201
  overview 176–7
  privatization of health care 222–3
  short-comings of tripartite approach 197–8
  to 'take steps' 177–8
  targeted measures
    importance 218–19
    throughout childhood 219–20
  use of tripartite typology
    fulfilment obligation 194–7
    overview 185–6

All appropriate means (*cont.*)
    protective obligations 190–7
    respect for right to health 186–9
Availability of health care 138
    abortion services 161–7
    forms of technology 273–4
    medicines 357
    natal care 260
    resource limitations 58, 63, 70, 252
    specialist health services 159–61
    state resources 341
    water for hygiene 259
    World Health Report 2008 266
Awareness and access to information
    see also Education
    African Charter Art 14 380
    basic knowledge and information 293–6
    CRC text 291–3, 376
    overview 291–3

'Basic' interest theory 52–4
Benchmarks 212–14
'Blind spots' 114–15
'Burdens of inertia' 114

Catholic values 21–2
Children
    see also Convention on the Rights of the Child (and its Committee); Infant and child mortality; Natal care; UNICEF
    abolition of harmful traditional practices
        contested concept 306–7
        cultural bias in identification 310–11
        gender bias in identification 311–14
        identification by list 307–10
    absence of substantive engagement in health rights 374
    African Charter Art 14 379–80
    consent to medical treatment
        assessing capacity to consent 148–51
        developing an appropriate test 146–8
        refusal of life-saving treatment 151–3
        sterilization 153–8
    impact of privatized health care 222–3
    Millennium Development Goals 87, 103
    sexual and reproductive freedom of adolescents 133–43
    targeted measures
        importance 218
        throughout childhood 219–20
        vulnerable children 220–1
Circumcision *see* Female genital cutting; Male circumcision
Class rights 19–20
Coherence
    global institutional reform 344
    importance 7–8

    intellectual property rights 364–6
    international cooperation 331, 369
    interpretation
        in reasoning 100–4
        system coherence 104
    interpretation of treaties 373
    methodology of interpretation 104–10
    'other appropriate measures' 186, 198
    resource allocation 226, 234
    respect for right to health 189
Collaboration *see* Participatory strategies
Collectivism
    see also Public health
    historical impact 19–22
    overview 15
Communist ideology
    dismissal of rights 21
    overview 15
    relevance 42
Communitarianism
    see also International cooperation; Participatory strategies
    effective people participation
        instrumental and normative foundations 214–15
        scope and limits of participation 216–17
    impact of Industrial Revolution 37
    individualized stereotyping 70
    methodology of interpretation 81–5
    rejection of State influence 86
Conceptual foundations
    challenges to legitimacy of health
        formulation objections 65–7
        libertarian objections 60–3
        relativism 67–9
        resource allocation dilemma 69–73
    cultural issues 59–60
    dignity 56–7
    incomplete theorized agreements 49–50
    instrumentalism 57–9
    interest theories
        absence of comprehensive moral theory 52–4
        social interest theory of rights 54–5
    nature of rights 50–2
    necessity of inquiry 47–9
    objections are without foundation 73–4
    overlapping consensus of right to health 372
    overview 44–7
    practices prejudicial to health of children 306–7
Conduct obligations 245–6
    see also Specific measures
Consent to medical treatment
    acceptable health care 172–4
    children 146–53
    complexities 145–6

disabled persons 377
female genital cutting 317
highest attainable standard of health 169
male circumcision 313
problematic inclusion 144–5
scientific experimentation 189
sterilization of women and children 153–8
Context sensitivity
global institutional reform 344
importance 7–8
international cooperation 331, 369
interpretation
global sensitivity 113–18
local sensitivity 111–13
overview 110–11
interpretation of treaties 373
'other appropriate measures' 198
resource allocation 226, 234
respect for right to health 189
Contraception *see* **Family planning**
Convention on the Rights of the Child (and its Committee)
see also Children
abolition of harmful traditional practices
contested concept 306–7
cultural bias in identification 310–11
gender bias in identification 311–14
identification by list 309
overview 287–9
progressive recognition 305
specific measures 318–21
terminology and labelling 315–16
acceptability and quality 172–3
access to treatment 168–72
all appropriate means
conclusions 224
data collection 209–11
effective participation 214–15
fulfilment obligation 191–2
indicators and benchmarks 212
justiciability 204
legislative measures 179
margins of appreciation 178–9
multisectoral initiatives 218
other measures 200
privatization of health care 222–3
protective obligations 191–2
respect for right to health 186–90
targeted measures 219–21
awareness and access to information 292–6
dignity 56
disease and malnutrition
application of available technology 272–4
clean drinking water 279, 281
definitions 269
mitigation of environmental factors 282–4

overview 268
provision of nutritious foods 274–5
family planning 299–301
formulation objections 66
freedom from non-consensual medical treatment 146–53
full text of Art 24 376–7
infant and child mortality
general comments by CRC Committee 257–8
treaty text 7, 376
international cooperation
conclusions 368–70
fulfilment obligations 341, 344, 346–8
nature and scope of obligation 329
overview 326
promotion and encouragement 329–31
protective obligations 339
interpretation of obligations 105
natal care 288, 290
parental guidance 299
preventative health care 296–8
progressive recognition of right to health
cooperation between States 231–2
maximum available resources 226–9
minimum core obligations 242, 247–52
social factors 230
recognition of multiple actors 83
sexual and reproductive freedom
justifications for international approach 140–3
model advanced under international law 136–9
specific measures
medical assistance and health care 263
overview 255
primary health care 263–4
sterilization of women and children 154
Cooperation *see* **International cooperation**
Core obligations *see* **Minimum core obligations**
Corporal punishment
cultural bias in identification 310–11
overview 13, 304
Cultural factors
see also International Covenant on Economic Social and Cultural Rights (and its Committee)
abolition of harmful traditional practices
female genital cutting 314–23
impact of non-state actors 190
necessary measures 12
need for culturally sensitive approach 323–4
overview 303–4
practices prejudicial to health of children 306–14
progressive recognition 305–6

Index

Cultural factors (*cont.*)
  access to treatment 167
  all appropriate means
    tripartite typology 185
  application of available technology 272–3
  conceptual foundations 59–60
  effective participation 214
  international cooperation 350
  interpretation of obligations 111–18
  prevention of HIV/AIDS 271–2
  primary health care 266–7
  relativism
    challenges to legitimacy of health 67–9
    harm to a child's health 323
    male circumcision 311
    objections without foundation 74

Data collection
  abolition of harmful traditional
    practices 320
  indicators and benchmarks 212–14
  problematic necessity 209–11
  specific measures 268

Dignity
  Catholic teachings 21
  conflicted and problematic role 56–7
  disabled persons 377
  idea of a human right 51
  implications of liberalism 39
  provision of clean drinking water 278
  social interest theory 59
  sufficient foundation for the right to
    health 73
  trade related rights 334
  UDHR 30
  UNDR 328

Disabled persons
  CRPD Art 25 377–8
  definition of health 208
  Latin American commitment 26
  non-discrimination 168–9
  recognition of the right to health 195
  specific measures 255
  targeted measures 218, 219

Disease
  counter swing towards humanitarianism 9
  CRC text 376
  defined 269–70
  historical role of public health 35
  impact of Industrial Revolution 38
  neglected diseases 269
  San Salvador Protocol 380
  shift towards instrumentalism 9
  specific measures
    application of available technology 272–4
    clean drinking water 278–81
    general measures 270–2

  mitigation of environmental factors
    281–5
  overview 267–8
  provision of nutritious foods 274–7

Economic and social rights
  see also International Covenant on Economic
    Social and Cultural Rights (and its
    Committee)
  ambiguity in international treaties 75
  class of rights is without justification 45
  current challenges 371–2
  development of the modern welfare state 42
  emergence within Latin America 40
  impact of Industrial Revolution 38
  inalienability 15
  inclusion in major declarations 17–18
  insufficiently specified counterpart
    obligations 224
  judicial deference 218
  justiciability 188, 201
  legal recognition 33
  legitimacy 123
  limitations 181
  negative and positive dimensions 117
  neglect during cold war 32
  origins of the right to health 19–23
  problems of implementation 175–7
  resource allocation dilemma 69
  State obligations 225
  status objections 63–5
  vanishing point of human rights law 371
  widespread disagreement as to status 48

Education
  abolish harmful traditional practices 12
  African Charter Art 14 380
  collective health/ measures 35
  conflation of right to health 132
  CRC text 7, 376
  formulation objection 66
  historical importance 17, 25
  impact of non-state actors 190
  interpretation of obligations 113
  libertarian theory 61
  macro/micro resource allocation
    dilemma 71
  measures to raise awareness and access to
    information
    basic knowledge and information 293–6
    overview 291–3
  need for State action 43
  San Salvador Protocol 380
  sexual and reproductive freedom 140–3
  withholding information 106

Effectiveness principle
  concerns over malnutrition 268
  core principle of public health ethics 209

enforcement of non-discrimination 207
evidence based measures to prevent
   disease 270
interference with human rights 183
interpretation of obligations 114–15
legislative measures 184–5
participation of children 215
prevention of disease 270
sexual and reproductive freedom 133
targeted measures 235
Enlightenment 36–7
Environmental protection
conflation of right to health 130–1
CRC text 7
formulation objection 65
highest attainable standard of health 108
ICESCR text 18
international regulation 107
libertarian theory 61
meaning of health 125
San Salvador Protocol 380
specific measures 281–5
Experimentation 122, 133, 144, 189–90

Family planning
see also Abortion services
CRC text 7, 376
impact of non-state actors 190
non-discrimination 377
physical accessibility 169
sexual and reproductive freedom
   justifications for international
      approach 140–3
   model advanced under international
      law 136–9
   strong case for inclusion 133–5
specific measures 299–301
US restrictions 349
Female genital cutting
see also Male circumcision
criminalization 85, 180
education through technology 274
effect on adolescent health 191
identification by list 308–9
interpretation of obligations 85
measures to abolish harmful traditional
   practices 314
nature and consequences of practice 316–17
need for zero tolerance 304
problems of classification 315–16
specific measures 317–23
Food and water
CRC text 376
minimum core obligations 248–9
specific measures to combat malnutrition
   application of available technology 272–4
   clean drinking water 278–81

general measures 270–2
'malnutrition' defined 269
mitigation of environmental factors
   281–5
overview 267–8
provision of nutritious foods 274–7
'targeted life cycle approach' 276
Formulation objections
challenges to legitimacy of health 65–7
conclusions 74
importance 372
Freedoms associated with health
freedom from medical experimentation 144
freedom from non-consensual medical
   treatment
   children 146–53
   complexities 145–6
   problematic inclusion 144–5
   sterilization of women and children
      153–8
overview 132–3
sexual and reproductive freedom
   justifications for international
      approach 140–3
   model advanced under international
      law 136–9
   strong case for inclusion 133–5
Fulfilment obligations
all appropriate means 194–7
international cooperation
   controversial duty 340–3
   forms of assistance 343–4
   need for global institutional reform
      344–8
   overview 327
   process by which assistance should be
      provided 348–51

Genital mutilation *see* Female genital cutting;
   Male circumcision
Great Depression 25, 40

Harmful traditional practices *see* Abolition of
   harmful traditional practices
Health and safety at work *see* Occupational
   health and safety
Highest attainable standard of health
associated freedoms
   freedom from medical
      experimentation 144
   freedom from non-consensual medical
      treatment 144–58
   overview 132–3
   sexual and reproductive freedom 133–43
definitions of 'health' 125–6
distinct nature of international
   formulation 123–4

Highest attainable standard of health (*cont.*)
  formulation objections 65
  ICESCR 18
  inclusion of entitlements 130–2
  interpretation of obligations 108
  introduction by WHO 27–30
  meaning and scope of interest
    conclusions 173–4
    distinct nature of international
      formulation 123–4
    inclusion of determinants such as
      food 130–2
    meaning of 'health' 125–6
    need to move beyond biomedical
      approach 126–30
    overview 121–3
  need to move beyond biomedical
    approach 126–30
  overview 121–3
  qualitative nature of entitlements
    access to treatment 167–73
    availability of health care 159–67
    overview 158–9
  recent formulation 44–5
  recognition in international treaties 50
History of right to health
  insights into contemporary
    understanding 33–4
  origins
    adoption of UDHR 30–1
    links with class rights 19–20
    links with economic and social rights
      21–2
    nexus with war and peace 23–7
    WHO and highest attainable standard of
      health 27–30
  overview 14–16
  recognition of inalienable right 16–19
  role of public health
    humanitarianism 38–9
    impact of Industrial Revolution 37–8
    mixed motivations 35–6
    rise and fall of Enlightenment 36–7
    social concern throughout history 34–5
    USSR and USA approaches
      distinguished 39–41
  value of 'prior languages and practices' 41–3
HIV/AIDS
  abolition of harmful traditional
    practices 312
  access to treatment 172
  all appropriate means
    data collection 210
    effective participation 215
    fulfilment obligation 195
    judicial review 203–4
    legislative measures 180

  targeted measures 220–1
  clear and practical approach to
    interpretation 99
  effect of sexual and reproductive freedom of
    adolescents 135, 138
  intellectual property rights 367
  preventative measures 271, 297
Humanitarianism
  conclusions 374
  counter swing towards 9
  emergency situations 263
  growing political movement 38
  international conduct obligation 246
  interplay of factors 41
  interpretative methodology 77
  League of Nations 23
  minimum core obligation 248
  need for a persuasive methodology 10
  provision of charity and welfare 35
  response to human suffering 33
  UDHR 55

Inalienable rights
  ICESCR 51
  nexus between war, rights, health, and
    peace 23–7
  omission of health by Jefferson 37
  origins and development 16–19
  rejection as foundation for the right to
    health 52, 73
  UDHR 20, 30, 51, 56, 58
Indicators 212–14
Industrial Revolution
  driving forces 37–8
  historical impact on health 38–9
Infant and child mortality
  African Charter Art 14 379
  CRC text 376
  cultural factors 111
  general comments by CRC
    Committee 257–8
  historical backdrop 255–7
  importance of 'social visibility' 259
  indicators and benchmarks 213
  lack of ICESCR guidance 261
  need for indicators 258–9
  need for multidisciplinary
    practices 260–1
  need for risk assessment 259–60
  state's international obligation 349
  treaty text 376
Initiation ceremonies 307
Instrumentalism
  conceptual foundation 57–9
  emergence of the right to health 43
  Industrial Revolution 38
  swing towards 9

Index

Intellectual property rights
  conclusions 369
  impact on access to medicine 350–3
  justifications for TRIPS
    legitimacy of aims 354–6
    limitation of objectives 356–8
    minimal impairment principle 359–64
    proportionality of assessment 358–9
    rational connection test 359–64
    reasonableness 354
  need for system coherence 364–6
  overview 327
  respect for right to health 335–6
Interdisciplinary initiatives
  all appropriate means 218
  primary health care 267
Interest theories
  absence of comprehensive moral theory 52–4
  social interest theory of rights 54–5
    cultural system 59–60
    objections are without foundation 73–4
International cooperation
  see also Communitarianism
  conclusions 368–70
  CRC text 376
  intellectual property rights
    adjusting and reviewing expectations 366–7
    impact on access to medicine 350–3
    justifications for TRIPS 354–64
    need for system coherence 364–6
  nature and scope of obligation
    fulfilment obligations 340–51
    history and development 327–9
    promotion and encouragement 329–31
    protective obligations 337–9
    respect for right to health 332–7
    specific measures 331–2
  overview 325–7
  progressive recognition of right to health 231–2
International Covenant on Economic Social and Cultural Rights (and its Committee)
  abolition of harmful traditional practices
    contested concept 306
    overview 287
    progressive recognition 306
  access to treatment 167
  all appropriate means
    accountability mechanisms 201
    conclusions 224
    fulfilment obligation 194
    indicators and benchmarks 212
    justiciability 204
    legislative measures 179

  margins of appreciation 179
  overview 175–6
  respect for right to health 186–90
  to 'take steps' 177–8
  tripartite typology 185
  appeals to natural law 51–2
  cultural system 59–60
  dignity 56
  formulation objections 66
  freedom from non-consensual medical treatment 144
  instrumentalism 58
  international cooperation
    conclusions 369–70
    fulfilment obligations 341, 343, 348
    nature and scope of obligation 328–9
    overview 325–6
    protective obligations 338–9
    respect for right to health 332–4
  interpretation of obligations
    on demand medicine 85
    recognition of multiple actors 82
    system coherence 105, 108
  progressive recognition of right to health
    cooperation between States 231–2
    maximum available resources 227
    minimum core obligations 238–52
    overview 225–6
    prioritization of resources 232–8
  reclusive state during Cold War 31–2
  resource allocation dilemma 72
  'right to highest attainable health' 18
  sexual and reproductive freedom 137
  specific measures
    awareness and access to information 291
    clean drinking water 280
    disease and malnutrition 267–8
    infant and child mortality 261
    medical assistance and health care 261–2
    mitigation of environmental factors 281–2
    natal care 288
    occupational health and safety 286–7
    overview 255
    preventative health care 297
    primary health care 263–4
Interpretation *see* **Methodology of interpretation**

Justiciability
  accountability mechanism
    comparative examples 205–7
    limits of litigation 207–8
    problematic transfer of case law 204–5
    role of civil and political rights 202–4
  civil and political rights 188
  CRC Committee 201

Justiciability (*cont.*)
  importance 1
  progressive recognition of right to health 253
  reluctance to embrace the right to health 5
  separate norm 102

Latin American philosophy
  historical impact 20–2
  overview 15
League of Nations 23–4, 327–8
Legislative measures
  abortion services 162
  'blind spots' and 'burdens of inertia' 114
  economic and social rights 64
  effectiveness principle 184–5
  explicit recognition of the right to health 3
  justifiable interferences with other rights 181–4
  margins of appreciation 201
  need for broad and diverse approach 179–80
Liberalism
  historical impact 19–22
  overview 15
Libertarian objections
  challenges to legitimacy of health 60–3
  conclusions 74

Male circumcision
  see also Female genital cutting
  cultural and gender bias 13
  gender bias in identification 311–14
  overview 304
Margins of appreciation
  abolition of harmful traditional practices 306, 317–23
  all appropriate means 178–9
  female genital cutting 314
  historical impact on international commitment 39–41
  international co-operation 331
  interpretation of obligations 112–13
  legislative measures 201
  prevention of HIV/AIDS 271–2
  requirement for safeguards 223
  scope and limits of participation 216
  specific measures
    awareness and access to information 293
    conclusions 301–2
    disease and malnutrition 271
    family planning 300
    infant and child mortality 258
    medical assistance and health care 263
    mitigation of environmental factors 283
    natal care 289
    occupational health and safety 286
    overview 254

  preventive health care 298
  primary health care 263
Maximum available resources
  construction of necessary institutional structures 230–1
  cooperation as source 231–2
  ICESCR 235
  open-ended vision 226–30
Meaning of health
  see also **Methodology of interpretation**
  associated freedoms
    freedom from medical experimentation 144
    freedom from non-consensual medical treatment 144–58
    overview 132–3
    sexual and reproductive freedom 133–43
  conclusions 167–73
  definitions of 'health' 125–6
  distinct nature of international formulation 123–4
  fundamental challenges 372–4
  inclusion of entitlements 130–2
  need to move beyond biomedical approach 126–30
  overview 121–3
  qualitative nature of entitlements
    access to treatment 167–73
    availability of health care 159–67
    overview 158–9
Medical experimentation 122, 133, 144, 189–90
Medicines *see* **Access to health**
Methodology of interpretation
  see also Meaning of health
  acceptable health care 172–4
  changing approach towards persuasion 78–80
  clear and practical approach 97–100
  coherence 100–4
    in reasoning 100–4
    system coherence 104–10
  conclusions 118–20
  context sensitivity
    global context sensitivity 113–18
    local context sensitivity 111–13
    overview 110
  fundamental challenges 372–4
  moves towards communitarianism 81–5
  overview 75–8
  principled interpretation
    care in drafting 95–7
    human rights treaties 92–4
    intention of parties 94–5
    overview 88
    VCLT 1969 89–92
  transparency 86–8

Migrant workers
  International Convention Arts 25, 28, 43, 45, 378
  non-discrimination 168–9
  normative commitment to the right to health 18
  recognition of the right to health 195
  specific measures 255
  targeted measures 219
Millennium Development Goals
  Child and Maternal Health 87, 103
  coherence 102
  impact on right to health 2
  intellectual property rights 367
  international cooperation 325
  provision of nutritious foods 276
  public health policy 103
Minimal impairment principle 359–64
Minimum core obligations
  genesis and conflation 238–41
  need for practical content
    conduct 245–6
    overview 243–5
    results 246–52
  need for principled basis 241–3
  weak/strong interpretation 117
Multisectoral initiatives
  all appropriate means 218
  primary health care 265

Natal care
  African Charter Art 14 379
  CEDAW Art 12 377
  CRC text 376
  impact of non-state actors 190
  infant and child mortality
    cultural factors 111
    general comments by CRC Committee 257–8
    historical backdrop 255–7
    importance of 'social visibility' 259
    indicators and benchmarks 213
    lack of ICESCR guidance 261
    need for indicators 258–9
    need for multidisciplinary practices 260–1
    need for risk assessment 259–60
    state's international obligation 349
    treaty text 376
  Millennium Development Goals 87, 103
  specific measures
    meaning of 'appropriate' 289–91
    progressive or immediate obligation 287–9
National plans, programs and policies
  accountability mechanisms 199–201
  African Charter Art 14 380
Natural law 51–2

Non-discrimination
  abortion services 143, 164
  access to treatment 167–8
  CEDAW Art 12 377
  CRPD Art 25 378
  ICESCR 109
  migrant workers 378
  respect for right to health 186
Non-governmental organizations
  abolition of harmful traditional practices 319
  African Charter Art 14 380
  competency and capacity 33
  inclusion of rights within the UDHR 68
  indicators and benchmarks 213
  international cooperation 344
  interpretative role 76, 82, 118
  protective obligations 192–4
Normative expressions of health
  all appropriate means 175
  chronological overview
    humanitarianism 38–9
    rise and fall of Enlightenment 36–7
    social concern throughout history 34–5
  effective participation 214–15
  formulation objection 65–7
  grounding rights in interests 52
  international cooperation 365–6
  international treaties 18
  meaning of health 101–9
  minimum core obligations 249
  obligation of states 11
  prelude to identifying rights 1
  progressive recognition of right to health 241
  recognition of the right to health 182
  rules of interpretation 88
  scope of the interest in which the right to health is grounded 123

Occupational health and safety
  impact of Industrial Revolution 38–9
  San Salvador Protocol 380
  specific measures 286–7

Parental guidance 298–9
Participatory strategies
  all appropriate means 214–17
  children's sexual and reproductive health 138
  conduct obligations 245
  construction of the multilateral treaties 95
  CRC 172, 187
  criticisms 6
  female genital cutting 322
  internal system coherence 109
  local context sensitivity 111

412   *Index*

Participatory strategies (*cont.*)
  meaning of health 99
  minimum core obligations 245, 248
  narrow biomedical approach 129
  planning and implementation of malaria controls 271
  primary health care 251, 263
  'rights based approach' 350
  specific measures 261, 265
Peace *see* War and peace
Persuasion
  changing approach from intentionalism 78–80
  clear and practical approach 97–100
  coherence
    in reasoning 100–4
    system coherence 104–10
  context sensitivity
    global context sensitivity 113–18
    local context sensitivity 111–13
    overview 110
  principled interpretation
    care in drafting 95–7
    human rights treaties 92–4
    intention of parties 94–5
    overview 88
    VCLT 1969 89–92
  role of interpretation 77
  transparency 86–8
Philosophical foundations *see* Theoretical and philosophical foundations
Poverty
  children 170
  clamour for public health measures 15
  counter swing towards humanitarianism 9
  impact of Industrial Revolution 38
  San Salvador Protocol 380
  shift towards instrumentalism 9
  specific measures 277
  'targeted life cycle approach' 276
Practicality
  access to education and information 292
  current challenges 371–2
  global institutional reform 344
  highest attainable standard of health 137–8, 140–1
  importance 7–8
  indicators and benchmarks 212
  international cooperation 331, 339, 369
  interpretation of treaties 373
  minimum core obligations 243–7
  'other appropriate measures' 186, 198
  preventive health care 297
  promotion and encouragement 330
  resource allocation 226, 234, 252
  sexual autonomy and non-consensual medical treatment 174

  vulnerable children 220
Preventative health care
  African Charter Art 14 380
  disease 271
  highest attainable standard of health 155
  need for indicators 258
  San Salvador Protocol 380
  specific measures
    development commitments 298
    open ended obligations 207–8
    overview 296–7
Primary health care
  African Charter Art 14 379
  CRC text 376
  difficulties of interpretation and implementation 264–6
  ICESCR and CRC distinguished 263–4
  international conference 31
  local context sensitivity 266–7
  minimum core obligations 249–52
  resurgent commitment 266
  San Salvador Protocol 380
Principled approach
  decision-making process 237
  free health care 172
  global institutional reform 344
  highest attainable standard of health 137–8, 140–1, 157, 160
  importance 7–8
  indicators and benchmarks 212
  international cooperation 331, 339, 369
  international treaties 49
  interpretation
    care in drafting 95–7
    conclusions 119
    human rights treaties 92–4
    intention of parties 94–5
    overview 88
    VCLT 1969 89–92
  interpretation of treaties 373
  minimum core obligations 239–43
  'other appropriate measures' 186, 198
  promotion and encouragement 330
  rebuttal of objections 372
  resource allocation 226–9, 234, 252–3
  respect for right to health 189
  sexual autonomy and non-consensual medical treatment 174
  vulnerable children 220
Prioritization of resources
  addressing allocation dilemma 235–8
  children's health 149
  conclusions 252–3
  essential medicines 351
  impact of IP rights 358
  infant mortality 258

macro/micro resource allocation
    dilemma 71
need for dialogue 232–5
participatory and collaborative
    approach 215, 217
safe drinking water 279
sanitation services 274
Privatized health care
centrality and prominence of issue 6
compatible with right to health 75
flagging threat 191
impact on children 222–3
impact on right to health 4
Progressive recognition of right to health
abolition of harmful traditional
    practices 305–6
maximum available resources
    construction of necessary institutional
        structures 230–1
    cooperation as source 231–2
    open-ended vision 226–30
natal care 287–9
overview 225–6
prioritization of resources
    addressing allocation dilemma 235–8
    need for dialogue 232–5
respect for right to health 335
Proportionality
health and IP 356–8, 363
justifications for TRIPS 358–9
local context sensitivity 112
recognition of the right to health 181–3
Protective obligations
international cooperation
    overview 327
    specific measures 337–9
need for more persuasive account 190–2
non-state actors 192–4
Public health
communication strategies 322
ESC Committee 238
historical role
    humanitarianism 38–9
    impact of Industrial Revolution 37–8
    mixed motivations 35–6
    rise and fall of Enlightenment 36–7
    social concern throughout history 34–5
    USSR and USA approaches
        distinguished 39–41
integrated approach 251
interference with other human rights
    180–4
nexus with human rights 101–3
overview 15
physical accessibility 169
preventive health care 298
primary health care 249

specific health needs of children 220
TRIPS 355

Qualitative nature of entitlements
access to treatment
    acceptability and quality 172–3
    financial accessibility 169–72
    non-discrimination 167–8
    physical accessibility 168–9
availability of health care
    abortion services 161–7
    specialist health services 159–61
CRPD Art 25 377
four elements 11
overview 158–9
TRIPS 361

Rational connection test 359–64
Reasonableness
decision-making process 237–8
justifications for TRIPS 354
Relativism
challenges to legitimacy of health 67–9
harm to a child's health 323
male circumcision 311
objections without foundation 74
Religion
historical impact of Catholic
    values 21–2
interplay of factors 41
provision of charity and welfare 35
replacement as motive for public
    health 36
Reproductive health *see* **Family planning**
Resources
African Charter Art 14 380
allocation dilemma
    conclusions 252–3
    distorted allocation 69–70
    importance 372
    macro/micro dilemma 71–3
    prioritization of resources 235–8
    relative scarcity 69
maximum available resources
    construction of necessary institutional
        structures 230–1
    cooperation as source 231–2
    open-ended vision 226–30
mitigation of environmental factors 285
prioritization of resources
    addressing allocation dilemma 235–8
    need for dialogue 232–5
Respect for right to health
all appropriate means 186–9
international cooperation
    overview 327
    specific measures 332–7

Result obligations
  food and water 248–9
  minimum core obligations 246–7
  primary health care 249–52
Ritual initiation ceremonies 307
Roosevelt, FD 15, 24–5

Sexual and reproductive freedom
  justifications for international
    approach 140–3
  model advanced under international
    law 136–9
  strong case for inclusion 133–5
Sickness
  Advisory Committee for Child Welfare
    (LON) 24
  CRC text 7
  impact of Industrial Revolution 38
  Latin American commitment 26
  meaning of health 85
  normative commitment to the right to
    health 18
  primary health care 262
  shift towards instrumentalism 9
Social factors
  see also International Covenant on Economic
    Social and Cultural Rights (and its
    Committee)
  all appropriate means 185
  application of available technology 272–3
  class rights 19–20
  effective participation 214
  interpretation of obligations
    global context sensitivity 113–18
    local context sensitivity 111–13
    overview 110
  libertarian objections to health rights 60–3
  meaning of health
    conclusions 173–4
    'health' defined 125–6
    inclusion of determinants such as
      food 130–2
    need to move beyond biomedical
      approach 126–30
    qualitative nature of entitlements 158–73
  primary health care 266–7
  progressive recognition of right to
    health 230–1
  using history to understand health 33–4
Social interest theory of rights
  cultural system 59–60
  objections without foundation 73–4
  underlying principles 54–5
Specific measures
  abolition of harmful traditional practices
    female genital cutting 314
    margins of appreciation 317–23

  nature and consequences of particular
    practices 316–17
  terminology and labelling 315–16
  conclusions 301–2
  disease and malnutrition
    application of available technology 272–4
    clean drinking water 278–81
    general measures 270–2
    mitigation of environmental factors
      281–5
    overview 267–8
    provision of nutritious foods 274–7
  family planning 299–301
  infant and child mortality
    general comments by CRC
      Committee 257–8
    historical backdrop 255–7
    importance of 'social visibility' 259
    lack of ICESCR guidance 261
    need for indicators 258–9
    need for multidisciplinary practices 260–1
    need for risk assessment 259–60
  international cooperation
    'concrete implications' 331–2
    fulfilment obligations 340–51
    protective obligations 337–9
    respect for right to health 332–7
  medical assistance and health care 261–3
  natal care
    meaning of 'appropriate' 289–91
    progressive or immediate obligation
      287–9
  need for creative synthesis 374–5
  occupational health and safety 286–7
  overview 254–5
  parental guidance 298–9
  preventative health care
    development commitments 298
    open ended obligations 207–8
    overview 296–7
  primary health care
    difficulties of interpretation and
      implementation 264–6
    ICESCR and CRC distinguished 263–4
    local context sensitivity 266–7
    resurgent commitment 266
  raising awareness and access to information
    basic knowledge and information 293–6
    overview 291–3
  San Salvador Protocol 380
State obligations
  abolition of harmful traditional practices
    need for culturally sensitive
      approach 323–4
    overview 303–4
    practices prejudicial to health of
      children 306–14

progressive recognition 305–6
  specific measures 314–23
 international cooperation
  conclusions 368–70
  intellectual property rights 351–67
  nature and scope of obligation 327–51
  overview 325–7
 progressive recognition of right to health
  conclusions 252–3
  maximum available resources 226–32
  minimum core obligations 238–52
  overview 225–6
  prioritization of resources 232–8
 specific measures
  conclusions 301–2
  disease and malnutrition 267–85
  family planning 299–301
  infant and child mortality 255–61
  natal care 287–96
  occupational health and safety 286–7
  overview 254–5
  preventative health care 296–9
  primary health care 261–7
 use of all appropriate means
  conclusions 224
  legislative measures 179–84
  margins of appreciation 178–9
  overview 176–7
  to 'take steps' 177–8
  treaty monitoring bodies 197–223
  use of tripartite typology 185–97
Status objections 63–5, 372
Sterilization of women and children 153–8

Targeted measures
 allocation of scarce resources 70
 child mortality 260
 ICESCR 178
 importance 218–19
 life cycle approach to hunger 276
 margin of appreciation 271
 throughout childhood 219–20
 vulnerable children 220–1
Technology
 African Charter Art 14 379
 combating disease and malnutrition 268
 CRC text 7, 268, 376
 highest attainable standard of health 265
 measures to combat disease and
  malnutrition 272–4
 prevention of infant mortality 261
 primary health care 250, 264
 recognition of the right to health 193
Theoretical and philosophical foundations
 challenges to legitimacy of health
  formulation objections 65–7
  libertarian objections 60–3

  status objections 63–5
  complexities and potential harm 47
  dismissal of health by some 45
  evaluation of rights 3
  formulation objections 67
  interest theories
   absence of comprehensive moral
    theory 52–4
   social interest theory of rights 54–5
  justification for a right to health 44–7
  national differences 39
  objections without foundation 74
  overlapping consensus of right to health 372
  overview 15
  scornful approach to health 4
Traditional practices *see* **Abolition of harmful
  traditional practices**
Transparency
 decision-making process 12
 exercise of discretion 374
 impact of TRIPS 335
 methodology of interpretation 86–8
 progressive recognition of right to
  health 237
TRIPS *see* **Intellectual property rights**

UNICEF
 abolition of harmful traditional
  practices 305, 321–2
 assertion of role 2
 awareness and access to information 291,
  293–6
 breastfeeding 276
 cause of death among children 259
 child specific indicators 213
 definition of health 208
 elements for effective participation 216
 female genital cutting 85
 fulfilment obligations 344
 internal system coherence 109
 international cooperation
  conclusions 368
  fulfilment obligations 346
 interpretation of obligations 109
 methodology 76
 natal care 290
 preventive health care 296
 primary health care 31, 250, 265
 provision of adequate nutritious foods 274
 public health policy 103
 use of water 248
 water supply and sanitation 279
 world military spending 261
Universal Declaration on Human Rights
 adoption and its aftermath 30–2
 appeals to natural law 51–2
 cultural relativism 68

Universal Declaration on Human Rights (*cont.*)
  cultural system 59–60
  dignity 56
  elevation of individual status 43
  inalienable rights 20
  inclusion of medical care in first draft 27
  instrumentalism 58
  international cooperation 328
  recognition of the right to health 181–2
  resources 16
  scientific advancement and its benefits 343
  treatment of health 17–18
'Urgent' interest theory 52–4

Vulnerable groups
  targeted measures
    children 220–1
    importance 218–19

War and peace
  emergence of human rights after WWII 16
  impact of Cold War 30–2
  nexus with health
    rebirth of rights after WWII 24–7
    WWI 23–4
Water *see* **Food and water**
Welfare state
  affirmation of values by Roosevelt 15
  development of economic and social rights 42
  emergence of economic and social rights 20
  expansion during Cold War 20
World Health Organization
  abolition of harmful traditional practices 315, 319, 321
  abortion services 165
  access to medicines 353
  assertion of role 2
  awareness and access to information 296
  breastfeeding 276
  cause of death among children 259
  clean drinking water 280
  disease and malnutrition 269–70
  elevation of individual status 43
  establishment after WWII 23–4
  female genital cutting 85
  human rights principles 103
  impact of Cold War 32
  international cooperation
    fulfilment obligations 343
    overview 325
    protective obligations 339
    respect for right to health 337
  introduction of highest attainable standard of health 27–30
  mitigation of environmental factors 281, 285
  natal care 290–2
  preventive health care 296
  primary health care 31, 264–6
  provision of nutritious foods 274, 276
  public health policy 103
  water supply and sanitation 279